HELL
IN A
VERY
SMALL
PLACE

THE SIEGE OF DIEN BIEN PHU

HELL
IN A
VERY
SMALL
PLACE

THE SIEGE OF DIEN BIEN PHU

BERNARD B. FALL

A DA CAPO PAPERBACK

Library of Congress Cataloging in Publication Data

Fall, Bernard B., 1926–1967.
  Hell in a very small place.

  (A Da Capo paperback)
  Reprint. Originally published: Philadelphia:
Lippincott, 1967.
    1. Dien Bien Phu, Vietnam, Battle of, 1954.
I. Title.
DS553.3.D5F35   1985   959.704′2   84-29203
ISBN 0-306-80231-7

This Da Capo Press paperback edition of *Hell in a Very Small Place:
The Siege of Dien Bien Phu* is an unabridged republication of the
first edition published in New York in 1967. It is reprinted by
arrangement with Harper & Row Publishers, Inc.

Published by Da Capo Press, Inc.
A Subsidiary of Plenum Publishing Corporation
233 Spring Street, New York, N.Y. 10013

Manufactured in the United States of America

To Dorothy

who lived with the ghosts of Dien Bien Phu for three long years

Preface

THERE HAVE been, even in recent history, many sieges which lasted longer than the French Union garrison's defense of a small town in the northeastern corner of Viet-Nam with the unlikely name of "Seat of the Border County Prefecture," or, in Vietnamese, Dien Bien Phu.

The French reoccupation of the valley lasted a total of 209 days, and the actual siege 56 days. The Germans held Stalingrad for 76 days, while the Americans held Bataan for 66 days and Corregidor for 26; British and Commonwealth troops defended Tobruk once for 241 days. The record World War II siege was no doubt that of the French coastal fortress of Lorient, held by German troops for 270 days from 1944 until VE-day. Many of the major sieges of recent years involved large numbers of troops on both sides: there were 330,000 German troops encircled at Stalingrad at the beginning of the siege, and the Soviet troops which encircled them numbered over one million. In comparison, Dien Bien Phu, with a garrison which barely exceeded 13,000 men at any one moment, and a Viet-Minh siege force totaling 49,500 combatants and 55,000 support troops, could hardly qualify as a major battle, let alone a decisive one.

Yet that is exactly what it was, and in a way which makes it one of the truly decisive battles of the twentieth century—in the same sense that the First Battle of the Marne, Stalingrad, and Midway were decisive in their times: although hostilities continued after the particular battle—sometimes for years—the whole "tone" of the conflict, as it were, had changed. One of the sides in the conflict had lost its chance of attaining whatever it had sought to gain in fighting the war.

This was true for the French after they had lost the Battle of Dien Bien Phu. The French Indochina War had dragged on indecisively since December 19, 1946, and reluctantly—far too reluctantly to derive any political or psychological benefit from the gesture—the French granted the non-Communist regime of ex-emperor Bao Dai some of the appurtenances but little of the reality of national independence. In fact, as the war bit deeper into the vitals of the French professional army and consumed an ever-rising amount of France's postwar treasure (it finally cost France about $10 billion, in addition to $954 million of United States aid actually expended in Indochina prior to July, 1954), it became increasingly clear that France had entirely lost sight of any clearly definable war aims. General Henri-Eugène Navarre, the unfortunate French commander-in-chief at the time of the Battle of Dien Bien Phu, was to argue later in his book *Agonie de l'Indochine* that there were two acceptable but contradictory war aims: France could be expected to fight the Indochina War alone but with all her might *only* if the Indochina States would accept a "special relationship" that would justify the expenditure in blood and money that would entail—and if they were willing to help in the fight to the utmost of their abilities. If, on the other hand, the Indochina War had become an integral part of the world-wide struggle, led by the United States, for the containment of communism, *all other* nations concerned with stopping communism had an obligation equal to that of France to participate in the struggle.*

It is because the United States herself now takes precisely that latter position that Secretary of State Dean Rusk and Secretary of Defense Robert S. McNamara went to Paris in December, 1965, to plead for greater and more direct support by America's NATO allies in the struggle the United States has been shouldering almost exclusively (with the exception of the South Vietnamese Army and minor contingents from a few small nations). The results, apparently, were negligible.

In contrast to the United States, France never had the strength for a large-scale unilateral commitment, and knew that public opinion at home, as well as war weariness among the nationals upon whose territory the war was being fought (a factor that appears to be too often forgotten now), demanded that a short-range solution to the conflict be found. Or, barring victory, that a situation be created in which the national armies of the Associated States of Cambodia, Laos, and Viet-Nam could deal with Communist guerrilla remnants once the French regulars had destroyed the enemy's main battle forces in a series of major engagements.

Contrary also to the American Chief Executive who is able to commit American troops in unlimited numbers in undeclared overseas wars, the French Parliament, by an amendment to the Budget Law of 1950, restricted the use of draftees to French "homeland" territory (*i.e.,* France and Algeria, and the French-occupied areas of Germany), thus severely limiting the number of troops that could be made available to the Indochina theater of operations. Caught in a web of conflicting

---

*"There was an incompatibility," said Navarre, "between these two possible war aims, because each of them required a political line and even a strategy of its own" (p. 67).

commitments and priorities—NATO and communism in Europe *vs.* containment in a peripheral area of Asia—the ever-changing governments of the French Fourth Republic shortchanged all of them: the French units in Europe, gutted of the bulk of their regular cadres, were unusable in the event of war, and the regulars sent to Indochina were scarcely more than skeleton units to be hastily brought up to strength by locally recruited troops. When General Navarre, upon assuming command in May, 1953, requested 12 infantry battalions and various supporting units, along with 750 more officers and 2,550 noncommissioned officers for his already understrength units, he finally received 8 battalions, 320 officers and 200 noncommissioned officers—and was told that the "reinforcements" were in fact an *advance* on the replacements he would have received the following year for 1953 combat losses.

In the meantime, the enemy was getting stronger by the day, particularly in well-trained, regular combat divisions that could take on anything the French could oppose them with. Twelve years later, the North Vietnamese were still unafraid to take on the best forces the United States can muster. With the Korean war terminated in a stalemate in July, 1953, Chinese instructors and Chinese-provided Russian and American equipment began to arrive in North Viet-Nam en masse. The enemy now had seven mobile divisions and one full-fledged artillery division, and more were likely to come rapidly from the Chinese divisional training camps near Ching-Hsi and Nanning. It therefore became imperative for the French to destroy at least a large part of the enemy's main battle force as rapidly as possible. This was feasible only if the French could induce the enemy to face up to them in a set-piece battle, by offering the Viet-Minh a target sufficiently tempting to pounce at, but sufficiently strong to resist the onslaught once it came. It was an incredible gamble, for upon its success hinged not only the fate of the French forces in Indochina and France's political role in Southeast Asia, but the survival of Viet-Nam as a non-Communist state and, to a certain extent, that of Laos and Cambodia as well—and perhaps (depending on the extent to which one accepts the "falling dominoes" theory) the survival of some sort of residual Western presence in the vast mainland area between Calcutta, Singapore, and Hong Kong.

This book is the history of that gamble. When the general editor for the Great Battles Series, the eminent military historian and writer Hanson W. Baldwin, approached me in 1962 with the assignment, I undertook it with great trepidation. I realized, from previous research on far less sensitive aspects of the Indochina War, that it would be extremely difficult to piece together a reasonably accurate picture of what actually happened at Dien Bien Phu without access to the existing military archives. A perusal of the available literature, with its obvious contradictions and errors, only increased my concern. In presenting the French authorities with my request for access to the documentation, I emphasized that any scientifically accurate account of what actually occurred at Dien Bien Phu would hardly constitute a complimentary picture of French political or military leadership in the Far East at that time. But, I argued, the myths and misinformation that had hardened into "fact" over the years would not only distort history irremediably but also prevent others who have a more immediate concern with Viet-Nam from understanding present-day events which in many ways are shaped by events at Dien Bien Phu in the spring of 1954.

Pending authorization for access to the official documentation, I proceeded to make my contacts with survivors of the battle. There were a relatively large number of French survivors available. Since Frenchmen held all command positions on the friendly side, they would be of prime importance in the telling of the story. But as I was to find out later, as is often the case when survivors retell their own experience to different listeners at different times, there were understandable gaps and biases in their accounts, some of them based on service rivalries. A paratrooper would feel that his units bore the brunt of the fighting; an officer from the Foreign Legion would be certain that it was his men who became the mainstay of the defense. There were officers of units that fared badly, according to most accounts, who were willing to affirm that such accounts were ill-founded. In addition, no account of Dien Bien Phu (including the one which follows) can remain totally uninfluenced by the bitter debate (which erupted in a court trial in Paris) between the then French commander-in-chief in Indochina, General Navarre, and his direct subordinate in North Viet-Nam, Major General René Cogny. Almost every survivor has taken sides in that dispute and, to a certain extent, the surviving archival documentation may have been affected by it.

I soon found to my surprise that no one apparently had sought to secure the views of the almost seventy per cent of the garrison who were not French: Legionnaires, North Africans, and Vietnamese. Here, also, I met with almost incredible kindness and understanding under most difficult circumstances. Less than one year after having won its independence from France in a bloody war that had lasted even longer than the Indochina War, the Algerian Republic permitted me to interview members of the Algerian armed forces who had served at Dien

Bien Phu and who, in many cases, had fought against France in Algeria. In 1962, in Communist North Viet-Nam, I had no difficulty in meeting men who would proudly speak of their victory over France. They were easily recognizable because they still wore, even on their civilian clothes, a special insignia awarded them by President Ho Chi Minh on the occasion of the victory. As it turned out, my own driver had been a machine-gunner there. In South Viet-Nam, and in France, a number of non-Communist Vietnamese survivors responded to newspaper advertisements I had placed. One customs official at Tahiti Airport had been at Dien Bien Phu; a German Foreign Legionnaire was found near Napoleon's Tomb; another was mentioned in a *New York Times* article dealing with travel in the Sahara.

When the authorization to consult the archives was finally granted in 1963 by Monsieur Pierre Messmer, the French Minister of the Armed Forces, I had been stricken by a near-fatal disease. But in 1964-65, thanks to a small research grant from Howard University, I was able to complete my documentary research. Let it be said from the outset that almost *all* the documents that were in Dien Bien Phu (war diaries, written messages from one unit to another, etc.) were destroyed before the fortress fell, or have since fallen into Communist hands. Also, only the Viet-Nam People's Army—the North Vietnamese Army which was still being referred to as the "Viet-Minh" in 1954—proceeded with a methodical interrogation of all the survivors immediately after the battle. Only General Vo Nguyen Giap, in Hanoi, is truly qualified to write this book, but because of his many other preoccupations, he has thus far published only a few superficial brochures on the subject.

The French archives, which are still being sorted out in part (the excellent staff of the *Service Historique de l'Armée* is minute and, in accordance with its own work schedule, is largely limited by the fifty-year rule on *in extenso* publication of recent documents), are fairly complete in terms of military plans, records of attempts to relieve the fortress, and its logistics for the period up to March 24, 1954, when the fortress was cut off from the outside world. Most documents after that date are copies of the radio traffic between Hanoi and Dien Bien Phu. An unknown quantity (said to be small) of documents is in the hands of the French government commission which investigated the Battle of Dien Bien Phu. Some documents not found in the archives, though of an official character, obviously are in the possession of some of the major actors in the drama, since they were published in certain French books which took sides in the Navarre-Cogny dispute. Finally, the separate archives of the French Navy and the French Air Force yielded much relevant data on the vital air-power aspects of the battle.

With that documentation in hand, the interviewing and, in many cases, later correspondence with most of the tactical commanders proved extremely rewarding. Unfortunately, except in rare instances, I was unable to interview two or more than two of the officers simultaneously —for the good reason that the survivors are now dispersed all over France. The collective-interview method, used particularly by the eminent military historian Brigadier General S. L. A. Marshall, is singularly helpful in reconstituting confused and swiftly changing actions—and there were many of them at Dien Bien Phu. In one particular instance, it took the concurring affirmation of several officers to pinpoint a position that had been erroneously located on the set of official maps prepared by the French Army after the battle. This does not mean that the present volume closes every information gap about the Battle of Dien Bien Phu; too many men have taken their secrets to the grave, too many documents are missing, and too many myths have already taken shape as facts. But my own notes and tape recordings of interviews were not seen, much less approved or censored, by *anyone*. All conversations and statements in the text are direct quotes, not my reconstructions of them. And if the trite phrase "telling the truth without fear or favor" has any meaning, it can in all fairness be applied here.

To give credit here to my numerous sources of information would be embarrassing to many in their present positions and would, in fact, ask them to share responsibility for the views I express here and which I must alone assume in full. But I must give thanks to the unfailing courtesy of the chiefs and personnel of the Historical Services of the French Army, Navy, and Air Force, for sharing their modest facilities with an outsider; to Major Jean Pouget, a retired French officer and author of the excellent *Nous étions à Dien Bien Phu,* who did not hesitate to place at my disposal some of his personal documentation; to Colonel Jules Roy, whose trail-blazing *La Bataille de Dien Bien Phu* proved often useful in cross-checking facts; to Hanson W. Baldwin for his deft and patient editing; to Mrs. Jewell Tait for struggling heroically with French abbreviations and Vietnamese place names while typing the manuscript; and to Dorothy for nursing me back to health and for putting up with a husband who mentally, for over three years, spent most of his time in a small and very green North Vietnamese valley.

Washington, D.C.   B. B. F.
New Year, 1966

Contents

Photographs

following page 204

Maps

The greatest writer of tragedy said that the evil men do lives after them, while the good is interred with their bones. In the lives of nations the opposite is often true. The good France has done in Indochina will endure. It is only the evil that was interred at Dien Bien Phu.

David Schoenbrun
As France Goes (1957)

Great battles, like epic tragedies, are not always staged or the product of human calculation; and disaster is less likely to derive from one gross blunder than from reasoned calculations which slip just a little.

Brig. Gen. S. L. A. Marshall
Night Drop—The American Airborne Invasion of Normandy (1962)

When a nation re-awakens, its finest sons are prepared to give their lives for its liberation. When Empires are threatened with collapse, they are prepared to sacrifice their non-commissioned officers.

Menachem Begin,
Leader of the Irgun,
The Revolt (1951)

I

Natasha

"CASTOR" was probably the first and last airborne operation in history in which the leading aircraft contained three generals along with the paratroop pathfinders. They were Lieutenant General Pierre Bodet, French Air Force, the French Deputy Commander-in-Chief in Indochina; Brigadier General Jean Dechaux, French Air Force, commander of *Gatac Nord,* the tactical air group that controlled all French air operations in northern Indochina; and Brigadier General Jean Gilles, commanding the French airborne forces in Indochina.

Their airplane, a twin-engine American-built C-47 crammed with radio communications equipment and loaded with sufficient gasoline for eight hours of flying, had taken off from Hanoi's military airport of Bach-Mai on November 20, 1953, at 0500. The mission of the lone transport aircraft was twofold: It was to make an appraisal of weather conditions over the valley of Dien Bien Phu and, if these were shown to be favorable, to drop the pathfinders—an elite group of paratroopers who were to jump on the designated drop zones a few minutes before the bulk of the troops and who were to earmark the zones with smoke markers.

Everything hinged on the weather conditions over the small valley that day, for it was impossible to maintain such a large concentration of transport aircraft for an indefinite period at Hanoi; they were badly needed elsewhere in Indochina.

When the airplane arrived over the valley at 0630, its visibility was almost completely blocked by the *crachin,* the dry fog that characterizes the weather in Viet-Nam's northwestern region even during the dry season. The ultimate decision for calling off or proceeding with the air drop now rested on the shoulders of Brig. Gen. Dechaux, a fifty-year-old leathery and tall military professional. Slowly the transport flew in wide circles above the valley shrouded in the fog. In the cramped cockpit, an officer from the Transport Command and an Air Force meteorologist calculated the chances of the fog's lifting in time for the drop. At 0700, the rays of the rising sun began to illuminate the upper layers of the clouds, which started to thin out noticeably. The weather officer walked back to where Gen. Dechaux was looking out of the airplane's windows on the valley below and said something to him that was lost in the noise of the airplane's engines. Dechaux went over to the radio operator, who was specially assigned to the aircraft to handle direct radio communications with Headquarters at Hanoi, and gave him a message.

The message reached Major General René Cogny, the commander of all French forces in North Viet-Nam, at 0720 and was immediately relayed by him to the commander of the Transport Air Force for Indochina who was waiting with his aircraft at the military airport at Bach-Mai. Operation "Castor" had begun.

For the crews of the French Air Force Transport Command, November, 1953, thus far had been sheer hell. The three Transport Groups normally available in North Viet-Nam, 1/64 ("Béarn"),* 2/64 ("Anjou"), and 2/63 ("Sénégal"), had constantly been engaged in supporting active combat operations directed against Communist Division 320 in the southwestern part of the Red River Delta. In fact, they had returned from that operation only on November 19 late in the evening and the Air Force mechanics had worked almost all night over the fatigued machines to make them ready for this morning's operation. But this was not the only worry of the commander of the Air Transport Command, Colonel Jean-Louis Nicot. He had been informed on November 10 under greatest secrecy that Operation "Castor" would take place on November 20 and had done his very best to scrounge the maximum number of airplanes and crews from the small transport force available inside Indochina. One of his problems was that at that particular moment there were fewer crews than airplanes in Indochina. Budgetary and political considerations in France had prevented the sending of additional air crews to Indochina despite the promises made to American military-aid planners that more French crews would be made available if the United States provided additional airplanes under its aid program. Yet, by mid-November, there were available to Nicot only 52 military crews for C-47's and 10 crews for the larger C-119 "Flying Boxcar" aircraft, while a theoretical total of 70 C-47's were available for operations. By frantically juggling his books, thinning out his crews, and putting on flying duty every staff officer (in-

*1st Group, 64th Squadron. For French military abbreviations and unit designations, see Appendix E.

cluding himself), Nicot succeeded in finding 65 air crews for the 65 aircraft capable of flying the mission of November 20.

At 0500, in the gray dawn of a dry-season morning, the air crews were picked up from their billets and the briefing began at 0550. Nicot himself conducted the briefing:

> Gentlemen, this is your mission: An airborne landing at Dien Bien Phu. This is an all-out effort with all available aircraft and crews. I personally will lead the first flight. The mission will take place in two serials; the first serial of 33 aircraft broken down in four platoons will take off from Bach-Mai Airport; the second serial of 32 aircraft grouped in four platoons will take off from Gia-Lam Airport. The first serial will be commanded by Major Fourcaut whose code name will be Yellow Leader. The second serial will be commanded by Major Martinet under the code name of Red Leader. My own code name will be Texas. Take-off spacing between serials will be three minutes, between the individual platoons one minute and between the three-plane sections will be ten seconds. Watch your timing, gentlemen, we must be extremely precise.
>
> Each plane will carry 550 gallons of gasoline at take-off. The second serial will do a second flight today, 24 aircraft will carry matériel and 8 will carry personnel. Another personnel drop will take place in the afternoon. The dropping of equipment should not take longer than 20 minutes.

The final navigational details were now worked out: The approach to the drop zone (DZ) was to be 170 degrees at an altitude of 2,900 feet. As soon as the dropping of equipment or men was completed, planes would exit from the drop-zone area by a 180-degree turn while climbing at the rate of 500 feet a minute. The estimated flying time was calculated at 76 minutes and 10 seconds.

Then came the technical details: climbing speeds, cruising speeds, approach speeds, parachuting speeds, navigational and operational VHF frequencies, the availability of emergency landing fields (none within a hundred miles) and coordination with the fighter-bombers and bombers which were also to operate around Dien Bien Phu at the same time.

The briefing was terminated at 0700, and at 0715 the air crews embarked in their airplanes in which the paratroopers and their equipment already had been loaded. Most of them scrutinized the cloudy sky intensely as they awaited the ultimate confirmation of the mission. Theoretically the engines were to begin to turn over at 0720 but the "go" order reached the Air Force Transport Command Headquarters at Bach-Mai only a few minutes before 0800. Then the radio earphones began to crackle in all 65 lumbering aircraft, engines sprang to life with a roar, red signal flares rose over the control towers at Bach-Mai and Gia-Lam airports, and one by one the heavily loaded aircraft roared down the runway and became airborne. At 0815 the whole air armada, having flown in slow circles until every airplane had been able to take its proper place in the flight pattern, changed directions and slowly headed on a westerly course towards the craggy mountains almost shining under their dark green jungle cover.

In Indochina, then as now, the impossibility of maintaining truly tight secrecy was the bane of all senior commanders.[1] Hence Gen. Cogny had not informed Gen. Dechaux of the impending airborne operation that he was going to command until November 12, a scant seven days before it was to take place. The order Dechaux had received was very laconic and simply provided for the occupation of the valley of Dien Bien Phu. In particular, the order prescribed (1) the creation of Dien Bien Phu of a "defensive system designed to insure the protection of the airfield to the exclusion of any system aimed at creating a belt of strong points around the airfield"; and (2) the eventual stationing of five battalions, two of which would roam throughout the surrounding area. The order was also communciated to Gen. Gilles.

It was already known to Gilles that there were Communist troops at Dien Bien Phu at the time and that, therefore, any dropping of troops on Dien Bien Phu would meet with at least some initial resistance. Ideally, he would have liked to parachute three airborne battalions simultaneously into the valley, in the hopes of encircling the Communist forces there and perhaps capturing their regimental commander. But the limited number of aircraft and crews available demanded that the operation take place in two separate phases, which would permit the airplanes to return to Dien Bien Phu and pick up the remaining troops and equipment for a later drop.[2] He decided, therefore, to drop two airborne battalions in the first phase and chose for this perilous mission the best units and commanders available in all of Indochina, the 6th BPC (Colonial Parachute Battalion) of Major Marcel Bigeard and the II/1 RCP (2nd Battalion of the 1st Regiment of Parachute Light Infantry) commanded by Major Jean Bréchignac. II/1 RCP had been a part of the First Free French Paratroops organized during World War II and in Indochina had participated in the operations of the "Street Without Joy."[3] The 6th BPC had been a commando battalion and had participated in every major battle since 1951. In particular, Bigeard had led it at the bloody sacrifice at

Tu-Lê, where the battalion had been offered as a bait in order to save the other garrisons of the T'ai highlands.[4] Together with the 1st BPC, which was to be parachuted on November 20 at 1400, the other two battalions formed Airborne Battle Group No. 1 (GAP 1) under Lt. Col. Fourcade. Commanded by Major Jean Souquet, the 1st BPC also was an elite unit; it had first arrived in Indochina in January, 1947, had later returned to Europe and had landed again in Indochina in June, 1953. Since then it had taken part in the battles for the Plain of Jars in Laos and most recently in Operation "Seagull" from which it had returned, like Col. Nicot's planes, the day before. As part of the first wave the 6th BPC and the II/1 RCP had 651 and 569 men respectively. In addition there were the 17th Company of Airborne Combat Engineers and a battery of the 35th Airborne Artillery Regiment which had jumped with Bigeard and the Headquarters group of GAP 1 and was to jump with Bréchignac's battalion.

Both Bigeard and Bréchignac had been called to see Gen. Bodet the day before the operation, to be briefed by him personally on the importance of their mission. Bodet had never been terribly happy about the operation and Bigeard distinctly remembered his last words:

> The way it looks, it ought to come off all right but if the situation is really too tough down there I leave you to judge as to what you have to do in order to save the maximum of personnel and to get out. In any case, if the weather is too unfavorable tomorrow, Dien Bien Phu will never take place.

And Bigeard was to add, years later, thinking back on what Bodet had said: "Oh, why did it not rain that day!"

But the key element of the briefing which Bigeard was to receive that day was given to him at a much lower level by Intelligence and dealt with the DZ for his battalion. Intelligence maintained 3,000 drop-zone files, each of which was neatly labeled with a number and a code name. Three major drop zones had finally been selected in the valley of Dien Bien Phu, two of them for personnel and one for equipment.

Each DZ file contained aerial photographs of the landing area and as much information about its topography and meteorology as could be found. The file number for Bigeard's DZ was 759 and its cover bore the name "Natasha." Bréchignac's drop zone was baptized "Simone" and the matériel drop zone was dubbed "Octavie." "Natasha," which was to become the key drop zone at Dien Bien Phu for months to come, deserves to be described more closely. It was situated 200 meters northwest of the village of Dien Bien Phu, had a total length of 3,900 feet (1,300 meters) and a total width of 1,350 feet (450 meters). It was pointed almost north-south, and was covered with semidry rice fields and a great deal of brush at its lower end and crossed by a little creek in its middle. The airfield of Dien Bien Phu—in fact, hardly more than a strip of packed dirt—lay 300 meters to the east of the drop zone. An aerial photograph of the valley taken on June 29, 1953, by a reconnaissance bomber of Overseas Reconnaissance Squadron (EROM) 80 shows Dien Bien Phu to have been an idyllic village, with almost all of its 112 houses neatly laid out in the midst of large plots or along the two main roads passing through it. A little river, the Nam Yum, could be seen meandering by the town on its way to the Mekong River. A sort of small commercial street had grown up on the other side of the Nam Yum facing Dien Bien Phu. Thick green shrubbery could be seen wherever there were no rice fields, and the streets containing houses were all tree-lined. The aerial photographs taken by EROM 80 also showed the proximity of the surrounding hill chains, forbidding-looking in the jungle darkness of their tree cover. And it also showed rain, for, as the French meteorological services well knew, the valley of Dien Bien Phu had fifty per cent more rainfall than any other valley in northern Indochina. An average of five *feet* of rain fell on the valley of Dien Bien Phu between the months of March and August of every year, and rain clouds would cover the valley for the better part of those months. Although all this could be read in File 759, rain was not Bigeard's major problem right now, since he was parachuting into Dien Bien Phu during the dry season. Yet it was to contribute to the doom of the fortress six months later.

Drop zone "Simone," located 400 meters southeast of Dien Bien Phu on the other side of the Nam Yum River, spread over part of the rice fields and hillocks that were later to become some of the key positions of the fortress. Drop zone "Octavie" was located farther to the south, well away from the personnel drop zones, in order to avoid (as almost happened by accident) the serious injuries that are likely to occur when paratroopers receive free-falling 100-pound bales of barbed wire or 200-pound bags of rice on their heads. As far as the paratroop commanders were concerned, there was no doubt that they would be able to carry out their mission victoriously. In addition to securing the airfield as rapidly as possible, which was the main aim of their operation, they also hoped to be able to capture the headquarters of Trung-Doan Doc-Lap (Independent Regiment) 148, a crack unit of the Viet-Nam People's Army specializing in mountain warfare and recruited from extremely well trained tribesmen from the area. This was all that was known about the enemy. It turned out to be too little.

At 1800, the battalion commanders called their officers together for a briefing and the troops were placed on airborne alert. However, secrecy was so well maintained that even the subordinate officers were not told the exact target of the next day's mission. But they were told to prepare for cold-weather fighting.

Many areas usually known as "tropical" contain vast mountain complexes that are extremely cold even when covered with jungle. In the Vietnamese and Laotian highlands the coexistence of lush jungle vegetation and winter temperatures of 30°F. is not unknown. The experienced troops of the 6th BPC and the II/1 RCP knew that this meant an operation in Northern Tonkin. At least one officer took no chance on the cold climate: Lt. Allaire of the 6th BPC prepared himself for the next day's jump by wearing his pajamas under his camouflaged combat uniform. He was to fight in them for three days.

At 0400, the 6th BPC left its quarters for Bach-Mai airfield. The premission briefing for the officers took place on the airfield itself at 0600. Bigeard's briefing was simple and direct: The battalion was to jump in one single wave at 1030 over DZ Natasha, reinforced by the 17th Company of Airborne Engineers and two batteries from the 35th Airborne Artillery. First Company was to cover a bridgehead west of the DZ facing the northern part of Dien Bien Phu; 2nd Company was to cover the DZ itself and the village of Muong Ten. Third Company was to support 1st Company and cover the northeastern end of Dien Bien Phu while 4th Company was to shield the northern extremity of the landing area. Battalion Headquarters and Headquarters Company, along with their mortars, were to install themselves at the southernmost corner of the landing area. The mission of the II/1 RCP was easier. It was simply to push northwestward in the direction of the town of Dien Bien Phu and thus insure that no major Communist elements would escape to the south. At the same time it was to give cover to the Headquarters Group of GAP 1 which was to jump with it. Jump-off time for both units was 1035. Special emphasis was placed by the battalion commanders on the greatest possible speed in leaving the aircraft; the company commanders nodded silently. Indeed, even if every paratrooper cleared the plane in five seconds and the lumbering C-47's flew at their minimal speed of 105 miles an hour, it would take two minutes for twenty-five fully equipped paratroopers to leave the airplane; and in two minutes, the airplane would cover more than three miles. In other words, the paratroopers would be spread over an area that was more than twice as long as the drop zone contemplated for them. As will be seen, this was to lead to a great dispersion of the parachuted units. At 0630 the embarkment of the troops into the transport aircraft began—and so did the seemingly interminable period of waiting for the take-off. It was with an incredible sense of relief that the news was finally received by the paratroopers at 0730 that the mission was "on." The flight itself was uneventful; some jokes flew back and forth and in a few planes some incorrigible optimists sang paratroop songs, with the deeper French voices clearly drowning out those of the lilting Vietnamese. For this first attack on Dien Bien Phu (contrary to later mythology, which attributed all the glories of the battle, if not of the whole Indochina war, to "German Foreign Legionnaires") was strictly a French-Vietnamese affair. Bigeard's 6th BPC contained more than 200 Vietnamese out of 651 men who made the jump, and Bréchignac's II/1 RCP reported at the beginning of November a total strength of 827 men, of whom 420 were Vietnamese. These proportions differed slightly from unit to unit but there was no strictly "French" unit in Indochina that did not have a large number of locally raised Vietnamese troops in their midst who acquitted themselves just as well as their French counterparts. The fact that such mixed French-Vietnamese units on the whole fought far better than purely Vietnamese units and also purely European units(who did not have the benefit of the knowledge of local terrain and language of their Vietnamese comrades) is an important lesson of the French-Indochina War that apparently was forgotten in South Viet-Nam ten years later.

By the time the paratroop transport armada reached the valley of Dien Bien Phu at 1030, the sun had burned away the last shreds of fog that covered the countryside. The headquarters aircraft with the three generals aboard was still flying its lazy circles high over the valley. The first flight of Yellow Leader now approached Natasha on a course of 170 with flaps down one quarter. In sixty-five aircraft the jumpmasters stepped to the open doors, twenty-five paratroopers in each craft stood up clumsily in full battle gear, hooked in their static lines to the guide wire which ran along the top of the fuselage and gave the line a few short tugs to verify that it was properly hooked on. Then they turned toward the door of the aircraft in the correct jump position, hands folded above the pack strapped on the chest. As the first wave of aircraft neared the drop zone, the pilots noticed a few tiny human figures running frantically away. The jump buzzers of the first wave began to ring at 1035.

Down in the valley of Dien Bien Phu, Friday, November 20, 1953, had begun like every other day. Dien Bien Phu had been in Communist hands since November 30, 1952, when a Laotian battalion had evacuated the whole valley without a fight and withdrawn into nearby Laotian territory. Most of its 13,000 inhabitants had stayed on. After all, there was very little likelihood that the incoming Viet-Minh were at all interested in confiscating their modest houses, their few buffalo, and their rice fields. If anything, the Viet-Minh were interested in seeing the economic activities of the Dien Bien Phu valley totally undisturbed: The valley grew almost 2,000 tons of rice a year and had long been known as one of the most important opium collection and processing centers in all Indochina. Raw opium of a value of more than 10 million piasters (then about $1 million) was collected there every year, and the Viet-Minh considered opium an important medium for illegal purchase of American weapons and European medical drugs on the black markets of Bangkok and Hong Kong.

The burden of Communist occupation had thus far been light on the T'ai tribal inhabitants of the valley. Independent Regiment 148 had made Dien Bien Phu its main operations base, but the bulk of its men came from other tribal areas farther to the north; it was fairly well received by the inhabitants. The 148th was an old elite regiment of the Viet-Nam People's Army. It had participated during November and December, 1952, in the bitter siege and unsuccessful assault against the French airborne hedgehog of Na-San, 70 miles northwest of Dien Bien Phu; then had taken part in the first Viet-Minh invasion of Laos in the spring of 1953, in which it had formed the central column of the three-pronged attack; and now was part of the Communist screening force that covered northwestern Viet-Nam against a possible French counterattack from Laos. Of the four battalions of the 148th Independent Regiment, Battalions 900, 920, and 930 were away from the Dien Bien Phu valley in an arc of jungle garrisons along the Laos-Viet-Nam frontier. But the regimental headquarters and Battalion 910 were present at Dien Bien Phu and French intelligence knew this. What French intelligence did not know was that Heavy Weapons Company 226 of Battalion 920 had remained at Dien Bien Phu with its mortars and recoilless rifles.

It had been joined there by a heavy weapons company of the 675th Artillery Regiment of the famous "Heavy Division" 351—the Soviet-patterned artillery division of the Viet-Nam People's Army—and by one infantry company of Regiment 48 of the 320th Infantry Division which, two weeks earlier, had been badly mauled by the French during Operation "Seagull." What had attracted Viet-Minh heavy weapons units to

Dien Bien Phu was exactly what had made the valley attractive to the French High Command also: wide open spaces in the midst of a mountain area whose unused airfield (the Viet-Minh, of course, did not possess a single aircraft) could be put to good use as both a firing range and a training ground for the troops. At the same time those troops, far away from any major French zone of operations, could take a full rest and eat their fill of gluey mountain rice while protecting the Viet-Minh's vulnerable rear areas.

And as luck would have it, on the morning of November 20, the bulk of the Communist troops in the valley of Dien Bien Phu were *not* concentrated near their headquarters, which was known to be in the center of town, but were going through their exercises and field problems near the airstrip of Dien Bien Phu, which had been neatly sabotaged against possible use by French aircraft with 1,200 deep holes dug all over its terrain. In fact, the bulk of the Communist mortars and machine guns were deployed in firing positions all over drop zone Natasha. The roving French twin-engine plane, which could be heard above the clouds and seen here and there when the cloud cover lifted, did not disturb the Communist soldiers to any great extent; if anything, it only added a note of realism to their exercise. Because the plane was alone, it was obviously a photo-reconnaissance aircraft, even if it did act a bit strange. The tribesmen and village people also went about their usual business, harvesting the late mountain rice with their short straight sickles and driving their buffalo to pasture. Two of them, Lo Van Don and his wife Lo Thi Un, from the village of Ban Bom La, two miles south of Dien Bien Phu, suddenly looked up from their work in the rice field along Dien Bien Phu's southern emergency airstrip when they heard the drone of numerous planes over their heads.

> I remember that morning only too well [Lo Van Don was to say to a foreign visitor one year later]. The morning mist had just cleared away when the planes came. All of a sudden they seemed to be everywhere at once, dropping clouds of white specks that looked like cotton seeds. But soon they opened up and we saw that soldiers were hanging from them. They seemed to cover the whole valley and within a few minutes they were on the ground, forming into groups . . .[5]

Lo Van Don and his wife had just witnessed the arrival of the first wave of Bréchignac's II/1 RCP. Farther to the north, however, where the men of Maj. Bigeard's 6th BPC were landing on Natasha, they were not received by surprised peasants but by Communist regulars who knew that they were about to face the best the French had to offer. They opened fire on the paratroopers as they were still dangling helplessly from their parachute shrouds. The doctor of the battalion, Captain André, whose first combat jump this was, died from a bullet that hit him squarely in the forehead. Another paratrooper, whose main parachute had failed to open and whose reserve chute had become entangled in the folds of the main parachute, bored into the ground with a sickening thud. Lt. Allaire, who commanded the 81-mm. mortar battery of the battalion, landed all by himself in the middle of the creek that crossed the DZ and by sheer luck, upon climbing out of the creek dripping wet, found the parachuted equipment pack which contained one of his mortars. Other groups were not as lucky; the whole 4th Company had been dropped much too far to the north of the DZ and had landed in thick brush in which it had a difficult time collecting itself, let alone helping the rest of the battalion. A part of 2nd Company suffered the same fate. The rest of the battalion, the Airborne Engineers and the Airborne Artillery detachment under Major Jean Millot, landed more or less within the general area of the drop zone but were immediately under small arms and mortar fire.

But as in almost all major airborne operations, the very chaos and dispersion of the drop pattern confused the enemy and prevented the immediate destruction of the dropped units. There was at first no clearly distinguishable center of effort upon which the enemy could concentrate its fire and troops. Most of the paratroopers of the 6th BPC now began to follow the old iron law of paratroop assembly: Walk "downward" against the general direction of the parachute drop and you will find the bulk of your comrades. A further complication was that both the French and the Viet-Minh were wearing the French paratroop camouflage uniform except for the flat woven palm-leaf helmet worn by Viet-Minh soldiers.

By 1040 part of 1st Company was deployed around Maj. Bigeard at the southern end of Natasha. By 1000, two more platoons of that company had regrouped and now faced westward toward the village of Muong Ten. That was the moment when Lt. Allaire arrived at Maj. Bigeard's command post.

"Is your piece ready, Allaire?" said Bigeard.

"Piece ready, boss!"

"All right, fire a series of ten rounds onto the edge of the village."

Allaire's reply that he had a mortar but had been unable to find shells for its was lost in the din of the battle. After a few minutes of searching among the cargo parachutes that were still raining down on the drop zone, he finally found three shells which he hoarded frugally for the next emergency.

The problem of unit identification was rendered even more difficult by the last-minute change in the color of the smoke signals assigned to each company and by the fact that since the last aerial photographs of Natasha had been taken, a senior T'ai chieftain had been buried in the middle of the drop zone and his tomb, clearly identified by several flagpoles festooned with tribal flags, was now being mistaken for a rallying point by errant paratroopers. This relative concentration of French troops at one particular point did not remain undetected by the Viet-Minh, whose mortars at 1130 unleashed a heavy barrage into the center of the drop zone. By that time, however, Bigeard had finally succeeded in establishing radio contact with all his companies but not with the command aircraft still circling above the valley. Slowly the battlefield began to take shape: 3rd Company had now reinforced 1st Company, which was still pinned down by heavy enemy fire; 2nd Company was holding its own to the west; 4th Company, in the process of assembling, was now progressing northward.

Bigeard's command post (CP) still was little more than a small hollow alongside a footpath across a rice paddy. There Maj. Bigeard himself, his personal code name "Bruno" shouted clearly over the radio waves, had taken command of the battle thanks to what an observer called "a whole pile of U. S. Army ANPRC-10 radio sets." His own command set's aerial had been shot to pieces by enemy fire, but at 1215 a tiny Morane-500 French Army observation aircraft appeared over the battlefield and with its radio equipment acted as a relay between the paratroopers on the ground and the outside world. This proved exceedingly fortunate since the mortars of the battalion were still without ammunition and the 35th Airborne Artillery was never to find its pieces until after the battle was ended. It was in this manner that air strikes against Dien Bien Phu were called for. Some B-26's had been standing by since the beginning of the air drop, awaiting the formation of a fixed line that would permit them to intervene without the risk of hitting their own men. The intervention now came with what the paratroopers would later call "surgical precision." A pall of black smoke began to rise along the east-west axis of the small village, and the intensity of enemy fire began to slacken considerably. Still, an attempt by 1st Company at 1530 to encircle Dien Bien Phu from the north failed when the Company was again pinned down under heavy fire from automatic weapons. Bigeard once more called for an air

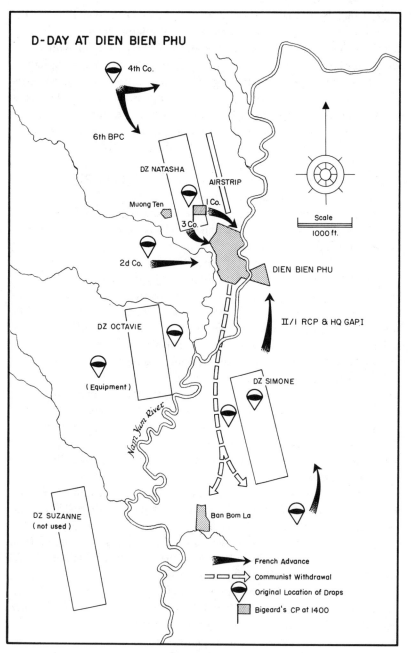

D-DAY AT DIEN BIEN PHU

4th Co.

6th BPC

DZ NATASHA

AIRSTRIP

Muong Ten

1 Co.

3 Co.

2d Co.

DIEN BIEN PHU

Scale

1000 ft.

DZ OCTAVIE

II/I RCP & HQ GAPI

(Equipment)

DZ SIMONE

Nam Yum River

DZ SUZANNE
(not used)

Ban Bom La

French Advance

Communist Withdrawal

Original Location of Drops

Bigeard's CP at 1400

strike, which now destroyed the whole center of Dien Bien Phu. At the same time his own mortars, which had finally found sufficient amounts of ammunition, began to plaster the enemy's likely route of withdrawal toward the south. Now, 3rd Company penetrated into the eastern half of Dien Bien Phu, while the left wing of 1st Company, in savage house-to-house fighting, moved along the town's main road toward the headquarters of the Viet-Minh 148th Independent Regiment, where the headquarters company of the 910th Battalion made a last-ditch stand in order to cover the retreat of the regimental staff. In this it was entirely successful.

In its final effort, 6th BPC was supported by the 1st BPC of Major Jean Souquet, whose troops had been ready in Hanoi since 0630. With a total of 911 men (of whom 413 were Vietnamese), the 1st BPC was probably one of the largest airborne battalions in Indochina. The battalion got ready to embark at 1330 in thirty C-47 transport aircraft, which carried 722 paratroopers[6] and 28 separate equipment bags. Its jump at 1500 on DZ Natasha, now fully held by the men of the 6th BPC, was largely uneventful, although one of the paratroopers of the 1st's 3rd Company was faced, upon landing, by a Viet-Minh soldier whom he killed, and four other paratroopers were wounded by wild shots while still in the air. Eleven men failed to make the jump on orders of the jumpmasters because of last-minute equipment difficulties.

Bréchignac's II/1 RCP had run into a difficulty which is always the bane of a massive paratroop assault: It had been largely misdropped and was spread over too wide an area. In addition, its mission of protecting the Airborne Battle Group Headquarters, which had jumped with it, slowed down its efforts to come to the aid of the other two battalions which were mopping up the enemy in and around Dien Bien Phu. Poor radio communications with the other units added to its lack of effectiveness. The result was that the heavily overgrown terrain along the Nam Yum River south of Dien Bien Phu was never successfully sealed off and the bulk of the Communist forces escaped in that direction. By nightfall, however, the II/1 RCP had closed in on the southeastern edge of Dien Bien Phu and had made its link-up with the other two battalions. Operation "Castor" had fulfilled its initial objective.

On the whole, the French High Command had every reason to be satisfied. Airborne Battle Group No. 1 had landed 1827 paratroops on a defended position 220 miles behind enemy lines, at the price of only 11 dead and 52 wounded, and had secured the position in less than six hours of fighting. The equipment drops on DZ Octavie already had begun in the afternoon of November 20. Command control, after an initial period of confusion that seems to be the normal accompaniment of air drops, was satisfactory. An Air Force liaison team, commanded by Captain Pierre Lorillon, had jumped with the 6th BPC and had set up shop near Bigeard's command post at the southern edge of Natasha. At 1602, the first two American-built H19-B helicopters hedgehopped in from nearby Lai-Chau bringing in two VHF and one high-frequency transmitter for the forward air controllers. This gave them direct communication with the transport aircraft, the B-26's of Bombardment Group 1/25 "Tunisie," and the SCR-300 radio sets of the paratroop battalions. On their return trip, the helicopters took with them the most seriously wounded.

French equipment losses had been minimal and were mostly due to the dispersion of the equipment parachutes. The missing mortars and recoilless rifles were found the following morning, but thirteen radio sets had been smashed on landing, which accounted in part for the difficulties in communications among the various units. On the Viet-Minh side, ninety dead in full uniform were found on the battlefield; but faithful to their well-established habit of hiding their losses even in the thickest of fighting, the Communists had carried away almost all of their wounded with the exception of four who were taken alive by the French. Subsequent discovery of graves hurriedly dug at the edge of the valley indicated that Communist losses might have been greater. The French also found only one automatic rifle and ten submachine guns, an indication of the discipline of the enemy troops. On the other hand they captured in one neat pile the hundred field packs of Company 226 and most of the document files of Regiment 148, abandoned in its headquarters inside Dien Bien Phu.[7] As night fell, the three battalions installed themselves in a tight ring around Dien Bien Phu. Bigeard himself had established his command post inside the village. The 1st BPC, now reinforced by two batteries of airborne artillery[8] and a company of 120-mm. heavy mortars, protected Natasha. An airborne surgical team had set up shop there, and Father Chevalier was comforting the wounded and administering the last rites to the dying and dead. Thus ended the first day of the Battle of Dien Bien Phu.

On November 21, 1953, Airborne Battle Group No. 2 and the Command Headquarters for the whole Dien Bien Phu operations under Gen. Gilles were parachuted into the valley. The forty-nine-year-old Gilles had carefully stashed his glass eye in the breast pocket of his jump suit and made an uneventful landing in the stubble of a harvested rice field. The commander of GAP 2, Lieutenant Colonel Pierre Langlais, who jumped at 0800 with the 1st BEP (Foreign Legion Paratroop Battalion), badly injured his left ankle on landing and had to be evacuated next day to Hanoi by airplane, cursing his bad luck; after all, he was going to miss all the fun of the fight for Dien Bien Phu.[9] The 1st BEP had only four other, non-fatal jump casualties out of a total of 653 paratroopers (including 336 Vietnamese) who made the jump. Having folded his parachute neatly, according to regulations, Gen. Gilles walked slowly over to the temporary command post of his friend, Maj. Bigeard. On the way, he greeted two Army photographers, André Lebon and Daniel Camus, who had jumped into Dien Bien Phu the day before with the II/1 RCP. Lebon was later to lose one of his legs at Dien Bien Phu. Camus was to march in May, 1954, on the murderous trek to the Communist prison camps. With the arrival at Dien Bien Phu of Gilles and his command group, Operation "Castor" was now commanded from Dien Bien Phu itself.[10]

Another interesting feature of this second day at Dien Bien Phu was the beginning of the heavy equipment drops at DZ "Octavie," although sometimes not precisely in the way they were planned. Two seven-ton bulldozers were to be parachuted from C-119 "Flying Boxcars." It was a magnificent sight as the small extracting parachute appeared between the tail booms of the first aircraft, followed by the main parachute, with its close to 9,000 square feet of canopy, and the palette carrying the bulldozer. For some unknown reason, the first bulldozer worked its way free from the parachute and nose-dived with an earth-shattering crash into an open rice field into which it buried itself under ten feet of earth. The other bulldozer arrived in a more conventional way and was promptly put to use filling in the holes of Dien Bien Phu's main airstrip.

Civilian air crews now began to fly the Dien Bien Phu run. With the French Air Force notoriously short of planes and personnel, it had become habitual in Indochina for civilian airlines to provide supplementary planes and crews even in combat zones on a temporary basis, and "Castor" was to be no exception. At 0600 of November 21, the crews had been briefed at the headquarters of Transport Group 1/64 "Béarn" at Hanoi's Gia-Lam Airport. The civilian air crews were composed of veteran bush pilots who had accumulated tens of thousands of flying hours in Indochina's incredible working conditions: small packed-mud airfields at the bottom of deep valleys, no navigational aids, few and inaccurate weather reports, and hit-or-miss maintenance. Since the flights to Dien Bien Phu required tight-formation flying, a type of work to which the civilian pilots were hardly accustomed, the briefing was particularly thorough.

Having explained the operation itself, the French Air Force colonel turned to the pilots and said:

"And now I would like to talk to your navigators, gentlemen."

There was a collective horselaugh. In Indochina the civilian pilots did their own navigating.[11]

By the time the 8th BPC (Parachute Assault Battalion) had its 656th man and 19 cargo parachutes dropped over the valley at 1305, the air space above it had become a veritable carousel of slowly circling aircraft: four-engine *Privateers* of French Navy Squadron 28.F, whose long range equipped them particularly well for the bombardment of Communist approach routes to the valley; faster and smaller B-26's and *Bearcats* which were helping the paratroopers push through the retreating elements of Regiment 148; and, finally, lumbering transport aircraft which were to disgorge 190 tons of air-dropped freight during those first two days. The 8th BPC likewise had five light jump casualties and immediately left from DZ "Natasha" to participate in the rebuilding of the airfield. On their way there, the men passed a small row of neat white crosses planted at the head of freshly dug graves. Behind them stood a newly erected flagpole for the French tricolor. Earlier that morning, the casualties of the day before had been buried. The parachutes that had borne them into the valley had served as their shrouds.

On Sunday morning, November 22, the last of the paratroop battalions that were to make up the initial garrison of the valley were parachuted in, along with Colonel Dominique Bastiani, who was to take command of the valley and replace Gen. Gilles. On the same "stick" with the command group of the 5th BPVN (Vietnamese Paratroop Battalion), which also contained Bastiani and his staff, was Mlle. Brigitte Friang. Brigitte was well known in Indochina since she was the only woman reporter in the whole command who held a military parachutist's diploma and a record of five combat jumps, including that of the 6th BPC's desperate rear-guard action in November, 1952, at Tu-Lê.[12]

The hustle and bustle inside Dien Bien Phu was taking on a semblance of order. General Gilles, equipped with a paratroop scooter, could be seen traveling from his own headquarters to the various battalion command posts while the lesser-ranking officers made do with bicycles. A few of the more enterprising junior officers had simply taken to the T'ai mountain ponies. Quite a few were found tethered under T'ai peasant houses, which are all built on stilts. Intensive spade work had made part of the airfield ready to receive small aircraft and the combat engineers began to lay long rows of prefabricated PSP's (pierced steel plates) to form what was eventually to become a steel runway 3,500 feet long. Throughout the valley, the air smelled of burning wood as the troops began to clear the approaches to the airfield and the hills and plains which later were to become part of the various strong points. There was now a total of 4,560 troops in the valley. As for the T'ai inhabitants, quite a few of them had fled in fright into the nearby mountains from where they observed the strange goings-on in their villages. But since they had had a long association with the French, they now began timidly to return to their homes. Soon a brisk trade began with soldiers and villagers exchanging canned rations for fresh fowl and vegetables, while small T'ai children, with uninhibited curiosity, formed groups around paratroopers going about their pursuits. The radio operators, with their squawking sets, proved the main attraction.

The first outside visitor to arrive at Dien Bien Phu was the commander of the northern theater, General René Cogny. He emerged early on Sunday afternoon from a small Canadian-built *Beaver* liaison aircraft otherwise loaded with bicycles. A blue-eyed giant of a man, Cogny was France's youngest major general. A heavy knotted cane helped him to cope with a severe limp—a reminder of the general's treatment at the hand of the Gestapo when he led a Resistance group against the Nazis during World War II. This earned him Gestapo torture and a two-year stretch in the infamous death camps of Buchenwald and Dora, from which he was liberated only after VE-day. Much will be said later about Cogny's role in the planning of the Battle of Dien Bien Phu and his overall command of it. As he landed at Dien Bien Phu, he was already aware of the fact that many senior officers of his command, notably Bastiani and Gilles, had been opposed to the idea of establishing another airhead behind Communist lines. A few months earlier, on August 12, Na-San, an airhead far closer to Hanoi than Dien Bien Phu, had finally been evacuated because it had tied down more troops and more air transport than it was worth. At that time, everyone had agreed that sealed-off "hedgehog" positions were hardly worth the cost of maintaining them. But, as will be seen, Dien Bien Phu was picked *precisely* because the valley (the largest in all of Indochina's northern mountain areas) was far too large to become a hedgehog position in which the French troops could be sealed off. Here, there was space for maneuvering. Tanks could be employed if they could be brought in by air, as indeed they were, later. General Gilles, particularly, who had personally conducted the difficult defense of Na-San for six long months and had earned his general's stars there (in the French Army, brigadier generals wear two stars), did not want to go through the same sort of experience again.

"I'll be pretty happy," he was to say privately to Cogny that afternoon in the Catalan-accented French that was spoken in his home district in the Pyrenees, "when you will have found a successor for me here. At Na-San I spent six months of my life like a rat. Make use of me somewhere where I am going to be in fresh air."

"It's a promise," said Cogny. "It's just a matter of days."[13]

While Cogny and Gilles were talking, the first flight of three Morane-500 observation aircraft of the 21st GAOA (Aerial Artillery Observation Group), nicknamed *Crickets* because of their grass-hopping ability and their high landing-gear struts, had also landed on the airstrip. Gradually reinforced to a total of six aircraft, they were to become the eyes of the fortress.

In the meantime another facet of the battle of Dien Bien Phu was taking place about sixty miles to the north in the airhead of Lai Chau. Lai Chau had been the capital of the whole T'ai Federation and the seat of the federal president, Deo Van Long. Like Dien Bien Phu, Lai Chau had been cut off from the outside world for more than two years. Its tiny airstrip, bounded on one end by a river and on the other by the first houses of the small town, was far more exposed than the airstrip of Dien Bien Phu. In fact the pilots used to say that Lai Chau was the only airport in the world where flying aircraft could be shot down by antiaircraft machine guns firing *down* on them. Gun positions hidden in the high hills commanded this last toehold of French territory inside the Communist zone. Late in 1953 it became obvious that even a modest effort on the part of the Viet-Minh forces could result in military disaster at Lai Chau, a military setback that could be complicated by the political consequences of losing the last government seat in the mountain areas. It was this political consideration which had weighed heavily in the French decision to reoccupy another stronghold in the T'ai tribal zone. On November 4, 1953, it was decided to evacuate Lai Chau and to transfer the government of the T'ai Federation to the new airhead at Dien Bien Phu. The French commander at Lai Chau, Lt. Col. Trancart, was informed of the planned evacuation of Lai Chau (dubbed Operation "Pollux")[14] on November 13. Trancart immediately ordered the withdrawal to Dien Bien Phu of the 1st T'ai Partisan Mobile Group (GMPT 1), led by the Eurasian son-in-law of Deo Van Long, Capt. Bordier. The withdrawal of the 700 men through terrain which they knew well did not at first present any special problems. However, roving units of Regiment No. 148 finally caught up with them when they were two days' march away from

Dien Bien Phu, and the last leg of their march became a continuous battle against well-laid Communist ambushes. These had to be broken up with mortar fire and continuous counterattacks. General Gilles ordered Bréchignac's II/1 RCP to head north on November 23 at 0630 until it had linked up with the T'ai Partisans. Reporter Brigitte Friang went northward with the paratroops. They met GMPT 1 at the village of Ban Na Ten, seven kilometers north of Dien Bien Phu, without encountering the slightest enemy opposition. Most of the French and the T'ai officers were mounted on sturdy local ponies. The tribesmen themselves were dressed in French army fatigues and wore slouch hats. They seemed hardly the worse for wear after their week-long trek and almost continuous fire fights. As the T'ai entered the valley, their officers made them assume a sort of military order and the unit flags were unfurled. The GMPT 1 carried the French flag and the flag of the T'ai Federation: three vertical stripes of blue, white, and blue with a sixteen-pointed red star (representing the sixteen *Chau*, or feudal baronies, of the T'ai Federation) in the center of the white field. No Vietnamese flag was in sight. Bréchignac's paratroops presented arms as the tribesmen filed by them.

In Paris, the news of Operation "Castor" came after almost all Friday newspapers had already been "put to bed." But on Saturday, November 21, most papers carried banner headlines whose uniformly overstated figures indicated that French official sources had deliberately provided the press with exaggerated statistics. A typical headline, that of *Paris-Presse* read:

> Lightning-like Operation in Tonking—Parachuted from 150 Dakotas, Thousands of French-Vietnamese Paratroopers Conquer Dien Bien Phu . . . "This is not a raid. We've taken the place and we shall stay there," declares General Cogny.

Aside from the Communist press, to which the attack on Dien Bien Phu was merely another act of "colonialist aggression," only the reliable *Le Monde* was a great deal less sanguine about the operation. Eschewing the black headlines, it gave a restrained account of the operations (including the same figures that had been fed to all the other papers) but added the following cautionary note:

> It is not certain, however [that the enemy], will not soon react. The whole area of Dien Bien Phu, and the whole T'ai country in general, is a major opium-producing area, from which the Viet-Minh draws many of its resources and particularly the means of paying the deliveries in matériel, arms and ammunition from Com-

munist China. Ho Chi Minh also uses clandestine sales of opium in
all of Indochina to finance his intelligence services and his propaganda and to pay his troops.[15]

This view of the situation at Dien Bien Phu proved to be entirely correct. In itself, as a rich valley providing a ready access route to Laos,
Dien Bien Phu was a desirable piece of real estate. When French planning
put into that valley numerous French troops operating with relatively
little artillery and armor and at the extreme range of their combat aircraft, the Communist high command began to find the valley of Dien
Bien Phu most attractive.

11

Base Aéro-Terrestre

"Dien Bien Phu" is not really a place name. It actually designates a T'ai village whose true name is Muong Thanh, but all of the villages in the valley are not necessarily T'ai. Those located high up on the slopes are inhabited by dour-looking Meo tribesmen. It is they who specialize in the growing of opium poppies; the T'ai, who control the valleys, are mostly the middlemen who market it. Until a hundred years ago, the valley had been largely isolated from the outside world but gained some importance as a roadway into the Mekong basin during the period when Chinese Ho pirates began to invade northern Laos in the 1870's. When the Ho pirates nearly overran all of northern Laos in 1887, the enterprising French consul there, Auguste Pavie, asked for the help of French troops in Tonking to pacify the northern approaches of both Laos and Viet-Nam. On April 7, 1889, Pavie personally signed a protectorate agreement with the powerful leader of the Ho, Deo Van Tri, at Muong Thanh. Since the village was located at the limit of the area controlled by the Vietnamese administration, it came to be known in Vietnamese as the "Seat of the Border County Prefecture," which in Vietnamese is translated as Dien Bien Phu.

For the next fifty years, the people of the valley led uneventful lives. The valley was eventually connected with the outside world on the Vietnamese side by Provincial Road 41, which was accessible to sturdy automobiles during the dry season. In fact, its motorable part ended at Dien Bien Phu. A rough track, known as *Piste Pavie* (Pavie Track), connected Dien Bien Phu with the seat of the T'ai tribal territory at Lai Chau. The sum total of the French colonial presence in the valley was a junior civilian resident administrator whose key job was to control the size of the opium shipments, since the sale of opium in formerly French Indochina was a state monopoly. There was also a small detachment of the locally recruited *Garde Indochinoise* in Lai Chau. When aviation came to Indochina in the late 1920's, the French government began to clear small airstrips in hundreds of places throughout the jungles of the country, inasmuch as the fragility of the airplanes of the time required that they make frequent emergency landings. The advent of World War II did not change the Shangri-La pace of Dien Bien Phu. The valley's very remoteness made it an asset to the Allied cause, since French Air Force planes (theoretically under Vichy French and Japanese control but in fact working covertly for the Allies) were able to use the Dien Bien Phu airstrip to receive Free French envoys and officers from Calcutta. On two occasions French aircraft used Dien Bien Phu to smuggle out American flyers who had been compelled to bail out from their crippled planes over Japanese-controlled areas of Indochina.

When the Japanese attacked the remaining French forces in Indochina on March 9, 1945, Dien Bien Phu became, for almost two months, the headquarters of last-ditch French resistance against Japanese aggression. Small aircraft from the U. S. 14th Air Force of General Claire L. Chennault landed at Dien Bien Phu with supplies for the French, and two obsolete French Potez-25 fighter planes, using the airstrip as a temporary base of operations against the advancing Japanese, flew 150 hours in forty days before they had to withdraw to Free China.[1]

Although the Japanese occupied Dien Bien Phu for less than two months, they were not remembered with fondness. It was later said that the Japanese had great plans for the Dien Bien Phu airstrip, including making it a major strategic air base for further operations against the key American air bases in nearby Yunnan. In any case, the Japanese never had time to carry out their grandiose schemes and limited their activities at Dien Bien Phu to lengthening the existing grass strip with the help of local unpaid forced labor. When the Japanese departed soon after VJ-day, they were replaced by Chinese Nationalist forces, whose job it was, according to decisions reached in July, 1945, at Potsdam, to occupy all of Indochina down to the sixteenth parallel and to intern the Japanese troops there. As in other places in Indochina, the Chinese proceeded to rob the countryside bare and are even less fondly remembered than the Japanese. Returning French units found Chinese Nationalist forces reluctant to give up the good life they were leading. A mixed column of French paratroopers and T'ai partisans stood eyeball to eyeball with the Chinese forces in Dien Bien Phu for a few unpleasant days in the spring of 1946 until the latter finally decided to obey the orders of their own government and withdraw to China.

The people of Dien Bien Phu were ready to return to their leisurely way of life, but times had changed. Deo Van Long, the successor of Deo Van Tri to the chieftaincy of the T'ai Federation, decided to remove Lo Van Hac, the able district chief of Dien Bien Phu, and to give his job to one of his own sons. In anger, Lo Van Hac joined the Viet-Minh guerrillas who had begun to operate in the mountain areas. Deo Van Long, in return, imprisoned Lo's wife. The fact that Deo Van Long was a White T'ai and Lo Van Hac was a Black T'ai exacerbated the quarrel. Further, the presence of pro-Communist Viet-Minh was to have serious effects later on.[2]

With the onslaught of Communist regular forces on the highlands as of October 14, 1952, matters changed. The Viet-Minh 308th, 312th, and 316th divisions, reinforced by Independent Regiment No. 148, crossed the Red River on a broad front and overran the first line of French defensive positions in less than a week. Only temporarily slowed down by the deliberate sacrifice of French paratroops, the Viet-Minh reached the French main line of resistance along Provincial Road 41. There, French resistance centered on the airstrip of Na-San. Thanks to a continuous stream of airlifted troops and artillery, Na-San was hastily transformed into what the French called a *Base Aéro-Terrestre*—an "air-land base"— or, in American military parlance, an "airhead." In the case of Na-San, the defenses around the airstrip comprised two complete rings of strongpoints, whose automatic weapons were mutually supporting; these, in turn, were supported by the howitzers of the airhead's artillery. A motley garrison, hurriedly scraped together by French Commander-in-Chief General Raoul Salan, consisted of paratroop remnants, Moroccans, Vietnamese, Foreign Legionnaires, and two battalions of T'ai mountaineer riflemen. The Communist commander, General Vo Nguyen Giap, no doubt inspired by the then current success of "human wave" attacks in Korea, concentrated both the 308th and 312th divisions on Na-San in order to overrun that strongpoint before the French had a chance to consolidate their position. Although the outer strongpoint line was twice breached, the French garrison beat back the attacks successfully. Na-San held and became the shining symbol of French ability to withstand a massive Communist assault on an organized position.[3] The victory at Na-San, unfortunately, also provided the theoretical underpinning for a whole new approach to the fighting in Indochina; an approach that was to become the official military strategy of Salan's successor, General Henri Navarre.

While Giap laid siege to Na-San, a part of his forces bypassed the

French "hedgehog" and plunged deeper into the T'ai territory, sweeping aside the light screen of small outposts which stood between them and the border of Laos. The French high command suddenly became aware of the new danger and hurriedly marched a Laotian light infantry battalion from San Neua to Dien Bien Phu. But is was obviously no match for all of the Viet-Minh's 316th Division plus the 148th Independent Regiment. Dien Bien Phu was evacuated without a fight on November 30, 1952. The retreating French-Laotian troops destroyed a small bridge across the Nam Yum River. For the first time, the Viet-Minh's red flag with a five-pointed gold star in the center flew over the yellow stucco building of what had been the residence of the French administrator. It was not to be the last time.

In the grim picture of the situation in northwestern Viet-Nam at the end of 1952, the loss of Dien Bien Phu was considered a minor incident, The French briefing officer of the Northern Command in Hanoi explained it to assembled reporters:

> Dien Bien Phu is not a strategic sector. At times in the past, rebel bands have penetrated it but have let it go again. Their occupation of this hole-in-the-ground isn't yet the invasion of Laos.[4]

While technically his statement was true, since the jungle-going Viet-Minh forces were quite capable of invading Laos through places other than a convenient river valley (as indeed they did later), the journalists and other observers knew that the loss of the whole highland area, save for the airhead of Na-San and the province of Lai Chau, constituted a severe French defeat. The occupation of Dien Bien Phu in particular gave the Viet-Minh an open door into northern Laos. General Salan, despite what his press officer said, was perfectly aware of the importance of the valley of Dien Bien Phu. In a top-secret directive (No. 40) issued exactly one month after the occupation of the valley by the Communists, he ordered a counterattack for January 10, 1953. In his directive, Salan stated:

> The reoccupation of Dien Bien Phu must constitute in the forthcoming period the first step for the regaining of control of the T'ai country and for the elimination of the Viet-Minh from the area west of the Black River.[5]

Directive 40 was passed down from the high command for execution by the northern commander, General René Cogny. His staff in turn, on January 7, 1953, issued to participating commanders Note No. 14 detailing certain aspects of Directive 40. In Note 14, the aims of the new counteroffensive directed at Dien Bien Phu were somewhat more limited: they were to "(a) Deprive the rebels of a base and communications hub; and (b) Permit the mopping-up of the province."

Because of the French Army's urgent commitments in the Red River Delta, where the situation had badly deteriorated, and the diversion of large French forces to Na-San and Operation "Lorraine,"[6] Salan never was able to assemble the troops necessary to implement the reconquest of Dien Bien Phu. The retrieval of the whole T'ai territory, between the Black and Red rivers, was out of the question. Nevertheless, the idea of Dien Bien Phu as a major strategic base in the North Vietnamese highlands, covering Laos and at the same time threatening the Viet-Minh's rear areas, began to take hold. Salan was soon to return to France after a tour of duty of almost four years in Indochina. He had served as deputy to the late Marshal Jean de Lattre de Tassigny and, after de Lattre's death from cancer in January, 1952, became commander-in-chief in his own right. Before Salan left Indochina, he addressed two *aide-mémoires* to his civilian superior in Paris, the minister in charge of relations with the Associated States, in which he emphasized Dien Bien Phu's importance.

On February 28, 1953, Salan underlined the possibility of a defense of the highlands from strongpoints such as Na-San, Lai Chau, and "eventually Dien Bien Phu"; while in his communication of May 25, 1953 (after his successor had already arrived in Indochina, but three days before Navarre took effective command) Salan underlined the usefulness of a reconquest of Dien Bien Phu as a stepping stone to the relief of the garrison of encircled Na-San. There can therefore be no doubt that the importance of Dien Bien Phu had become ingrained in French military thinking. Since Gen. Salan is serving a life sentence for attempting mutiny in Algeria in April, 1961, it has been impossible to determine whether, upon his return to France in June, 1953, he continued to advocate a strategy based on the creation of more air-supplied hedgehogs. In view of what came later, it is certain that Salan's Directive 40 and his efforts to implement it must have made it easy for his successor to follow in his footsteps.

Lieutenant General Henri Navarre, who took command of the destinies of Indochina on May 28, 1953, and who, rightly or wrongly, will be remembered in history as the man who "lost" the battle of Dien Bien Phu, is a complicated man. An article published in a French Army magazine in Indochina while Navarre was commander-in-chief contains the following revealing passages:

The Commander-in-Chief of the French Union Forces advanced toward the small group of officers standing at attention who had come to greet him and coldly shook the hands of two or three of them. . . . General Navarre is the happy owner of a Persian cat . . . and hides from no one the fact that he adores cats "because they prefer to be alone and because they have an independent way of thinking." And Navarre, who is extremely sensitive, belongs to the category of people who are not afraid to be alone, who work alone and find their strength within themselves. . . .

His own subordinates find him to be "a good boss" because he never comes to bother them while they are executing an order: "Navarre is master of his nerves; Navarre won't stand for a job sloppily done; and Navarre never admits extenuating circumstances." . . .

It is said that he has kept, from the years he spent in intelligence, the respect for secrecy and a taste for mystery.[7]

Major General René Cogny, his subordinate commander in North Viet-Nam at the time of the battle of Dien Bien Phu, was to say of him ten years later:

That "air-conditioned" General froze me. . . . As for his way of thinking, it disconcerted me like an electronic computer which I do not succeed in feeding the necessary basic data, and which, unperturbed, bases its reasoning on I-don't-know-what. . . .

Perhaps I am better inspired in remembering the [professional] deformation of the man who served in intelligence and whose reasoning finally becomes crooked because he must deal with so many crooked people. . . .[8]

And the French author Jules Roy, whose views of Navarre were to involve him in a public exchange of letters with the general, described him as "physically and morally a feline" and "simultaneously cordial and distant, debonair and icy." *Time* magazine, which devoted a cover story to Navarre on September 28, 1953, provided American readers with the kind of quotable gems about him which are the trade-mark of that publication when it decides to give a favorable build-up to a "good guy":

There is an 18th-Century fragrance about him. He is a portrait on a cameo from the time of Louis XV. One almost expects ruffles and the powdered wig . . . He is the hardest general I know— clever and ruthless. He believes in nothing but the army.

Time also found an anonymous official in Washington willing to provide Navarre with an American accolade:

> In our opinion, Navarre is a man of courage, energy and imagination. He knows his business and has military and political guts of a high order . . . [he] is leading a new team which looks pretty good to us.

And *Time* ended its profile of the new commander with another quotation:

> "A year ago none of us could see victory. There wasn't a prayer. Now we can see it clearly—like light at the end of a tunnel."

But Navarre's character came through perhaps more clearly, in a friendly press interview that he gave almost ten years after the battle of Dien Bien Phu, in response to the reporter's passing allusion to the alleged fact that after the battle of Dien Bien Phu a group of French officers in Indochina had sent him a beautifully lacquered box with a loaded pistol inside—a clear reference to the tradition that a senior commander should not survive a major defeat. Navarre's remarks were as follows:

> I would not have done it in any case. Aside from any other consideration, to commit suicide would have meant absolving everybody else from any responsibility by recognizing myself guilty. *I have a very strong feeling of responsibility for Dien Bien Phu. I have no feeling of guilt.*[9]

Contrary to public mythology, Navarre's career was not entirely spent at desk jobs in various rear headquarters. As a nineteen-year-old cadet he had fought on the Western front against Germany from May, 1917, onward. Immediately after the war he went to Syria where he spent two years in anti-guerrilla fighting against Arab rebels. After a stay with French occupation forces in Germany, and studies at the French War College, Navarre spent four years, from 1930 to 1934, in the "pacification" campaigns in Morocco. He began to serve with French Army Intelligence in 1937, and during the fateful years of 1938-40 was the head of its German section. During the German occupation of France, Navarre served in the intelligence branch of the French underground; but, in November, 1944, after France was liberated, he led an armored regiment, the 5th Spahi, into Germany. After a regional command in Algeria and a staff position in Germany, Navarre became commander of the 5th French Armored Division in Germany. He was later appointed chief of staff to the commander of NATO's

Central European land forces. When he was hand-picked for his new post by French Prime Minister René Mayer at the recommendation of Field Marshal Juin (France's then highest-ranking officer) Navarre was, by all standards of military judgment, an officer who was exceptionally well qualified for the position. While without field experience in Indochina, he was nonetheless experienced in counter-guerrilla operations. The absence of prejudice toward operations in Indochina was considered, in fact, an asset. Moreover, his recent position in a high-ranking NATO command enabled him to see the Indochina War in the over-all scheme of things. His experience must also have given him respect for the value of reliable intelligence.

While Salan's departure from Indochina also brought about departures at other levels, it cannot be assumed that Navarre had to work with an entirely inexperienced assemblage of subordinate commanders. In any case, had he desired it, he could have demanded that Salan's subordinates stay on, at least temporarily. On the contrary, Navarre seemed quite happy to be able to put men of his own choice into key posts. For example, he in no way opposed the departure from Indochina of the commander of the key northern region, Major General Francois Gonzalez de Linarès, and his replacement by a considerably younger French brigadier general who, until then, had commanded the *2nd Division de Marche du Tonkin* (2nd DMT) and who, to all appearances, was a study in physical and psychological contrasts to Navarre: Cogny, then forty-eight and a muscular six feet four inches tall, was probably the only French general who was both a graduate of France's most prestigious engineering school, École Polytechnique, and holder of a diploma in political science and a doctorate in jurisprudence; the latter two acquired on a "bootleg" basis when the army had sent him on special duty to acquire additional military engineering training while he personally preferred political science and law. Well liked by his troops and irresistible to women, he had been one of the favorite subordinates of the late Marshal de Lattre de Tassigny and had inherited from him a taste for military pomp and circumstance.[10] An officially approved biographical article stated that "if a sudden furor takes hold of him, he lets it explode, masters it very rapidly and does not bear any grudges."[11] A favorable, if unofficial observer, Jules Roy, says of Cogny that he was detested by his superiors for arguing orders, and confirms his thin skin:

> A single word can wound Cogny deeply; in that case he does not forgive. . . . He will charge head down on the person whom

he thinks responsible for the wound and will try to trample him.[12]

From Cogny's remarks about Navarre ten years later, in what he calls "a free confession," the latter character trait seems fairly well documented.[13] Yet this was the man whom Navarre personally picked on May 21, 1953, to direct what surely was to become the decisive phase of the eight-year-long Indochina War. On that day also, Navarre made Cogny a major general.

Navarre made several changes and innovations within his own general staff. He strove for a greater integration of the naval and air commands and the ground forces, ordering his new chief of staff, Maj. Gen. Gambiez, radically to streamline his command structure. Perhaps in an attempt to imitate the dash and drive with which the late Marshal de Lattre had inspired the Indochina command,[14] Navarre, sometimes at great personal risk, visited literally every sector of Indochina in the space of a few weeks. He was particularly interested in the Lai Chau and Na-San airheads. His airplane was hit in several places by Communist antiaircraft fire while visiting the latter base. Navarre even visited a mountain tribal guerrilla base deep inside Communist territory, something no other commander-in-chief in Indochina had done. It was during his visit to Na-San that Navarre met the commander of that base and of Mobile Group 7, Colonel Louis Berteil. Berteil was an officer who, even prior to Dien Bien Phu, had few friends among his peers. A graduate of the General Staff College, he had literary aspirations and his preciousness of expression had provided the senior officers' messes in Indochina with a vast array of quotable quotes, some erroneously attributed to Berteil, others directly traceable to him. One of the more memorable was his characterization of the airhead of Na-San as offering an "indirect and bivalent protection of both Laos and the Red River Delta."[15] Berteil caught the attention of Gen. Navarre at Na-San and soon found himself on Navarre's staff as deputy chief for operations. Cogny, Berteil's immediate superior at Na-San, was to say of him ten years later that he was "pregnant" with a vast theory on the uses of fortified airheads. Cogny also asserts that it was Col. Berteil who eventually convinced Navarre not only of the usefulness of Dien Bien Phu, but also of the over-all correctness of the "air-land base" as a panacea for the dilemmas of the Indochina War.[16]

What made the air-land base concept so attractive was that it seemed to provide a solution to one of the key problems which faced the French commanders, one which still faces the South Vietnamese and their American allies more than ten years later: how to spread a sufficient degree of insecurity into the enemy's own rear areas so as to compel him in turn to disperse his troops for the purpose of protecting those areas. Since successful infiltration of Communist-held areas could be attempted only with hand-picked French and Vietnamese special forces units, conventional military means had to be found for something more massive than infiltration. This turned out to be strongly defended hedgehog positions resupplied by transport aircraft and supported, in case of direct enemy attack, by combat aircraft.

In the spring of 1953, Navarre was content to take stock of the situation and to present to Paris a coherent scheme for French operations during the following year. At a conference held with regional commanders in Saigon on June 16, 1953, Navarre presented an outline of the battle plan he intended to submit one month later to the National Defense Committee, the French equivalent of the American National Security Council. It is not clear whether the occupation of Dien Bien Phu was discussed at that meeting, or whether Navarre had decided to shelve Gen. Salan's Directive No. 40. It is now established, however, that Navarre had by then been convinced of the military and political uselessness of the airhead of Na-San. Militarily, Na-San tied down the effectives of a light division and an important share of the available air transport tonnage without tying down even its own equivalent in enemy manpower. Politically, it was nothing but an abstract point on the map—neither a tribal provincial capital nor a geographically important communications hub, as Lai Chau and Dien Bien Phu were. General Cogny, therefore, did not object to the evacuation of Na-San since it would provide him with first-class troops sorely needed elsewhere. At the same time (and this is likely to have taken place at the commanders' conference of June 16) *it was he who suggested the reoccupation of Dien Bien Phu.* Cogny was to express his reasoning in the following words ten years later:

> I suggested the occupation of Dien Bien Phu to install there a simple mooring point (*môle d'ammarrage*) for our military and political activities in northwestern Tonkin. We thus would derive an advantage from the hostility of the T'ai mountaineers against the Viet-Minh from the plains who seek to subject them to their yoke. Unfortunately, the capital of Lai Chau cannot even be defended against a modest attack. . . . I felt a certain degree of urgency in preparing the eventual transfer of the T'ai capital to Dien Bien Phu so as to be able to face a probable increase of the local danger, but also and above all in order to present an addi-

tional argument in favor of the evacuation of Na-San, which I insistently requested from General Navarre.[17]

Much now hinged on how Navarre and Cogny would define their respective concepts of whether Dien Bien Phu was an air-land base or a "mooring point." Navarre would argue to the last that, indeed, it was Cogny who had proposed the occupation of Dien Bien Phu; and Cogny would argue with equal insistence that the rationale for occupying Dien Bien Phu hinged entirely on his own concept of Dien Bien Phu as a resupply point for tribal guerrilla units who were to operate in the Viet-Minh's rear areas. The presence at Dien Bien Phu of Deo Van Long's T'ai federal administration would provide political competition for Ho Chi Minh's own administration. It may be pointed out that the two explanations are not mutually exclusive. Cogny himself admits that he *did* propose to Navarre what amounted to an implementation of Gen. Salan's Directive No. 40, of whose existence he surely was aware. There is no evidence in any available documentation (including the French military archives and the heated public controversy between Generals Navarre and Cogny, which resulted in a lawsuit in 1955 and a series of highly emotional articles and open letters in 1963) affirming that Gen. Cogny had clearly expressed to Navarre his own interpretation of what he meant Dien Bien Phu to be. Nor is there any evidence to show that Gen. Navarre had made clear to Gen. Cogny *at that time* that he meant Dien Bien Phu to become a jungle fortress designed to withstand a regular siege.

On July 17, Navarre presented his plans to the French Joint Chiefs, presided over by Marshal Juin, who approved them with the reservation that all the additional forces and equipment that Navarre required might not become available.[18] On July 24, Navarre addressed the whole National Defense Committee, composed of the Joint Chiefs, the Prime Minister, the ministers of Foreign Affairs, Finance, Interior, Defense, Overseas Affairs, and Indochina Affairs, the service secretaries, and presided over by the President of the Republic.

That meeting was crucial in deciding the fate of northern Indochina in general and that of Dien Bien Phu in particular. Navarre insisted later that "after long and confusing discussions, no firm decision was taken on any of the questions raised." In his own memoirs on the subject, Joseph Laniel, who was then Prime Minister in one of the Fourth Republic's "musical chairs" governments, and who had become Premier on July 3, 1953, commented on Navarre's assertion by saying that the stenographic transcript of the meeting clearly showed that he had received instructions to abandon Laos if necessary and that he had objected to those instructions on the grounds that they would have created an unfavorable psychological effect in Indochina.[19] Navarre in turn asserted that (1) he did not know that a transcript had been kept of the meeting until he read about it in Laniel's book; (2) the transcript, if it existed may well have been tampered with; and (3) in any case the transcript was ambiguous.[20]

General Georges Catroux, who headed the French government's 1955 commission investigating the Dien Bien Phu disaster (the report to this day is a state secret), and whose own writings are far from tender toward Gen. Navarre, tends to side with the commander-in-chief on this point. Since Dien Bien Phu made sense only if the French government desired to hold Laos, or at least large parts of it, Navarre's argument hinges primarily on whether or not he had been fully informed as to the French government's *intentions* about Laos. As Catroux described this situation on the basis of all the testimony his commission had heard or received, it appears that the French Joint Chiefs, after having heard Navarre, had recommended to the National Defense Committee that "no obligation be put upon him to defend Laos."[21] This recommendation was apparently communicated only by indirection to Navarre at the July 24 meeting, and was not then embodied in the form of a governmental directive. Catroux' investigation commission found, in fact, that it had taken the French government until November 13, 1963, to express its view on Laos in a formal directive addressed to Navarre's theoretical civilian superior, the Secretary of State for Associated States (*i.e.,* Indochina) Affairs, M. Marc Jacquet! According to Catroux, Navarre received this communication only on December 4, two weeks after the first wave of Bigeard's paratroopers had landed on DZ "Natasha." No explanation for this incredible delay in transmitting a vital directive was ever offered.

Dien Bien Phu itself had been mentioned at the July 24 meeting of the National Defense Committee, but only in passing since in Navarre's mind an operation at Dien Bien Phu was to have a purely secondary character and was, in any case, entirely within his sphere of responsibility as military commander in Indochina. Moreover, he had already made up his mind about it. On the following day, July 25, his staff in Saigon issued Directive No. 563, which represented the first formalized document providing for the occupation of Dien Bien Phu. It presented the operation as a "preventive action" against the Communist thrust through the upper Mekong River (*i.e.,* Northern Laos).[22] The political stage was now set for the military drama that was to follow.

Henceforth, the planning of the battle of Dien Bien Phu took on the preordained air of a Greek tragedy. On August 12, 1953, the airhead of Na-San was successfully evacuated by the French. The Communists were so totally surprised by that evacuation that even the last of the rear guard of the 9,000-man garrison were picked up by air without enemy interference. This rear guard comprised a company of T'ai Partisans commanded by a French lieutenant with the unlikely name of Makowiak, who, with his straw-blond hair, bluish eyes, and square build, fully looked the part of a Polish peasant from the plains of Poznan. "Mako," as he was known to his intimates, had been given the delicate job because of his perfect familiarity with both the terrain of the T'ai country and the tribal languages there. Those two capabilities were to stand him in good stead later during the battle of Dien Bien Phu. The rapid evacuation of Na-San permitted the safe withdrawal of all men and weapons, but compelled the French to leave behind many of the fixed installations, large stocks of reserve ammunition, and the precious pierced-steel mats with which part of the airfield was covered. The vast mine fields which covered the various strongpoints were also left behind and later carefully dug up by the Viet-Minh and used against the French elsewhere. The French sabotaged as much of the matériel as possible and the French Air Force bombed many of the remaining installations, but a great deal nevertheless fell into Communist hands. Inasmuch as Gen. Cogny regained control of nine battalions and of a great deal of airlift capability, the evacuation of Na-San was considered a clear success. Unfortunately, it also heightened the confidence within Navarre's general staff[23] in the ability of the French forces to occupy such an airhead and to evacuate it successfully when it was no longer useful.

On October 22, 1953, France signed with the then (and often later) Prime Minister of Laos, Prince Souvanna Phouma, a treaty of association and several conventions which simultaneously reaffirmed the independence of Laos and its membership in the French Union. Particular importance was attached to this treaty because Laos was first of the three Indochinese states (the others being Viet-Nam and Cambodia) to complete signing such a treaty with France. While the treaty did not contain a hard-and-fast clause making it mandatory for France to come to the defense of Laos, the commitment was clearly implied. Indeed, there was no other reason for Laos to sign the treaty. This further reinforced Navarre's conviction that in the case of a second Viet-Minh invasion of Laos (the first, it will be recalled, took place in the winter and spring of

1953.) an all-out attempt would have to be made to defend that country. Indeed, as was shown, Navarre argued in 1955 (as well as in 1963) that he had not received an explicit directive from the French government at home as to whether to abandon Laos or not—a decision, Navarre avers, that was entirely political and thus had to be made by Paris and not by him.

> Suppose [said Navarre in 1963], that I had . . . abandoned Laos on my own initiative and opened to the Viet-Minh the road toward total victory: I would be branded today as the man who had betrayed the honor of his country.[24]

As was shown earlier, Navarre's doubts were resolved by the French governmental directive of November 13, which he received after the beginning of the attack on Dien Bien Phu. In the meantime, however, the signing of the French-Laotian Treaty may have reinforced Navarre's impression that Laos had to be defended and that the valley of Dien Bien Phu was the place from which to defend it. On November 2, 1953, Navarre's operations chief issued Directive No. 852 outlining the command channels for the forthcoming operation.[25] General Cogny as the commander of ground forces in North Viet-Nam became the over-all commander of the operation, which was to be carried out between November 15 and 20, or not later than December 1. The initial number of troops to be used was to be limited to six battalions, later to be reduced to five.

If one is to judge from the memoranda submitted to Cogny by his subordinates on November 4, the effect of that directive on Cogny's staff in Hanoi was that of a bombshell.

Couched in the first person singular, since they were to be addressed by Cogny to Navarre, they were unanimously and even vociferously opposed to the whole operation:[26]

> . . . It seems that to the general staff (EMIFT), the occupation of Dien Bien Phu will close the road to Luang-Prabang[27] and deprive the Viet-Minh of the rice of the region.
>
> In that kind of country you can't interdict a road. This is a European-type notion without any value here.
>
> The Viets can get through anywhere. We can see this right here in the Red River Delta.
>
> The rice surplus provided by Dien Bien Phu will only feed one division for three months. Therefore, it would only make a fractional contribution to an [enemy] campaign in Laos . . .
>
> *I am persuaded that Dien Bien Phu shall become, whether we*

like it or not, a battalion meat-grinder,* with no possibility of large-scale radiating out from it as soon as it will be blocked by a single Viet-Minh regiment (see example of Na-San).

While a clear-cut threat exists against the [Red River] Delta which becomes more evident every day, we will immobilize 300 kilometers from Hanoi the equivalent of three regimental combat teams. They represent all the reinforcements which we have received . . . which permit us to inflict losses upon the enemy. . . .

The consequences of such a decision can be extremely grave and EMIFT must know this.

A second memorandum went into details of the cost of an operation at Dien Bien Phu. It emphasized that being cut off from the rice of Dien Bien Phu would be only of minor importance to the enemy in any case; that French-led guerrilla units in the area were not yet effective; and that an early operation at Dien Bien Phu could well bring about their destruction. The memorandum also pointed out that effective interdiction through aerial bombardment of the main access roads to Dien Bien Phu would absorb three fourths of all the combat aircraft available in Northern Command. It further underlined that the five battalions initially planned for Dien Bien Phu would soon have to face at least nine Communist battalions readily available in the area and that these, in turn, would have to be matched by more French units withdrawn from the Red River Delta. The memorandum ended with a request on the part of Cogny for more troops and air transport "if, against the clearly unfavorable opinion which the Commanding General of the Ground Forces in North Viet-Nam admits himself to respectfully express," the decision to carry out the operation was maintained by the GHQ in Saigon.

The last note merely emphasized the difficulty of withdrawing the garrison of Lai Chau toward Dien Bien Phu and prophesied that the Viet-Minh forces would be able to establish a strongly defended road-block position between the two airheads.

This wholly negative appraisal of what was to become Operation "Castor" was followed two days later by a personal letter from Cogny to Navarre which was a great deal less clear-cut. Navarre gave the necessary orders to his staff to prepare the launching of the operation for November 20. Observers who otherwise were almost totally sym-

---

*The French expression is *gouffre à bataillons,* which means literally an "abyss for battalions," *i.e.,* a position which will devour troops without any significant advantage. I find that the expression "battalion meat-grinder" renders the French meaning more adequately than a direct translation.

pathetic to the viewpoint of Cogny nevertheless felt that in this instance his position had been ambiguous.[28] Prime Minister Joseph Laniel was to explain that attitude by what he called the "umbrella politics" of certain French senior commanders who, according to Laniel, were concerned with covering themselves more against personal responsibility than against enemy attacks.

> That concern leads them to an excessive usage of memoranda, reports, and to the refusal to undertake any initiative without a written order. It also leads them to request means that go far beyond what can be provided so as to have, in case of failure, the excuse of not having been listened to.[29]

In a recent rebuttal to such views and to the suggestion that his deep disagreement with Navarre should at that point have led to Cogny's resignation (or at least the offer of resignation) from the command of a zone which was about to engage in an operation with which he personally was in apparently complete disagreement, Cogny argued that, once he had presented his objections to the operation, discipline demanded that he execute the given orders. While he could have "tip-toed" away from the forthcoming disaster with his major general's stars safely on his shoulders, he felt that he had an "obligation" toward his own troops in Tonkin to remain at his post.[30] He was to use the same argument also to explain why he did not resign later on when Navarre almost unilaterally decided to transform the valley of Dien Bien Phu from a guerrilla force "mooring point" into a set-piece jungle fortress. It is probable that this total breakdown of rapport between Navarre in Saigon and his key commander in Hanoi (and, to all appearances, between their immediate subordinates) had a decisive if not fatal effect on the manner in which plans were eventually implemented.

As was shown earlier, Cogny in turn informed his subordinate air force and paratroop commanders on November 11 and 12 of their part in the forthcoming operation, and in his orders to paratrooper Gen. Gilles, he once again emphasized his understanding of the Dien Bien Phu airhead as "a mooring point" for guerrilla operations by instructing Gilles that the defense of the Dien Bien Phu airfield would *"exclude* any system designed to provide a belt of strongpoints for the airfield." The commander at Lai Chau, Lt. Col. Trancart, was informed on November 13 that his command would have to be sacrificed. But he was ordered at the same time to "repress" any rumors about the fact that this was going to take place.

On the following day, November 14, Gen. Navarre issued final operational instructions (known in French Military parlance as IPS, or "personal and secret instructions") to the regional commanders who would have to co-operate with one another in the matter of the Dien Bien Phu operation: Gen. Cogny in North Viet-Nam and Colonel Boucher de Crèvecoeur, the commander of all French forces in Laos.[31] For, as Cogny was to emphasize ten years later, Dien Bien Phu was located a mere eight miles from the Laotian border and much that was going on in its hinterland obviously concerned the commander in Laos as much as the commander in North Viet-Nam. Yet, since all the logistical support bases for the battle of Dien Bien Phu were located in the Red River Delta, and the troops stationed in Dien Bien Phu were to come from Gen. Cogny's command, most of the decisions were finally made in Hanoi. It is unclear to what extent the lack of a single over-all command at Dien Bien Phu hampered the eventual direction of the battle, but there is doubtless a certain measure of justification in Cogny's assertion that Dien Bien Phu had become the key to the battle for all of northern Indochina and thus should have been under a single over-all commander.

In the IPS of November 14, Navarre again outlined the political and strategic importance of maintaining inside the T'ai tribal territory a French position which would cover Laos as well. The operation, set for November 20, provided for the creation of an airhead at Dien Bien Phu that would establish a land link with French forces in northern Laos and would provide support for Lai Chau until its eventual evacuation. The three directives of November 14 contained a special appendix dealing with political and administrative problems, since the evacuation of Lai Chau implied the transfer of the whole T'ai Tribal Federation's administration to Dien Bien Phu.

With only five days to go, Cogny's staff shifted into high gear. There were difficulties to be surmounted, inasmuch as the bulk of the troops and aircraft to be involved in the operation were still heavily engaged in the southern part of the Red River Delta. Still, those of Cogny's aides who were doubtful about the whole operation were given another, final opportunity to express their misgivings to the commander-in-chief. On November 15, Marc Jacquet, the Secretary of State for Associated States Affairs, arrived in Saigon, apparently unaware that his office in Paris had received on the previous day the important directive of the National Defense Council inviting Navarre to modify his strategy. Two days later, on November 17, Navarre, Jacquet, the French civilian High

Commissioner in Indochina, Maurice Dejean, and Vietnamese Prime Minister Nguyen Van Tam, flew to Hanoi and were briefed on the general outlines of the forthcoming operation. None of them objected in any way to it and Marc Jacquet, by all accounts, felt no particular need to inform Paris by telegram of this military move. While this routine briefing was held for the civilians, the more dramatic military discussion took place among Navarre, Cogny and their respective staffs. Last-minute intelligence information had shown that Dien Bien Phu was far from undefended and was in fact held by parts of Communist Regiment 148. Also, an important shift had taken place in the movements of People's Army Division 316. The 316th Division was not the best of all Communist outfits, but it was excellently suited for operations in the highlands because two of its three infantry regiments, the 176th and the 174th, were recruited from among tribesmen who spoke the same language as the inhabitants of the T'ai highlands.

In addition to its three infantry regiments, Division 316 also had an artillery battalion, the 980th, equipped with recoilless rifles and heavy mortars. On the basis of this intelligence, it should have been obvious to the French that Dien Bien Phu was an unlikely choice as a mooring point for light, mobile guerrilla forces.

In the face of a full-scale assault by a regular Communist division which could be reinforced by additional heavy elements, the French at Dien Bien Phu had two choices: either to evacuate the valley altogether or to make it impregnable by transporting into it an adequate garrison supported by vast amounts of firepower. As it turned out, the French High Command never had enough troops at its disposal even to occupy the approximately seventy-five square miles of valley bottom, let alone defend and hold the line of surrounding hills. The valley, with its minimal perimeter of about fifty miles, would easily have required the presence of as many 700-man battalions as there were miles. And since only six such battalions were available for the operation, it was a foregone conclusion that any compromise between the two alternatives was bound to be unsatisfactory, if not altogether disastrous. The orders issued by Gen. Cogny's headquarters on November 30, 1953, had already begun to show the effects of that compromise.

At Dien Bien Phu, where the Airborne Division Command Element (EDAP) of Gen. Gilles had been replaced by the headquarters of the Paratroop Operational Group (GOP) of Col. Bastiani, the news meant that the lightly armed paratroop forces would have to be replaced by normal field units of excellent quality and that the light field entrench-

ments around Dien Bien Phu would have to be replaced by permanent
field fortifications. In effect, the new directive gave the GOP of Dien
Bien Phu the mission to (1) "guarantee at the very least the free usage
of the airfield," (2) "gather intelligence from as far away as possible,"
and (3) proceed with the withdrawal to Dien Bien Phu of the units
from Lai Chau.[32] The directive gave specific and detailed instructions
as to how each of those missions was to be fulfilled. The "free use" of
the Dien Bien Phu airfield was explained to mean that the whole "defensive position" of Dien Bien Phu was to be held "without any thought
of withdrawal" (*sans esprit de recul*). In effect, the troops at Dien Bien
Phu were to maintain freedom of movement within a radius of eight
kilometers around the airfield. Correctly enough, Gen. Cogny's headquarters foresaw that the major enemy effort would come from the east
or northeast, and it ordered the commander at Dien Bien Phu to concentrate his defensive efforts in that direction.

As to the directive's second point (offensive stabs from Dien Bien
Phu to the north and northeast in direction of Ban Na Tau and Tuan
Giao) the garrison was also to use "at least one half of its strength"
in operations designed to inflict heavy losses on the enemy and to delay
his laying a tight siege ring around the valley. At the same time, Dien
Bien Phu was directed to operate a link-up through the roadless jungle
with Col. de Crèvecoeur's French-Laotian forces advancing toward
Dien Bien Phu from Muong Khoua. Lastly, the evacuation of Lai Chau
was to take place at the order of Gen. Cogny and was to be covered by
French-led guerrilla formations who were also to continue their activities
in the Lai Chau area after the withdrawal of all French regular units.

There were two major aspects of the November 30 directive that can
only be characterized as unrealistic. The first was the supposition that
a garrison of 5,000 men, in terrain that was largely jungle-covered and
impassable, could defend a roughly circular area with a perimeter meas-
uring about thirty-one miles (that is, a radius of eight kilometers around
the airstrip). As past experience in Indochina had shown, an average
700-man battalion could hold a line of no more than 1,500 yards, or
even less. The second was the clear implication that sophisticated field
defenses were to be constructed even though the directive specifically
prescribed that "at the very least" one half of the garrison was constantly to be away on patrol! As will be seen later, the garrison's command obeyed this provision of the November 30 directive to the letter,
with the result that only scant attention was paid to a thorough in-depth
defense of the terrain until long after the siege ring had tightened.

And this had to be done with a garrison constantly weakened by having its most aggressive units far away in the field. As several of the commanders of the strike units reported later, their men scarcely had the heart for extensive spadework after returning from exhausting combat reconnaissances deep in the hostile jungle.

While the final strategic decisions had now been taken to gird for battle at Dien Bien Phu, a new event in the Red River Delta almost changed the fate of Dien Bien Phu. French radio intelligence had suddenly picked up strong evidence that the enemy was shifting key elements of his battle force—notably the 308th and 312th Infantry Divisions and the 351st Heavy Division—from staging areas in the triangle Phu-Tho - Yen Bay - Thai Nguyen toward the northwestern mountain areas. Among the intercepted messages were orders for Communist engineering units to build bridges on the Black River and to prepare ferry facilities across the Red River at Yen Bay for 6,000 troops per night as of December 3. As soon as the information was fully confirmed, Gen. Cogny sent a radio message to Gen. Navarre suggesting a diversionary stab into the Communist base area in order to slow down the Viet-Minh build-up around Dien Bien Phu.[33] Much was said later by Cogny and Navarre and their respective apologists about Navarre's refusal to consider the possibility of a large-scale diversionary attack from the Red River Delta into the enemy's rear areas. The idea of relieving the pressure on Dien Bien Phu in this manner was to remain ever-present in the minds of Cogny's staff officers throughout the battle of Dien Bien Phu, with new documents being added to the plans for the contemplated operation until late in April of 1954.[34] In short, three alternatives were seriously being considered, each of which had the advantage of having been tried once before, and it was likely that many of the troops that had participated in the earlier operations would be available for a repeat. The first suggested operation was an attack against the major Viet-Minh administrative headquarters at Thai Nguyen, in whose limestone caves Ho Chi Minh and his war cabinet, as well as Gen. Giap and his staff, were housed. An operation with the same objective had been undertaken by the French in October, 1947, under the code name "Léa." The second alternative was an armored stab of almost one hundred miles (in comparison Thai Nguyen was only fifty miles from Hanoi) toward the major Communist supply center at Yen Bay. A similar operation, code-named "Lorraine," had been tried in November, 1952. The third alternative consisted of a smaller-scale paratroop operation along the lines of Dien Bien Phu itself, but close enough to the French battle line in the Red River Delta for the paratroops to be rescued within a few days by an armored battle group. This operation would be pretty much a copy of Operation "Swallow" (*Hirondelle*) undertaken by the French against Lang Son in July, 1953.

A decade later Gen. Cogny was still unable to overcome the bitterness with which he had received Navarre's disapproval of the latter type of operation:

> The very hour when I learned that the Viet battle force was following the traces of the 316th Division in direction of the northwest, I initiated the idea of an attack from the [Red River] Delta, including the necessary reconnaissances and troop movements. [Colonel] Vanuxem[35] would command the shock forces which would grapple with the rear columns of the Viets and would force Giap to turn around with at least a part of his forces. We would break contact and would attract the Viets into the immediate approaches to the Delta where we would have been in the best condition to defeat them.
>
> General Navarre refused by invoking some mediocre arguments about the availability of the necessary forces.[36]

An impartial examination of Cogny's arguments shows that Navarre may have had compelling reasons for rejecting an alternate attack against the enemy's centers of strength north of the Red River. The record of previous French operations in that area was hardly promising. Operation "Léa" had involved the use of seventeen battalions, including three airborne and three armored battalions, for over three weeks. Yet while it succeeded in conquering Thai Nguyen and some other Communist-held cities, it nevertheless failed entirely in its key purpose of capturing the enemy leaders, or destroying large bodies of enemy troops. Operation "Lorraine" was even more disastrous: Although involving close to 30,000 men, including several airborne and armored battalions, it not only ran out of steam before it was able to reach Yen Bay but on the return to the delta, a part of the French troops fell into a large-scale ambush at the gorges of Chan-Muong and sustained heavy losses. "Lorraine," too, had been mounted in good part for the purpose of compelling the Communist divisions that had begun to invade the T'ai highlands to fall back in order to rush to the defense of their own rear areas. The strategy had failed because Giap had never departed from his strategy of leaving smaller units to fend for themselves even at great costs because he was absolutely certain, thanks to his excellent intelligence network, that such French offensive operations would always sooner or later run out of steam. In fact, he could assume with a great deal of certainty that the greater the size of the initial French stab, the more likely that the troops which had been scraped together for it from various commands and theaters would soon be badly needed again. Usually, a few Communist attacks in the areas from which these troops had been temporarily withdrawn would suffice to put enough pressure on the French High Command to call off the large-scale offensive in order to save large tracts of hard-won territory from being totally subverted again by Communist infiltrations.[37]

In justifying his decision, Navarre asserted (and Gen. Cogny never contradicted him on this score) that Cogny had requested a deep stab into the enemy's rear areas requiring a total of six motorized regimental combat teams, two armored regimental combat teams, and two airborne regimental battle groups. In addition, Cogny asked for three to four combat teams to keep lines of communications open, and two additional armored combat teams and one airborne battle group to remain in reserve inside the Red River Delta.[38] This force exceeded by perhaps one third *all* the mobile ground forces available throughout the whole Indochina theater, and by one hundred per cent the total of armored units available. To be sure, Cogny could always have executed short "round-trip" operations of the type of Operation "Swallow" in July or "Seagull" in October, 1953, but neither of them had tied down a large amount of enemy troops. On the other hand, they had caused a great deal of strain on the already badly overworked French air potential in Indochina. Navarre explained this to Cogny when he flew to Hanoi from Saigon on Saturday, November 28, 1953. On the following day, Cogny accompanied Navarre on the latter's first visit to Dien Bien Phu.

Cogny was worried about the fact that the enemy would now be able to concentrate the overwhelming bulk of his battle force on a single, lightly defended airhead, and his later assertion that he made an eloquent plea for the preservation of a "satellite" position somewhere in the mountain area (preferably at Lai Chau) is certainly understandable. But so was Navarre's reasoning. If one was short of elite troops for a major operation such as the defense of Dien Bien Phu, there was little point in diverting whatever was left of French mobile forces for yet another difficult breakthrough operation whose ultimate effect on a battle taking place 300 miles away was at best doubtful. General Cogny must have finally agreed with his superior, for he issued his famous Directive of November 30 on the day after his inspection of Dien Bien Phu with Gen. Navarre.

What followed next has never been satisfactorily explained by the former French commander-in-chief. While he had been at Dien Bien Phu with Gen. Cogny, his own staff in Saigon had worked out the details of the future battle for Dien Bien Phu. According to officers familiar with the situation, that plan had been entirely worked out by Navarre's key planner, Col. Berteil. It was communicated to Cogny on December 3, 1953. Navarre had made the final decision to accept the battle in the faraway mountains of northwestern Viet-Nam.

> . . . I have decided to accept the battle in the Northwest under the following general conditions:
>
> 1.   The defense of the Northwest shall be centered on the air-land base of Dien Bien Phu which must be held at all costs.
>
> 2.   Our occupation of Lai Chau shall be maintained only inasmuch as our present forces there shall permit its defense. . . .
>
> 3.   Ground communications between Dien Bien Phu and Lai Chau (until we eventually evacuate our forces from there) and with Laos via Muong-Khoua shall be maintained as long as possible.
>
> In view of the remoteness of the northwestern theater of operations [from his main bases] and the logistical obligations of the Viet-Minh, it is probable that the battle will be fought according to the following scenario:
>
>> The *movement phase*, characterized by the arrival of the Viet-Minh units and their supplies in the Northwest; whose duration may extend over several weeks.
>>
>> An *approach and reconnaissance phase*, in the course of which enemy intelligence units will make efforts to determine the quality and the weaknesses of our defenses and where the [enemy's] combat units will proceed with the positioning of their means of attack. That phase may last between six to ten days.
>>
>> An *attack phase* lasting several days (according to the means employed) and which must end with the failure of the Viet-Minh offensive.

Mission of the Air Force

1.   The mission of the Air Force shall be, until further orders, given priority and with the maximum of means at its disposal, to the support of our forces in the Northwest.

2.   The Commanding General of the Air Force in the Far East will, to that effect, reinforce the Northern Tactical Air Group. . . . [39]

Future events were to show how grossly mistaken Navarre's staff was in estimating the Viet-Minh ability to marshal forces and prosecute the attack on Dien Bien Phu. While the movement phase indeed covered several weeks, the approach and reconnaissance phase, instead of lasting six to ten days, lasted almost one hundred days, until March 13, 1954; and the attack phase, instead of lasting "several days," lasted a hellish fifty-six days and nights. And instead of failure, it ended in victory for the Viet-Minh.

Even though Navarre's view of the forthcoming battle was somewhat overoptimistic, he harbored no illusions as to its difficulty. The French forces at Dien Bien Phu were to be beefed up to a total of nine battalions, including three airborne battalions; five batteries of 105-mm. howitzers (a total of 20 field pieces), and two batteries (8 pieces) of 75-mm. recoilless rifles; and one company of heavy mortars. But that force, even if it had been in amply fortified positions on favorable terrain (neither of which was the case) would have been in no position to resist the onslaught of a regular enemy battle force three times its own size. All available sources—and Gen. Navarre has not contradicted them since—indicate that the French commander-in-chief *knew* since at least November 28 (when he met Gen. Cogny in Hanoi) that the bulk of the enemy's battle force was in the process of getting ready for the long march into the T'ai hill country. If anything, an order of the day issued by the enemy commander-in-chief on December 6, which spoke of "developing the victories of the winter campaign of 1952," should have put Navarre on further notice that the Viet-Minh indeed was determined to stand for battle in the jungle valley.

Yet, December 12, 1953, Navarre issued his Instruction No. 964 in which he notified his subordinate commanders of his decision to launch his long-planned offensive in south-central Viet-Nam regardless of the fact that he already had decided to face the enemy at Dien Bien Phu! Although the complete battle plan for Operation "Atlante" was to cover ten full pages, the gist of it was contained in the following few lines:

> The essential objective which I expect to reach [in 1953-54] is the disappearance of the Viet-Minh zone which spreads from south of Tourane [Danang] to the north of Nha Trang and eastward to the Southern Mountain Plateau; that is, the destruction of the military forces of Lien-Khu V . . .
>
> In view of the considerable strategic and political results which one is entitled to expect from the complete execution of that operation, I have decided to *subordinate* to it the conduct of the whole

Indochina campaign during the first semester of 1954.

According to the details and appendices attached to the instruction, "Atlante" was to be subdivided into three phases code-named "Arethuse," "Axelle," and "Attila." The troop requirements for the first phase were to be twenty-five infantry battalions, three artillery battalions and two engineering battalions. For the second phase, these requirements were to be increased to thirty-four infantry battalions and five artillery battalions. And for the third phase, Navarre expected that he would need forty-five infantry battalions and eight artillery battalions. In other words, the same commander-in-chief who had refused Gen. Cogny the use of perhaps twenty battalions for an offensive which might have at least in part alleviated the pressure on Dien Bien Phu, now was willing to use twice as many troops in a sector whose conquest at that time by the French (or whose continued control by the Communists) was in no way vital to the outcome of the war.

The Viet-Minh had controlled the "Inter-Zone" (*Lien-Khu*) V since 1945 and had transformed it into a strongly defended bastion that contained almost 3,000,000 people and about 30,000 Communist troops, including twelve good regular battalions and six well-trained regional battalions. As Navarre, in apparent contradiction of Instruction 964, was to say in his own book a few years later, the Communist forces of the Fifth Inter-Zone were, in view of their light armament, not particularly inclined to undertake a major offensive in the plateau area.[40] It is hard to understand Navarre's decision to undertake Operation "Atlante" at a moment when the chronic French shortage of troops was strongly felt because of the battalions tied down at Dien Bien Phu. When one considers the fact that his request for massive reinforcements from France had been turned down by the French government and he had been invited, as we have seen earlier, "to adjust his operations to his means," one fails to see how he could think he could conceivably undertake "Atlante."

In defense of his plan, Navarre was to argue later that the very size of the Communist bastion (230 miles in length along the Vietnamese shore, and with an average depth of forty miles) compelled him to maintain a large force in the area anyhow. Temporary reinforcement by units "not employable" in northern Viet-Nam, would suffice to liberate over 10,000 square miles of territory, to free the sensitive plateau area of the threat of Communist invasion, and provide the demoralized Vietnamese government in Saigon with a sorely needed boost in morale. Yet this argument was, at least in part, specious. While units made up of local tribesmen could hardly be employed except on their own home ground, there were at least two full-fledged regimental combat teams (the North African 10th and the French 100th, the latter being made up largely of French troops who had returned from Korea) which could have been easily used in the north. Navarre's further allegation that the aircraft used in supporting Operation "Atlante" could not have been used at Dien Bien Phu because of their type or state of repair,[41] also does not withstand serious examination. Granted, some of these aircrafts no longer had the range required to fly missions to Dien Bien Phu. Nevertheless, they could have been used by Gen. Cogny within the Red River Delta while some of the more airworthy craft were used in support of Dien Bien Phu.

The ultimate judgments as to whether "Atlante" was justified or not, and whether it had a negative influence on the battle of Dien Bien Phu, rest upon its outcome. After an initially successful landing at Tuy-Hoa behind Communist lines on January 20, 1954, the operation bogged down completely. The Vietnamese troops who were to receive their baptism of fire in the beachhead either gave a poor account of themselves or settled down to looting. The Vietnamese civil administrators who began to pour into the newly liberated areas were, if anything, worse than the military units. Presently, the Viet-Minh forces of the Inter-Zone, unimpeded by the French "Atlante" beachhead, went on the counteroffensive on the southern mountain plateau, destroying Regimental Combat Team 100 and compelling Navarre to summon from North Viet-Nam airborne troops which had been located there as theater reserves for Dien Bien Phu.[42]

In retrospect, the first week of December, 1953, was the decisive moment when the fate of Dien Bien Phu was sealed. Thanks to a vast increase in the American military aid budget for Indochina, more French troops had become available and there was plenty of American matériel on hand to arm them. Tens of thousands of new Vietnamese recruits were joining the French Union forces. The French forces held the initiative throughout Indochina and the enemy seemed for once uncertain as to what to do next. In fact, the leader of the Viet-Minh, Ho Chi Minh, had given an important interview to the Swedish newspaper *Expressen* on November 29, in which he declared that the "government and people of the Democratic Republic of Viet-Nam are ready to discuss French propositions for an armistice and a settlement of the Indochinese question by negotiations."[43]

Militarily, Navarre, during the first week of December, still had the choice of completely withdrawing the garrisons of Lai Chau and Dien Bien Phu by airlift and—having shielded the major part of northern Laos by means of the air-land base of the Plain of Jars with its three easily-defended airstrips—concentrating the bulk of his battle force for a major offensive against the enemy's main logistical centers while carrying out, if he wanted to, his original plan of eliminating the large Communist pocket in the south.

In fact, as was his duty as commander-in-chief, Gen. Navarre foresaw the theoretical possibility of a fighting withdrawal from Dien Bien Phu under overwhelming enemy pressure. On December 29, 1953, in top-secret Directive No. 178/EMIFT, he ordered Gen. Cogny to work out such a plan in cooperation with his colleague, the commander of French Union forces in Laos. The plan was to take the appropriate code name of Operation "Xenophon,"* and was supplemented by an alternate plan named "Ariane."†

One of the problems in working out the plan was that Navarre had ordered his subordinates to keep it a secret from the commanders at Dien Bien Phu lest it affect their morale. Cogny, therefore, told them that what they were in effect planning was a "pursuit" of retreating Viet-Minh forces. Yet, in transmitting the completed plan to Navarre on January 21, 1954. Cogny, departing for a moment from his earlier reserve with regard to the battle that was shaping up, "respectfully insist[ed] that Dien Bien Phu be held at all costs." Cogny was to argue later that his plea for the stand at Dien Bien Phu merely expressed a *preference* to the alternative of a fighting breakout with its expected high losses—and not an approval of fighting a battle at Dien Bien Phu. It that was so, it does certainly not appear in his reply to Navarre of that date.

But Navarre himself had second thoughts. On January 1, 1954, as he addressed his yearly report to his government in Paris, Navarre wrote that "with the arrival of new means [from Red China], I can no longer guarantee a successful outcome . . ." Yet, he also did not draw what should have been the logical consequence of the various elements of information which now filtered into his office: a massive influx of Chinese and Soviet logistical support to the Viet-Minh forces; the rapid closing-in of several Viet-Minh divisions on Dien Bien Phu; and the lack

*Xenophon was a Greek general who led the retreat of 10,000 of his troops from Persia across Turkey to Greece, in 401-400 B.C.

†Ariane was the daughter, in Greek mythology, of King Minos of Crete, and led Theseus out of the Minotaur's labyrinth.

of additional reinforcements from France for his own depleted troops. Far from reducing the scope of "Atlante" or of canceling it altogether, he went ahead with it.

At that crucial juncture, Navarre became unfaithful to his own policy of economy of forces, which he had practiced since he had assumed command in July. Thus Dien Bien Phu became, instead of a daring but relatively safe play, a desperate gamble. As seen from Navarre's vantage point, even the loss of Dien Bien Phu was an acceptable risk if it first fulfilled its role as what the French call *abcès de fixation* (an untranslatable French military term which designates small forces that act as "bait," or poles of attraction, for the enemy while their parent force makes its retreat toward a better position or prepares itself for a counterthrust elsewhere).

To Cogny, the battalions that were going to be offered up for sacrifice at Dien Bien Phu were not impersonal pawns upon a chessboard, but flesh-and-blood units of his own command. In fact, they were the *best* troops available in all of Indochina. The realization that they were going to be used as bait for the enemy's main battle force seemed to Cogny not only a military mistake of first magnitude, but also rank betrayal. This feeling dominates Cogny's writings ten years later; while Navarre's reflect incomprehension of Cogny's argument. Navarre later invoked a number of sieges in which the besieged force had succumbed, but by its struggle had bought time for the main force to fight on to victory. Indeed, had Dien Bien Phu been played as a *Kriegspiel* on a set of computers, no doubt the computers would have confirmed Navarre's view that the loss of the garrison of Dien Bien Phu was strategically acceptable. But his very brilliance as a military theorist prevented him from seeing that the loss of some of the best units of the French Army in Indochina would probably break the back of combat morale in Indochina itself, and erode political support for the war effort in France.

All this still does not explain what led Navarre to accept the fantastic proposition that nine French infantry battalions (only three of which could be considered elite troops) could withstand, inside a ring of hastily built field entrenchments, the assault of three Communist divisions solidly supported by artillery firepower unprecedented in the annals of fighting in Indochina. Navarre, as it behooves a commander-in-chief, accepted full responsibility for his decision, but his gesture does not satisfactorily explain the basis on which his decision was made. Many French officers then in Navarre's entourage tend to blame Col. Berteil for surrounding the commander-in-chief with an atmosphere of un-warranted optimism. Yet this cannot possibly suffice to explain the risk taken at Dien Bien Phu. According to Gen. Catroux, the chairman of the investigating commission, Navarre's lack of firsthand knowledge of jungle warfare in the marshes of Indochina was the principal cause of a fatal flaw in reasoning: On the basis of intelligence provided him, Navarre felt that the Viet-Minh could hardly concentrate more than one division at Dien Bien Phu within a month's time and that it would be impossible for the enemy to maintain more than a two-division siege force at Dien Bien Phu even for a limited period in view of the severe pounding of his communication lines by the French Air Force. In other words, what Navarre and his general staff in Saigon planned was a repetition of the siege and attack on Na-San the year before, with each side operating on a somewhat larger scale but with the French eventually carrying the day because of their superiority in ground and air firepower.

The underestimation of the Viet-Minh's capabilities was perhaps the only *real* error made by the French commander-in-chief in planning for the Indochina campaign of spring, 1954. Yet it was a strategic error and had strategic consequences. This view was enunciated by Gen. Catroux when he stated in 1959 that Gen. Navarre had been acting under the influence of preconceived ideas which his staff had pro-claimed as eternal truths; *i.e.,* that the enemy had reached his apex of strength and that he was unable to launch large-scale operations in view of his logistical limitations.[44] A major study of the battle of Dien Bien Phu, prepared at the French War College, held that the high command in Saigon had "substituted the preconceived idea it had of the Viet-Minh for the facts; that is, for intelligence based upon the verified information it had received." The supercilious rejection by the general staff of unpopular facts reported to them by the fighting men in the field was to remain a constant factor in the Vietnamese situation.

The Viet-Minh high command shared, at least in part, the views of Gen. Navarre and his staff. In his book on the battle of Dien Bien Phu, General Vo Nguyen Giap makes this abundantly clear. His own logisti-cians, apparently, were afraid that they would not be able to supply a large siege force so far away from their major centers of supply. Some of the field commanders, mindful of the disastrous experience when they attacked the French "Marshal de Lattre Line" in 1951, and the field fortifications of Na-San in 1952, were not particularly inclined to attack Dien Bien Phu in a brief massive rush.

As the Viet-Minh well knew, their troops were inexperienced in the destruction of well-entrenched and mutually supporting strongpoints. Thus, a series of headlong rushes against such French fortifications could well result in extremely heavy losses and a perhaps crippling deterioration of morale. Failure could set back the over-all Communist plan for a general offensive by a year, after which the new influx of extremely large amounts of American aid would make itself felt in Indochina and would permit the French vastly to expand the native Indochinese armies. Thus, Dien Bien Phu became a momentous gamble for the Viet-Minh as well. General Giap's decision was not easy. Surely he must have encountered much resistance within his own staff and among the political leaders of the Viet-Minh. But, says Giap:

> . . . we came to the conclusion that we could not secure success if we struck swiftly. In consequence, *we resolutely chose the other tactics: To strike surely and advance surely.* In taking this correct decision, *we strictly followed this fundamental principle of the conduct of a revolutionary war: Strike to win, strike only when success is certain; if it is not, then don't strike.*
>
> In the Dien Bien Phu campaign, the adoption of these tactics demanded of us firmness and a spirit of resolution. . . . As a result not everybody was immediately convinced of the correctness of these tactics. We patiently educated our men, pointed out that there were real difficulties, but that our task was to overcome them to create good conditions for the great victory we sought.[45]

In the deadly guessing game that is grand strategy, the little Vietnamese history professor with his largely self-taught military science had totally outguessed the French generals and colonels with their general-staff school diplomas. As the divisions of the Viet-Nam People's Army swiftly began to close in on the garrison of Dien Bien Phu, and the latter made no move to evacuate the valley, Giap knew that the final victory in the battle was to be his. A few months after the battle, Giap summed up his view of the situation in a few simple phrases:

> The French Expeditionary Corps faced a strategic surprise—it believed that we would not attack and we did attack; and with a tactical surprise—we had solved the problems of closing in, of positioning our artillery, and of getting our supplies through.[46]

The Battle of Dien Bien Phu was lost during the brief fortnight between November 25 and December 7, 1953. It was not lost in the little valley in Viet-Nam's highland jungles but in the air-conditioned map room of the French commander-in-chief. Once Giap had decided to accept trial by battle at Dien Bien Phu, it remained only for 15,000 French and 50,000 Viet-Minh troops to act out the drama in pain and blood and death.

Sorties

WHILE THE FATE of Dien Bien Phu was being decided at a higher level in Saigon and Hanoi, its garrison was busily engaged in transforming the verdant valley into the messy terrain characteristic of modern warfare. Small tent cities sprang up on hillocks where only a few days before broad-horned buffaloes grazed. Large brush fires had been set in many places by the paratroopers to clear away vegetation from prospective fields of fire, and the 17th Airborne Engineers had dismantled several of the native houses to build emergency bridges across the Nam Yum and the small creek which separated the airfield from the town. On November 25, at 1130, the first Dakota cargo plane landed on the rebuilt airstrip. The wash of its propellers left a long trail of reddish sand behind it. The sand, churned up by thousands of landings and take-offs, was soon to cover Dien Bien Phu.

Even though the arrival of the first T'ai mountaineer units three days later added a certain amount of "local color" to the operation, it still rested mainly on lightly armed airborne troops who had not been trained to build and defend fixed positions. The paratroopers knew that they were not going to stay in Dien Bien Phu and, understandably, they did not go about the business of building field fortifications with the sense of urgency they no doubt would have displayed had they known that the valley was soon to be attacked by vastly superior forces. For a few brief days, the whole operation had the air of a vast Boy Scout jamboree. The multinationality of the French forces: French, Foreign Legion, Vietnamese, Arabic, and African, living in pup tents and cooking over small camp fires, only added an air of unreality.

On November 28, Dakota aircraft unloaded the eight 105-mm. howitzers of the Autonomous Laotian Artillery Battery (BAAL). This unit, airlifted in from Laos as a stopgap measure, never endeared itself to the garrison because the Laotian gun crews were obviously terrified at the thought of having to fight in a valley far from home. Furthermore, its pieces, American hand-me-downs that had been given to the Laotians when the French and the Vietnamese no longer found them dependable, were so obviously worn out that their effective range barely exceeded 1,500 yards. In December, to everyone's relief, the Laotians were transferred back to Laos. Better-qualified artillery units had become available.

In the meantime, two other key men were to enter the unfolding Dien Bien Phu drama. The first was the man who was to command the fortress throughout the battle, if in name only; the second was the man who would lead it, in fact. As we have seen, Gen. Cogny had promised to relieve Gen. Gilles of his command at Dien Bien Phu so that he could resume his post as commander of all French airborne forces in Indochina. Several senior colonels in Indochina had been offered the Dien Bien Phu command but chose to turn down the offer. At least one of them stated openly that he felt that the defense of Dien Bien Phu would be an open invitation to disaster. According to a version of an incident which neither of the participants has denied, both Navarre and Cogny had agreed upon the choice of Col. de Castries during their joint trip to Dien Bien Phu on November 29, and Gen. Gilles had agreed with their choice.[1]

Navarre had reasons for favoring that choice. He had known de Castries personally for almost twenty years, when the latter served as a sergeant and Navarre as a lieutenant in the 16th Dragoons. Later on, during the victorious dash into Germany in 1944-45, de Castries had been the commander of an armored squadron in the 3rd Moroccan *Spahis* (Cavalry), whose regimental commander again was Navarre. The commander-in-chief, therefore, was fully aware of the various traits which made de Castries stand out even among the other highly individualistic French senior commanders in Indochina.

Colonel Christian Marie Ferdinand de la Croix de Castries, born in Paris in 1902, looked every inch the blue-blooded aristocrat he was. As his official biography showed (the French Army's public information office had soon realized how very much this impressed American journalists) the de Castries' ancestors had served France with the sword since the Crusades. They included a field marshal; a general, Armand de Castries, who had served with Lafayette in America; eight other generals; an admiral; and four royal lieutenant-governors.

De Castries had disdained the routine way of becoming an officer, particularly for a man of his social status. Instead of entering the Army through the military academy, he enlisted as a cavalryman at twenty and rose through the ranks to sergeant before being posted, in 1925, to the Saumur Cavalry School as an officer candidate. Throughout the 1930's de Castries' life appears to have been a *dolce vita*. As a member of the French international riding championship team from 1927 to 1939, de Castries could be seen at every fashionable event of Paris high society. A daredevil pilot since 1921, holder of two world championships for horseback riding (the high jump in 1933 and the broad jump in 1935), the young nobleman with the profile of a Roman emperor was irresistible to women. His close brushes with the outraged husbands of his female conquests were countless. A reckless gambler, he was also debt-ridden.

His impetuousness led him to request service with the famous *Corps Francs* (a commando-type force) at the outbreak of the war in September, 1939. One of his subordinates recalled how de Castries and his small troop of men had operated in German territory in the Sarre far beyond the Maginot Line in order to take German prisoners. One day, having accomplished his mission behind the German lines, de Castries had the church bells rung in the small German village which he had infiltrated. When two of his men were killed by retaliatory artillery fire of the Germans, another curious character trait of de Castries came to the fore: he seemingly "withdrew" from the situation. He was to say later that he did not like to come into contact with things that were not beautiful. To see pain or death made him feel uncomfortable. When he commanded his own armored squadron in 1944-45, he allegedly avoided contact with the dead and wounded of his own unit, and almost never visited the squadron's dressing stations.

This did not reflect upon his personal courage. In June, 1940, he fought for three days with sixty men against a whole German battalion, reinforced by tanks, and was taken prisoner only after he was wounded and his men were out of ammunition. In Germany, he made three unsuccessful escape attempts. Then, on March 31, 1941, he succeeded in digging his way out from Oflag IV-D, a maximum-security camp deep in Silesia, along with twenty other officers. After a hair-raising trip across the breadth of Germany, he returned to France. He promptly crossed the Spanish border illegally and joined the Free French Forces in Africa.

Wounded a second time in Italy (where his jeep hit a mine), de Castries nevertheless participated in the landing in southern France and in the final campaigns against Germany. He was first assigned to Indochina in 1946. As a commander of a light armored squadron group in Cochinchina, he soon acquired a solid reputation as a *baroudeur* (a "fighter"). In 1951, after a tour of duty at the War College in Paris and a promotion to lieutenant colonel, Gen. de Lattre de Tassigny recalled de Castries to duty in Indochina and gave him command of the critical Red River sector. De Lattre, who liked officers who combined guts with "style," took an immediate liking to the dashing cavalryman with his bright-red *Spahi* cap and scarf, his magnificent riding crop and his combination of easygoing manners and ducal mien, which made him as irresistible to women in Indochina in the 1950's as he had been to Parisiennes of the 1930's.

Seriously wounded in a large-scale ambush, in which both his legs were badly fractured, de Castries was repatriated to France for an assignment with SHAPE. Though still limping from his wounds (he was to use a cane henceforth) he managed, through an effort of iron will, to participate in horse-jumping events during November, 1952. With the appointment of his former regimental commander as commander-in-chief in Indochina, de Castries wasn't happy until he was assigned to Indochina once more in August, 1953, and given the choice command of a mobile group in a difficult sector of the Red River delta. At fifty he was a full colonel, Commander of the Legion of Honor, wounded three times, and mentioned eighteen times in dispatches.

Therefore, his appointment to the command of the fortified camp at Dien Bien Phu was not entirely illogical. A man was needed there who enjoyed the confidence of the commander-in-chief, who had an eye for the use of armor and mobility, and who had sufficient prestige to be followed and obeyed by his soldiers as well as by the senior officers who were to become his immediate subordinates during the battle.

The other key officer in the defense of Dien Bien Phu was Lieutenant Colonel Pierre Charles Langlais. In almost all respects, Langlais was the opposite of his commander. De Castries, though Paris-born, originated from the strongly Latinized parts of southwestern France. Langlais, who was born in 1909 in Brittany, looked, with his angular features over a wiry body, every inch the Celt. De Castries affected not to be serious even in the most difficult situations and never lost his exquisite courtesy. Langlais, who was never known to refuse a stiff drink, was also famous for his towering rages and his unflagging devotion to his men. De Castries had approached his army career as a dilettante and had risen through the ranks. Langlais had passed the stiff entrance examinations to the French military academy at St. Cyr and was therefore a full-fledged regular. De Castries had chosen to serve in a "fashionable" cavalry regiment, never too far from the fleshpots of Paris. Langlais had, with equal deliberation, chosen what was probably the loneliest military assignment the prewar French Army had to offer: the *Méharistes*—the prestigious corps of camel-riders that patrolled the Sahara Desert, engaging in constant scrimmages with marauding Arabic tribes. In the Méhariste units a young French officer would often spend months in the open desert with his native camel-riders without ever returning to a fixed base, facing constant hunger and thirst (there were no portable radio communications available then) as well as sandstorms and the risk of being drawn into a deadly ambush by the desert-wise tribesmen. This hard school was to stand Langlais in good stead when, after campaigning during World War II in Italy, France, and Germany, he first went to Indochina with the 9th Colonial Infantry Division in October, 1945.

As a young battalion commander, he participated in the first battles of the Indochina war in December, 1946, notably in the bitter house-to-house fighting that accompanied the French reoccupation of the city of Hanoi in the spring of 1947. He returned to Indochina for a second two-year tour of duty in 1949. Assigned to the Chinese border, he witnessed at first hand the defeat of the last remnants of the Chinese Nationalist forces on the mainland. Later, he was given other difficult assignments in central Viet-Nam and northern Laos. Upon his return to France, Langlais took command of the 1st Colonial Half-Brigade of Paratroop Commandos, which had been commanded by his friend Jean Gilles. In order to take this assignment, Langlais became a paratrooper. Returning to Indochina for yet another tour of duty, he was given the command of GAP 2 and, as we have seen earlier, participated, with unfortunate consequences to himself, in the first air drop on Dien Bien Phu.

Langlais knew de Castries, since they had come to Indochina at almost the same time in 1945. There was a great deal of mutual esteem between the two men. Even a decade after the battle and, despite what was to take place later at Dien Bien Phu, Langlais never lost his friendly attitude toward de Castries.

On November 30, 1953, Langlais, who had been nursing his ankle at Hanoi's choicest hotel, the Métropole, met de Castries on the staircase as the latter was hurrying to a last-minute briefing at Gen. Cogny's headquarters prior to taking his new command at Dien Bien Phu.

De Castries informed Langlais that Gen. Gilles had designated him (Langlais) as the commander of the airborne forces in the valley. Langlais pointed at his plaster cast and said:

"In that case, Colonel, you will have to make do with a clumpfoot as a commander for your paratroops. I won't be able to walk normally for another month."

"Oh well," said de Castries, "we'll find you a horse."[2]

On December 12, Col. Langlais arrived at Dien Bien Phu. But this time he took the precaution of using a transport aircraft. As de Castries had promised, there was indeed a snow-white T'ai pony awaiting Langlais in the valley, and thus the paratroop colonel rode into battle, as he would have in 1914, astride on his charger.

In the meantime, at Dien Bien Phu, the airborne battalions had begun their sorties as soon as they had received Gen. Cogny's Directive 739 of November 30. Elements of the 8th Parachute Assault Battalion under Captain Pierre Tourret, reinforced by Captain Guilleminot's company of T'ai mountaineers from the 3rd BT, were to penetrate deeply into the jungle to the north of Dien Bien Phu and make contact with the French-led tribesmen who operated as guerrilla units throughout the mountain areas. These guerrillas were intended to create insecurity behind the Viet-Minh's lines, just as the Communists had done behind the French lines.

Little was known about the French commando units. They operated directly under the jurisdiction of the French Central Intelligence services, just as ten years later the U. S. Special Forces in South Viet-Nam for a time were to operate directly under the responsibility of the Central Intelligence Agency. Their commander, Major Roger Trinquier, had a great deal more authority than his lowly military rank would indicate, since he and his free-wheeling subordinates could operate largely on their own. Officially these guerrilla units were known until December, 1953, as *Groupements de Commandos Mixtes Aèroportés,* or GCMA; *i.e.,* Composite Airborne Commando Groups.[3] In December, 1953, their name was changed to *Groupements Mixtes d'Intervention* (GMI) or Composite Intervention Groups; but their mission remained the same: to set up native *maquis* behind enemy lines and report back as much intelligence as possible. The French members of the GCMA's were hand-picked for this mission and usually spoke one or more of the mountain dialects perfectly. They were also capable of getting along with a minimum of western conveniences for several months, if not years, on end. Ideally, Dien Bien Phu should have become a permanent base where such GCMA groups could come for a much needed rest or to which they could withdraw if the pressure became too great. That had been the basis for the idea of the airborne "mooring points," and the sorties of the airborne units from Dien Bien Phu were to provide the field test for this theory.

Tourret, who commanded the whole operation, decided to give his paratroops the maximum benefit of the mountaineers' knowledge of local conditions. Hence the task force was reorganized so that each of the paratroop companies had one mountaineer platoon attached to it; Capt. Guilleminot commanded the lead element of the small force. The objective of the force was not only to make contact with the *maquis* elements in the area (notably the Meo tribesmen at Ban Phathong) but also to push as far as the important road junction of Tuan Giao, about fifty miles northeast of Dien Bien Phu (see map, p. 60). Tuan Giao was the major Communist supply staging area near Dien Bien Phu and, as soon as Lai Chau had fallen into Communist hands, had also become the terminal for the shortest supply road between the battle-field and Communist China. Possession of it was therefore vital for both sides.

For two days, Tourret's paratroopers and Guilleminot's T'ai moun-taineers hacked their way northward via Ban Tau and Muong Pon into the 6,000-foot-high Phathong Mountain ridge. So far, aside from the physical strain of the operation, they had encountered no difficulties and, more importantly, had made no contact with the enemy. Tourret radioed back to Dien Bien Phu that he needed silver coins for the partisans (the latter wisely had no confidence whatever in the various types of rapidly depreciating paper currency which the French, the Communists, and the native governments issued) and that he also needed maps for his push on Tuan Giao. He agreed to a rendezvous with one of the Cricket aircraft from Dien Bien Phu, an appointment the latter faithfully kept on December 5 at 1000. While Tourret was clawing his way into the hills north of Dien Bien Phu, Maj. Souquet's 1st BPC and parts of Bréchignac's II/1 RCP pushed forward directly along Road 41, a bare three miles northeast of the center of Dien Bien Phu itself.

At that point, there existed along the road a small T'ai tribal village called Ban Him Lam. The road to Ban Him Lam twisted through a narrow valley overshadowed on both sides by hills in the 1,200-foot range; and the paratroopers, confident that no enemy force would oper-ate that close to Dien Bien Phu at that time, advanced along the road without any particular precautionary measures. But at 0945, the 1st

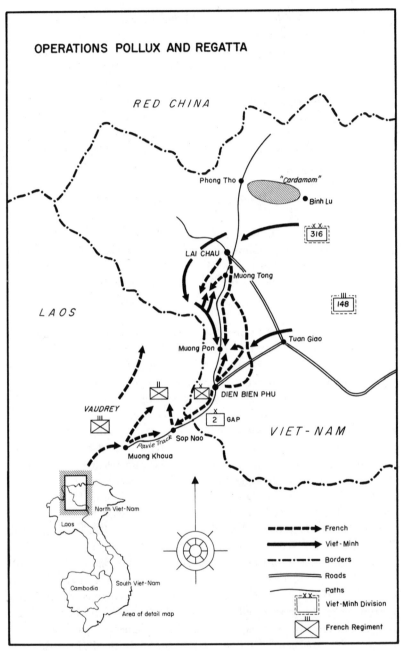

OPERATIONS POLLUX AND REGATTA

Company of the 1st BPC radioed back that it saw suspicious signs of enemy troops nearby.

Hardly had the message been transmitted when murderously accurate Communist mortar and grenade-launcher fire completely enveloped 1st Company. The lead platoon was virtually wiped out within a matter of seconds. The rest of the company, with the sound discipline that can only be developed by well-trained regulars, immediately formed a hedgehog position as screaming waves of Communist infantrymen emerged from the thickets. The battle soon developed into bitter hand-to-hand fighting with commando daggers, machetes, and hand grenades. Over the din of the battle, the Communist troops could be distinctly heard appealing to their Vietnamese brothers who were fighting as members of the paratroop battalion. They appealed to them not to lay down their lives for the "French Imperialists." For a brief moment, the Communists' appeals seem to have had some effect, as a few of the Vietnamese paratroopers ceased firing and began to look for a way to crawl out from the fight. Only the providential arrival of the rest of the task force, as well as some artillery fire laid down by the main position's howitzers, finally saved 1st Company of 1st BPC from total destruction. Even so, its losses had been heavy—fourteen dead and twenty-six wounded lay bleeding on the terrain. As usual, the enemy had disappeared as suddenly as it had come and had taken almost all its casualties with it. But not all of them. A quick search of the pockets of some of the dead enemy soldiers confirmed what their quilted mountain uniforms already had revealed: they were not part of a passing guerrilla unit that had encountered the French paratroopers by sheer chance; on the contrary, they were part of Battalion 888 of the 176th Regiment of the enemy's 316th People's Army Division. The first links in the Communist siege ring around Dien Bien Phu had begun to appear.

Yet on the same day, Gen. Cogny, in the course of a visit at Dien Bien Phu, had decided in accord with Gilles and the recently arrived de Castries, to establish a strongpoint at Hill 506, which controlled Road 41, three hundred yards to the west of the village of Ban Him Lam. Gilles, to all accounts, was not too happy about Hill 506 and argued that it was overshadowed by Hills 781 and 1066 looming on the nearby horizon. Finally, the choice was made to fortify Hill 506 because it offered the best communication lines with the main position at Dien Bien Phu itself (the other two hills would have been immediately cut off from Dien Bien Phu because they were located in the middle of the jungle) and because it was hoped that the Communists would never be able to bring their artillery in close enough to take advantage of the controlling hill line. And even if the Viet-Minh were to place artillery pieces on those heights, the French fighter bombers and the heavy 155-mm. howitzers that Cogny had decided to have brought to Dien Bien Phu would silence them in short order. General Cogny was, after all, an artillery general. His judgment prevailed over that of his commanders in the field.

Another offensive stab was launched along Road 41 on December 7, this time in sufficient strength to discourage the kind of ambush that had cost the 1st BPC an entire platoon. This time, the whole GAP 1 of Col. Fourcade (1st BPC and 6th BPC), reinforced with recoilless rifles and mortars and covered by fighter bombers flying overhead, deployed itself in the direction of Ban Him Lam and pushed forward to Ban Na Loi, a good four miles beyond Hill 506. On December 9, the Viet-Minh once more tried to ambush the advancing paratroopers, but this time it found them prepared. Unmoved by the Communist appeals to surrender, the Vietnamese paratroopers held their ground alongside their French comrades. Battalion 888 never got close enough for hand-to-hand fighting. Having sufficiently freed the immediate environs of Hill 506 to permit the movement of trucks carrying building materials between Dien Bien Phu and the new strongpoint, GAP 1 methodically withdrew to the main base. On December 10, Hill 506 received its official name. It has been rumored that all the fortified positions of Dien Bien Phu had been given the names of Col. de Castries' mistresses. That rumor has remained unverified. In any case, a few of the positions did not have girls' names: Hill Gabrielle was at first known as *Le Torpilleur* (the "torpedo boat") because of its shiplike shape; another strongpoint was known as *Opéra,* after a Paris subway station; and yet another strongpoint was known as *Epervier,* or "Sparrowhawk." But 506 was baptized *Beatrice.*

The success of Tourret's four commando groups in infiltrating the valley twenty miles from Dien Bien Phu and of GAP 1 in marching ten miles into enemy territory should not have overshadowed the stark fact that each thrust had failed to attain its objective—the disruption of Communist road traffic close to the new position and the creation of viable *maquis* forces inside Communist territory. In fact, the disaster which was to strike the units retreating from Lai Chau at that very moment was only a harbinger of things to come. Dien Bien Phu indeed had ceased to fulfill its mission even before the French had a chance to build the sort of defenses that would have made it a true fortress.

The gauntlet run by elements of the garrison of Lai Chau pointed up one fallacy in thinking of Dien Bien Phu as an offensive base. As early as December 5 it had become apparent to Gen. Cogny that the capital of the T'ai highlands would become untenable.* The city itself was located at the bottom of a valley at the confluence of the Black River and the Nam Na. A small dirt airstrip, which often tended to be covered by flood waters, was Lai Chau's only means of communication with the outside world aside from a narrow jungle path which could not even accommodate jeeps in most places and in some places was even difficult for mules. It went by the name of *Piste Pavie,* or Pavie Track, in honor of Auguste Pavie, the French official who signed a protectorate treaty with the T'ai tribes in the 1880's.

As an air-land base, Lai Chau had been very important after the almost total occupation of northwestern Viet-Nam by the Communists. It had served as a mooring point for various GCMA *maquis* groups, some of which, it was said, even penetrated into Red China. Here and there, they could be seen at their base on the edge of Lai Chau; a few French sergeants, one or two junior officers and a few score tribesmen, always staying together and not mixing with the other troops of the garrison. But with the withdrawal to Dien Bien Phu of Capt. Bordier's GMPT 1 in the last days of November, it became obvious that no attempt would be made to defend the valley against the thrust of the whole 316th Division. General Cogny made the decision on December 7 to launch Operation "Pollux," along with a high-speed airborne pull-out of the regular units and civilians from the little valley under the cover of the GCMA units and the remaining sub-groupments of GMPT 1.

On December 7, Gen. Cogny, accompanied by his wife and daughter and Gen. Gilles, landed for the last time at Lai Chau and personally brought the bad news to Deo Van Long, the president of the T'ai Federation. Deo Van Long accepted the news impassively. Is his lifetime he had seen Lai Chau occupied by Chinese pirates, French soldiers, Chinese Nationalists, the Viet-Minh, and, once more, the French. On the next day, the old leader and his entourage of graceful princesses and ballet dancers embarked on a C-47 transport plane for Hanoi. He was to die in exile in France a few years later.

In 183 flights to Lai Chau, French aircraft removed the 301st Vietnamese Infantry Battalion (BVN), a paratroop company, parts of the 2nd Moroccan Tabor (Battalion), the 7th Company of the 2nd T'ai

---

*I had been to Lai Chau a few weeks earlier, and the impossibility of its prolonged defense seemed obvious.

Battalion, and finally the 327 men of the Headquarters Detachment (ZONO),[4] made up entirely of Senegalese. That air operation, baptized by the code name "Leda" (the mythological mother of Castor and Pollux) ended successfully; Lt. Col. Trancart himself left the almost deserted city on December 10, as 300 tons of ammunition and forty vehicles which had to be left behind began to blow up and burn. A few rear-guard elements still stalked through the ghost town. There also were about 400 mules and pack horses, roaming freely through the abandoned fields and streets. They had belonged to the French Army and should have been shot to keep them from being used for the enemy's own transportation: Apparently no one had the heart to do the job. Regiment 174 of the 316th People's Army Division was on the march toward Lai Chau, but it, too, had been held up by the roadless jungle as well as by occasional attacks by French fighter bombers. Also, it had to cross the *maquis* zone "Cardamom" stretching between Phong-Tho and Binh Lu. When the 316th entered Lai Chau on Saturday, December 12, 1953, they found the French tricolor flying high over the dead city. The French had left it for the Communists to cut down.[5]

The twenty-odd T'ai Irregular Light Companies (CLST) (there may have been as many as twenty-nine) now had to fight their way south to Dien Bien Phu or west to Laos. In either case, more than sixty miles of roadless jungle awaited them, for it was a foregone conclusion that the best-known tracks and paths were already under Communist control. These light companies usually comprised about 110 men armed with rifles and submachine guns and perhaps a few 60-mm. mortars. In most cases they were commanded by a native leader seconded by a French sergeant. Even a whole group of such companies would "rate" only a French lieutenant in command, so scarce were experienced cadres and specialists able to fulfill such a mission.

A deadly chess game was to develop now over 6,000 square miles of jungle between 2,100 T'ai tribesmen and thirty-six Europeans on one side, and the 316th Division, reinforced by parts of Regiment 148, on the other. Prior to the official start of "Pollux," Trancart had begun to pull back the T'ai light companies in the direction of Dien Bien Phu or Lai Chau, telescoping one unit into another so as to avoid their becoming hopelessly dispersed in the jungle. All the T'ai units were given American "694" radio sets to permit them to keep contact with each other, and were provided with whatever spare portable armament could be found at Lai Chau (such as more 60-mm. mortars).

Exactly what happened to the T'ai light companies during the desperate ten days between the evacuation of Lai Chau and the arrival of their last remnants at Dien Bien Phu will never be known. Too few unit commanders survived and some units were completely destroyed in the jungle, never to be heard from again. At the start of the evacuation, there apparently were four company groups of GMPT 1 in the Lai Chau area. Three of them were commanded respectively by Lts. Ulpat, Guillermit, and Wieme, and the fourth was commanded by Sgt. Blanc. Originally the sub-groupments Ulpat and Guillermit were supposed to stay inside Communist territory and form guerrilla groups just as the GCMA had done in the "Cardamom" area, but this soon proved unworkable. To establish a guerrilla zone, one must have time to become acquainted with the local terrain and the local populace and to set up base areas. This was no longer possible in view of the approaching Communist units. Between December 5 and December 11, three French sergeants, Guizier, Bonhil, and Lahalle, had shielded with their units (the 388th, 282nd, and 295th Light Companies respectively) the retreat of the remaining forces from Lai Chau to Partisan Pass.

But as the T'ai tribesmen began to realize they were going to leave their homeland, and often their families and villages, in enemy hands, they became unsure of themselves and some of them silently slipped way from their units. On December 10, fifty-two men of the 547th Company left their unit with four automatic rifles and a 60-mm. mortar. On the following day, Ulpat's sub-groupment received a radio message to pick up the remaining units in the Lai Chau area (Deo Van Long's palace guard and some of their family members had insisted on staying behind until the Communists reached the town). Then it was the turn of the 273rd Company to desert to a man with the exception of its native noncommissioned officers.

After receiving an air drop of food and ammunition and having reorganized his remaining six companies, Lt. Ulpat began his march south in a wide detour to the east to avoid the Communist ambushes which the faithful Cricket spotter planes already had reported to him along the Pavie Track. His progress was slowed by the fact that his column contained women and children. Nevertheless, on December 17 the sub-groupment had reached Pou Koi, about midway between Lai Chau and Dien Bien Phu to the southeast. There it received another air drop of supplies. Thus far, contact with the enemy had been limited to sporadic encounters with what seemed to be enemy scouts. Hope increased that

Ulpat would reach nearby Laos, where a relief column of Laotian mountaineers and French commando forces under Lt. Col. Vaudrey[6] was clawing its way through the jungle in the direction of the light companies.

But on December 18, at 1000, a murderous mortar barrage, followed by swift infantry attacks of Viet-Minh regulars and pro-Communist tribesmen, shattered that hope. Within a few hours, sub-groupment Ulpat had ceased to exist. Lieutenant Ulpat, five French noncommissioned officers, a T'ai lieutenant from the 301st BVN, and six tribesmen found each other after wandering in the jungle for four days. They were spotted by French helicopters from Dien Bien Phu on December 22 and picked up at 1700.

Sub-groupment Guillermit had been under constant attack since December 8 and never succeeded in shaking the enemy. Faithful to his mission of defending as long as possible the approaches to Lai Chau, Guillermit and his seven companies hung on grimly to Pa Ham Pass. Finally, under intense mortar and rifle fire from the surrounding heights, Guillermit requested permission to make a last stand on *Piton Para* (Paratroop Hill) two miles northwest of the pass. The permission was granted but too late to save Guillermit and his men. Under violent attack for almost two days, the force was overrun on December 10 at 0910 by a Communist reinforced battalion. One French sergeant, Arsicaud, and about 150 men succeeded in breaking out from the massacre and reached Muong Tong, fourteen miles south of Lai Chau, on the afternoon of December 11.

What the gallant Sgt. Arsicaud did during the next seven days deserves a whole book in itself. Muong Tong had become the rallying point of the remnants of every light company in the area, with the result that Ariscaud soon commanded a 600-man force which, according to its size, should have been commanded by a major. He diligently organized an air drop of supplies, succeeded in getting a helicopter for five serious casualties he had been carrying with him, and led his force to the south without stopping. It is surprising that the French Army, which was to maintain helicopter contact with the Arsicaud force to the end, never thought of lightening his command burden by bringing in some higher-ranking officers. Arsicaud kept driving his men south. His aim was to catch up and rendezvous with the Ulpat force at Pou Koi, but the constant pressure of Communist units made his column's progress an endless agony.[7]

At 1600, December 15, Sgt. Arsicaud reached Muong Cha under

heavy fire. A new isolated company, the 546th, and forty men from
the 547th, joined his column but only for a short time. The Communists,
like hungry wolves attacking the stragglers of a caribou herd, pounced
on the newcomers during the night and destroyed them. It had now
been four days since the Arsicaud force had received its last air drop
of supplies. The men were exhausted from hunger and thirst, as Arsicaud made known on December 16 in a laconic radio message. A
rendezvous was made for an air drop on December 17 in the afternoon
at a clearing near Ban Nam Cha. By now, the Arsicaud force was a
mere day's march behind the slower-moving Ulpat force. As the
sergeant's battalion established its bivouac at Ban Nam Nhié on the
evening of December 18, the harassed men re-established radio contact
with the base at Dien Bien Phu, only to receive the shattering news that
the Ulpat force had been crushed and that their most direct road to the
south was already sealed off. At 2130 there was a brief message from
Ariscaud that he was under attack. However, a message from GMPT 1
at Dien Bien Phu ordering him to turn around and head northwestward
into Laos apparently was never received.

When a French reconnaissance plane flew over the battle area on the
following day at 1600 it suddenly spotted Arsicaud and a handful of
men. They were still armed and they still carried a radio. The spotter
plane gave them a rendezvous point for the next day where they
could be picked up by helicopter. Arsicaud agreed that he would be
there and disappeared into the jungle after a last wave at the circling
aircraft. He and his men were never seen again.

Sergeant Blanc's group, comprising the 416th, 418th, and 428th
Light Companies, as well as the remaining headquarters elements of
GMPT 1 and dependents from the 301st BVN, never had a chance.
Encircled at Muong Pon, seventy kilometers south of Lai Chau, the
sub-groupment was constantly under heavy attack. Five wounded were
evacuated by helicopter in the afternoon of December 11 and Sgt.
Blanc attempted to push the women and children southward in the direction of the rescue forces from GAP 2, which were fighting their way
northward against strong opposition. Blanc failed in his attempt. The
three companies disappeared completely in the course of Communist
attacks during the night of December 12-13, 1953.

Only sub-groupment Wieme was lucky. Pushing resolutely eastward
into enemy territory rather than westward into the expected pursuit
area, the 431st, 432nd, and 434th Light Companies (with the 434th
under M/Sgt. Cante making its way separately from the main column)

arrived at Hill 836 six miles northeast of Dien Bien Phu as early as December 15 and reached the valley without further losses.

Other dispersed units had varying degrees of luck. The 388th Company received orders on December 12 to fall back to Partisan Pass. It sought to reach Laos via the Nam Meuk Valley. On December 14 and 15 it received air drops of supplies, and orders to march in direction of Dien Bien Phu. The order was acknowledged and the little band was seen changing directions. It disappeared during the night of December 16-17 and was never heard from afterward. The T'ai Mule Transport Company and the 248th Light Company had better luck. Already enroute southward when Lai Chau fell, they passed through Muong Pon before Sgt. Blanc's sub-groupment was encircled there and arrived at Sop Nhom on December 16, where they found a survivor of one of the commando forces of the 8th BPC and some escapees from the destroyed garrison of Muong Pon. Until then, the Mule Company had dragged along its faithful beasts. But during the night of December 16-17, the path the unit had chosen (and wisely for it led them in a wide swing around the Muong Pon battle area) became so abrupt that the mules had to be abandoned. On December 18, the Mule Company and the 248th emerged from the deep jungle and established radio contact with Dien Bien Phu. An airdrop of emergency supplies permitted the starved survivors to regain energy for the final trek. They arrived in the valley of Dien Bien Phu on December 22.

The agony of the "Pollux" force had not taken place in isolation. In fact, it was to become a first test of the ability of Dien Bien Phu to play its contemplated role as a mooring point for deep offensive stabs; a role whose importance had been underlined once more by a new directive from Gen. Cogny on December 8.[8]

The operation involved pushing the whole reinforced GAP 2 to Muong Pon, one third of the way along the Pavie Track to Lai Chau. This was no minor operation, since it involved the 1st BEP, the 5th BPVN, all the remaining elements of the 8th BPC, and two batteries of 105-mm. howitzers. The force also had one Cricket reconnaissance plane and four B-26 bombers at its disposal.

The force was alerted on December 10 at 1630 and left the valley at 0200 with Tourret's 8th BPC in the lead. Eight hours later, at 1000, Tourret reported that "progress was slow but normal." This report was confirmed by the spotter plane. Nevertheless, at 1130, just as Tourret's lead elements penetrated the seemingly abandoned village of Ban Tau, deadly accurate infantry fire suddenly erupted from the surrounding hills. With practiced speed the paratroopers fanned out into a defensive perimeter and began to engage the invisible enemy. Within a few minutes, the 8th BPC had suffered eleven casualties. It slowly began to hack its way toward a hill which would give it a better defensive position should the enemy decide to rush the small force. The newly arrived Langlais joined the column astride on his pony, but the latter soon had to be abandoned when it proved unable to advance on the narrow paths hacked out of the jungle. Grimly restraining his pain, Langlais gave a first lesson in leadership to his new command: holding on to an enlisted paratrooper and to Lt. Singland of the Heavy Airborne Mortar Company, he hobbled along with his troops for the rest of the whole mission.

In the meantime, at 1530, the Muong Pon garrison under Sgt. Blanc, hard-pressed by the enemy, kept calling for an early breakthrough of the rescue forces. It requested napalm on the surrounding enemy positions.

The advance of the bulk of GAP 2, however, had ground to a complete halt. With Tourret still pinned down on his hill, the GAP 2 made preparations for an all-around night defense. Beginning its progress again at 0300 of December 12, the bulk of GAP 2 reached Tourret at 1400 against light enemy opposition. But in order to avoid falling into yet another ambush of the type which had held up the 8th BPC, the whole GAP 2 now took to marching along the hill line running parallel to the Pavie Track. While militarily a sound solution, it proved physically agonizing. The hill line was totally covered by six- to nine-foot-high elephant grass which had to be cut with machetes. In full battle gear with no sources of water within reach, the paratroopers hacked their way forward at a rate of 200 yards an hour. Many of them collapsed from the effects of dehydration. Grimly, the men marched on throughout the night of December 12-13, spurred on by the radioed pleas of the hard-pressed garrison of Muong Pon.

On December 13 at 0800 and with Maj. Leclerc's 5th BPVN in the lead, the GAP's march on Muong Pon continued, this time within earshot of the battle for Muong Pon where Sgt. Blanc's depleted T'ai light companies were still holding out. But there remained an agonizing four kilometers to cover at the cost of thousands of machete blows against an almost impenetrable wall of high grass. As the noon hour approached, the fire at Muong Pon suddenly began to die down. A few minutes later the little reconnaissance Cricket confirmed the bad news: Sgt. Blanc's gallant little garrison had been overrun, the village was in flames and apparently crawling with Viet-Minh regulars. Nonetheless, the GAP pushed on in the hopes of being able to rescue some of the survivors. It was again the paratroopers of Tourret who were in the lead. When they reached Muong Pon at 1400, its ruins were deserted save for the bodies of the T'ai tribal soldiers who had fallen. The survivors and the civilian population had been carried away by the departing Communists. Tourret and his men fell back on the main column at 1530, having found no survivors.

There was yet another act in the dramatic attempt at rescuing the light companies. The four earlier-dispatched commando groups of the 8th BPC, reinforced with one company of the 3rd T'ai Battalion had, upon the news that the garrison of Muong Pon was in desperate straits, hacked their own way through the jungle east to west from their raid on the road to Tuan Giao. They had remained in radio contact with the 5th BPVN and also had reached the Muong Pon area at almost the same time as the vanguard of Capt. Tourret. They had learned by radio that the garrison at Muong Pon had succumbed. The paratroop commandos, fleshed out with tribesmen who were native to the area, truly showed what an elite force could do even under trying physical circumstances: in contrast to the sluggish progress of the paratroopers of GAP 2, who were hauling along on their march everything from medium mortars to 105-mm. howitzers and who were not accompanied by native T'ai tribal forces, the mixed T'ai and paratroop force had approached Muong Pon in harrowing forced marches. They, too, had to hack their way through the jungle with machetes. Instead of being able to follow a ridge line, they had to walk *across* several ridge lines whose valley bottoms were often 2,000 feet below the crests. For three days in a row, they kept moving for seventeen hours a day, only to be faced with the heartbreaking fact that the whole effort had been in vain. In fact, one of the last ironies of the situation was that some of the commando elements had come across the path of advance of GAP 2 and, thinking it newly hacked out by the advancing Viet-Minh, had thoroughly mined it. When the 8th BPC was apprised of the fact that the Vietnamese paratroops of the 5th BPVN would have to use the pass for their withdrawal, Sgt. Benzeck, who had placed the mines, had to turn back and undertake the dangerous job of defusing his own booby traps.

While the attempt at rescuing Muong Pon had failed, the battle was far from over for the 2nd Airborne Group. Major Leclerc's and Capt. Tourret's spearhead forces had barely begun their withdrawal southward when at 1650 their column was raked by heavy enemy fire. As the report of GAP 2 was to show later, the Viet-Minh had succeeded in installing its heavy weapons within 500 yards of the last nighttime bivouac of the paratroopers' weapons (they were undetected by both French aerial reconnaissance and the paratroop patrols) and they were able to blanket the paratroopers with utmost precision. Within a few minutes, the paratroopers were taking heavy losses and calling for an air strike by the B-26 bombers which were at their disposal. The prompt intervention of the bombers probably saved the 5th BPVN from almost total destruction. Even so, the battalion's losses were serious: three dead, twenty-five wounded, and thirteen troopers missing.

This was not the end. The Communist forces, no longer held up by the roadblock of Muong Pon, now began moving in on the whole airborne group. On December 14 at noon, the howitzers began firing in support of the rear-guard elements of the GAP 2 formed by the paratroopers of the 1st Foreign Legion Parachute Battalion (BEP). As on the previous day, the Viet-Minh sought to close in with their target as rapidly as possible in order to avoid the destructive strikes by the French Air Force. At 1450 the 1st BEP reported that it was heavily engaged in hand-to-hand fighting with Communist regulars. Again the French Air Force intervened, this time getting a foretaste of what fighting would be like at Dien Bien Phu. At 1500 one of the reconnaissance *Crickets* reported that it had been hit by enemy antiaircraft fire and at 1600 one of the fighter-bombers reported hits.

The Legionnaires in the meantime were taking a serious pounding. When the enemy finally broke off the attack at 1830, the 1st BEP had twenty-four wounded and twenty-eight dead and missing to report. It also had lost a great deal of equipment: four automatic rifles, twelve submachine guns, one .30-cal. machine gun, and three radio sets. The 5th BPVN lost another three dead and twenty wounded in its last clash. On December 15 at 0735, the last elements of GAP 2 re-entered the valley of Dien Bien Phu. Its first raid in force and reconnaissance in depth had ended in failure. In addition, the destruction of the T'ai light companies had shown that it was almost impossible to maintain any kind of regular units behind Communist lines in the face of determined Communist clearing operations. As the situation now developed, the forces at Dien Bien Phu had ceased to be a mooring point for offensive operations within one week after the fall of Lai Chau. It was equally obvious that heavy paratroop forces were not the ideal tool for this sort of operation. On the other hand, small raiding parties or guerrilla units such as Tourret's commandos or the GCMA "Cardamom" force were unable to inflict upon the enemy the kind of damage that would prevent it from carrying out its major strategic intentions. For such small forces to become truly effective would take months, if not years, of political preparation of the terrain. This the French had failed to do when there was time for it. Now it was too late; five years' neglect could not be repaired in a few weeks.

There now remained the task of adding up the losses of the past week of mobile operations. When the "Pollux" force had set out from Lai Chau on December 9, it numbered 2,101 men including three French lieutenants and thirty-four French enlisted men. When the last survivors of the T'ai Mule Company and the 248th Light Company reached Dien Bien Phu on December 22, a total of ten Frenchmen, including Lt. Ulpat, and 175 tribesmen were accounted for. Almost 2,000 armed men and several hundred civilian dependents along with two French officers and fourteen sergeants had disappeared on the trek. In addition, the Communists had captured enough weapons to arm a regiment.

In his hard-hitting post mortem of the operation, the newly arrived commander of the GAP 2, Lt. Col. Langlais, noted the incredible ability of the enemy to camouflage his gun positions and camps so as to render them invisible to aerial observation and ground reconnaissance. In contrast, Langlais noted, the French paratroopers would establish their bivouacs without much concert about camouflage and, like any "rich" Western amy, would drop along their path empty cigarette packs and ration containers "to leave a track like Hansel and Gretel," for Communist patrols to follow.

This first serious setback—remarkably enough, it received almost no publicity whatever[9]—seemed to have made no impression on the French Northern Command in Hanoi, which had been responsible for the conduct of the battle.

With Lt. Col. Langlais in the lead, despite his barely repaired ankle, the GAP again made for the hills at midnight of December 21, 1953. Not that the eight intervening days had been spent by the Airborne Group in idle rest and recuperation; on the contrary, it had been busily engaged building the headquarters bunkers of Dien Bien Phu, and the 5th BPVN was hacking out the brush about three kilometers northwest of the airfield around two small hills which were to become later strongpoint "Anne-Marie."

The terrain which the second reconnaissance raid was to traverse was if anything even more difficult than that encountered on the attempt to reach Muong Pon. Moreover, even if it succeeded in reaching the French-Laotian forces of Maj. Vaudrey, the mission would have no tangible aftereffect; neither Vaudrey nor the garrison at Dien Bien Phu had sufficient troops to spare to make the link-up permanent. In addition, to make the jungle track between Dien Bien Phu and Sop Nao (the nearest Laotian town) accessible even to light vehicles would have been a feat of road engineering that could not have been dreamed of under prevailing conditions. To give but one practical example, it took the United States Army in nearby Burma nearly eighteen months to build the famous 120-mile-long Ledo Road—and that without enemy interference and with all the engineering equipment that American ingenuity could muster. The fifty-mile-long jungle track between Sop Nao and Dien Bien Phu was cut by deep ravines, crossed a 6,000-foot-high mountain range of sheer limestone cliffs, and was located hundreds of miles away from the nearest French heavy equipment bases. The engineering aspects of the problem alone were nearly insoluble. When one considers that such a road would have to have been built in the face of constant Communist attacks by full-fledged regular divisions, the futility of a ground link-up with Laos for other than psychological reasons ("to prove" that Dien Bien Phu was not hopelessly sealed off from the outside world) was obviously futile.

The operation had a double code name: "Ardèche" (a French department known for its deep valleys) for the forces coming from Laos and "Régate" (Regatta) for Langlais' forces coming from Dien Bien Phu. The "Ardèche" force was composed of the 5th Battalion of Laotian Chasseurs commanded by Maj. Vaudrey and the 5th Moroccan *Tabor** commanded by Maj. Coquelet. The whole force was commanded by Maj. Vaudrey. "Ardèche" had begun only a few days after operation "Castor" and had involved a harrowing 200-mile march in the face of constant harassment by Laotian pro-Communist Pathet Lao guerrillas. It was also known that all of Battalion 920 of Viet-Minh Regiment 148 was awaiting the "Ardèche" force at the key river crossing of Muong Khoua (see map, p. 60). Muong Khoua had already been the site of an epic battle during April and May, 1953, when the French ordered a light Laotian battalion to make a last stand there in order to gain time for the defense of central Laos.[10]

Now the roles were reversed. Battalion 920 was holding fixed positions and it was the French and Laotians who were on the offensive and in the jungle. They reached the heights overlooking Muong Khoua on December 3, 1953. The Viet-Minh, who had been expecting the attack for days, were ready to receive them with well dug-in automatic weapons, pre-set mortar aiming points, and even mine fields, quite probably the same the French had left behind when they were overrun six months earlier. The combined Laotian-Moroccan-French force pressed on. By 1630 it

*A battalion-size unit of Moroccan semi-regular *goumiers* in the French Army.

had captured a key hill overlooking the main positions and the battle became a carbon copy of the earlier one, except that for once the Communists and not the French were cornered into defending a fixed position. The 920th was a solid force and grimly held on throughout the whole next day in the other two bunker positions. Its last survivors escaped across the Nam Ou River during the following night.

A lesson could have been learned here for Dien Bien Phu: there is little point in defending a fortified position if adequate firepower and personnel are not available to beat off the assault force. This lesson had apparently been learned by the Communists after Muong Khoua. It was not learned by the French.

With Muong Khoua solidly in hand as a rear base, the "Ardèche" force was ready for its final dash toward Sop Nao, where it was to meet the paratroopers from Dien Bien Phu. This force consisted of the 2nd Battalion, 3rd Foreign Legion Regiment, which reached Muong Khoua after a forced march of twenty-one days and looked, according to one observer on the ground, "like concentration-camp inmates. Its young doctor has lost twenty-two pounds. Several men are dying of typhus."[11]

The trek to Sop Nao, although only twenty-five miles away, proved miserably difficult. As the path led across an almost uninhabited mountain chain, no water was available and the men chewed leaves from the opium-poppy flowers to still their thirst. There was also one Frenchwoman in the force; she was one of the top combat reporters in the Indochina war, with a splendid record in the French Resistance Movement during World War II. Mlle. Brigitte Friang had been parachuted to the "Ardèche" force before it reached Muong Khoua and was to follow the whole operation on foot all the way to Dien Bien Phu. On December 21, the force reached Nga Na Song, a bare eight miles from Sop Nao. As Communist forces were reported in the area, the Moroccans of the 5th Battalion set up a defense perimeter around it while Vaudrey and the Laotians made the final dash for Sop Nao. The small airstrip at Nga Na Song had been completely destroyed by the Viet-Minh, who had made the population construct dikes across it. Throughout the night, in the light of the burning vegetation, the Moroccans flattened out all the obstructions on the field with picks and shovels parachuted to them at 2100 by the supply aircraft. Colonel de Castries, who desired to be on hand when the "Ardèche" and the "Régate" forces met in the middle of the Laotian jungle and in the presence of previously flown-in newspaper men and camera operators, landed at 1400 on the following day on the small strip in his own *Cricket* liaison craft.

One last fire fight with the retreating Communists still awaited Vaudrey and his Laotians as they entered Sop Nao. A rear-guard force of Regiment 148 had laid an ambush across the path; it had to be destroyed with mortar fire and gun fire from the 57-mm. recoilless rifles that had been painfully dragged along through the jungle. But at noon on December 23, 1953, Maj. Vaudrey and Lt. Col. Langlais shook hands in front of the cameras in the middle of Sop Nao. For public consumption, the myth that Dien Bien Phu could become the mooring point of free-wheeling raiding forces had been established. The paratroopers of the 8th BPC and 1st BEP, who had reached Sop Nao with no incident other than the repeated crossing of deep icy rivers with all their equipment, looked somewhat bedraggled in their dripping wet uniforms: their last bivouac had been at Houei Houn, three miles from Sop Nao but across yet another river.

The return to Dien Bien Phu was even worse than the approach march. Unseasonal rains had fallen and the already swift mountain rivers were even harder to cross. Christmas was spent in wet uniforms in the middle of the jungle. Because large elements of Regiment 148 were now reported in the surrounding area, Lt. Col. Langlais had decided to follow a new path, and air drops of additional supplies were forbidden in order not to give away the new route of the "Régate" force. The path became so impracticable that it was decided to destroy part of the heavy equipment. A Legionnaire paratrooper had his arm torn off when a sabotaged mortar exploded prematurely. He was evacuated by a helicopter which also brought in an American journalist, Dixie Reeds, who was to follow the last two days of the march to Dien Bien Phu in a business suit with a pair of American loafers on his feet. Finally on the morning of December 26, a cry went up among the lead elements of the column: "Dien Bien Phu!" The valley had finally been reached.

But the Viet-Minh gave the returning force a last reminder of how closely it had been shadowed. As the French crossed the last hill line in full view of the fixed positions in the valley, an isolated rifle shot was heard and one of the paratroopers crumpled in a heap. He was to die a few hours later.

As the exhausted paratroopers stumbled into camp, Brigitte Friang noticed a "Christmas tree" in front of one of the dugouts—a tree that might have come straight out of Goya's *Disasters of War*. The trunk was a pole used to hang barbed wire; it was crowned with an enemy helmet and carrying for ornaments a well-worn GI boot, empty bottles, and smashed cans of army rations.

Thus ended the last deep penetration of French forces from Dien Bien

Phu into the hinterland. In his official report written on the following day, Langlais showed that he had no illusions as to the possibility of regular communications with the nearest friendly post in Laos.

"The jungle is so thick," said Langlais, "and the terrain is so fragmented that to establish a straight-line connection between Dien Bien Phu and Sop Nao, for example, would in all likelihood take several months."

This left the French High Command in Hanoi and Saigon with two choices for Dien Bien Phu. One of them was to recognize that the valley could never play its role as a mooring point for offensive operations. Where such operations were feasible, they could be carried out by the infiltrated commandos of the GCMA or by much stronger forces such as those of the "Ardèche" type, whose operations were similar to those of the British and Americans in Burma in 1942-44.[12] The other alternative was to construe Dien Bien Phu's role as that of becoming a center of attraction for strong Communist forces at a point far away from the most sensitive French targets in the Red River Delta, while they were being readied for the major 1955 campaign which Navarre had originally envisaged.

As it was, the French did neither. Extensive raiding operations were continued, bringing few results in terms of intelligence and being extremely costly in terms of human losses. At the same time no all-out effort was made to put Dien Bien Phu's fortifications in shape to withstand a major Communist assault. Long-range reconnaissance operations of the "Régate" and "Pollux" type left the participating units unable to fortify their positions.

The reconnaissance missions continued, although they now were limited to the immediate environs of the valley. How close the enemy now was became clear when de Castries' chief of staff, Lt. Col. Guth, was killed on December 28 by eighteen tommy-gun bullets during a patrol only a few hundred yards north of strongpoint Anne-Marie. On the following day, parts of Major Paul Pegot's 3rd Battalion of the 13th Foreign Legion Half-Brigade (3/13 DBLE) opened the road beyond the village of Ban Him Lam only to run immediately into heavy resistance, and on December 30, the 2nd Moroccan Battalion, pushing southward from strongpoint Isabelle, ran into enemy opposition at the village of Ban Cang, five kilometers to the south. Again, the French suffered losses.

But the High Command thought (and this turned out to be a correct assumption) that the heaviest attacks would come from the northwest along the road from Tuan Giao, from which the bulk of the Communist supplies would have to come. Therefore, de Castries decided to push the whole 8th BPC as far along the road toward Tuan Giao as it could go without encountering heavy enemy resistance. To make the mission even more fruitful, the 8th decided to follow a route across the mountains so as to bypass, if possible, a Communist roadblock or outpost likely to exist in the little town of Ban Na Loi, four kilometers north of strongpoint Beatrice. Some of the tribesmen still living in the valley had been taken along to serve as guides, for they had said that they knew which path should be taken by the paratroopers. Yet when the column entered the jungle on the afternoon of January 6, there began a great deal of inconclusive marching to and fro. The "guides" began to disagree as to which path was to be taken and finally admitted that they had "forgotten" the exact path.

Captain Tourret decided to hack his own path northward, and the column emerged the following day on Road 41 north of Ban Na Loi. The 8th had barely reached the road when it was greeted by an intensive barrage of well-aimed infantry fire. The well-trained paratroopers rapidly took cover and then counterattacked. They lost only five wounded and were able to capture a wounded Viet-Minh soldier. All six casualties were loaded on stretchers, but the Viet-Minh prisoner and one of the wounded T'ai died two days later when almost within sight of Dien Bien Phu. With their presence now discovered, Tourret felt that the chances of progressing further were slim, and he ordered the return of the battalion via Ban Na Loi. As expected, Ban Na Loi was held by the Viet-Minh, who met the French column with mortar fire. Tourret finally called for air strikes from Dien Bien Phu in order to break the roadblock. The fighter-bombers reduced Ban Na Loi to a shambles and the 8th BPC returned to Dien Bien Phu on January 8 at 1200. It had again failed in its long-range reconnaissance mission, although it had once more clearly documented the fact that the Communist siege ring was tightly wound around the valley and was getting tighter by the day.

Undeterred by these reverses, de Castries kept on trying to fulfill his primary mission of offensive mobility. On December 13, 1953, he had written to Gen. Cogny to ask for a "minimum of twelve battalions" with which he "could simultaneously control a battlefield of forty square kilometers while being able to launch reconnaissances-in-force and raids with effectives of about three battalions."

Hanoi indeed did its level best to improve de Castries' manpower position by relieving some of the least reliable or most fatigued units such as the 301st BVN or the 2nd Moroccan *Tabor* and replacing them with better troops. Yet this did not improve the results of the offensive stabs outside the valley. A raid carried out on January 12, 1954, on the village of Ban Huoi Phuc three kilometers southwest of Isabelle by all of GAP 2 yielded nothing but some more casualties. A massive attack was once more led by the much-harassed GAP 2, reinforced by the 3rd Battalion of the 3rd Foreign Legion Infantry Regiment, against Hill 683, a Communist position within 2,000 yards of strongpoint Gabrielle. It lasted from January 31 to February 2, 1954, and for the first time ran into strongly fortified Communist positions. The advancing troops saw nothing until they suddenly were fired on almost directly from under their feet. The Viet-Minh, incredibly successful masters of the art of camouflage, had built bunkers directly into the ground and underbrush; their firing slits, hardly wider than a mail slot, barely revealed themselves even when the bunker crews used their weapons.

Resistance had become so strong and knowledge of the terrain so essential that Langlais decided to include in his task force the 2nd T'ai Battalion (BT) of Major Maurice Chenel. The 2nd BT, which the year before had fought with distinction in defense of the northern part of the T'ai territory (its home area), had shown a distinct decline in combat morale since it had arrived in Dien Bien Phu. Chenel, a Foreign Legion officer who knew the T'ai uplands well, was aware of this. He requested time to take his battalion in hand again, but felt that he could not refuse an order to participate in a sortie. On February 1, with the primary mission of finding and destroying enemy artillery positions and bunkers already a failure, parts of 2nd BT found themselves in a rear-guard position when, at 1530, heavy Communist fire enveloped the platoon of Lt. Nègre. Within a few minutes seventeen tribesmen and Lt. Nègre lay dead on the battlefield. Only a rapid turnabout of the paratroopers saved the 2nd BT from annihilation.

While the losses in men were serious, a more ominous stroke of bad luck attended their death. Lieutenant Nègre had carried with him on that raid a large-scale map of the valley of Dien Bien Phu which had just been completed by the French Army from the most recent aerial photographs. With the map in their hands the Communists were able to adjust their artillery fires with utmost precision. The Viet-Minh artillery, until then more often talked about than actually seen and felt on the battlefield, no longer was a myth. On January 31, the mountain ring around Dien Bien Phu had echoed for the first time with the sharp bellow of American 75-mm. pack howitzers and 105's bombarding the Dien Bien Phu airstrip and strongpoints Eliane and Dominique. An aircraft parked on the strip was damaged. French combat aircraft intervening in the ground battles, as well as the lumbering transports that landed in a steady stream on the dust-covered airfield, also experienced something that until now had been a rarity in the Indochina war—Communist antiaircraft artillery. A few days later French intelligence identified the enemy as the 45th Artillery Regiment and the 367th Flak Regiment.

As of February 6, until the actual outbreak of the battle on March 13, the primary mission of the reconnaissance elements was to destroy the Communist artillery, which to all appearances was invulnerable to counterbattery fire from the increasingly large artillery available to the French at Dien Bien Phu. The B-26's and *Bearcat* fighters with their rockets, bombs, and napalm canisters proved equally ineffective. The very size of the sortie elements involved—they often comprised more than half of the total garrison—indicated the high priority the French commanders now assigned to the problem.

On February 6, Lt. Col. Langlais and GAP 2, the 2nd BT, the 1st Battalion of the 4th Moroccan Infantry, a Foreign Legion flame-thrower detachment, and a platoon with explosive charges from the 31st Engineering Battalion assaulted the highest mountain in the immediate vicinity of Dien Bien Phu—Hill 754-781. Though the target was located four kilometers due west of Dien Bien Phu, the Langlais task force used Road 41 as far as Ban Him Lam and then turned southeastward. Langlais left the 1st BEP at Ban Him Lam in reserve to cover the withdrawal of his task force. For eight hours, progress was smooth. The enemy seemed to have evaporated and by 1115 the Moroccans of Major Jean Nicolas had almost arrived at the crest of 781.

Contrary to the widely accepted myth that only the paratroopers and the "Germans of the Foreign Legion" fought the battle of Dien Bien Phu,[13] the Moroccans had acquired a solid reputation as "road openers." They regularly exercised this specialty on the dangerous part of the Pavie Track between Dien Bien Phu and Isabelle, six kilometers to the south. This explains why on a dangerous mission such as this they formed the lead element of the stab. It became obvious that the artillery, contrary to expectations, was not on the reverse slope of 781 (where, according to the artillery manuals, it should have been) but was probably on the forward slope facing Dien Bien Phu. Once this had been ascertained, the Langlais task force began to move forward again. Immediately, it was hit by a Communist infantry counterattack as violent as it was sudden. At 1300, 3rd and 4th companies of the Moroccan Battalion were hit and at 1345 the attack engulfed the already mauled 2nd BT. But the Moroccans were undeterred. Sergeant Lahcen Ben Khlifi of 1st Company, despite heavy enemy fire from automatic weapons, immediately led his squad in an assault on the high ground on Hill 781 and held it long enough to permit an orderly withdrawal from the murderous trap. Captain Girard and his 3rd Company also held in spite of heavy losses. Sergeant Cante and his platoon held off two Communist attacks while Cante himself dragged back the body of M/Sgt. Pierron. The acts of individual heroism were many that day atop Hill 781, but few equaled that of Private Mohammed Ben Miloud who, seeing two Viet-Minh soldiers drag a wounded Moroccan into the jungle, jumped from his cover, killed the two enemy soldiers and dragged the wounded man back with him.

While the Moroccans held, the T'ai tribesmen of 2nd BT were virtually disintegrating and had to be "sandwiched" between the Moroccans and the paratroopers of GAP 2 to be kept in line. At 1820 the order came to fall back to Ban Him Lam and at thirty minutes past midnight, the exhausted Langlais task force returned to camp. It had accomplished nothing but had lost ninety-three men, including three officers and twelve sergeants. The 1st Moroccan Battalion (1/4 RTM) alone had lost one dead, fifty wounded (some of them to French artillery shells which had fallen short), and five missing. One wounded company commander, the Moroccan captain, Fassi, was to die on February 11.

On February 9, an infantry task force composed of Foreign Legionnaires of the 1/13 DBLE and 1st Battalion, 2nd Foreign Legion Infantry (1/2 REI), a company of White T'ai[14] and a mixed company of the 1/4 RTM explored Hill 273 at Ban Hong Lech Cang, about five kilometers due west of Dien Bien Phu. As it approached the deserted village, the lead unit was met by a well-deployed paratroop company easily recognizable by its distinctive French camouflage uniforms. The fact that the unit was made up exclusively of Vietnamese was not surprising, either. After all, each of the Foreign Legion and even of the mainland French paratroop units had been "yellowed" up to fifty per cent of its strength. That the task force had not been notified of the presence of other friendly units in the area was also not surprising since each day one strongpoint or another would send out local reconnaissances, or foragers, to find construction wood for bunkers and trenches.

This was what made the first volleys fired by the Communists wearing French camouflage uniforms (probably captured from a misdropped airborne cargo load) so murderous. It was fortunate that there were no paratroop units on the French side and they therefore were wearing jungle green instead of camouflage dress. Otherwise, in the confusion the

French forces would have shot at each other. Even so, the engagement degenerated into hand-to-hand combat at 1230. At 1600, reinforcements had to be called to permit the disengagement of the reconnaissance forces, who returned to camp with seven dead and twenty-one wounded. From that day onward reconnaissance outfits were issued distinctive strips of colored material torn from the parachutes. A specific color was worn around the left or right arm by all troops participating in a given operation. Enemy intelligence was so good, however, that even this measure did not entirely eliminate traps of the kind which had occurred at Ban Hong Lech Cang.

The main danger to the French position was to come from the dominant hill lines to the north and northeast, occupied by the enemy's 308th and 316th divisions, and, on January 23, by the 304th division. Frantically, the twelve French battalions dug in to withstand a first assault, which French intelligence announced for January 25. Contrary to expectations, however, the enemy attack did not materialize. Instead, the 308th Division left the siege ring and made yet another stab deep into Laos in the direction of the royal capital of Luang-Prabang, just as it had done in the spring of 1953. In fact, both de Castries at Dien Bien Phu and Gen. Navarre in Saigon feared that the Viet-Minh had altogether abandoned the idea of attacking Dien Bien Phu head-on and would bypass the strongpoint just as it had bypassed Na-San one year earlier.[15]

On January 29 and 30, 1954, the French High Command ordered de Castries to undertake further powerful reconnaissance missions;[16] and on February 2, Navarre and his chief advisers in Saigon felt so certain of the enemy's change of intentions that they recommended to Gen. Cogny that the garrison of Dien Bien Phu be reduced to nine or even six battalions.[17] Cogny objected firmly to that idea and argued that even with the departure of the 308th Division the enemy retained a two-to-one manpower superiority over the French garrison. Moreover, the repeated failures of the reconnaissance forces to break out from the tight siege ring laid around the valley by the Communists augured ill for a reduction in the size of the forces stationed there. The alternative would have been total evacuation of the valley.

This was the reason the Communist forces held on to all their observation posts on the high ground around Dien Bien Phu. On December 25, the French had intercepted a message sent by the forward element of the Viet-Minh forces' intelligence services to the Communist high command. It contained the following significant passage:

If we let the enemy pull out without noticing it, as happened at Na-San, we will bear the responsibility for it before the [Political] General Delegate of the Army.

Retrospectively, this gives the battle of Dien Bien Phu new dimensions. The first battle lost was that of the long-range penetrations designed to dislocate the enemy's rear areas. The second battle was now under way. Its design was to dislodge the enemy from his dangerous northern and northeastern look-out posts from which the whole valley and the so-essential airfield could be constantly watched. The French were now in the process of losing this battle.

On February 10, Langlais' GAP 2, reinforced by a company of the Algerian 5/7 RTA under Lt. Botella, and Maj. Pégot's 3/13 Foreign Legion Battalion, once more attempted to clear Hill 674, 1,200 yards east of Gabrielle. By 1000 all progress had stopped in the face of heavy enemy resistance from excellently camouflaged bunkers and trenches. Artillery fire was called for. It came promptly, but fell far short of its targets and landed in the midst of the advancing French force, killing fifteen Algerians. For the time being, this stopped the attack in the direction of 674.

In the meantime, another prong of the same operation sought to clear once more the ever-tightening encirclement around strongpoint Beatrice. A light battalion formed from the 9th, 11th, and 12th companies of the 3rd Battalion, 3rd Algerian Rifle Regiment (3/3 RTA), under Captain Jean Garandeau, reinforced by the 3rd Battalion, 3rd Foreign Legion Infantry (3/3 REI), under Major Henry Grand d'Esnon, attempted to clear the hill line to the southeast of 674. The 3/3 RTA had been continuously in Indochina since November, 1950, and had participated in the difficult clearing operations north of Saigon until 1952, when it had been sent to fight its way through the infamous "Street Without Joy."[18] It had gone directly from there to the Plain of Jars in Laos to fend off yet another Communist offensive and thence to North Viet-Nam where it had suffered severe losses in clearing operations in the Red River Delta early in December, 1953. As its diary noted tersely, the battalion had had ten days of rest in the five months prior to its transport to Dien Bien Phu. On January 30, one of its outposts east of strongpoint Dominique, commanded by a French sergeant, had been mysteriously wiped out by a Communist commando, leaving only one Algerian survivor. At Dien Bien Phu, the 3/3 RTA was considered an outfit whose long battle experience had, through wear and tear, turned into battle fatigue.

The 3/3 Foreign Legion, on the other hand, was a solid battalion composed largely of Germans but with some Italians, Spaniards, and Yugoslavs. Two of the company commanders were named Rossini and Gatti, and a third company was commanded by Lieutenant Alain Gambiez, the son of Gen. Navarre's chief of staff. There was also a Lieutenant Rajko Cibic and Sergeants Magnono, de Biasi, Jorge Saez, and Ahmed Subasic.

The Algerians and the Legionnaires ran into a heavy ambush along the northwestern approaches to Hill 781 at 1315 on February 11. Within a few minutes, the Algerians lost eighteen men. Again, the Communist positions seemed invisible under the deep canopy of trees and thick underbrush. The 3rd Foreign Legion Battalion also suffered heavy losses, and at 1700 the order was given for both units to fall back on Ban Kha Chit, a small village about 2,000 yards south of Beatrice and due west of 781.

The 9th and 12th companies of the Algerian battalion covered the withdrawal under heavy fire and lost another eleven men and one field radio set in the process. In the meantime, Langlais' main thrust against 674 also had stalled in the face of enemy small arms and artillery fire. On February 13, the reinforced Airborne Group once more slashed forward, but this time behind a carpet of bombs laid down by B-26's which had flown in from Hanoi. While the actual results of the air strike on the Communist positions was almost nil, it gave the French forces the needed boost in morale for yet another push forward. In bitter hand-to-hand fighting in which no quarter was given and French, Vietnamese, and North African lives were lost each foot of the way, the Langlais task force finally cleared Hill 674 as well as Hills 633, 632, and 626; destroying each of the well-camouflaged Communist blockhouses and bunkers with flame throwers and explosive charges.

Yet even this partial victory was hollow, for it had been won at the price of heavy losses and the temporary commitment of everything movable within the garrison. Hill 674 was so far removed from the main centers of French strength that its permanent occupation (or rather, the securing of supply and communication lines between it and the rest of the valley) would have been too costly to contemplate. Nevertheless, the repeated failure of the French before 781, which was even closer to the vitals of the fortress than 674, might in the end prove fatal. There, the hard-pressed Algerians and Legionnaires had received orders to fall back to Road 41, since it was obviously impossible for two weary battalions to take a strong position defended by the better part of a Communist division. The withdrawal itself proved a delicate matter and required help from the newly constituted French tank squadron, whose ten vehicles, as will be seen later, had laboriously been put together by hand in the middle of the battlefield. On the evening of February 15, de Castries called off the whole operation and the Langlais task force returned to the valley.

That evening an agonizing stock-taking was in progress at de Castries' headquarters and in Hanoi. According to the latest statistics provided by Dien Bien Phu the losses incurred by the garrison amounted, from November 20, 1953, to February 15, 1954, to a total of 32 officers, 96 non-commissioned officers, and 836 enlisted men, or about ten per cent of all the officers and eight per cent of all the troops available in the valley. In other words, the French had lost the equivalent of one full battalion of infantry and the cadre of two full battalions. These losses did not include those of the "Pollux" force.

It was up to Gen. Cogny in Hanoi to make up for the losses, since they were suffered in his command. On February 17, he made the fateful decision that henceforth attacks launched by the Dien Bien Phu garrison would be limited to "light reconnaissances" to be carried out by "commandos made up of restricted amounts of personnel."[19] The order made quite clear that it had been given in view of the "losses incurred whose importance is without any relation to the ascertainable results." This decision came in the wake of two other developments, each of which was minor but which had impact on the development of this crucial phase of the battle. On February 4, the French 4th Bureau (Supplies) in Hanoi had informed Dien Bien Phu that it would have to reduce its over-all ammunition consumption rate in view of the attack of the Communist 308th Division on Laos. On February 6, Gen. Cogny sent a personal directive to de Castries informing the latter that his depleted ammunition stocks would remain that way for another eight days in view of other priorities. Thus, the offensive stabs against Hills 674 and 781 had been sparingly supported by the French artillery and almost no artillery fire was available to pounce on the Communist artillery positions when the latter were being installed and were thus relatively vulnerable!

With the loss of the battle for control of the heights around Dien Bien Phu, the last raison d'être of Dien Bien Phu had evaporated. The slash of the 308th Division to within twenty kilometers of Luang-Prabang and the simultaneous stab into central and southern Laos by the 325th Division and one regiment of the 304th, amply demonstrated that Dien Bien Phu had lost its last shred of usefulness. In Hanoi, Gen. Cogny's sharp-eyed deputy chief of staff, Lt. Col. Denef, had clearly recognized the situation one month earlier and had written in a short and brutally frank note for his commander:

It is too late to throw the machine into reverse gear. To break out, we would need four battalions to act as rear guard and four battalions as flank guards, and they would be by and large offered up for sacrifice. Since the three T'ai battalions[20] are unusable for such a mission, we would have to sacrifice the bulk of the force to save four battalions, three of whom would be T'ai. . . . That battle will have to be fought on the scale of the whole Indochinese peninsula or it will become a hopeless retreat.

In transmitting this report to Gen. Cogny, Col. Bastiani, the chief of staff, added a note of his own which was deeply significant:

I fully agree . . . in either case, it will have to be the battle of the Commander-in-Chief. I think he must have foreseen the necessary requirements before letting himself into that kind of hornet's nest.

This was the ultimate excuse of a staff officer: the situation was hopeless, the action taken made no sense, but there might after all be a higher reason for all of this.

"The Führer must know what he is doing." This phrase had been repeated a hundred times over by the German defenders of Stalingrad as they senselessly fought on toward catastrophe. The same rationale now began to prevail among the French senior commanders as they contemplated developments in the faraway valley. Even the small commando reconnaissances confirmed what now was known to everybody—that Dien Bien Phu was tightly encircled by a vise of at least four Communist divisions.

Nevertheless, de Castries did not altogether give up the idea of powerful reconnaissance stabs. After all, he had been entrusted with the command of the valley precisely because of his predisposition for offensive operations. Thus, on March 4, a mixed force of T'ai tribesmen of the 3rd T'ai Battalion (Major Léopold Thimonier) and of the 5/7 Algerian Rifles of Major Roland de Mecquenem, from Gabrielle, sought to dislodge an enemy force which had entrenched itself a bare kilometer north of Gabrielle, on Hill 633. As might have been expected, the French force was almost immediately caught in a cross fire of well-camouflaged enemy weapons and had to withdraw with heavy losses. On the following day, the 1st BEP under Major Maurice Guiraud once more attempted the deadly climb of 781. It might as well have saved itself the trouble. Major Guiraud's battalion found the enemy heavily entrenched almost all the way to Road 41, and around three sides of strongpoint Beatrice. On March 6, Gen. Cogny once more warned Col. de Castries against losing too many men in costly reconnaissance missions.

Finally on March 11, 1954, Lt. Col. Langlais, for the last time, led the 2nd Airborne Group on a large-scale reconnaissance. The objective was not the Communist forward supply base at Tuan Giao, nor even nearby Sop Nao or Muong Pon. It was only Hill 555, two miles away from the center of the fortress. Here the enemy was digging trenches in open daylight, directly overlooking Hill 506, on which Beatrice was located. GAP 2 could not even make a dent in the Communist positions. At 1700 it began to fall back to Dien Bien Phu, carrying its dead and wounded with it.

The battle of Dien Bien Phu was exactly forty-eight hours distant.

Siege

WHILE LANGLAIS' paratroopers and the infantry battalions of the perimeter were fighting the last phases of the battle for the hill line, a struggle of a different sort was going on in the depths of the valley.

As was shown earlier, the French High Command had realized only belatedly that Dien Bien Phu would have to be organized defensively. Like the other phases of the battle of Dien Bien Phu, the battle to fortify the valley was going to be lost in Hanoi and Saigon. And this defeat was not, as commonly supposed, in the field of intelligence or aerial supply, or even in that of artillery, but in *combat engineering.*

As long as Dien Bien Phu was considered a guerrilla mooring point, the preparation of permanent field fortifications had been kept to a minimum. Until December 4, 1953, the 17th Airborne Engineering Company had concentrated on making the airfield usable for cargo aircraft and rebuilding the wooden bridges connecting the airfield with the town of Dien Bien Phu and Route 41. At the same time, each of the battalions of the original landing force had dug some sketchy defensive positions in a narrow perimeter around Dien Bien Phu. The 5th BPVN dug in on the hill line east of the Nam Yum River overlooking the town of Dien Bien Phu, where strongpoint Eliane was going to be constructed later. Bigeard's paratroopers covered the northern approaches and the airstrip, where strongpoint Huguette would appear. The remaining elements of GAP 2 covered the southwestern approaches of the base until airlifted ground troops became available to relieve them.

With the arrival of the 3rd Company, 31st Engineering Battalion, on December 4, and the consequent relief of the lightly equipped Airborne Engineers, engineering work began on a larger scale. Yet it was still concentrated primarily on the infra-structure of the base itself rather than on preparation of the valley for a prolonged defense against massive attacks. First priority was now given to covering 6,600 feet of the airstrip with American-designed PSP's—pierced steel plates that can be fitted together like a gigantic puzzle and constitute an acceptable substitute for concrete airstrips—and to the improvement of roads and bridges within the valley itself. These tasks alone soon outstripped the capabilities of the 3/31st Engineers. By December 21, 2nd Company, 31st Engineers, had also been airlifted into the valley. They were shortly to be followed by the whole complement of the 31st Engineering Battalion under Major André Sudrat, who also became the chief engineering adviser to Col. de Castries.

By the end of December, it had become obvious that there would soon be a direct clash between the force defending Dien Bien Phu and the vastly superior and heavily armed Communists. A light tank squadron was airlifted in in mid-December. Since one of the tank platoons was to go five miles southward to strongpoint Isabelle, the Engineers were given the onerous task of building bridges capable of supporting the eighteen-ton tanks. As a constant stream of artillery pieces and infantry units was disgorged onto the Dien Bien Phu airstrip, Maj. Sudrat began to warn his superiors of the engineering problem that was rapidly becoming insoluble.

On December 26, Col. de Castries issued an order to all units in the valley that their positions were to be fortified to resist artillery shells of 105-mm. caliber. The engineering manuals of every modern army have a standard answer to this problem: two layers of wood beams at least six inches in diameter, separated by three feet of closely packed earth topped off by sandbags to absorb splinters. No such protecting roof was to cover an unsupported area more than six feet in width. Time-tested in two world wars in which the 105-mm. had been the standard field-artillery weapon, the average tonnage of engineering materials necessary to protect a unit of a given size was known to the last ton. To protect one squad against enemy artillery, thirty tons of engineering materials were required. Building a combat bunker for one automatic weapon required twelve tons. To entrench a full battalion, fifty-five squad dugouts and seventy-five automatic weapons bunkers were required—a total of 2,550 tons of engineering materials plus 500 tons of barbed wire and accessories. Sudrat thus calculated that in order to satisfactorily fortify Dien Bien Phu for the initial garrison of ten infantry and two artillery battalions he needed 36,000 tons of materials. The only way to reduce the logistic burden was to substitute local materials for those to be brought in by airlift.

The hope of finding suitable construction wood within the valley or on the surrounding hills soon evaporated. Even by literally taking apart every building and shed in the town and the surrounding villages (a measure which the population rightly considered a barbarism and which threw it automatically on the Communist side), only a few hundred cubic yards of construction wood could be secured. The high bamboo stands found in the valley were excellent for kindling wood but of no value whatever for construction that had to resist heavy loads. Woodcutting parties sent into the surrounding hills proved about as impracticable as the reconnaissance raids of GAP 2. The woodcutting parties would be ambushed and soon required large bodies of protective troops. Once the wood was cut, the small pool of transport vehicles was hardly suitable for heavy transport—even if it were possible to get the trucks far enough into the roadless jungle to pick up the wood.

Nevertheless, between the dismantled tribal houses and the wood cut along the rim of the valley, Sudrat succeeded in collecting about 2,200 tons of construction wood. This left Dien Bien Phu about 34,000 tons short of minimal engineering requirements. The chances for a successful defense of Dien Bien Phu under direct attack could be expressed in one frightening equation: 34,000 tons of engineering equipment represented the cargo loads of about 12,000 flights of C-47 transport aircraft, the standard aircraft then available in Indochina. About eighty aircraft were deployed on the daily run to Dien Bien Phu. At that rate, and assuming that *nothing else* but engineering materials were flown into Dien Bien Phu, five months would have been required to make the forlorn valley into a defensible field position! Sudrat, as well as his superiors, knew that they would not have five months and that there would not be 12,000 C-47 flights.

When Sudrat presented his calculations to de Castries' staff he met with incredulity bordering on derision. With heavy battles going on in Laos, Dien Bien Phu's airlift allocation barely reached the 150 ton/day level necessary to maintain the normal supply requirements. Orders, as we have seen, had been given to cut down on ammunition expenditure. Undeterred, Sudrat continued to argue that he had been given the responsibility not only of preparing Dien Bien Phu for a long siege but also of providing the fortress with two airfields (a second airfield was being prepared north of strongpoint Isabelle), two heavy-duty bridges, and electrical power and purified drinking water for over 10,000 men. Yet there was just so much that could be squeezed into the airlift. De Castries and presumably Gen. Cogny and his staff made the decision to allocate about 4,000 tons of engineering materials to the fortress. Roughly, this tonnage was broken down as follows: 3,000 tons represented barbed wire and accessories; 510 tons represented PSP's for the two airfields; 44 tons were made up of Bailey bridge elements; 70 tons were devoted to five bulldozers (one of which had participated in the Italian campaign of 1943) and 23 tons represented mines and other explosives. A total of 118.5 tons represented the allocation of wooden beams for the construction of protected foxholes and bunkers for the troops. The Engineers were thus about 30,000 tons short of minimal requirements.

"That leaves us with exactly enough materials to protect the headquarters command post, the signal center, and the X-ray room of the underground hospital," said Sudrat. "The rest of Dien Bien Phu will have to get on as best it can."[1] And that was exactly what happened.

Engineering was not the only problem that would make the construction of adequate defenses at Dien Bien Phu an almost hopeless task. In addition to the tonnage requirements which the engineering manuals demanded, there were the approximate time and manpower requirements for the construction of field fortifications. Thus, to construct a squad dugout capable of protecting ten men against field artillery, a forty-man platoon would have to put in eight days of work. To construct a bunker for automatic weapons, the same platoon would require five days. A whole battalion would have to work at nothing else but its protection for about two months to insure itself against the kind of artillery bombardment that Dien Bien Phu was led to expect, and which, indeed, it got. Additional time would have to be allotted for the construction of communication trenches, the laying of mine fields, and the building of adequate protection for the lightly manned service units that could not possibly spare men for the task: headquarters units, artillery, air control, armor, and quartermaster and maintenance. Yet the available manpower obviously could not be devoted entirely to the task of position building. The GAP 2 was almost constantly engaged in reconnaissance operations, and most of the other infantry units were so often engaged in close-in combat operations that they were able to devote scarcely any time to a fortification program that had to be pushed with the utmost energy if it was to be successful.

Furthermore, the many hesitations and counterorders emanating from Hanoi and Saigon until almost thirty days before the onset of the actual battle, were not conducive to a co-ordinated fortification effort. After all, there was Gen. Cogny's long-standing hope that, thanks to wide-swinging offensive operations centered on the valley, an actual duel inside the valley would not last long enough to make permanent fortifications worth-while.[2] This opinion, it will be remembered, was shared by Gen.

Navarre. Added to this was the opinion of both the artillery specialists and the Bomber Command that any strong concentration of enemy artillery would undoubtedly be knocked out before it could do serious damage. Lastly, there was the fact that until late February there had been no clear idea as to where the field fortifications were to be constructed and how many men were going to occupy them.

Indeed, by messages of February 3 and 6, Hanoi told de Castries to undertake studies for a modified position at Dien Bien Phu held by only six battalions for the duration of the monsoon season, *i.e.*, from April to September.[3]

The reply which de Castries sent Cogny on February 15, based on studies made on the spot by Maj. Sudrat and his engineers, was equally frank in commenting on the position as it then existed and in what it implied about its fate, should the battle occur during the rainy season.

> The work on the present defensive system is practically completed. In any case, the lack of materials (barbed wire) does not permit me to pursue certain improvements, particularly the construction of internal enclosures between the strongpoints. . . .
> The same shortage of materials permits only the barest sketching-in of interval strongpoints between the eastern hills destined to insure the close-in defense of the supply dump zone. . . .[4]

De Castries furthermore expressed the fear that his supply dumps, now located in the valley bottom near the Nam Yum, would be flooded when the rains started for good and sent Cogny a map overlay clearly showing how much of his then held position would be under water (see maps, p. 92). Farther south, as de Castries noted, strongpoint Isabelle would be almost totally flooded, and he recommended that it be abolished altogether.

Lastly, said de Castries, "Since the flooded areas cover the whole southern and western part of strongpoint Claudine, the whole strongpoint will have to be pushed northward and a new bridge will have to be constructed across the Nam Yum since the present bridge will disappear under an expanse of water of 300 meters." De Castries also recommended that further fortifications, instead of being dug into the ground where they would be necessarily flooded, be constructed above ground.

What is amazing about this communication is that it contains, on de Castries' part, the simultaneous affirmation that his defense works are "practically completed" and that he lacks construction materials to such an extent that there was not enough barbed wire to seal off the various internal parts of each strongpoint from one another and to build the vitally

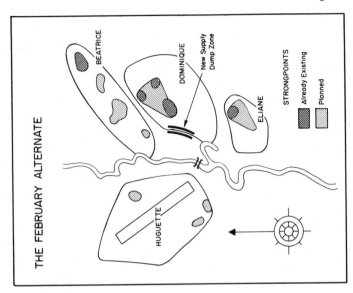

THE FEBRUARY ALTERNATE

BEATRICE

DOMINIQUE

New Supply
Dump Zone

ELIANE

HUGUETTE

STRONGPOINTS

Already Existing

Planned

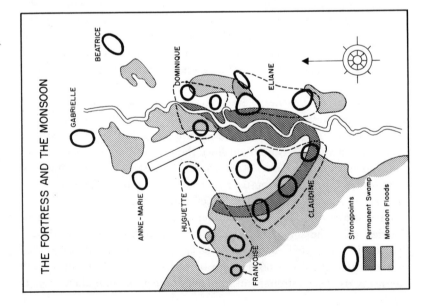

THE FORTRESS AND THE MONSOON

GABRIELLE

BEATRICE

ANNE-MARIE

DOMINIQUE

ELIANE

HUGUETTE

FRANÇOISE

CLAUDINE

Strongpoints

Permanent Swamp

Monsoon Floods

important interval strongpoints that would prevent enemy infiltrations between the key hill positions covering the northeastern face of the fortress. Both shortcomings were to prove decisive once the battle was joined. The absence of sufficient barriers inside the strongpoints made it difficult to seal off the Viet-Minh whenever they achieved a breakthrough; and during the crucial battles of March 30-April 3, 1954, important positions of Hills Dominique and Eliane were lost to lateral infiltrations which interval positions could have blocked.

As it was, the project of "getting Dien Bien Phu out of the water," as the saying went, never materialized for lack of time and materials. When the rains came in April (that year they were both earlier and heavier than usual) nearly all strongpoints immediately took water and Isabelle in particular almost disappeared in the quagmire. The rains also weakened the already flimsily built bunkers and trenches. There was hardly a man in Dien Bien Phu who did not at least once find himself buried under his collapsed dugout.

Another surprising element in the preparation of Dien Bien Phu for battle was the absence of any attempt at concealment and camouflage. The urgent needs for construction wood led, to be sure, to the almost immediate felling of all the trees in the position area. The trees were followed within a short time by all the bushes, which were used as fuel for the hundreds of cooking fires of the garrison. The constant marching to and fro of 10,000 men, 118 vehicles, ten tanks, and five bulldozers took care of the grass. Within a few weeks, even the slightest slit trench or the smallest bunker entrance inside Dien Bien Phu outlined itself against the brown earthy background of the valley like a Chinese ink drawing. Each artillery piece and mortar could be seen from far away, glistening in its wide-open firing position. And since there was neither space nor materials available for alternate gun positions, enemy observers hidden in the hills were able accurately to pinpoint every heavy weapon in the fortress. In some cases, the very meticulousness of the job done contributed to the defenders' difficulties. The Foreign Legion always prided itself on the workmanlike execution of its fortifications. As one of the officers of the 31st Engineers was to observe, the firing slits of the dug-in automatic weapons soon acquired a telltale dark powder color against the surrounding sand and earth, and soon it became the habit of some of the particularly ambitious weapons crews to actually paint the firing slits black. No doubt the fortifications impressed the high-ranking French, American, British, and Vietnamese generals and other civilian dignitaries who kept visiting Dien Bien Phu in a steady stream, but unfortunately they left absolutely nothing to the imagination of the enemy. Little wonder, then, that the enemy artillery, once the battle began in earnest, immediately registered in on the most sensitive targets with devastating effect. Another dead giveaway of important positions at Dien Bien Phu was the tall radio whip aerials gently swaying in the wind over every command post and battery position. Of the 1,400 sets within Dien Bien Phu, at least 300 required outside aerials, and in some places they were as dense as the bamboo hedges which had been destroyed to make place for them.

The answer given to visitors who wondered at the absence of any kind of camouflage was that enemy observers in the hills were capable of seeing everything that went on in the valley. The answer is not fully satisfactory. Camouflage nets over some of the most important communications trenches and battery positions would have at least prevented the enemy from obtaining exact timetables of French troop rotations and patrol reliefs. In some cases, they would have delayed the enemy's immediate observation of the damage his fire had caused.

In certain instances, the bareness of the terrain was unavoidable. Most of the artillery pieces, for example, had to be capable of firing in all directions and therefore could not be dug in; and the battalion strong-point commanders were haunted by the thought, based on dire previous experience elsewhere in Indochina, that the slightest shred of vegetation would be used by the enemy to camouflage his approach prior to an assault. As it turned out, the enemy instead chose to drive approach trenches as close as possible to the French positions, from which they emerged at the opportune moment under the cover of their own artillery fire.

There were other major engineering tasks to be accomplished inside Dien Bien Phu. Since early December, Dien Bien Phu had also been host to an ever-increasing detachment of observation and fighter aircraft, notably six light observation aircraft of the 21st Artillery Air Observation Group (GAOA) of Captain Robert Durand and a flight of fighter bombers from the Fighter Group 1/22 "Saintonge" under Major Jacques Guérin, who was also to become the senior air officer in the fortress. Since they realized that these aircraft would become essential in a prolonged defense of Dien Bien Phu, the French had constructed veritable "dugouts" away from the airstrip itself, where the aircraft would be parked during the night or when not in service. Major Sudrat's engineers had built another bridge leading from the airfield to the dugout area, which the airplanes easily crossed under their own power. A third bridge was built at strongpoint Isabelle to provide access to the southern airstrip located to the east of Road 41, on the far side of the Nam Yum. To save precious building materials, Sudrat had bulldozed the river bank into the Nam Yum to a distance of twenty feet in order to build a narrower bridge span. As it turned out, the southern airstrip, located in the midst of a plain which was completely undefended, was never used. Major Guérin landed an empty C-47 transport aircraft on it to test the feasibility of landings on the unimproved strip. But as long as the PSP-covered main airfield was available, there was no reason for using the southern strip. When the northern airfield became unusable, the southern strip was already under enemy fire.

Finally, when it became clear that the battle for Dien Bien Phu might be a prolonged one, a last-minute attempt was made to save the large supply depots of the fortress from flooding by digging new supply emplacements along the steep western edge of Hill Dominique. The new depot emplacements required that 2½-ton trucks would have access to the other side of the Nam Yum, so Sudrat had to build a 44-ton Bailey bridge across the river to connect the depot area with the rest of the valley. Again, the backbreaking labor proved useless. With the other urgent commitments inside the fortress, the depots were never transferred to Dominique. The bridge soon came under such intensive fire that it was useless for communications. It was much safer and easier to ford or swim across the Nam Yum. Since much of Dominique fell into Communist hands as early as March 30, it turned out to be fortunate that the project was not carried out.

Another major task of the engineers was to provide drinking water for 15,000 men. The Nam Yum and its tributaries, like all tropical rivers, were heavily polluted; anyone drinking the water was certain to become a victim of amoebic dysentery. Hence the engineers installed four water purifiers weighing a total of sixteen tons, which provided drinkable water for the garrison. The main water purifier, heavily dug in and operated by a single man, provided water to the central strongpoints until the end of the battle. Yet as the fighting grew in severity the water-carrying parties suffered heavy losses, and the men began to resort to drinking the relatively clean rain water, of which there soon was more than anyone wished.[5] Another major problem for the engineers was providing Dien Bien Phu with the necessary electrical power. There were fifteen power generators and five battery chargers at Dien Bien Phu providing electric light to the main strongpoints and command posts and power for the various radio and telephone installations, as well as to the X-ray room and operating room of the underground hospital. Here also, engineering miracles were accomplished by repair teams who kept the main generators going throughout the battle and kept the power wires (which had to be laid into the soggy ground and were often lying in pools of water) in operating condition. In fact, so urgent were the needs for power that two generators were parachuted into the fortress while the battle raged. One of them smashed on landing while the other landed upright and undamaged, but proved, in view of its weight, unmovable by hand under fire.

Aside from the fortifications, two other factors were to play a decisive role in the defense of Dien Bien Phu: the tanks and the artillery. As it became clearer that the battle would have to be fought in the valley, de Castries counted firmly on the massive use of firepower and the relative mobility of his forces to destroy the enemy before he could decisively harm the garrison. In fact, on December 19, de Castries had sent a message to his subordinate commanders in which he traced the outlines of the battle as he saw it:

> . . . the battle of annihilation which I expect to lead in the valley of Dien Bien Phu rests essentially:
>
> 1. On an ensemble of five centers of resistance which form the infrastructure of the static defense and which shall define on the terrain the area of the desirable battlefield;
>
> 2. On the ability to concentrate on every point of the battlefield at least four fifths of all the firepower available to me;
>
> 3. And on a full scale of prepared counterattacks . . .
>
> The mission of the centers of resistance which, at certain moments, could be completely encircled, is to hold without any thought of withdrawal even if one of their constituent strongpoints were to be taken by the enemy. It will be their task, under the best of circumstances, to reoccupy the lost strongpoint by a local counterattack; or, at the very least, to neutralize it by their proper fires and by calling upon the means at the disposal of GONO.
>
> The counterattacks will, as a matter of principle, be led by the commander of the 2nd Airborne Group. . . .[6]

De Castries, who had been selected for the Dien Bien Phu command on the strength of his reputation as an armored cavalryman, did not lose sight of the possibility of using tanks. Early in December, he requested that a light squadron of M-24 "General Chaffee" tanks be airlifted to Dien Bien Phu. This request implied that the tanks would have to be dismantled in Hanoi and rebuilt from scratch inside the fortress. Ten of the eighteen-ton vehicles (they were factory-new and had recently been delivered to the French by U. S. Military Aid) were brought to Dien Bien Phu during the month of December in a small separate air-lift. The shipment of each tank required five C-47's and two British built Bristol freight aircraft with frontal clamshell doors that accommodated the tank hull, weighing four tons.

Within a few days, the mechanics of the 2nd Automobile Repair Company of the 5th Foreign Legion Regiment (2/5 CRALE), under Lt. Bugeat, had laid out what seemed to be a small-size reproduction of the original tank assembly line in Detroit, save for the fact that it was located in the midst of a jungle valley with sand winds reaching gale force. Each piece of equipment, particularly the engines, had to be cleaned a hundred times from the all-pervasive sand before it could be installed. The only heavy tool available for the assembly line was a lifting rig (the Legionnaires had borrowed it from the artillery) which was used to place the huge engines into the tank hulls. Everything else was done by hand. One fully assembled tank was produced every two days. On Christmas Day, 1953, an armored platoon of three tanks under the command of Master Sergeant Aristide Carrette, from the Moroccan Colonial Infantry Regiment (RICM), became operational.

On December 29, de Castries sent a routine message to Hanoi requesting that a third tank platoon be assigned to Dien Bien Phu and that the small squadron be given its own command staff. In the files of the French Army, this message bears a handwritten inscription scribbled across one of its corners signed by Lt. Col. Denef, Gen. Cogny's deputy chief-of-staff: "Take a captain from the 1st Regiment of *Chasseurs* [1 RCC], Captain Hervouët." And thus the fate of a man was sealed.

Captain Yves Hervouët, who was to command what became the 3rd Squadron of the 1st Regiment of Light Infantry at Dien Bien Phu, had until recently been in Morocco as the aide to Field Marshal Alphonse Juin, and had volunteered for combat duty in Indochina. He had recently been assigned to the 1st RCC in the Red River Delta. A quiet and studious-looking young man with his glasses half-rimmed in gold, Hervouët was well liked by everyone, but particularly by Lt. Col. Langlais, with whose GAP 2 Hervouët was to cooperate very closely in the last reconnaissance battles prior to the outbreak of the Viet-Minh attack. When he was assigned to Dien Bien Phu, Hervouët had just had an accident and commanded his tanks with his left arm in a plaster cast and sling. Wounded in the other arm as he led his tanks into battle during the Communist thrust against Eliane on March 30-31, he continued to command his "Bisons" (as they were affectionately known at Dien Bien Phu) to the last day. Hervouët was to die of exhaustion on the death march to the Communist prison camps in June, 1954.

By January 17, all three tank platoons had become operational. Hervouët, his little staff, and two of the tank platoons under Sgts. Carrette and Guntz stayed in the main fortress. The 3rd Platoon commanded by Lieutenant Henri Préaud, went southward to reinforce strongpoint Isabelle. On February 1, Hervouët's tanks fought their first engagement northeast of Hill Gabrielle.

As it became clear that the battle for Dien Bien Phu was going to be a slugging match, the French High Command decided to provide Dien Bien Phu with sufficient heavy firepower to enable it to destroy the enemy's field pieces by counterbattery fire, and to smash his infantry attacks against the strongpoints by withering protective fires.

In addition to the artillery inside the fortress, there was the firepower of the fighter-bombers and B-26's of the French Air Force and Navy. Above all, there was the cumulative experience of the French artillery commanders. Ever since Napoleon, the French (not unlike the Russians) had prided themselves on the efficiency and know-how of their artillerists. In World War I, the French "75" not only outstripped its German equivalent, but it became the standard field gun of the U. S. Army as well. In Indochina, many of the senior commands were in the hands of artillerymen, such as Gen. Cogny. The deputy commander of Dien Bien Phu was forty-eight-year-old artillery Colonel Charles Piroth. Piroth's jovial exterior and friendly round face hid a sensitive personality. He was an excellent choice for the job. Although seriously wounded in Italy in 1943, where he had lost his left arm almost to the shoulder, Piroth had remained on active duty. In Indochina he had commanded the 69th African Artillery Regiment, notably in the "Street Without Joy" operation of 1953. In Cogny's view, Piroth the artilleryman would be an excellent complement to de Castries the cavalryman.

Piroth assumed command on December 7, the day the first major artillery unit of what was to become the permanent garrison began to be airlifted into the valley. It was the 3rd Artillery Group of the 10th Colonial Artillery Regiment (III/10 RAC) under the command of Maj. Alliou. The III/10 RAC had been the organic artillery battalion of the 13th Foreign Legion Half-Brigade (DBLE), which was also being transferred to Dien Bien Phu, and thus it was familiar with the infantry units with which it would have to fight. With its full three batteries of four American 105-mm. howitzers each, the III/10 RAC represented quite an impressive fire element. It was reinforced by mid-December with the 2nd Group of the 4th Colonial Artillery Regiment (II/4 RAC), commanded at first by Maj. Hourcabie and later, during the actual battle, by Maj. Knecht.

The 4th RAC was one of France's oldest artillery units permanently stationed in Asia. Its shell-scarred flag bore the battle streamers of the conquest of Tonkin of 1883-85 and of the Boxer Rebellion of Peking in 1900. It fought in the hopeless rear-guard actions against the Japanese in 1940 and in 1945, and a handful of its men fought their way into Nationalist China rather than surrender to the enemy. In 1951, a new 4th Artillery Group[7] was added to the normal complement of three groups of the regiment and that unit was equipped with brand-new American 155-mm. medium howitzers served by Moroccan gun crews. The 155's were the largest field pieces available in Indochina and their booming voices often spelled the end of a Communist attack on outlying posts in the Red River Delta. In addition, there were three heavy mortar companies equipped with French 120-mm. (4.2-in.) mortars whose plunging fire should have been capable of destroying most of the enemy's entrenchments. Relatively small and easy to handle, the 120's did not require the complicated firing pits necessary for the howitzers. On the other hand, they did not have the range of the latter, nor their precision. The 1st Foreign Legion Airborne Heavy Mortar Company, commanded by Lieutenant Erwan Bergot, took up positions on strongpoint Claudine; the 1st Composite Mortar Company of the 3rd Foreign Legion Infantry took up positions on Anne-Marie; and the 2nd Composite Mortar Company of the 5th Foreign Legion Infantry[8] transported its eight pieces of 120-mm. and four of 81-mm. to strongpoint Gabrielle on December 27, 1953.

Finally, at the suggestion of an American officer, Maj. Vaughn, who had witnessed their devastating effect in Korea and had, in Hanoi, mentioned it to the commander of the French antiaircraft artillery, two quadruple mounts of .50-caliber machine guns were transported to Dien Bien Phu. In Korea, the "quad-fifties," as they were nicknamed, had done a terrifyingly effective job of hacking to pieces massed attacks of Communist infantry. They were to do the same job at Dien Bien Phu. Electrically swiveling on their mount, they would fire two of their four barrels at once, while two barrels were always in reserve. Many Communist attacks, having smashed through the French infantry and silenced the French artillery, would be stopped by the throaty staccato of Lt. Redon's "quad-fifties." In spite of many close calls, they remained effective until the end of the battle.

Under the command of Col. Piroth, the artillery of Dien Bien Phu was split into two major groups: Groupment A, which comprised the III/10 RAC and two mortar companies; and Groupment B, which included the II/4 RAC, the battery of 155's, one mortar company, and the "quad-fifties." As strongpoint Isabelle was installed to the south of Dien Bien Phu, Piroth decided to provide it with a fairly large amount of artillery designed to smash any possible enemy attacks against the southern part of Dien Bien Phu itself. Thus, on December 24, the 8th Battery of the III/10 RAC (Capt. Reis) was transferred there, followed on January 23 by the 7th Battery and a fire control center under Capt. Noël.[9] Captain Libier became the over-all commander of the artillery at Isabelle. Finally, when the battle of Dien Bien Phu was already raging and Isabelle was nearly cut off from the rest of the valley, the 9th Battery of the III/10 RAC (Capt. Rencoul) fought its way toward Isabelle under cover of a sortie of Isabelle's tank platoon and 3rd Battalion, 3rd Foreign Legion Regiment. This distribution of artillery apparently was justified by two factors. First was the size of the central position which, at its largest, measured hardly more than a square mile and already contained twelve medium field guns, four heavy field guns and twenty-four heavy mortars as well as enormous stocks of ammunition.[10] Second was the fact that both the southeastern strongpoint Eliane and the southwestern strongpoint Claudine were considered particularly vulnerable and in need of additional fire protection, which Isabelle, located 5.5 kilometers to the south, could easily provide. Both de Castries and Piroth had foreseen that the brunt of the initial attack would be borne by the outlying strongpoints Gabrielle and Beatrice. Gabrielle, therefore, had its own heavy mortar company. Beatrice, on the other hand, had its normal complement of 81-mm. mortars, which were deemed sufficient for close-in defense against the surrounding Communist hill positions, and could of course count on the support of the field guns from the main position.

Herein lay the tragedy. When the battle unfolded on March 13, Communist artillery fire rapidly neutralized the main artillery positions inside Dien Bien Phu itself, while the field guns stationed at Isabelle found themselves beyond effective range of the northern strongpoints and thus were incapable of taking the place of the muzzled main artillery positions. As Gen. Catroux was to say later in his report:

It is possible to estimate that if the site chosen to establish Isabelle had been closer to the central position, its artillery would have been capable of supporting those essential strongpoints and could also have been reduced by a [infantry] battalion which could have reinforced the reserves.[11]

There were other weaknesses. To spot enemy targets the artillery had to rely on its observation posts (OP's) placed on the peripheral hill positions and on its own small squadron of six observation aircraft. Both the hilltop observation posts and the observation aircraft were lost during the first forty-eight hours of the battle. It was then too late to provide Dien Bien Phu with such electronic aids as target acquisition radars. In any case, it would have been doubtful that such delicate instruments would have long withstood the constant pounding of the Communist artillery. In a report written after the battle by the surviving artillery commander, he simply noted that "the artillery became progressively blind."

Its only resource from then onward was the information provided by spotter planes from the 21st and 23rd Artillery Air Observation Group who would brave the three-hour round trip from the small Laotian airstrip at Muong Sai as well as the Communist flak over the valley— it had been reinforced by deadly 37-mm. pieces on February 11, 1954— to provide a measure of information about enemy movements. Reconnaissance aircraft of the French Air Force, along with daily aerial photography of the valley, provided additional information. But soon all this would become largely irrelevant as the artillery pieces concentrated on Communist troops and trenches often a mere thousand feet away from their own pits. But none of this was known to de Castries and Piroth in December and January, 1953-54.

In fact, Piroth had worked out a plan for the destruction of the enemy's artillery which he happily recited to each of the high-ranking visitors who called on the staff of the fortress:

"Firstly, the Viet-Minh won't succeed in getting their artillery through to here.

"Secondly, if they do get here, we'll smash them.

"Thirdly, even if they manage to keep on shooting, they will be unable to supply their pieces with enough ammunition to do us any real harm."

There is some evidence that Piroth was not entirely taken in by his own high spirits. In a personal letter of December 16, 1953, to his direct superior in Hanoi, Col. de Winter, Piroth argued the fact that he had in Dien Bien Phu less artillery and manpower than that normally allocated to an infantry division, "yet I need more men and more firepower." He was right. The garrison of Dien Bien Phu, with its twelve battalions, would have been entitled to three full artillery groups of 105-mm. guns and one full group of 155's. The heavy mortars, which were supposed to fill the gap, could hardly be considered an adequate replacement. Yet on the following day, when Gen. Navarre visited Dien Bien Phu with Gen. Cogny and the commander-in-chief of the French Far Eastern Air Force, Gen. Lauzin, Piroth was his old self again. The generals, accocmpanied by de Castries and Piroth, had visited the freshly built strongpoint Beatrice where Lt. Col. Gaucher and part of his impeccably aligned 13th Foreign Legion Half-Brigade did the honors. Navarre had climbed on top of the command post bunker of Beatrice and was looking directly back along Road 41 into the heart of the valley, where the low hillocks of Dominique and Claudine could be seen as though they had been drawn on a map. Clearly, Navarre was worried: Beatrice was surrounded by impenetrable jungle hills which could conceal scores of enemy heavy guns, and once Beatrice was in enemy hands, it was obvious that much of Dien Bien Phu was going to be under enemy fire. Pierre Schoendoerffer, a young reporter with the French Information Service in Indochina, who stood with the official party atop the bunker, distinctly recalled Piroth's reply:

"*Mon Général,* no Viet-Minh cannon will be able to fire three rounds before being destroyed by my artillery."

Navarre looked at him, looked back at the vista of the valley beyond and then said quietly:

"Maybe so, but this won't be like Na-San."

The same scenario was repeated on January 26, 1954, when Marc Jacquet, the French Secretary of State for Associated States Affairs, visited Dien Bien Phu. He had been impressed by Piroth's presentation of his counterbattery fires, but as a former air force officer, he was worried about the amount of protection available for the vital airstrip on which the survival of Dien Bien Phu eventually would have to depend. He also had been impressed by reports of massive use of American artillery to break Communist human wave attacks in Korea. As Jacquet was leaving Piroth's command post, he turned back and said to the artillery commander: "Colonel, I know that there are hundreds of unemployed artillery pieces around Hanoi. Take advantage of the fact that a member of the government is here to get yourself some extra pickings of them."

Piroth was alleged to have answered with indignation that, as he had shown the Secretary of State on his plans of fire, he had more guns then he could handle. And to Gen. Blanc, the chief of general staff of the French Army, who had come with Jacquet and who was an artillery-man by origin, Piroth said: "If I get thirty minutes of advance warn-ing, my counterbattery will be effective."[12]

By the end of January it had become obvious that the excellent camouflage of the enemy artillery and even of the enemy's infantry positions was going to be a major problem during the battle. In fact, Piroth was visibly preoccupied by the fact that his guns could not provide effective support for the sorties of GAP 2 and of the other battalions. Later Major Jean Nicolas was to remember how Piroth came, with tears in his eyes, to Nicolas' Moroccan rifle battalion on strongpoint Eliane to present his apologies to the men for the shells from his guns that had fallen short on February 6, injuring several Moroccans as they participated in the attack on Hills 754 and 781. The Moroccans, assembled by the embarrassed Nicolas, had listened to Piroth's apology in stony silence.

Other signs of impending disaster appeared by mid-February, 1954. A Communist prisoner had been captured with drawings of underground artillery firing positions of an unorthodox design, which in effect would leave unprotected only the very small area of the firing tube itself. Basically, the process was not new. It presupposed that the artillery pieces would not have to be moved very often and would be able to cover only a relatively small zone within the target area, as had been the case during the stalemate years of the Korean War. The American forces, with a superabundance of bombers and artillery, had found it difficult to locate and destroy such guns, although in most cases the Korean terrain was barren of any sizable vegetation.

Around the valley of Dien Bien Phu, on the other hand, vegetation was available in lush abundance. The French Air Force had long known that it was unable to photograph it by conventional means and had requested American assistance with newly developed infrared film. Between January 23 and March 2, 1954, a Captain Hill of the U. S. Air Force had been on temporary duty in Hanoi to experiment with this infrared film and with newly developed camouflage-detection film as well. Both had worked effectively in Korea. In Viet-Nam, they were total failures.

All this had not been the case at Na-San the year before. There, the French positions formed two complete rings around the airstrip and covered all the high ground, and for miles around the terrain was fairly open and the sparse Communist artillery was easily detected. At Dien Bien Phu, Piroth still clung to the hope that any kind of digging such as would be required fo rthe shellproof camouflaging of a large artillery force, could not go undetected. It did.

The French Air Force had picked up here and there evidence of the passage of heavy equipment. In fact, it is surprising how deadly accurate its estimates were. As early as December 27, 1953, French Air Force intelligence estimated that the enemy's total strength would be about 49,000 men, including 33,000 combatants; figures which would turn out to be within ten per cent of reality. As early as January 9, aerial photography had shown that 105-mm. howitzers had left Communist rear-base areas in the direction of Dien Bien Phu. Whatever else it was, Dien Bien Phu was not an example of a failure in French intelligence.

In fact, as early as February 16, 1954, *Le Monde's* veteran correspondent Robert Guillain reported from Dien Bien Phu all that had to be known about the Viet-Minh's siege techniques: "Without us seeing it, the Viets built their positions right under our eyes," said Guillain, "and not on the reverse slope but on the one facing us." Guillain, who had been to Korea, correctly stated that similar situations had existed there, but that fantastically dense American air strikes usually overcame the obstacle and neutralized such positions. And he likewise identified— one month before the battle began and four months before it was lost— the key French weakness: airborne fire power.

Guillain bluntly doubted that fire-suppression missions flown by *two* fighters could seriously impede the enemy's activities and called them "simili air strikes." What Guillain knew, others knew as well. The French knew that in a set-piece battle it is preferable to hold the high ground, but they had counted on their fire power to compensate for their unfavorable positions. It was one of their key mistakes.

On January 30, 1954, Maj. Privat, the French chief cartographer in Indochina, informed Navarre's headquarters in Saigon that the French large-scale maps for the Dien Bien Phu area were fairly inaccurate and scarcely usable for the precision maps required by the artillery. In Privat's words, "The maps are bad and the artillerymen in particular will notice it soon." A new large-scale map (which, as this writer knows from personal observation, also had its share of inaccuracies), hastily drawn from aerial photographs, was distributed at Dien Bien Phu, but it promptly fell into enemy hands during the abortive raid of Maj. Chenel's 2nd T'ai Battalion.

When it became apparent at the beginning of March that the French counterbattery was totally ineffectual in silencing the Viet-Minh artillery, Piroth and his superiors in the artillery command in Hanoi sought to rectify the situation by last-minute measures. General Cogny, an artillery-man himself, ordered a full-scale review of the artillery situation in Dien Bien Phu during the first week of March, 1954. By then, sufficient Communist artillery fire had been received from enough different places to give an approximate idea of the enemy's capabilities. In addition, the deciphered Communist logistics code had given the French a com-plete view of the number of Communist artillery shells already in place within the battle area: 44,000 shells of 37-mm., 5,000 of 75-mm., 21,000 of 81-mm., 15,000 of 105-mm., and 3,000 of 120-mm. Appar-ently, there were also some Russian 1943-model superheavy 160-mm. mortars in the Dien Bien Phu battle area.

Prepared in the cool atmosphere of a staff office in Hanoi, far away from the exhilarating atmosphere of a garrison which had been waiting now for four months to measure itself against an enemy who refused to come out into the open and fight, the new report of the artillery situation presented an all too accurate picture of what was going to be the fate of Dien Bien Phu:

> . . . total neutralization fire requires about fifty rounds per hour per hectare [2.5 acres] of terrain. The Viet-Minh is capable of delivering approximately thirty-three rounds per minute for a duration of five hours on the totality of the headquarters posi-tions, the artillery and the mortars; while partially neutralizing Isabelle as well. . . .
>
> The Viet-Minh artillery is as numerous as ours and its observa-tion is better.

The report reached Gen. Cogny in person on March 9. The archive copy bears in the left corner, along with his initials, the scribbled ques-tion: "Why wasn't that study made earlier?"

The fortress of Dien Bien Phu began to take final shape during the last weeks of February, 1954, behind its thousands of tons of barbed wire, around its unprotected gun emplacements bristling with artillery and heavy mortars, and under the cover of its shoddily built bunkers and foxholes, animated with the hope that its ten light tanks and its handful of fighter-bombers would keep the enemy at arm's length.

One of the more curious aspects of Dien Bien Phu is the fact that the various errors committed in the physical construction of the fortress apparently remained hidden from the constant stream of French and foreign notables who inspected the valley in some detail prior to the outbreak of the battle. It was with understandable feeling that Gen. Navarre was to write later that . . .

> . . . not a single civilian or military authoritative person, including French or foreign ministers, French service chiefs, or American generals . . . ever, to my knowledge, admitted any doubts before the attack on the ability of Dien Bien Phu to resist.[13]

This seems to have been true. Rarely had a front line position deep behind enemy lines been the object of more high-level visits. As will be recalled, Gen. Cogny himself first landed at Dien Bien Phu two days after its occupation, to be followed on November 24 by the British military attaché, Brig. Gen. Spears. On November 29, Cogny returned to Dien Bien Phu and brought with him the commander-in-chief, Gen. Navarre, as well as the chief of the United States Military Assistance Advisory Group (MAAG), Major General Thomas Trapnell. Cogny returned again on December 4, and was followed on December 11 by his own Air Force commander, Gen. Dechaux, who inspected the air facilities at Dien Bien Phu. Cogny himself returned on December 12, accompanied by Navarre's deputy, Gen. Bodet; the commander of French forces in Laos, Col. de Crèvecoeur; and the British writer Graham Greene. On December 19, Gen. Trapnell, escorted by his own staff, returned to Dien Bien Phu and again expressed nothing but admiration for the job being done there.

On Christmas Eve, Navarre and Cogny and a large part of their respective staffs arrived at Dien Bien Phu and spent Christmas with the troops. Navarre personally inspected one strongpoint after another and then attended midnight services in the midst of his soldiers on the open terrain. Four days later, Gen. Bodet, escorted by the commanding general of the French Far Eastern Air Force, Major General Henri Lauzin, and the Inspector General for the French Artillery in Indochina, Brig. Gen. Pennachioni, as well as Gen. Cogny, again visited Dien Bien Phu. Each general had brought his own experts along, and they, in turn, had had long talks with their counterparts inside the fortress.

One of the officers present kept a partial record of the subjects covered when Gen. Bodet visited Dien Bien Phu. General Bodet apparently underlined the "absolute necessity to maintain the airfield in working order at any price" and asked whether the strongpoints around it permitted the effective defense of the airstrip. He was reassured on that score by Col. de Castries. General Lauzin, looking toward the north where strongpoint Gabrielle stretched its shiplike shape, wondered aloud whether it would not be "extremely dangerous" to have to parachute supplies on Gabrielle if it were to be cut off. Bodet, who also was an Air Force officer and who apparently had second thoughts about the efficiency of the airlift operations into Dien Bien Phu, stated that he would have liked to have a French air operations officer at Dien Bien Phu who had participated in the Berlin airlift of 1948.

In contrast with Gen. Navarre's claim, both Air Force generals present, and in particular Gen. Lauzin, seemed uneasy about some of the tactical decisions made in the valley. Lauzin worried about Isabelle's probable inability to observe enemy antiaircraft artillery which could be concealed in the hills. He suggested that helicopters place observation teams along the whole crestline.

Colonel de Castries, exhibiting the selective memory that often afflicts officers when faced with high-ranking superiors, seemed, according to the record, to have forgotten about his abortive attempts at breaking through to the hill-line. He argued that he was "too poor in helicopters" to afford the risk of losing them on such missions. But, said de Castries, he would entrust the job of observing the crestline to native scouts.

Lauzin then made one of those suggestions which, for a brief moment, clearly showed a lapse into another war and another era. He suggested that Isabelle could perhaps be equipped with a *captive balloon* for the purpose of spotting the enemy's flak. He apparently forgot that if the flak was accurate enough to be dangerous to his aircraft, it would surely quickly dispose of the captive balloon.

It was also Lauzin who, while visiting Isabelle later that day, commented on the distances between the auxiliary southern airstrip and the surrounding mountains (the record shows that he received "various" answers). He pointed out that some of the ammunition dumps were situated too closely to the parking area of the aircraft (they were later hit by enemy fire and blew up with some of the aircraft), anl let it be known that he was "skeptical" about strongpoint Gabrielle. The record does not show that Lauzin's recommendations were acted upon, or that he expressed his reservations to his own commander-in-chief.

In the meantime, the steady stream of high dignitaries continued. By now, de Castries had refined their visits to a well-rehearsed maneuver: the reception at the airfield by an honor guard of Moroccan riflemen in gleaming white turbans and webbings; a visit to the outlying strongpoints (preferably to the well-turned-out Legionnaires at Beatrice) in de Castries' own jeep driven by himself; lunch at de Castries' own command mess on an impeccably gleaming table service; a thirty-minute briefing at his headquarters; and, usually, a brief glimpse of "Dien Bien Phu at war"—either a brief artillery demonstration impeccably fired by the African cannoneers of one of the batteries at Claudine or a combat reconnaissance combining Capt. Hervouët's brand-new Chaffee tanks and Col. Langlais' lithe paratroopers.

In January, 1954, the visits of the high civilian dignitaries began. On January 3, Navarre and Cogny escorted the French High Commissioner in Indochina, Ambassador Maurice Dejean, for his first visit to Dien Bien Phu. On the 14th there was another visit by Gen. Trapnell, who beamingly hovered over this French military enterprise like a mother hen: His concern becomes somewhat more understandable when one realizes that the American equipment inside the fortress represented a donation of well over ten million dollars by American taxpayers. The day after Trapnell's visit there was one by Cogny and, on January 22, one by Navarre. The latter came this time to prepare for the earlier mentioned visit by the French Secretary of State for Indochinese Affairs, Monsieur Marc Jacquet, who was also escorted by the chief of staff of the French Army, Gen. Blanc. On February 2, the highest-ranking American visitor, Lieutenant General John ("Iron Mike") O'Daniel, arrived. He was United States Army Commander in the Pacific. O'Daniel inspected Dien Bien Phu with an important retinue of American officers, including some who had experience with Communist antiaircraft artillery in Korea. While O'Daniel's reports to Washington have thus far not been published, President Eisenhower released their gist in his own memoirs in 1963. In reply to a report from the late Secretary of State, John Foster Dulles, to the effect that the French government had informed him that the war was going badly, President Eisenhower wired Dulles (who was then in Europe) on February 10, 1954, that "General O'Daniel's most recent report is more encouraging than that given to you through French sources."[14] In other words, O'Daniel, like the others, had been fooled by Dien Bien Phu. On that very same day, in Saigon Gen. Blanc gave a top-secret oral briefing of which at least one stenographic record has remained. Given before both his civilian superiors, Pleven and Chevigné, Blanc apparently was blunt: by April 15 the fortress would be "a marsh" drowning in the monsoon rains, and to destroy the enemy's main battle force there was a "pure illusion." That oral briefing at best led to a few more incisive questions on the part of Pleven when he reached the fortress himself, but to little else. And Gen. Navarre did not hear of it until 1964.[15]

Yet, at least three Americans *were* stationed at Dien Bien Phu almost until the battle was joined: one U. S. Air Force officer and two U. S. Army officers. The Air Force officer, Captain Robert M. Lloyd, was assigned by the U. S. Pacific Air Force (PACAF) to study the effects of Communist antiaircraft artillery on French air operations; while Lieutenant Colonels John M. Wohner and Richard F. Hill, from U. S. Army, Pacific (USARPAC), observed the preparations of the battle from the vantage point of Colonel Jules Gaucher's Foreign Legion's 13th Half-Brigade. In other words, American observation and advice were available to the French at all levels. There is no evidence whatever that the French were either advised against fighting at Dien Bien Phu or advised against any specific aspects of the defensive system of the valley. If such advice was ever given—*i.e.,* comments going beyond doubts expressed by one American observer to another, or to their own superiors—it is still cloaked in the secrecy of American archives.

On February 7, it was the turn of France's Secretary of Defense, Chevigné, to visit the valley, escorted by Cogny. The Secretary returned to Dien Bien Phu a week later, this time escorted by the Chairman of the French Joint Chiefs, General Paul Ely. Chevigné did not take his tour lightly but stayed overnight and carefully visited every one of the strongpoints. A former regular army colonel, he was conversant with military problems in general. His visit was a reconnaissance for the visit of his Minister of Defense, Monsieur René Pleven, on February 19. By then, both Cogny and Navarre were commuting forth and back between Dien Bien Phu and Hanoi, for both of them had been in the valley on the previous day in company with the French Army Surgeon-General, Dr. Jeansotte, and the commanding medical officer for North Viet-Nam, Col. Terramorsi, M.D. With Pleven's visit, it seems, the high point of Dien Bien Phu's period of outside inspections had been reached. True, the Honorable Malcolm McDonald, Britain's High Commissioner for Southeast Asia, visited Dien Bien Phu on March 6, 1954, when its airfield already was under intermittent Communist fire. Generals Navarre and Cogny made a last joint trip to Dien Bien Phu on March 4. But most of the other visits now were by lower-level specialists working frantically just before what they knew would soon be the full-scale attack.

On Friday morning, March 12, Gen. Cogny's command aircraft landed for the last time on Dien Bien Phu's main strip, already lined with the burned-out hulks of several aircraft destroyed by Communist artillery.

Cogny made a last visit to Beatrice, showing obvious signs of concern for its welfare if it were not properly supported by powerful counterattacks. Throughout the day isolated Communist shells, thus far fired from 75-mm. cannon and 120-mm. mortars, fell in a random pattern on many points in the valley, seemingly avoiding the parking area of the airfield, where Cogny's C-47 had stood all day. Other transport planes hurriedly trundled down the runway, dropped their loads, and took off again. At 1530, Cogny returned to his aircraft, escorted by de Castries and his staff. Perhaps Cogny believed that this had merely been another of his inspection tours at Dien Bien Phu, but many of the men who stood at respectful attention as his tall silhouette disappeared inside the aircraft knew that they would not see him again before the end of the battle.

As both engines of the airplane slowly turned over, a volley of 105-mm. howitzer shells crashed into the parking area, virtually boxing in the escort party now lying flat on the pierced steel plates of the taxi stand, and setting afire two *Cricket* reconnaissance planes parked nearby. The C-47 took off in a cloud of dust and pulled in its wheels as soon as it was airborne. At 1730, an F8F *Bearcat* fighter bomber undergoing repairs was riddled by shrapnel. By the next day, six F8F's of the 1st Group of the 22nd Fighter Wing (GC 1/22 "Saintonge"), would have disintegrated under enemy fire.

Meanwhile, French intelligence had picked up a valuable bit of information: the Communist political commissars had told the population in the villages to clear the valley by noon Saturday, March 13, 1954. Captain Noël, the intelligence officer, had brought the news to Col. de Castries after his return from the airfield. Previous experience suggested that the enemy would attack at an hour when it would still be light enough for him to register his artillery fires, but too late for the French fighters based at Dien Bien Phu effectively to intervene in the battle, and for those based in Hanoi to intervene at all. March nights fall early in a deep valley located 21° north of the equator.

At the regular briefing of the senior commanders prior to dinner, de Castries went through the routine announcements, listened to the usual remarks, read a telegram from Gen. Lauzin exhorting all pilots participating in the battle of Dien Bien Phu to take "exceptional risks," and then ended the briefing with the simple sentence: "Gentlemen, it's for tomorrow at 1700."

As the French garrison readied itself for the showdown at Dien Bien Phu, it is useful to describe once more the final order of battle.

As seen from the air or from the surrounding hills, Dien Bien Phu now looked like some gigantic primitive village whose population, not having mastered the art of building houses, had preferred to take shelter in holes in the ground. Inside the main center of resistance and on top of the main outlying positions, the last shreds of vegetation had completely disappeared. Only near Anne-Marie and along the western flank of Claudine was there still any evidence of the original rice fields that had once existed there. There was no longer any trace of what had been the cluster of small hamlets and villages around the little town of Dien Bien Phu itself. The stately house of the pre-war French Resident had stood on what was now strongpoint Eliane 2, now occupied by Maj. Nicolas' Moroccans. The buildings had been dismantled stone by stone to construct bunkers. Nicolas himself had used part of the cellar for his own command post—a move which led to the pleasant surprise of finding a small cache of twenty-year-old bottles of French wine. A whole new road system, traced into the soil by the vehicles and tanks of the garrison, now connected the various strongpoints. Each strongpoint was more or less surrounded by barbed-wire entanglements. At night the roads and paths between them were closed with mobile barbed-wire barriers. The peripheral positions had, in addition, been surrounded by conventional mine fields and with electrically detonated "bouncing mines" designed to devastate onrushing waves of enemy infantry after they had come through the barbed wire. In addition, the French engineers had dug into the slopes of the steeper hills ten-gallon drums of "nagel"—jellied napalm whose fiery flow, detonated by electrical triggers, would smother the attackers in flames and would transform them into human torches. Finally, key French positions had been equipped with "sniperscope" rifles whose infrared rays could spot an advancing enemy soldier on the darkest of nights.

The strongpoints were connected to their own higher headquarters by wire and radio. All were similarly connected to de Castries' command post. In January, 1954, de Castries had reorganized the whole position into three subsectors: the northern subsector, composed of strongpoints Anne-Marie and Gabrielle, under the command of Lt. Col. Trancart (who had commanded the abandoned Lai Chau); a central subsector, comprising the main positions of Dien Bien Phu and outlying strongpoint Beatrice, under the command of Lt. Col. Gaucher; and a southern subsector, under Lt. Col. Lalande, comprising strongpoint Isabelle and the outlying patrol strongpoint Marcelle. Marcelle had led such a fugitive existence within the organization of Dien Bien Phu that all the other accounts of the battle have thus far ignored it. Created on

January 12, 1954, by a detachment of the 3/3 REI just south of the village of Ban Loi almost halfway between Isabelle and the main positions at Dien Bien Phu, Marcelle was later garrisoned by the 434th T'ai Company, under M/Sgt. Cante, until March 14, when he and his small unit fell back to Isabelle as enemy pressure began to build up around Ban Loi. Françoise, another such outlying position located 500 yards west of Claudine and held by the 414th White T'ai Company under M/Sgt. Comte, held its position until it was abandoned during the night of April 2 by the demoralized tribesmen, who left behind them their weapons and noncommissioned officers.

On the left flank of the northern sector, there was strongpoint Anne-Marie, occupied by the 3rd T'ai Battalion under Maj. Thimonier. Gradually reinforced since it was first occupied on December 7, 1953, Anne-Marie was composed of a half-moon-shaped hill position whose horns faced the enemy hill-line. Together, they formed Anne-Marie 1 and 2. The two remaining positions, Anne-Marie 3 and 4, were located in the dishpan-flat rice fields between the northern tip of the airstrip and Anne-Marie (AM) 1 and 2. Both AM 3 and 4 were laid out in a curious triangle formed of three positions shaped like arrowheads grouped around a central headquarters position. AM 4 served as a connecting link between the northern hill position and the rest of Dien Bien Phu. AM 3, on the other hand, rested like a little dot capping the long "i" of the airstrip itself. It also lay athwart the Pavie Track leading to Gabrielle.

While it is convenient for purposes of illustration to give the strongpoints at Dien Bien Phu the amoeba-shaped contours with which they are usually depicted, they were quite different. There was neither a connecting trench system nor a common belt of barbed wire nor even mine fields which connected all the positions of a strongpoint. This was particularly true early in the battle, when the newspapers as well as the French Army's information services attempted to make the world believe that the French "fortress" of Dien Bien Phu encompassed the whole valley. In the case of Anne-Marie, AM 1 and 2 were connected with each other, since they were located on one and the same hill, but the other two positions were little worlds of their own, each inhabited by one company of about 130 tribesmen, a few French noncoms and one French officer: Capt. Gendre on AM 3 and Capt. Désiré, on AM 4. Désiré, whose wife was expecting their first child (the baby girl was born in France on May 4 and promptly baptized "Anne Marie"), had acquired a T'ai horse for which his men had dug him a pit. He could be seen going for the unit's mail and to briefings gaily trotting through the dust on his charger.

Like all the other battalions inside the valley, the 3rd BT had its normal complement of four 81-mm. mortars as well as some lighter 60-mm.'s and its machine guns. While Anne-Marie was not rated as an excellent position, it had the advantage of solid backing from almost all sides. To the north, the heavy mortar battery of Gabrielle could cover all of Anne-Marie with its supporting fires, and the tank squadron would simply have to barrel down the length of the airstrip to reach it with supporting paratroops in case of real trouble. In addition, while Maj. Thimonier was not as popular with his men as the departing Maj. Archambault, the company commanders were men with considerable experience. In addition to Gendre and Désiré, there were Capt. Guilleminot and Lt. Makoviak. The later fate of the 3rd BT left the indelible impression that the unit had always been worthless. An investigation of its background shows that this was not so.

The year before it had fought very well in the fortified camp of Na-San where its 12th Company under Makoviak had formed the rear guard when the camp was evacuated. Although there had been uncertainty among the unit's mountain tribesmen when it appeared that their native region was to be abandoned to the Communists, only twenty men deserted. The rest of the battalion had performed extremely well during the difficult and costly mop-up operations, "Flanders" and "Pike," in the southern part of the Red River Delta. The 3rd BT had particularly distinguished itself in October, 1953, during Operation "Seagull," in which it was for a time the lead element in a multi-regiment operation that badly mauled the 320th People's Army Division in the limestone hills and crags around Phu Nho Quan. In that operation, it had worked under the command of Col. de Castries and side by side with the 3/13 DBLE. Thus, when it replaced the thoroughly demoralized 301st BVN in December, 1953, there was no reason to believe that the unit would not give a good account of itself. If anything, its morale was expected to rise since it was again being committed in its own T'ai hills.

This appeared to be the case. The battalion began fraternizing with its fellow tribesmen from the neighboring villages of Ban Kéo and Ban Long Thong. Some intelligence reports cautioned that the T'ai tribesmen in the garrison of Dien Bien Phu might be subverted and demoralized through their contacts with the local population, but this was readily discounted by the French officers who worked with them and who knew them. Furthermore, as long as the population lived in the valley it was virtually impossible to enforce a ban on fraternization. Such a ban would also run against the French policy of attempting to win over the populace to the Nationalist side.

There was no such problem on stark, abrupt strongpoint Gabrielle. Although no longer called the "Torpedo Boat," Gabrielle, now totally denuded of all vegetation, looked more like a warship than ever, an effect heightened by its eight-gun battery of superheavy 120-mm. mortars and the battalion's own battery of four 81-mm.'s. The Algerians of the 5/7 RTA had truly worked hard in preparing their position. In an inter-strongpoint competition proposed by Col. de Castries, in which a team of outside officers would judge each position on the base of the solidity of its construction and the excellence of the tactical layout, Gabrielle had won hands down. Its men had been given a large cash prize by de Castries. The battalion "blew" it in an enormous *nouba* (a Moslem festive dinner) on January 28, 1954, to which it invited de Castries and most of his senior staff officers.

Indeed, it was the only strongpoint which had two complete defensive lines. Its mortars were well dug in and were well registered on all their most likely targets. The four rifle companies were also well protected. The 5/7 was solid: it had arrived in Indochina in the middle of the first heavy Communist offensives of the spring of 1951 and had then been thrown into combat without any heavy weapons. For two long years it had been in charge of the defense of one of the vital sectors covering the approaches to Hanoi from the north and had acquited itself of its task with high marks for competence and courage. It had Frenchmen and Algerians among both officers and NCO's and, prior to its arrival at Dien Bien Phu on Christmas Day, 1953, it had been reequipped with new uniforms and weapons, including infrared sniperscopes. The 5/7 RTA could be relied upon to give a good account of itself. This reliance was, it turned out, fully justified.

The battalion's commanding officer, Major Roland de Mecquenem, had his unit well in hand. After a tour of duty with the NATO Standing Group in Washington from 1950 until 1952, de Mecquenem had spent two years with the Algerians in the Red River Delta and was shortly to be returned home. In fact, his replacement, a Major Kah, had arrived on Gabrielle on March 2, but de Mecquenem had insisted upon staying on so as to be able to instruct his successor in all the details of the defense of the position. Both officers were still on strongpoint Gabrielle when the battle started. Finally, one of the T'ai auxiliary companies, the 416th, also had been assigned to Gabrielle; but thoroughly demoralized after its harrowing trek from Lai Chau, the 416th was assigned little more than housekeeping functions. It melted away once the battle began.

The central sector, with its cluster of main strongpoints and its outlying satellite strongpoint Beatrice, was of course the heart of the fortress. It fell into two major subdivisions: the hill positions east of the Nam Yum River and the flatland positions to the west of it. So long as Beatrice was in French hands, Communist artillery could be kept at arm's length from the airfield, and as long as the hill positions of Dominique and Eliane were in French hands it was possible to move with a certain amount of safety within the fortified camp. On the western side, the Communist hill-line positions were far enough away from the heart of Dien Bien Phu—which the French soon began to call the "Center of Resistance" (CR). The full weight of French firepower was expected to keep Communist assault troops sufficiently far away to prevent them from becoming too dangerous.

Thus, much, if not all, depended on Beatrice. Little wonder, then, that its defense and the over-all command of the central sector as well had been entrusted to Col. Gaucher's Mobile Group 9. This unit had been built around the 13th DBLE and included the 3/3 RTA on Dominique, and another Moroccan battalion which had not been brought into the valley.

The 13th DBLE was one of those legendary units of the French Army which had never lost a battle even during the worst days of World War II. As part of the Free French forces in Africa, it had fought along with the British Eighth Army in Libya. In fact, it had been entrusted with the difficult mission of covering the retreat of that army into Egypt when it was pursued by German Field Marshal Rommel's Afrika Korps. At a desert oasis called Bir-Hakeim it made a last-ditch stand despite several offers to surrender. Only after it had bought the time necessary for the Eighth Army to take up new positions did the 13th break out of the encirclement.

With this to live up to, Beatrice was obviously in excellent hands. The position itself, though considered well built by everyone who had visited it, was overshadowed by neighboring jungle hills. There simply had not been time enough to burn down tens of square miles of surrounding jungle. Hence, a Communist unit could approach Beatrice to within a few hundred yards with almost total impunity. The position itself was made up of three round hills grouped in the form of an irregular triangle. Beatrice 2 and 3 overlooked Road 41, while Beatrice 1 faced the jungle hills to the north. All three positions comprised several well dug-in bunkers, and the command-post bunkers were placed in the center of the triangle. A small outpost bunker stood somewhat apart on a little knob to the west of Beatrice 1. Slit trenches connected the various positions with each other and well dug-in automatic weapons covered all the likely approaches to Beatrice. These were also placed in a manner to be able to give mutually supporting fires to the defensive positions within the strongpoint.

By early March, 1954, Major Paul Pégot, the commander of the 3/13 atop Beatrice had done all that was possible to fortify the strongpoint with the means available. Yet he could not prevent the steady drain on his forces necessary to keep the road open from Beatrice to the main position at Dien Bien Phu. When the attack on Beatrice actually began on March 13, the total strength of the battalion had been reduced to about 500 men (instead of 700), and most of its platoons were commanded by sergeants. In fact, one French intelligence source maintains that there was only one officer left per company, plus a very small battalion staff.

Strongpoint Dominique contained the highest terrain features of the main center of resistance. Its-peripheral positions D1 and D2, 530 and 560 meters high respectively, towered by about 200 feet above the valley bottom and dominated by almost 100 feet neighboring strongpoint Eliane. This meant that Dominique also included important artillery observatories for the whole fortress. The trouble with Dominique was that it was too widespread and incoherent for an effective defense. The 583 soldiers, ninety non-coms, and fifteen officers of the 3/3 RTA, whose mission was to defend Dominique, were strung out over a position whose maximum length was almost two miles and maximum width almost one mile. And while D1 and D2 were hill positions straddling Road 41, D3 was in the flatlands along the Nam Yum (where the depots were supposed to have been dug in) and D4 was altogether on the west bank of the river. Here again, the egg shapes reassuringly drawn on the maps around those isolated positions meant nothing: there were no continuous barbed-wire entanglements of mine fields between D1 and D4 (see map, p. 117) and there was plenty of low underbrush and open space in the ravines around the Nam Yum for the enemy to infiltrate. In the engineering reports, Dominique was the only position rated as "bad," and Capt. Garandeau's Algerians were, like the Moroccans on neighboring Eliane, just as good as their leaders. They fought when well led, but were likely to collapse if their unit commanders were

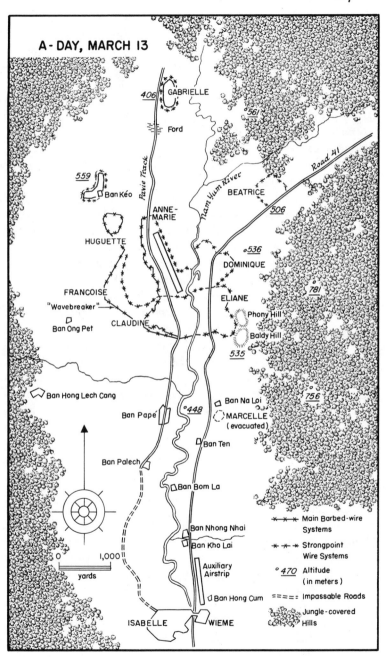

A - DAY, MARCH 13

Main Barbed-wire Systems

Strongpoint Wire Systems

°470 Altitude (in meters)

Impassable Roads

Jungle-covered Hills

killed or wounded.[16] In the case of Dominique there existed several re-assuring factors. The position was shielded from almost all sides by peripheral strongpoints and it was within easy reach of the paratroop battalions of GAP 2, whose role would be to back up the faltering garrisons of the outlying strongpoints. When it became clear that the battle would soon be joined, Dominique was reinforced accordingly. D1 was held by the 9th Company of the 3/3 RTA and an artillery observation detachment. It was reinforced in March by a battery of six 120-mm. heavy mortars from Col. de Castries' headquarters reserve.

On outlying D2, Capt. Garandeau had set up his own command post with 11th Company and Headquarters Company. D2 was further reinforced on January 9, 1954, by the arrival of the 425th CSM, one of the T'ai auxiliary companies. D3 was held by 12th Company with the exception of one platoon which acted as Col. de Castries' honor guard at his own headquarters. Finally, D4 was held by 10th Company. A new strongpoint, baptized D5, was inserted between D2 and D3 on March 7, and was occupied by 5th Company of the 2nd T'ai Battalion. Finally, on March 15, when the battle had already begun, it became apparent that the defense of Dominique was vital to the survival of the fortress. A new strongpoint, D6, was therefore hastily inserted between D1 and D2. But this is part of the later story.

To the south of Dominique lay Eliane. If any part of the battle of Dien Bien Phu earned a place in the annals of human heroism, it was the single-minded defense, to the last cartridge and the last man, of these two blood-drenched hillocks. It is not without reason that the Viet-Minh forces, after the battle was over, built the monument commemorating their dead atop Eliane 2, although that position was overshadowed both in height and size by many others. But for none other had the battle raged for so long and so bitterly, and none other had cost as much in dead and wounded.

Eliane had first been occupied by the 3rd BT and the 5th BPVN. Prior to the outbreak of the battle, it had become the home of the Moroccans of the 1/4 RTM. Its flatland rear area housed one of the engineering companies and a company of paratroopers from the 8th BPC. When the battle developed, Eliane would subdivide like an amoeba and sprout new strongpoints. But two of the most important features of Eliane were not even located inside its position. They were two hills situated to the east of Eliane 2 which had not been included in the French defensive perimeter because they would have added little to its strength. The northernmost hill, however, had been equipped with a rudimentary defensive position in order to deceive the enemy as to French intentions in that sector. Actually, it was held during daylight by an outpost garrison and at night by three-man patrols. In view of its fictitious character, the hill became known as *Mont Fictif;* in English, perhaps, "Phony Hill," or "Phony Mountain." The other hill soon became no man's land and was, in view of its bareness, referred to as *Mont Chauve,* which translates as "Baldy Hill," or "Baldy Mountain." Both Phony Hill and Baldy Hill were to play roles in the drama of Eliane.

On the left flank, beyond the Nam Yum, lay the hard core of Dien Bien Phu; that is, the bulk of its garrison, the airfield, and all the artillery with the exception of two batteries of 105's of the II/4 RAC located near Dominique 4. The two strongpoints which covered that area, Huguette and Claudine, were military abstractions without any salient terrain features. This is best shown by the maps and aerial photographs of the first few days of March, 1954, none of which agree as to the exact outlines of the positions.

For example, some of these maps show the headquarters area as being part of Claudine, while others show the various headquarters installations in a sort of no man's land in the center of the strongpoint cluster. Only during the battle, when one strongpoint after another (and often a particular position within a strongpoint) had to fight for its life, were the various positions of Huguette and Claudine to take on an individual character of their own. Both strongpoints had another special feature in common, at least at the begnning. They were both garrisoned by Foreign Legion infantry battalions. Claudine was held by Maj. Coutant's 1/13 DBLE, while Huguette was defended by the 1st Battalion, 2nd Foreign Legion Infantry, of Maj. Clémençon. Like all the other strongpoints, both Claudine and Huguette had their share of T'ai mountaineer auxiliary companies: two of them on Claudine and three on Huguette. On the side facing the enemy, Claudine, tucked away behind the elaborate barbed-wire "wave-breaker," looked like a normal strongpoint; her inner side facing the core of the fortress looked more like a strange factory producing weird machinery in shops without a roof and without walls. Here was the major depot and headquarters zone of Dien Bien Phu, with its repair shops, its power generators, motor pools, and hospital. This was Main Street, Dien Bien Phu. Close to Claudine 1 there were the main artillery and mortar positions, comprising sixteen 105's and the 155-mm. guns of the counterbattery, plus Lt. Bergot's Airborne Mortar Company with its eight 120's. At the eastern edge of Claudine, where the position abutted on the Nam Yum, was the head-

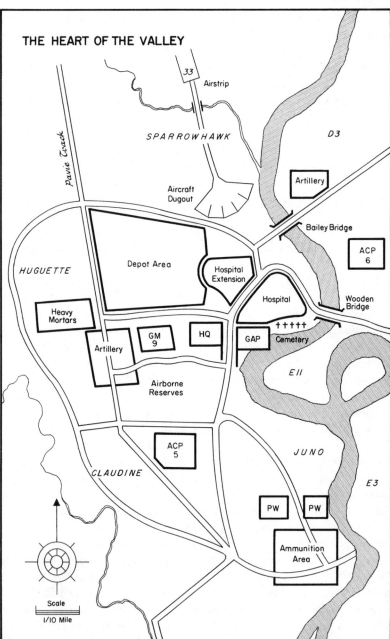

THE HEART OF THE VALLEY

quarters of the armored squadron. Here the engineers had dug deep pits from which the turrets of the tanks emerged with their cannon like so many menacing war elephants.

Just to the north of C1 and C2, where the Pavie Track joined Road 41, were the heart and soul of Dien Bien Phu—Col. de Castries' own headquarters with its corrugated steel roof (the only one at Dien Bien Phu) deeply buried under layers of beams and sandbags. Across the road, on a slight rise along the Nam Yum, was Col. Langlais' GAP 2, next to which was Dien Bien Phu's main hospital.

The hospital began as a comfortably small affair with forty-four beds for seriously wounded, and well-appointed dugouts for the operations, X-ray, and recovery rooms. This was before it became clear that not one wounded man would leave the hell of Dien Bien Phu by air. The hospital with its forty-four beds soon cared for perhaps 3,000 wounded and, from a model field installation, it became an apocalyptic charnel house in whose dark recesses the wounded would lie in the muck and stench of their own blood and excrement. The main hospital was run by Major Paul Grauwin, M.D., a reserve officer who had served in Indochina for over ten years and who, with his completely bald head, looked like a Roman emperor with rimless glasses.[17] Grauwin commanded the Mobile Surgical Detachment (ACM) 29, reinforced in February, 1954, by the Vietnamese Army's ACM 44 under Lt. Gindrey, M.D. Each surgical detachment had enough personnel to supervise a small field hospital and to perform all the chores of the surgery room. In addition, of course, each one of the battalions inside Dien Bien Phu had its own doctor and male nurses and corpsmen, yet all this was ridiculously inadequate and the local medical personnel knew it even before the battle. On January 19, 1954, Capt. Rives, M.D., then the chief medical officer at Dien Bien Phu,[18] sent a report to de Castries stating that the small number of available hospital beds was "beneath comment."

The result was that three complete Airborne Surgical Teams (ACP), complete with their doctors and operating-room equipment, had to be parachuted into Dien Bien Phu in the midst of the battle. ACP 3 was parachuted onto isolated Isabelle, while ACP Nos. 5 and 6 were parachuted into Dien Bien Phu itself. No. 6 was installed on shell-smothered Eliane, where it kept operating and treating the wounded under incredible conditions until the last day of the battle. As losses piled up and wounded could not be evacuated, two complete blood banks were parachuted in on April 15 and 18, as well as an X-ray machine, to replace the one in the main hospital which had been destroyed. All this was installed in the central recesses of strongpoint Claudine, as well as signal companies, gasoline depot units, ammunition detachments, a quartermaster unit, a military police detachment, an army post office (No. 74.144), and small detachments of operatives of the French equivalent of the Central Intelligence Agency—referred to as "Section 6"—and D.O.P. The latter employed their own force of Meo tribesmen, who were quartered near de Castries' headquarters in their own dugouts and disappeared into the nearby mountains on their mysterious errands.[19] The women and children of the Meo intelligence agents lived with them inside the fortress, for there was a heavy price on their heads if the Viet-Minh captured them. In a depression near the Nam Yum, between GAP 2 and the hospital, huddled Dien Bien Phu's cemetery. Soon, the number of dead required that graves be dug with the help of the bulldozers. And soon thereafter, the dead would simply be buried where they fell, in shell holes or collapsed dugouts and trenches.

Strongpoint Huguette's key job was to protect and keep open the bulk of the airfield. With Anne-Marie 3 holding the northernmost edge of the strip and Dominique 4 insuring the defense of its parking area and taxi stand, Huguette 1 straddled the Pavie Track at a point about 2,700 feet from the beginning of the runway. H2 was also located on the Pavie Track, but only 900 feet to the northwest of the beginning of the runway. H3 was inserted a few hundred feet farther to the south when the increasing pressure and boldness of the enemy showed, in January, 1954, that his attack would be a serious one and that the airfield would be one of his prime targets. That is what led Col. de Castries, on the recommendation of Maj. Clémençon, to provide Huguette with an advanced first line in the form of two outlying strongpoints, H4 and H5, about 1,500 feet farther to the west of H1, H2, and H3. On the aerial photographs taken at the time they appear as mere squiggles of trenches and a few bunkers within the irregular star shape of their mine fields and barbed-wire entanglements. Yet the battle for the Huguettes was to become as merciless and bloody as that for the Elianes. Still farther to the west, in the flattened ruins of what used to be the small T'ai village of Muong Ten, there was the already mentioned strongpoint, Françoise, which could hardly be called a "strongpoint." It was more what the French called a *sonnette*, a "doorbell" designed to warn the units behind it of the arrival of the enemy.

Finally, barely visible through the haze of the valley bottom, lay, far to the south and all by itself, strongpoint Isabelle. Installed on a small hillock in a loop of the Nam Yum, Isabelle was organized in four strongpoints located on the west bank of the river and in a fifth located across the river at the base of what was to have become Dien Bien Phu's auxiliary airstrip. If all of Dien Bien Phu was fated to be drowned in the monsoon rain and mud of late April and May, this problem scarcely arose on Isabelle. Constructed in the middle of a swamp for the single purpose of providing artillery protection and hardly more than 2,000 feet long at its widest spot, Isabelle's troops lived in the water from the beginning of the battle. The two infantry battalions, the artillery battalion, the tank platoon, and the T'ai auxiliaries lived like animals in a cage in total isolation for forty days. Even the hell of the main position of Dien Bien Phu, with its 10,000 troops, seemed like a small paradise in comparison.

On Isabelle, there was no escape from anything—the shelling, the humidity, the wounded, and the dead. The four western strongpoints of Isabelle were tightly grouped in the fashion of a loose mosaic around the headquarters cluster in the center. To the east, there was the famous bridge for whose construction Maj. Sudrat had in part filled in the Nam Yum, and beyond that bridge, which was surrounded on the eastern bank of the Nam Yum by a narrow neck of trenches, was the strange world of Isabelle 5, an even more isolated subsatellite whose official nomenclature was soon forgotten in favor of the name of the young lieutenant who commanded the 431st, 432nd, and 434th T'ai Auxiliary companies. And so it was that Isabelle 5 became the only position in the valley to be named after a human male and one who was part of the garrison at that: Strongpoint Wieme. Shaped like the blade of a pickax whose handle would be the north-south line of the Pavie Track and whose arrow point would focus on the Nam Yum bridge, strongpoint Wieme jutted out into the no man's land where the enemy roamed, until the last day of the battle; but scores of men paid with their lives just to supply and relieve it regularly, for the Nam Yum bridge was under constant observation and fire by the enemy.

But in those bygone days of mid-March, 1954, the thoughts of the garrison at Isabelle were not yet geared to the possibility of having to fight on alone. Between Isabelle and Claudine there lay the open flatlands of the valley bottom with its little midway post, Marcelle, and the seemingly unstoppable power of Capt. Hervouët's armored "Bisons," which would surely be capable of plowing through any kind of Communist infantry force. Any kind, that is, except one solidly entrenched and dug in with sufficient antitank bazookas. Registration fires of the artillery pieces of the III/10 RAC had shown that Capt. Libier's guns could easily reach the southern part of Dien Bien Phu and place any would-be attackers of Eliane under murderous flanking fires. Conversely, the heavy artillery from Claudine could box in Isabelle under its own fires on a moment's notice. And to the south, hardly a mountain chain beyond the valley, was friendly Laos.

Though the immediate border areas were occupied by Viet-Minh forces just as the T'ai highlands of Viet-Nam were, there still existed throughout the Laotian mountain areas the French commando forces of the GCMA whose radio operators quietly cut into the radio traffic at Isabelle and who constituted a sort of reassuring external presence. Everyone agreed even before the battle started that if Dien Bien Phu were to be crushed by overwhelming Communist forces, the best road to salvation lay to the south, beyond Isabelle.

There had been a few rain squalls on March 13, 1954, over the valley of Dien Bien Phu, but the air transport traffic had not been impeded by them. Nor had the intermittent Communist harassing fires been any worse than usual. Almost a decade later I was to sit in the Museum of the Revolution in Hanoi, where the North Vietnamese government keeps its mementos of past struggles, watching a film put together by Roman Lazarevich Karmen, the Russian cinematographer, and to see through the eyes of an anonymous Viet-Minh cameraman what the battlefield looked like that fateful late afternoon. The particular sequence had apparently been taken from the mountain hills overlooking Claudine and Huguette, clearly visible in their sandy outlines against the lush green of the surrounding rice fields. The whole French position looked, as so many observers had already stated, like a huge Boy Scout jamboree, with its tents, the rising smoke of the many cooking fires, and the laundry laid out to dry over the strands of barbed wire. For a few seconds the camera seemed to "zoom" in on the flapping laundry and on a jeep racing like a little toy on the dusty road between Claudine and Huguette.

And then this whole bucolic scene suddenly dissolved in what seemed to be a fantastic series of ferocious black tornadoes which completely covered the neat geometrical outlines of the French positions. The Communist bombardment of the French fortress of Dien Bien Phu had begun. It was March 13, 1954; the hour was 1700.

V

Assault

ON THE VIET-MINH side March 13 was the payoff for almost five months of backbreaking labor: the transportation through hundreds of miles of jungle of thousands of tons of supplies, and the gamble of Gen. Giap and his able chief of staff at Dien Bien Phu, General Hoang Van Thai.

The Viet-Minh's previous experiences, attacking French fortified positions had not been encouraging. The attack on the "Marshal de Lattre" line, in the face of French artillery and fighter bombers in 1951-52, had been a failure. During the previous summer the French garrison at Na-San, after again beating off a concentrated Communist attack, successfully slipped out from the encirclement and was evacuated by air. Considering how long it took the Viet-Minh logistical system to build up supply depots with human carriers and its small pool of Russian trucks, a last-minute French decision to pull out from Dien Bien Phu by air would leave the bulk of the Communist battle force almost in the middle of nowhere, while the French would be free, thanks to their high airborne mobility, to concentrate their troops for an attack on the Viet-Minh's sensitive rear bases to the north of the Red River Delta. Fortunately for Gen. Giap, he was able to compel his French opposite number, Gen. Navarre, to depart from his erstwhile policy of economy of forces. Through daring raids of the 308th Division into northern Laos and of the newly formed 325th Division in the direction of the Mekong in December, 1953, and January, 1954, Giap led Navarre to fritter away his last mobile reserves into a series of smaller airheads at Muong Sai and Séno. Those airheads not only absorbed whatever reserve tonnage the French Air Force Transport Command could make available, but also prohibited, as was seen, an adequate supply build-up at Dien Bien Phu during that crucial phase and rendered impossible a timely evacuation of the French forces there—had such a decision ever been made.

Yet, to judge from the slowness of the Communist build-up at Dien Bien Phu, the chances for a successful evacuation might have been good in mid-December, 1953, and again in mid-January, 1954. After the retirement of Independent Regiment 148 from the Dien Bien Phu valley, only a light screen of Communist regional forces remained in the area. Seven battalions of General Le Quang Ba's 316th Division, reinforced by the division's Artillery Battalion 980, arrived in the general area of Dien Bien Phu only around December 17, having been delayed by the destruction of the T'ai light companies. General Vuong Thua Vu's crack 308th Division, composed almost entirely of volunteers from Hanoi and the province of Vinh-Phuc-Yen, started its march toward Dien Bien Phu on November 28 under a steady pelting by French fighters and bombers which, to all appearances, had little effect. The division arrived in the Dien Bien Phu area during the last days of December, inflicted some severe losses on the reconnaissance stabs of GAP 2, but then moved on for its raid toward Luang-Prabang. It was to return to Dien Bien Phu only late in January, 1954, and its arrival gave rise to the French Intelligence estimate that the general attack on Dien Bien Phu was to begin on January 25. Finally, Regiment 57 of the 304th Division under Colonel Hoang Khai Tien reached Dien Bien Phu on January 24, after a forced march of ten days across more than 200 miles of jungle from Phu-Tho.

Thus, a total of twenty-eight infantry battalions with 37,500 combatants constituted the hard core of the infantry siege force. As the battle wore on, the Communist high command threw another 10,000 reserves— some of them almost raw recruits—into the fight. It also brought in three more regular battalions from the 304th and 316th divisions and from Regiment 148.

But this was not all. Had the Communist force been made up entirely of infantry, the French garrison, though one third the enemy's strength, could probably have withstood the assault, thanks to its massive firepower and air support. What really broke the back of the French resistance at Dien Bien Phu was Gen. Vu Hien's 351st "Heavy Division." The concept of the Heavy Division was one which the Viet-Minh had inherited from its Chinese Communist and Russian mentors. It was this type of massive utilization of concentrated artillery fire which time and again smashed the German front in Russia. In Viet-Nam, where relatively few well-trained artillerymen were available, the concentration of such firepower in a single large unit made a great deal of sense.

The 351st had come a long way since its humble beginnings in 1945,

when the Viet-Minh artillery was equipped with some antiquated French
and Japanese mountain guns. One by one its battalions had gone through
the Chinese Communist artillery training camps at Ching-Hsi and Long
Chow. At first equipped mostly with American 75-mm. howitzers captured from the Chinese Nationalists, the division received forty-eight
American 105-mm. howitzers in 1953, mostly from freshly captured
Korean stocks. By mid-December, 1953, the 675th Artillery Regiment
(probably equipped with twenty-four pack howitzers of 75-mm. caliber
and twenty heavy mortars of 120-mm.) arrived in the Dien Bien Phu
area in the wake of the 308th Division. During the first week of January,
the 45th Artillery Regiment, equipped with nine batteries of four
105-mm. howitzers each, also arrived in Dien Bien Phu, followed shortly
by the 367th Antiaircraft Regiment, equipped with thirty-six Russian flak
pieces. Later on, at least parts of the 237th Artillery Regiment, equipped
mostly with heavy mortars, was also reported in the Dien Bien Phu area.
In addition, the infantry divisions which were part of the siege ring also
brought along with them their normal complement of heavy weapons and
mortar battalions as well as their own light antiaircraft pieces.

While exact figures will no doubt remain forever unknown, French
ground and air observation (which was far from perfect) estimated that
the enemy finally fielded at Dien Bien Phu at least forty-eight field howitzers of 105-mm. caliber, forty-eight pack howitzers of the 75-mm. caliber,
forty-eight heavy 120-mm. mortars, and at least as many 75-mm. recoilless rifles (whose effect became murderous as the Communists began to
occupy the outer edge of Dominique), and at least thirty-six heavy flak
guns. Finally, as the battle reached its climax, Viet-Minh began to em-
ploy Soviet-built "Katyusha" multitube rocket launchers. In all, then, the
Communists possessed at least 200 guns above the 57-mm. caliber. On the
French side, the maximum number of such guns ever available amounted
to sixty and dropped to an average of less than forty within a week after
the battle had begun.

Since the French Air Force and naval aircraft could not hope to make
up for a four-to-one inferiority in artillery, the disparity in firepower is
almost sufficient explanation of the outcome of the whole battle.

The real surprise to the French was not that the Communists had that
kind of artillery. In fact, its existence had been known for a year. What
surprised the French completely was the Viet-Minh's ability to transport
a considerable mass of heavy artillery pieces across roadless mountains to
Dien Bien Phu and to keep it supplied with a sufficient amount of ammunition to make the huge effort worth-while. The French artillery special-

ists inside the fortress later estimated that they had been hit by approximately 30,000 shells of 105-mm. artillery and probably by over 100.000 shells of other calibers. This represents roughly 1,300 to 1,700 tons of munitions delivered to the valley between December, 1953, and May, 1954.[1] In addition, about 6,500 tons of other supplies were brought to the valley by the Viet-Minh.

Essentially, then, the battle of Dien Bien Phu was won along the communications lines leading from the Chinese border at Mu Nam Quan over Provincial Road 13-B to the Red River, and thence via Provincial Road 41 to Dien Bien Phu. The total length of that trek from the border, with all its detours, deep fords, substitutions for blown bridges, and alternate bypasses, was over 500 miles. It is difficult for the Western observer to imagine what it means to keep open 500 miles of jungle road in the face of the constant threat of aerial bombardment and strafing. It would have been extremely difficult had there been available modern road-building machinery and adequate protection against air attacks, as had been the case when American engineers built the Burma Road during World War II. The road to Dien Bien Phu required nearly 20,000 coolies and tribesmen impressed from the nearby villages, who slaved for three months to rebuild the shattered remains of Road 41 and to widen its turns to accommodate the artillery pieces and the 800 Russian-built Molotova 2½-ton trucks which were to become the backbone of the conventional supply system.

The greatest challenge was met in the last fifty miles of the road, from the main supply dumps at Tuan Giao to the valley. On this stretch, the road had simply ceased to exist and had to be rebuilt from scratch. There, also, it was closest to the French airfields and, for obvious reasons, most subject to French aerial surveillance. Yet, by what a French observer was to call the "veritable mysticism of the Road,"[2] everything was subordinated to the one gigantic, single-minded effort of feeding the front. It was co-ordinated by a top-level Government Front Supply Commission, which had full powers to requisition all men, machines, and draft animals available. The slogan "Everything for the Front, Everything for Victory" could be heard hundreds of times a day over the Viet-Minh radio network and could be seen on posters and inscriptions throughout the Viet-Minh zone. In a new edition of his small work on Dien Bien Phu, Gen. Giap himself describes that effort:

> Our troops opened the road and hauled the artillery pieces into our lines . . . during seven days and seven nights . . . our troops razed hills, cut roads into the mountainsides and opened the

road to the artillery in the prescribed time. The secret was well
kept thanks to excellent camouflage, and the roads were kept open
until the end of the battle. . . .

Night and day, the enemy bombed those very difficult roads
and nonetheless our transports got through on the whole. Hundreds
of thousands of *dan cong* [civilian coolies], women as well as
men, surmounted perils and difficulties and spent more than three
million work days in the service of the front, in an indescribable
enthusiasm.[3]

In actual fact, popular enthusiasm was backed by several solid regiments of combat engineers. The 151st Engineer Regiment of the 351st
Division worked on Road 41 since early December, 1953. It was reinforced in January, 1954, by Regiment 88 of the 308th Division, which
concentrated on the road stretch between Tuan-Giao and Dien Bien Phu.
Furthermore 10,000 coolies were sent to work on the same stretch in February, reinforced by 5,000 raw recruits of Regiment 77. As the monsoon
rains and intensified French bombardment began to have some effect on
the Communist supply system, another regiment of engineers, the 154th,
was sent from the north-central Vietnamese province of Nghé-An.

Contrary to later allegations,[4] the French High Command was fully
aware of the fact that *all* depended on whether the Communist supply
system could be effectively disrupted. Unfortunately, on the basis of the
devastating effect of aerial bombardment on conventional supply lines in
Europe (and a myth sedulously fostered in the early 1950's by the American proponents of heavy-bomber warfare and used against the Ho Chi
Minh Trail in 1965-66), the French Air Force shared the belief of its
American colleagues that round-the-clock bombardment of the one Communist communication axis with Dien Bien Phu would actually succeed.
Apparently, the United States Air Force had failed (at least by late
1953) to inform its French colleagues in the Far East of the highly ineffective American aerial interdiction operations in North Korea in
1951-52, known under the code name of Operation "Strangle."

"Strangle," as its name suggests, consisted of round-the-clock aerial
bombardment of every road and rail line, of every tunnel and culvert,
likely to be able to support the North Korean and Chinese supply system
leading to the Korean front line. When faced with that challenge, the
Communist in Korea simply switched, as would their Vietnamese comrades, to hundreds of thousands of human carriers who did not depend
upon bridges and tunnels and other obligatory passage points. To the
best of anyone's knowledge, the Communist supply system in Korea never

failed its front-line soldiers, whereas the road-bound and mechanized American supply system on the other side was often affected by poor roads and bad weather. To this day, French Air Force sources agree that they had not been informed of the severe limitations of U. S. Air Force interdiction in Korea. Thus, they looked forward with confidence to a mission in which, for the first time, they would find the enemy in a clearly identified target area from which, to all appearances, he could hardly deviate.

There were, then, in other words, *three* battles of Dien Bien Phu: the first, fought by Col. Langlais' GAP 2 and the T'ai light companies around the edges of the highland valley; the second, fought by the French Air Force against the Viet-Minh combat engineers and coolies along Road 41; and the third, fought by the siege force around Dien Bien Phu against the garrison in the valley. The first battle, as we have seen, was lost probably by late December, 1953, and, in any case, by February, 1954. Now it was the turn of Air Force General Jean Dechaux and the Northern Tactical Air Group (GATAC Nord) to try their luck. For that mission, Dechaux provided, until the beginning of April, 1954, a theoretical maximum of 107 aircraft (32 fighters, 45 fighter-bombers, and 30 bombers). This meant the French had an effective maximum, considering combat losses, repair and maintenance, of about seventy-five aircraft. This is a pitifully small force when one considers that the United States, in its air operations against North Viet-Nam in 1966, easily fielded 200 combat aircraft in a *single* raid. Yet the French force represented seventy-five per cent of all the combat aircraft then available in all of Indochina.[5]

In addition to that pure interdiction force, some of the heavy "Flying Boxcar" C-119's of Transport Group 2/63 were used to deliver deadly cargoes of six tons of napalm on targets around Dien Bien Phu and along the communication lines. The total effort, under the command of Lt. Col. Dussol's Bombardment Sub-Group, was shared by both the French Air Force and the French Navy. On the Air Force side, Bomber Group 1/25 "Tunisia" used B-26's while the two fighter groups (1/22 "Saintonge" and 2/22 "Languedoc") used *Bearcat* F8F's. The French Navy was at first represented by the aircraft carrier *Arromanches* (Capt. Patou), followed in April, 1954, by the American-built aircraft carrier *Belleau Wood* loaned to the French Navy and manned by French personnel (Capt. Mornu). Until the arrival of the *Belleau Wood,* the *Arromanches* carried the 3rd Carrier Assault Squadron equipped with SB2C *Helldivers,* and the 11th Carrier Fighter Squadron equipped with F6F *Hellcats.* In addition, the French Navy also possessed the only aircraft in Indochina approaching long-range bombardment capability: six heavy *Privateer* bombers of Squadron 28F.[6] Designed for long-range antisubmarine patrols, the *Privateers* were the ideal aircraft for deep penetration along the Communist supply lines to Dien Bien Phu and were capable of delivering about four tons of bombs on their target. During the battle of Dien Bien Phu, they also had been equipped with new American "Lazy Dog" antipersonnel bombs, whose thousands of razor-sharp splinters have a deadly effect on unprotected humans caught in the open by them. The LD's, as they were called, were also to be used later by the United States in its air operations in Viet-Nam.

Two alternative techniques existed for the interdiction of the Communist supply routes: the creation of one single major cut and its repeated bombing by daily waves of aircraft, or the creation of multiple cuts all along the Communist routes of march. Both methods were tried by GATAC Nord on Roads 13 and 41—and both failed. To assume that one could permanently interdict Communist supply lines to Dien Bien Phu by one single large cut would have implied that the Viet-Minh was incapable of hacking alternate routes through the jungle. As the French had found out during previous experience with road interdiction, the Communists had been capable of quickly rebuilding roads that had been hacked into sheer cliffs by extremely perilous skip bombing. Also, the single-cut method would have permitted the Viet-Minh to concentrate all its coolies in a single bypass area and to protect that point with the antiaircraft artillery which had become available in increasing numbers. Hence, the decision was made to concentrate on the aerial interdiction on a few major points: the Red and Black river crossings, the junction at Co-Noi between Roads 13 and 41, and the depot zone at Tuan Giao. Also, it was planned to maintain smaller cuts all along the length of the road so as to compel the enemy to maintain numerous repair crews and bypass systems.

As for the effectiveness of the enemy's antiaircraft artillery, it had long gone beyond that of the isolated enemy machine-gunner taking aim at a low-flying aircraft. As early as December, 1952, French air reconnaissance had spotted 170 different flak positions in North Viet-Nam and had reported fifty-five aircraft hit. In 1953, the number of such positions found was 714, and the French reported 244 aircraft hit and then shot down. As Gen. Giap built up his supply system for Dien Bien Phu, the whole length of the road became a veritable "flak corridor" along which the French aircraft had to run the gauntlet. The effectiveness of the Communist fire at the beginning of the battle for Dien Bien Phu is illustrated

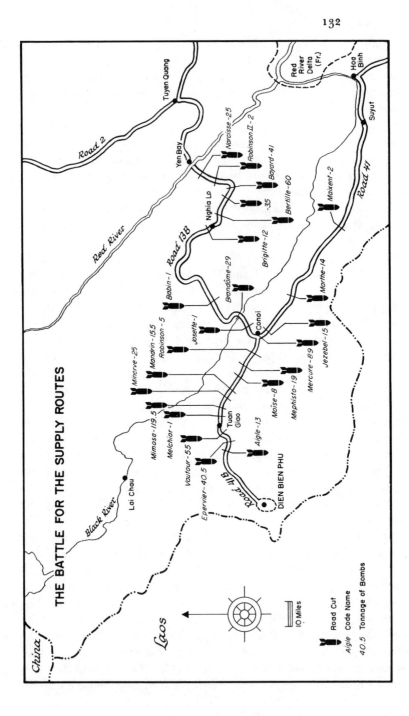

THE BATTLE FOR THE SUPPLY ROUTES

by the fact that during the two weeks beginning with November 24, 1953, forty-five French fighter-bombers out of fifty-one that had been bombing and machine-gunning the Viet-Minh engineering regiments along Roads 13 and 41 had been hit by Communist antiaircraft fire. One fighter-bomber and two reconnaissance Crickets had been shot down.

The situation worsened during the months of December, as French aircraft began to attempt the interdiction of Communist supplies closer to the Chinese border and farther away from their own bases. A total of 367 combat sorties were flown[7] and forty-nine aircraft were hit. On December 26, the decision was made to divert increasing amounts of fighter-bombers and bombers to flak-suppressing missions in order to be able to interdict at least some of the flow of Communist supplies without suffering unacceptable losses.

Day after day, until the last day of the battle for Dien Bien Phu, the exhausted Navy and Air Force pilots dived into the flak corridor of Roads 13 and 41, spraying coolie columns and the rare trucks that could be spotted through the camouflage. At certain points the Viet-Minh had actually tied the tall treetops together until they formed a tunnel of vegetation. We shall never know how many thousands of coolies and mountain tribesmen impressed into the *dan cong* died under the strafing, the napalm, the delayed-fuse bombs and the hail of "Lazy Dogs," but Giap's siege force never ran out of ammunition. As Giap was to say later to a French visitor: "We did construct our supply roads; our soldiers knew well the art of camouflage, and we succeeded in getting our supplies through."

Inexorably, like hundreds of little streams joining together to form a major river, the flow of Viet-Minh coolies, trucks, thousands of hand-pushed bicycles, and pack animals converged on the valley. By December 27, 1953, the ultimate enemy build-up at Dien Bien Phu was estimated at 49,000 men, including 33,000 combatants. This estimate was revised upwards after the enemy feint of January 25 and the return to Dien Bien Phu of the 308th Division from its stab into Laos.

When the battle finally began on March 13 enemy *combatant* strength in the Dien Bien Phu area was estimated at 49,500 men, with 31,500 logistical support personnel. Another 23,000 Communist support troops and personnel were strung out along the communication lines. On the French side, there was a total of 13,200 men in the valley, of whom about 6,600 to 7,000 could be counted on as front-line combatants, and of very unequal quality, at that. Thus, in addition to enjoying firepower superiority, Gen. Giap's forces also enjoyed a superiority in manpower of five-to-one. And since it is accepted that three-to-one superiority will generally achieve victory in an infantry breakthrough, Giap's forces had met the conditions prescribed by the Viet-Minh slogan, "Certain attack, certain progress."[8]

"A" Day—March 13, 1954

March 13 had begun in a routine manner in the fortress. Yet two major problems had arisen. First, strongpoint Beatrice now was so tightly surrounded that on March 11 and 12 it had required a battalion reinforced by two tank platoons for the Legionnaires to get drinking water from the nearby Nam Yum. On the morning of March 13, Major Jean Chenel's 2nd BT had reopened the road to Beatrice in fierce hand-to-hand combat, but only after the roadsides had been liberally napalmed by French fighter bombers. As they went along the road, the T'ai tribesmen finished off the burned enemy soldiers with their bayonets.

Second, Dien Bien Phu's airfield was now constantly under Communist fire. In fact, a single enemy 75-mm. mountain howitzer had been zeroed in on the airfield since February 1. It had damaged and destroyed almost a dozen aircraft without being located by the French. Now the situation was far more serious, since there were perhaps a dozen enemy pieces firing at the airfield from several directions, and with telling effect. On March 11, one of the large American "Flying Boxcars" (which had had to remain at Dien Bien Phu overnight for engine repairs) was shot to pieces. It burned late into the night like a warning torch. On the following day Communist 105-mm. pieces opened up on the airstrip. The second round destroyed one of the *Cricket* reconnaissance aircraft. The fourth round destroyed another reconnaissance aircraft. At the same time, enemy artillery began to search for the other combat and reconnaissance aircraft parked in dugouts south of the field.

The aviators were now clearly worried, as it became increasingly obvious that it would be impossible to maintain the fighter-bombers and reconnaissance aircraft on which the French had counted so heavily to counteract the enemy's fire superiority. Since February, Dien Bien Phu's tiny control tower and air traffic control center, commanded by Captain Jean Charnot and known officially as "Air Base 195," had been hit eight times by Communist shells. Each time a hit tore a hole in the pierced-steel plates of the field, the combat engineers had to weld the break in full view of the enemy.

What made the situation particularly awkward was that on March 12, eleven *Bearcat* fighter-bombers at Dien Bien Phu were immobilized prevailing winds combined with the high humidity at Dien Bien Phu could have caused the trouble that day. Throughout the night of the 12th the mechanics worked frantically to make the aircraft operational for the following day. But the enemy was aware of the prize within his grasp, and all night long Communist shells fell in the aircraft pit area. One *Bearcat* was destroyed by a direct hit from a white phosphorus shell while others sustained lighter damage which had to be repaired. Two of them, piloted by Sgts. de Somow and Barteau, were operational in the morning, and flew ten support sorties during the day. In the evening they escaped to the French airfield at Vientiane, Laos.

Other troubles were in store for Air Base 195 that day. A large C-46 Curtiss *Commando* aircraft which the French had used a year earlier to deport the nationalist Sultan of Morocco, was shot to pieces by Viet-Minh artillery at 0830 as it prepared to depart. Until it was completely destroyed late in April, the Curtiss became a landmark for units fighting in the airfield area and distances were often measured in meters beyond the Curtiss or south of the Curtiss. Shortly thereafter, a C-47 landing with supplies was shot to pieces while rolling on the ground and early in the afternoon another C-47 was hit, a fighter destroyed, and another damaged, until at about 1600, air-base control broadcast a "QGO" message. In the international communications code, the letters "QGO" stand for "Interdiction to Land at Airport." Dien Bien Phu was sealed off from the outside world for the first time. The last French premise upon which a victorious defense of Dien Bien Phu was based—continued availability of uninterrupted air support— had proved false.

At 1510, two reporters landed in the last *Dakota* that landed safely. Both André Lebon and Jean Martinoff were old Indochina hands and even Dien Bien Phu hands, since Lebon had jumped into the valley with the first wave on November 20 and Martinoff had participated in the GAP 2's march to Sop Nao. Lebon already had been wounded twice in earlier operations and looked forward to the big battle, which obviously was only hours away. He was an old acquaintance of the 1st Battalion, 2nd Foreign Legion Regiment, on Huguette, and took a ride down to the strongpoint to get a general view of the situation "at ground level." At the little officers' mess, there was talk only of the attack expected for that night.

"What do you think, fellows?" said Lebon. "It's going to be the great show this time."

"You can say that again," said one of the lean Foreign Legion officers. "The curtain-raiser already has begun. Giap's boys are already giving us their best cards: 81-mm. mortars, 120-mm. mortars, 105-mm. howitzers—the whole works."

"It's going to be like Na-San, only ten times bigger."

"Or almost Verdun! This time they'll put all their big artillery here and will show us what they have learned about big-war fighting."[9]

The friendly din of the mess was suddenly overshadowed by the heavy explosions of the 105's on the airfield. Lebon decided that this was as good a time as ever to take a close look at what the enemy's firepower looked like. Both he and Martinoff raced back to the airstrip, now barren of any human activity, with the enemy's shells methodically proceeding with the destruction of a *Cricket* reconnaissance plane and a damaged *Dakota.*

"Get down into the ditch," said Lebon to Martinoff. "I'll shoot a sequence on the destruction of the *Dakota.*"

Then three shells fell almost simultaneously. Martinoff died on the spot. Lebon lost his right foot and was evacuated the same evening aboard one of the ambulance aircraft which had braved the enemy fire. His stay at Dien Bien Phu had been somewhat less than six hours.

At headquarters, impending attack had not changed routine. The daily intelligence report received from Beatrice by radio on the morning of March 13 simply confirmed what already had been known; to wit, that Beatrice was now completely encircled by enemy approach works, some of which were within fifty meters of the first French positions. After the road had been reopened during the day by the BT 2 and the tanks, Lt. Col. Gaucher, the commander of both the central sector of Dien Bien Phu and of the 13th Legion Half-Brigade, drove to Beatrice in his open jeep for a last talk with Maj. Pégot. Pégot told Gaucher that his men were tired; in fact, not only tired, but nervous.

Gaucher once more looked over the position and at the enemy, who now could be clearly seen on the facing slopes in spite of the intermittent French artillery fire, and, in his deep voice grunted: "This is no time for nerves, because it's for tonight for sure."

This was known to every Legionnaire on Beatrice. In fact, to judge from the account of a survivor, Sgt. Kubiak, the men were less nervous than their officers:

> The day seemed to start like all the other days. We were busy with the eternal reinforcement of our positions. Orders rained down from every side and to judge from the nervousness of our

officers it seems that something is in the air . . . as we comment upon this state of affairs, a Legionnaire comes over and asks me that Lt. D. wants to see me. Received the order to verify my machine guns, to be sure that they would fire the evening without jamming. In a few words Lt. D. informs me about the situation.

I am flabbergasted, but nonetheless it seems that the nerves of the lieutenant hold up less well than mine. He simply announces to me that the Viets will attack tonight at 1700!

I salute, go away thinking: "There must be quite a few nervous people in this world and even a few nuts."

Indeed we would have to consider as crazy the Viets who would have the idea to try and dislodge us from our Hill Beatrice, well fortified and defended by a whole Foreign Legion battalion. Believe me, it would be no simple walk in the sun for them!

Well, I am a model sergeant—at least I try to be under such special occasions—and I went to verify my machine guns.

That did not stop me from feeling pangs of hunger and with the afternoon going by without bringing any change in the situation, I decided to visit with my friend M/Sgt. N. at 1600. Since, as you imagine, he is the mess sergeant, his was about the only place where I could hope to find something to drink before the battle—that is if the battle was to take place. . . .

At 1655, still occupying that excellent position which is N's trench, I have a last drink with my buddy. Then I walked back toward my bunker to recuperate in peace. . . .

We are all surprised and ask ourselves how the Viets have been able to find so many guns capable of producing an artillery fire of such power. Shells rained down on us without stopping like a hailstorm on a fall evening. Bunker after bunker, trench after trench, collapsed, burying under them men and weapons.[10]

And that was how it began. Within a few minutes the battle would also begin for the rest of the valley of Dien Bien Phu. To the west of Beatrice, on Gabrielle, intermittent shelling by mortars and 75-mm. howitzers had been taking place for over a week. As in the case of Beatrice, communications with the rear at Dien Bien Phu had become increasingly difficult. On March 12, the strong reconnaissance force under Lt. Botella had lost ten men at the small river crossing of Ban Khé Phai, which was the obligatory passage point from Dien Bien Phu for any potential rescue force. At the same time, Lt. Moreau proceeded with a company-sized force northward to clear out the nearest Communist trenches. On the basis of documents found by the combat patrol and by their visual observations, de Mecquenem was able to establish a fairly accurate map of the trench system around Gabrielle. He sent that map, which showed Communist approach trenches to the north and northwest within less than 200 meters of his position, to de Castries' headquarters on March 13 in the morning. In the same report, de Mecquenem also mentioned that his patrols had seen on March 11 Communist mortars being installed on Hill 701, overshadowing his own position, and he estimated enemy strength immediately available around Gabrielle at a full three infantry battalions. In the meantime, both Botella's and Moreau's outfits had returned to Gabrielle in good order, but not without taking further losses from Communist mortar fire. At 1600 the battalion doctor, Lt. Chauveau, had been wounded and was replaced within the hour by Dr. Dechelotte, who braved the ever-increasing shelling in an open jeep and reached Gabrielle without incident.

At 1700, as the bombardment began on Beatrice, the men on Gabrielle were treated to yet another ominous spectacle: on Hills 633, 674, and 701, a few hundred meters to the north and west of them, hitherto unrevealed and undetected enemy antiaircraft batteries began to attack the remaining planes frantically trying to take off from the airfield. Placed perfectly in the take-off axis of the airstrip, they would be capable of executing a veritable turkey shoot on any aircraft foolhardy enough to brave them.

At this point, Majs. Kah and de Mecquenem (who, it will be remembered, was to have handed over command to his replacement that week) had other problems. Their heavy mortar battery, which in part was assigned to give supporting fire to Beatrice, was being smothered, along with the rest of the position, by extremely dense and accurate Communist artillery fire, followed at 1900 by some enemy infiltrations of the first line. These cost the 5/7 RTA a few destroyed bunkers and twenty casualties, including the newly arrived Dr. Dechelotte. The latter was replaced late on the following day by Sgt. Soldati, a Foreign Legionnaire who turned out to be a full-fledged Czechoslovak M.D. A few minutes past midnight of March 13, the first attack on Gabrielle had been beaten off and its garrison of Algerians and Frenchmen grimly settled down to watching the agony on nearby Beatrice.

At the headquarters of GAP 2, March 13 had been a routine day. Colonel Langlais had returned from a late afternoon briefing at de Castries' command post. At 1700 he was in the process of taking a shower under an old gasoline barrel which his men had rigged up on top of four poles, when suddenly he heard the opening blasts of the enemy artillery in the hills, followed by the ear-rending crash of the shells nearby. Dripping wet, Langlais grabbed his uniform in one hand and ran stark naked toward his command post. As he dressed, earth and dust kept falling from overhead as the enemy shells fell increasingly closer.

Langlais immediately attempted to contact Guiraud and Tourret, the commanders of the 1st BEP and the 8th BPC, but the two telephone lines had already been hacked to pieces by artillery shells. His line to head-quarters still worked and a staff officer there told him breathlessly that strongpoint Beatrice already was under heavy attack. A few minutes later, Langlais established radio contact with his two paratroop battalions. Everything was under control there; although theoretically in reserve for a counterattack, both battalions also held a sector of front because of the shortage of personnel. Thus far, they had been spared by the enemy's shells. At 1730 the roof of Langlais' dugout sustained a direct hit. The eight men in the dugout were buried under the sand and the fallen timber but escaped unharmed. They had barely risen to their feet when they heard the screeching of a second shell, followed by a sudden silence broken by the voice of someone saying: "Look, Colonel, we're in luck." The second shell had followed the path of the first shell through the roof, missed the shoulder of one of Langlais' staff officers by a few inches and penetrated in the rear wall of the dugout where it could be plainly seen—unexploded.[11] At 1950, the telephone rang. Colonel de Castries himself was on the line:

"Is that you, Langlais? Gaucher has just been killed with his whole staff. You are taking over as commander of the central subsector . . ."

At Gaucher's command post, the battle had begun without undue excitement. Everybody was at his post, the colonel and his aide in one underground dugout while his chief of staff, Major Michel Vadot, and his aides worked in an adjoining dugout. They had agreed that they would not stay together so that they would not become simultaneous casualties in case of a direct hit. Under the swinging light of the bare electric bulbs hanging from the low ceilings, the radio operators kept up their quiet chatter with Beatrice, the artillery positions, and head-quarters. Here and there one could hear the crackling voice of the radio operator on Beatrice calling *"Soleil à Soleil autorité"* (Sun to Sun Command) as he called Gaucher's command post by its code name.

By 1815, the assault units of People's Army Regiments 141 and 219 of the 312th Division were pressing hard against the outer perimeter of Beatrice and Maj. Pégot requested final protective fires; *i.e.,* artillery as close as possible to his own lines. In the open gun pits outside, the French and African gun crews raced to their pieces under the heavy bombardment while the fire-direction officers called out new fire orders. However, the enemy counterbattery took a heavy toll: within a few minutes, two 105 howitzers were knocked out and most of the gun crews suffered severe casualties. But the fire was kept up.

At 1830, the command bunker on Beatrice took a series of direct hits, killing Pégot and his whole staff, an occurrence that was going to become familiar during the next few days. Gaucher, however, succeeded in re-establishing contact with the individual companies of strongpoint Beatrice which were now fighting by themselves but still taking a heavy toll of the enemy's assault forces. In fact, a Communist source shows the last French barbed-wire entanglements around the strongpoint were breached by explosive charges only sometime after 2030, and only at the price of very heavy losses. One of the Viet-Minh soldiers who led the assault on the northeast bunker of Beatrice, squad leader Phan Dinh Giot, was to become the first hero of the Communist siege force. When a French machine gun firing from the bunker endangered the assault wave through its enfilading fire, Phan Dinh Giot threw his body against the bunker's firing slit. He was torn to shreds by a machine-gun burst but blocked the gun long enough for the assault wave to pass.[12]

In Col. Gaucher's command-post bunker, the problem of appointing an acting commander for Beatrice had to be solved immediately, for it was impossible to continue to direct the battle by radio. The telephone rang in Maj. Vadot's dugout across a small corridor from Gaucher's own and Gaucher himself asked Vadot to come over to his office to decide, with Maj. Martinelli (Gaucher's deputy), which of the company commanders on Beatrice would make a suitable temporary battalion commander. Vadot walked into the small office of his superior, already crowded by the presence of Gaucher, Martinelli, their aides, and a radio operator. Looking for a place to sit down, Vadot finally decided to fold his tall frame onto Gaucher's bunk in the corner of the office. This probably saved his life. At the very moment when Gaucher was to open the conversation, an enemy artillery shell hit the dugout's air-shaft, penetrated Gaucher's room and exploded literally in front of the colonel. When the smoke cleared the two aides lay dying, Martinelli was wounded and Vadot, aside from a few scratches and the stunning blow of the explosion, was unscathed. But Col. Gaucher was lying on the floor under the debris of his desk, with both his arms torn off, his legs mashed, and his chest torn open. Yet he was conscious when the brigade chaplain, Father Trinquand, entered the dugout, and he asked the chaplain to wipe his face and give him something to drink. An ambulance jeep from the hospital braved the artillery fire to bring Gaucher to the surgery room, but in vain. He died in the arms of Father Heinrich, Dien Bien Phu's chief chaplain, after two Foreign Legionnaires carried him in. Now the key central subsector was leaderless.

From Beatrice, the bad news continued to trickle in via the radio waves. By 2030, 10th Company holding the northeast of Beatrice ceased responding to the radio calls. A few minutes before 2100, 11th Company said tersely that the "Viets were all over the place" and that it was fighting around the CP bunker. It was its last message.

By now, not a single able-bodied officer was left on Beatrice. It was commanded by master sergeants and squad leaders. The 9th Company was still holding out around the blasted remains of the CP with Sgt. Kubiak. Incredibly, it stopped the enemy for another two hours, thanks in large part to the heavy artillery fire of Col. Piroth's howitzers. But at eleven o'clock, the Vie-Minh assault units had regrouped for the final attack. Their artillery was now falling heavily on the remaining strongpoint, where defenders were running out of ammunition. It also had become obvious that, contrary to what they had been led to expect, there would be no immediate counterattack from Dien Bien Phu. At 0015 of March 14, 9th Company's radio went off the air. As Sgt. Kubiak told it, the last message of the radio operator had been a request for artillery fire directly on the remaining bunker. The radio operator was cut in two by one of the French shells. At 0200, Kubiak and the remnants of the 3rd Battalion, 13th Foreign Legion Half-Brigade, abandoned Beatrice and hid in the nearby jungle until daybreak. They knew very well that, should they attempt to approach the French main lines at night, they would be taken for enemy soldiers using a ruse and would probably be killed before they could identify themselves.

At 0225 of March 14, the radio teletype at Gen. Cogny's headquarters in Hanoi began to tap out a brief message from Dien Bien Phu: "Without liaison with Beatrice since 0015. By listening in on internal radio net assume all of strongpoint in Communist hands. Colonel Gaucher dead." Thus ended the first day of the battle of Dien Bien Phu.

Sunday, March 14, 1954

Rain clouds hung heavily over the valley the next morning, completely preventing the arrival of supply aircraft and aerial reconnaissance in the immediate surroundings of the fortress as well. The combat commanders prepared to counterattack and retake Beatrice. When Sgt. Kubiak and the 100-odd survivors of the 3/13th staggered into the valley, they already found the paratroopers of the GAP ready to move out. Without much ceremony, the survivors were handed carbines, bandoliers of ammunition, and pouches of hand grenades and were immediately reassigned to the assault companies heading for Beatrice. Supported by tanks, they began to move out at 0730 along Road 41 and almost immediately came under heavy enemy fire. Obviously, the Viet-Minh expected a counterattack and were ready and waiting. While the French were regrouping for a second attack, a wounded Legionnaire officer suddenly staggered toward them from the other side. It was Lt. Turpin of 11th Company. He was seriously wounded and heavily bandaged and carried a message from the commander of the Viet-Minh 312th Division, offering the French a truce from 0800 to 1200 to pick up their wounded from Beatrice.

De Castries called Gen. Cogny on the radiotelephone in Hanoi and asked whether the truce could be accepted; and Cogny, after referring the matter to GHQ in Saigon, authorized de Castries to accept. In the world press, the French represented this generous gesture as a sign of weakness of the enemy by intimating that it was the Communists who had asked for a truce to pick up *their* dead and wounded. The result was that further humane gestures were not repeated on a large scale by the Viet-Minh until after the battle. A few minutes before nine o'clock a small convoy, composed of a jeep flying a large Red Cross flag, a 2½-ton truck, and an ambulance, bypassed the waiting paratroopers and took the road to Beatrice. In the lead jeep were the 3/13th's own doctor, Capt. Le Damany, and the brigade's chaplain, Father Trinquand. Sergeant Kubiak asked to be among the dozen or so unarmed soldiers who had volunteered to go and pick up the casualties. The road was seemingly deserted until they reached the foot of Gabrielle itself where a small group of Viet-Minh soldiers and officers was waiting for them. After an exchange of impeccable salutes, the grim search began. For all practical purposes, the whole defense system of Beatrice, so laboriously built over the past three months, was completely plowed under by enemy shells and explosive charges. The Communist casualties already had been removed, along with all equipment that was in working order. The stench of the close to 300 dead Legionnaires lying in the broiling sun, was overpowering. Finally, eight wounded survivors were found, one of whom died on the spot after Father Tringuand had administered the last rites. By 1000, the small convoy had returned to camp. When the final count was in, it turned out that two lieutenants and 192 men out of a garrison of 750 had survived the eight-hour battle. The remnants of 9th and 10th Companies went to strongpoint Huguette with the 1/2 REI, while the remnants of 11th, 12th, and Headquarters Companies were assigned to Half-Brigade Headquarters. Their morale was badly shaken. On March 17 two Legionnaires of the 10th Company deserted from Huguette without their weapons. During the first days of April ten more Legionnaires of the 3/13th went over to the enemy.

There still remained the question of the counterattack on Beatrice. Was it really worth it? In view of what had happened the night before, and in view of the shattered condition of the hill's defenses, it would be almost impossible to hold the strongpoint unless it were permanently connected with the rest of the main center of resistance. That would mean, as far as de Castries was concerned, the commitment of his reserves of airborne battalions, tanks, and artillery to the defense of a position whose usefulness was highly doubtful. There were other factors involved. Most important was the fact that the first night of artillery dueling had cost the French 6,000 rounds of 105-mm. howitzer shells, or about one fourth of their stock. Since the airfield was under fire and the monsoon-laden clouds lay heavily over the whole valley, air traffic was nearly at a standstill and quick resupply of the stocks was unlikely. De Castries also urgently needed an airborne battalion to replace the destroyed 3/13th in order to have enough troops available for an immediate counterattack on Hill Gabrielle. There was no doubt in anyone's mind that Gabrielle would now be the enemy's next objective. Hence, de Castries decided, in accord with Cogny, to postpone the counterattack on Beatrice until a later date. In fact, it was never attempted.

Meanwhile, the whole camp was making feverish preparations for the next round. At the hospital, Maj. Grauwin had requested an emergency shipment of six liters of fresh blood from Hanoi and the parachuting of an Airborne Surgical Team on the auxiliary airstrip near Isabelle. At 0800, Major Claude Devoucoux, commander of Air Liaison Squadron (ELA) No. 53 at Hanoi, dropped his little single-engine De Havilland *Beaver* through the clouds to a short roll on the airstrip. He left the precious containers of blood and picked up four seriously wounded and Paule Bourgeade, Col. de Castries' secretary. She had been the only European woman permanently assigned to Dien Bien Phu and departed after protesting the direct order of her chief. At 1500, the Airborne Surgical Team under Lt. Rézillot, M.D., was misdropped into the barbed-wire entanglements of the main position of Dien Bien Phu. Under intermittent Communist artillery fire, the men slowly extricated themselves from the barbed wire and reported to Dien Bien Phu. Then they boarded a truck for the perilous five-mile ride to Isabelle.

In the meantime, the main airstrip at Dien Bien Phu had become untenable. Artillery fire had registered on it and on the airplane revetments where the maintenance crews were frantically working at getting their seven remaining *Bearcat* fighter-bombers airborne. At about 1400, three of the aircraft were, as far as could be judged, airworthy. The pilots, Lt. Parisot and Sgts. Fouché and Bruand, revved up their engines in the dugouts and came roaring out of them at maximum speed. They were airborne before the Communist artillerymen could recover from their surprise. They reached Cat-Bi Airport near Haiphong without further incident. Communist artillery now began to concentrate on the remaining aircraft and the airport installations. The last six *Bearcats* were riddled with shells and eventually destroyed, the control tower was partially destroyed, and the radio beacon essential to planes trying to find Dien Bien Phu at night or through the clouds was completely destroyed. One helicopter was seriously damaged at the airfield and another lightly damaged as it attempted to pick up wounded near the hospital. At 1930 the last *Cricket* reconnaissance aircraft was set afire. Thus, one day after the battle had begun, Dien Bien Phu had lost all its local air support.

Nevertheless, the garrison had a boost in morale when at 1445 wave after wave of transport aircraft dropped Major André Botella's 5th Vietnamese Parachute Battalion (BPVN) from a 600-foot altitude on the old familiar drop zones Natasha, Octavie, and Simone. While enemy flak was quite inaccurate (and the dispersion of the drop on three different drop zones helped to confuse it) the enemy's artillery proved effective in covering much of the landing areas with its fire. Some of the little Vietnamese paratroopers died before they reached the ground. The 1st Company and Headquarters Company, dropped on Natasha near the main airstrip, suffered particularly severe losses. By 1800, the battalion had regrouped on the other side of the Nam Yum on strongpoints Eliane 4, 1, and 2. Many of the men, who had marched ten miles under artillery fire since they had been parachuted, were exhausted when they reached their positions across the river on Eliane. Yet they immediately had to begin to dig a few rudimentary trenches to protect themselves from the intermittent enemy artillery fire. The rainstorms which had begun that afternoon further added to their discomfort. By 2000, with its mortar batteries dug in, the 5th BPVN began to participate in the developing battle for Hill Gabrielle, whose silhouette was clearly outlined against the night sky by the enemy artillery bursts on top of it. Within a few minutes, the Communist artillery had the range of the airborne mortars. At 2100, in brief succession, three of the mortar crews were destroyed by enemy direct hits.

In the meantime, Maj. de Mecquenem's 5th Battalion, 7th Algerian Rifles, got ready to meet the attack which was sure to come that night. Gabrielle was the best-built strongpoint of all, and the only one which had a second line of defense. In the previous weeks, some of its officers had dryly noted that its over-all dimensions of 500 meters by 200 meters corresponded exactly to the standard fire dispersion pattern of 105-mm. howitzers firing over medium distance; and that the position was so full of troops and mortars that any shell which fell upon it was bound to cause casualties. However, Col. Piroth, the one-armed artillery commander, had laughingly assured de Mecquenem that his position wouldn't even be "scratched" by enemy artillery.

Methodically, de Mecquenem and his replacement, Maj. Kah, verified the positions of their men. During the morning of the 14th, the ration and ammunition levels on Gabrielle had been increased to permit four days of continuous fighting. De Mecquenem asked his artillery liaison officer, Lt. Colin, to have the batteries of the II/4 RAC register on the narrow valley neck north of Gabrielle and on the deep new approach trenches dug by the Communists at the foot of Gabrielle. There was a feeling of utter confidence among the Algerians and French atop Gabrielle. After all, the Algerians were professionals, and prided themselves on being at least as good, if not better, than the Foreign Legionnaires. They knew that their strongpoint was better built than Beatrice and easier to get at from the rear. How high the *esprit-de-corps* was among the Algerians was perhaps best illustrated by Sergeant Major Abderrahman Ben Salem (whom I met nine years later as a major in the Algerian National People's Army), a platoon leader in Capt. Narbey's 1st Company on Gabrielle. Abderrahman had been wounded in January by grenade splinters in both thighs. He had been evacuated to Hanoi, but when he received letters from his friends telling him that an attack on Gabrielle was likely, he had defied his doctors and smuggled himself aboard an aircraft to return to Gabrielle on March 12.

At 1500, de Mecquenem ordered the evacuation of the Communist PW's—the PIM's—who had served as orderlies and laborers on the strongpoint. They reached their camp at Dien Bien Phu without incident. At 1700, Sgt. Soldati, the new Czech doctor and the third to serve on Gabrielle in as many days, arrived from Dien Bien Phu, the last man to do so before the battle began. The two majors now ordered a distribution of a full meal of warm food for everybody. The officers also settled down for a last meal together. De Mecquenem and Kah gave their orders. They had been assured by the French Air Force that a C-47 "flare ship" would be available to light up the battlefield during the night. Plenty of artillery support was assured them. In order to prevent the command echelon of the strongpoint from being destroyed by a single chance hit, a secondary command post with a radio set was installed in the officers' mess. De Mecquenem pointed smilingly toward several bottles of champagne nestling in a cooler in a corner of the mess: "We're going to drink them together after the battle is over and the Viets are clobbered," said he.

At 1800 promptly, the enemy bombardment began with a battalion of enemy 120-mm. heavy mortars opening up from Ban Na Ten, less than two kilometers away. This barrage was followed within the hour by the fire of a battery of 105-mm. howitzers situated three kilometers north of the strongpoint. Gabrielle's bunkers had been designed to withstand some artillery fire, but few field fortifications could have withstood continuous bombardment of the kind which now fell on the area. By 2000 the heavy-weapons bunkers in Lt. Moreau's 4th Company area had collapsed. By 2200, the CP of 4th Company was destroyed. Lieutenant Moreau (whose wife had arrived in Hanoi only a few days earlier as a member of the French Women's Army Corps) died in the debris of his dugout. Two of the battalion's 81-mm. mortars were also destroyed. The heavy 120-mm. mortars assigned by the 5th Foreign Legion Regiment to Gabrielle now were also under heavy fire. Within the first few salvos, their commander, Lt. Clergé, found his radio set damaged. He laid on all final protective fires and went to the officers' mess to use the radio set there to contact artillery headquarters.

The real danger lay with 4th Company. After the destruction of Moreau's CP, enemy infantry began slowly to infiltrate its position. This was no human-wave assault. The Viet-Minh were apparently unwilling to pay the heavy price they had paid the night before at Beatrice. As discovered later, all of Regiments 88 and 102 of the 308th People's Army Division participated in the attack, and were probably reinforced at dawn by elements from two more regiments. This insured superiority over the French defenders of at least eight to one. By midnight, de Mecquenem and Kah decided to commit their last reserves for a counterattack to rescue 4th Company. Sergeant Major Lobut and a T'ai mountaineer platoon of the 416th CSM, and Sgt. Rouzic with a platoon from 2nd Company led it. Rouzic, in civilian life, had been the driver of the getaway car of France's most famous postwar gangster, *Pierrot-le-Fou* (Pierre the Crazy One) and had decided to join the French Army in Indochina when the French police began to close in on his employer. That night, on Gabrielle, he stood up to his reputation. Slowly fighting their way forward, Rouzic, Lobut, and their men cleared the second line of 4th Company with tommy guns and hand grenades, closed the breach that had opened in the 3rd Platoon area of 4th Company, and, with the surviving Algerians, settled down grimly to a night of close-in fighting. When, totally outflanked, Rouzic pulled back at 0730 of March 15, he had exactly seven men left. Meanwhile, Piroth's artillery sent volley after volley of 105's and 155-mm. shells crashing into the Communist first line, apparently with devastating results. As suddenly as it had begun, the Communist artillery fire on Gabrielle ceased on March 15 at 0230. So did the attacks of the enemy infantry. The Algerians had already lasted longer than the elite troops of the Foreign Legion on Beatrice. De Mecquenem, after surveying his heavily battered but largely unbreached position, made a brief radio report to de Castries' headquarters and then crawled into his dugout for a brief rest after having passed command to Kah.

Monday, March 15, 1954

The respite granted the defenders of Gabrielle was to be of short duration. Precisely at 0330, the Communist artillery bombardment began again, with two more enemy batteries, firing from the northeast, revealing themselves. The enemy now renewed its attempts at infiltrating along the north-south ridge of Gabrielle separating the positions of 1st and 4th Companies (see map, p. 148), an attempt which was made relatively easy by the fact that the crest itself hid the penetration until the first-line trenches of 1st Company received flanking fire from the advancing Viet-Minh. What apparently stalled the Communist advance was the machine guns firing from 1st Company's northernmost bunker. But Viet-Minh gunner Pham Van Tuy, who had dragged a hand-built 75-mm. wheeled bazooka to within 150 yards of the bunker, scored three direct hits on it and silenced its guns. He later received a first-class and third-class combat star for his feat.[13]

It is not clear whether it was Pham Van Tuy's lucky shots or the renewal of the withering enemy artillery barrage which caused the death of

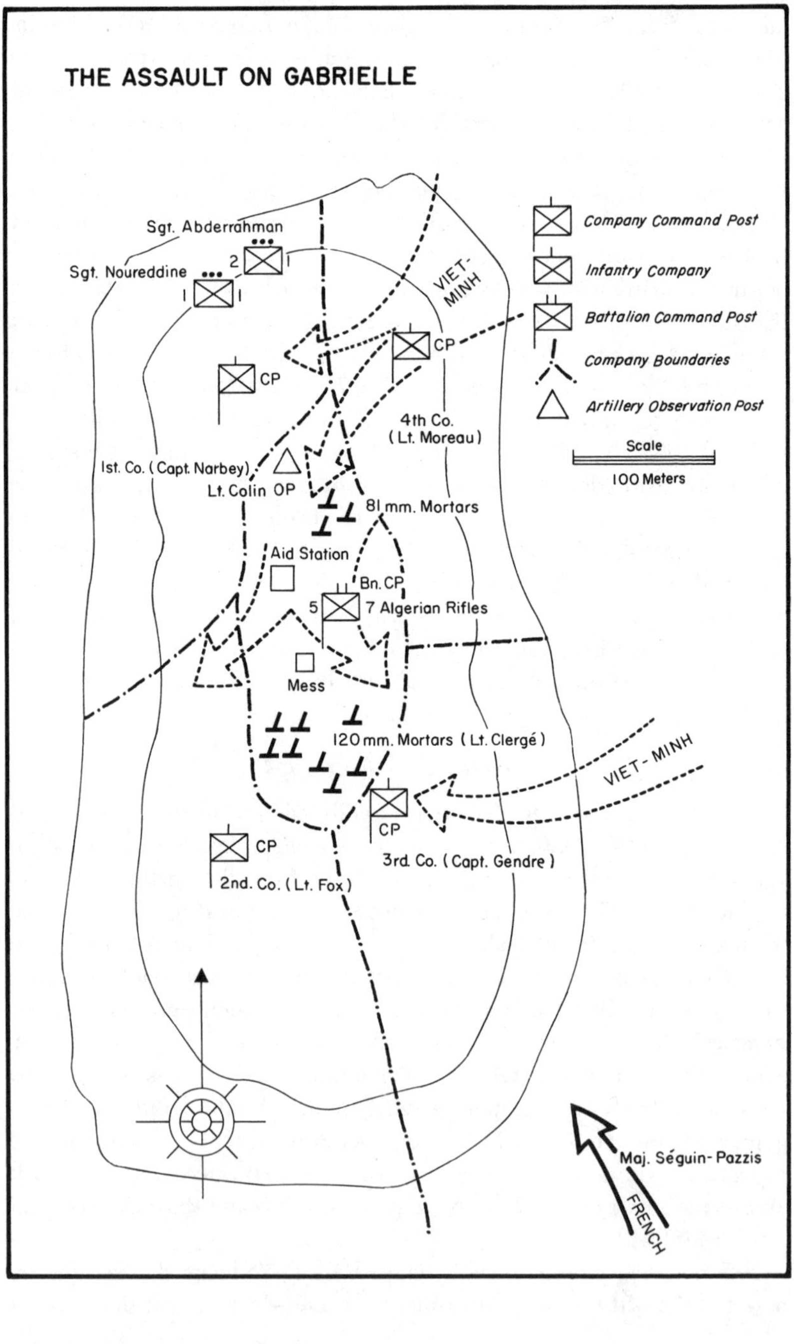
THE ASSAULT ON GABRIELLE
Company Command Post
Infantry Company
Battalion Command Post
Company Boundaries
Artillery Observation Post
Scale
100 Meters
Sgt. Abderrahman
Sgt. Noureddine
VIET-MINH
CP
CP
4th Co. (Lt. Moreau)
Ist. Co. (Capt. Narbey)
Lt. Colin OP
81 mm. Mortars
Aid Station
Bn. CP
5
7 Algerian Rifles
Mess
120 mm. Mortars (Lt. Clergé)
VIET-MINH
CP
CP
3rd. Co. (Capt. Gendre)
2nd. Co. (Lt. Fox)
Maj. Séguin-Pazzis
FRENCH

Capt. Narbey, 1st Company's commander and wounded the only other officer of the company, Lt. Roux. The fact remains that by four o'clock 1st Company was left in the hands of two Algerian platoon commanders, Noureddine and Abderrahman. In a few minutes the enemy had also knocked out the remaining 81- and 120-mm. mortars of Gabrielle, whereupon the artillery officer, Lt. Colin, requested final defensive fires all the way to the second line of defense. De Mecquenem, who was awakened by the sound of the artillery fire at about four o'clock, spoke with de Castries on the radio and was promised all available artillery fire, including the 155's. He was also assured that infantry and tanks would be made available for a prompt counterattack, should the need arise. With that news, de Mecquenem returned to the combat CP where Maj. Kah and the battalion staff were leading the fight.

As all the senior officers of the strongpoint were standing together with their radio personnel and staff, an enemy shell with a short-delay fuse hit the CP with devastating effect. One of Maj. Kah's legs was torn off (he was to die in Communist hands on March 27), de Mecquenem was riddled with splinters and knocked out by the blast, and both his aide and the artillery liaison officer were seriously wounded. At the same time all the radio sets connecting the CP with the infantry companies, and the strongpoint itself with Dien Bien Phu, were knocked out. Gabrielle had become leaderless. Why were the leading officers of the strongpoint in the command post at the same time? The answer was given to me personally by de Mecquenem (then a colonel) nine years later. He said that the meeting of all the senior officers was a matter of sheer chance and was to last only a few minutes. There is an Arabic term widely used in the French Army to designate wild luck: *barakka!* Colonel de Mecquenem was to say to me later: "I always believed in my *barakka*." It had apparently run out for strongpoint Gabrielle at 0430 on March 15, 1954.

With the two majors wounded, command on Gabrielle fell to the captain who was de Mecquenem's deputy, but that officer lost his nerve. But another officer, young Capt. Gendre, the commander of 3rd Company, assumed temporary command sometime before 0500. Lieutenant Clergé, the mortar battery commander who had survived the destruction of his pieces, took over as artillery liaison officer although he was already wounded. The defense of Gabrielle now was led from the command post of 3rd Company. Gendre immediately requested a powerful counterattack with infantry and tanks from the center of the fortress. That counterattack was promised him and he was told to hold out at all costs. In the meantime, the Algerians of 1st Company were bearing the brunt of the battle. The sergeants, seeing themselves outflanked, had withdrawn the company to the second line in fairly good order, but Noureddine's 1st Platoon had been in large part buried by enemy artillery shells which pulverized the whole trench system. Abderrahman, however, after discovering that he no longer had radio contact with his battalion headquarters, found himself, much to his surprise, in direct liaison with de Castries' command net, which had been listening in on the radio channels of the individual companies. He was told to hold on to his position as he would soon be reinforced by tanks and paratroopers.

The next phase of the battle for Gabrielle was lost at de Castries' headquarters in Dien Bien Phu. While the battle was raging over the hill position, the Viet-Minh had launched a diversionary infiltration between strongpoints Eliane and Dominique on the east flank of the fortress, while maintaining intermittent fire on Claudine, Dominique, and faraway Isabelle. It is not clear today whether, at about 0400, the infiltrations on the east flank were mistaken as the prelude to a second full-scale attack which would, in combination with the attack on Gabrielle already under way, take Dien Bien Phu into a huge pincer and perhaps cut it in two. Some of the French officers involved, whose arguments are obviously emotional, felt that the decision eventually made represented the "selfish" desire of the past commander of the airborne forces, Lt. Col. Langlais, to preserve most of his own men from an action he felt was sure to lead to heavy losses. It must be remembered that Langlais had only the previous day taken over the command of the whole central sector. His chief-of-staff, the tall and gentlemanly Major Hubert de Séguin-Pazzis, had simultaneously taken over as commander of the GAP. While Langlais was supposed to take an over-all view of the battle, he was in fact still deeply involved with the fate of his paratroopers. This is apparently what led him to choose the newly arrived and dead-tired 5th BPVN as the mainstay of the counterattack rather than the far more experienced 1st BEP and 8th BPC. At a hurried meeting in de Castries' bunker it was suggested that the Vietnamese of the 5th BPVN could hardly be expected to find their way through the maze of barbed wire and mine fields. Langlais accordingly accepted the addition of Captain "Lulu" Martin's company from the 1st BEP to the task force which Séguin-Pazzis was to command. The tank squadron of Capt. Hervouët was to lead the counterattack.

One can imagine the feelings of the Vietnamese paratroopers, sopping wet in their newly dug trenches and already under intermittent artillery fire, as they crossed almost the entire width of Dien Bien Phu and half its length at a quick pace toward the flaming hell which they had been able safely to observe earlier. The overconfidence of the whole Dien Bien Phu command now began to show undesirable dividends. While Capt. Hervouët had reconnoitered the road for his tanks by jeep in earlier days, the tank commanders and their cumbersome vehicles had never taken the path themselves, and certainly not at night under artillery fire. Neither had anyone paid much attention to the Communist road-block previously set up at the river ford near Ban Ké Phai. The counter-attack started at 0530 with Martin's reinforced Foreign Legion company in the lead behind the tanks, and the Vietnamese of Major Botella bringing up the rear. Séguin-Pazzis, who had been detained for last-minute orders at de Castries' headquarters, raced the length of the airfield in a jeep under heavy Communist fire and caught up with his troops as they were about to enter the critical passage. At 0700 the task force had reached the ford of Ban Ké Phai and the hard-pressed defenders on Gabrielle could hear the rumble of the tank engines through the din of the battle. But all of a sudden hell broke loose on the left flank of the paratroop column. What seemed to be at least a battalion of enemy troops and extremely well-registered artillery fire opened up on the area of the river ford. As seasoned troops familiar with the terrain, the Foreign Legion paratroopers quickened their pace, stuck closely to the tanks, and got through the ford without undue difficulty. They were followed by 3rd Company, Headquarters Company, and parts of 2nd Company of the 5th BPVN. But Lt. Ty of 2nd Company froze in his tracks and with him all of 1st and 4th Companies. From this moment, the counterattack of the Séguin-Pazzis force had become hope-less. It was 0730.

On top of Gabrielle, in the meantime, the situation had deteriorated further. At 0600, the enemy infiltration of the 4th Company area devel-oped into a breakthrough which affected 1st Company as well. There, Sgt. Abderrahman and one of the riflemen attempted to carry the wounded Lt. Roux to the infirmary on top of the central platform of Gabrielle. As they arrived in the early dawn they were confronted by Viet-Minh infantrymen progressing slowly toward the CP. The two Algerians dropped the stretcher, threw themselves on the ground and rolled down the hill to their own position. Lieutenant Roux himself rolled off the stretcher into a nearby trench. He played dead for a whole day and, dragging himself more than 400 meters through the brush, was picked up by the French on March 16 at 0400.

By now, 1st Company was at the end of its tether: not only was it short of ammunition but the French counterbattery fire, now directed, on Capt. Gendre's orders, on the first forward line, tended to fall short and began to cause casualties among the Algerians. Abderrahman radioed to de Castries' headquarters to lift the artillery fire but his set sustained a hit before the end of the message. By 0730, the helmets of the Viet-Minh regulars began to appear on all sides. Sergeant Noureddine and his platoon fell back on the last existing blockhouse, but the Viet-Minh began to throw grenades into the trench from the top of the hill which they already occupied. Slowly, the men began to stand up, leaving their weapons on the ground. Very rapidly, a Viet-Minh officer, recognizable only by his map case, ordered the dazed remnants of 1st Company to march down the hill northward toward the Viet-Minh lines. This meant crossing both the French barbed wire and the mine fields. When the Algerians hesitated, the Viet-Minh told them to step on the bodies of the Communist casualties, who at certain spots virtually carpeted the barbed-wire entanglements. Prodded in the ribs by the tommy guns of their guardians, Abderrahman and his men began to move. Suddenly, Abderrahman came to a dead stop. Ahead of him, sliced open from side to side and with his intestines hanging in the barbed wire in a bloody mass, was a Viet-Minh rifleman, still alive. In fact, as he saw the approaching column of prisoners his eyes widened and his lips moved as if to speak. The Viet-Minh officer rapidly picked his way forward to the head of the column to see what had stopped it. He then motioned Abderrahman forward and said: "You can step on him. He has done his duty for the People's Army."[14]

The hour had also come for 2nd and 3rd Companies. Capt. Gendre had been listening in on the progress of the Séguin-Pazzis force and had become a witness to the set of contradictory orders it received from headquarters during the progress of the operation. The first order had clearly been for the column to advance to Gabrielle, relieve the pressure on the garrison, and to pursue the enemy into his own lines. When the task force was intercepted at Ban Ké Phai, it received the order to push as far north as it could in the direction of Gabrielle in order to facilitate the withdrawal of the remnants of the garrison. Finally, at about 0700, Séguin-Pazzis received a third set of orders directing him to push to Gabrielle and there to decide whether to hold or to evacuate. As can now be imperfectly reconstructed (for he died of dysentery in a Communist prison camp), Gendre received only the second set of orders on his radio set and gave orders to 2nd and 3rd Companies to begin their withdrawal in the direction of the paratroopers at 0800.

Until then, the men had fought under the impression that the position would be held and reinforced. Now it was obvious that the position would be abandoned and that further losses for its defense would be meaningless. Parts of 3rd Company stampeded. Second Company, now under the orders of Capt. Carré, began to abandon its position between 0715 and 0730, without regard for the remnants of 1st and 4th Companies and of Battalion Headquarters, still holding some of the forward trenches. In fact, much of what happened in the forward area bordered on both the heroic and the incongruous. At 0730, the wounded de Mecquenem entered a bunker in the area where 1st Company was sorely pressed, only to find a French sergeant meticulously filling forms at his typewriter while the battle was raging all around him. In one furious gesture the major flung the typewriter on the ground and told the sergeant in no uncertain terms to get out and help the Algerians in the fire fight. The sergeant died later in a Communist prison camp. His major personally helped to dig his grave. De Mecquenem briefly re-entered the officers' mess where Maj. Kah was still lying on his stretcher with the wounded. He told Kah that he would try to crawl south and get reinforcements from 2nd Company which was apparently still secure. Kah quietly looked at his colleague and said: "*Au revoir,* old man, get going. You've got a lot to do."

But as de Mecquenem began to run south along the communications trench, two enemy soldiers fell upon him and took him prisoner. He never drank the victory champagne he had left to cool in his command post.

At a point near the top of Gabrielle, the Foreign Legionnaires of the Heavy Mortar Company, whose pieces had been knocked out, were fighting as infantrymen. The surviving mortar officer, Lt. Clergé, and his remaining fifteen men began to fall back in the direction of 2nd Company with most of their radio sets and equipment. Two Legionnaires, Pusch and Zimmermann, opened the way with hand grenades. Clergé attempted to contact Dien Bien Phu for more fire support but found out that his batteries had run low and crawled back into his old position with two other Legionnaires to pick up spares under the feet of the first enemy assault wave. With the northern sector of 3rd Company now a complete shambles, the handful of Legionnaires found themselves in an impossible position. Yet the seemingly indefatigable Pusch and Zimmermann had picked up automatic rifles in an abandoned position and were laying down a withering defensive fire on the Communist assault waves. Within a short time, they had beaten back two assaults and the barbed wire ahead of them was covered with enemy bodies. Still the enemy came on. Just as they were about to be submerged both men and an Algerian sergeant threw eight hand grenades in quick succession and hacked their way in the direction of Dien Bien Phu. For the rest of the small band, the end had come. At 0745, an artillery shell knocked out Clergé's last serviceable radio set at the instant he and his men could see the tanks and paratroopers of the rescue force emerging from the smoke and monsoon rain. As they began to withdraw they were engulfed by a volley of hand grenades, followed by hordes of enemy infantry.

At 0830, the remnants of 2nd and 3rd Companies, 5th Battalion, 7th Algerian Rifles, joined the paratroopers and tanks at the foot of Gabrielle. The latter were also pinned down by heavy enemy fire and were taking serious losses. One of the tanks had been hit by a Viet-Minh bazooka and Sgt. Guntz, commander of the 3rd Tank Platoon, was killed. The retreat from Gabrielle in full daylight, under direct observation from the enemy who now held the crest of Hill Gabrielle, was sheer agony. The crossing at Ban Ké Phai was still blocked by enemy fire and even the large volume of French counterbattery shells failed to show any noticeable effect. Still, by 0900 of March 15, the survivors of the 5/7 RTA and the battered Séguin-Pazzis task force re-entered the protective perimeter of strongpoints Anne-Marie and Huguette. Far away, where Hill Gabrielle lay in the morning mist, a few shots rang out where isolated French and Algerians were fighting their last-ditch fight.

The fight for Gabrielle had been bitter and the losses had been heavy. Almost 500 men were missing from the 5/7 RTA, of whom at least 80 were dead. Both battalion commanders had been taken prisoner. The 416th CSM had also ceased to exist; only a handful of Legionnaires from the mortar company had made good their escape. Moreover, there were heavy losses in the rescue force. Captain Martin's Foreign Legion Paratroop Company had lost one fourth of its effectives, and Martin himself had a bullet in one arm. One tank was severely damaged, and the newly parachuted 5th Vietnamese Airborne Battalion had for all practical purposes disintegrated. In all, the French probably lost close to 1,000 troops that night. Following the loss of Beatrice, the loss of Gabrielle, known for so long as the best built of all the strongpoints at Dien Bien Phu, had a disastrous effect on the morale of the garrison. But it was the failure of elements of the 5th BPVN under Capt. Botella to cross the ford at Ban Ké Phai that bore the brunt of Col. Langlais' criticism. White with rage, Botella lined up his men by the companies and proceeded to purge ruthlessly from their ranks all officers and men whose conduct had not been above reproach. They were dismissed from the battalion on the spot and left to fend for themselves as coolies in the camp.[15]

On the Communist side, the battle for Gabrielle had not been easy, either. According to French aerial estimates the Viet-Minh had lost probably over 1,000 dead and perhaps between 2,000 and 3,000 wounded, from some of the best units available. Enemy radio traffic picked up by the French that day indicated that Gen. Giap was in urgent need of troop replacements for his depleted divisions and, above all, more ammunition from the rear depots in Tuan Giao. But the *Bo-Doi* (infantrymen) of People's Army Regiments 88 and 102 of the 308th Division had cause for rejoicing. They had fulfilled the promise made to President Ho Chi Minh when their division political commissar handed the leading assault group of Regiment 88 a new red banner said to have been offered by Ho Chi Minh himself, inscribed with the stitched-in motto "To Fight and to Win." A twenty-five-year-old sergeant named Tran Ngoc Doan planted the flag on top of Maj. de Mecquenem's command bunker at about 0700 of March 15. Four other men of his platoon had been wounded trying to do so. The Communist forces knew Hill Gabrielle as Doc-Lap, a Vietnamese word which can be translated as either Independence, Isolation, or Loneliness.

Despite the low clouds and almost nonexistent visibility, two fighter-bombers that were still undergoing repair at Dien Bien Phu attempted to intervene in the battle for Hill Gabrielle. But flight "Savart Blue" was taken almost immediately under heavy and extremely accurate antiaircraft fire. "Savart Blue" Leader dropped its bombs about 6.5 kilometers north of the airstrip, while Blue No. 2 dropped his at about 5 kilometers. Then Blue Leader seemed to disintegrate in mid-air as it was hit almost simultaneously by several antiaircraft shells. Its pilot, Sergeant Ali Sahraoui, an Algerian from Squadron 2/22 "Languedoc," died instantly. "Savart Blue" No. 2 succeeded in escaping, but Lt. Lespinas, piloting a Navy dive-bomber from Squadron 11-F, became the second pilot casualty of the day. With the clouds continuing to hang low over the field, the control tower shot to pieces, the VHF beacon out of commission, and the shell craters on the airstrip itself, only 12.5 tons of supplies were parachuted on Dien Bien Phu that day. This was far too little to make up even in part for the huge expenditure of ammunition and other supplies.

But air support and logistics were not the only problems which Dien Bien Phu had to face on March 15. Colonel de Castries' staff was cracking under the strain of the battle. Colonel Piroth, the jovial one-armed artillery commander, had spent a good part of the night before witnessing the gradual neutralization of his firepower as deadly accurate Communist shellfire blanketed the artillery positions. Two 105-mm. howitzers had been destroyed together with their crews. One of the four 155's was out of commission, and the whole heavy mortar company on Gabrielle had been wiped out. As far as could be observed, the results of the French counter-battery had been negligible except on attacking enemy infantry. There was no evidence that Piroth's cannoneers had silenced even a small part of their opposite numbers. From buoyant overconfidence, Piroth now fell into extreme despair. He went from one command post to the other, under heavy enemy fire, to apologize for what he considered to be the failure of his command. The commander of the northern sector of Dien Bien Phu, Col. (later Gen.) Trancart, who was a personal friend of Piroth's, later recalled how the latter walked into his dugout where he was watching the agony of Gabrielle and said to him with tears in his eyes:

"I am completely dishonored. I have guaranteed de Castries that the enemy artillery couldn't touch us—but now we are going to lose the battle. I'm leaving."

Trancart recalled that, preoccupied as he was with the battle, he had given Piroth some sort of a noncommittal answer. But some other officers recalled that when Piroth made a similar remark to the exhausted Lt. Col. Langlais, who now had to bear the responsibility for the defense of the whole central sector, the latter had turned sharply and said something to the effect that indeed an expiration for the failure of the artillery would be in order.

Without another word, the old colonel walked out of the command bunker and over to his own dugout. Being one-armed, he was not able to cock his service pistol. But it was not difficult for him to find a hand grenade in an ammunition box. Probably at dawn of March 15, Col. Piroth lay down on his field cot, pulled out the safety pin of the hand grenade with his teeth, and then held the explosive charge against his chest. Colonel de Castries was undoubtedly informed immediately of the death of Piroth, but to judge from the telegrams first sent to Hanoi, there seems to have been an attempt at covering up Piroth's suicide. The initial message, which appears to have been sent three days after-ward, seems to have stated that Piroth had died, like the unfortunate Gaucher one day before him, from a direct enemy artillery hit on his bunker. This version was replaced in one message text which seemed to indicate that Col. Piroth had been reported "missing" while being sent as an emissary to the enemy for a negotiation whose purpose was never made clear. An officer of the French central intelligence service who had his own radio communications with the outside world, informed his superiors on March 20 that Piroth had been missing for the last three days along with a jeep and that only three officers had been told what really happened. Piroth unquestionably died by his own hand sometime between March 15 and 19.[16]

Meanwhile, Col. de Castries' chief of staff, Lt. Col. Keller, had suffered a nervous breakdown and could be seen sitting in the deepest dugout of the headquarters complex, wearing a steel helmet. In a brief exchange of telegrams with Gen. Cogny, de Castries proposed that Keller be relieved and returned to Hanoi for "briefing." The episode was camouflaged so as (in de Castries' words, in one of the telegrams) "not to hurt Keller's career." Thus, de Castries was deprived of his whole first command echelon of officers, precisely the men upon whom he had relied, and who were best acquainted with the planning of the fortress and the thinking of its commander.

The day was to end with yet another piece of bad news. At 2000, Capt. Guilleminot's 12th Company of T'ai riflemen on Anne-Marie 3 began to abandon its weapons and slip through the barbed wire entanglements and mine fields in the direction of the nearby hills. The T'ai mountaineers of the 3rd BT had been recruited from faraway Son-La and Nghia-Lo. Their families already were in Communist hands. They now were fighting in an area not under the jurisdiction of their own tribe. As far as they were concerned, it was no longer their war. The Communist propaganda directed at them during the previous weeks was obviously beginning to pay off and the destruction of the garrison of Hill Gabrielle under their eyes had done the rest. The French officers and sergeants and a few T'ai noncoms and soldiers who had remained faithful spent an uncomfortably lonely night awaiting the Communist attack that would surely submerge them. Fortunately, it never came.

At Gen. Cogny's headquarters in Hanoi high optimism had been replaced by deep gloom. Off the record, on hearing of the failure of the counterattack on Gabrielle, Cogny had declared to a group of his staff officers as well as to two journalists, Lucien Bodard and Max Clos, that for "several months" he had told Gen. Navarre that Dien Bien Phu was nothing but a "mouse trap." And on the same day he sent an urgent top-secret note to his commander-in-chief in which he informed the latter that a "disaster" at Dien Bien Phu must now be considered a distinct possibility. In this event, Cogny continued, his northern command in the Red River Delta would require three Mobile Groups of which two would have to be on the spot within eight days. In Cogny's view, the balance of forces in the vital Red River area was as follows: The enemy had at his disposal the whole reconstituted 320th People's Army Division plus six regular independent regiments, for a total of thirty-nine battalions, of which twenty-four were regulars. In addition, there were more than 100 local companies infiltrated in the Delta and about 50,000 Communist village militiamen. On the French side, Cogny had eighty French and Vietnamese battalions and twenty so-called "Light Battalions," but much of that force was tied down on guard duty in the fixed positions of the Marshal de Lattre Line and in guarding the numerous airfields, bridges, and towns in the lowlands. This meant that only twenty-seven of the 100 battalions were available for mobile warfare, and of those only sixteen were massed in the hard-hitting Mobile Groups necessary to stand up to large enemy regular units. In his message Cogny also suggested that Navarre call off Operation "Atlante" in southern Viet-Nam in order to save equipment and manpower for the serious fighting in the north.

Since Navarre was in Hanoi on March 15 and spoke to Cogny that day, it was obvious that the memorandum was written for the later historical record rather than for immediate action. This explains why Navarre allowed fifteen days to pass before replying to it in the curtest possible way compatible with administrative courtesy: "I fully understand your viewpoint but cannot take it into account." Obviously, communication between both men had, for all practical purposes, already broken down.

Tuesday, March 16, 1954

At 0109 Dien Bien Phu informed Hanoi that the southern part of the airstrip should be used as a DZ that day and that the personnel for a whole artillery battery should be included among the reinforcements, as at least six 105's and eight complete gun crews had become casualties during the past forty-eight hours. At 0448, Dien Bien Phu reported medium to heavy rain and at 0630 it established a priority system for the day's air drops: personnel first, then a new VHF radio beacon, followed by medical supplies, to be dropped on the main DZ. Dismantled artillery pieces and howitzer ammunition was to be dropped on DZ Octavie west of Isabelle, followed by infantry ammunition and food. Ammunition, suddenly, had become a priority item as Dien Bien Phu had fired almost five days of ammunition in less than three: 12,600 rounds of 105 out of 27,000; 10,000 rounds of 120-mm. mortars out of 23,000; and one-fifth of its 3,000 rounds of 155-mm. medium howitzer ammunition. Dien Bien Phu also warned Hanoi that "neutralization of antiaircraft artillery cannot be guaranteed."

The problem of dropping reinforcements involved not only protecting the drop and landing zones from enemy artillery fire, but also securing them from occupation by enemy troops. This was particularly true in the case of DZ Octavie, which was finally occupied by a sortie from Isabelle at about 0900. But the enemy had realized what was afoot. Fairly dense artillery fire fell on the DZ's and LZ's all day long. Finally, at 1105, as the sun dispersed the rain and fog which lay in thick layers over the valley, the first waves of transport aircraft began to drop the first "sticks" of Maj. Bigeard's 6th Parachute Battalion.

This was the second drop of Bigeard's battalion at Dien Bien Phu. Yet the battalion was now neither as big nor as fresh as it had been the previous November. Since then it had fought in the battles for southern Laos and had been pulled back into airborne reserve at Hanoi, and at Haiphong's Cat-Bi Airport, only to be involved in a vicious night fight with a Communist commando force, led by Captain Minh Khanh, the deputy commander of People's Army Battalion 204. During the night of March 7, Khanh had entered the heavily guarded air base and attached explosive charges to six *Cricket* reconnaissance aircraft and four B-26 bombers. The pursuing paratroopers caught some of the saboteurs but this was small consolation for the losses suffered by France's already slim air force in North Viet-Nam.

Even so, the 613 paratroopers (332 of whom were Vietnamese) who now were dangling in their parachute harnesses over Octavie were a welcome sight to the weary defenders of Dien Bien Phu. They were also followed by another 100 replacements for the 1st BEP and the 8th Assault; three complete gun crews from the 35th Airborne Artillery completed the day's personnel drop. In spite of the artillery fire, the drops went surprisingly well—no doubt because they were dispersed over a fairly wide area on two drop zones, which the Communist artillery could not cover very well simultaneously. The 6th BPC, moreover, was an experienced elite force familiar with the terrain. Hence, only two casualties, one dead and one wounded, were attributable to enemy action. The only two jump casualties were Maj. Bigeard himself and the medical officer of the battalion, Lt. Rivier, both of whom suffered ankle sprains. Bigeard hobbled over to nearby Isabelle and obtained a jeep which brought him in a zig-zag course to de Castries' headquarters. By 1630, the whole battalion and the other reinforcements, escorted by tanks from Capt. Hervouët's squadron, had safely reached Dien Bien Phu. One company of the 6th moved for the time being to depleted Anne-Marie while the rest of the battalion crossed the Nam Yum under fire and installed itself on the slopes of Eliane 1 and 4. At 1858, Dien Bien Phu reported all drops terminated and successfully hauled to safety.

The Viet-Minh artillery fire continued to do damage. The last two operable *Cricket* reconnaissance aircraft were destroyed that day and a direct enemy hit ignited the depot containing napalm bombs. Though hurting no one, the fire covered the camp with a depressing mushroom cloud of smoke. On the ground, there were Communist infiltrations on the western, northern, and eastern sides of Anne-Marie. Late in the afternoon pressure again increased on Dominique. Yet such was the reputation of Bigeard and the 6th BPC that the beleaguered men, from the commanding officer to the wounded in Maj. Grauwin's underground hospital, began to take heart again: After all, Bigeard had been in the most desperate situations in Indochina and had always walked out alive from them. During the afternoon of March 16, de Castries issued an order of the day, which was transmitted to all units in the valley and was probably addressed as much to the enemy listening in as to them:

> We are undertaking at Dien Bien Phu a battle in which the whole fate of the Indochina War will be decided.
>
> We have taken some pretty hard blows and have been losing many men, but those have been replaced immediately by two airborne battalions. There are five more of them ready to jump in.
>
> Our artillery is intact and ready for all protective fire missions. Guns as well as artillerymen have been parachuted in.
>
> Hence, the reinforcements which have arrived amply make up for our losses. The Viets can't say as much about their own.
>
> You may perhaps be surprised at not seeing more bombers [but] it must be understood that the present weather does not permit all sorts of missions.
>
> At the very first clearing of the sky all of the airpower available in Indochina will be above Dien Bien Phu.
>
> Everything rides on us here. A few more days, and we shall have won and the sacrifices made by our comrades shall not have been made in vain.
>
> (signed) de Castries.

De Castries' personal feelings were expressed in a two-line telegram which he sent at 1730 to Hanoi: "Personal to General Cogny. Present

situation requires permanent stationing of one battalion on airborne alert.
(signed) de Castries."

Cogny replied at 2225 in an equally laconic message informing de Castries that he had only one more parachute battalion left in North Viet-Nam and that there were only two more available throughout Indochina.

The atmosphere on that third day of the battle was described on pieces of paper a French combat photographer added to rolls of exposed film that left Dien Bien Phu during the next few days on one of the ambulance aircraft. The photographer, Jean Péraud, was a survivor of the Nazi concentration camps and a seasoned observer not given to overstatements and dramatics. His reaction to Dien Bien Phu on March 16 was as follows:

> Air drop of March 16 — Viet-Minh bombardment of DZ and of GONO — Cavalcade of soldiers under fire — Our artillery smashed up by Viet-Minh — Attempt at embarkation of wounded under fire of Viet-Minh 105's — Tragic — Many wounded.
> — Gloomy atmosphere reminds of German concentration camps
> — Catastrophic.

The notes were supposed to have been delivered in Hanoi to another journalist, François Sully, who later reported another Viet-Nam war for *Newsweek,* but Sully never received the note and only parts of the film. I found the notes ten years later in the French military archives, marked with a red rubber stamp and the word *Saisi* ("Seized") (see p. 162). The French military censors in Hanoi had decided that their immediate release would have been too demoralizing.

Earlier that evening a Communist officer under a flag of truce had approached strongpoint Anne-Marie and left a letter addressed to de Castries stating that on March 17 in the morning, eighty-six wounded survivors from Gabrielle would be left to be picked up 600 meters to the north of Anne-Marie 2. This offer, as well as others which were to follow at least for a while, put de Castries in a cruel dilemma. It was obviously impossible for purposes of morale to refuse to take back his own wounded, but on the other hand the limited medical facilities of Dien Bien Phu were already hopelessly overcrowded and the chances of evacuating anyone were almost nil. Even though they performed incredible feats of courage, the flimsy and underpowered helicopters of the period were capable of picking up only a handful of wounded and, as will be seen, the transport planes would soon be unable to land.

Titre : Compte non discrétion —

1	~~Bobine~~ relatant évacuation samedi. du 17. Catastrophique — sous tir V.M. Essai infructueux.
2	retenté le 18 à 2 reprises, mais toujours sous tir V.M. bien que Croix rouge apparente —
3	Ambiance d'angoisse, de terreur même — cris, pleurs — ruelle des blessés vers la porte —
4	n'ai pas vu pareille chose depuis camp de concentration —
5	Me garder SVP clichés, car sans doute très intéressants. Moral toujours très haut même
6	sous tir V.M. — Suis toujours intact. dire à M. NÉVILLE que son cousin est vivant — lui ai remis sa lettre

The enemy knew this as well as de Castries did. Hence, the return to French lines of French casualties was coupled with not only the Viet-Minh's refusal to allow the landing of ambulance aircraft but also their refusal to accept the return of their own wounded! General Giap fully realized the burden which the mass of casualties would create for the French command and had made the decision that the wounded, Viet-Minh and French, would also have to play their role in the battle.

In view of the appalling conditions in the hospital area which, in spite of the Red Cross flags which marked it, had become a favorite target of the enemy artillery, Maj. Grauwin on March 17 attempted to propose to de Castries the establishment of a neutral "medical village" between Dien Bien Phu and Isabelle where French and Viet-Minh medical personnel would impartially care for the casualties of both sides. The idea was forwarded by de Castries to Hanoi and apparently rejected. It is not clear to this day whether that decision was made unilaterally by the French or after rejection by the enemy high command.

Wednesday, March 17, 1954

In the morning, before the fog began to lift, a brief message came in from the artillery officer stationed at an OP on Anne-Marie 2 saying: "The T'ai are getting the hell out of here." Indeed, without fuss and without much noise the T'ai mountaineers of Anne-Marie 1 and 2 were slipping away through the barbed wire and the openings in the mine fields toward their beloved mountains on the horizon. The action had come so suddenly and so quietly that the French officers and NCO's and the few remaining faithful T'ai had not been able to hold them back. Indeed, why hold them back at all? Obviously, they would have

---

TRANSLATION OF OPPOSITE PAGE

Counting on your discretion — Film shows medical evacuation of 17 [March] — Catastrophic under Viet-Minh fire — Attempt fruitless — Tried again on 18 twice, but still under V.-M. fire, though Red Cross [markings] apparent — Atmosphere of anxiety, terror even — Screams, crying — Rush of the wounded to the [airplane] door — Haven't seen anything like it since the concentration camps — Please keep proofs for me as pictures must no doubt be very interesting — Morale is still very high, even under V.-M. fire — Am still hale. Tell Mr. Neville that his nephew is alive — I gave him his letter.

(signed) J. Péraud

disintegrated under the first serious attack. As leaflets found in the trenches were to show, the Communists had done their propaganda job through the best possible channels, the civilian population. Incredible as it may seem, many of the villages surrounding the French positions had not been fully evacuated (on orders of de Castries, they were to be fully evacuated by March 20). It was a daily occurrence to see womenfolk from the partisan units, from the two mobile field bordellos,[17] and from the Meo tribesmen of the French central intelligence detachment, do their marketing at Ban Co My or Ban Loi. There they would be met by other tribesmen from the Communist areas who brought Communist propaganda with them. Needless to say, some of these tribesmen were trained spies who found it simple to re-enter Dien Bien Phu with the returning civilians. The partial desertion of the 3rd BT, soon followed by the total demoralization of the 2nd BT and of many of the men of the remaining T'ai light companies, was a major victory of Communist psychological warfare, for it cost the French almost one fifth of their garrison without the Communists' having fired a shot.

Anne-Marie 4, held by Capt. Désiré's 9th Company, was the only one which stood fast, as the remaining French and T'ai elements from AM-1 and AM-2 began to fall back at about 1400. From AM-3, Capt. Guilleminot telephoned Désiré to tell him things weren't going well but that he could hold with the Legionnaires. On questioning from HQ GONO, Désiré affirmed that he could guarantee the defense of AM-4 for at least twenty-four hours. By nightfall, the question as to whether the northern positions of Anne-Marie were to be retaken and held by the newly arrived paratroopers had become academic. The Viet-Minh now rapidly pushed forward to seize the last shreds of high ground which the French held to the north of the airfield. In fact, because of the artillery bombardment that had been maintained all day on the northern sector of Anne-Marie, the retreating French cadres had been unable to take with them the heavy weapons of the battalion installed in the forward positions.

It is curious that the 3rd BT, which had fought extremely well the previous year in the fortified position of Na-San and had distinguished itself in operations against the 320th Division in difficult terrain only a few months before, now fell apart after scarcely two days of fighting at Dien Bien Phu. The fact that the battalion's dependents were now partly in Communist hands may have played a part. However, it is more than likely that the recent change in battalion commanders, Communist psychological warfare, and the unaccustomed pressure of continuous enemy artillery bombardment in a fixed position (there was Viet-Minh artillery at Na-San, but not remotely of such density) must have played a decisive role. The final question that remains is why de Castries did not use part of his reconstituted airborne reserve to retake the precious piece of high ground which had been lost under far less honorable conditions than either Beatrice or Gabrielle.

De Castries' answer appears to have been that the defense of Anne-Marie might have cost him heavy casualties,[18] which he could not have readily replaced since Cogny had informed him that he could, for the time being, count only on one more airborne battalion. Furthermore, there was strong evidence that the next push might be against the vital remaining high ground east of the Nam Yum, where Algerian and Moroccan troops also were showing signs of battle fatigue. De Castries and Langlais therefore decided not to make a fight for Anne-Marie 1 and 2 but to attach Anne-Marie 3 and 4 to strongpoint Huguette as of 2000 that night. Anne-Marie 3 became known as Huguette 6 and Anne-Marie 4 became Huguette 7.

March 17 had also been a bad day in the air. The poor weather had kept aerial resupply at a minimum and the Communists were now covering all possible drop zones with intermittent artillery fire. The last remaining repairable *Cricket* reconnaissance plane had finally been found in its pit by the enemy gunners and set afire, and the Air Force's gasoline and ammunition storage dumps had been exploded by enemy artillery. At 1500, however, the exhausted medical personnel of Dien Bien Phu were relieved to see the flawless drop of Airborne Surgical Team (ACP) No. 6, under Lt. Vidal, M.D. Their arrival permitted Dr. Grauwin to install a hospital annex on the other bank of the Nam Yum, thus saving the seriously wounded a dangerous trip across the open bridge. But Dr. Grauwin's big problem still was the wounded who could not be evacuated. Here the enemy had selected his action for maximum effect. He would hold his fire until the trucks, with huge Red Cross flags flying, would arrive on the airfield and approach the ambulance aircraft wheeling to a standstill. Then, when both the airplane and the wounded were at their most vulnerable, Communist artillery would open up in full force and the airplane would roar off either empty or loaded with the more able-bodied wounded, or even some unharmed cowards trying frantically to leave the valley. Even so, two C-47's made it. One, piloted by Capt. Cornu, rapidly dumped off essential medical supplies and picked up thirty-two men instead of the twenty-four the plane was supposed to carry. The other aircraft, commanded by Capt. Darde, landed in the

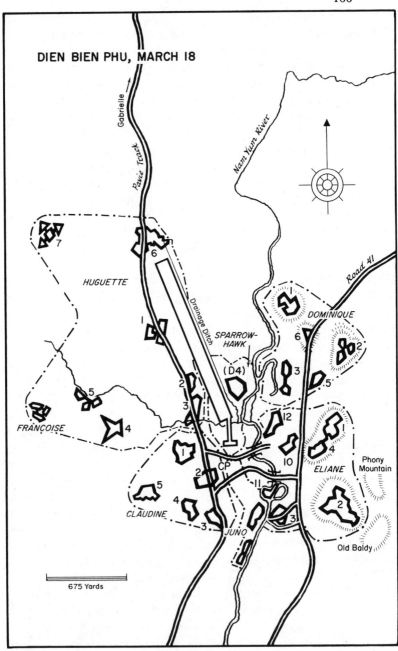

DIEN BIEN PHU, MARCH 18

675 Yards

middle of a heavy artillery barrage at 1900 and waited for five minutes on the ground before taking off again empty. Not one of the ambulance trucks had been able to approach the airstrip.

At noon, Dien Bien Phu had had a visitor: Gen. Cogny had flown over the fortress for a full half hour observing the battle. It was said later that the sight of the martyred fortress plowed under by the constant rain of Communist shells (and to judge from the tenor of its command communications, in an obvious state of low morale), inspired Cogny with the idea that he should land, when possible, and direct the battle, just as his own mentor, the late Marshal de Lattre, had done in 1951 during the battle for Vinh-Yen. At Vinh-Yen, de Lattre had landed in a *Cricket* reconnaissance aircraft in the middle of a French encircled unit and, faced with the pleas of his chief-of-staff that he was in mortal danger, had superbly replied: "Come and get me out." In defending Cogny's ultimate decision not to do so, Jules Roy has argued that Dien Bien Phu was not Cogny's work but Navarre's. To risk his life for it would have been tantamount to admitting that he was "responsible" for Dien Bien Phu.[19]

This argument, in my view, is specious. As commander of the northern theater, where Dien Bien Phu was located, Cogny *was* responsible for its defense even *if* he had not personally picked Dien Bien Phu. The deployment of the artillery, the improvised character of the counterattacks, the poor use of the reserves, and the poor choice of the units assigned to Dien Bien Phu were *his* responsibility, and his alone. The available documentation and statements subsequently made by Cogny or Navarre in no way change this fact. As soon as Cogny had made his choice not to resign but to continue to lead a battle of which he apparently now fully disapproved, he assumed a historical responsibility which can be evaded only with difficulty.

Thursday, March 18, 1954

The supply problems that Dien Bien Phu faced turned from bad to worse. The enemy artillery now crowned all the heights around the valley and Communist 37-mm. antiaircraft guns began to fire directly into the take-off and landing patterns of the airstrip from the newly conquered positions on top of Gabrielle and Anne-Marie. One of the major problems of nighttime supply drops was that the garrison was not yet geared to the complicated problem of collecting and distributing over 100 tons of diverse cargo within a few hours. At 0125 of March 18, Dien Bien Phu suggested to Hanoi that henceforth it would be simpler to parachute supplies directly on the strongpoints rather than on the DZ's. The fog-shrouded morning hours always provided the weary garrison with some respite, since there was light enough to do the most essential chores without being seen by the enemy observers. First Company of the 5th BPVN, under Lt. Rondeaux, took advantage of the fog to relieve Capt. Désiré's 9th T'ai Company on what was now Huguette 7, and Désiré, on holding a roll call for his men, noticed with satisfaction that only three were not accounted for. Methodically, his men packed up for the ten-kilometer march southward to Isabelle, their new assignment.

On the airfield, the Moroccans of the 31st Engineering Battalion used the morning respite to repair the pierced steel plates of the airfield. Enemy shells had hacked it to pieces until there were only 600 meters of it left. After some hasty hammering and welding under intermittent, if blind, artillery fire, the airfield was again usable to the 1,000-meter limit. On March 19, further exposed scraping and patching would make it again operable to the 1,500-meter limit. The work of the combat engineers paid off. At 1055 an ambulance aircraft piloted by Lt. Biswang succeeded in landing and picking up twenty-three wounded who had been lying in open slit trenches along the taxi strip. Major Darde came in close behind and had begun to roll on the field when he was boxed in by a salvo of mortar explosions which riddled the rear of the aircraft and seriously wounded a doctor who was aboard. Two helicopters from the 1st Light Helicopter Evacuation Company suffered a similar fate. The first landed directly near the main hospital and was able to embark one wounded man. Another helicopter attempted a landing at the CP of Mobile Group 9, where Lt. Col. Gaucher had been killed five days earlier, but was waved off before it could land.

That night, Major Jacques Guérin hit upon a solution to the night landing problem which temporarily permitted the evacuation of a large number of wounded. One French C-47 would act as a "decoy" and fly a low-level air-drop pattern over the valley which was sure to attract the attention of most of the enemy's antiaircraft gunners. At the same time a blacked-out aircraft would attempt to "glide" into the airport with propellers almost feathered and with only very few directional lanterns to guide him on the strip. Among the pilots, there were heated arguments as to whether it was more dangerous to play decoy or to land on the darkened airfield in the middle of artillery fire. Yet the ruse worked until March 27, when a parachute flare, fired from a mortar of Huguette 6 at the wrong moment, brilliantly lit up the runway and gave away the scheme to the Communists. At least 223 wounded had been picked up in this manner and 101 were evacuated by helicopters, providing the sorely taxed hospitals of the valley with at least a brief respite.

On the ground, Communist pressure had changed in character. With the outer defenses of Dien Bien Phu solidly in Viet-Minh hands, Gen. Giap decided to switch to more economical siege techniques. Thousands of coolies began to arrive in the valley and were soon at work digging the huge communications trench system designed to eventually surround the fortress completely. At 1525, de Castries informed Hanoi that trenches dug only one kilometer south of strongpoint Eliane now had reached the Nam Yum, thus cutting off the best direct road between Dien Bien Phu and Isabelle. As night fell and the artillery fire slackened off, the French outposts could hear the noise of picks and shovels around Dominique 1 and 2, northwest of Eliane and again to the south of it. The noise of entrenching also came closer to Huguette and Claudine in the west as well as to the north of Isabelle. Until now, Isabelle had operated as a dependency of Dien Bien Phu and had relied heavily on the daily convoys which continued to hack their way through Communist ambushes, bring in wounded and picking up supplies. Now the sealing off of Isabelle became highly likely.

Friday, March 19, 1954

During the night, helicopters and C-47's had evacuated a total of thirty-six wounded under heavy fire. The heavy C-119 "Flying Boxcars" of the American-operated Civil Air Transport Company now were dropping huge pallet loads of one ton or more, and while this was efficient in terms of utilization of aircraft and pilot potential, the huge loads proved totally unmovable by hand under fire. The problem was further complicated when such a load, usually containing ammunition and other explosives, fell into a mine field and blew up together with it, or when, because of a parachute failure, the load plowed into a French entrenchment or dugout with all the impact of a heavy bomb. As a result, Dien Bien Phu requested at 2038 that henceforth only smaller loads be dropped whenever possible. These, it was proposed, should be limited to individual packages of 100 kilograms or less.

On the ground, strangulation began. New trenches were discovered 600 meters west of Claudine and now even the smallest patrol sorties ran into heavy infantry fire. The effect on the morale of the lonesome de Castries can be guessed from a message which he sent at 1500 on a top secret and personal basis to Gen. Cogny. He envisaged the early fall of Dien Bien Phu "which would be shortly followed by the inevitable fall of Isabelle." De Castries then requested authorization for Lt. Col. Lalande and his men at Isabelle to blow up their artillery and to make a break in the direction of Muong Khoua and Muong Sai in Laos.[20]

Cogny's reply message was noncommittal on the issue itself, and contained a modicum of encouragement for the future:

> You are right in envisaging at your command level even the most catastrophic hypotheses. Shall give you the indications concerning same. But am quite certain that you shall be successful thanks to your will to resist on the spot, communicated to the important effectives [under your command] in their improved positions, and to your spirit of aggressiveness communicated to the internal counterattack forces as well as to those devoted to preventive outside action [sic] whose aim it is to hamper enemy forces on their line of departure. In warm friendship, Cogny.

Here again, one may well suspect that the message was sent for purposes of being inserted in the future historical record, or simply to help de Castries over a very difficult psychological moment. Nevertheless, it was obviously unrealistic in terms of conditions inside the fortress. While the effectives were important, they were at most one fourth those of the enemy. The French positions, far from having been improved, except in the sense that under heavy Communist artillery fire everybody now was digging deeper and better trenches and dugouts, had lost most of the vital high ground that had made Dien Bien Phu viable. And as for counterattacks and "preventive outside action," these would have taken more men and more artillery and more air support than de Castries could have mustered in his wildest dreams. Yet it was obvious that Cogny now realized the gravity of the command crisis at Dien Bien Phu. He was to return to the same theme during the following days. He also would provide de Castries with senior officers to replace those lost during the first week of the battle.

On the night of March 19 a small squadron of five transports, led by Lt. Col. Descaves, succeeded in picking up ninety-five wounded, the largest number thus far. Earlier during the day, another rescue operation had taken place. Helicopters marked with Red Cross insignia had picked up the uninjured pilots of Fighter Group 1/22 "Saintonge," isolated at Dien Bien Phu since their airplanes were destroyed in mid-March.

This clear-cut violation of the Red Cross convention certainly did not escape the Viet-Minh forward observers. The commander of the French helicopter group was later to remark that the Viet-Minh had at first abstained from firing on "Med-Evac" helicopters or aircraft, until they saw the pilots embarking. Then immediately began firing on the second wave of helicopters. "That serious violation [on the French side]," said the report, "was to cost us later two helicopters and crews and was used as pretext [by the enemy] for firing on other Red Cross planes."[21] Yet the violations continued, as the French brought in Lt. Col. Ducruix (de Castries' new chief-of-staff), Lt. Col. Lemeunier (the new commander of GM 9), and Col. Vaillant (the artillery commander replacing Piroth) by ambulance helicopter or aircraft. While it is doubtful, as the Viet-Minh charged, that ambulance aircraft attempted to land everything but medical supplies, the verified violations of the Red Cross rules gave the Communists a welcome pretext for ignoring them as well.

On March 23, when Gen. Navarre addressed an open radio message to Giap (in which he called him "General" for the first time) asking for protection of medical aircraft and, if necessary, their inspection by an International Red Cross commission, his offer was met with stony silence from Giap. Moreover, "Voice of Viet-Nam" propaganda broadcasts charged the French with bringing in ammunition in ambulance planes.

Late that night, de Castries decided to expel the T'ai population from the surrounding villages in the valley as of March 20, both to save it from the increasingly heavy bombardment and to prevent further infiltration of intelligence agents into the camp. This did not end the presence of civilians on the battlefield or even inside Dien Bien Phu. The 8th Commando Group (GC 8) of Capt. Hébert, which was the local unit of the French central intelligence services, supervised a small group of Meo tribal operatives, whose wives and children were no longer able to slip back to their native areas. The evacuation of the wives and families of the men of GMPT to Hanoi also was no longer possible. Finally, there were two *Bordels Mobiles de Campagne,* Mobile Field Brothels. One was made up of Algerian girls from the Oulad Naïl tribe, the other of Vietnamese girls. Both shared the trials of the garrison. The presence of civilian elements was to add to the tensions inside the camp and in the end, the fate of the civilians was to be far worse than that of the soldiers.

During the night of March 19 to 20, leaflets in French and Arabic fell on strongpoint Dominique, inciting the Algerians of the 3/3 RTA to abandon the cause of the "French imperialists."

Saturday, March 20, 1954

March 20 was a calm day, save for intermittent artillery fire. In Hanoi, Gen. Cogny continued to be concerned by what he felt to be a morale crisis among the senior commanders at Dien Bien Phu. Early in the morning, he sent de Castries a new five-point directive, of which, curiously enough, two somewhat different versions exist. The first was provided by Cogny to Roy,[22] and the second is contained in the French War Archives. The directive, with alternate modifications, reads as follows:

1. Above all one must keep in view the success of the battle.
2. An Airborne [Regimental] Group is being speedily activated, but its commitment must be reserved to the exploitation of the success.
3. The only immediate possibility is to reinforce you by one battalion in order to compensate your losses suffered during the counterattacks; but even the dropping of that battalion can only be permitted on the condition that the integrity of the fortified camp be guaranteed.
4. Any strongpoint upon which the Viet-Minh would set foot must be retaken from the enemy on the spot. [Alternate text: "be retaken by an immediate counteroffensive with your own means at hand."]
5. In the unfortunate and infinitely improbable hypothesis which has been considered [here, the alternate text specifically refers to de Castries' telegram of the previous day], an eventual operation for the rescue of the break-out force has been studied.

Here again, the difference between the situation at hand and its appreciation in Hanoi is striking. "A guarantee" of the integrity of what was left of the position of Dien Bien Phu was totally meaningless under the circumstances. The dictum to retake any lost strongpoint "on the spot" (softened to "immediately" in the text apparently transmitted to Dien Bien Phu) also meant very little in view of the vastly superior enemy infantry and firepower that overwhelmed strongpoints Beatrice and Gabrielle. It has been said that the messages of March 19 and 20, and those which followed within the next few days, were designed to lift the spirits of the local command. If this was so, they failed. The recipients were to say later that they were irritated by what they thought was a lack of appreciation of the precariousness of their situation.

The opening of the road between Isabelle and Dien Bien Phu ran into relatively little trouble at the Communist roadblock at Ban Kho Lai. Yet, it cost five dead, two missing and five wounded, including 2nd Lieutenant Alain Gambiez, son of Gen. Gambiez, Navarre's chief of staff. By chance, Gen. Gambiez that same evening flew over Dien Bien Phu in the headquarters aircraft making its daily rounds over the valley, co-ordinating supply flights and air support. Gambiez insisted that his son not be the object of particular solicitude but be flown out only when his proper turn came.

At 2243, with most of the urgent radio traffic out of the way, Personnel at Dien Bien Phu reminded Personnel at Hanoi that is was still in urgent need of more artillery specialists, particularly a crew for a 155-mm. howitzer that had been wiped out by Viet-Minh counterbattery fire.

Sunday, March 21, 1954

A sharp blast awoke the camp at 0300 as a Viet-Minh commando unit, which had sneaked right past the patrols and strongpoints of Huguette, blew a hole in the airstrip near Huguette 1. Patrols had been seen on the airfield before, but not so close to the central position.

On Dominique, things had been unquiet. Enemy leaflets had been replaced by "Open Letters" addressed by name to the Algerian sergeants. Later, leaflets and loud-speaker appeals in German were to follow. The enemy was trying to soften up the non-French elements of the garrison. Moreover, the listening posts (*sonnettes,* or "doorbells") far out in the no man's land beyond Huguette, Dominique, and Eliane began to report contacts with enemy patrols.

To the south, at Isabelle, the Legionnaires had another arduous day attempting to break through to the main position. Slowly, the enemy stranglehold at Ban Kho Lai and Ban Nhong Nhai became increasingly tighter. It now took the tank platoons of both Warrant Officer Carette and Lt. Préaud to effect the breakthrough at 1655, instead of the usual noon hour.

Nevertheless, de Castries, mindful of Cogny's exhortations, and personally willing to stay on the offensive as long as possible, decided to attempt major forays for the following day. A strong task force centered on the 1st BEP under the command of Capt. Vieulles, supported by the now-grounded French Air Force detachment of Capt. Charnod fighting surprisingly well as infantry, and by Algerians with tanks from Isabelle, attempted to mop up the Ban Kho Lai roadblock. In addition to artillery support, the Air Force had allocated eighty-eight combat missions for the operation.

Even before the sortie began on Sunday evening, Maj. Bigeard had taken his veteran 6th BPC northward out of Dominique along Road 41 on an armed reconnaissance, to verify reports of a dangerous enemy build-up in the area.

The day ended where it had begun—on the airfield. At 2200, a patrol of bearded Legionnaire sappers from 1/2 REI's headquarters company ran into a Viet-Minh patrol and engaged it in a fire fight without notice-able results. At midnight, after a C-47 from Transport Group 2/64 "Béarn" made a successful blind landing and was in position for take-off with a full load of wounded, when Viet-Minh infiltrators shot the pilot, Lt. Arbeley, in the legs. Both he and his cargo of wounded were returned to Dr. Grauwin's hospital.

At 2300, a patrol consisting of a corporal and two Legionnaires dis-appeared in the no man's land between Huguette 7 and tiny Françoise. It was never heard from again.

Monday, March 22, 1954

By dawn, Bigeard's paratroopers were under heavy pressure. They had run into strong enemy elements very close to Dominique and were pinned down. Casualties would be severe if the enemy found them in the open after the morning fog had lifted. Soon the battalion mortars were involved in the fight, followed by the howitzers of the II/4 RAC. Bigeard now carefully extricated his men from the trap.

To the west, a patrol from 1st Company, 5th BPVN, reported enemy occupation of the abandoned strongpoints Anne-Marie 1 and 2, which brought Huguette 7 into full enemy view. The siege ring was apparently airtight throughout the whole northern area. How tight it was to the south would be disclosed later in the day.

In the meantime, the foggy morning hours were being put to good use elsewhere in the camp. Lieutenant Arbeley, his legs heavily swathed in bandages, was rolled back to the airport along with the men wounded the night before, and managed to get his aircraft back to Hanoi despite Viet-Minh fire. A fifteen-man group of artillerymen from the 35th Airborne Artillery Regiment, led by Lt. Yziquel, was air-dropped on Isabelle as reinforcements for the III/10 RAC.

The mop-up operation at the Viet-Minh blocking position of Ban Kho Lai began at 0730. At first it proceeded with incredible smoothness. No enemy opposition could be found. However, as the leading elements reached Ban Kho Lai, the strangulation tactics of the enemy were dra-matically revealed. Each day the Viet-Minh around Dien Bien Phu added to what was to become a ring of trenches surrounding the fortress. It soon became clear that the 1st BEP, even though reinforced by a tank platoon under Sgt. Ney, would not be able to force the blockade alone. Elements of the 2/1 RTA (Algerian Rifles) from Isabelle were thrown into the fight, followed by Isabelle's tank platoon and riflemen from the T'ai Sub-Groupment Wieme. Nevertheless, the two enemy companies dug in at Ban Kho Lai fought to the last ditch. It was only when the French committed the remaining four tanks of the squadron at Dien Bien Phu that they finally succeeded in joining hands with the Isabelle force at 1200. It was the first French victory in the valley of Dien Bien Phu. The enemy had paid for it dearly: There were only nine survivors of one of the companies of Regiment 57 which had held the trenches at Ban Kho Lai. On the French side, losses had also been heavy: 151 dead, including three Foreign Legion paratroop lieutenants, 72 wounded, and one man missing. At 2305, Airborne Surgical Team No. 3 at Isabelle radioed for an urgent drop of three gallons of fresh blood, 50 pair of surgical gloves, 100 tubes of catgut and more surgical equipment. Obviously, the road to Isabelle was becoming a meat-grinder operation which the French could not indefinitely afford.

At de Castries' command post and Gen. Cogny's headquarters in Hanoi, the "mosaic" of aerial photographs of the valley taken daily by reconnaissance aircraft of the 80th Overseas Reconnaissance Squadron (EROM) began to tell the story of the tight network of trenches that were beginning to strangle Dien Bien Phu. Older officers, who had served in World War I, recalled their knowledge of trench warfare, mine galleries, and countermines dug under the enemy's trench systems. Cogny ordered de Castries to prepare to wage countertrench warfare. In a personal telegram on the afternoon of Monday, March 22, de Castries informed Cogny that he lacked specialists and combat engineering equipment for trench warfare. On the following day he requested four copies of regulations on the defensive organization of terrain and other documents on trench warfare. It was only on March 23 that de Castries issued orders that all strongpoints had to be interconnected with communications trenches and that light nighttime reconnaissance parties should mine and booby-trap the newly dug enemy trenches.

Tuesday, March 23, 1954

The following day, two helicopters from the Laotian base at Muong Sai attempted to pick up wounded from Isabelle in the midst of an artillery barrage. The pilot of the first landed right on top of the hospital because he had a letter for Dr. Rézillot. In view of the heavy artillery fire falling, he was told to leave immediately without waiting to pick up any wounded. As he lifted off, the second helicopter of the flight (apparently neither of them checked in with Dien Bien Phu air control before making their approach) settled down on the landing area just vacated by the first helicopter. Its pilot, Warrant Officer Henri Bartier, ran into the hospital dugout and picked up Lt. Gambiez. He was lifting off when a volley of enemy shells disintegrated the lead helicopter. The same fragments also hit the rear fuselage of Bartier's craft which descended heavily and broke into flames. Bartier, who had recently flown his one thousandth combat mission in Indochina, and who had rescued 250 men with his helicopter, was pulled from the helicopter. But it was too late for Lt. Gambiez. The magnesium alloy of the aircraft burned fiercely and the young lieutenant was incinerated with it. Still another helicopter landed at Dien Bien Phu and succeeded in bringing in a new senior officer, Lt. Col. Voinot, who was to command the western sector of Dien Bien Phu; *i.e.,* Huguette and Claudine.

Later that day, Lt. Col. Langlais escorted the newly arrived Col. Lemeunier and Col. Voinot on an inspection tour to Isabelle. Escorted by Capt. Jeancenelle's Algerians from Isabelle, they had no trouble with Communist roadblocks that day: Apparently People's Army Regiment 57 was still licking its wounds. Late in the afternoon the garrison was treated to the French Air Force's Operation "Neptune"—a massive napalm bombardment of the enemy trench positions around Dien Bien Phu. While the sheets of flame and black smoke creeping over the hills were impressive, the application of napalm on a waterlogged rain forest seemed of dubious efficacy. A few minutes after the end of the barrage, ground observers reported that the napalm had burned but had not set spreading fires. The following morning, headquarters at Dien Bien Phu reported laconically that the effort had "not yielded observable results." Undeterred, the Air Force launched Operation "Eole" on the stretch of Road 41 leading into the valley of Dien Bien Phu. This effort did not yield observable results, either.

Wednesday, March 24, 1954

At 0710 in the morning of March 24, Lt. Col. Keller, de Castries' chief of staff who had broken under the strain, was embarked on an ambulance aircraft. De Castries now had to face the battle with an entirely new group of subordinates. Yet this had become irrelevant since de Castries was no longer leading the battle. He had withdrawn from his men and even from his staff. While it is untrue, as some people later asserted, that de Castries sat in his well-protected bunker wearing his steel helmet (as Keller had done), it is nonetheless a fact that he rarely left his underground headquarters. Jules Roy was to say of de Castries that he acted "as if a spring had broken inside him." When Langlais appeared before the French Government Commission investigating the battle of

Dien Bien Phu, in 1955, he described de Castries' role in the battle laconically: "He transmitted our messages to Hanoi."

What happened at Dien Bien Phu on March 24 has never been fully explained, but it seems that Langlais' reply to the investigation commission was not a quip; it was the truth. According to senior officers who were eyewitnesses to part of the drama, Lt. Col. Langlais, flanked by the fully armed commanders of the paratroop battalions at Dien Bien Phu, entered de Castries' office and bluntly told him that henceforth the effective command of the fortress would be in his own hands, but that as far as the outside world was concerned de Castries would retain the appearance of command and would serve as an intermediary between the paratroop commanders and Hanoi.

It is odd that until now, this situation, which was well known to a fairly sizeable group of senior officers both at Dien Bien Phu and in Hanoi, has remained publicly unmentioned. None of the published works on Dien Bien Phu mentions it, although Langlais, at the end of his own book, makes a significant reference to the scope of his own responsibilities which would be excessive were it not for the fact that he had *de facto* command of Dien Bien Phu after March 24:

> Though I was only a simple paratroop lieutenant colonel at the beginning of the battle, *I had directly under my orders 10,000 men;* but nobody in Hanoi or elsewhere sought to deprive me of that handsome command. It would nonetheless have been easy to get to Dien Bien Phu with a parachute on one's back; or, up to March 29, even by landing there. I was in the damned valley up to my neck and I stayed in it to the bitter end.[23]

In view of the subsequently excellent personal relations between Langlais and de Castries, it is difficult to describe what happened on March 24 as a "mutiny" or a *Putsch* by what some staff officers called the "paratroop Mafia" or "Langlais' Brain Trust." Actually, there was no formal take-over of constituted authority, nor did de Castries protest the change. To paraphrase a senior officer who was there, GAP 2 logically took the place of a command organization that no longer existed, and exercised prerogatives whose effective usage the commander of the fortress had ceased to exercise.

Only one senior officer, the newly arrived Col. Voinot, attempted to resist the reorganization of the command structure rammed through by Langlais. Langlais walked into the map room and allegedly threw a glass of whiskey in Voinot's face and told him, and everyone else within earshot, to come outside and settle the matter man to man if he disagreed with the reorganization. No one did. Langlais later apologized to Voinot for the rashness of his gesture and the two worked together in harmony until the end of the battle. The same courtesy and friendship prevailed between Langlais and de Castries. To the end, Langlais remained, along with Lemeunier and Voinot, one of de Castries' nighttime bridge partners.

The reorganization of the Dien Bien Phu command[24] established the following structure: Langlais was now in charge of the whole defense, and Lemeunier was his deputy. Dien Bien Phu itself was subdivided into two subsectors whose limit was the Nam Yum. The key eastern subsector (Dominique and Eliane) was directly commanded by Langlais from the headquarters of Mobile Group 9, while Lt. Col. Voinot took command of the western subsector (the lowland part of Dien Bien Phu) from the headquarters of the former command post of Col. Trancart's northern sector. Trancart, whom Langlais blamed for the loss of Gabrielle and Anne-Marie, remained at the disposal of de Castries. Séguin-Pazzis retained command of GAP 2 while the tough Bigeard became Langlais' deputy for "intervention," *i.e.*, the counterattacks. Langlais reserved for himself the use of the tanks and the quad-fifties. All counterattacks had to be cleared with him.

The mission assigned to the western subsector was to maintain the integrity of the lowland strongpoints—to "give itself air during the day and ears at night" (that is to stay on the offensive during the day and to be watchful at night) and to insure the protection of the airstrip and of the aircraft attempting to land on it.

Signed by de Castries himself, this order was one of the last written documents to reach Hanoi before Dien Bien Phu was sealed off forever. From the marginal comments made by Cogny's headquarters, it was obvious that its real portent was misunderstood. To be sure, Hanoi was surprised by Langlais' increased responsibility, but only for bureaucratic reasons, such as the fact that in his functions of commander of the eastern subsector, Langlais would theoretically be under the command of Lemeunier, his own deputy junior in rank by one year. The staff noted that the order did not spell out any combat directives for the eastern subsector, which Langlais was to command himself, and an unknown hand wrote on the original document: "Langlais himself must have written that order." The comment, as Langlais was to tell this writer ten years later, was correct.

It is difficult to this day to assess what effect the change of command had on the battle itself. Looking back from the distance of a decade,

Séguin-Pazzis felt (and Langlais was to confirm this to a certain extent in his own writings) that de Castries exercised a beneficial influence on the conduct of the defense. Between Langlais, who saw salvation only in staying constantly on the offensive no matter how high the cost, and de Castries, who saw salvation in lasting long enough to be rescued from the outside, the battle alternated between obstinate defense, as best shown in the ensuing battle for the Huguette positions, and determined offensive, as in the battles for the Eliane hills. A constant example of the compromises between de Castries and Langlais was the use of flare ships (aircraft dropping parachute flares) over the battlefield. Langlais often demanded that the flare ships stop their work because they interfered with "his battle," while de Castries just as insistently demanded that they continue to operate at the same time because they facilitated "his logistics." When the choice had to be made between airplane tonnage for troops or for supplies, Langlais usually opted for troops, observing that ammunition would do him no good without combatants; while de Castries, with equal justice, would argue that troops without ammunition would do little good either. In any case, the opposing forces in the battle of Dien Bien Phu were finally led by a French lieutenant colonel who, in effect, commanded a whole division, and by a Vietnamese history professor who, in effect, commanded a whole army.

The day also brought another long letter from Gen. Cogny for Col. de Castries which merely underlined the world of unreality that prevailed in Hanoi. It was another document to be on file for the historical record. In it, Cogny assured de Castries that the enemy had suffered heavy losses, was finding it difficult to find replacements for his depleted units, and was experiencing logistical difficulties particularly in the field of ammunition and rice.

"The rainy season, now close at hand," said Cogny, "will compromise his communication lines and will oppose a major obstacle of mud to the development of his field fortifications."

The exact opposite was true. The monsoon rains gave Communist supply convoys added protection against roving French aircraft and further compromised the efficacy of the French supply system, which now depended entirely on parachuted reinforcements and supplies. The Communist trenches and field fortifications around Dien Bien Phu were in every case either far higher on the mountain slopes than those of the French or at least, as south of Claudine and Eliane, at the same level with them. The Communist artillery, deeply buried in the hillsides, occupied positions that could not be weakened by waterlogging, whereas the

French dugouts and underground shelters would collapse more readily from the effects of rain than from Communist artillery shells.

Cogny reiterated his promise to de Castries of an airborne battalion, but hedged his additional promise of another airborne battle group until "the enemy, disintegrating from or exhausted by your aggressive resistance, shall abandon the game." As for the problems of airborne resupply for Dien Bien Phu, Cogny felt that even continued occasional landings of aircraft, particularly light aircraft and helicopters from Muong Sai, would remain feasible.

Cogny also suggested that the enemy's attack plans on Dien Bien Phu be kept off balance as much as possible and that his intelligence about the French order of battle be confused by the building of phony artillery positions and the periodical displacement of field pieces to alternate gun pits.

When this order reached Dien Bien Phu, the landing of helicopters and light aircraft had become nearly impossible. The last C-47 to take off intact from Dien Bien Phu became airborne on March 27. The last helicopter or light aircraft left the valley on the last day of the month. As for the digging of phony gun emplacements and confusing enemy intelligence estimates, it made little sense in a position in which every available yard of terrain was already crammed with infantry, depots and artillery pieces. Moreover, every available French infantryman and combat engineer was frantically working to maintain or improve existing field fortifications. Also, Communist observers with ordinary field glasses could read every French daytime movement like an open book, and, in any event, a steady trickle of prisoners and deserters assured enemy intelligence of a constant flow of fresh information. "And thus," continued Cogny, "you will repel the attack until the day when the [monsoon] season will make it impossible." Cogny then went on to explain to de Castries that in order to avoid strangulation he should, as a matter of first priority, try to suppress the enemy flak and should attempt offensive infantry stabs, "to push further back those too audacious artillerymen and those too enterprising infantrymen."

Cogny must have realized that the French at Dien Bien Phu would also suffer from the rains. Yet with a blitheness of style that is hard to render in translation, he recommended that de Castries transfer the center of gravity of the whole position from the lowlands west of the Nam Yum to the hill line on the east, as if the battles for blood-drenched Beatrice and the steep jungle hills to the east of Eliane had never occurred, and as though the 312th and 316th People's Army Divisions were mathematical abstractions. As for the French artillery at Isabelle, Cogny made one recommendation: since the guns were emplaced to fire towards Dien Bien Phu, it would be easy to protect them by burying them deeply in the ground in casemates. The fact that there was not a spare plank of wood available at Isabelle apparently never occurred to Gen. Cogny. Moreover, Isabelle was under constant artillery fire. Lastly, he admonished de Castries constantly to keep two full battalions in reserve, if not possibly three. This recommendation was made when Langlais had exactly one mixed company of Foreign Legionnaires and paratroopers under Capt. Philippe as his total reserve for all of Dien Bien Phu.

Cogny concluded by assuring de Castries that the full application of the directive would assure him of victory:

> You shall therefore win. You shall delay the attack, you shall win the defensive battle and you shall break out of Dien Bien Phu. You will then go over to the exploitation phase for, at the very least, you will be able to reduce the strength of your organization and to proceed with the relief of the units who will have well merited it.

The second phase of the battle was about to begin. On the morning of the 24th, the Foreign Legionnaires of the 1/2 REI had discovered Communist trenches approaching the barbed wire of Huguette 6 to a distance of barely fifty meters and had gone out with tanks to fill them in. Later in the day, the 6th BPC, supported by the tank platoon of Sgt. Ney, again proceeded with the opening-of-the-road ceremonial in the direction of Isabelle, only to be caught in yet another Communist roadblock at Ban Ong Pet. This time the Communists were ready to deal with the tanks. A well-aimed rocket from a Viet-Minh bazooka damaged tank "Posen," which had to be towed back to base.

At 1600, a transport aircraft was caught by enemy flak and crashed in a rice field. The entire crew was lost. Later, a depot of 120-mm. mortar shells was hit by enemy fire and exploded with an earth-shaking roar.

Thursday-Saturday, March 25-27, 1954

When dawn broke on the 25th of March, the Communist trenches around Dominique had grown tentacles, particularly around D1 and D6. D6 had become so precarious that Langlais decided to pull out the depleted 2nd Company of the 5th Vietnamese Parachute Battalion and to cover the area by flanking fire from the higher positions of D1 and D2. On March 24, Viet-Minh soldiers arrived on top of D6. A counterattack by 4th Company of the 5th BPVN, after a short artillery barrage, re-occupied it. On March 25, D6 was further reinforced by 3rd Company which took up a position on it to cover the flank of Maj. Tourret's 8th Parachute Assault Battalion, which was attempting to clear the approaches to D1. A fire fight ensued when the enemy attacked the paratroopers. To the south of Dominique, Guiraud's 1st BEP and the rest of Botella's 5th BPVN, supported by Ney's tank platoon, also were in the process of clearing Viet-Minh penetrations from around Eliane 4. Péraud, the French Army photographer, participated in the action and his photographs of it were probably the last French pictures to leave the valley. His scribbled notes of the day clearly indicate an improvement in the morale of the garrison:

> Assault of the trench with hand grenades—brought on a barrage of Viet-Minh grenades—firing by our tanks—terrific atmosphere! I must have some very nice photos. Ran out of 35-mm film. Two Dakotas shot down by VM antiaircraft guns . . . films [for me?] no doubt given to pilot of second shot-down plane—morale excellent . . .

Farther to the south, it was the turn of Maj. Nicolas' Moroccans to open the road to Isabelle. Near Ban Loi they found Viet-Minh bunkers, and Warrant Officer Carette's tank platoon was summoned. It finally took the arrival also of the tank platoon from Isabelle to reopen the road to the south.

Far to the north where the airfield lay, an endless desert in comparison to the cramped quarters of the rest of Dien Bien Phu, an Air Force detachment under M/Sgt. Peyrac frantically inched its way forward in broad daylight to one of the transport planes which had been shot down but which had not burst into flames. Of the six men in the rescue squad, four, including Peyrac, were wounded by Communist shell fragments. Yet they succeeded in pulling the dazed crew out of the aircraft before the Communist gunners destroyed it.

Beyond the airfield, Huguette 6 and 7 were leading their solitary existence three kilometers from the center of Dien Bien Phu, and separated from it by the lonely expanse of the airfield. Viet-Minh trenches were now closing in. In fact, the situation had become so critical that on the 26th, two companies of the 1st BEP, reinforced by the two full tank platoons, counterattacked to fill in the trenches strangling Huguette 6. On the 27th, H7 had to be cleared in the same manner by the T'ai mountaineers of 2nd BT under Maj. Chenel. Unlike the T'ai of 3rd BT who had abandoned Anne-Marie a week earlier, 2nd BT was still firm. However, its position on the inner flanks of Eliane had never been as exposed as that of 3rd BT, and it had not been as exposed to Communist propaganda as 3rd BT.

But while the battle ground on; so did the smaller wheels of military bureaucracy. Very little that happened at Dien Bien Phu gave rise to humor, but two amusing events took place on March 26. The French Army in Indochina, in deference to its many Moslem servicemen, had for years run a small airlift to the Moslem holy city of Mecca. Since, according to the Moslem faith, a man who had accomplished the *Hadj* (pilgrimage) was assured of a partial remission of his sins in the here-after and of the consideration of his fellow soldiers and citizens in the mean-time, these pilgrimages were much sought after. It was therefore not entirely surprising when Sgt. Sadok, a Moroccan from the 31st Engineers, received a routine telegram informing him that he had received leave to go immediately on a pilgrimage to Mecca. Grenier, another sergeant in the same battalion, had a different problem. His term of enlistment had expired and, in view of the situation at Dien Bien Phu, he was not of a mind to extend it. He therefore refused to re-enlist. The French Army, on the other hand, found it difficult to repatriate him. Never-theless, the sergeant adamantly refused to sign up. He thus became the only "civilian" doing combat duty there. The personnel section in Hanoi sent a bureaucratic radio message to the Engineers on March 26 to the effect that although "Sgt. Grenier has arrived at the term of his enlistment; his refusal to extend his tour of duty does not seem to call for administrative action right now." The unfortunate man received a shell fragment in his chest on April 16.

Finally, that day, the 155's of the counterbattery scored heavily: three out of four 75-mm. howitzers of a Communist battery, dubbed by the French "YJ" and situated two kilometers east of Isabelle, were destroyed by direct hits. There would be few such lucky hits throughout the battle.

Meanwhile, the massacre of transport planes continued. One *Dakota* piloted by Capt. Boeglin was shot down west of Huguette on the evening of March 26, but its crew was saved. The aircraft itself burned like an enormous funeral pyre for hours. On March 27 at 0700, Capt. Dartigues succeeded in landing his *Dakota* No. 267 and taking on a full load of wounded. He brought them safely to Hanoi and imme-diately started for a second run, only to be shot down at 1000 on the approach run across Eliane. The whole crew perished. At 1750 another *Dakota* from Transport Group 2/63 "Sénégal" plowed into the ground west of Claudine. It burned like a torch. Sergeant Peyrac and his

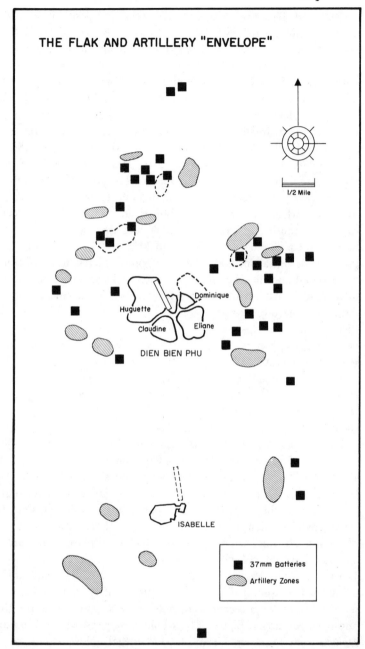

rescue crew raced under shellfire across the airfield, the barbed wire, and the mines around Claudine, dragging their carbon dioxide fire extinguishers, but they were too late. The entire crew had perished. Later that evening, one last transport aircraft, piloted by Capt. Bourgereau, managed to land at Dien Bien Phu and to pick up nineteen wounded who had been waiting anxiously in the drainage ditch near the airfield's taxi stand. The plane took off in a rain of mortar shells. Its crew (which, like all the ambulance aircraft in Indochina, included a French Women's Air Force nurse) did not know it, but theirs was the last flight to take off safely from the fortress.

That evening two men made decisions about the tragic situation of the transport aircraft over Dien Bien Phu. One of them was Col. Nicot, the Air Transport commander in Hanoi; the other was Col. de Castries. Nicot fired off a message at 1930 to Gen. Lauzin, the commander-in-chief of the French Far Eastern Air Force:

> It is hardly necessary to insist on the necessity of stopping that carnage. But the air crews, in addition to an obvious physical fatigue, have suffered a psychological shock. . . . It is necessary to immediately stop low-level parachute drops and I have given the order to do so as of tonight.

For the C-47's, this meant that the daytime parachute drop altitudes went from 2,500 feet to 6,500 feet and later, as enemy flak became even more proficient and largely equipped with Soviet 37-mm. guns, to 8,500 feet. In turn this meant that parachuted loads had to be equipped with powder-train delays whose small explosive charge would open the parachutes at a pre-set altitude. The first experiences with the delayed drops were disastrous because complete loads either fell into enemy hands or the delay failed to open at all and the cargo impacted inside Dien Bien Phu like a bomb.

De Castries also had to face the fact that Dien Bien Phu was going to die, and die rapidly, if he did not succeed in temporarily silencing the enemy's antiaircraft fire which was reducing his whole logistical support system to a shambles. It is not clear whether de Castries acted on his own initiative or upon an admonition from Hanoi, but on March 27, at 1900, he called in Maj. Bigeard for the planning of a limited offensive against a nest of Communist light flak near Ban Ong Pet, about 2.5 kilometers west of Claudine.[25] With gentlemanly understatement, de Castries said to the barrel-chested major whom he did not yet know too well:

"My little Bruno [Bigeard's alias from French resistance days], you will have to go out and get me that Viet flak out west."

"When do you want it?"

"Tomorrow. You have *carte blanche*. Take everything you need and orchestrate the business any way you wish."

"All right," said Bigeard. "I'll do it, but I would like to make a few remarks: You'll have to accept some pretty serious losses among the best units you've got; and you are leaving me very little time to put together in black-on-white an operation of that nature which has to be precise, delicate, and rapid and where everybody has to be fully briefed on his own mission."

Bigeard settled down in a corner of the headquarters command post (his own command post not being equipped for such mundane affairs as making plans and writing field orders) and worked frantically for the next six hours. At two o'clock in the morning of Sunday, March 28, he was ready to brief the unit commanders who would participate in the operation four hours later.

Sunday, March 28, 1954

The briefing held by Bigeard at 0200 was remarkable in many ways. He was a major commanding a battalion, who was "orchestrating" an operation involving five battalions, requiring air support that was to come from bases more than 200 miles away, and the firepower of more than two full artillery battalions commanded by a full colonel. Yet this was Bigeard and the place was Dien Bien Phu, and no one seemed to mind. In fact, at Dien Bien Phu all senior officers had decided, by common accord, to do away with the normal military formalities and to call each other not only by their first names but also by the familiar French *tu*. Bigeard's briefing included not only the men directly concerned with the operation—the three airborne battalion commanders, Tourret from the 8th Assault; Guiraud from the 1st Foreign Legion Paratroops; Capt. Thomas who now commanded the 6th BPC since Bigeard had been appointed commander of the counterattack forces; and Clémençon, commanding the 1st Battalion, 2nd Foreign Legion Infantry on Huguette—but also the gentle and scholarly-looking Capt. Hervouët, who still commanded his tank squadron with both arms swathed in plaster casts; Col. Vaillant, who now commanded the artillery after Piroth's suicide and, finally, the cadaverous-looking (for he was badly afflicted with amoebic dysentery) Air Force Maj. Guérin.

The mission would be difficult. A regiment of the 308th Division—probably the combat-experienced, tough Regiment 36—had been assigned to the defense of the flak positions. In the dishpan-flat terrain on the west, salvation would lie in total surprise: a short but murderous artillery barrage which the advancing infantry and tanks would follow as closely as possible, a rapid exploitation of the resulting chaos, and an equally quick withdrawal before the enemy could adjust his fire to the new situation. For, as the French had discovered, the only remaining weakness of the Communist forces lay in their relatively inexperienced artillery commanders who were not yet capable of shifting targets rapidly. Also, since the positions at Dien Bien Phu were stationary, the Communists had dug in most of their fieldpieces so that they would cover a given sector and could not rapidly be trained elsewhere if the situation required it.

Bigeard's plan was simple. The 6th and the 8th Battalions would be on their line of departure in 0530 and ready to jump off at 0600, with the 8th facing Ban Ban and the 6th directly opposite Ban Ong Pet, having approached the target to a distance of 300 meters. Clémençon's Foreign Legionnaires would stand by at 0500 in a back-up position. The 1st BEP would remain in reserve at 0800 on a five-minute alert basis. The artillery command had guaranteed Bigeard the use of twelve 105's, two 155's, and twelve 120-mm. mortars to deliver a massive rolling barrage, in five-minute waves, as of 0600. At 0615, one half of the artillery fire would begin to concentrate on the frontage of the 8th Assault Battalion and the other half on that of the 6th BPC. Tank platoon Carette would support the advance of the paratroopers and the Air Force fighters, on call as of 0630, would seal off the battlefield and pin down the Viet-Minh reserves.

The whole operation came off without a hitch. To be sure, the Air Force fighters were delayed until 0900 by the extremely low clouds and poor visibility, but they very effectively attacked the two villages and the hills behind them. The enemy's resistance around Ban Ong Pet was stiff enough temporarily to pin down the 6th BPC. Then Préaud and his tank platoon from Isabelle joined the fray and slammed into the southern flank of the Communist position. Two of the tanks were slightly damaged by Communist bazookas, but by 1500 the wild melee was over and the paratroopers looked around in amazement. The enemy was retreating in disorder and the French remained masters of the battlefield. Moreover, the bodies of 350 Vietnamese Communists littered the area, leaving intact five 20-mm. antiaircraft cannon, twelve .50-caliber antiaircraft machine guns, two bazookas, fourteen automatic rifles, and hundreds of other weapons.

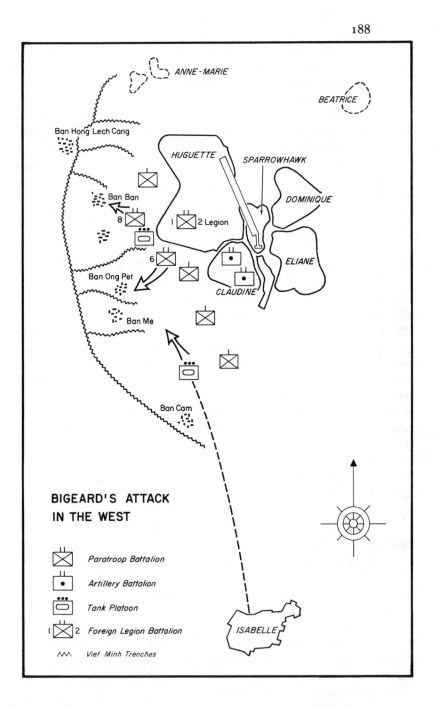

ANNE-MARIE

BEATRICE

Ban Hong Lech Cang

HUGUETTE

SPARROWHAWK

DOMINIQUE

Ban Ban

8

1 ⊠ 2 Legion

6

ELIANE

Ban Ong Pet

CLAUDINE

Ban Me

Ban Cam

**BIGEARD'S ATTACK
IN THE WEST**

⊠ *Paratroop Battalion*

⊡ *Artillery Battalion*

⊟ *Tank Platoon*

1 ⊠ 2 *Foreign Legion Battalion*

∧∧∧ *Viet Minh Trenches*

ISABELLE

Ten prisoners were later to tell their captors of the surprise and shock the enemy had experienced at seeing the supposedly demoralized French go over to the attack. Yet there weren't enough troops to hold and defend the conquered ground at Ban Ong Pet and Ban Ban, particularly since it was overshadowed by the hill line behind it. Soon after three o'clock, Bigeard gave the order to withdraw to the main line of resistance. While the boost in morale had been tremendous (even the defeatists in Hanoi who, for days, had been going around saying that the garrison was *foutue*—"cooked"—took heart again), the price of the small sortie had been heavy. The 6th BPC had had two lieutenants (Vigouroux and Jacob) and fifteen paratroopers killed and one officer and thirty-five paratroopers wounded. The 8th Assault had lost three paratroopers killed and four officers and fifty paratroopers wounded. With the other casualties suffered by the garrison during the relative lull during the second week of fighting at Dien Bien Phu, the total still amounted to 522, or almost a full batallion. These losses, despite the reassurances of Gen. Cogny, had not been made up by parachuted replacements. French Intelligence officers reported a total of 284 enemy dead for the week prior to the battle of Ban Ong Pet. Hence, the losses had evened out numerically, but the Communists had five times as many troops on the line as the French,[26] and were in a much better position to replace their losses.

Far to the north, where 1st Company of the 5th BPVN had held Huguette 7 under constant enemy harassing fire since March 18, its commander, Lt. Rondeau, was seriously wounded that day—he would stubbornly hang on to life until after the end of the siege—and replaced by Capt. Bizard, who had been parachuted into Dien Bien Phu on March 26. The situation had seriously deteriorated at the two northern Huguettes covering the airstrip. On March 27 Maj. Séguin-Pazzis had been forced to lead the better part of the 1st BEP and the 5th BPVN in a full-scale clearing operation, in the course of which 3rd Company of the Vietnamese Paratroopers, reinforced by a company of the 8th Assault, pushed as far north as the ill-fated ford at Ban Ké Phai on the road to Gabrielle.

At 0200 of March 28, Air Force Capt. Tournois of Transport Group 1/64 "Béarn" planned to take off from Hanoi's Gia-Lam Airport as command pilot on aircraft *Delta Coca* No. 434. At the last minute, Tournois was replaced as senior pilot by Maj. Blanchet, the deputy commander of Group 1/64. This was a familiarization flight for Blanchet, since he had not yet participated in night landing missions of ambulance aircraft. The rest of the crew was already aboard including the Women's Air Force nurse, Geneviève de Galard-Terraube, when Blanchet climbed into the craft. As they approached the Dien Bien Phu strip at 0345, the enemy flak was at its most violent. In all likelihood, the ground personnel did not expect another landing that night for the few minute landing lights which were usually left on to guide incoming aircraft were turned off. Blanchet nonetheless succeeded in landing his plane safely, but as it rolled toward the taxi stand it veered into a barbed-wire entanglement and developed an oil leak. Unable to work at it in total darkness and aware that the Communists would start firing at the aircraft at first light, the mechanics hit upon an ingenious stratagem: they pushed a wrecked C-47, with which the Communist artillerymen already were familiar, to the location of the disabled *Delta Coca,* and put the *Delta Coca* in the place of the wrecked craft. They hoped that the Communists would concentrate their fire on the wreck and leave the new arrival alone until it could be repaired. The ruse almost worked. During the early morning hours the French assault on Ban Ong Pet diverted Communist attentions to other matters. But the heavy fighting also prevented the mechanics from working on the aircraft. By noon, however, the hole in the oil tank was patched up. Twenty-five stretcher cases were again lying in the mud of the nearby airfield drain along with their nurse. Then the moment of truth came: the engines of the aircraft had to be started for testing and a brief warm-up before the wounded could be loaded. The starting of the engines and the turning of the propellers could not be hidden even from the most obtuse Viet-Minh artillery observers. With unerring precision, the shells began raining down on the aircraft. At 1300, hit by the third shell, the aircraft began to burn. Fortunately, Maj. Blanchet and his crew escaped the burning plane.

On hearing this news, Capt. Tournois attempted to land at Dien Bien Phu the following night, but heavy rainstorms prevented a landing. During the next night, the second enemy assault on Dien Bien Phu began. Major Blanchet became the deputy to Dien Bien Phu's Air Controller, Maj. Guérin. The other crew members joined Capt. Charnod's Air Force detachment with 4/1 BEP. The nurse, Geneviève de Galard-Terraube, joined Maj. Grauwin's hospital. She was a modest girl, with blue eyes, brown hair, and a ready smile. To her, Dien Bien Phu was just an ambulance mission that aborted. No one there ever called her the "Angel of Dien Bien Phu." This name was given to her by rear-echelon press agentry. To the men at Dien Bien Phu she was known as Geneviève.

VI

Strangulation

Monday, March 29, 1954

The enemy now has adopted a new defensive system: He has abandoned the system of isolated strongpoints in favor of large centers of resistance, whose attack will require the commitment of important forces.

Henceforth, the battalion shall not fight alone but within a larger unit in cooperation with other friendly elements. Its successes or failures will have great repercussions throughout the whole regiment, the whole division and sometimes upon the whole campaign. . . .

These were the first few lines of the new field manual on the attack of fortified positions by infantry battalions issued by the Viet-Minh high command shortly before the Dien Bien Phu offensive.[1] The manual also stated that in order to attack such positions an over-all manpower superiority of three-to-one and a firepower superiority of five-to-one were necessary.

After the opening of the first breach one must immediately penetrate into the interior of the enemy fortified system and hold that penetration to the bitter end . . . with a sufficient concentration of forces on the principal point of effort we are assured of being able to press home the attack to our advantage, no matter how strong the enemy defense is, thanks to successive assault waves.[2]

That would be Gen. Giap's attack tactic throughout the battle of Dien Bien Phu. It had already been used on Beatrice and Gabrielle. Now it was going to be employed on a large scale in what later became known as the Battle of the Five Hills—Dominique 1 and 2, and Eliane

1, 2 and 4. Ever since March 20, Maj. Nicolas' Moroccans had had difficulty in keeping patrols and outposts on top of Old Baldy and Phony mountains. Many men on patrols simply disappeared, or the next patrol found their bodies stabbed and stripped of their weapons and equipment. The French frequently had toyed with the idea of occupying Old Baldy in strength, but the idea was finally abandoned for lack of building materials and troops. In any case, the French artillery commander had assured de Castries that the enemy could be permanently kept off these strategic outlying hills by firepower alone. This proved to be another mis-calculation.

Lieutenant Colonel Langlais instinctively felt that Bigeard's attack had proven French strength and firepower in the lowland areas. He therefore believed the main Communist effort would be redirected to the French hill positions. These were now all located east of the Nam Yum. If this high ground fell, the fate of Dien Bien Phu would be sealed. Hence, a desperate last-minute effort was made to reinforce the hill-line. Dominique was reduced to its strongpoints 1, 2, 3, and 5 (D6 no longer being held), while Dominique 4 became an independent strongpoint held by the 8th Assault Battalion of Maj. Tourret along with one platoon of the quad-fifties. This new strongpoint was baptized *Epervier* (Sparrowhawk). At the southernmost point of Dien Bien Phu's main position, Claudine 6 had been detached from the main position and had been transformed into a separate strongpoint known as Juno. It was placed under the command of Maj. Guiraud and held by a mixed bag of the 1st BEP's Foreign Legion paratroopers, White T'ais, the remaining two quad-fifties of Lt. Redon, and, finally, the Air Force detachment of Capt. Charnod.

But it was the Elianes that had received the heaviest reinforcements. In addition to the whole 1/4 Moroccan Rifles which held Eliane 1, 2 and 3 (the latter also being defended by two companies of T'ai auxiliaries under Lt. Martinez), there were now two companies and the head-quarters of the 5th BPVN on Eliane 4. In the small plain between the river and the hill-line, a large part of the 6th BPC lay in reserve behind E4 and E12, E10 was held by a company of the 8th BPC under Capt. Pichelin, E11 was held by a company of Combat Engineers, and E12 was held by parts of 2nd BT.[3]

The elite airborne battalions had lost much of their combat strength in the counterattacks of late March and no one knew whether the tribes-men of 2nd BT would melt away if they were given the chance. But the Algerian and the Moroccan battalions were counted as solid units, although the Moroccans did not think too highly of the Algerians on their left flank.

This seemed also to be the opinion of the new commander of the whole central redoubt, Lt. Col. Langlais. The loss of an Algerian battalion on Gabrielle probably influenced them more than the loss of a Foreign Legion battalion on Beatrice affected the remaining Legionnaires. Therefore, Langlais decided to stiffen the key positions of the Five Hills with paratroops from the reserves. Fourth Company of the 5th BPVN was alerted to reconnoiter D1 in preparation for relieving a company of the 3/3 RTA on the following day. A company of the 6th BPC moved to Eliane 4, now held by Capt. Botella and two of his companies.

That day the monsoon rains fell heavily on the valley, hampering supply drops and aerial reconnaissance. Isabelle's garrison succeeded once again in breaking through to Dien Bien Phu with an ambulance truck carrying five seriously wounded patients for the main hospital. ACP No. 3 was now cleared of serious cases, but Grauwin had 175 seriously wounded men awaiting an air evacuation that never came. Nor did the men on Isabelle know that there would be no more convoys to Dien Bien Phu. The siege ring had become too tight.

As night came and the artillery fell silent, Langlais and Vadot climbed out of their dugout for a breath of fresh air. Beyond Claudine and Huguette, the sky still glowed red—not from the setting sun but from the napalm fires smoldering in the forest. But beyond the Five Hills, to the east, an incredible sight confronted the two officers: like thousands of glowworms, torch-bearing columns of enemy soldiers or porters could be seen leaving the valley. To this day it is not clear whether they were coolies who had brought supplies forward or soldiers relieved from duty in the first line. Either way, the strange ceremony was a radical departure from the enemy's usual caution and concern with concealment.

"Look," said Vadot to Langlais, "they're getting the hell out of here. They're going to steal our battle away from us."

Tuesday-Wednesday, March 30-31, 1954

The night of March 29 was calm save for light harassing fire by enemy artillery. Rain fell continuously. The troops in the open trenches of Claudine and in the drainage ditch of the airfield began a forty-day trial of knee-deep mud, wet clothes, and human excrement. Combat rations were eaten cold.

Shortly before dawn, Lt. Thélot, who commanded a platoon on Huguette 7, had gone 150 meters north of the position for the almost daily routine of flushing the enemy from the trenches dug during the night. He and his men had been in the habit of leaving some mines and booby traps for the Viet-Minh to locate and defuse during the evening, but this time the work was proceeding with greater difficulty than usual. Apparently the Viet-Minh were learning from experience. They zeroed in several 120-mm. heavy mortars on their own work site, which was also covered by the direct fire of a 57-mm. recoilless rifle. Nevertheless, Thélot once again succeeded in his mission and returned to Huguette 7 at 0900 with only a few slightly wounded men.

The calm continued throughout the day, with the rain hampering the enemy flak and the French supply planes in about equal measure. The antiaircraft did not hit any of the planes, but the planes misdropped many of their supply loads. Langlais was worried, feeling that the situation at Dien Bien Phu was totally misunderstood in Hanoi. He therefore decided, with de Castries' agreement, to attempt to hitch a ride on one of the ambulance planes which was supposed to land that night. Langlais would see Cogny in Hanoi and obtain firm commitments for the all-out defense of Dien Bien Phu. He would fly back and parachute in on the following day.[4] The plan never materialized. The battle would be fought with what was at hand.

Langlais now decided to pay one last personal visit to each of the eastern strongpoints from north to south. At the headquarters of the Algerian battalion, he found the commander, Captain Jean Garandeau, down with the flu but confident that he could withstand even a sizable attack. Langlais went along with him until he discovered that parts of the flanks of D2 were held by T'ai auxiliaries, and D5 by elements of the 2nd BT. Langlais exploded in fury and ordered Garandeau immediately to replace the T'ai unit with his own regulars. He found the Algerians downtrodden and soggy in the rain. They did not inspire confidence. Yet there was nothing Langlais could do about it now. He could not commit his precious paratroop reserves to holding the line and then risk finding himself without reliable troops for immediate counterattacks.

Langlais felt much better about Eliane. It had three battalion commanders present and paratroopers interspersed with the Moroccans. The vital cornerstone position of the entire defensive system, Eliane 2, appeared well defended. Nicolas, the commander of the 1/4 Moroccan Rifles was well situated in the concrete cellar of the French Governor's house. The ruins of the house, it will be remembered, had been used to build some of the works of E2. With its steep sides, the hill seemed almost unclimbable. The headquarters strongpoint dominated a flat stretch of terrain connecting it with the southeastern end of the hill. This flat stretch had been dubbed the *Champs-Elysées*. What concerned Langlais about the southern part of Eliane 2 was that it came fairly close to Old Baldy, whose round back to a great extent hid what went on behind it. At the same time, the French had been forced to abandon the patrolling of Phony Mountain. As the French artillerymen had predicted, the Communists never succeeded in establishing themselves *on top* of Phony Mountain. Instead, they had burrowed long tunnels right *through* it. The result was that while nothing changed on the observable surface of the hill, it had become a veritable honeycomb of Communist automatic weapons and recoilless rifles. On E2 also, Langlais wanted to make certain that the best available men were in the forward positions. He decided to reinforce the 2nd Company, 1/4 Moroccan Rifles, of Capt. Nicod with a company of tough paratroopers from the 1st BEP. A first platoon from Lt. Lucciani's company arrived late in the afternoon, looked at Old Baldy looming close by, then looked with utter disgust at the shallow trenches dug by the Moroccans. They immediately began to dig deep. The going was slow, however, as the hill contained just about the only rocks available around Dien Bien Phu.

With the forces at his disposal, Langlais had done his best. The key strongpoints had been provided with at least a thin veneer of first-class troops. The bulk of the paratroop reserve now was on the eastern side of the Nam Yum and would not have to cross its bridges under fire. Ney's tank platoon was ready to go into action, and even the quad-fifties from Juno had registered their redoubtable eight barrels from a thousand meters away on the flanks of E2. By 1800, orders had been given to the battalions to see to it that all men received warm food that evening and that the food be brought to the men before 1800. On Dominique, this schedule was being strictly adhered to. On D1 food was being distributed and the paratroopers from 4th Company, 5th BPVN, were in the process of moving in with their weapons and equipment to take the place of the Algerian company there. The men were bunched up in the communications trenches collecting their equipment and other paraphernalia. This was the precise moment that the murderous Communist artillery barrage began to land on all the Dominiques, Elianes, and the Headquarters area. The battle for the Five Hills had begun.

Within a few minutes, the world seemed to be coming apart on top of Dominique and Eliane. The assault waves of two Communist divisions began to follow the rolling barrage. Lieutenant Reboul's 2nd Foreign

Legion Medium Mortar Company on D1 took heavy casualties before its gunners could fire their first volley.

It was the final hour for D1 and D2. Thanks to its careful preparatory work, the enemy infantry emerged from its approach trenches and blasted its way through the mine fields and barbed wire so rapidly that the prearranged French defensive fires fell far beyond the Communist assault waves. On D1, the Algerians and T'ai partisans disintegrated. In order to stop the panic, the commander of the relieving paratroop company of the 5th BPVN, Lt. Martinet, ordered his men to shoot anybody who fled.[5] Completely sealed off, the paratroopers, the Algerian noncommissioned officers, and the survivors of the mortar company fought on to the last man. Their sacrifice against an enemy at least ten times more numerous bought time for the rear area of Dominique. At 2150, D1's radio fell silent.

On D2, disaster came even more swiftly. At 1900 Bigeard radioed Langlais, who was following the battle from Gaucher's headquarters, that the Algerians with Capt. Garandeau had broken completely and were running away in direction of the Nam Yum. Langlais had believed in the intrinsic strength of D2 and was impressed by the assurances of its commander. This now proved to be an error. Garandeau, as it behooved him, stayed in the debris of his strongpoint and disappeared with it at 2000. Tiny Dominique 5, rather symbolically held by 5th Company, 2nd BT, obviously was in no position to stop anything. Everything now hinged on D3. If it fell, the whole Eliane position would be outflanked and Communist assault troops would cross the Nam Yum River within hours and overrun the unprotected headquarters area. The battle for Dien Bien Phu would be over.

Yet, all there was on D3 in the way of infantry was yet another company of Algerians whose morale was, if anything, lower than that of the garrisons of D1 and D2. The Algerians had witnessed their compatriots' destruction and had felt the impact of Communist artillery. There was another unit on D3: the African artillerymen of Lt. Brunbrouck's 4th Battery, 2nd Battalion, 4th Colonial Artillery Regiment. With night closing in, Algerian riflemen fleeing in all directions, and the green-clad waves of Communist infantry clearly visible against the flaming outlines of Dominiques 1 and 2, the gallant gunners in their open pits depressed their fieldpieces to minimum elevation and began to fire volley after volley point-blank into the massed infantry. And a miracle happened. The 312th People's Army Division was too close for artillery support from its own pieces. The assault waves halted and recoiled from the blazing guns. Then the quad-fifties on Sparrowhawk began firing. Their murderously effective slugs began to trace fiery lines in the night sky as they began to find their mark on the slopes. The lines of Communist infantrymen stopped, wavered, and began to seek protection in the narrow valley behind D6. In their panic they ran straight into a new mine field which Langlais had laid a few days earlier. Two hundred Viet-Minh perished there.

While the battle was being contained on Dominique, Eliane was under heavy attack by the bulk of the 316th Division. At the sight of the collapse of the Algerians, the two Moroccan companies on Eliane also began to waver. By 1900 Botella reported from E4 that Moroccans fleeing from E1 were crossing his position, but that his own men were holding up well under fire. Farther to the south, Eliane 2 had been under fire since the beginning of the battle and was being plowed under by Communist artillery. The Communist recoilless rifles and heavy machine guns buried in the sides of Phony Mountain now revealed themselves with devastating effect. Almost nothing was left of the *Champs-Elysées* trenches, and by 2100 there were only a corporal and six Foreign Legion paratroopers left of the force than had dug in at the southern tip of E2 four hours earlier. At 2150 the fire suddenly lifted on E2. French flare shells spread their ghostly light over the no man's land between Old Baldy and Eliane. It was crawling with enemy infantry rising out of the ground. At 2210 there was nothing left of the French garrison in the southern half of E2. The surviving Moroccans grimly held on to battalion headquarters in the ruins of the French Governor's residence.

At 2300 Maj. Nicholas' radio on E2 ceased to answer the anxious queries from Langlais' command post. There, Langlais was fighting a complex struggle against a conflicting set of high-priority demands, since, in addition to the battle for the Five Hills, a Communist stab by elements of the 308th Division developed against dangerously exposed Huguette 7. Young Lt. Thélot and Sgt. Cloître had been killed by a direct hit of a 57-mm. shell through the porthole of their bunker. The rest of 1st Company, 5th BPVN, seemed in serious trouble as Viet-Minh infantrymen began to pour into the gap left temporarily by the silent northern bunker of H7. Langlais curtly turned down a request from Maj. Clémençon on Huguette for a company to counterattack on H7. The battle for the Five Hills had to command his attention, for if Eliane fell that night, whatever happened on Huguette would be academic.

One question remained. Should Langlais retake the lost positions immediately through night counterattacks, or should he await daylight?

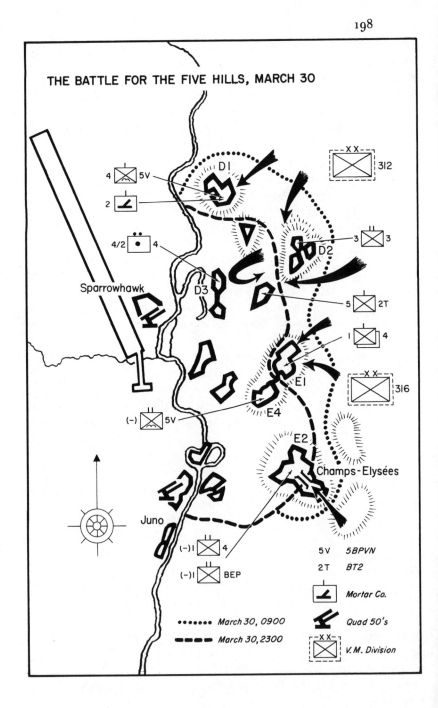

THE BATTLE FOR THE FIVE HILLS, MARCH 30

Sparrowhawk

Juno

Champs-Elysées

D1
D2
D3
E1
E4
E2

312
316

5V   5BPVN
2T   BT2
Mortar Co.
Quad 50's
V. M. Division

•••••• March 30, 0900
■ ■ ■ March 30, 2300

It is interesting, on such an occasion, to witness the tricks a man's memory can play upon him. Colonel Langlais himself affirms in his account of the battle that if Dien Bien Phu was not lost that night, it was due largely to the fact that the enemy, surprised by the rapidity with which it had reached objectives for which it expected to fight all night, had been unprepared to exploit its initial breakthrough. Langlais also felt that "a night counterattack on the lost positions was impossible. It would be done tomorrow, if there was going to be a tomorrow."[6]

The facts as described in unit diaries, by other participants, and the record of radio messages sent by de Castries' headquarters to Hanoi, seem to indicate otherwise. In actual fact, Lt. Lucciani and the remaining paratroopers of his company had begun to counterattack in the direction of the summit of E2 shortly after midnight. In brutal hand-to-hand fighting this mixed force of Frenchmen, Moroccans, and Foreign Legion paratroopers threw back the enemy and pushed him downslope along the *Champs-Elysées*. As the counterattack progressed, two tanks from Platoon Ney joined the fray, reinforced by parts of yet another company of the 1st BEP, led by Lt. Fournier. As morning dawned the haggard defenders of Eliane could look down at the carpet of enemy bodies covering the slopes all the way from Eliane to Old Baldy. That counterattack might well have failed at a particularly crucial moment shortly before midnight, when Langlais, exhausted and under the terrific strain of the emergency radio messages from five infantry battalions and the artillery, assumed that the silence of Nicolas and the 1/4 RTM on top of Eliane 2 meant that the unit had been destroyed. In actual fact, there seems to have been a temporary error in wave-length setting, for while Langlais could not hear Nicolas, the latter was heard very clearly by Bigeard sitting in a foxhole on Eliane 4. Fortunately, Bigeard listened in both on the channel of E2 and on Langlais' command channel, where around midnight he picked up Langlais' order to the artillery to keep up a continuous barrage on the center of E2, precisely where Nicolas and his Moroccans were making their last stand.

"Hold everything," said Bigeard. "This is Bruno speaking. Nicolas is still holding, and if you can't hear him, it's because your set is off channel, but he can't hold out till daybreak by himself. I am sending him one of my companies."

Bigeard thereupon dispatched Lt. Trapp and his company to Eliane 2. Not that he wasn't under attack, for E4 was now in the front line. Third Company, 5th Vietnamese Paratroops, was bearing the brunt of the battle. This company lost what it could least afford to lose: three of its French officers.[7] Its whole weapons platoon was wiped out. Finally, on H7, a surviving platoon noncom, Sgt. Tournayre, had taken over the defense of the northern bunker and, in bitter hand-to-hand fighting, had sealed the Viet-Minh breakthrough. At 0530, Huguette 7 was once again in French hands. While the casualties had been heavy (the French would lose 2,093 men between March 28 and April 2), they had once more averted disaster. It is difficult to assess now whether Col. de Castries did not play a particularly meritorious role that night of March 30-31, when, according to various eyewitnesses, it was he was decided not to wait until the morning for the counterattacks on Eliane 2 and threw in the hastily assembled paratroop and Foreign Legion companies. Apparently, the disastrous lessons of Beatrice and Gabrielle had not been lost on the French: the later the counterattack, the more time the enemy would then have to consolidate the conquered position, to cover it with his artillery fire, and also to reinforce it with fresh troops.

The biggest job still remained. Dien Bien Phu would never again be secure if Dominique 2 and Eliane 1 remained permanently in Communist hands—particularly D2 which, with its 505-meter altitude, dominated the whole position. Before collapsing from lack of sleep (he had been on his feet since dawn of March 30) Langlais, together with de Castries, Séguin-Pazzis, and Bigeard had decided to launch a full counterattack in the afternoon of March 31, including practically the whole GAP 2 (6th BPC, 8th BPC, parts of the 5th BPVN), reinforced by Maj. Grand d'Esnon's 3rd Battalion, 3rd Foreign Legion, which would make its approach march all the way from Isabelle, along with Lt. Préaud's tank platoon. Captain Hervouët's "Bisons" would also be thrown into the fight, and so would all the artillery that could be spared. The artillery had suffered frightfully under the enemy's fire. On March 30, there had been twenty-one out of twenty-four 105-mm. howitzers available, along with three heavy 155's. On March 31, there remained eighteen howitzers, two 155's, and seventeen out of thirty-two 120-mm. heavy mortars. On April 1, at 0430, when the losses of the previous day had been tabulated, Dien Bien Phu notified Hanoi that the artillery was in "very bad shape." With the destruction of three more heavy mortars during the day, its effectiveness was one half of what it had been. It had also suffered eighty-five casualties, which depleted the gun crews almost to the point where they no longer could service the available field pieces. Furthermore, the artillery on March 31 had nearly exhausted its ammunition: the seventeen 105's fired an incredible 13,000 rounds that day, while the heavy mortars fired 1,200 rounds, and the remaining 155's expended 855 shells.

March 31 brought an improvement in the weather. The rains ceased during the day and the C-119's, with their American pilots, and the French *Bearcats* and *Helldivers* began to appear in the sky. What de Castries and Langlais and Bigeard were anxiously awaiting, and upon which the success of the counterattack hinged, failed to come: airborne reinforcements. The last French parachute battalions available in Indochina were now assembled in Hanoi. They were also perhaps the best, made up of mainland Frenchmen and Foreign Legionnaires with a solid admixture of little Vietnamese, and reinforced by the remaining elements of the 35th Airborne Artillery (RALP). Despite the fact that the units had recently participated in severe combat operations in Laos, they had been reinforced by newly arrived replacements and were at full strength. The first of these battalions to be parachuted into Dien Bien Phu, the 2nd Battalion of the 1st Parachute Light Infantry Regiment (II/1 RCP), had a tradition of daring paratroop operations going back to the British red-beret Special Air Service of World War II. It was commanded by tough, aggressive Major Jean Bréchignac (known as *Brèche*, "the Breach," by everybody) who recently had established his reputation by capturing the whole headquarters of the Communist 325th Division in Laos. The next battalion slated for Dien Bien Phu was Major Hubert Liesenfelt's 2nd BEP with its mixture of ex-Nazi Germans, ex-Anarchist Spaniards, and wholly nonpolitical Vietnamese. Lastly, there was the 1st Colonial Parachute Battalion under young Captain Guy de Bazin de Bezon. This was a veteran outfit which had first landed in Indochina in February, 1947, and now was on its second tour of duty in Viet-Nam. With its 911 men, of whom 413 were Vietnamese, it was the largest airborne battalion in Indochina.

As early as the evening of March 30, de Castries had requested the parachuting of an additional battalion but had been temporarily turned down, apparently because Hanoi could not make up its mind as to whether Dien Bien Phu was worth the additional sacrifice of a battalion, or whether it should be allowed to die with what it already had. Yet no satisfactory reason has been provided for what was to happen later.

At dawn, the 3/3 Foreign Legion and Préaud's tanks left Isabelle for the planned breakthrough to Dien Bien Phu. Scarcely two kilometers north of Isabelle, they fell on the Communist blocking position at Ban Kho Lai and Ban Nhong Nhai. There was no way of making an end run around this position; to go closer to the mountains on either side of the valley would have invited sure disaster at the hands of the enemy artillery. To cut across the flooded rice fields off Road 41 would have slowed down the operation to a crawl. People's Army Regiment 57 was ready and waiting for the Foreign Legion task force when it reached the enemy position. Recoilless rifles and bazookas now disclosed themselves, and two enemy infantry pincers appeared on both sides of the battalion. By 0900 the unit was completely pinned down and tank "Neumach" had sustained a direct bazooka hit and had to be towed back. By 1150 the 3/3 Foreign Legion was fighting for its life. Far from supporting the main effort at Dien Bien Phu, the Legionnaires now had to divert artillery fire to cover their withdrawal, with Viet-Minh infantry in hot pursuit. Only the tanks prevented the retreat from becoming a disaster. Even so, the battalion lost fifteen dead and missing and brought back fifty wounded to overcrowded Isabelle. This operation confirmed the fact that breakthroughs to Dien Bien Phu would henceworth be impossible. Isabelle was alone.

The paratroop counterattack on Eliane and Dominique began at noon with Bigeard commanding the operation from E4. Anxiously, the senior commanders scrutinized the radiant sky for "Banjos" (the code name for troop-carrying airplanes) in the hope that a last-minute effort from Hanoi would give them the extra manpower needed. In the meantime, Tourret, of the 8th Assault, would be responsible for the main push on D2. Whereas Bigeard's own 6th BPC, under Capt. Thomas, and parts of the 5th BPVN would retake Eliane 1, the main weight of the counterattack fell to the 8th Assault, which had to cross almost 400 meters under fire, climbing a rise of 150 meters over the distance. They left their line of departure at 1330, with Capt. Pichelin's company in the lead. Pichelin, his American carbine flung over his right shoulder and his steel helmet overshadowing his long angular face, climbed silently upward behind the barrage of French artillery and mortar shells which now obscured the summit of D2. One of his friends used to say of him that Pichelin was "a purebred who will gallop until his heart bursts."[8] At 1430 Pichelin and his men, quickly followed by the bulk of the 8th Parachute Assault Battalion, entered the smoking hell that was the top of Dominique 2. Nothing recognizable remained of the French positions of the day before. Hundreds of Viet-Minh and French bodies covered the hill. Hit time and again by shell fragments, they had begun to rot in the sun. With the French and the Communists in close combat on top of the position the artillery on both sides ceased firing on the hill. The enemy, almost a regiment strong, immediately regrouped for the counterattack. Yet Capt. Pichelin, in his last moments on earth, had the satisfaction of knowing that the 8th Assault had retaken D2. He died a few minutes later from an enemy machine-gun burst.

On Eliane 1 the little Vietnamese of the 5th BPVN, whose heroic conduct of the last few days had made up for their failure at the ford to Gabrielle on March 15, had determinedly pushed onward to E1 along with the 6th BPC. E1 had been even more thoroughly devastated after twenty hours of continuous shelling than D2. There were no shelters, no dugouts, no barbed wire—just the pockmarks of shells, the shattered bodies, and the stench of rotting human flesh. As soon as the Communists were driven from the position, Viet-Minh counterbattery fire slammed into the reconquered hills. The paratroop battalions were winning their battle at a heavy price. It was now time for the reserves to relieve them. At 1500 Bigeard reported to Langlais that all objectives had been reached but that now reinforcements were absolutely essential to retain the gains of the day.

"No news from Brechignac?"

"Nothing from Hanoi. We don't know what the hell they are doing."

What Hanoi appeared to have been doing was attempting to make up its general-staff mind. As far as can be established, Gen. Cogny had had a social engagement, which had taken up part of his evening, and did not even bother to meet his commander-in-chief when the latter arrived at Hanoi on March 31 at 0115. Navarre was briefed on the situation during the night. According to Roy, whose views are not unsympathetic to Cogny, the latter finally arrived at his office at 0745 and gave the waiting Navarre a briefing based on the information received before midnight the day before.

"Then," Gen. Navarre later told Roy, "I exploded. I bawled him out. And he in return told me to my face all that he had been telling others for sometime."[9]

It was theoretically still possible to dispatch the II/1 RCP, on airborne alert in the paratroop barracks near Gia-Lam Air Base, save for one fact: the density that enemy daytime flak had reached over the valley. One C-47 aircraft which tried to come in low on March 31 was promptly shot down. Even the speedy Navy *Helldivers* from the aircraft carrier *Arromanches* (who were loved by the paratroopers for the risks they took, and for which they paid a higher price in lives than the Air Force) found it almost impossible to get through. During the morning of March 31, the squadron leader of Carrier Squadron 3-F, Lt. Andrieux, and his gunner, Petty Officer 2d Class Jannic, were caught in the crossfire of several flak batteries near Beatrice. Their plane was destroyed and both men were killed.

It had therefore been decided not to risk massive daytime paradrops, which could result in excessive casualties. Nevertheless, there is little doubt that Cogny's presence during the night of March 30 could have resulted in a decision to order the timely parachuting of the II/1 RCP into Dien Bien Phu before dawn of March 31. This timetable would have given it ample time for rest and orientation before the noontime attack.

The two paratroop battalions that had bled all day to hold the high ground had now reached the end of their tether. There would be no relief force. There would be no reinforcements from the rest of Dien Bien Phu, where Langlais had already scavenged everything that could be depended upon not to disintegrate as soon as it was put into the line. From his open hole on top of E4, where he had been living for the last forty-eight hours amidst the continuous crashing of mortar shells and the unnervingly persistent waterfall noise of his radio sets, Bigeard had to make the agonizing decision voluntarily to give up his conquests of the day or to lose his remaining troops and the terrain within hours.

"I've got no reserves for you," he radioed to Tourret, who was still clawing his way through the last enemy pockets of resistance atop D2, "If you can't hold it, pull out."

At 1530, the 8th Assault did just that.

There was an audible triumphant chatter as the first waves of Viet-Minh infantry again swarmed over the top of D2. Under the circumstances, any attempt to defend little D5, hopelessly overshadowed by D2, became pointless. Bigeard ordered Tourret to pull back the T'ai for a final stand on D3. There was no point in further exposing the three remaining howitzers of Lt. Brunbrouck to the oncoming enemy infantry. As dusk set in, the tall Africans lifted the heavy field pieces out of the mud, and with the help of the remaining trucks, towed them under fire across the Bailey bridge over the Nam Yum toward strongpoint Claudine. With D2 gone, E1 was again badly outflanked. At 1800 with a heavy heart, Bigeard ordered his troops to pull back to E4.

At headquarters even the indomitable Langlais was overcome by the hopelessness of the situation. There were no reserves left. Ammunition reserves, even if the remaining cannon could sustain the fantastic firing rate of the past day without bursting, were barely sufficient for another day's fighting. Moreover, on the evening of March 31, Dien Bien Phu had exhausted its hand grenades and 81-mm. mortar shells.[10] The cruelest blow came in the form of a brief message from Intelligence. General

General Gilles *(left)* and General de Castries. *(Photo French Army)*

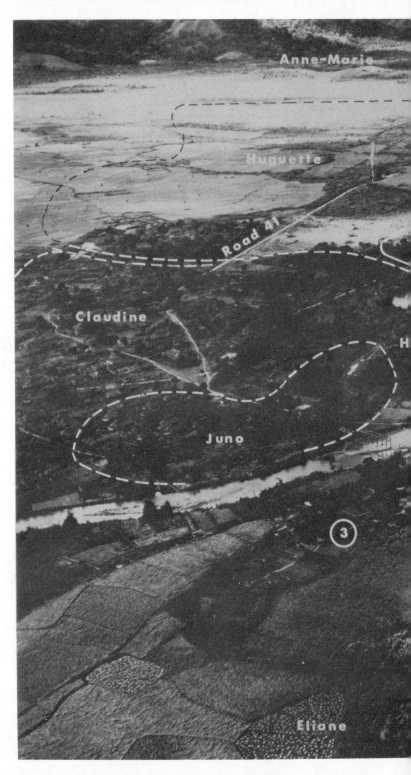

Dien Bien Phu before the battle. *(Photo French Army)*

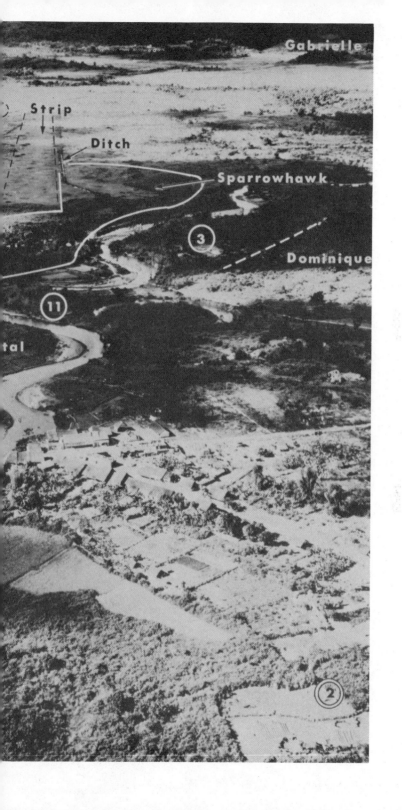

Gabrielle: the end of the beginning. *(Photo French Army)*

Eliane 2: the Governor's House disintegrates. *(Photo French Army)*

The losers: General de Castries *(left)* and General Navarre.
(Photo French Army)

The futile breakout: Operation "Regatta" to Sop Nao, December, 1953.
(Photo French Information Service)

Major Tourret of the 8th Parachute
Assault. *(Photo French Army)*

The cliffs at Dominique: home of the Rats of the Nam Yum. *(Photo French Army)*

Confidence: de Castries and Defense Minister René Pleven. *(Photo French Army)*

The American CATs flew C-119's. (*Photo French Army*)

The Strip. The control tower is at right. *(Photo French Army)*

Viet-Minh transport on the road to Dien Bien Phu.
(Photo Viet-Nam People's Army)

Planning the attack: Ho Chi Minh *(center)* and General Giap *(right).*
(Photo Viet-Nam People's Army)

A Viet-Minh bamboo bridge. *(Photo Viet-Nam People's Army)*

Bicycle transport. *(Photo Viet-Nam People's Army)*

American General O'Daniel *(right)* visits Dien Bien Phu. *(Photo French Army)*

Major Bigeard of the 6th Colonial Parachute. *(Photo French Army)*

Colonel Langlais *(center)* of the 2nd Airborne Battle Group. *(Photo French Army)*

Major Guiraud, the 1st BEP's commander *(left)*. *(Photo French Information Service)*

The Strip, with its napalm-loaded fighters. *(Photo French Information Service)*

Colonel Godard of Condor Force.
(*Photo French Army*)

Major Vadot of the Foreign Legion.
(Photo French Army)

The view from Sparrowhawk. E2 is under fire. At right, the Bailey bridge.
(Photo French Army)

e paratroop "Mafia": *(left to right)* Guiraud (1st BEP), Botella (5th BPVN), Bigeard
h BPC), Tourret (8th Assault), Langlais (GAP 2), and Séguin-Pazzis (Chief of Staff).
hoto French Army)

The beginning: the assault on Beatrice, March, 1954. *(Photo Viet-Nam People's Army)*

A few minutes' fighting: shell casings after an artillery barrage. *(Photo French Army)*

Captain Pichelin. He died for D2. *(Photo French Army)*

The last take-offs under artillery fire. *(Photo French Army)*

Lieutenant Fox *(left)* and Captain Gendre. Fox died on Gabrielle, Gendre in a Viet-Minh prison camp. *(Photo Colonel de Mecquenem)*

The deadly error: Colonel Piroth, the artillery commander who killed himself. *(Photo French Army)*

Captain Hervouët of the "Bisons." He died in a prison camp. *(Photo French Army)*

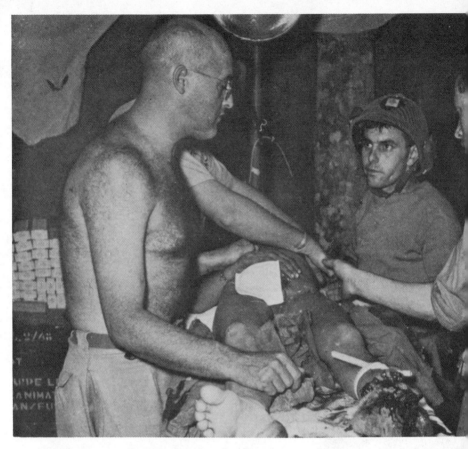

Dr. Paul Grauwin, Chief Surgeon *(left)*. *(Photo French Army)*

Entrance to the bunker hospital. A corpse awaits burial.
(Photo French Army)

The last helicopter evacuates the wounded under shellfire.
(Photo French Army)

The men who stayed for good: the cemetery at Dien Bien Phu.
(Photo French Army)

The victor: General Giap *(center)* at his CP near Dien Bien Phu.
(Photo Viet-Nam People's Army)

A Viet-Minh prisoner of war.
(Photo French Army)

General Van Tien Dung of the Viet-Nam
People's Army. *(Photo French Army)*

Giap inspects antiaircraft artillery. *(Photo Viet-Nam People's Army)*

A paratrooper dies on Eliane 2. *(Photo French Information Service)*

Counterattack: the 5th BPVN passes a napalm-burned Viet-Minh. *(Photo French Army)*

T'ai survivors of Lai Chau. *(Photo French Army)*

Enemy assault on E2. *(Photo Viet-Nam People's Army)*

Useless sacrifice: French Navy fighters on their way to Dien Bien Phu.
(Photo French Army)

Viet-Minh artillery units in victory parade in Hanoi.
(Photo Viet-Nam People's Army)

French wounded awaiting evacuation after the battle.
(Photo French Embassy, Press and Information Div.)

Viet-Minh soldiers atop de Castries' bunker. *(Photo Viet-Nam People's Army)*

Two more losers: General Salan *(left)* and General Cogny.
(Photo French Information Service)

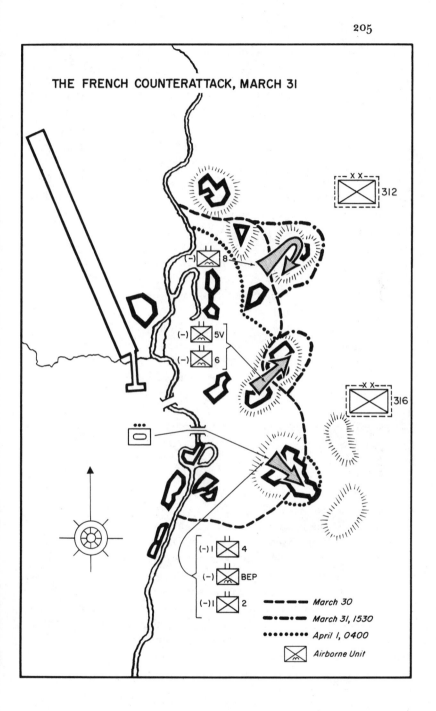

THE FRENCH COUNTERATTACK, MARCH 31

March 30

March 31, 1530

April 1, 0400

Airborne Unit

Giap had arrived in the valley and had personally taken over command of the battle from General Hoang Van Thai. A Chinese general, Li Cheng Hu, said to be Giap's adviser, was reputed to have arrived with him. The enemy had apparently decided to finish off the hill positions that night. Giap was fully aware of the crucial importance of the eastern hills. In the revised edition of his book *Dien Bien Phu,* Giap notes that "Hill A1, the most important of the Five Hills, is the last defensive bastion of the central sector and the struggle for it was particularly fierce."[11]

At about 2200, Langlais informed Bigeard that he was free to judge for himself whether the remnants of Dominique and Eliane could be held for the night. Everything now hinged on the decision of a relatively junior officer who, for the past week, had been discharging the responsibilities of a brigade commander under the worst possible conditions; and who, for the past 48 hours, had barely eaten and scarcely slept. Bigeard's answer came over the AN/PRC 10 radio circuit, on which most battalion commanders (as well as the Communists, who were fully equipped with captured radio sets) could listen in:

"Mon colonel, as long as I've got one man left alive I'm not going to let go of Eliane."

Eliane now meant Eliane 2. As night fell, the dark-green hordes of Communist infantry began to emerge from behind Old Baldy, poured over the destroyed barbed-wire entanglements of the southern end of E2, and began to mount the blood-drenched *Champs-Elysées* corridor. Lieutenant Lucciani and his mixed bag from the 1st BEP, Moroccans from the 1/4 RTM, and Lt. Rancoule's composite outfit of Legionnaires and T'ai from the 1/2 REI were ready for them. The situation now seemed hopeless. The numerical superiority of the enemy infantry (there were probably almost two enemy regiments committed to the attack) was so overwhelming that the French garrison would obviously be trampled under the wave of humanity surging at it.

At this moment, precisely at midnight of March 31, the throaty rumble of Capt. Hervouët's M-24 tanks was heard churning across the Bailey bridge and clattering over Road 41 into the hills. But the enemy was prepared. Determined 57-mm. recoilless rifle teams were waiting for the tanks. A Communist source has given us a vivid description of the tank counterattack on E2. It takes the form of a Viet-Minh forward artillery observer reading off firing indications in a simple code language that surely could have fooled no one who bothered to listen in:

"Customers right on red line. Request manager to settle ac-

counts. Two of my customers' oxen have knocked down coffeeshop.
Request boss deliver at once pumpkins, gourds, melons. . . ."
  Immediately after his calls, shells of all sizes rained on the black
swarm of infantry and roaring tanks which were climbing uphill.
  The smoke cleared off, the black enemy swarms thinned out sub-
stantially. Another attack was repelled.[12]

The Communist narrator was not exaggerating. In Sgt. Ney's leading
tank platoon the tanks "Ettlingen" and "Smolensk" were hit by 57-mm.
shells—the first, six times and the latter, twice. But both were able to continue the fight. At 0400, Hervouët himself, with both arms in plaster casts,
decided to lead the remaining tanks of Warrant Officer Carette's platoon
into combat. This time the mass of armor, small though it was, succeeded
in blunting the enemy's attack and in holding it back. But the enemy's
troops were also elite forces, and they did not yield easily. The command
tank "Bazeille" sustained a direct bazooka hit in its vitals and exploded
into flame, wounding Hervouët, Carette, and Sgt. Salaun. Tank "Mul-
house" also sustained a bazooka hit, but stayed in the fight to the end.
As dawn broke, Lucciani and his mixed bag of troops still held on to the
high part of Eliane 2. Bigeard and the rest of the 6th Colonial Paratroops still held Eliane 4 and the 8th Paratroop Assault battalion still
held Dominique 3. On top of E2, the black carcass of tank "Bazeille"
would become a landmark like the lone banyan tree which stood near
the ruins of the French Governor's residence, whose bare limbs pointed
skyward like the hand of a skeleton.
  On Huguette 7, the heavy mortars of the 312th Division had maintained the gaping breach in the northern bunker where Sgt. Tournayre
was still holding on with the survivors of Lt. Thélot's platoon. Unable to
get reinforcements, Capt. Bizard decided to exploit the apparent inability of the Viet-Minh regulars to adjust to an unforeseen situation.
Bizard pulled out from the northern and central portion of the strongpoint and withdrew into the two southern bunkers that were still left
intact. At 2300, the enemy began its assault with mechanical precision,
shelling the abandoned northern bunker and then entering the central
portion of the strongpoint, in which there was little room for maneuver.
At this moment, the French artillery plastered the area with high
explosives. As April 1 dawned, 1st Company, 5th Vietnamese Paratroops, led by a French captain, rose from its bunkers and holes and
charged with a loud yell into the remnants of the Viet-Minh force. By
1035 that morning all of Huguette 7 was again in French hands.

Thursday, April 1, 1954

April began with cloud cover over the valley. On Eliane 2, a company of the 6th BPC and Lucciani's surviving Foreign Legion paratroopers once more barreled down the *"Champs-Elysées* in an attempt to improve their hold on the hill. But the enemy was back in force and his artillery and mortars had again zeroed in on the lost terrain. The attack was stopped after the BEP had lost yet another 16 dead, 27 wounded, and 4 missing. Indeed, both paratroop battalions had suffered heavy casualties during the past week. The 6th BPC had lost 46 dead and 183 wounded, and the 1st BEP had paid for the toehold on Eliane with 40 dead, 189 wounded, and 8 missing, including five officers and eleven sergeants. Nonetheless, the counterattack permitted the recapture of a French 120-mm. mortar and the improvement of the position in the direction of E1. That day Bigeard, for valor on E2, raised Corporal René Sentenac to the rank of sergeant. Sentenac was to die four years later from an Algerian Nationalist bullet in the sands of the Sahara, still fighting alongside Bigeard.

Lieutenant Rancoule's mixed-bag Foreign Legion Company, which had suffered heavy losses on E2 the night before, returned to its home battalion on Huguette. There another mixed company under Lt. Spozio began the dangerous trek north to relieve the badly exhausted 1/5 BPVN on Huguette 7. After their victory of the previous night, the little Vietnamese paratroopers of Capt. Bizard bore themselves proudly as they marched across the whole camp under intermittent artillery fire. They had proved that they could fight just as well as the next paratroop outfit if well led and given a clear mission. At 1400, a radio message came in from outlying position Françoise, one kilometer west of Huguette, where for the past two weeks Warrant Officer Cante had commanded two small T'ai auxiliary companies. As on Anne-Marie, the T'ai, frightened by the continuous artillery fire, the constant trickle of losses on patrols, and swayed by enemy propaganda, were disintegrating. In contrast to what happened on the forward positions of Anne-Marie, on Françoise the process was gradual enough for 1st and 2nd Companies of the 1/2 REI to move out and pick up the mortars and machine guns of the little strongpoint before falling back with its French and T'ai cadres. Langlais was disgusted with the performance of the T'ai auxiliaries, although it must be remembered that they were not trained for trench warfare. He ordered that all save the noncommissioned officers be disarmed and used as coolie labor.

In fact, the T'ais were not much use as laborers, either. They melted into the maze of abandoned dugouts and trenches in the cliffs of Dominique and the banks of the Nam Yum where they joined hundreds of Algerian, Moroccan, and Vietnamese deserters who had left their units on the battle line and were now living on a separate island within the dying fortress. They made nightly forays, stealing parachuted supplies and even weapons and ammunition. They operated a brisk black market, and unit commanders in some cases had to beg them to surrender precious misdropped special foods for the hospital, or batteries for the radio sets. At one time or another, Langlais thought of actually attacking the "Rats of the Nam Yum," as they were known in the camp, but he abandoned the idea when it became clear that such a fire fight inside the camp could lead to the complete collapse of some North African and Vietnamese units who were hanging on with their French and Foreign Legion comrades to the bitter end. Every prolonged siege has known the phenomenon of "internal desertion," and Dien Bien Phu was no exception. At one point, the paratroopers and Legionnaire neighbors of the Rats of the Nam Yum neatly solved the problem of their somewhat negative contribution to the defense of Dien Bien Phu by sealing off the communications trenches around the deserters' area—thus compelling them, in case of an enemy attack, either to fight it out in order to preserve their skins, or to leave their rat holes and surface, thus insuring their destruction.[13]

At 0900 an important conference took place in Hanoi to assess the new situation at Dien Bien Phu. It included Gen. Cogny and his deputy for logistics, Brigadier General René Masson, Gen. Dechaux from the French Air Force, and several of the key staff officers of the Northern Command.

Cogny was concerned with the possibility of using once more one of the southern drop zones, such as "Simone" and "Octavie" (cf. map, p. 13), which had been suggested by Dien Bien Phu as alternates to the murderously difficult approach to the main DZ's inside the perimeter. Col. Nicot, the commander of Air Transport, argued heatedly that his planes would have to fly a prolonged course at a 300-meter altitude in the face of heavy flak and would be "massacred." And Col. Sauvagnac, in charge of all paratroop replacements, added that the same argument held for his paratroopers, who would be at the total mercy of enemy fire for a full five minutes before they could be regrouped.

Dechaux also argued against the southern DZ's for another reason: their exact location had been compromised by being described over the radio, without any attempt at concealment, by Dien Bien Phu to a command aircraft, on March 31. Instances of similar laxness in communications security were picked up in mid-April by French press observers flying over Dien Bien Phu,* and must be taken into account as one of the reasons for the incredible precision of Communist flak fire.

Sauvagnac then proposed what, to him, was "the only possible solution: the nighttime dropping of personnel by single planes coming in at irregular intervals." He argued against the massive drop of complete battalions, however, both because of the possibility of high losses and because of the "overwhelming worries [*soucis écrasants*] of the supply problem there is no point increasing it for a very uncertain advantage." Most of the other senior officers present approved the idea immediately—thus depriving Dien Bien Phu of the massive reinforcements which would have been its only salvation and which would have, on the previous day, saved the Dominiques.

In characteristic fashion, Cogny approved the opinion of his subordinates and concluded that a massive airdrop of reinforcements "could reasonably take place only outside the valley either in the form of a battalion which could attempt at joining Dien Bien Phu; or by an extension of the battle through acting on [the enemy's] rear areas." In other words, Cogny, on April 1, had abandoned all hopes of reinforcing the garrison as such, but was still willing to risk perhaps 30,000 of his troops for a diversionary operation from the Red River Delta.

Both of those decisions, the record of the conference shows, were left for the commander-in-chief, Navarre, to make. The only decision that Northern Command had taken upon itself to execute in full in the meantime was to starve the garrison of reinforcements, or to dribble them in parsimoniously. The results were obvious.

Inside Dien Bien Phu, every man willing and able to fight became a prized commodity. Units were shuffled squad by squad to reinforce existing positions. The arrival of the 1/2 REI's flame-thrower team on Eliane 2, on the night of April 1, was considered a significant reinforcement. At last, at 2030, the drone of transport aircraft was heard over the valley: the "Banjos" were bringing in the II/1 RCP.

Suddenly, all hell broke loose. The Viet-Minh flak opened up on the lumbering transports, which had to come in on a prescribed course directly over the lower end of the airstrip. The DZ had shrunk to less than 500 meters in length and barely covered the width of the taxi strip. In addition, it was cluttered with the jagged wrecks of over a dozen aircraft. And it was impossible to parachute the men faster than one half a stick

---

*Charles Favrel, in *Le Monde,* April 22, 1954, after a supply flight to the valley, spoke of his "amazement at hearing transmitted in the clear messages and orders to aircraft arriving on bombing missions or bringing in reinforcements or matériel!"

at a time. The strain on the pilots, compelled to fly a steady pattern in a narrow valley in which they were buffeted by the blasts of the friendly artillery, was incredible. While the rest of the transport group flew a holding pattern, 4th Company of II/1 RCP, under Lt. Subrégis and Warrant Officer Rebroin, plus a command element of the battalion and a gun crew from the 35th Airborne Artillery, succeeded in hitting ground at the price of seven casualties, five of them sustained in mid-air. The rest of the battalion had to return to Hanoi because the slowness of the troop drops prevented the dropping of the urgently needed ammunition and other supplies.

At Langlais' command post, the results of the air drop of that night were considered catastrophic. If men were to be fed into the fortress at that rate, there was no way to make up for each day's losses, let alone reinforce the depleted battalions. And depleted they were. The BEP and the 6th BPC had four small 100-man companies each, and that day Botella had reorganized his decimated 5th BPVN into three companies with the strength of about two platoons each. Something had to be done, and done quickly. In the view of Langlais and the other airborne officers, this meant the abandonment of the conventional rules of what constituted a proper drop zone for paratroopers. They would simply have to be dropped all over the fortified camp, regardless of barbed wire, gun positions, and radio aerials. This was to become the object of an incredibly bitter procedural fight between the combat commanders at Dien Bien Phu and the paratroop bureaucrats in Hanoi, notably the commander of the airborne replacement command, Col. Sauvagnac. To the end, Sauvagnac insisted on properly established DZ's to be used only by properly qualified paratroopers with the requisite amount of training jumps. On the other hand, Langlais insisted that basically a parachute was just a handy way of getting out of an aircraft in mid-air and could be used by any reasonably agile man who had jumped off a streetcar. Langlais turned out to be right.

The most critical attack of the day came late at night. At 2200 the 312th Division renewed its attack on unfortunate Huguette 7, whose star-shaped layout had long since disappeared under the pockmarks of Communist and French artillery. At 2330, the second prong of the attack by the 312th Division clamped on to Huguette 6. If both H6 and H7 cracked, Dien Bien Phu would lose control of its airfield. Having failed to achieve swift victory on the Five Hills, Giap was now determined to attain it by destroying Dien Bien Phu's lifeline. The battle for the Huguettes was about to begin.

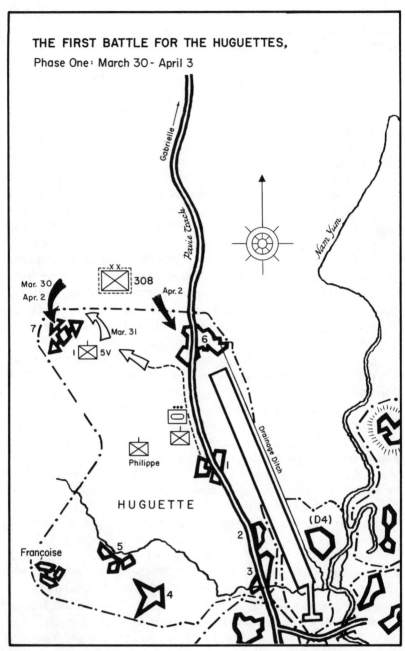

THE FIRST BATTLE FOR THE HUGUETTES,

Phase One: March 30 - April 3

On April 1, Dien Bien Phu had expended 4,500 artillery shells. Most of the ammunition dropped that day fell into enemy lines, and twenty-five per cent of the air resupply missions aborted. The improved weather permitted the French Air Force and Navy to fly ninety-nine combat missions.

Friday, April 2, 1954

As the night progressed, enemy pressure on the northern Huguettes also increased. A deserter from the Communist side (incredibly enough, there were a few Viet-Minh who still believed in the possibility of a French victory) had told the French that rumors had been going around his outfit that if the French held until April 15, the Viet-Minh would give up its attempt to crush them. Yet the evidence was that Giap was trying to be sure that he would not have to keep that promise.[14]

By 0400, swarms of enemy infantry were inside H7. This time the Viet-Minh artillery made sure that they would not again fall into another trap. All French battery positions came under intense enemy fire and the Viet-Minh *Bo-Doi* saw to it that no French infantrymen would be left over in the dugouts to offer resistance. But in bitter hand-to-hand fighting, Lt. Spozio's mixed-bag company of Foreign Legionnaires, Vietnamese and T'ai held out throughout the night in one of the corner bunkers against the full weight of more than two Communist battalions. In spite of the heavy Communist artillery fire, Maj. Clémençon had ordered Capt. Bizard to break through to H7 with whatever troops he could scrape together. These amounted to two platoons of the 1st Company, 5th BPVN, and one remaining platoon of 4th Company, 1/2 REI, which was pulled off H1 while passing through. Accompanied by three of the now badly damaged tanks of the wounded Carette, commanded by Sgt. Boussrez, the small band of 100 men began to dog-trot across the seemingly endless plain west of the airfield. It touched base on hard-pressed H6, which could still fend for itself, and then pushed on to flaming H7. There the situation was desperate. On one corner of the position one could still hear the throaty staccato of some French automatic weapons, countered by the sharp blasts of Viet-Minh recoilless rifles. Yet once more the psychological shock value of the tanks and the Legionnaires did the trick. The enemy infantry began to fall back and, much to their own surprise, the French remained in possession of H7. Lieutenant Huguenin, the deputy of Spozio, had disappeared, but in the last remaining bunker there was Spozio, seriously wounded, with thirteen survivors and three dead men.

Nothing was changed by this small victory. The abandoned hills of Anne-Marie 1 and 2, now bristling with enemy recoilless rifles and mortars, were still looking down the throat of Huguette 7, which was now so completely plowed under that it would have to be reconstructed under enemy fire and supplied with endless transfusions of infantry. But there was simply no infantry around for that purpose. From the results of the previous night's air drop, which had finally yielded four miserable "sticks" of paratroopers from the II/1 RCP, it would have been suicidal to attempt to provide enough replacements to feed both the battle of the Five Hills and that of the Huguettes. Agonizing as the choice was, Langlais made the decision to abandon H7 at 0805. The survivors withdrew with their remaining weapons. One platoon was left behind as additional reinforcement on H2. Bizard returned to the main position by noon. The first round of the battle for the Huguettes had gone to the Viet-Minh.

The Communists were also doing well in the artillery battle. At 0845, Dien Bien Phu reported to Hanoi that the gun crews at both Isabelle and Dien Bien Phu had been decimated, and that the French Air Force and Navy fighters would have to take over counterbattery fire against the Communist artillery positions near Beatrice. By then, there were exactly four serviceable 105's left at Isabelle and eight at Dien Bien Phu. After seventy-two hours of continuous fighting, their gun crews were in a catatonic state. To be sure, the artillerymen had trained a few of the infantrymen around them in the use of the field pieces, but they could not hope to replace the dying and wounded gunnery officers and noncoms who were being wiped out like flies in their open pits.

On Eliane 2, Lucciani's mixed crew of Moroccans, Legionnaires, and paratroopers was still grimly gnawing away at the Communist toehold on the *Champs-Elysées.* French artillery had finally found its mark on the Communist fire base on Old Baldy, and Bigeard released the major part of the 1st BEP for a head-on attack down the middle of E2, while French combat aircraft, including napalm-laden C-119's, successfully interdicted D1, D2 and E1. As night fell, E2 was almost entirely in French hands and what remained of the Communist infantry was back in the ravines between Phony Mountain and Old Baldy, being pounded by the French artillery. But the price of that victory had again been heavy. The 1st BEP had lost 13 dead, 9 missing and 23 wounded including its battalion commander, Maj. Guiraud. His job was now taken over by Captain François Vieulles. The 6th BPC was down to fifty per cent of its strength.

With the French back in their original position, Communist artillery

commenced an intensive bombardment of E2. Caught in the open in the
badly disorganized positions they had just retaken, the paratroopers again
had to fall back at 1930 as Communist infantry once more began to seep
over the eastern slope of E2. Finally, at 2230, the enemy artillery lifted
off E2, but the methodical gnawing of the Viet-Minh infantry continued.

At 1830, as night fell, the troop transports of Operation "Banjo" re-
appeared in the sky over Dien Bien Phu and began their slow dribbling
of reinforcements over the airfield. Bulldozers of the Engineers had
cleared off the aircraft wrecks which had littered the field. Despite the
entreaties of Langlais that it would be safer to drop the men all over the
central position than on the airfield which the Communists kept under
continuous fire, paratroop regulations continued to prevail. The result
was that the build-up of the II/1 RCP was agonizingly slow—the more
so as absolute priority had to be given to the reconstitution of the decimated artillery crews. Thirty-two men from the 35th Airborne Artillery,
led by Lieutenant J. M. Juteau, jumped into Dien Bien Phu that night,
along with seventy-four reinforcements and three equipment bags for 4th
Company, II/1 RCP, of Lt. Subrégis, which then became strong enough
to be installed as a separate unit on E3.

A stick of twelve Vietnamese from the battalion apparently was misdropped and was not heard from again. Stick No. 11 was misdropped on
top of enemy-held Dominique 2, 1,500 meters northeast of the "T" of the
drop zone, and lost all but three men. Such errors were unexplainable
that night because the DZ was clearly marked and a Navy *Privateer* had
verified the visibility of the markers; but the reason was obvious—some
pilots were more impressed by enemy fire than others. It was clear that it
would be impossible to continue the battle with a replacement rate of
fifty men a night. In fact, de Castries' staff had calculated that even with
a net drop rate of 100 men a night Dien Bien Phu could hold out for
only another fifteen days, even assuming that the enemy would not continuously stay on the offensive. How gratuitous that assumption was,
was shown that very night, as heavy pressure again developed on E2 and
then suddenly reached its paroxysm in a large-scale attack on H6. The
radio message to Hanoi sent by the command transmitter at Dien Bien
Phu at 0215 had become so routine that it was not even marked with a
special operational priority: "Last reserves committed on E2."

Saturday, April 3, 1954

The night of April 2-3 had been arduous on Huguette. Not only was
H6 severely attacked, but at 0500 Communist infiltrators blew up

Bangalore torpedoes in the outer barbed wire of H1. H1 was, for all practical purposes, almost completely encircled by Communist trenches. But there was no doubt that the object of the next big Communist attack would be H6, with its small garrison of 100 Foreign Legionnaires under Lt. Rastouil. If anything, H6 was even more exposed than H7 had been, lying as it did at the end of the completely open runway of the airstrip. For the past fifteen days the small garrison did little else but hang on to its position, counterattacking where it could and filling in Communist feeler trenches inexorably groping their way forward to the strongpoint.

The garrison of H6 also had the grim example of the fate of H7 right in front of its eyes. At noon the Viet-Minh added to the demoralization of the garrison by a small but neat bit of psychological warfare. Opposite H6, a Communist regular stood up under a white flag and informed the French that a short truce would be offered for them to come over and pick up the wounded from the battle for Huguette 7. M/Sgts. Katzianer and Sterzing volunteered to go into the Communist lines with a group of stretcher bearers to pick up their comrades. On the Communist side, there were indeed four stretchers waiting for them, but instead of the expected wounded, they contained bodies of four dead men, disfigured beyond recognition. It was perhaps the sight of those disfigured bodies which provided the final psychological shock, for that same afternoon twelve Legionnaires from H6 left their weapons behind, crawled through the barbed wire, and deserted to the Communist side. There also were minor disasters that day. The two water tanks which until now had provided the garrison with a handy supply of pure drinking water, and thus kept intestinal diseases under control, were both pierced by enemy shells, adding to the other physical miseries of the men.

At 1925 the Communist assault began against H6. Dien Bien Phu immediately requested air intervention to stand by on thirty minutes' notice. The new attack developed on the eastern flank of H6 and at first gained ground fairly rapidly. Langlais then decided to commit his last preciously-hoarded reserve: Capt. Desmont's company from the 8th Assault on strongpoint Sparrowhawk. Led by the three tanks of Sgt. Ney, the small band sprinted under heavy fire across the bare airfield, caught its breath under the illusory protection of the wreck of the C-47 transport, and slammed into the southeastern flank of the Communist spearhead of Division 312. This time the enemy was caught in the open by superior firepower and the three "Bisons" had a field day among the disorganized Communist infantry. Within thirty minutes, as suddenly as he had come, the enemy began to fall back, pursued by the fire of the tanks.

The latter remained, like faithful watchdogs, until late at night. When it was certain that the enemy had no immediate plans for another attack, they and Desmont's paratroopers began the slow march southward.

The greatest success of the night was the parachuting of an appreciable segment of Bréchignac's II/1 RCP. This followed a Homeric exchange of words between Langlais and the senior Air Force officer commanding Operation "Banjo." At 2000 the troop transports were flying a holding pattern over Dien Bien Phu awaiting the slowing down of the battle for H6 (and the extinction of the parachute flares which were being dropped in support of the counterattack). The despairing Langlais again foresaw only a trickle of the reinforcements if the Air Force insisted upon landing them only on the authorized DZ. The alternative was to ignore air-drop regulations and to dump the men over the central position itself. Langlais lit a gasoline barrel as a drop-zone marker at the edge of the Nam Yum and told the drop commander to begin the air drop. When the latter once more objected that the DZ "was not according to regulations," Langlais simply said:

"*Merde!* you can tell Colonel Sauvagnac that I'll take the responsibility for the drop-zone violations. Drop those men!"

This time Langlais fully prevailed. The bulk of the II/1 RCP began to land all over the inside of the fortress. Mishaps occurred, of course, but to a far lesser degree than could have been expected. When the air drops had to stop at dawn, April 4, 305 men of the II/1 RCP and sixteen equipment bags (that is, the bulk of the headquarters and Headquarters Company, 3rd Company, and one half of 2nd Company) had safely landed inside Dien Bien Phu. Total casualties were two dead from enemy gunfire and ten wounded, most of whom had only minor jump injuries. The battalion commander, Maj. Bréchignac, himself landed in the barbed wire near Langlais' dugout and joined the latter after having abandoned his trousers in the wire. His deputy, Capt. Clédic; fell north of Sparrowhawk in front of Lt. Allaire's mortar company. But not one man was misdropped to the enemy.

In addition to the paratroopers, non-parachutist reinforcements needed for the various technical services of the position were also air-dropped. On this point there had been a long and acrimonious debate between Dien Bien Phu and the paratroop bureaucracy in Hanoi. At first the latter simply refused to parachute anyone who had not gone through the complete cycle of jump training. Langlais held that the fortress would be devoid of radio specialists, artillery gunners, and tank crews by the time Hanoi combed Indochina for men who had the required skills; were qualified for jump training, and who had volunteered for duty at Dien Bien Phu. At first, Langlais' plea to let unqualified technical personnel jump into the valley fell on deaf ears. But as the battle devoured complete units and specialists of all sorts, it became clear that the Airborne Replacement Training Center was unable to deliver qualified paratroopers in sufficient numbers. The rule requiring qualification jumps was waived. The "Book" went out the window. Moreover, it is a known fact that the second and third parachute jumps are psychologically more difficult than the initial one. The problem of having to jump immediately after parachute training into a flaming valley crisscrossed by machine-gun and artillery fire and from planes buffeted by flak, often resulted in a great number of last-minute jump refusals.[15] As it turned out, the jump casualties among the nonjumpers who "hit the silk" for the first time above Dien Bien Phu were as low as those among fully qualified paratroopers.

A total of 4,277 reinforcements were air-dropped into Dien Bien Phu, of whom 3,596 were qualified parachutists and 681 were nonqualified jumpers. The latter had been culled from a pool of 2,594 *volunteers* drawn from units all over Viet-Nam and comprised of 2,048 Europeans, 451 North Africans and Africans, and 95 Vietnamese. At Dien Bien Phu, courage apparently had no nationality.[16]

Along with the paratroopers, two young officers from the armored forces, 1st Lt. Adenot and 2nd Lt. Mengelle, jumped into Dien Bien Phu that night. They replaced the wounded Capt. Hervouët and Warrant Officer Carette.

Sunday-Monday, April 4-5, 1954

The night was fairly calm except for some Communist patrols roving around Claudine 4 and 5 in the west. Between 0330 and 0530 Maj. Coutant's Legionnaires of the 1/13th Half-Brigade fired upon some of the *Bo-Doi* in the process of cutting through the barbed wire and drove them off.

As dawn broke, the sleepless, bearded defenders of Dien Bien Phu were briefly treated to a spectacle to which they had become unaccustomed for almost a month: the paratroopers of Bréchignac's II/1 RCP, fully assembled, standing erect in their still-neat camouflage uniforms, field packs rigged as per regulations, impeccably cleaned submachine guns and carbines slung across their chests or over their shoulders, breaking into a long single file as they began their march across the whole camp to their new quarters on Eliane 10 and D3. For a brief instant it seemed as if time itself had stopped. The monsoon rains had lifted and

only a few clouds were hanging around the mountaintops on the edge
of the valley. The air was light and dry and even the Communist artillerymen seemed to be taking a rest. And at 1400 there came another piece of
good news: the Viet-Minh were leaving E2, quietly and deliberately,
pulling back into the ravines at the foot of it. The whole hill stank with
the sickly smell of death as 1,500 Communist and 300 French corpses
rotted in the sun. Slowly, French patrols began probing down the
Champs-Elysées to the east slope without encountering enemy opposition.
But Bigeard decided to leave the lower part of E2 a no man's land since
it would be impossible to garrison it effectively as long as the enemy had
its guns dug in on Old Baldy and Phony Mountain.

Far to the south, Lt. Col. Langlais' garrison on Isabelle had been fighting off strangulation for the last three days. It seemed that the Viet-Minh
were testing the siege techniques which they planned to use later on on
the main position of Dien Bien Phu. Communist trenches crept slowly
toward Isabelle, to be followed by veritable bunkers which would have
to be destroyed by dive bombers or tanks in costly close-in attacks. On
April 2, Lt. Préaud's tank platoon had gone on such an operation, losing
M/Sgt. Cancilieri in the process. On April 4 the three tanks had again
smashed into the enemy trench line and destroyed Viet-Minh bunkers
with point-blank cannon fire.

As night fell, the monsoon rains started again with devastating force.
Hanoi promptly informed Dien Bien Phu that no personnel drops would
be made that night. The 212 remaining troops of 1st and 2nd Companies,
II/1 RCP, would have to spend another twenty-four hours in Hanoi.
However, the enemy had decided not to wait to press home his attack on
the decimated garrison of H6. At 2015 Huguette 1, 5, and 6 reported
that they were "seriously probed." At 2200, as Langlais returned from
dinner with Lemeunier and Vadot via the underground tunnel system
which now connected most of the central headquarters dugouts (and
which had been appropriately given the name of *Métro,* after the Paris
subway), he was informed by Maj. Clémençon that Huguette was under
heavy artillery fire and that a massive assault against H6 was building up.

Indeed it was. The Communist high command had apparently decided
to smash into the French defensive system over the outposts in the valley
bottom, where the massive Viet-Minh superiority and manpower could
be fully brought to bear against the French, and where all French reinforcements would have to run the gauntlet of the open airfield rather than
use the protection of the hill-line and the high eastern bank of the Nam
Yum. The new attack was entrusted by Le Trong Tan, the commanding

general of the 312th People's Army Division, to Col. Thuy's 165th Infantry Regiment with its four battalions, reinforced by the 401st Heavy Weapons Company of the 308th Division with its 120-mm. mortars. In addition most of the enemy howitzer batteries on the western flank of Dien Bien Phu were now working over the northern part of Huguette and the airfield.

What happened during the next few hours on Huguette 6 was a perfect example of what raw courage and determined leadership can do even in a desperate situation. When the second battle for H6 began its garrison counted exactly eighty-eight Legionnaires and two lieutenants: Rastouil, whose tour in Indochina had ended, and his replacement, Lt. François. Shortly after 2200 (it will probably remain forever impossible to retrace fully the exact sequence of events[17]), Clémençon committed Capt. Viard's Composite Intervention Company from the 1/13 Half-Brigade to the help of H6. As the battle developed, the various strongpoint commanders were anxiously listening in on the command net and thus heard within a few minutes that Viard's small band was being hacked to shreds along with the remaining Legionnaires on H6. At 0030 of April 5, H6 reported that it was being attacked simultaneously from the west, north, and east and that its survivors were withdrawing into the southern part of the strongpoint.

French reserve units now were thrown in piecemeal as they became available. At 0115, the Special Air Service Company of the 8th Assault, under Lt. Bailly, began to move northward inside the airfield drainage ditch, accompanied by tanks "Conti" and "Ettlingen" under Lt. Mengelle. But this time the Viet-Minh were prepared for the arrival of the tanks and a heavy barrage of artillery shells and bazooka rockets greeted their appearance. Nevertheless, they and Bailly's weak company kept inching forward and finally reached the southwestern corner of the strongpoint, where the Communists had dug in their forward base of fire. This is where tank "Conti" blew up a mine, wounding among others the gallant Sgt. Ney, who had led the platoon since the beginning of the battle. Tank "Ettlingen" also sustained a bazooka hit but stayed in the fight. Bailly split his company into two parts, one of which succeeded in breaking through to the garrison while the other, with the help of the remaining tank, kept the Viet-Minh's mortars temporarily pinned down. It was clear, however, that this was not enough to save the survivors of H6, let alone hold on to the position. At 0315 the under-strength 2nd Company, II/1 RCP, under Capt. Clédic, was committed to the battle. Clédic had arrived at Dien Bien Phu only the day before but, installed with his men on top of E2, he had been able to survey the battlefield quite thoroughly. Clédic decided to take his men right across Sparrow-hawk to the drainage ditch, only to be informed by Bailly that further progress along the ditch would be impossible. But Clédic was not going to be pinned down. In one flying leap he and his company crossed the wide-open airstrip, whose metallic runway plates shone like a mirror in the greenish light of the parachute flares, and rushed head-on into the southernmost Viet-Minh elements covering the encircled strongpoint on its southern face. Clédic never gave them the chance to take aim. At 0420 he closed in with them and in a vicious hand-to-hand fight mowed them down and broke into the ruins of H6 where about twenty survivors were still holding on to one bunker. Without breaking pace, Clédic's men began to mop up the peripheral trenches of H6.

While Clédic had staved off disaster, Langlais had called on the indefatigable Bigeard to mount one of his instantaneous operations. At 0500, Bigeard arrived at Langlais' headquarters from Eliane 4 with his deputy, Maj. Thomas, one intelligence officer, a map officer, and his unit clerk. In less than one hour, Bigeard had orchestrated a counterattack to be led by two companies of his own 6th BPC, with Vieulles' 1st BEP standing by in reserve. The French Air Force promised a major effort as soon as the weather permitted it, probably early in the morning. At 0600, the lead company of the 6th BPC, under Lt. Le Page, reached the line where the 8th Assault had dug in. It was immediately followed by a second company. Considering that both companies together numbered less than 160 men, they could hardly be considered a match for the more than 3,000 *Bo-Doi* committed to the fight by the other side. Yet they arrived exactly as the enemy committed a fourth battalion (14/165) to the battle for one last furious counterattack. But he had waited too long. Daylight had come and the French artillery now began taking a frightful toll of the attackers. As they began to recoil at 0830, the first French fighter-bombers appeared in the morning sky and began their deadly carousel over the enemy infantry, caught completely in the open and far away from the protective shelter of the jungle.

At 1015 Clédic and the other junior officers who were now masters of Huguette 6 surveyed the battlefield around them. There were the bodies of more than 500 dead Viet-Minh, many of them perhaps sixteen years old or younger, sprawled in grotesque positions inside the ravaged breast-works of Huguette 6. In the barbed wire and mine fields around the posi-tion, 300 more bodies could be counted and at least as many wounded must have been taken along by the retreating enemy. Twenty-one Com-

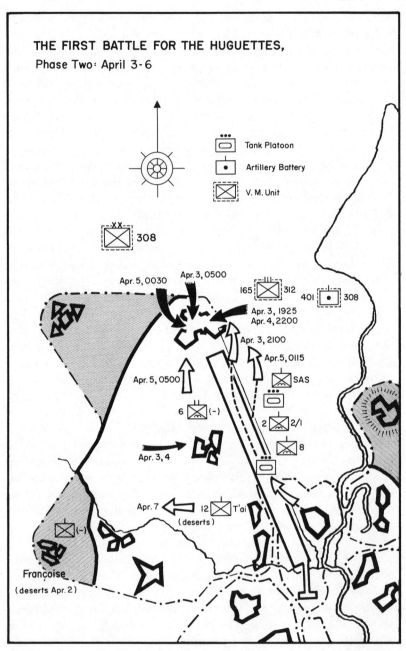

THE FIRST BATTLE FOR THE HUGUETTES,
Phase Two: April 3-6

Tank Platoon

Artillery Battery

V. M. Unit

308

Apr. 5, 0030   Apr. 3, 0500   165   312   401   308

Apr. 3, 1925
Apr. 4, 2200

Apr. 3, 2100

Apr. 5, 0500   Apr. 5, 0115

SAS

6   (-)

2   2/1

8

Apr. 3, 4

Apr. 7   12   T'ai
(deserts)

Françoise
(deserts Apr. 2)

munist prisoners, all very young and jabbering from shock, were found among the dead and later on sent to the prisoner-of-war camp which Dien Bien Phu still maintained in its midst. The 312th Division, for the time being at least, had lost the use of at least one full regiment. On the French side, the losses had also been heavy, and irreplaceable. Of the four small paratroop companies committed during the night, more than 200 men, including four officers, had become casualties. Miraculously, Clédic's outfit had suffered less than ten. The Foreign Legionnaires who had garrisoned H6 had practically ceased to exist. Had Dien Bien Phu's ability to receive reinforcements by air been unimpeded, these losses would have been acceptable. But in the face of a trickle of reinforcements which, over the whole duration of the battle, averaged only seventy-five men a night, the losses were extremely serious. French Intelligence soon picked up urgent radio messages from Gen. Giap to his own rear services to provide him with replacements from his 25,000-men reserve pool dispersed in well-camouflaged camps throughout North Viet-Nam. At the same time messages to Red China were intercepted, requesting delivery to the Viet-Minh forces of another flak regiment with sixty-seven guns of 37-mm. caliber.

The second Viet-Minh offensive against Dien Bien Phu had been weathered. While the French had "won" the battle, it had been won at a price in men, equipment, and lost terrain that was to insure ultimate defeat.

As for Lt. Col. Langlais, he had directed the battle from Clémençon's command post on H3, which he had reached in pitch blackness with his jeep, accompanied by Bigeard and his small staff. By an effort of iron will he had abstained from intervening in Bigeard's orchestration of the counterattack and had spent part of the night reading a book about the life of a yacht in his beloved home province of Brittany. ("Escape" reading was very much the vogue at Dien Bien Phu; Maj. Séguin-Pazzis recalled that he was reading Han Suyin's famous novel *A Many Splendoured Thing* alternately with a book on the Korean War.)

The battle for the Five Hills and the northern Huguettes had been expensive in other ways. Only four tanks now remained in working order at Dien Bien Phu, with two more still operating on Isabelle. Moreover, the American 105-mm. howitzers proved extremely vulnerable to counter-battery fire because their hydraulic recoil mechanisms kept being pierced by shell fragments. Major Alliou's III/10 RAC alone found six of its 105's disabled during the previous night's battle and had to switch to the far less satisfactory heavy mortars for the support of the infantry. Early in the afternoon of Monday, Lt. Minaud's company of the II/1 RCP, reinforced by a platoon from the 8th Assault, replaced Clédic on H6 while a detachment of disarmed T'ai tribesmen and Viet-Minh prisoners under Air Force Warrant Officer Lafon began the grim task of clearing the corpses from the position.

In the face of the French successes on Eliane and Huguette, another Communist probe against the triangle of Huguettes 1, 2 and 5, and aerial photographs now showing Communist trenches within 100 meters of Isabelle, could for a time be disregarded. Even the fact that at 1400 a lumbering "Flying Boxcar" dumped its whole cargo of six tons of storage batteries and two 75-mm. recoilless guns into enemy lines, was greeted with only mild expressions of disgust. The radio operator at Dien Bien Phu added: "We'll try to destroy it with artillery and Air Force." In fact, Dien Bien Phu did better than that. On April 6, a strong reconnaissance force of Foreign Legionnaires pushed a full three kilometers southward to Ban Co My without encountering any enemy resistance, except at an observation post where three men were killed, and entered the deserted village. The force miraculously recovered not only the two lost recoilless guns but also a cargo of fresh human blood still in its refrigerated container.

VII

Asphyxiation

THE Viet-Minh did not consider the battle for the Five Hills and for the Huguettes an unmitigated victory. To be sure, the Communist forces were in a far better position to replace their losses at Dien Bien Phu, but Gen. Giap was also concerned with the whole Indochina peninsula. While Dien Bien Phu absorbed perhaps five per cent of the French battle force, including eight to ten top-notch battalions, the same battle tied down fifty per cent of the Communist forces and an overwhelming share of the military supplies provided by Red China. French intelligence estimates were to show later that of the total of perhaps 23,000 Viet-Minh casualties suffered during the battle of Dien Bien Phu, more than 10,000 had been suffered by April 5; *i.e.,* the conquest of the outer hill positions had been terribly expensive and had thus far failed to be decisive. General Giap's own view of the battle clearly indicates that a revision of the tactics for the next siege phase was taking place:

> Our offensive on the eastern hills of the central sector has obtained important successes, but had failed to reach all the assigned objectives. . . . We have therefore decided to continue to execute the tasks foreseen for the second phase of our offensive: To advance our attack and encirclement lines, improve our positions and occupy new ones; progressively tighten further our stranglehold so as to completely intercept reinforcements and supplies . . . utilizing trenches which have been driven forward until they touch the enemy lines, the tactic of gnawing away at the enemy piecemeal.[1]

Every morning, new aerial photographs and maps told the story of this siege technique. A *Bearcat* reconnaissance fighter from EROM 80 would sweep low over the camp and free-drop to de Castries a bag containing official correspondence, mail for the troops, and the newest set of developed and interpreted aerial photographs and maps showing the seemingly unstoppable progress of the enemy's trench system throughout the valley.

Tuesday-Friday, April 6-9, 1954

April 6 was a day for stock taking. The picture that emerged was not a pretty one. Artillery ammunition had shrunk to 371 rounds of 155-mm., 7,500 rounds of 105-mm., and 1,500 rounds of 120-mm. mortar shells, or about what Dien Bien Phu's artillery would fire in one night of fairly serious combat. There were no more mines left to put in front of the rear area strongpoints such as Huguette 1 or the newly created "Lily," carved out of Claudine 1, and a newly dug bunker system between H4 and Claudine 5 (see map, p. 263). On April 7 this position was occupied by the remnants of the 1/4 Moroccan Rifles of Maj. Nicolas. There were also no 60-mm. shells left for the small mortars of the forward infantry units. On the evening of April 6, the fortress also ran out of flare shells for its 81-mm. mortars. The despair of the garrison was therefore readily imaginable when yet another flight of C-119's, apparently disoriented by the enemy flak, misdropped its cargo of eighteen tons of howitzer ammunition behind Communist lines near Ban Co My. Another infantry breakout had to be mounted on the following day to collect at least part of it.[2] In fact, the ammunition losses through misdrops had become so heavy that one of Langlais' officers suggested deliberately misdropping ammunition packages containing booby-trapped shells. These, upon being loaded into the enemy howitzers, would cause them to explode— which, considering how invulnerable they were to French counter-battery fire, surely would cause them greater casualties than the French artillery and Air Force together and might discourage the Viet-Minh from reusing misdropped shells.[3] The idea was never accepted by Hanoi, which did not wish to divert scarce supply space to yet another untried experiment. In all likelihood some of the planners feared that ammunition drops designed to be misdropped would manage to fall with utmost accuracy *inside* Dien Bien Phu and blow up French artillery pieces.

Not counting the sealed-off garrison of Isabelle, which on April 3 totaled 1,613 men, the main garrison at Dien Bien Phu was now reduced to five paratroop battalions, none of which (with the exception of the II/1 RCP which had received another 177 men on April 5) had more than 300 men; two Foreign Legion battalions with a total of about 600 men; and the unreliable debris of the T'ai and North African units, for a total of less than 2,600 infantrymen. In fact, this tiny infantry force still held a perimeter almost ten kilometers in length and also protected over a thousand wounded and 2,200 Communist prisoners of war held inside the camp. This force also guarded the "Rats of the Nam Yum," the deserters and forcibly disarmed T'ai mountainers, to the end of the battle. In addition to lacking good infantrymen, Dien Bien Phu also continued to bleed to death slowly because of the lack of specialists. The battle devoured tank crews, artillery gunners, observers, and radiomen at an incredible pace. At 1930 of April 6, Dien Bien Phu requested three tank commanders, two tank gunners, one driver and one radioman.

Yet even this calm day was not without its minute of excitement, for one very last airplane that day landed at Dien Bien Phu. It was a reconnaissance Morane-500 *Cricket* of the 23rd Artillery Observation Group based on the Laotian airstrip of Muong-Sai, about 120 kilometers southwest of Dien Bien Phu. The tiny aluminum-and-cloth reconnaissance craft of the 21st and 23rd Observation Groups of French army aviation continued to fly the gantlet of enemy flak to provide a minimum of information to the artillery at Dien Bien Phu, which had been without observation posts since the loss of the French hill positions. Since the appearance of the unarmed *Crickets* over the battlefield was usually followed by improved French artillery fire, they had become a priority target for enemy antiaircraft fire. It was the 21st Group that lost seven planes at Dien Bien Phu and another six through sabotage on March 7 during a daring Viet-Minh commando raid on the French air base of Cat-Bi. Many of its pilots were now sharing the aircraft of the 23rd Group. Thus, it was Sergeant-Pilot Ribière of the 21st Group who was at the controls of *Cricket* VG and flying with Lieutenant Choue de La Mestrie, an artillery observer from the 23rd. Enemy flak had been particularly quiescent that uneventful afternoon and perhaps the pilot of the *Cricket* had become overconfident and had gone lower than he should have; but all of a sudden the little aircraft found itself framed by the black clouds of Communist antiaircraft fire, followed by the tracer bullets from 50-caliber machine guns. Within a few seconds, Ribière reported that de La Mestrie was badly hit and that he would attempt an emergency landing at Dien Bien Phu. Losing altitude rapidly, the little plane plunged earthward almost vertically and began its short landing roll on the southern end of the strip. A rescue crew from the Air Force detachment raced toward the plane in an attempt to save not only the crew but the aircraft, but it was too late. With unerring precision the Communist guns had already switched back to their favorite target, and began to hack the little aircraft to shreds. Lieutenant de La Mestrie died on the spot, but Sgt. Ribière was pulled alive from the wreck. Within a few minutes the *Cricket* was burning fiercely.

Outside Dien Bien Phu, negotiations with the United States for a major bombing operation on the Communist siege force around Dien Bien Phu were in the process of bogging down (see Chapter IX), and General Navarre now began to make plans for a diversionary operation from Laos in the direction of Dien Bien Phu, designed, if unable to break through to the besieged force, at least to divert from it parts of the Communist divisions holding the valley. Navarre had decided to entrust that operation to the commander of French forces in Laos, Colonel Boucher de Crèvecoeur, an old Indochina hand with almost twenty years' experience in the country. The new task force was to be composed of three battalions reinforced by a series of French commando groups. When Navarre spoke to Crèvecoeur at the southern Laotian airbase of Séno on April 6 at 1300, he harbored few illusions as to the ultimate success of the operation, but he ordered its beginning as of April 13. Its code name was to be "Condor." Crève-coeur, by the way, translates into English as "Heartbreak."

On April 7, the unnatural calm at Dien Bien Phu continued. More and more trenches now appeared around Isabelle. These had to be cleared again in a costly hand-to-hand counterattack beyond Isabelle 5. On Huguette 2, another minor disaster occurred in the form of the desertion of what was left of Capt. Guilleminot's 12th Company of 3rd BT. Guilleminot had been wounded a few days before, after which the tribesmen felt their bond of fidelity to the French had been severed. To them, war was a very personal affair: they were fighting for Guilleminot, not for some abstract government in Saigon (a city of which they had never heard), or the abstraction of a struggle between the "free world" and "Communism." Fortunately for the French, H2 was not yet on the firing line and, while the men deserted with most of their individual weapons, the situation was rapidly taken in hand. Captain Bizard and his little tough Vietnamese paratroopers of 1/5 BPVN moved in on the remainder of the company, disarmed it and sent it to join the "Rats of the Nam Yum." Those who voluntarily stayed on were transferred to the artillery. Interspersed with the African gun crews, they could do no further harm.

At 1050, de Castries sent a brief personal query to Hanoi: "I've got 60 Communist wounded on my hands. Can I give them back to the enemy?" Indeed, the problem of the Communist wounded in French hands was an additional cross which the garrison had to bear. Contrary to the practices of 1961-67, in which both sides acted as if there were no rules of warfare and conventions on the treatment of prisoners, both the

French and the Viet-Minh made some effort at fighting the war within at least a few humanitarian rules. Hence, Hanoi had no objections to de Castries' addressing a radio message to the other side with the following text:

> To the Commander of the People's Army siege force. We inform you that twenty of your wounded will be brought on stretchers to Ban Ban tonight at 2200. The men who will bring them shall not be armed. No action or firing shall take place in that zone until midnight.

The exchange took place. As the French stretcher bearers, led by a master sergeant, arrived at Ban Ban there was a group of Viet-Minh stretcher bearers standing there in complete silence. Without exchanging a single word with the French, the Viet-Minh picked up their wounded and disappeared in the night.

In view of this experience, on April 9 de Castries sent a captured Viet-Minh officer with a white flag at the head of a small truck convoy with the remaining Communist wounded. The convoy entered enemy lines 800 meters south of E2. The Viet-Minh officer was let through by the enemy outpost, but the French medics and their wounded charges were left to wait in the open, untouched and in silence. When the Viet-Minh officer failed to return and it became clear that no one on the Communist side was going to make a gesture to take over the wounded, the French also returned to their lines. Later that night a radio message arrived from the enemy side:

> We have received your message concerning the wounded. We are awaiting instructions from higher up and hope to be able to give you tomorrow an exact hour for the meeting. The commander, People's Army Regiment east of Dien Bien Phu.

The Viet-Minh command proposed an exchange of wounded, with the French wounded to be left two kilometers north of Dominique while the Communist prisoners would be brought through south of Claudine. The return of the French wounded to Dien Bien Phu, while in human terms unrefusable, would of course have canceled out whatever alleviation of the overcrowded hospitals inside the besieged fortress had been hoped for. Still, it had to be accepted. After the French counterattack on E1 of April 10, however, the Viet-Minh high command informed de Castries curtly that further exchanges would not take place. According to the recollection of Langlais,[4] it was de Castries who finally decided against an alternative—simply to leave the Communist wounded at a given point in the no man's land—for fear that the Communists would deliberately leave them to die unattended. Either way, to be wounded at Dien Bien Phu was an unenviable fate. On the Communist side the wounded faced days of portage and scant medical care. The Viet-Minh had only one full-fledged surgeon, Dr. Ton That Tung, and six not too well informed medical practitioners, to take care of the needs of almost 50,000 men. On the French side there were nineteen doctors and facilities for surprisingly excellent surgery, but the wounded had to face an indefinite stay under fire in an underground dugout with the chance of being killed or wounded by Communist shells while lying in the hospital.

On April 8, Capt. Bizard and his small company from the 5th BPVN once more returned to H6 in order to relieve Capt. Minaud and his mixed company from the II/1 RCP. Minaud and almost all the other company officers of the II/1 RCP (Lieutenants Subrégis from the 4th Company, Chardiny from the 2nd, and Ruiter from the 3rd) had been wounded during the counterattack of April 5. Minaud, however, had remained at his post. Bizard's small band was reinforced during the day by another ragtag company, assembled from units of the 1/2 REI, under the command of Lt. François. Yet the Viet-Minh seemed to have tired of frontal attacks on H6. Instead, the aerial photographs dropped the following day disclosed that the enemy was driving a prong of trenches around either side of H6 with the obvious intent of choking off the position.

The initiative for the next round of the battle did not belong to the Viet-Minh, but rather to the indomitable Maj. Bigeard. In view of the garrison's unexpected survival of the battle of the Five Hills and the Huguettes, Gen. Cogny now agreed to parachute into Dien Bien Phu yet another paratroop battalion, but not until he apparently once more tried to substitute some of his less desirable Vietnamese troops for the remaining elite paratroops. De Castries—or Langlais, over de Castries' signature—had fired off a curt telegram directly to Navarre at 0925 of April 9, with the following text: "Want the 2nd Foreign Legion Parachute Battalion [you] promised, and not 1st Vietnamese Parachute Battalion. Prevent that swindle."

It is rumored that the two battalion commanders had drawn lots for the honor of jumping into Dien Bien Phu first. Major Hubert Liesenfelt, of the 2nd Foreign Legion Parachute Battalion (BEP), won.

Assured of replacements, on April 6 Bigeard made the decision to retake Eliane 1. With E1 in the hands of the Viet-Minh, the other hill positions were almost untenable. No one could move on E4 without being immediately shot at by elite marksmen installed on E1. Even rifle grenades landed in the trenches day and night. Bigeard, his men from the 6th BPC, and one company of 5th BPVN, lived like troglodytes in narrow grottoes and tomblike burrows. On the evening of April 8, Langlais approved Bigeard's plan. Anticipating the approval of his senior commander, Bigeard (copying the methods of the enemy) had had his men dig approach trenches at night from E4 in the direction of E1. In order not to give away the impending attack, Bigeard decided to begin the artillery preparation with the battalion's own 81-mm. mortars and the 120's of Lt. Allaire. In addition, every available 105-mm. howitzer in *all* of Dien Bien Phu, twelve in Dien Bien Phu proper and eight at Isabelle; would open fire on E1, delivering 1,800 rounds in ten minutes. The mortars would fire a rolling barrage twenty meters ahead of the first infantry wave and the artillery would fire a dangerously close forty to one hundred meters ahead of the French. But this was not all. As soon as the artillery lifted, the remaining four tanks, drawn up on the road below E4, would take the hilltop of E1 under direct fire, as would the quad-fifties from Sparrowhawk. Lastly, the six machine guns and twelve automatic rifles dug in on neighboring E2 would pin down anything that still moved on top of E1. It was Bigeard's intention to husband the manpower he could not afford to lose by high-volume, well-aimed firepower. In fact, the infantry force devoted to the undertaking consisted of what was left of the 6th BPC. This was not much, even though a trickle of parachuted reinforcements had permitted the reconstitution of three rifle companies and a headquarters company. (Each of those so-called companies numbered only eighty men.) Everything depended upon whether Hanoi would deliver the spare paratroop battalion.

On April 9 almost 180 tons of supplies had been dropped over the valley, with only a ten per cent loss to the enemy. That night monsoon rains began to interfere with the dropping of the 2nd BEP. Nevertheless, the battalion's 7th and 8th Companies and part of Headquarters Company managed to land inside the fortress without a hitch. They were immediately assigned to D3.

The evening before, a small action that had taken place on the airfield indicated the high morale of the garrison. Captain Charnod and his men from the Air Force detachment had mounted a small commando operation across the airfield in order to drag the charred remains of Lt. de La Mestrie out of the carcass of the downed observation plane in order to give him proper burial.

Out to the west, between Claudine and Huguette, the Moroccans were building a new strongpoint called Lily or Liliane. Claudine 1 became Lily 1, Lily 2 was entirely new; and Huguette 4 became Lily 3. Placed under the command of Maj. Nicolas, it became fully operational by April 14.

At 1800 of April 9, two *Helldivers* off aircraft carrier *Arromanches* piloted by Lt. de la Ferrière and Ensign Laugier, roared in right "on the deck" along Road 41, looking for Communist supply convoys near the battlefield. The nest of flak machine guns around Beatrice opened up and its tracers seemed to follow Ensign Laugier's airplane almost all the way to the ground. He crashed too far behind the enemy's line to be reached by Charnod or by anyone else.

Saturday-Sunday, April 10-11, 1954

The dawn of April 10 witnessed the French assault on Eliane 1, exactly as planned by Bigeard. Bigeard's term "orchestrating an operation" meant exactly that. To direct the attack on E1, Bigeard had had his men dig a hole on the slope facing the objective, into which he moved half a dozen radio sets, each within reach. There he would huddle for the next ten hours, covered with the sand and debris of nearby enemy hits and "playing" the whole battle on his radio transmitters as though they were ungodly musical instruments. He listened in on his infantry companies and on their calls to their platoons; he talked to the artillery commander and to the forward air controller, the mortars, and the tanks.[5]

Bigeard had personally briefed all the company commanders the evening before: Lieutenants Trapp, Le Page, Perret, and Datin for the infantry, and Allaire for the mortars. On returning to their units, they in turn briefed their platoon commanders. H-hour was set at 0550. Contrary to established doctrine, Bigeard deliberately used commando tactics. The infantry was committed in very small units advancing as rapidly as possible, leaving enemy pockets that had not been destroyed by the artillery to be mopped up by the second or third commando wave. The solid advantage of this technique, at least in this instance, was that the Viet-Minh commander was unable to organize his defensive fires because the French troops were completely intermingled with his own. At 0610, as soon as a series of smoke shells marked the end of the French barrage, Lt. Trapp's leading company began climbing the steep slopes of Eliane 1 while French dive bombers, right on schedule, began working over the enemy positions to the rear of the Elianes and Dominiques, thus sealing off the battlefield completely. Presently, however, the Viet-Minh boxed in the French rear with a counterbarrage. Trapp's company was pinned down high up on the western slope of E1. Bigeard now committed Le Page's company along with a flame-thrower team and an automatic rifle team. With Le Page also went a new officer, Lt. Combaneyre, who had been parachuted in on April 8. The new company cleared the enemy 120-mm. mortar barrage in long leaps, but with heavy losses. The automatic rifle group was completely annihilated and Lt. Combaneyre received a severe head wound. But Le Page and the flame-thrower team got through. Within seconds the western bunker of Eliane 1 disappeared in a river of flame soon followed by a black cloud and the smell of charred human flesh. At 1400 Trapp and Le Page and the survivors of their two companies were on top of E1 and looking down on the east slope in direction of Phony Mountain where the *Helldivers* from French Navy Squadron 3-F were finishing off what was left of the full Viet-Minh battalion that had held the hill. At 1600 Bigeard replaced his two companies on top of E2 with two fresh companies from Bréchignac's II/1 RCP under the command of Captains Minaud and Charles. The new companies were digging frantically into the loose sand on top of E1 when the enemy began to lay down a heavy counterbarrage of mortars and artillery on the strongpoint.

When 6th BPC called the roll that evening, its losses had been 13 dead, 26 wounded (including three officers), and 10 missing. This represented one third of the total force committed. There were also six Vietnamese paratroopers in the attack who, having survived the shock of the assault, promptly deserted.

The two companies had hardly had time to become acquainted with what was left of the position when an enemy counterattack began at 1845. It was preceded by a violent artillery barrage not only on E1 itself, but also on the headquarters area and the artillery positions. General Giap was apparently willing to pay the price for E1: a full Viet-Minh regiment —the 98th Infantry of the 316th Division—with three battalions was involved from the beginning. Charles and Minaud and their small band of defenders were now in an impossible situation. Although fully equipped with automatic weapons, they were incapable of mowing down the onrushing waves of enemy infantry fast enough. By 2000, the French on E1 were fighting on in isolated small groups as the vanguard of the Viet-Minh reached the crest of the hill.

Shortly after 2100, both the company commanders were wounded (this was Minaud's second wound in five days), and E1 was leaderless. Bigeard, who had watched the agony of the position from Eliane 4, decided to make a stand for it. Frantic radio calls went out to the counter-

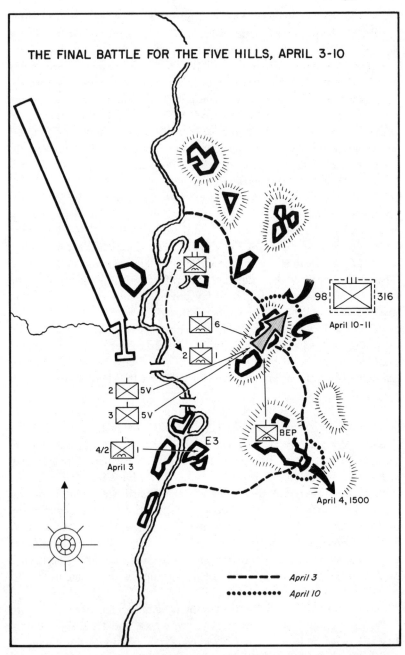

THE FINAL BATTLE FOR THE FIVE HILLS, APRIL 3-10

attack companies, organized on a stand-by basis by all the paratroop battalions. The first unit to respond to the call was the 1st BEP, which sent two small companies of fifty men each under Captains Michel Brandon and "Loulou" Martin into the blazing furnace atop E1. Simultaneously, Gen. Giap threw a fourth infantry battalion into the battle.

Then something very strange happened. Something which, in the recollection of the thousands of men who heard it that night, had rarely happened before in Indochina. As the hundred Legionnaires and French paratroopers stormed across the low saddle between E4 and E1, they began to sing. Some of the French paratroop songs are in fact translations of German paratroop songs, and now, as they stormed forward, the German Legionnaires were singing in their grave Teutonic accents while the French were singing in their own language. For a moment there seemed to be a brief lull in the battle—even the enemy seemed to attempt to identify the strange new sound. But the song and singers melted away in the firefight atop Eliane 1 and Bigeard decided to throw in the last available ready reserves: 2nd and 3rd Companies, 5th Vietnamese Paratroops. This was the same battalion that had covered itself with shame at the ford of Ban Ké Phai on March 15. Purged of their unreliable elements, and reinforced by some of the French cadre left over from the disintegrated T'ai battalions, they had given a good account of themselves in the previous battles for Huguette and the Five Hills. Yet somehow they had never again been taken seriously. Now their turn had come to be offered up for sacrifice on Eliane 1. Unflinchingly, the little Vietnamese paratroopers and their French cadres began the climb, and they, too, sang. In 1954, the Vietnamese Army was still a young army. It had flags of its own and a national anthem. But so far, no one had yet found the time to provide that army with a rousing marching song that could be shouted at the top of one's lungs if only to drown out one's fright. But there was one song which was then still in the cultural inventory of every Vietnamese schoolboy, and that was the French national anthem, the *Marseillaise*. As the Vietnamese paratroopers in turn emerged on the fire-beaten saddle between the hills there suddenly arose, for the first and last time in the Indochina War, the *Marseillaise*. It was sung the way it had been written to be sung in the days of the French Revolution, as a battle hymn of the French Republic. It was sung that night on the blood-stained slopes of Hill Eliane 1 by Vietnamese fighting other Vietnamese in the last battle France fought as an Asian power.

By midnight, the remnants of the RCP, the Foreign Legion Paratroopers, and the Vietnamese had again cleared E1 in hand-to-hand fighting. The Viet-Minh began to fall back, stunned. As dawn broke Bigeard fed into E1 the newly arrived 7th Company, 2nd BEP, of Capt. Delafond. The captain had been killed earlier that evening by a Communist shell and the company, now led by Lt. Lecour-Grandmaison, had witnessed the whole battle from its reserve position on Dominique 3. It had also directly witnessed the counterattacks of the 1st BEP and of the 5th BPVN and knew what to expect. But the enemy fire had slackened off on E1 and the unfolding daylight revealed the shambles of the position. Perhaps 400 Communist dead lay intermingled with the heavy casualties of the French. Of the two small companies of the II/1 RCP, one had ceased to exist, counting 10 dead, 21 missing and 66 wounded, including Lt. Ruiter. The 1st BEP and the Vietnamese also had about 100 casualties. Yet they had taken and held E1 and they were going to hold it now grimly for twenty full days and nights of fighting. Companies would stay forty-eight hours on E1, be bled white and pulled back for rest. The next company would then be hacked to pieces on top of the hill. The bodies of friend and foe on E1 were covered with a light layer of sand and sandbags and used as revetments, only to be torn up again and again by the incoming shells. The French were to stay on Eliane 1 almost until the end. When E1 finally fell, Dien Bien Phu had only a few days to live. Meanwhile, like the "band of brothers" in Shakespeare's *Henry V,* the French paratroopers at Dien Bien Phu had had their Saint Crispin's day.

After the successful counterattack on E1, Langlais once more reorganized the defense of Dien Bien Phu. Rank and seniority no longer counted. The only criterion for command responsibility was the net worth of the officer. A number of lieutenant-colonels and majors found themselves unemployed or relegated to minor tasks having nothing to do with their rank or past experience. On the other hand, the actual conduct of the battle was now completely in the hands of the "Paratroop Mafia." Langlais divided the whole main position of Dien Bien Phu into five *quartiers* (districts), and assigned one of his most trusted associates to the command of each, Bréchignac was named to the command of the Five Hills; Chenel, of 2nd BT, commanded the lowland areas east of the Nam Yum; Guiraud, though wounded, took command of the northern part of Dien Bien Phu proper; Tourret commanded on Sparrowhawk; and Vadot took over the west and south of Dien Bien Phu. Bigeard now officially became Langlais' deputy for counterattacks, and henceforth shared his command post. A briefing took place every morning at 0900 which was attended by the five *quartier* commanders, plus Langlais, Bigeard, Col. Vaillant (the artillery commander), the officer in charge of supply operations (usually Maj. de Brinon), Guérin from the Air Force and an officer representing Col. de Castries.

The progressive alienation, if not estrangement, of de Castries from the battle was part of a process which to this day is not clearly understood even by the men who witnessed it. To be sure, every day Bigeard made it a point of reporting personally to de Castries on the decisions made by the command group during the morning briefing. Apparently his even temper sat better with de Castries than that of the more ebullient Langlais. Usually, these reports left little for further decision-making by the nominal commander of the fortress, except perhaps to couch the often brutally direct messages forwarded by the paratroop commanders into terms more amenable to the refined ears of the rear-echelon command in Hanoi. On April 11, 1954, there were, in addition to Langlais, six lieutenant-colonels in the Dien Bien Phu perimeter and perhaps twenty majors. Yet the fate of Dien Bien Phu and indeed of the whole Indochina war, rested in the hands of Langlais and his little "band of brothers." Later Bigeard was to say that the morning briefings not only served to recapitulate the situation in the camp, to plan counterattacks and establish supply schedules, but also (and, perhaps, above all) to serve as a precious boost to morale. He put it in simple terms: "Our comradeship was excellent—and after all, we were fighting for our skins."

The enemy had also reappraised the situation. It was clear to Giap that to conquer Dien Bien Phu by frontal attacks at the price of destroying a large part of his regulars would play into the hands of the French High Command. To many of Giap's subordinates the situation at Dien Bien Phu, after the initial easy but costly victories over the French, now dangerously resembled some of the other battles which the PAVN had fought against the French in prepared positions and which had cost it extremely heavy losses. There is no question but that the week of April 11-18 was one during which combat morale on the Communist side was lowest, and that on the French side, highest. In fact, French radio intelligence in the fortress picked up agitated messages from lower-unit commanders reporting that certain units refused to obey orders. Prisoners openly admitted that in some instances they had been made to advance by actual threats of being shot from behind by their own guns.[6] Hence, Giap decided to revert to tried-and-true trench warfare tactics of the Ypres salient of World War I. With tens of thousands of coolies available from the road-building jobs on the supply lines, every French position was soon surrounded by a spider web of approach trenches, many of them carefully burrowed underground for long stretches until they emerged inside the French barbed wire or even at the French bunker line. In some cases, mine galleries would be dug, particularly in the Five Hills area, where Regiment 98 of the 316th People's Army Division held the line. The 98th had been recruited largely from among the Vietnamese of the Dong-Trieu area, which is one of the major coal-mining areas of North Viet-Nam. Many of the men from the 98th were former coal miners and were familiar with the digging of shafts and the preparation of explosive charges. One day, the surprised Langlais was informed from Hanoi that he would receive a shipment of "geophones." Indeed, a few days later there was parachuted a load of flat French Army wine canteens with medical stethoscopes, along with a short notice on how to listen for the noise of underground digging. Hanoi also was full of good advice on how to build countermines—that is, assuming that one had an unlimited amount of construction wood, manpower, and dynamite.

In the case of Dien Bien Phu, precious airborne cargo space had to be used at times to parachute in the minimum amount of construction materials necessary merely to keep in existence some of the strongpoints, which were rapidly crumbling away under the combined effects of the monsoon rains and enemy artillery. But when the nights were calm, the defenders of Elianes 1 and 2 could hear the clinking of picks and shovels almost under their feet. And they could hear it without using the "geóphones." That day, also, the Viet-Minh began to tighten its hold around Huguette 1 which, until now, had been to the rear of the battle line. In fact, the counterattack on Five Hills and the bloody struggle for E1 had completely obscured the total deterioration on Huguette. There, what was left of Clémençon's 1/2 Foreign Legion was being bled white at a fast clip. On April 8, the last remnants of 1st and 3rd Companies were merged into a *compagnie de marche* (provisional company) under Lt. François, and the NCO training unit was dissolved and formed into *Compagnie de Marche* "3/13"—in memory of the battalion which had been slaughtered on the first day of the battle on Beatrice. That company was commanded by Capt. Philippe. On April 9, a new reorganization took place as the battle for E1 drained off the last reserves. François' company relieved Clédic's company of the II/1 RCP on Huguette 6, and Huguette 4 was yielded to a mixed Moroccan company and became part of the new strongpoint Lily under the name of Lily 3. Finally, the already wounded Capt. Bizard relieved Minaud and his 4th Company, II/1 RCP, from H6 so that they could participate in the assault on E1. Bizard took command of H6 and Philippe and his deputy, Lt. Legros, installed themselves with the newly formed 3/13 Company on Huguette 2. This left Lt. Spozio, who already had been wounded during the fight for H7 on April 2, with his badly weakened 2nd Company, 1/2 REI, to hold Huguette 1. And on that Sunday, Spozio's men made an attempt once more to clear the tentacular Communist trenches which were in the process of encircling them. They were virtually submerged by three Viet-Minh companies that seemingly emerged from nowhere. Within a few minutes, one platoon from H2 and another from 4th Company were committed to save Spozio's outfit from being swallowed up. The 105's from Claudine chimed in and a few minutes later again the two tanks available for combat at the moment entered the fray under the command of 2d Lt. Mengelle. But the new strangulation tactics of the Communists seemed to work perfectly. One of the French tanks sustained a bazooka hit, and both Spozio and Legros were badly wounded; while Spozio could still be dragged back by his men, Legros had to be abandoned to the Communists, in whose hands he died a few hours later. But that was not the worst of it: 2nd Company had not succeeded in shaking off the encirclement and for the first time the Communists held on to approach trenches in broad daylight. This augured ill for the future.

Monday, April 12, 1954

As night fell on Sunday, Communist artillery again opened up on Eliane 1, followed within a few minutes by Battalions 215 and 439 of the 98th People's Army Regiment. This time, General Vu Manh Hung was determined to conquer and hold E1 for good. In view of the lack of any kind of obstacles in front of the first trenches on E1, the whole fight degenerated almost immediately into hand-to-hand combat. With Communist infiltrators seeping in between E1 and E4, Bréchignac ordered Trapp's and Le Page's companies from the 6th BPC into the fight; and on it went, man against man all night long in the trenches and bunkers of Eliane 1. By 0700, Regiment 98 had had enough; what was left of the two first-wave battalions (Nos. 215 and 439) engaged in the assault began to roll back down the eastern slope of E1, pursued again by the mortars and the artillery of Dien Bien Phu. According to the Viet-Minh manual on the assault of fortified positions, a three-to-one superiority of the assailant over the defender was required. In that night attack, the Viet-Minh had a seven-to-one superiority, but the thin line of paratroops held. Again their losses had been heavy. The two small companies of the RCP alone had lost nineteen killed and sixty-six wounded, including two officers, while the BEP had had forty-seven casualties. That meant that the 154 reinforcements for the 2nd BEP, who had been parachuted into Dien Bien Phu that night, merely made up for the night's losses but did not represent an increase of strength. The 3rd and 4th Companies of the II/1 RCP were now so depleted that Bréchignac dissolved them and formed them into a *compagnie de marche* under the command of 2nd Lt. Leguère. That left 1st Company, II/1 RCP, under Lt. Périou as the last ready reserve. Just before noon, Bréchignac committed it to the defense of Eliane 1. With Périou on E1 and Clédic now in reserve on E4, the II/1 immediately solved one of its major problems, that of secure voice radio communications. With the Communists being plentifully equipped with captured American radio sets of exactly the same type as those which the French had, secure radio communications (except for the top-secret Z.13 ultra high-frequency radio telephone link between de Castries and Hanoi and the messages sent in code) were nonexistent and often the Viet-Minh would successfully jam French communications or simply horn in on them; in any case, they would be constantly listened to. This was particularly bothersome when the communications involved exact relief hours for unit changes. In some cases, such as in communications between de Castries and Lt. Col. Lalande on Isabelle, English was used, since both officers spoke it fluently and, at least in 1954, the chances of the Viet-Minh's having trilingual radio operators were almost nil. The same system was used in communications between Clémençon and Bizard, since the latter had been educated in London. The North African units often would converse in Arabic as a way of throwing off indiscrete listeners, but in the case of Clédic and Périou, conversations were totally foolproof Both were Bretons; their language, which resembles Welsh, was incomprehensible not only to the Viet-Minh but also to other Frenchmen (except other Bretons). These conversations in a totally strange language were of course also picked up by French radio intelligence and resulted in at least one urgent message informing Hanoi that radio traffic "in an unknown Asian language" had been picked up near Dien Bien Phu.[7]

If the news was not too discouraging on the ground, air support remained the main worry of the garrison that day. At 1130, a French Navy *Privateer* four-engine bomber of Squadron 28, which was plastering enemy positions with the newly arrived American "Lazy Dog" bombs,[8] was hit by enemy antiaircraft fire northwest of Anne-Marie and disintegrated. Its chief pilot, Ensign Mankanovsky, died with the aircraft to give the other two men, Petty Officers Carpentier and Kerrones, a chance to jump. They parachuted safely and were taken prisoner. A few minutes later, at 1200, a B-26 dive-bombed Sparrowhawk by mistake, which, aside from the damage it caused to the strongpoint, gave Lt. Col. Langlais a severe jolt. For one fleeting moment of panic he thought that the Red Chinese Air Force had intervened in the battle. This, as far as Dien Bien Phu was concerned, would have meant death on short notice. As Langlais tells the story, he left the commander of Sparrowhawk, Maj. Tourret, somewhat perplexed when, on being apprised by him over the telephone that his strongpoint had been bombed by a French airplane, Langlais exclaimed: "Thank God, it's one of *ours!*"

But that was only the beginning of a particularly jinxed air support operation. Things were to get for worse on the following day.

Tuesday, April 13, 1954

While the ground war slackened for a time, Dien Bien Phu was again beset with airlift problems. Too much of the precious deliveries simply were misdropped to the other side. The effect was felt not only in the supply gaps of the garrison but also in such unnerving situations as the intensive shelling, during the night of April 12-13, of much of the Dien Bien Phu area by brutally effective 105-mm. shells equipped with new American short-delay fuses that came directly from misdropped supplies. Many of the French dugout and underground positions which had thus far successfully resisted enemy artillery fire were now pierced by the shells and destroyed. French-American cooperation in the supply operations also left something to be desired. Twenty-four of the twenty-nine C-119's flying as part of the French supply operations had American crews under contract to the Taiwan-based Civil Air Transport Corporation (CAT). Officially, the crews were all "civilian" but in actual fact some American military pilots had been quietly detached to CAT to familiarize themselves with the area in case of American air intervention on behalf of the French.

Since the crews spoke no French and most of the French air control personnel spoke no English, communications were often difficult, particularly so in the forward combat area. Dien Bien Phu, with its limited radio facilities, often had to deal simultaneously with thirty or forty aircraft operating near and over the valley. Rather than engage in lengthy and sometimes fruitless conversations with the ground, the U. S.

crews often tended to follow their own experience or their own flight leaders. That also had happened during the night of April 12-13, and at 0930 of April 13, de Castries bitterly complained that the "American crews refused to take into account at all the indications given by our own air liaison headquarters down here." When later in the day the French Air Force added injury to insult by bombing some of the French-held strongpoints three times, and Dien Bien Phu also found out what exactly had been the content of the cargo lost by the C-119's during the previous night, de Castries in person sent another radio message to Hanoi informing it of the bombing and of the fact that the five full plane-loads of ammunition represented "at least 800 rounds of artillery ammunition. No comment. (signed) De Castries."

And the day was to continue like this. At 1425 a fighter-bomber dropped its bombs between strongpoints H1 and H6 while another dropped its bombs on a French ammunition depot inside Dien Bien Phu, which blew up, killed several soldiers in the area, and destroyed close to 1,000 rounds of precious 105-mm. howitzer ammunition. And while this went on another C-119 again managed to drop its whole cargo of 105-mm. ammunition on the northeastern slope of Communist-held Dominique 1.

And again, as in earlier weeks, there was the gnawing need for specialists. The GAP 2, for example, had a signal organization originally designed to operate with three independent battalions. Now the GAP was in control of six airborne battalions but had, if anything, lost signal personnel rather than added to it. What was left of the two Foreign Legion outfits in the main center of the fortress was hardly large enough for one single battalion, let alone a half-brigade, and de Castries insisted that Foreign Legion replacements be dropped in. (At the news, a complete Foreign Legion battalion in the Red River Delta volunteered, included its commanding officer.) Yet the replacements who had come in during the previous night amounted to only seventy-one men, including another Airborne Surgical Team (ACP No. 5) under Capt. Hantz, which was installed in the area of the Half-Brigade's headquarters— hardly enough to make up for the day's losses.

Finally, at 1915, for no apparent reason, the Communist artillery again opened up with a violent bombardment of the headquarters area and the artillery positions on Claudine. The gun pits of the 4th Battery, II/4 RAC, seemed to be singled out for particular punishment. The enemy volley finally hit its mark, destroying completely one howitzer and setting afire the ammunition depot. The battery commander, gallant

Lt. Brunbrouck who had saved Dominique 3 two weeks earlier, lay dying in his half collapsed command post, his back torn open by shell fragments but still conscious. "Keep firing!" said Brunbrouck to one of the crew chiefs standing next to him, "We've got to show them . . ."

Still conscious when Father Trinquand crawled over from headquarters to give him absolution, he died calmly a few minutes later.

Wednesday, April 14, 1954

As the fog cleared on April 14, the first French patrols on their way to strongpoints Huguette 1 and 6 suddenly encountered an obstacle whose creation during the past night had been drowned in the noise of the artillery bombardment. A Communist commando force had infiltrated the airfield and had blasted a trench almost completely across the southernmost third of the airfield about halfway between H1 and H2. Almost simultaneously, at 1020 H1 reported that it was almost completely surrounded on its western perimeter by occupied Viet-Minh trenches, as close as fifteen meters from its outer barbed wire. The latter also had been blasted during the night by Bangalore torpedoes and a three-meter gap had been blasted into it which reached all the way to the innermost strands. At 1200, elements from the 6th and 8th BPC attempted to break through to H1 but found themselves blocked north and west of H5, east of H2, and north of Sparrowhawk by new mine fields placed across the airfield area and by extremely dense Communist mortar fire. This meant in effect that both H1 and H6 were now almost completely sealed off from the rest of Dien Bien Phu. If both fell, Dien Bien Phu would lose about twenty per cent of its area, including two thirds of its airfield. Not that the latter was important *per se,* but its loss would mean that the Communists could install antiaircraft machine guns in closer to the main center of Dien Bien Phu and the parachute aircraft would have to run a flak gauntlet even tighter than before. And thus began the second battle for the Huguettes.

Indeed, as the battle in the northwest of the fortress was beginning to take shape, there were other signs that the enemy, far from relinquishing his hold on Dien Bien Phu if he failed to take it by April 15, was in fact reinforcing his position. Messages intercepted and decoded by the French indicated that Battalions 910 and 920 of the famous Mountaineer Regiment 148 were being recalled from Laos, along with Battalion 970 of Regiment 176 of the 316th Division; all three of which had been operating in Laos as "advisers" to the indigenous Pathet Lao rebels. Giap also ordered that Battalion 900 of Regiment 148, which was a mixed elite outfit providing support for the regimental headquarters of the 148th, detach for duty at Dien Bien Phu such additional units as the 523rd Signal Company and the 121st Heavy Company, with its six recoilless cannon and its four mortars. In addition, Regiment 9 of the 304th Division received orders to join its sister regiment 57/304 in the siege ring at Dien Bien Phu; and, finally, Red China was asked to provide immediately an additional 720 tons of ammunition and one more complete flak regiment with sixty-seven 37-mm. antiaircraft guns. What with the thousands of individual reserves called up from rearward training camps, the Viet-Minh siege force had been able to more than make up its earlier losses—even if some of the new replacements were inexperienced and often extremely young.

As the final struggle for the airstrip now began, Gen. Giap still could field at least 35,000 front-line troops and 12,000 artillerymen and engineers. The French—even after the successful air drops of the first half of April—still had less than 5,000 fighting men at their disposal. Indeed, the arrival of two airborne battalions and other individually parachuted replacements was slim consolation in the face of the statistics compiled by Maj. Grauwin for the field hospitals inside Dien Bien Phu: from April 1 to April 15, 751 wounded had been admitted, of whom 310 required surgical operations, and 76 had died. Those figures, of course, did not include the hundreds of men relatively lightly wounded again and again, or those who died at their positions. As for the conditions under which the wounded had to live, they merely deteriorated from the atrocious to the intolerable as the monsoon rains began to seep into the underground dugouts in mid-April. The consequences of this new catastrophe for the wounded soon became evident—on April 17, the hospitals reported their first cases of gangrene.

But the major problem for Grauwin was lack of space. Like an octopus, the hospital had continued to grow in all directions. Every night, the available Moroccan sappers of the 31st Engineering Battalion were at work digging new tunnels into the ground in order to make room for the wounded. Finally, there simply was nowhere else to go but into the dugouts of other units. Here the requirements of the hospital also inflamed a long-standing vendetta between Langlais and French Central Intelligence. Ever since the beginning of the battle, Langlais had felt that Central Intelligence's local unit, Commando Group (GC) 8, had become totally useless and that its operatives should be included among the infantry of the fortress, just as the aviators were. Since the detachment commander, Capt. Hébert, was in fact not under the command of anyone inside Dien Bien Phu but (as is the case with other intelligence agencies) responsible only to his own superiors in Hanoi and Saigon, Langlais was in no position to make the order stick. He thereupon issued an official note to all paratroop units on March 22, informing them that Hébert and his unit had preferred to remain burrowed in comfortable dugouts rather than join the fight. Langlais went even one step further when, on March 28, as senior paratroop officer in the valley, he ordered Capt. Hébert (who was also a paratrooper) to stop wearing the hallowed red beret of the Colonial Paratroops.

Langlais, whose impulsiveness was well known, was being somewhat unjust to GC 8. Hébert, far from being a "chair-borne" intelligence officer, had earned his paratrooper wings during dangerous behind-the-lines missions in World War II, in the course of which he had been severely wounded; as a result one of his legs was seven centimeters shorter than the other. Nevertheless, in October, 1953, he had volunteered to be parachuted into enemy territory in Indochina with one of the GCMA outfits and had been made a knight of the Legion of Honor for his achievements. Now, Langlais seized an opportunity for liquidating once and for all what he called "that state within a state" of the Central Intelligence station. Faced with the urgent requirements of Grauwin's hospital for more space, Langlais walked into the dugouts of GC 8 on April 9, escorted by a few of his armed paratroopers, and simply ordered the Meo tribespeople to vacate them. They at first tried to pass through the enemy siege ring even at the risk of being captured and tortured by the Viet-Minh. Two of them were killed during the night of the 10th and another during the night of the 11th while many others, including women and children, were wounded by the fire of both sides. In a radio message to his own superiors in Hanoi, Hébert argued that "everybody here is afraid of Langlais" and requested support. A mild rebuke to Langlais by de Castries only increased the fury of the latter against Central Intelligence and, on April 14, Langlais actually sent a squad of tough Foreign Legionnaires into the GC 8 area with direct orders to clear the premises, if need be, with hand grenades.[9]

It finally took a direct order from Gen. Cogny and a threat of "grave personal sanctions" for Langlais to leave the last remnants of GC 8 alone. But he did succeed in providing Grauwin's hospital with enough bunker space for over 200 wounded, even though the area was separated from the hospital by the much-traveled segment of Road 41 that passed right through the camp. The indefatigable 31st Engineers solved this problem one night by digging a complete trench through the road and covering it with wooden beams and steel plates from the airfield. This left Grauwin with just one more problem. The constant extension of the graveyard near the hospital (one of the remaining bulldozers did little else during the relatively safe night hours but dig vast trenches for the next day's cargo of dead) had brought about a pullulation of huge slimy white maggots which now infiltrated the tomblike galleries where the wounded were lying and which soon could be found crawling about the open festering wounds. There was simply no way of holding them back or of exterminating them. In the long list of pressing air-drop priorities, medical supplies often had to accept a secondary position to ammunition and gasoline.

It was simply impossible to find space for the hundreds of pounds of disinfectants that were required when fresh blood, plasma, and even simple items such as wound alcohol came in carefully measured quantities. Grauwin explained to the wounded that the maggots fed only on dead or putrescent bone and flesh and, for all their unwholesome aspect, contributed to keeping wounds clean. It is not known whether his explanation made anyone feel any better, but at least it calmed the panic of those wounded who believed that the appearance of the maggots in their bandages was a sure sign of coming death.

Yet another problem which had become acute on April 14 was that of food. Supplying an isolated force of 16,000 men for fifty-six days under combat conditions was a feat, which, over a similar length of time, had been equaled only at Stalingrad.[10] To realize how complicated the food supply problem for Dien Bien Phu was, it must be realized that there were six different types of food rations allocated: European, North African, African, Vietnamese, T'ai Auxiliary, and "PIM"—the PW's. For example, it was impossible to feed the standard pork meat of American or French canned rations to the pork-shunning Moslems. The Europeans could not subsist indefinitely on rice, but all Vietnamese considered rice a staple. As it became less and less possible to cook, the men began to rely more and more on canned combat rations. There was therefore a strong possibility that much of the garrison would fall victim to diseases connected with the lack of vitamins, such as scurvy or beriberi. Hence, a concerted effort was made to have all the men eat raw onion and fruits even during the worst of the battle. A brief list of the major consumable supply items shows what this meant in actual practice. It also showed some of the peculiarly "French" aspects of the problem:

Rice	791 tons
Frozen meat	195 tons

Dried bread	473 tons
Fresh vegetables	25 tons
Individual combat rations	623,194
Survival rations	22,760
Wine	49,720 gallons
Wine concentrate	7.062 gallons
Mustard	60 kilograms

Among the other items parachuted, one may note a total of 2,952 tubes of toothpaste and only 16,460 razor blades. Even if one admits that the smooth-skinned Vietnamese among the garrison hardly ever needed a shave, this still meant that over the three months of battle hardly more than two to three razor blades were consumed by each man.

The tightening of the siege ring around the drop zones compelled both Hanoi and the command at Dien Bien Phu to make an agonizing daily choice between the airplane space accorded to reinforcements, munitions, and medical supplies, and that allotted to food. The result, obviously, was that food took the lowest priority and that units were, at critical moments, compelled to live off survival rations ordinarily to be consumed only in dire emergencies. Thus it happened that on April 7, Dien Bien Phu ran out of food rations except for those already distributed to the individual units. While the battle raged for E1 and the northern part of Huguette was in the process of being sealed off, the combat units were authorized on April 11 to consume one day's worth (of the three they had theoretically in stock) of survival rations.

The following days brought some relief as the air drops on April 13-14 climbed to the never-again-to-be-reached height of 217 and 229 tons. But on the evening of April 14 events were to smash all hope of building up adequate reserves. As the surviving trucks and jeeps collected the food in the headquarters area to insure its proper distribution, a rain of Communist artillery shells set fire to the unprotected mound of easily combustible food. More than 300 kilograms of cheese, 700 kilograms of tea, 700 kilograms of coffee, 450 kilograms of salt, 110 kilograms of chocolate, and 5,080 individual rations were lost. This disaster matched another, a few days earlier, in which the whole camp's tobacco reserve was set afire, an incident which caused Langlais to say that "all of Dien Bien Phu smelled as if it were smoking a gigantic pipe." From April 14 onward, Dien Bien Phu remained on short rations, and on April 29 it actually went on half rations. Not only was the garrison being bled white by the enemy and short of ammunition, it was fighting most of the time on empty stomachs as well.

On April 14 also, the struggle between Langlais and the paratroop bureaucrats reached its highest level on both sides. In a telegram which had obviously been prepared by Langlais for de Castries' signature, the latter told Cogny in no uncertain terms what the exact situation inside the fortress was and began his message with what turned out to be an incredibly accurate prophecy:

> 1. Reference your telegram 19-31 [dealing with the dropping of non-parachutists]. The fate of GONO will be sealed by May 10 regardless of parachute training regulations. Inform you that effectives 1/13 Half-Brigade, 1/2 REI, 3/13 Half-Brigade holding west flank are respectively 354, 380, 80. I/4 RTM with two combatworthy companies holds southwest. Airborne battalions' total effectives approach 2500 hold the other flanks and constitute the reserves. Stop.
> 2. Evolution of [enemy] works threatens Huguette 1 and Huguette 6. Attempt at clearing Huguette 1 this morning fell upon numerous mined zones between Huguette 1, Huguette 3 and Huguette 5 and mortar and artillery fire. Will be attempted again at nightfall at the same time as repairs on landing strip. Stop.
> 3. At 0800 transmitter of Regiment 102 [308] announced to its subordinated units to "stand by for important news." Stop.
> 4. Insist once more upon dropping each night five aircraft of personnel. Stop. End.

> (signed) de Castries[11]

Otherwise, little else happened at Dien Bien Phu that day. One electric generator urgently needed to provide the fortress with electric power for its transmitters, water purifiers, and minimal illumination, was parachuted but so poorly packed that it shattered on landing; and somebody in Hanoi had not yet heard about the pressure effects of a brutal air drop on a completely filled gasoline jerry-can. Instead of allowing space for the gasoline to slosh around in, the dropped jerry-cans were filled to the rim and promptly burst upon landing. De Brinon, a Foreign Legion major who had been pulled out from the 1/13th to serve as air-drop controller at de Castries' headquarters, sent a brief message on the subject to Hanoi: "Tell the air-supply companies to do their job right. Now we don't have enough gasoline to keep our tanks going."

Indeed there were things wrong with the French air-supply system. Prior to the battle of Dien Bien Phu, nobody apparently had dreamed that so large a garrison would have to be fed by air drops. Only a steady stream of American parachutes from Japan kept the air-supply effort from collapsing. Until late in the battle, only the Airborne Supply Center in Hanoi was capable of preparing and folding cargo parachutes, with the result that the chutes arrived in Haiphong by air or sea, had to be transported to Hanoi for folding, and then shipped back to Haiphong to be attached to cargo loads. A French mission from Indochina went to visit supply operations at the 8081st Quartermaster Airborne Supply and Packaging Company of the U.S. Army at Ashyia Air Force Base and had returned amazed not so much at the efficiency of the American supply operation (which, at Ashyia, represented nothing out of the ordinary) but at the marvelous layout of the entire base. Less national pride and more willingness to learn from an ally would have helped the French a great deal. However, their unwillingness to devote extensive attention to quartermaster problems dated back more than a decade.[12]

It was also surprising to see that it took until April 14 for Dien Bien Phu to request the bulletproof vests that had first made their appearance in great numbers during the Korean War. Distributed to the artillerymen and other personnel fighting in fixed positions, they could well have saved Dien Bien Phu hundreds, if not thousands, of casualties. The initial request was processed by the United States forces in Japan within five days. It took the French supply system another eight days to parachute the first load into Dien Bien Phu, and this fell straight into Communist hands. A second load of 200 bulletproof vests finally arrived at Dien Bien Phu on April 27, while another hundred was parachuted the same day on Isabelle. This shipment could have saved half of the fortress's artillery crews had it been requested a month earlier.

That day also, patrols of the 1/13th pushed as far west as Ban-Ban and Ban Pa-Pé. And on battered Huguette 6 three of the platoon commanders, Lts. Rastouil, François, and Méric had been down on their haunches with Capt. Bizard for a brief talk on the situation while they ate meager combat rations, when a heavy shell smashed right into the dugout, killing Rastouil and seriously wounding Méric. Bizard and François were barely scratched. H6 had become a veritable hell: With its dugouts almost completely smashed, the garrison was constantly exposed either to the monsoon rains or to the blazing sun beating down on the flat plain. Thirst now had become a major problem. Bizard had begun to dig a well in the middle of the position, but thus far nothing but dirty, oily mud had come to the surface.

Thursday, April 15, 1954

There were three ways of reaching Huguette 6 from the main center of resistance at Dien Bien Phu. One was straight up along the open expanse of the airfield over 1,500 meters of billiard-like plain mercilessly beaten by enemy artillery—clearly a suicidal operation. The second approach was west of the airfield along what remained of the Pavie Track, which entailed running the enemy gauntlet of its now solidly held trench system around H1. Third, there existed an approach halfway between the two others, which consisted of following the airfield drainage ditch out of strongpoint Sparrowhawk to a point north of the H1 bottleneck, but on the other side of the airfield, at which point it was necessary to race across the width of the airfield and reach the relative safety of the communication trenches leading northward from H1 to H6. All trails to H6 were rough.

The needs of Capt. Bizard's small band were simple: water and ammunition. Food in the form of individual combat rations and emergency rations was available but the broiling heat brought on dehydration that could kill a man in twenty-four hours (and which still gave trouble to U. S. Marines at Danang in 1966). Every man had to drink at least a half-gallon of liquid a day. For the approximately 200 men of the garrison, this meant 100 gallons a day, or twenty standard five-gallon jerrycans that had to be carted for over three kilometers under fire. That was the job of the poor miserable PIM's, the Communist PW's of whom there had been, on March 13, 2,440 inside Dien Bien Phu. "PIM" stood for *prisonnier-interné militaire,* a term coined by the French Army to designate Viet-Minh captives who had normal prisoner-of-war status in contrast to Communist civilian prisoners who were turned over to the Vietnamese authorities and who usually suffered a barbarous fate, not unlike that which they still suffer in 1967 in full violation of the appropriate articles of the Geneva Convention on War Victims of August 12, 1949. The PIM's were treated more or less according to the regulations and their camps were subject to inspection by Monsieur Durand, the one-armed Swiss representative of the International Red Cross, or even by representatives of the other side, such as Gen. Giap's own brother, who resided in the French-held zone. But this being a civil war, adherence to the Geneva Conventions was more often honored in the breach, with the results that the PIM's actually fell into three informal categories: the regular PIM's duly registered in a camp, the PIM's informally detained by the unit which captured them and used by it as coolie labor, and the "converted" PIM's who had volunteered to join the French union forces as regular soldiers. In the latter case, a small scenario was usually adhered to, in the course of which the PIM was first reported as having "escaped," and then the enlistment of a new Vietnamese soldier would be reported under a name different from that of the escapee.

The 31st Engineers used PIM's for basic construction work. While it could be argued that the building of bridges and roads and cantonments was not, as such, military activity prohibited under the Geneva Convention, there is no doubt that the building of battery positions and of underground dugouts was a violation, as was the use of PIM's during the battle for the collection of air-dropped supplies and carrying water and ammunition under the fire of their own brothers-in-arms.

The PIM camp was located between Juno and Claudine and the PIM's were distributed every day at 0730 and at 1130 to the various units as requested. The word "distributed" was to have unfortunate consequences when a Viet-Minh political commissar, Khanh, discovered the distributions hours still posted at the camp gate after the battle: "Distribution! Can you imagine?" said the commissar. "You mean you are distributing people like issue items, like beans or biscuits?"[13]

The prison camp at Dien Bien Phu was under the control of a kind young French officer, Lt. Patrico, who headed a guard detachment of eight North Africans, led by a Tunisian sergeant. Initially, the PIM's were supposed to have been flown out before the battle began, but this became impossible. It was also impossible to release them and thus provide the enemy with another regiment of well-fed troops with the immense advantage of being thoroughly familiar with the fortress. Hence, they shared the fate of the French to the last day of the battle. Since they were not allocated any construction materials for their camp, the PIM's soon devised, with typical Vietnamese ingenuity, a new type of dugout which was soon adopted by the combat troops. It consisted of a deep vertical shaft at the bottom of which the PIM's dug a narrow tunnel just sufficiently wide for one prone body. If one was not prone to claustrophobia, this kind of individual dugout was as good as any built at Dien Bien Phu.

The faithfulness of the PIM's at Dien Bien Phu to their captors remains a mystery to this day. Only thirty actually made a deliberate and successful attempt to escape while between the lines collecting dropped supplies. Patrico distinctly recalls the following conversation between a PIM and a Moroccan guard who had panicked under the artillery fire and was running away from his guard detail. The PIM ran after the

Moroccan and brought him back to where the PIM's were "sweating out" the barrage, and said to him: "You Moroccan here to guard PIM; you stay here." In the course of their supply-collecting assignments, the PIM's often came upon freshly parachuted weapons or found fully-loaded weapons on the battlefield. There was no known case of the PIM's trying to hide such weapons. It was not uncommon for PIM's to be separated from their guard while they were between the lines and mine fields on the look-out for dropped cargo; more than once one of the outposts suddenly radioed that he was being approached by "some Viet-Minh carrying our supplies."

Under such living and working conditions, the losses suffered by the PIM force amounted to more than fifty per cent. When the PIM infirmary was finally crushed one day by one of those one-ton cargoes whose parachute failed to open (killing twelve patients) the other PIM's and all other incoming prisoners were treated at Maj. Grauwin's ACM 29 and in the proper order of the urgency of their wounds. After the fall of Dien Bien Phu, the Viet-Minh made a special point of verifying that its own wounded prisoners had received proper medical attention. To everyone's relief, the enemy high command found no cause for complaint. But the supreme test of the feelings of the PIM for their captors also came at the end of the battle. The Viet-Minh had vowed that they would try as war criminals French officers who had worked with the T'ai guerrillas, the GCMA, Intelligence, and any who had been part of the PIM guard detachment. Hundreds of the PIM knew Lt. Patrico by sight and quite a few knew him by name. Not one denounced him. Major Coldeboeuf, whose name ("Beef-Neck") exactly translated his build and stature, also commanded a large PIM detachment, as deputy to Maj. Clémençon. As he in turn, his hands tied tightly behind his back with telephone wire, marched off to prison camp after the battle, he passed by chance in front of his own PIM detachment awaiting transportation by the wayside. One by one the PIM rose and gave him the military salute. One of them who spoke French said, *"Bonne chance, mon Commandant."* They were booted away by their own liberators. Little is known as to how the Viet-Minh treated its own returning prisoners. Perhaps they were treated, like those of the Soviet Union in 1945, as cowards and deserters.

But in mid-April, 1954, there still remained for the PIM's the final agony of the battle and the arduous task of supplying faraway Huguette 6. During the night of April 14-15, the better part of the 1st and 2nd BEP attempted the passage via the Pavie Track with a supply carrier detachment of about fifty PIM's. They were pinned down for almost four hours between H1 and H2, separated by only 200 meters of open terrain, fired on not only by the enemy artillery but also by enemy infantry still holding the trench blasted into the airfield. In addition, there now was an enemy machine-gun nest in the carcass of the destroyed Curtiss C-46 *Commando* aircraft. In the dishpan-flat plain, that relative elevation of about six feet was enough to give the machine gun a commanding field of fire. It was to cost the French dearly later. Finally, at 0240, the supply convoy got through to Bizard. The operation had cost the French a heavy price in casualties and a good part of the supplies had been lost en route. Now the covering force had to face the grim prospect of the return trip in the face of an enemy who was fully aware of its presence. Langlais thereupon decided to confuse the Viet-Minh by launching two diversionary attacks. The first was led by Lt. Bailly's company of the 8th Assault across from Sparrowhawk against the Viet-Minh trench on the airfield. The second was led by Capt. Philippe's composite Foreign Legion company against something new in the Viet-Minh siege arsenal—a regular enemy strongpoint (see map, p. 254). Indeed, the Viet-Minh had, within the space of a single night, connected the trench system it had built during the previous days with a series of combat bunkers and firing positions in front of which there even was some barbed wire and some of the mines collected from other French strongpoints.

Undeterred, Philippe and his company of the 13th Half-Brigade pressed forward, only to be pinned down by the enemy's automatic weapons and mortars. The company began to take heavy losses. Clémençon was finally compelled to commit his last reserve unit, 2nd Company, to the fight. It finally extracted the remnants of Philippe's company from the trap but also lost ten men in the process. At the airfield trench, Bailly kept trying all day long to clear it in bloody hand-to-hand fighting but was taking losses as every one of his men had first to race the gantlet of the open field before reaching the Communist trench. Finally, at 1615, with the other two attacks a failure and with the supply convoy at last back inside the French lines, the elements of the 8th withdrew back to the drainage ditch east of the airstrip. One half of the airfield and one fifth of the total remaining area of Dien Bien Phu, along with some 400 of its best combat troops, now were in deep jeopardy. On April 15, the supply runs to Dien Bien Phu reached their all-time high. In a steady drone of American-piloted C-119's, and civilian and military C-47's and 46's flown by French Air Force and civilian crews, nearly 250 tons were dropped into the valley, almost as much as the daily maximum reached by the German Air Force at Stalingrad. Even though at least fifteen per

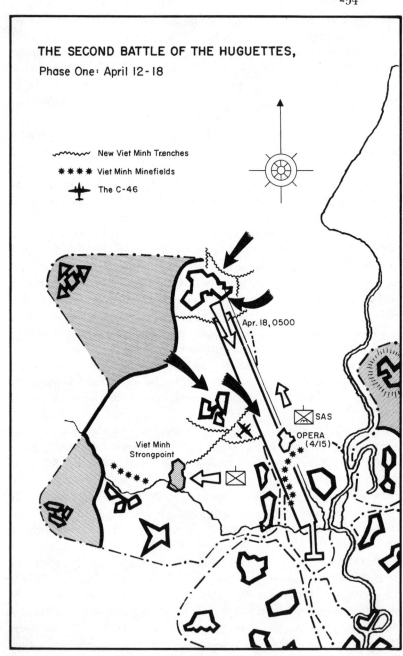

THE SECOND BATTLE OF THE HUGUETTES,
Phase One: April 12-18

New Viet Minh Trenches

Viet Minh Minefields

The C-46

Apr. 18, 0500

SAS

OPERA
(4/15)

Viet Minh
Strongpoint

cent (and, according to Pouget, almost one half) fell into Communist lines, it permitted the hard-pressed fortress to replenish its reserves at the following levels: two days of food, five days of 105-mm. shells, and six days of 120-mm. mortar shells. With the air drops now being so large and so vital to the survival of the fortress, the Communists made it a habit to register machine guns on some of the most conspicuous parcels and to await the dark of night in silence until some movement on the French side showed that an attempt was being made to collect them. Then the enemy machine guns would open up on the collection crews (often made up of the hapless PIM's) with devastating results.

At 1700, a fighter-bomber from the carrier *Arromanches* was to drop a brand-new complete set of aerial photographs of the valley, *including all the French positions,* and a set of maps especially drawn in Hanoi on extra-large 1 : 25,000 scale showing all the new French positions as well as all the detected enemy antiaircraft positions. In addition, it carried a smaller-scale 1 : 100,000 map of all of North Viet-Nam with all the French code names of enemy targets and detailed notations of enemy transportation bottlenecks. As the plane approached the center of Dien Bien Phu for the free drop of the pouch, the pilot pushed back his heavy glass canopy, but at that moment enemy flak began to open up on him. At the last moment the pilot attempted evasive tactics and went into a wing-over-wing barrel roll. The heavy pouch, marked clearly for easier identification, fell right out of the cockpit and into enemy hands. Now Gen. Giap not only knew almost as much about Dien Bien Phu as de Castries did, but he also knew exactly what the French knew (or did not know) about his armed forces. This meant that French codes had to be changed throughout Indochina, and perhaps dozens of infiltrated French agents paid with their lives for the nervousness of one pilot. To make matters worse, more packages of photos were lost from another airplane on the following day.

On Isabelle, the much-battered T'ai Sub-Groupment Wieme, which had held its improvised strongpoint against heavy enemy pressure since the beginning of the battle without breaking or deserting, was finally relieved by Capt. Désiré's 9th T'ai Company, the one outfit of 3rd BT that had not disintegrated. The enemy detected the suspicious movement on Wieme and hit the position at the dangerous moment when one unit was not yet installed and the other unit had not yet withdrawn; there were losses among both the new arrivals and the departing tribesmen.

Friday, April 16, 1954

Good Friday began with yet another costly breakthrough operation to H6. Again almost sixty PIM's were escorted by elements from both the two BEP's and from the 6th BPC. By now, the operation had become a death march in which the PIM's with their clanking jerry-cans or ammunition boxes, simply did not have a chance. They had set out with 700 liters of water and a half-dozen boxes of small-arms ammunition. According to the official report of the day, 42 PIM's were killed or wounded in the breakthrough and only seven water carriers with five jerry-cans of water made it safely to H6. This left every man of the garrison with about one pint at the most, instead of the two quarts needed. It was clear that the French could not afford to supply H6 indefinitely.

Around H1 also, the situation had seriously deteriorated. At 1020, Dien Bien Phu reported that Communist trenches around H1 now reached the airfield and that the strongpoint was thus completely surrounded. On H2, where two companies from Claudine's 1/13 Half-Brigade under Lieutenants Viard and Chounet had relieved the exhausted troops of the 1/2 REI, the decision was made to make an attempt at beating the Viet-Minh at their own game. Instead of attempting to force their way into H1 through costly assaults, the Legionnaires would now try to patiently dig their way forward toward H1. The problem of course was that at one point the north-south trench of the Legionnaires would encounter the Communist west-east trench south of Huguette 1. Being Legionnaires, they would cross that bridge when they reached it.

But among the logisticians at Dien Bien Phu, the old and never-resolved struggle between supply and personnel requirements continued. To be sure, that mid-April period was to witness some of the best days of air transport, what with the relatively good flying weather permitting effective fighter and fighter-bomber protection for the defenseless supply carriers. April 16 was another day where the supplies loaded at Haiphong and Hanoi reached 215 tons (with a misdropped percentage of ten per cent and an effective collection ratio of perhaps two to one) but de Castries complained in bitter terms that he now needed mechanics and electricians to keep the last remaining vehicles and, above all, the precious electric generators and water purifiers going. And, finally, the artillery gun crews were reaching, after thirty-two days of constant duty in the open gun pits, a state of total physical and psychological breakdown. The accuracy and speed of the counterbattery fire now began to suffer. The men still went through the motions but it was no longer possible to get from them the reaction, speed, and accuracy necessary to utilize the few guns and the now closely rationed artillery shells with maximum effectiveness. De Castries once more requested that the remainder of the 35th Airborne Artillery be dropped into the valley. Of the forty-nine officers and men of the 35th RALP who had been parachuted in during the month, only twenty-seven would be fit for duty on April 24 and the remaining airborne gun crews outside the valley were sorely needed in other areas as well.

Hanoi had no encouraging answers to any of those questions. All it had to offer that day was the news that Col. de Castries had been promoted to brigadier general and that most of the other senior commanders in the fortress had been advanced one notch on the promotion list. Langlais and Lalande were now full colonels, Bigeard became a lieutenant-colonel, and the many captains who in fact had commanded battalions for months were now promoted to majors. In a comradely gesture, the higher-ranking officers passed on their old rank insignia to the newly promoted lower-ranking officers; thus, Col. Langlais inherited Col. de Castries' five stripes, but since the latter, as a cavalryman, wore them on a red background, Langlais had to use india ink to dye it black. Major General Cogny, in Hanoi, who had still been a brigadier general the year before, had his own brigadier's stars parachuted to de Castries along with a bottle of champagne. They fell outside the French lines into Communist hands.

Saturday, April 17, 1954

As night fell on the 16th, another column of paratroopers from the 6th BPC and the two BEP's escorted yet another convoy of water carriers to the hell of H6. In almost routine fashion, the supply group met a Communist roadblock near the Communist trenches south of Huguette 1, ran the gauntlet of the machine-gun nest installed in the wreck of the Curtiss "Commando" and, after a small firefight, finally reached H6 at 0125 with only minor losses. This time the convoy had succeeded in bringing in enough water not only for the garrison's minimal water ration but also for it to drink to de Castries' general's stars and to the Officer's Cross of the Legion of Honor, which 29-year-old Capt. Bizard just had received for his gallant defense of H6.

But even this small success begged the question as to whether holding H6 was worth the price. Langlais had calculated the cost of maintaining open communications with H6 during the preceding week, and it amounted to more dead and wounded than the whole counteroffensive for the conquest of Eliane 1. Against this, two factors could be thrown into the equation. First was the fact that during the past night a total of only eighty reinforcements had been parachuted in. Second, the northern part of the airfield was, in view of the Communist trenches which now pierced it, useless as a drop zone anyway. General de Castries accepted Langlais' reading of the situation and at 1820 decided to evacuate Huguette 6 during the following night. At the same time he requested a maximum air effort from Hanoi in support of the evacuation operation. It is difficult to judge if the amputation of H6, as of April 18, was a serious flaw in reasoning. The decision was apparently made by two ground-force officers without consulting the air operations officer, Maj. Guérin. The loss of H6 was almost immediately followed by a closing in of the enemy antiaircraft artillery and machine guns onto the runway. This made the flying of a set course by the transport aircraft even more hazardous than before and thus materially affected the ability of Dien Bien Phu to survive.

Aside from the elements of the II/1 RCP which again faced a determined Communist probe on E1 and counterattacked later in the day, Bigeard committed at 2000 the bulk of the 1st BEP and elements of the 8th Assault and detachments from the 1/2 REI along with two tanks to the breakthrough to H6. At 2200, Bigeard and his task force had reached the enemy trench blocking the airfield at the latitude of Huguette 1. In fact, the word "trench" no longer was applicable here, because the Communists had dug a veritable trench system composed of several separate lines facing both the encircled strongpoint and the main center of resistance from which the counterattacks would come. At 2200 the task force had finally fought its way through two trench lines but now was, in the words of Col. Langlais, "out of breath, of ammunition, and of men."

Easter Sunday, April 18, 1954

Four hours later, at 0200 of April 18, after Bigeard had thrown in every unit that could be scraped together—namely, a weak company of his own 6th BPC and another one of Moroccan riflemen from the 1/4 RTM—the attack bogged down completely. The breakthrough force, caught in part on the open airfield and in part in the newly occupied Communist trenches, began to take heavy losses. As dawn broke, the French pulled back toward a bunker system now being set up by the Engineers in the airfield drainage ditch, called "Opéra," which provided a small measure of protection against enemy shells in spite of the fact that flooding was a severe problem. Another part of the breakthrough force had withdrawn westward beyond H1, where the Engineers were also installing a new small holding position at the crossroads north of H2. At 0730, even the tough Bigeard, the man who probably believed longest that Dien Bien Phu had a fighting chance of surviving, was ready to concede that the attempt at rescuing H6 had failed and that a new attempt might devour men and supplies far beyond any benefits that could be derived from rescuing even a few of the defenders of H6.

Bigeard left Maj. Clémençon the unpleasant task of informing Bizard by radio that he would have to attempt his own breakout, if possible, but that no one would blame him if, in view of the number of wounded, he had to abandon them or, in view of the pitifully small chance at H6 he had of breaking through; he chose to surrender to the enemy. In order to be sure that the Communists would not understand what had been said, the whole radio conversation between the two officers had taken place in English. But for young Bizard and his mixed bag of Foreign Legionnaires and French and Vietnamese paratroopers, there was no question of surrendering. He informed Clémencon that a breakout would be attempted at 0800 sharp. The decision was made to break out on a broad front, using mainly hand grenades, while abandoning all wounded and all heavy equipment to the enemy.

In order to protect themselves from the effects of their own grenade splinters most of the men slung sandbags partially filled with earth over their chests and backs[14] as they lined up, facing southward, in their own forward trench only thirty meters away from the first Communist line. They knew that the breakout would be difficult but Bizard's men at least enjoyed the tactical advantage that the Viet-Minh fully expected the breakthrough of rescue forces from the south while it did not believe that the battered survivors of H6 would, in their weakened state, attempt anything as desperate as a breakout. And since the Communists themselves fully expected to use their trench for the final assault on H6, there were no barbed wire or mines between them and the French garrison. Moreover, early morning fog which, as usual, covered most of the valley hid the movements of the French troops on H6 from the enemy.

Finally, on a shouted order of Bizard, the thin line climbed over the trench parapet. Under the cover of their own hand grenades and of one last automatic rifle, manned by Foreign Legion Sgt. Ganzer who, being wounded, had volunteered to stay behind and cover his comrades (and who was to die a few minutes later from enemy fire), they vaulted clear over the Communist trench and the heads of the Viet-Minh and began racing southward in the direction of the French first line 300 meters away. On the right flank, the platoon of Sergeant Josef Franz fell upon a trench filled with Viet-Minh soldiers and came to a dead halt. For a brief moment there was a dead silence as, suddenly, no one fired. Then a voice on the Viet-Minh side said in French: "Put your weapons down! Surrender!" That broke the spell: on the French side a Legionnaire yelled *"A l'assaut!"* and threw a grenade into the tightly packed enemy trench. Franz's mesmerized platoon jumped over the trench, lost a few of its men, and joined the rest of Bizard's force.

The fog was now lifting rapidly and survival lay in outracing the enemy's fire while French heavy mortars, firing over the heads of the escapees from H6, kept the enemy machine-gunners pinned down. Lieutenant Bergot, the commander of the 1st Foreign Legion Airborne Heavy Mortars Company on Claudine, distinctly recalls that Bizard's men were yelling and singing as they raced southward on the totally bare steel plates of the airfield, with some of the Spanish Anarchists singing a children's ditty which could be clearly heard:

Si tù madre	(If your mother
Quiere un rey	Seeks a king
La barajo	The deck of cards
Tiene Cuatro	Has four of them)

It is not certain how many men tried to break out, as it was difficult to count them and it was not clearly known how many of them were wounded or killed during the final rush. But when Bizard collected his men at 1040 on Huguette 2, the exact dimensions of the bloodletting became clearly visible: the small force had lost 106 dead, 49 were wounded, including Lts. Cousin and Weinberger, and 79 men were missing. Among the dead were two of the lieutenants, François and Donadieu, who had been part of Huguette 6's garrison for almost a month and who had, just the day before, received battlefield promotions to the rank of captain. They never had the chance to wear their new insignia. Captain Bizard and the artillery FO, Lt. Lagarde, miraculously escaped without a scratch. Of the total of sixteen officers who had served on Huguette 6 at one time or another, only five survived.

The battle for H6 was over. The agony of H1 now began. But the evacuation of H6 had left a sour taste in the mouth of Bigeard and de Castries, as is clearly apparent from the latter's radio messages to Hanoi on that Easter Sunday. According to de Castries, the breakthrough operations had been severely hampered by Hanoi's failure to replace the aerial photographs lost during the previous days, for the French assault force had no clear idea of the Communist trench layout which it was about to penetrate. Direct observation also had been hampered in the various positions of the valley bottom by the fact that there existed no trench periscopes at Dien Bien Phu and that requests made for them on April 13 had simply not been answered by Hanoi.

Some of the units were now running out of platoon commanders: the valiant 6th BPC no longer had any able-bodied platoon commanders left and neither had 3rd Company of the 31st Combat Engineers. Another officer of that company, Lt. Maury, was wounded on April 21 by shell fragments while personally installing a mine field in front of the new strongpoint in the airfield drainage ditch. Work on Opéra was further hampered, as de Castries pointed out to Hanoi on April 18, by directly observed enemy fire from Dominique 1 and the river bend of the Nam Yum. Neutralization by aerial attack was requested. In addition, the constant harassing fire of the enemy artillery was taking its toll. At 1600 two enemy howitzer shells fell into the pit of a 155-mm. gun of Capt. Deal's battery, knocking out the piece and killing part of its crew. That left Dien Bien Phu now with only two 155's. At 1800, other enemy shells damaged heavily two of the lighter 105-mm. howitzers.

In the meantime, however, the battle for Huguette 1 already was taking shape and the new strangulation methods tested by Giap's generals on H6 had now reached a level of deadly perfection. This is why it was decided to relieve the battle-weary 4th Company of the 1/2 REI by Capt. Chevalier's 4th Company from Maj. Coutant's 1st Battalion, 13th Foreign Legion Half-Brigade. Stationed thus far on the relatively quiet strongpoint Claudine, the 1/13 was in better shape than most other units and what was in store for Huguette 1 required soldiers of the first quality.

Chevalier and his men began the dangerous trek northward shortly after nightfall, after having eaten one last warm meal on Claudine. By now, most of the communications trenches in the central part of the fortress had been roofed over. As the airfield had become useless its steel plates were ruthlessly "cannibalized" as construction material. Hence, supplies, reinforcements, and wounded, would circulate in the almost total darkness of what now indeed had become a "subway," whose stops were represented by exits toward the various combat strongpoints or other underground command posts. Chevalier's men were now groping their way forward from Claudine 2 past Lily 1 towards Huguette 3, where they were taken in charge by an officer from the 1/2 REI which held that strongpoint. They were then funneled through Huguette 2 and finally emerged from cover into the open approach trench which the Legionnaires of 1/2 REI had dug in the direction of the Communist transverse trench cutting off H1 to the south and breaching the airfield as well. As they came to the end of the French approach trench they now also were under the fire of the Viet-Minh strongpoint which the enemy had inserted east of Huguette 5. In the past few weeks the Communists not only had learned how to dig in artillery to the point where it became invisible and invulnerable, but apparently they had also learned how to build defensive trench and bunker systems that could hold their own with the best. Twelve years later, underground bunker systems built by South Vietnamese guerrillas would similarly withstand high-explosive bombs dropped from American B-52 bombers. The lessons of Dien Bien Phu were not forgotten, at least on one side of the fence.

In Hanoi, Mme de Castries told Associated Press reporter Larry Allen that her husband had told her over the radio-telephone that he would resign from his command unless he was immediately promoted to the rank of brigadier general.[15] The French Army attempted to retrieve that statement (as many others made by Mme de Castries, or at least attributed to her), but to no avail.

Easter Monday, April 19, 1954

Thirty minutes past midnight, Chevalier's company was completely pinned down on its line of departure and Chevalier requested concentrated artillery fire and air support to smash through the last 200 meters to H1. With creditable precision and speed the weary gunners threw their heavy fieldpieces around and delivered concentrated fire on the small strip of terrain between Opéra, H2, and H1, followed at dawn by the *Bearcats* and *Helldivers* of the French Navy. The Navy pilots had already earned a citation from Gen. de Castries on April 10 for the precision of their close air-support work and their willingness to take higher risks in low-level missions than, reputedly, their compatriots in the French Air Force.

At 0645 the enemy was sufficiently softened up for the breakthrough. By 1000, 4th Company of the 1/13 was in place inside Huguette 1 and 4th Company, 1/2 REI, had withdrawn southward, with both outfits taking losses while doing so. It had taken Chevalier's unit about fourteen hours of bitter fighting and exhausting crawling to cover the 1,500 yards between its old position and H1. The strongpoint in more than one way resembled the ill-fated Huguette 6. Whatever field fortifications it had were completely plowed under by enemy fire; much of its defensive works such as barbed wire and mine fields already had been destroyed by the previous weeks of fighting; and enemy approach trenches in many places

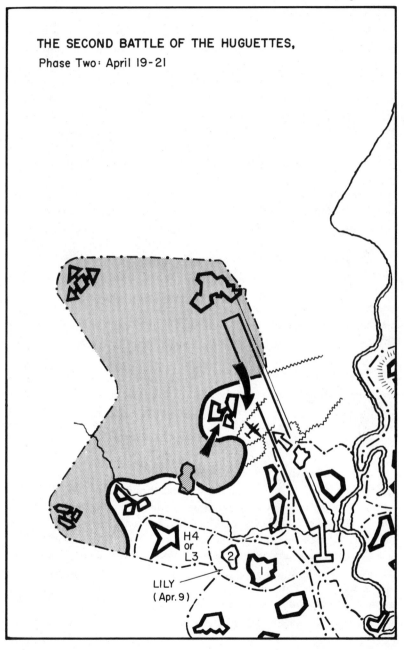

THE SECOND BATTLE OF THE HUGUETTES,
Phase Two: April 19-21

H4
or
L3

2

LILY
(Apr. 9)

had penetrated the French wire entanglements. The problem of water was as bad on H1 as it had been on H6, but the garrison at least had the slim psychological consolation of not being in the middle of nowhere at the end of a seemingly boundless airfield.

Colonel Langlais used the temporary respite offered by the enemy during the day to relieve some of the other units which had been on the firing line for several days. Not that there was anywhere to go inside Dien Bien Phu where one could sleep soundly in the knowledge that one would not be buried under tons of earth and beams. But at least on most of the inner strongpoints one was at least safe from the thousands of small arms, machine guns, and light mortars that made life on the Five Hills and on the outer Huguettes a permanent nightmare. Second Company of II/1 RCP was relieved on E1 by 7th Company, 1st BEP; on Opéra, Bizard's reconstituted 2nd Company, 5th BPNV, relieved 1st Company of the same battalion, commanded by Vietnamese Captain Pham Van Phu; while 3rd Company of the same battalion, commanded since April 16 by the barely healed (for he had been wounded on April 3) Capt. Guilleminot, stayed in reserve. Early in the evening, at 1800, 1st Company of 1/13 relieved much of what remained—except Clémençon himself and his command staff—of the 1/2 REI from Huguette 3. The much-battered Foreign Legionnaires from Huguette took up second-line positions on Claudines 2 and 3. The relief by Chevalier of 4th Company, 1/2 REI, earlier that morning had cost two killed, six wounded, and six missing.

Still, the French kept fighting offensively. At 1400 that day a mixed force of Legionnaires and Moroccans pushed southward on a strong reconnaissance as far as Ban Co My, almost halfway to Isabelle, until they met with strong resistance.

As usual, the real problem was air support. Throughout the whole night of April 18-19, no supplies had been dropped on Dien Bien Phu and on Monday only about 100 tons were delivered. Officially, the reason was that the weather over the Red River Delta had made take-offs impossible even though the weather was quite good over Dien Bien Phu. The general impression among the garrison was that the outside world was celebrating Easter and did not give a hoot as to how Dien Bien Phu was faring. Dien Bien Phu, that day, was short of mines and barbed wire for the new strongpoint Opéra, and it now lacked officers for the 1st BEP and for both the surviving Foreign Legion infantry battalions. When air drops finally resumed at 2200 on Monday evening, the already tense relationship between the garrison of Dien Bien Phu and the French Air

Force further deteriorated when the first two aircraft completely mis-dropped two "sticks" of nonparachutist volunteers deep into enemy ter-ritory. Most of them were exterminated before they were even able to extricate themselves from their parachute harnesses. A few of them, how-ever, managed to find their way back to Dien Bien Phu. One bearded Moroccan is forever remembered for his first remark as he finally reached a French outpost.

"I just don't understand it," said the bewildered man who was ob-viously unacquainted with the unreliability of air drops. "Do you have any idea why we were dropped on the Viet-Minh?"

Tuesday, April 20, 1954

What was particularly upsetting about the situation was that many of the officers of de Castries' staff began to blame the hapless Air Force Major Guérin for the shortcomings of the French Air Force in Hanoi. There is no question that enemy flak over Dien Bien Phu was heavy. During the month of April alone, Communist flak shot down eight air-craft and severely damaged forty-seven; the total included two B-26 bombers that were shot down on April 26 from an altitude of almost 10,000 feet. Indeed, some of the older pilots who ten years earlier had flown in raids on Germany swore that the density of Communist flak over Dien Bien Phu often exceeded that faced over heavily defended industrial targets in Germany. On the night of April 19-20, 1954, both the French and the American pilots of the transport aircraft refused to come down to a lower parachute altitude because of enemy flak—pre-cisely at the very moment when, for reasons unknown, enemy flak com-pletely failed to materialize. Apparently the pilots had mistaken the clearly visible artillery ground fire for flak and refused to take the word of the ground personnel when it reported that no flak was in evidence. This attitude was to give substance later to the ground commanders' charges of excessive prudence if not cowardice by the French Air Force (they explicitly excepted the pilots of the aircraft carriers). The bitterness of de Castries' staff is pointed up in a message sent at 1000, when the results of the previous night's air-supply operations became apparent:

> During the last two days we should have received sixty C-119 aircraft. In reality only twenty-three came and three threw their stuff on the Communist side. The situation with regard to food becomes critical. Units only have one more day of food left. We still have not received any tropicalized rations; our requests are not being taken into account. The 1/2 REI has only 300 men and seven officers left.

But on the other side, the war was also taking its toll. At 1220, as Capt. Clédic and some men of his company of II/1 RCP on Eliane 1 looked down over the sun-baked slopes of the strongpoint toward the Communist lines, they suddenly noticed a single *Bo-Doi* racing madly in their direction. When he came close enough to be clearly distinguished he began to wave a white handkerchief. He was sent down for interrogation to headquarters and the story he told about conditions in the 312th Division had a familiar ring to the battle-weary defenders inside the fortress.

According to the deserter, he had been a soldier in the 209th Regiment of the division. Since its heavy losses during the battle for the Five Hills, the 312th Division had been filled up with raw recruits who apparently now composed one half of it. Supplies of all kinds were hard to come by because of the effects of French aerial bombing on Road 41. If anything, the rains made living conditions thoroughly uncomfortable in the hills around Dien Bien Phu as well, and French artillery still carried a fearsome punch when it suddenly opened up on an exposed enemy infantry unit. The deserter said that the new recruits were pretty despondent about the toughness of the struggle and its length, but he also said that his political commissar had told him that the attack on Dien Bien Phu would continue regardless of losses and that coolies would make up for the supply difficulties caused by French bombardment of truck transport. But the deserter also brought news of a more unwelcome nature: there were Chinese Communist advisers with each 37-mm. antiaircraft gun, which beyond a doubt accounted for the deadly accuracy of that type of weapon in the hills around Dien Bien Phu. Chinese advisers wore the same uniforms as the Viet-Minh forces with the exception of a small cloth insignia showing a sun.

It was perhaps not coincidental that on the same day, at 0315, Col. Lalande's forces on Isabelle made a successful tank-supported counterattack beyond strongpoint Wieme, in the course of which Battalion 265 of the 57th People's Army regiment took losses and abandoned many weapons. And at 0345, an attack against the as yet unfinished strongpoint Opéra with its small garrison of Vietnamese paratroopers was easily fended off by artillery and, above all, by Lt. Redon's quad-fifties from Sparrowhawk. Apparently, in that latter part of April, 1954, both sides of Dien Bien Phu were in the position of punch-drunk fighters, each determined to outlast the other in the hope of winning the battle by a technical knockout, if by no other way. It was not, however, without irony that the Viet-Minh would eventually achieve that TKO not by overwhelming manpower but by massive firepower—a prerequisite usually associated with a Western military establishment. At Dien Bien Phu the hard casualty statistics pointed the other way: seventy-five per cent of all French losses were attributable to artillery fire rather than infantry combat.[16]

At 1000 on April 20, Dien Bien Phu again radioed to Hanoi that it was being badly hurt by directly-observed fire on the headquarters and battery area from 75-mm. recoilless rifles on Communist-held Dominique 1. "We again ask with extreme urgency that D1 be permanently and rapidly *matraquée* ["clobbered"] by the Air Force or we shall soon find our whole artillery shot to pieces and our depots on fire." Indeed, a shell hit an ammunition depot at 1430, and Capt. Charnod and M/Sgts. Diringer and Peyrac of the Air Force detachment (and, therefore, more familiar than the ground troops with fire-fighting equipment) succeeded in extinguishing the fire before it became a major disaster.

Late in the afternoon seven T'ai auxiliaries, including a noncom-deserted from strongpoint Juno, taking along with them three French submachine guns. No doubt, when interrogated a few hours later by a Communist intelligence officer, they told him the same story in reverse that the Viet-Minh deserter had told French intelligence officers in Dien Bien Phu.

Wednesday-Thursday, April 21-22, 1954

The pattern of H6 now began to repeat itself on H1 with desperate monotony. During the night of April 20-21, Communist probes against H1 were perfunctory but just strong enough to insure that no supplies would get through to H1 from the south. Still, the Legionnaires from the 1/13 and the Vietnamese from Opéra, reinforced by two of the four tanks remaining in operable condition, again attempted to break through with supplies. In bitter hand-to-hand fighting, they finally succeeded in opening a narrow funnel between 1045 and 1130, and at 1400, Langlais ordered the cessation of the effort for the time being. It was simply getting too costly in terms of men and munitions.

In other sectors, however, the French had not abandoned their earlier aggressiveness. During the night of April 20-21, a company of the II/1 RCP had raided Dominique 6, lost to the enemy for more than a month and no doubt deemed totally secure by it. The paratroopers fell upon the unsuspecting Viet-Minh like the proverbial bats out of hell, killed nineteen of them and captured three, destroying in the process four enemy bunkers whose accurate automatic-rifle fire had made life miserable in the French positions below; and also brought back with them two of those automatic rifles and four submachine guns. On Claudine, the 1/2 REI had taken over most of the positions held by the 1/13 Half-Brigade and also had begun long-range patrolling in the direction of Ban Co My. Parts of the 6th BPC remained on an alert basis on H2 and worked at reinforcing the position under artillery fire. Even this innocuous occupation cost it eleven dead and fifteen wounded that day.

Again the airborne reinforcement in men and supplies came in at a slow pace, further hampered by extremely heavy flak. Of the 135 tons of supplies programmed for that day, 19.4 per cent fell into Communist lines, with much of the rest being used directly by the strongpoints on which the load fell. When the battle began, there had been forty-four jeeps, forty-seven ¾-ton trucks, twenty-six 2.5-ton trucks, one ambulance, and three bulldozers at Dien Bien Phu. The mechanics from the various maintenance units, and in particular the Air Force detachment, had made heroic efforts to keep at least a few of the jeeps running so that they could be used for the picking up (or often, towing) of the heaviest of the air-dropped loads. Unfortunately, unlike the German *Volkswagen* jeeps of World War II which were equipped with air-cooled engines, the French at Dien Bien Phu had only American vehicles with the usual front-mounted engines and their highly vulnerable water-filled radiators, which were being constantly pierced by shrapnel or small-arms fire. The result was that when Communist artillery fire destroyed the last three trucks of the fortress during the night of April 21-22, the collection of more than 100 tons of bulky supplies by hand became virtually impossible and also exhausted the troops. Soon any attempt at maintaining an orderly centralized logistical support system inside Dien Bien Phu completely broke down. But the most serious negative effect on combat morale was due less to the inadequacy of supplies than to the dribbling number of personnel replacements which almost never covered the daily losses.

On April 21, an unfortunate young parachutist volunteer whose parachute had opened too fast became hooked on the tail assembly of his transport aircraft and swung helplessly from it for seemingly endless minutes as the aircraft circled over the valley in the hope of shaking the man loose before his parachute tore to shreds. The attempt failed, however. A few minutes later, the volunteer plummeted to earth somewhere inside the Communist lines. That night, the commander of Gia-Lam air base, an experienced lieutenant-colonel who pitched in as relief pilot on the supply airlift, suddenly found his airplane "framed" by the streak of ten rockets three miles east of Dien Bien Phu. A shiver went down the spine of French planners. If the enemy had flak rockets in any quantity, Dien Bien Phu was doomed inside 24 hours. As it turned out, there were very few such rockets—at least then. But they would be there in quantity, for the Americans, twelve years later.

The following day was like the calm before the storm. At 0840, a task force from H2 successfully broke through for a short time to H1 after a whole night of fighting and one company of the 6th BPC executed a raid on D5, destroying a Communist bunker and capturing its weapons. Headquarters was still complaining about not receiving any periscopes— they were never received—and begged for any of even the most rudimentary kind.

On H3, Sgt. Kubiak, the survivor of the 3/13th on Beatrice, quietly celebrated his twenty-fifth birthday. In keeping with Foreign Legion traditions, he had been given the day off and some of his best friends had brought him their ration of "Vinogel," the French Army's newly developed and awful-tasting wine concentrate. But he was not going to be able to enjoy a full day's rest in his dugout: a sergeant who was to have headed a supply detail to H1 that night was wounded at 1700 by a shell from the nest of recoilless rifles on D1 and, as night fell, Kubiak, ten Legionnaires, and fifteen PIM's picked up their jerry-cans of drinking water and the ammunition boxes and began the trek to fire-beaten Huguette 1.

What Sgt. Kubiak did not know was that there was another Kubiak at Dien Bien Phu—and that he fought on the other side. He was Major Stefan Kubiak, a Pole born in 1923 in Lodz. The son of a poor weaver, Kubiak had joined the Communist Polish Army after World War II. A good party member, he had been posted to the Army Political Commissars School. When he found that his wife was having a love affair with one of his superiors, Kubiak deserted from the Polish Army, drifted to West Germany and eventually enlisted in the Foreign Legion. Sent to North Viet-Nam in 1947, he soon was disillusioned with the French and deserted from the Foreign Legion in 1947 at Nam Dinh in the Red River Delta.

Received at first with distrust by the Viet-Minh, he soon rendered them important services by training their troops in using and servicing the American weapons which they captured from the French. This was particularly important since the Viet-Minh did not have, until early in 1950, good direct overland communications with the Red Chinese. Kubiak distinguished himself for his bravery during the battle for the Hoa-Binh salient,[17] in 1951, and was "adopted" by Ho Chi Minh himself and given the Vietnamese name of Ho Chi Thuan. Promoted to the rank of captain, and then major, Kubiak served at Dien Bien Phu with the 312th Division and had personally participated in the attack on Beatrice in which, unknowingly, he had probably faced his French namesake. This was to occur again when during the last days of the battle some of the Foreign Legionnaires were also thrown into the Five Hills area.[18]

In the meantime, still being unfamiliar with the labyrinth of tunnels and communications trenches leading northward, Sgt. Kubiak's supply group lost its way for a moment, ran right into the field of fire of the quad-fifties on Sparrowhawk, retraced its steps to Huguette 3, and then followed the sound of the guns northwestward toward where H1 was agonizing. On H2 it picked up its escort from the 1st BEP and finally arrived at the usual stopping point about 150 meters south of H1. There, a shell fragment the size of a fist pierced one of the jerry-cans Kubiak was carrying.

But the water was no longer of any importance, for Huguette 1 was dying. At 0210, Capt. Chevalier had informed battalion headquarters on H3 that while he was not being seriously attacked, "the Viet seems to be getting through all over the place." Indeed, small groups of *Bo-Doi* were coming out of an infinity of small approach trenches (aerial photographs were to identify about thirty of them on the next day) and throwing themselves forward against the French position. Many of them would get mowed down by French fire only to be replaced by yet another small group of green-clad men. This wasn't a "human-wave" attack, for the enemy came in very small groups of perhaps five to eight men. Even the word "infiltration" did not convey what was happening as well as the phrase "seeping in." Some of the Viet-Minh trenches had been driven forward as far as the middle of the French barbed-wire entanglements, and thus some of the enemy infantrymen would suddenly spring up in the midst of the wire like a jack-in-the-box, fire a volley, and disappear again in their little trench. At 0230 the last radio message came through from Chevalier, urgently asking for help.

Friday, April 23, 1954

It already was too late for help. As Kubiak and his supply group made ready for the final dash to H1, one of the sergeants on outpost duty returned and told them there was no point in going onward and that H1 had fallen. At 0700 a few Foreign Legionnaires from H1 succeeded in crawling back to H2 and said they had seen Capt. Chevalier standing on top of his own bunker with a last square of ten Legionnaires and dying on the spot.[19] Sergeant Kubiak had witnessed the end of H1 from his vantage point in the communications trench north of H2. When he was asked as to whether there were many prisoners who had fallen into Viet-Minh hands, the sergeant from the Legion outpost said in what was meant to be a reassuring tone: "No, they are surely not prisoners. It looks as if it has been a real massacre."[20]

The loss of H1 was ominous for two reasons: first, because it demonstrated the effectiveness of the new Communist "siege-by-seepage" tactics; and second, because it gave the Viet-Minh virtual control of ninety per cent of the airfield making relatively safe, accurate parachuting of reinforcements all but impossible. As soon as the seriousness of the situation was grasped by Langlais and Bigeard on one hand, and by de Castries on the other, a dramatic conference took place at the latter's command post.

The problem was deceptively simple, for it left the French with only two agonizing choices—attempt to retake H1 at the cost of heavy and surely irreplaceable casualties (during the night of April 22-23, only thirty-five men arrived at Dien Bien Phu while sixty-seven had been lost that day, not including the garrison of H1), or accept the loss of H1 and thus save some scarce elite troops for the decisive assaults that were sure to come.

Cogny's headquarters had sent an extensive questionnaire to Dien Bien Phu a few days earlier, asking de Castries what he required to save Dien Bien Phu from drowning in the rising monsoon rains. His staff had worked at the problem over the preceding two days and on April 23, by sheer coincidence, the answer for Hanoi was ready. It was more or less a re-edition of the plan submitted in February, 1954: As foreseen, Huguette 5, Lily 3, and major sectors of Claudines 3, 4 and 5, as well as Juno and the north of Sparrowhawk, already were partly flooded and their occupants lived in a constant agony of two feet of mud, dripping and slippery trench walls, and collapsing waterlogged dugouts. Merely to get the wounded, the depots, and the artillery out of the quagmire would have required a counteroffensive involving the recapture of at least all the original Dominique position and preferably its further expansion. Consideration also was given to bringing in the whole garrison from Isabelle, which would provide the main garrison with over a thousand troops, the more so as Isabelle also faced a serious flooding problem. As Maj. Grand d'Esnon, the former commander of the 3/3 REI on Isabelle, was to tell me almost a decade after the battle, by late April the nonflooded area of Isabelle was limited to a few tens of square meters. However, de Castries at that point was against the evacuation of Isabelle because it would have meant the abandonment of its artillery, which was still giving useful support to Eliane and Claudine through flanking fires.

In all, de Castries foresaw also that the full reoccupation of the Dominiques would provide Diem Bien Phu with a large drop zone which would no longer be under directly observed close-range fire of enemy mortars. To carry out that operation, it was estimated that the parachuting of the complete 1st Airborne Group, now being assembled in Hanoi from a steady stream of paratroop reinforcements from France, would be necessary. It is not clear whether de Castries explained this "big picture" with sufficient clarity to Langlais and Bigeard to make them commit themselves to the reconquest of Huguette 1 with the same drive and energy they had devoted to the counterattack on the Five Hills. Langlais makes it clear in his book that he was dead set against the operation on H1 because it would be a serious drain on the strength of his last constituted reserve unit, the 2nd BEP.[21]

The same argument was presented in greater detail to de Castries by Bigeard. According to him, even the 2nd BEP was now reduced to 380 men and committed to the defense of Eliane. Considering the state of general fatigue of the garrison, there was a good chance that the operation would fail; and even if it succeeded there would be no troops left to hold H1 successfully.

It was clear that these words were not spoken by the "old" Bigeard who barely a month ago had sworn to defend Eliane to the last man. Hence, the alternatives to the manner in which the counterattacks on H1 were organized and led constitute one of the many fascinating might-have-beens of the battle of Dien Bien Phu.

At about 0900, in the face of the objections by Langlais and Bigeard, de Castries maintained his order that the "impossible" must be done to retake H1 before 1600 that afternoon. Langlais, as was proper in his role as commander for the defense, followed precedent and left the organization of the counterattack to Bigeard. The latter went to work with his usual speed and competence. As a first step he ordered the disengagement of the 2nd BEP from Eliane and its replacement by the alert units of the II/1 RCP, 6th BPC, and 1/2 REI. Then, Maj. Guérin requested from *Gatac Nord* in Hanoi a "credit" of twelve fighter-bombers and four B-26's to work over the Communist trench system around H1 as of 1345. Another four B-26's were to stand by as of 1400 to strike at targets of opportunity.

As soon as the air support finished its task, the artillery and mortars were to fire 1,200 rounds on Hugette 1, followed by smoke shells on the Communist artillery observation posts on Dominique and Anne-Marie, with the mortars of H2 and H5 and of Sparrowhawk taking over close-in support thereafter. The last remaining three operational tanks under Lt. Mengelle would support the southern prong of the infantry attack.

Then came the briefing of the infantry leaders. Here, Bigeard made the fateful decision not to command the operation himself but to leave its execution to Maj. Liesenfelt, whose battalion, after all, would bear the brunt of the attack. Many reasons were advanced later to justify or criticize that decision. It was said that Bigeard's over-all command of the counterattack on Eliane was justified because it had involved several different battalions and someone had to co-ordinate the various elements involved. In the case of the counterattack on H1, however, one single constituted unit was involved in the operation. Others said that Bigeard simply wanted to wash his hands of an operation which he disapproved of and was certain would fail. Bigeard himself felt that the operation, while difficult, was of the sort that the 2nd BEP already had experienced and that the unit could be trusted to handle it competently. Moreover, Bigeard felt that breathing down Liesenfelt's neck would be rightfully resented. It may also be added that Bigeard had stayed awake the whole previous night watching the agony of Chevalier on H1 and was, after weeks of poor food and little sleep, dead tired. He had personally briefed Liesenfelt, Mengelle, and the four paratroop company commanders, Lts. de Bire, Boulinguez, Pètre, and Lecour-Grandmaison, as to their role.

The way Bigeard saw it, the operation was to be conducted in the same manner as he had executed the counterattack on Eliane: lots of firepower and sparing use of infantry in small commando-like groups. At 1425, de Bire's 5th Company was to jump off from the communications trench north of H2, with Boulinguez' 6th Company standing by in reserve on H2 near the command post from which Liesenfelt was coordinating the operation. At the same time, east of the airfield, 7/2 BEP under Lecour-Grandmaison and the so-called CIPE under Pètre were to jump off from strongpoint Opéra across the airfield and past the enemy machine gun in the Curtiss C-46 wreck.[22]

The operation at first went like clockwork. The Viet-Minh company which now held Huguette 1 was, inside a few minutes, hacked to pieces and reduced to a dozen stunned survivors by the *Hellcat* dive bombers

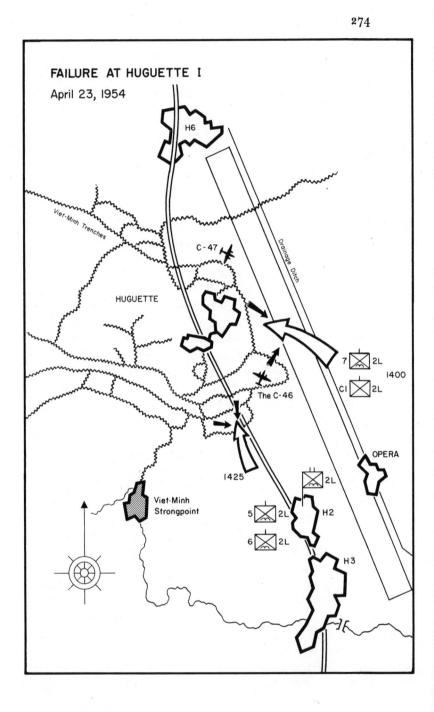

FAILURE AT HUGUETTE I
April 23, 1954

of Navy Squadron 11F. At 1400 the French, Legionnaires, and Vietnamese paratroopers emerged from their trenches, the tropical heat beating unmercifully down on them: the metal plates of the airfield were too hot to lie down upon. The two companies emerged in the open on the airfield when heavy machine-gun fire sprayed the men from the undestroyed Communist machine-gun nest in the nose of the Curtiss. Lieutenant Pètre was seriously wounded almost immediately and both 7/2 BEP and the Indochinese Company were taking heavy losses until, finally, some well-adjusted French artillery fire silenced the machine gun. On the southern flank, matters were worse. Fifth Company had, like Sgt. Kubiak and his supply convoy the evening before, gotten lost in the maze of underground tunnels and communications trenches and was not in place for the jump-off when the aerial bombardment lifted. When it and 6th Company were finally in place, the surviving enemy gunners had crawled out of their dugouts and, supported by some of the remaining Viet-Minh machine-gun nests in the no man's land north of H2, began to lay down an impenetrable defensive fire in the best traditions of trench warfare of World War I. For all practical purposes, the counterattack on H1 already had failed. The Communists now knew fully what was happening and their artillery, though in part shooting blindly, joined the fray, as did their flak which had already shot down a French Navy fighter-bomber.

Battalion Commander Liesenfelt knew nothing of all this. Ensconced in the command post of H2, Liesenfelt apparently meant to run his operation by radio just as Bigeard had done on Eliane, except that Bigeard directed it from the bare top of E4 and had an unimpeded view of his own assault units, just as the Communists had an unimpeded view of him. Having given his orders and knowing the truly undisputed excellence of his company commanders and, for that matter, his troops; Liesenfelt patiently waited for further radio contact with them.

Meanwhile, Bigeard had collapsed on his cot and was profoundly asleep in the belief that the 2nd BEP could be trusted to carry out its mission properly. Fortunately for the French, de Castries' headquarters had kept up its habit of listening in on the combat radio circuits and heard the desperate calls for help of the pinned-down companies of the 2nd BEP. When apparently no one but the artillery reacted to them, de Castries personally intervened in the battle. He had Bigeard awakened and in the quaintly understated British style which any proper French nobleman uses even under the worst of circumstances, de Castries told Bigeard:

"I have the impression that the attack doesn't carry the proper *punch*" —he used the English term in his phrase—"Go on over and have a look at what is going on."

Bigeard rapidly equipped himself and, disregarding the heavy enemy counterbattery shelling, raced one of the last few operable jeeps across the whole camp to H2, where he found Liesenfelt calmly in his dugout, awaiting events. To Bigeard's question as to how the operation went, the commander of the 2nd BEP answered: *"Ça doit coller*—it must be going all right; I'm not getting anything from my units." Bigeard turned to Liesenfelt's radio set, looked at it, fiddled with it, and in his own words, began to howl with rage. Liesenfelt's set was slightly off the proper wave length and he had been sitting in his dugout, deaf and mute, while his battalion was pinned down in the open.

Bigeard himself now took over the battle. Being the man and sound tactician he was, he knew it would be pointless now to reinforce defeat. At 1525 he called off the attack and ordered the survivors of the 2nd BEP to fall back at a quick pace to their line of departure. At the same time he ordered the four B-26's who were standing by to use their delayed-fuse bombs on the Communist machine-gun nests while the French artillery laid down yet another barrage on the eastern hills and on Anne-Marie. For the two companies who had crossed the whole open airfield under fire and, after the destruction of the machine-gun nest in the Curtiss, had worked their way to within fifty meters of H1, the withdrawal was as costly as the advance. Lieutenant Guérin, the deputy commander of the Indochinese company, had both his legs mangled by an artillery shell on the way back across the airfield. Rather than risk the lives of his men who began to crawl back onto the exposed strip to rescue him, he committed suicide by shooting himself in the head.[23]

The failure of the counterattack on H1 was the single largest disaster to hit Dien Bien Phu since the loss of the Dominiques, and the fact that it happened to an elite parachute battalion gave it considerable impact. A total of 150 men (almost two complete companies) had been killed or wounded, wiping out Dien Bien Phu's last operational reserve. Liesenfelt was relieved of command and the remnants of his battalion were merged with the already under-strength 1st BEP on April 25. The new unit was known as the *Bataillon de Marche, BEP,* or Composite Foreign Legion Parachute Battalion under the command of the recovered Maj. Guiraud.

To be sure, the enemy had paid dearly for his victory, as the regimental commander from the 308th Division was to admit candidly to Bigeard after the latter had been taken prisoner. Not only had the enemy company holding H1 been completely destroyed but the enemy troops in the communications trenches also had suffered and more of them were lost when they imprudently pursued the French into the open after they withdrew. The Viet-Minh were also surprised to see that the usually aggressive French tanks had failed to push forward during the attack; this was no doubt due to the fact that the tank crews, too, felt the absence of effective leadership. It is also likely that the crews, now largely composed of parachuted replacements unfamiliar with the terrain, were more hesitant to commit their worn vehicles—all of which showed large gashes in their armor from enemy shells—to an attack in which they obviously lacked infantry support. Instead of the allocated 1,200 rounds, the French artillery had fired 1,600 rounds of 105-mm., 1,580 rounds of 120-mm., and 80 rounds of 155-mm. ammunition.

On what was left of Huguette, the Foreign Legionnaires of the 1/13 continued to relieve the 1/2 REI. Capeyron's 3rd Company, 1/13, relieved 2nd Company, 1/2 REI, on Huguette 5. The rest of the 1/2 REI, reinforced by White T'ai tribesmen from Air Force Captain Charnod's strongpoint Juno, continued its patrol activities south and west of Claudine. The 31st Engineers was fighting its own mechanical battles elsewhere. A crate with impatiently awaited spare parts for the electric generators had fallen just outside the French lines and Communist marksmen soon registered on it. Without success, the French and Moroccan Engineers tried to secure the precious cargo but to no avail: before it could be dragged to the nearest French position, Communist shells had shot the package to pieces.

Among the daily fighter-bomber pilots who flew support missions that day on H1 was Lt. Bernard Klotz of Navy Squadron 11F. His code name for the day was "Savart Green" Leader and his flight mate was Petty Officer Goizet. Both had flown a complete circle around the objective at an altitude of 8,500 feet with their aircraft, each carrying two 500-pound bombs. At 1415 Klotz decided upon a dive-bombing run on H1. The stubby American-built aircraft nosed downward and began its dive but was immediately followed by heavy enemy flak from Anne-Marie, D1, and new flak positions just west of where strongpoint Françoise had been. As the plane reached the 6,000-foot level, Goizet saw that his flight leader's plane was on fire. Klotz calmly acknowledged the message and continued his run and launched his bombs right on target, then pulled up and veered left 180 degrees. The anxious Goizet stayed with his comrade until he saw Klotz pulling himself out of the airplane and attempting to open his parachute by hand. While Klotz was struggling with his chute, it opened suddenly and tore the ligaments of his arm. A few seconds later he landed in a wet rice paddy 400 meters south of Eliane 2. Now a race began between the garrison of E2 and the Viet-Minh from Old Baldy as to who would reach Klotz first. From his high vantage point, Petty Officer Goizet clearly realized what was afoot and in turn descended for a strafing run on Old Baldy. It apparently slowed down the Viet-Minh just long enough for a Foreign Legionnaire to reach Klotz first. That evening Dr. Grauwin set his shoulder in the hospital and on the following day, Klotz joined Majs. Guérin and Blanchet as an air controller and became the first French Navy representative inside landlocked Dien Bien Phu.

The battle for the three northern Huguettes was now over. It had lasted almost a full month and had cost the enemy a better part of three regiments in dead and wounded. At least a good third, if not more, of the Viet-Minh artillery had been constantly committed to the bombardment of the three tiny positions of Huguettes 1, 6, and 7. On the French side, the losses amounted to about 500 men, including many of the best men of the garrison, and one tank. Yet what Col. Langlais would call "three laughable squares of rice field" had made the enemy pay dearly for his gain of 800 meters of vacant airstrip.

In a passage of unusual frankness for a Communist military commander, General Vo Nguyen Giap showed clearly what the battle of Huguettes had cost his own forces:

> However, the principal trait of that phase of the battle has been the violent character of the combat . . . the battle having lasted a very long time, more troops—who had had to fight without interruption—become fatigued and are worn and are faced with great nervous tension. . . . Our forces have not been able to avoid decimation, which requires rapid reorganization and reinforcement.
> . . . among our cadres and combatants there appear negative *rightist tendencies,* whose manifestations are the fear of having many killed, the fear of suffering casualties, of facing up to fatigue, difficulties, privations. . . .[24]

It would take the Viet-Minh siege force until May 1 to recover from the battle of the Huguettes, to replenish some of its depleted front-line regiments, and to fill up its ammunition stocks for the final offensive.

Isabelle Alone

THE MAIN POSITION of Dien Bien Phu, even at the worst moment of the battle, measured almost a full square mile. Until the very last day the eastern hills masked at least some of the enemy artillery, and along the steep eastern bank of the Nam-Yum there was until the end a small measure of protection. Units could be moved from one hill to another and a long crawl through the seemingly endless "subway" system at least provided the illusion of relative mobility. There also were the women of Dien Bien Phu: the prostitutes of the two brothels, the families of the Meo tribesmen, and Mademoiselle de Galard. In a world gone mad, such pitiful remnants of normality did a great deal for the morale of the garrison.

None of this existed on isolated strongpoint Isabelle. Here, 1,809 men, eleven 105-mm. howitzers and three tanks lived on a patch of marshy river bend which at no time measured more than one-fourth of a square mile. On Isabelle, there were no terrain features behind which to hide, no bushes or trees to use for camouflage, no women even to look at from afar, and no tunnel system. The main position of Dien Bien Phu had until the last an offensive role and for that reason received extensive reinforcements of fully constituted units. Isabelle's twofold role was simple —to provide flanking artillery fires for the main position and to stay alive. There could be no massive counterattacks because there were not enough troops available to mount any. In fact, as it soon became obvious once the enemy began to deploy his troops in full strength and began to dig his all-pervasive system of trenches, there were not enough troops available at Isabelle and in the main position of Dien Bien Phu to keep the road link between the two positions open. Like the loss of the main airfield of Dien Bien Phu early in the battle, the loss of road communications between Isabelle and Dien Bien Phu after two weeks of fighting had not been provided for. As to the auxiliary airstrip which had been bulldozed just north of Isabelle, it had witnessed the landing of exactly two aircraft before it, too, was under Communist fire and became unusable. A special strongpoint had been built at the southern end of the airfield in order to serve as its link with the rest of Isabelle located on the other side of the Nam Yum.

The word "strongpoint" used in connection with the position at the airstrip was almost a joke. Officially dubbed Isabelle 5, it became known throughout Dien Bien Phu as "Strongpoint Wieme," after the young reserve lieutenant whose T'ai tribesmen from the 431st and 432nd Mobile Auxiliary Company occupied it. Built as an afterthought once the four other sub-strongpoints of Isabelle had been constructed, strongpoint Wieme was built on top of the bulldozed remains of a French prewar military guard post. Every tree and brush had been removed from Wieme's area to serve as construction material for the other positions of Isabelle. The result was that Wieme was composed of very little except four-foot-deep trenches dug directly into the earth and mud; since there was nothing to contain the earth, the trenches, when dug deeper, tended to collapse on top of the men. The bulk of the obstacles around Wieme were simply sharpened sticks of bamboo and a few mines, rather than barbed wire. That also had been absorbed by the main position. Isolated from the rest of Isabelle by the Nam Yum, Lt. Wieme, his four French sergeants, and the 219 T'ai of the two companies lived in total isolation, fighting a war of their own in the knee-deep mud and, like the Five Hills of the main position, connected to the rest of Isabelle only via a small bridge under constant enemy fire.

Indeed, it was the enemy artillery that became the major bane of Isabelle. Since its role was one of fire support for the main position of Dien Bien Phu, it was constantly the object of neutralization fires of the Viet-Minh, and the small size and total immobility of the target made every enemy shell a direct hit. Indeed, every survivor of Isabelle was to mention the unnerving effect of the constant thumping of the enemy artillery over everyone's head. The result was that, in contrast to what happened at the main position, the men at Isabelle could not even visit with their comrades in neighboring dugouts and any move from one place to another, whether it was for a briefing or to go to the infirmaries, to the hospital, or to relieve oneself, became a matter of life and death.

What saved the garrison from early physical destruction was beyond a doubt the fact that the commander of Isabelle, Lieutenant Colonel (promoted to full colonel on April 16, 1954) André Lalande had been an artillery commander during World War II and thus was fully aware of the necessity to dig in his troops, and dig them in deeply. Even ten years later, some of his subordinates recalled that Lalande had called them together before the battle even started and had told them: "The Viets have got 105's. You've got to put at least one meter of earth above your heads." And Lalande could be seen personally inspecting the construction of the strongpoints to see that they met his specifications. Some of his subordinates who, prior to March 30, had had the opportunity of visiting the main position at Dien Bien Phu, returned to Isabelle shaking their heads; for at Dien Bien Phu the construction of proper field fortifications was left largely to the imagination or sense of responsibility of the individual unit commanders. And very often the most spirited unit commanders—those who hoped the whole battle of Dien Bien Phu would be a highly mobile affair and thus considered the building of elaborate dugouts an unadmitted form of cowardice— cared least for the construction of solid field fortifications, even assuming that the proper materials had been available. As we have seen, most of the time they were not.

Lalande, a tall Foreign Legion officer with well-chiseled features, was forty-one years old when he took command of Isabelle and had behind him a glorious career of combat assignments. He had been part of the French expeditionary force to Norway in 1940 and commander of a ski reconnaissance outfit; he was severely wounded at Narvik and was one of the earliest followers of de Gaulle in the Free French movement. He fought on almost every battlefield of the Free French—and from January 1, 1942, always with the 13th Half-Brigade of the Foreign Legion. He had fought in Syria against the Vichy French, in Libya against Germany's Rommel, in Italy, and in France. In 1946, he was the top graduate of the French War College and, after an assignment to NATO Headquarters, he volunteered for Indochina in 1953 and received the command of the 3rd Foreign Legion Regiment and of Mobile Group 6. The fact that Isabelle was as well equipped for its mission as it finally turned out to be is no doubt to a great extent due to Lalande's own efforts. It was no doubt also due to the fact that the enemy gave the attack on the main position of Dien Bien Phu full priority over everything else.

Giap assigned the mission of immobilizing Isabelle to Lt. Col. Hoang Khai Tien's Regiment 57 of the 304th People's Army Division, reinforced during the battle by Battalion 888, Regiment 176, of the 316th Division. Both units fully succeeded in their mission, since by the end

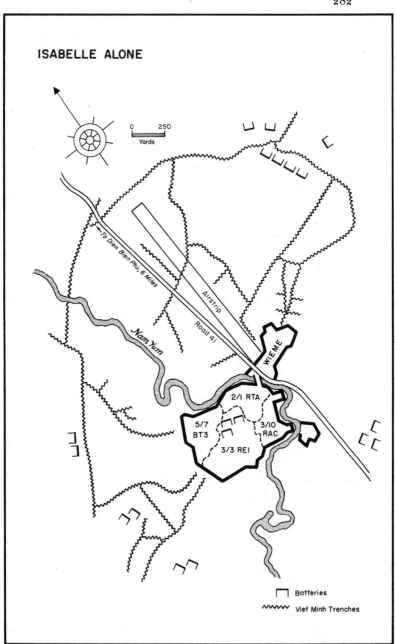

ISABELLE ALONE

of March, 1954, Lalande found it impossible to maintain open communications with Dien Bien Phu. On the other hand, the artillery batteries dug in around Isabelle (see map, p. 282) never succeeded in muzzling Capt. Libier's 3rd Battalion, 10th Colonial Artillery Regiment, whose last remaining howitzer became, on May 7 at 1700, the very last artillery piece still capable of firing in all of Dien Bien Phu. What beyond a doubt hurt Isabelle, aside from being completely sealed off even from the main position, was that prior to March 30 it had become the refuse heap for all units that had broken and run at Dien Bien Phu. Thus, the remaining 200-odd T'ai of 9th Company, 3rd BT, under Maj. Thimonier and Capt. Désiré, were transferred to Isabelle after they had broken and run on Anne-Marie on March 17 and 18. The fact that thirty of Lt. Wieme's T'ai tribesmen deserted on March 30 from Isabelle 5 may have had something to do with the arrival of the wobbly remnants of 3rd BT on Isabelle. During the last week of March also, Capt. Gendre's 120 survivors of 3rd Company, 5/7 Algerian Rifles, arrived on Isabelle after the brutal shock of the attack on strongpoint Gabrielle. What that did to the morale of Captain Pierre Jeancenelle's 2nd Battalion, 1st Algerian Rifles, can be easily guessed at.

The order of battle of Isabelle was as follows: Aside from strongpoint Wieme and another small bridgehead across the Nam Yam held by the Foreign Legion at the extreme south of Isabelle, its main position was subdivided into four sub-strongpoints. Isabelle 1 was held by the 2/1 RTA; Isabelle 2 by the remnants of 3rd BT and the 5/7 RTA; and the bulk of Isabelle 3 and 4 by the 3/3 Foreign Legion (REI). The slight rise in the middle of the central position held the command post, the hospital, and the bulk of the artillery battery positions. The platoon of three tanks commanded by Lt. Préaud was dug in not far from strongpoint Wieme since it was the strongpoint most likely to be in need of the tanks and since it also constituted, short of the landward west flank, the only exit from the bend of the Nam Yum, which encircled the strongpoint almost on three sides.

Friday, April 2, 1954

With the outbreak of the Viet-Minh attack on Dominique on March 30, Isabelle also was faced for the first time with intensive Communist neutralization fire against its battery positions. The effect was devastating, and at 0045 Isabelle reported that only four of its eleven fieldpieces were still capable of firing. In some cases this meant that the gun pit itself had been ravaged but that the gun was intact once it was dug out of the debris; in other cases it meant that the gun itself was partly damaged and that spare parts for it would have to be parachuted—an operation which, miraculously, worked almost to the end—and in some cases it meant simply that the gun crews had been annihilated. At Isabelle, it was the last that had taken place, for at 1035 the strongpoint reported nine guns capable of firing, but only six gun crews available, and requested the immediate parachuting of additional gun crews. At 2045 it again reported intensive artillery hammering. As the battle now began, Isabelle fielded the following units:

2/1 RTA	545
3/3 REI	426
T'ai	410
3/10 RAC	116
5/7 RTA	116
Miscellaneous	50
	1,663

Facing that force were about 3,500 first-class Communist troops.

April 4-April 11, 1954

On April 4, enemy pressure began to tighten around the western flank of Isabelle, where the Foreign Legionnaires began to notice the same deadly approach trenches which were about to strangulate the Huguettes six miles farther north. On April 5, those trenches had reached to within 100 meters of Isabelle, and the Legionnaires, like their comrades to the north, now began the costly chore of counterattacking in order to fill the approach trenches. In the northeast corner of Isabelle, Wieme's little T'ais were doing exactly the same thing, but under worse conditions. On March 30-31, they had fought off a strong attack by the Viet-Minh's Intelligence Company No. 63 which had lasted twelve hours and which had caused Wieme to request flanking artillery fires from Claudine to within 100 meters of his own position. His own battery of small 60-mm. mortars had fired 600 rounds that night at an angle of eighty degrees with no powder increments; that is, the shells were meant to fall just barely outside his own trenches. After this failure, Regiment 57 and its ample fire support settled down to grinding the position to pieces.

April 12-April 19, 1954

On April 15, with ten per cent of his men dead and forty per cent missing or prisoners, Wieme asked Col. Lalande temporarily to relieve his unit from Isabelle 5. Lalande agreed and 9th Company of 3rd BT, under Capt. Désiré, was sent to replace Wieme. But the relief had not passed unnoticed on the other side; it was greeted by intense artillery fire, and stocky, bearded Capt. Désiré was gravely wounded in the chest and legs while attempting to cross the Nam Yum. His deputy, Lt. Siauve, took command of 9th Company, 3rd BT, on strongpoint Wieme. From now on, the small strongpoint was to fulfill for Isabelle the same functions that the Five Hills fulfilled for Dien Bien Phu's main position. In doing so it became the object of constant attacks. In an attempt to give some room for maneuver to the garrison, Préaud's tank platoon, supported by Legionnaires from the 3/3 REI, made a sortie which proved fruitless and which was followed by yet another Communist attack on Wieme on April 19. A counterattack of T'ai and Legionnaires at 1700 that day nearly succeeded in clearing the enemy's penetration.

April 20-April 27, 1954

Lieutenant Siauve of 9th Company, 3rd BT, was killed on Wieme at 2215 of April 21. Like most French officers on that acre of fortified swamp, he had lasted about a week. But as in the case of E2 on the main position, the French had decided to make a stand for it, and like E2, Wieme would hold to the bitter end.

Isabelle, to a far greater extent than the main position, suffered from the problem of misdropped supplies. With the loss of control of the southern airstrip late in March, the only available drop zones left were those directly on the pitifully small target of the main strongpoints of Isabelle. A cargo aircraft, even flying at stalling speed, would cross all of Isabelle in about two seconds; hence, even the tiniest navigational error (and they were numerous and excusable as the pilots entered the flak gauntlet over the valley) meant that the supplies would fall outside the perimeter and be lost to the enemy. In the case of Isabelle this meant that the last warm food was eaten by all hands on April 19, and that the whole garrison completely ran out of food on April 20 in the evening—with the exception of the severely wounded who were put on minimal rations. At 1400 that afternoon, Lalande laconically reported his situation as follows:

2/1 RTA	490
3/3 REI	400
T'ais	370
5/7 RTA, etc.	140
	1,400

The strongpoint's small hospital now also housed 117 severe hospital cases that no longer could be evacuated to the main hospitals in Dien Bien Phu, let alone picked up by aircraft. Another 136 men had died in combat or were missing. The artillery still had eight howitzers, and two of the three M-24 tanks were still operational. In other words, the over-all casualty rate was around fifteen per cent. That, along with the constant artillery bombardment and the starvation of the last days, was bound to bring about a crisis. It broke out on April 26.

On that day, Lalande had given Jeancenelle the order to pick four of his best platoons for a counterattack against the Communist approach trenches northeast of strongpoint Wieme. According to Intelligence, the counterattack would involve the crossing of only one enemy trench. As it turned out, there were two enemy trenches, one behind the other, and the Algerians' attack ran into trouble on April 18-19. What saved the Algerians from total destruction was that Lt. Préaud threw his two remaining "Bisons" into the fight and covered the withdrawal of the Algerians back to Isabelle 4. The small company had lost six dead and twenty-two wounded in the fight.

What happened next remains difficult to reconstruct to this day, as almost all the participants are highly reluctant to tell the whole story.

Upon the return of the Algerian force to the main position, Col. Lalande felt that an example had to be set after this second unsuccessful attack in one week lest the other units be demoralized, and he decided to use a harsh last-resort measure only rarely employed in any army: execution for cowardice. Courts-martial for cowardice are extremely rare. Throughout all of World War II, the United States Army executed only one man, a Pvt. Slovik, in connection with such a charge. During the Korean War, there seems to have been only one such trial, and the defendant was allowed to plead to a lesser charge. In France, a large-scale mutiny of front-line troops in 1917 was severely dealt with and at least one unit was "decimated" in the literal sense of the word; i.e., every tenth man was executed as an example, regardless of his own individual guilt.[1] Lalande now decided to apply this ancient iron law to the company that had failed and ordered the platoon commanders to designate on their own two men each to be shot before a firing squad at 1800 that evening.

In the 2/1 Algerian Rifles there was a company commander of Algerian nationality, Lt. Cheik Belabiche, of 8th Company. He had not participated in the day's unfortunate operation, but one of his platoons had, and the bearded Algerian master sergeant, an old-time regular with fourteen citations for bravery, came to see him after the news of the punishment had spread.

"Lieutenant," said the sergeant, "I am not going to designate two guys from our platoon to be shot! We were all equally brave and we all tried just as hard. They can either shoot us all or they better not shoot anybody."

Belabiche first called Capt. Gendre to check the news. Gendre had heard about it also and thought that "someone had gone nuts." Soon thereafter Jeancenelle talked to Belabiche over the telephone and reviewed with him the aborted attack. Jeancenelle felt that, considering the mistake made by Intelligence, the operation had gone as well as could be expected; but when Belabiche then objected that the drastic punishment that was about to be meted out was therefore not called for, Jeancenelle simply replied:

"The colonel has made his decision. I can only approve him."

"Captain," said Belabiche, "have you foreseen the consequences of this?"

"I know the Algerian *tirailleurs* better than you do, lieutenant, and I know how to keep them on the leash."

Then Belabiche lost control of himself:

"Listen, Captain, the *tirailleurs* are standing right here with drawn submachine guns. If you wish to get them this will end up in us shooting at each other and the Viets will end up getting what's left. Think that one over!"

Thereupon, Belabiche decided to go and see Lalande himself. At first, Lalande insisted upon carrying out the punishment as decided. But then, Belabiche told him bluntly that when his own Foreign Legionnaires had failed to break through and in fact had "run like rabbits," nobody had been sent to the firing squad. None of the Algerians would ever understand why two different standards of judgment should be applied to the same act. Lalande calmed the young officer and finally Belabiche said softly:

"Do you think, *mon Colonel,* that we can afford to throw away the few troops we've got? I have received exactly one man in airdropped reinforcements for the sixty we have lost."

Lalande thought it over and then found a solution to the dilemma. He felt that he could not entirely back down without giving in to troops who were on the verge of mutiny—even though the situation might well have been created by his own action. He thereupon told Belabiche to return to the Algerian riflemen and tell them that a trial would be held, but that the men would be acquitted. With that assurance in hand, Belabiche returned to his troops.

And that evening, indeed, the fantastic scene took place. A formal court-martial had been convened, with three captains and three lieutenants, in one of the dugouts. The bewildered Algerian riflemen who had been selected for the trial stood in front of the board with their appointed defense counsel, a French officer from another battalion in the position. With Communist artillery shells bursting overhead, in the bleak light of a bare electric bulb dangling from a wire affixed to the roof of the dugout, the prosecutor presented his charges; the counsel for the riflemen presented his defense; and the jury briefly left the room to deliberate. It duly returned a verdict of "not guilty" and the riflemen, just as bewildered as before and barely comprehending what the whole ceremonial had been about, returned in the midst of the artillery barrage to their own dugouts.

Belabiche heaved a sigh of relief and as he returned to his own CP, he met Jeancenelle who told him that his Legion of Honor, for which he had been proposed weeks ago, had finally been approved. Belabiche thanked him and then added:

"I am glad to have it, but I really earned it just a few hours ago."

That evening, de Castries sent a personal telegram to Gen. Cogny in which the events of the day on Isabelle were not mentioned directly. In fact, it is doubtful that Lalande had reported them to de Castries at that time. But the telegram contained the following telling passage:

> Isabelle reports very strong lowering of morale among North African troops. They request that they also should be mentioned in the dispatches.

With the rains now falling, most of Isabelle became a swamp, and strongpoint Wieme in particular became little else but a knee-deep quagmire. A counterattack by Legionnaires and T'ai, on April 27, to eliminate the Viet-Minh penetration in the northeast corner of Wieme, failed just as miserably as had the attack by the Algerians on the previous day. And with the main position at Dien Bien Phu now facing its agony, there was little artillery support now available on Claudine (the howitzers of Isabelle itself being far too close to fire effective support) to help Isabelle in its own predicament.

Thursday, April 29, 1954

At 2225, a new threat developed against sorely tried Wieme when suddenly several powerful 75-mm. recoilless rifles appeared in the Communist forward trenches, coupled with murderous 105-mm. fire now using the brand-new American short-delay fuses from misdropped French artillery shells. Within a few minutes the rain-logged bunkers and dugouts of Wieme were a complete shambles in which the dazed survivors of 9/3 BT and some of Wieme's own T'ai were frantically seeking shelter. Within a few minutes Lt. Préaud's tanks entered the fray since their cannon were able to fire direct support. But the Communist gunners were also prepared for them. A rain of 105 shells fell on their position and soon tank "Ratisbonne," severely disabled, fell silent. This time, Regiment 57 seemed to be determined to finish off Isabelle, or at least to silence its artillery. A never-stopping rain of shells continued to hack away at the rest of the position.

Friday, April 30, 1954

The situation inside Isabelle was further worsened when the garrison saw the apparent unwillingness of the Air Force transports to take chances in resupplying them. At 0200, Isabelle radioed that seven C-47 aircraft were circling over the position with only very weak flak fire to oppose them, but that they were dropping their troops in almost meaningless dribbles. One plane turned back without dropping anything, a second plane dropped only four paratroops, and all the others finally dropped only a total of sixty-five men, of whom only one had an accident on landing.

But that was not the only trouble which faced Isabelle that day. Having run out of food the previous week, it now was running out of artillery ammunition. For the last ten days Isabelle had requested an average of 1,700 rounds of 105-mm. ammunition for each day as its howitzers, part of which were now well dug in as they were firing in only one direction, took over an increasingly important part in the defense of the eastern hills of Dien Bien Phu. Yet it had received only an average of 348 rounds every twenty-four hours. De Castries now requested that Hanoi build up a reserve of 8,000 rounds of ammunition on Isabelle, the more so as flak was relatively thinner near the southern strongpoint than around the main center of resistance at Dien Bien Phu. With a point of irony, de Castries conceded that "this will involve a few risks for the transport aviation but our situation here requires that they, too, assume some risks."

April 30 was also the traditional holiday of the Foreign Legion, "Camerone." On that day in 1863, a small Foreign Legion company had, in a manner reminiscent of the Alamo, fought to the death at the Mexican *Hacienda de Camerone* in order to cover the retreat to the coast of the French forces which had come to Mexico to prop up Austrian-born Emperor Maximilian. The ceremonial involves a reading of an account of the battle by the youngest Legionnaire, a festive dinner, and an induction to honorary membership in the Foreign Legion of particularly well liked non-Legionnaires.

Tradition was not broken on Isabelle. With the whole position constantly under fire since the previous day and with strongpoint Wieme breached in three places, Camerone Day was properly celebrated. Colonel Lalande himself sang the traditional Foreign Legion song *"Tiens, voilà du boudin . . ."* and the two clergymen at Isabelle, Reverend Pierre Tissot and Father Guidon, were made honorary privates first class in the Foreign Legion. Tissot was the only Protestant minister in all of Dien Bien Phu, and was at Isabelle by accident when it became impossible to reopen the road to the main position. Guidon had been a missionary with the T'ai tribesmen at Lai-Chau and in December, 1953, had trekked to Dien Bien Phu with them and also had become immobilized on Isabelle when it was surrounded. He went to the prison camps with the garrison and shared its fate to the end. Undaunted, he returned to missionary work later and in 1959 I met him in northeastern Thailand at Ubon-Rajthani, still spreading the Gospel.

Saturday-Monday, May 1-3, 1954

With the major attack now under way on the main position, the Communists now were also accentuating the pressure on Isabelle. During the night of May 1, they achieved their first real breakthrough in the northeastern corner of Wieme. On the other hand, the Legionnaires on the western side sallied forth to fill in Communist trenches and reached a point 200 meters northwest of Isabelle, where they made a strange discovery: a dead African in Communist uniform. Since he had no identification papers on him it was impossible to tell whether he was a turncoat French African soldier taken prisoner by the Communists, or whether he was a Chinese-trained "volunteer."

In the meantime, however, the Communist attack on Wieme continued. At 0200 of May 2, Regiment 57 succeeded in gaining a foothold in the position, now defended by 11th Company, 3/3 REI, the Algerians, and two tanks. At 0830, the French could count 100 Viet-Minh bodies in the barbed wire. By noon, only six of the original eleven howitzers were still firing.

At 1220 the French again counterattacked on Wieme but were stopped once more; but a third counterattack at 1610 finally got a foothold. What was left of strongpoint Wieme was just an incredible quagmire of rotting bodies, destroyed ordnance, and shell craters. There was no recognizable position. Lalande decided to leave an alert patrol on it but not to attempt to garrison it. At 2400 Communist artillery shells again began to rain on martyred Wieme. The survivors of the patrol began to fall back. The day had cost the French five killed, one missing, and twenty-two wounded.

On the following day, the Foreign Legion again fought its way through the barbed wire on the western flank into the Communist forward trenches, which had to be cleared in hand-to-hand combat. The Legionnaires counted eight Communist dead and wounded many others and brought back with them nineteen submachine guns and two rifles. On Wieme, the patrol captured a Communist 75-mm. recoilless rifle. If anything, these last operations tend to show that, contrary to some accounts, isolated Isabelle did not accept its ultimate fate passively.

Tuesday-Thursday, May 4-6, 1954

Despite the never-ending bombardment, in which some 75-mm. pack howitzers now also participated, the Foreign Legionnaires mounted another operation on the Viet-Minh trench system west of Isabelle in the midst of a monsoon storm. This time, however, they fell upon an enemy ready and waiting for them.

When the Legionnaires finally fell back late at night, they had lost two dead and thirty wounded, including two of their officers. On that day also, Rev. Tissot was wounded by Communist shell fragments.

On May 5, Lalande received a top-secret message informing him of the contemplated breakout operation code-named "Albatross." As will be seen later, the plan involved a breakout southward into Laos via Isabelle, with the latter having to play for a few hours the unenviable role of a holding position and rear guard. I was told later that Lalande felt that to communicate the plan to the troops or even the subordinate commanders might have a demoralizing effect. He decided to keep it to himself for the time being, with the result that when he and his own troops were left to attempt "Albatross" by themselves, they had to do it without any rehearsal.

On May 6, Isabelle disappeared under a permanent cloud of exploding mud. Communist batteries, intent upon neutralizing what last help Libier's howitzers could give to the main position, maintained a steady bombardment of the whole strongpoint. Wieme had given become no man's land, but Isabelle's garrison could take a small measure of pride in the fact that to the end no Viet-Minh unit ever succeeded in permanently holding on to a shred of the strongpoint. At 2200 a succession of heavy explosions shattered Isabelle as Communist shells found their mark and three of the remaining 105's were destroyed with their ammunition and crews. By midnight, there remained but one last howitzer on the position. Third Battalion, 10th Colonial Artillery, had done its duty to the end.

Friday, May 7, 1954

Throughout the night of May 6 to 7, the enemy artillery bombardment never let up on Isabelle. By listening to the radio traffic, Isabelle also realized that Dien Bien Phu was dying. By early afternoon of May 7, Lalande and his men could watch the explosions and fires of the depots on Dien Bien Phu, and around four o'clock Lalande received a radio call from de Castries. With Lalande having served with the Free French Forces alongside the British Eighth Army in Egypt, both men could easily converse in English for greater secrecy.

De Castries told Lalande: "I'm afraid I'll have to give up. You are now free to try 'Albatross.' "

De Castries also told Lalande that, instead of attempting to break out to the southwest, which seemingly was the shortest distance to friendly forces, but where Communist roadblocks would most likely await them, Lalande's troops should attempt to break out toward the southeast. Since that direction pointed deep into enemy territory, it was likely to be less well guarded. Also, small French and mountain tribal commando groups of the GCMA, operating far ahead of the "Condor" relief force of Colonel Boucher de Crèvecoeur, had cautiously worked their way to the very edge of the southern end of the valley. Very cautiously, their radio transmitter had made contact with Isabelle's command channel, and now that the Communist siege ring had become airtight, Lalande ordered Lt. Wieme and his T'ai Partisans to revert to their traditional role and attempt to break out in the direction of the French commando force code-named "Condor." From its vantage point in the hills near Ban Cang the commando force could see Isabelle quite clearly.

As one of the survivors of the lone southern strongpoint would say later, the defense of Isabelle had been "hell in a very small place."

IX

Vulture, Condor, and Albatross

THE AGONY of Dien Bien Phu was to become the object of an international disagreement between France, the United States, and Great Britain, the repercussions of which still make themselves felt more than a decade later. On the Communist side Dien Bien Phu represents the kind of military victory which has widespread political effect. On the western side, Dien Bien Phu, to the French, represents an extreme of American indecision and British callousness. In the United States, which in 1966 is deeply committed to insuring the survival of the Republic of South Viet-Nam, the ghost of Dien Bien Phu still haunts the minds of military and political planners. What remains important to this day is the byplay which led to the failure of allied action to stave off French defeat at Dien Bien Phu. Here, American actions in Viet-Nam since the deliberate bombardment of North Vietnamese territory as of February 8, 1965, eloquently show that some conclusions have been drawn from the previous experience.

Precisely because the political byplay which took place in those tragic days of spring, 1954, still has relevance today for the United States, it is difficult to obtain from American official sources a coherent picture of what exactly went on.[1] Fortunately, French and British sources no longer are bound by such restrictions. Several high officials of both countries (such as Britain's then Foreign Secretary, Sir Anthony Eden; and France's then Prime Minister, Joseph Laniel, among others) have published accounts which are substantially in accord with each other as to the sequence of events.[2] In the United States, the volume of memoirs published by President Eisenhower and certain press articles whose correctness were not denied by the late Secretary of State John Foster Dulles,[3] also contribute to the over-all picture.

In American foreign policy, the fates of Korea and Indochina were considered as intimately linked from the date of the outbreak of the Korean War in June, 1950, to the end of the Truman administration in January, 1953. This common concept of policies included as one of its basic tenets that none of the Western powers engaged in military operations against a Communist aggressor would negotiate a separate cease-fire since the immediate results would be an increased burden upon the others' theaters of operations. The *quid pro quo* of that agreement was that the French broke off negotiations under way with the Viet-Minh,[4] while the United States began to assume an ever-increasing part of the financial burden of the Indochina war. The closeness of the relationship between the Indochina and Korean wars becomes really clear when it is remembered that the 1954 Geneva Conference, though it dealt almost exclusively with Indochina, was still officially billed as a conference to settle both the Korean and the Indochina problem.

In actual fact, however, the administration of Dwight D. Eisenhower felt it important to honor its commitment to the American electorate to settle the costly Korean stalemate by some sort of a cease-fire. When the Communist powers agreed to an arrangement under the terms of which the two Koreas would remain divided at a battle line which more or less straddled the original 38th Parallel, the administration accepted, and the cease-fire was signed on July 27, 1953. The record does not as yet show whether the French government of the time made a strong effort either to prevent a unilateral cease-fire in Korea or to make it dependent upon similar indications of good will on the part of the Communists in Viet-Nam. But the then Prime Minister makes it clear in his book on the subject that he informed Navarre personally at the July 24, 1953, session of the French National Defense Committee (the equivalent of the American National Security Council) that the French government intended to begin negotiations for a cease-fire as soon as that in Korea was signed.[5] In any case, as I know from personal experience since I was in Hanoi during all of the summer of 1953, the increased weight of new matériel for the Communists and of Chinese instructors for the Viet-Minh forces made itself readily felt immediately after the Korean cease-fire. This cause-and-effect relationship between the end of the Korean War and the increase of the war burden on Indochina is readily acknowledged by President Eisenhower:

> Toward the end of 1953, the effect of the termination of hostili-
> ties in Korea began to be felt in Indochina. . . . The Chinese Com-
> munists now were able to spare greatly increased quantities of

matériel in the form of guns and ammunition (largely supplied by the Soviets) [6] for use on the Indochinese battle front. More advisors were being sent in and the Chinese were making available to the Viet-Minh logistical experience they had gained in the Korean War.[7]

Other contemporary American sources make it clear that this consequence of the Korean cease-fire had been clearly realized at the time, but it apparently was felt that the risk could be undertaken. The principal negotiator in Korea, Arthur Dean, who also had been a law partner of John Foster Dulles, testified before the Senate Foreign Relations Committee in January 1957 "that it was known in advance that a Korean truce would release Chinese troops to attack French Indochina."[8] When asked by the then Senator Hubert Humphrey if it was his impression that the Communists had accepted an armistice in Korea "in order to be free to move into Indochina," Dean replied that this was his opinion and went on to say that in June, 1953, the Administration had sent Lt. General John W. O'Daniel, then commander of U. S. Army forces in the Pacific, to make a survey of the situation in Indochina, and that he had returned from his mission with the view that the French could withstand the pressure with increased American aid. As in the case of Dien Bien Phu itself, General O'Daniel's optimism was not justified by later events. In the absence of any documentation from the Communist side, it is difficult to state whether Moscow, Peking (then still tightly aligned with it), and the Viet-Minh in the jungle took the unilateral Korean cease-fire as a "signal" that direct American help to the French, should the Indochina situation deteriorate further, would be anything but assured.

On the other hand, with the United States extricated from a military confrontation with Communism under conditions which could be criticized (and were) by right-wing elements as "appeasement," the Eisenhower administration no longer was particularly interested in fostering yet another situation in Indochina which could only lead to yet another accommodation with Communism on a basis that fell far short of a victory. This view led, in the fall of 1953, to a considerable hardening of the American position toward negotiation in Indochina. The immediate result of that new position was a considerable relaxation of pressure on France to grant or complete the granting of independence to the Indochina States; the granting of an additional $385 million to France for the specific purpose of implementing the Navarre Plan, and an exchange of letters on September 29, 1953, which provided for greater consultation between the two governments with regard to Indochina that was interpreted in the French Parliament to mean that France could not negotiate an Indochina cease-fire with the Viet-Minh or Peking without prior American approval.[9] In France itself, the new American encouragement to seek an improved military situation prior to negotiations was well received by the conservative coalition which then was in control of the French government. An offer made by Ho Chi Minh via Sweden on November 29, 1953 (that is, hardly a week after the first French landing at Dien Bien Phu), of direct negotiations with France based on a simple battlefield truce, was never given an official answer.

Throughout the winter of 1953-54, little transpired that would make Paris or Washington adopt a different reading of the situation. According to his own memoirs, President Eisenhower still felt in January, 1954, that United States ground forces would not be required in Southeast Asia and that American air strikes in support of the French against Communist forces deployed in the jungle would be of little effectiveness and, in his words, "would create a double jeopardy; it would comprise an act of war and would also entail the risk of having intervened and lost." In any case, such American support was, for the time being, considered a mere hypothesis. As was shown earlier, American military observers in whom the President had the greatest personal trust readily discounted the pessimistic statements made even by the French senior officials who were in the best position to know how their military were faring in Indochina. How badly misinformed the administration in Washington was became clear after the first attacks on Dien Bien Phu. Even a decade later Eisenhower still wondered about the pessimism displayed by the French after the fall of strongpoints Beatrice and Gabrielle since in his view, the French, "well dug in," should have had no trouble in fending off even a more numerous attacking force. Apparently, General O'Daniel had failed to see, or failed to report, the obvious deficiencies of the Dien Bien Phu position, aside from its valley-bottom location.

But there was yet another problem that deeply worried the French: What if the Chinese threw their air force into the fight? Over the previous two years, French Intelligence had reported the presence of several Chinese airfields in the proximity of the North Vietnamese border. The then-modern MIG-15's had been spotted on those airfields and some of them assertedly bore Viet-Minh rather than Chinese insignia. During the earlier "Quinpart" conferences the possibility of a Chinese-Korean-type attack against the French in Indochina had been taken under consideration, and the French had worked out a contingency plan, fittingly code-named "Damocles," which provided for the immediate falling back of all French forces in North Indochina to a beachhead position in the Red River Delta and to the occupation of a defensive line across the narrow waist of the Indochina peninsula until American and other allied forces would become available. "Damocles" also provided for the immediate intervention of United States air power over Indochina. As will be seen, during the following few weeks Secretary of State Dulles, Vice President Richard M. Nixon, and the then Chairman of the Joint Chiefs of Staff, Admiral Arthur B. Radford, would use every means at their command to show that the conditions for unleashing "Damocles" had indeed occurred in Indochina, and particularly in the valley of Dien Bien Phu.

A three-week mission of investigation in Indochina by the French Minister of Defense, René Pleven, merely reinforced the pessimism of the French government. In the course of a meeting of the French National Defense Committee on March 11, 1954, Pleven informed the Prime Minister that in order to avoid any misunderstanding with the United States, which, in his words, still "seemed to count on the possibility of a fairly rapid military solution," he would send the Chairman of the French Joint Chiefs, General Paul Ely, to Washington.[10] General Ely had previously served in Washington as the senior French representative to the NATO Standing Group and was known for his feelings of friendship for the United States, and thus was a good choice for that mission, save for the fact that his understanding of the English language was somewhat limited.

When Ely arrived in Washington on March 20, hills Beatrice and Gabrielle had fallen after a brief struggle and Anne-Maries 1 and 2 had been abandoned three days earlier by the 3rd BT. Dien Bien Phu's airfield was under heavy fire and the evacuation of casualties, was in jeopardy when Ely began his conversations with Secretary Dulles, his brother Allen Dulles, then Director of the Central Intelligence Agency, Vice President Nixon, and General Matthew Ridgway, Chief of Staff of the U. S. Army. Ely also saw President Eisenhower and—a rare privilege for a foreign officer—attended a meeting of the U. S. Joint Chiefs. When John Foster Dulles saw Ely again on Tuesday, March 23, for a formal working session at the State Department, he prudently did not commit the United States to any support action on behalf of the French.

Two versions of the key points that were discussed are available. According to a memorandum prepared by Dulles for President Eisen-

hower, Dulles told Ely that the United States could not afford to engage
its prestige in a military operation "and suffer a defeat which would
have world-wide repercussions." According to Ely, a possibility of
American intervention in Indochina had been directly raised, but, says
Ely, "—and I insist on this point—would become conceivable . . . only
in the hypothesis of Chinese air action in Indochina."[11]

But while Ely was in the United States, the Viet-Minh at Dien Bien
Phu unveiled its new powerful artillery and, above all, its Chinese
antiaircraft batteries. Contrary to expectations, then, the Chinese intervention took on not the aspect of air strikes but of a fairly massive
specialized support on the ground, for which the contingency plans of
the old "Damocles" project had no answer. It became readily fore-
seeable that the Chinese flak would bring disaster to Dien Bien Phu just
as readily as Chinese MIG's. In the light of this new situation, Radford—
who already had, in previous conversations with Ely, suggested to the
latter that American military intervention would be feasible if the
French government formally requested it—now proposed to Ely the
possibility of brief American action against the Communist flak positions.
In Radford's view, this would merely be, to use a term much in vogue at
present, a matching "escalation" for that undertaken by the Chinese in
providing North Viet-Nam with abundant artillery and logistical support. Here again, Ely insists that the initiative came from Admiral
Radford.

Ely had barely arrived in Paris on March 27, when Secretary Dulles,
on March 29, delivered a major address on Asian policy before the
Overseas Press Club in New York City. In language still used in 1966 to
explain the American position in South Viet-Nam, Dulles first ticked off
the details of Chinese Communist involvement with the Viet-Minh—
thereby compromising, according to the French, some highly precious
French intelligence networks in the Communist-held areas of Viet-Nam.
Then the Secretary of State went on to warn that "the imposition on
Southeast Asia" of Communism "should be met by united action. This
might involve serious risks. But these risks are far less than those that
will face us a few years from now if we dare not be resolute today."
Dulles also recalled that on March 24, President Eisenhower had stated
that Southwest Asia was of "transcendent importance" to the free world.
The speech, which was billed as having the advance approval of President Eisenhower, was received in Paris with considerable elation.

Prime Minister Laniel who, in the meantime, had organized a special
restricted "war committee" to decide on Indochina policy, made up of the

Joint Chiefs and some key cabinet members, met with Ely and the committee on March 29 to debate what appeared to be a firm American
offer. To the French, while tempting, the offer was not an undisguised
blessing: What would happen if a single such American raid, or even
a series, failed to destroy the Viet-Minh siege force but, on the other
hand, brought in its wake a massive Chinese intervention of the Korean
type, beginning with swarms of MIG fighters? Or, if such a raid brought
in its wake the destruction of all hopes of a peaceful solution to the
Indochina War at Geneva on April 26, should the Communist powers
decide to withdraw from the conference? Having scraped by several close
calls in Parliament on the Indochina problem, the broadening of the
war created by American intervention might cause the defection from
Laniel's coalition of the left-of-center parties it needed to remain in
power. Laniel and the war committee decided to send Col. Brohon, an
aide of Ely who had been with him in Washington and had attended
all the crucial conferences, to Saigon in order to sound out Navarre as
to whether he felt that Dien Bien Phu's situation was such that all risks
had to be taken to save its garrison.

When Brohon finally caught up with Navarre in Hanoi on April 2,
the first battle for the Five Hills had just taken a disastrous turn which
only a massive annihilation of the enemy flak could reverse.

Two equally authoritative French versions exist of the next act of the
drama. According to Colonel Jules Roy, whose account is based on
Gen. Cogny's recollection of the event, Brohon mentioned that the
project involved the use of "several A-bombs" in the Dien Bien Phu
area.[12] According to Major Jean Pouget, who then was Navarre's personal aide, the question of the use of atomic weapons was never raised
"even under a veiled form."[13] A similar discrepancy exists as to Navarre's
answer. According to Roy, the answer was negative. Pouget, on the other
hand, cites the full text of Navarre's reply to Ely sent by radio message
in his own personal code during the night of April 3-4:

> The intervention of which Colonel Brohon has spoken to me
> may have a decisive effect particularly if it comes before the Viet-
> Minh assault.

Other sources confirmed that view of the facts. Since no written notes
were kept of those top-secret sessions, it is not known who first gave the
projected operation its eventual sinister code name, but its first written
mention seems to have been in another message sent to Ely by Navarre
on April 6. That telegram began with the simple phrase: "The planned

intervention takes the code name 'Vulture.'"

While the French government and the French military were trying to hammer out a common policy in Paris, Saigon, and Hanoi, John Foster Dulles and Admiral Radford simultaneously prepared the U. S. Congress for the unleashing of "Vulture." On Saturday, April 3, 1954, eight senior legislators were called to the Department of State for a secret conference with Secretary Dulles, Admiral Radford, and some of their senior aides. The legislators were a bipartisan group including Senators Lyndon B. Johnson (then Minority Leader), Richard B. Russell, Earl C. Clements, William F. Knowland, and Eugene Millikin; and Representatives John W. McCormack, J. Percy Priest, and Joseph Martin.[14]

Dulles stated that President Eisenhower himself had asked him to call the meeting and that the President wanted Congress to pass a joint resolution permitting him the use of air and naval power in Indochina—in other words, a resolution granting him a far more restricted freedom of maneuver than that which President Lyndon B. Johnson was given in August, 1964. Radford then succinctly outlined the situation in Indochina and particularly the desperate straits of Dien Bien Phu. In language which was to be used again almost verbatim a decade later, Secretary Dulles warned that the fall of Indochina might well lead to the loss of all of Southeast Asia and that "the United States might eventually be forced back to Hawaii." He also added that failure by the United States to support the French and the local governments now might result in an abandonment of the war by the French. In his outline of "Vulture" Radford stated that it would be based on the two American aircraft carriers *Essex* and *Boxer*,[15] reinforced from land-based U. S. Air Force units from Clark Field in the Philippines. According to French sources, a total of sixty B-29 heavy bombers, each carrying nine tons of bombs, and about 450 fighter aircraft would be involved if the strike were to be made with conventional weapons. However, according to official American sources, a total of ninety-eight heavy B-29 Superfortresses, each of which carried fourteen tons of bombs, with two wings stationed at Okinawa, and one stationed at Clark Field, would bear the main burden of the mission. Also, close to 450 jet fighters were available to provide cover against possible forays of Chinese MIG's against the American bombers. Upon questioning, Radford allegedly stated that the action contemplated might put the United States "in the war" and that, if the initial strike did not bring full relief to the fortress, follow-up strikes were contemplated.

He hedged his reply as to the possibility of eventually committing

American ground troops in the war and admitted that none of the other military staff chiefs agreed in full with his plan. As is the custom, the Senate Minority Leader led off with the questioning of the Administration representatives, and he did so with great emphasis and vigor. In fact, as the also-present Chairman of the Senate Armed Services Committee, Richard B. Russell, was to recall later, "the discussion was vigorous and a bit of it might have been described as heated."[16]

According to Chalmers Roberts, "Lyndon Johnson put the other key question in the form of a little speech." The Senate Minority Leader stated that the Korean War had been financed and fought by the United States to an extent of ninety per cent and then asked Dulles whether any other allied nation (outside of the French, who already were committed to the war) had been consulted as to whether they would join the United States in intervening in Viet-Nam.

Retrospectively, this seems to have been the key question and the key stumbling point. When Dulles acknowledged that, in view of the urgency of the situation, he had not yet consulted any other allies, the eight Congressional leaders flatly turned down the idea of a joint resolution and told the Administration that Congressional support for "Vulture" or any similar operation would be contingent upon three conditions:

> (1) United States intervention must be part of a coalition to include the other free nations of Southeast Asia, the Philippines, and the British Commonwealth.
>
> (2) The French must agree to accelerate their independence program for the Indochina States so that the United States assistance would not appear as supporting colonialism.
>
> (3) The French must agree to stay in the war.[17]

That, for all practical purposes, killed all chances of rescuing Dien Bien Phu for it was obvious that it would be absolutely impossible to constitute anything resembling a "united front" of allied powers in sufficient time for the air strikes to become effective. The question then arises whether the subsequent activities of Secretary Dulles to establish such a front were simply an attempt to shift the blame on other hesitant allies, such as the British—a view that was openly expressed later[18]—or whether he in fact believed that such a united action, even if it failed to materialize in time to save Dien Bien Phu, might still come in handy for a subsequent American intervention in the war or as a diplomatic backstop for the coming Geneva Conference. In the absence of any published American documentation on the subject it is difficult today to assess whether that second alternative was then considered an acceptable fall-back position. The available testimony of all the French participants clearly shows that only the first alternative—that is, the rescue of hard-pressed Dien Bien Phu—was first and foremost in their minds and that they were not particularly interested in the second alternative which, even if successful, could only insure the failure of the Geneva Conference and an extension in time, or perhaps in scope, of the Indochina War.

During the same week-end, Col. Brohon was on his way back from Indochina to Paris. He arrived on Sunday, April 4, and he immediately spoke to Gen. Ely. He expressed to him the second thoughts which Navarre harbored about "Vulture," notably that it might lead to an unleashing of Red China; but at that very moment Navarre's top-secret telegram requesting U. S. intervention arrived in Ely's hands. Armed with the telegram and reinforced by Brohon's presence, Ely went to see the Defense Minister, Pleven, and the latter took both of them directly to the Prime Minister. Laniel in turn decided to call a meeting of the war committee for after dinner. In a dramatic late-evening session, fully conscious that their decision might bring about an expansion of the war and a shattering of all hopes of a *détente* with the Soviet bloc, the war committee decided to make a formal request for U. S. air intervention in the war. At midnight, Laniel requested that the United States Ambassador in Paris, Douglas Dillon, come to see him immediately at Matignon, the official residence of the Prime Minister. At 0100 of April 5—or at about the same time, making allowance for the differences in time zones, as the French at Dien Bien Phu retook Huguette 6 —the French Prime Minister explained the gravity of the situation at Dien Bien Phu to the American Ambassador. He underlined that only American heavy bombers could destroy the deeply dug-in Viet-Minh artillery in the hills around Dien Bien Phu and that only such an operation could still save the garrison. While the American Ambassador transmitted the telegram via his own channels to Washington, Ely also informed his own successor at the NATO Standing Group in the Pentagon, Gen. Valluy, of the decision made in order to accelerate to the utmost the military measures about to be undertaken by Admiral Radford. According to Ely, Valluy telephoned him from Washington early in the afternoon, Paris time (that is, in the forenoon, Washington time) that matters were progressing satisfactorily with the American military. At the same time, the French Embassy in Washington again reported that obviously inspired press releases and unattributed statements mentioned heavy Chinese intervention in Viet-Nam and seemed to be preparing

American public and Congressional opinion for an American intervention at Dien Bien Phu.

On the same day also, President Eisenhower wrote a long personal letter to Winston Churchill who, though eighty-five, had again assumed the Prime Ministership of his country. In his letter, largely made public in the President's first volume of memoirs, Eisenhower outlined to Churchill the new "united front" concept:

> The important thing is that the coalition must be strong and it must be willing to join the fight if necessary. I do not envisage the need of any appreciable ground forces on your or our part. . . .
>
> If I may refer again to history, we failed to halt Hirohito, Mussolini and Hitler by not acting in unity and in time. That marked the beginning of many years of stark tragedy and desperate peril. May it not be that our nations have learned something from that lesson? . . .
>
> With warm regards,
Ike

As is now known from the memoirs of Britain's then Foreign Secretary, Sir Anthony Eden, the American request was received with consternation. Sir Winston and British public opinion were, after almost seven years of cold war, dead set against any move which would jeopardize the prospects of the forthcoming Geneva Conference. Hence, Churchill took three days to reply to his good wartime friend, and his reply was simply that the British government would discuss the matter with Dulles in London on April 12. Two days after its formal launching the Dulles-Radford Plan already was encountering heavy resistance on several key fronts.

It is difficult to assess from the available records how long it took the French to become aware of the fact that operation "Vulture," as originally planned, was already in serious jeopardy. It must have been almost immediately after the telephone conversation between Valluy and Ely, because on April 7, Navarre replied negatively to a message from Gen. Ely asking him whether he would accept the use of fifteen B-29 heavy bombers to be operated out of Clark Field with French Air Force crews from Indochina. Navarre's refusal to accept the B-29's on that basis rested on at least three serious objections: First, there was a desperate shortage of air crews in the Indochina theater. There were more aircraft available than French pilots to fly them, and it would take France a month to replace the thirty multi-engine pilots who would be going to Manila. To deprive the already overburdened Dien Bien Phu airlift of thirty air crews would have been disastrous. Second, American estimates were that it would take even trained multi-engine pilots four months to become completely familiarized with the B-29's; by then the fate of Dien Bien Phu would have long been sealed and the whole project would have been largely irrelevant. Third, the sudden appearance of such a small heavy-bomber force with French insignia but without the requisite heavy fighter escort would have been an open invitation for the Chinese to score an easy victory by sending in a force of Chinese MIG's to shoot them down, thus precipitating operation "Damocles" but without any assurance of American support. It is difficult to assess how far the plans for this particular subvariant of "Vulture" were pushed. I was told, however, that B-29's with French tricolor bull's-eye insignia could be seen standing ready at Clark Field.

That the French were short on multi-engine pilots was as much their own fault as that of NATO planning. Since France had been assigned within the alliance a wholly defensive role in the field of aviation, French pilots were entirely trained for fighter-interceptor missions. In fact, a separate French bomber command did not even exist at the time of Dien Bien Phu, and during World War II the United States provided the Free French with no combat aircraft larger than the twin-engine B-26. The same problem arose in the field of air transport. Since NATO plans did not provide for a French role in that field, French Air Force tactical transport was reduced to a minimum. The net result of all of this was that, aside from the already committed French Navy *Privateer* bomber crews, there was no French personnel available to man the B-29; by the time the battle of Dien Bien Phu ended, there were in all of France only forty twin-engine transport crews left in reserve. It is unofficially admitted by the French that they had misinformed the United States about the state of readiness of French flying personnel. At Dien Bien Phu the consequences of that lack of candor now were there for everyone to see.

Realistically, Navarre understood that it would be folly to assume that "Vulture" in one form or another would be launched in the near future. Also, as has been seen, Navarre that very day began to undertake the planning for a diversionary operation against the Communist siege ring on the basis of a small T'ai-pronged relief force from Laos, of which more will be said later. The code name for that undertaking, in order to remain consistent with the bird motif chosen earlier for the raids on Dien Bien Phu, was "Condor."

But while Washington apparently had written off "Vulture," the

American planners in the field were going ahead in the full belief that the mission to rescue the French would be executed. At the beginning of April, 1954, Lieutentant General Earle E. ("Pat") Partridge, Commander of the U. S. Far Eastern Air Force (FEAF), had arrived in Saigon and begun talks with his French counterpart, Gen. Lauzin, as well as with Navarre. He had brought with him Brigadier General Joseph D. Caldara, then the chief of the FEAF Bomber Command—the man who would fly and command the "Vulture" missions.

The Americans had arrived at Saigon's Tan Son Nhut airport in a discreet B-17, so as not to alert hostile eyes to the unfamiliar configuration of the B-29 Superforts. From the beginning, the Americans were appalled at the total lack of French preparedness for anything like the control of a major saturation bombardment operation. For instance, Caldara soon found that there was not, in all of Indochina, short-range navigational radar (SHORAN) equipment which was absolutely essential to precision-guidance of heavy bombers which were supposed to hit an enemy closely encircling a friendly force: a hesitation of a few seconds, a minute guidance error, and hundreds of tons of explosive bombs would obliterate the French rather than the Viet-Minh.

Caldara decided to judge the situation for himself. On April 4, 1954, in the dead of the night, he flew his B-17 with an American crew over the valley of Dien Bien Phu, repeated the mission later with a French Dakota; and then once more with the B-17. In Hanoi, where he had met Cogny and Dechaux and found them very eager to see "Vulture" attempted, Cogny had suggested that three shoran ground parties could be parachuted into the jungle to guide the bombers, even if they had to be sacrificed. The Americans, however, felt that there were too many elements of chance involved in that approach. Instead, Caldara proposed contour-flying and bombardment by visual navigation, even if this entailed greater risks for the American air crews. Otherwise, the overall plan was simple enough: the two wings from Okinawa and the one from Clark would rendez-vous east of the Laotian capital of Vientiane, head for their target; and exit from Indochina via the Gulf of Tonkin. Strict orders were given that any disabled Superfort would do its utmost to crash in the open sea, rather than on the ground, where Communist discovery of B-29's and, worse, of live American air crews; could have appalling political repercussions.

Meanwhile, as the French began to realize that their American opposite numbers were stalling for time until Washington made up its mind, exchanges became more acrimonious, not only between the French and the Americans, but also between the American air commanders and their own diplomats on the spot, since the latter fully realized the implications of a French defeat at Dien Bien Phu.

When FEAF made known its requirements for ground-based shoran, the Saigon mission let it be known that it was disappointed to find that the Strategic Air Command (SAC) was not an "all-weather" force. The French themselves, at the highest political levels, seemed to have no idea of the awful destructive power of 98 Superforts and suggested that, if need be, the chances of killing some of the French defenders of Dien Bien Phu should not prevent the raid from taking place. Banging with his fist on the table, one of the American generals reminded his colleagues that saturation missions were not flown on that basis.

The American *chargé d'affaires,* Robert McClintock, sought to lighten the atmosphere by citing George Clemenceau's famous phrase that perhaps "war was too serious a business to be left entirely to generals." But this was no longer a time for jokes. Gen. Caldara wheeled around, looked at McClintock, and said quietly:

"If that mission takes place, I'm going to be riding the lead B-29 into the goddam' flak, and you're welcome to the right seat."

On April 8, Dulles finally informed the French that no American action on behalf of Dien Bien Phu could be undertaken without some sort of common Western position. That, of course, shifted the burden of decision from the American Executive to the allies, particularly the British. Eden's memoirs appear to make it clear that Britain was in no way willing to make even a token gesture that would lead the Red Chinese to believe that London was ready to support an American-French-"Allied" military undertaking before Geneva. Yet Secretary Dulles, to judge from Eisenhower's recollection, informed the President that he had succeeded in overcoming most of Britain's objections to joint action. That was, to say the least, a total misreading of the British position, but there is no doubt that upon continuing his journey from London to Paris on April 14, Dulles conveyed a similar reading to his French partners, Prime Minister Laniel and the radically activist French Foreign Minister, Georges Bidault. (Bidault, an ardent advocate of keeping Algeria French, later conspired against de Gaulle and now lives in exile in Latin America.)

It is in the course of that particular meeting that Dulles allegedly brought up the subject of using atomic bombs to save the French garrison at Dien Bien Phu. According to one extremely well-informed source, whose statement, when published, was never officially denied, Dulles said to Bidault in French: "And if we gave you two atomic bombs to save Dien Bien Phu?"[19] It should be underlined that Dulles, who had in his youth studied at the Sorbonne, spoke good French and that Bidault had, prior to entering politics, been a professor of English. Hence, the chances that either of them had misunderstood the other were minimal. Bidault was said to have replied that the use of such bombs would destroy the garrison as well as the Viet-Minh, and Gen. Ely, though denying that the use of A-bombs had ever been seriously considered, nonetheless spoke of the presence of the nuclear deterrent represented by the aircraft carriers of the Seventh Fleet in the Gulf of Tonkin.

It is perhaps immaterial at this point whether such a use of atomic weapons around Dien Bien Phu was feasible or even desirable—and this writer, for one, on the basis of his personal research, is certain that their use had been seriously considered at one point or another by the military planners involved—but the fact remains that even British Foreign Secretary Eden seems to have been persuaded that the use of such weapons was not entirely ruled out and that the weapons were readily available for use.[20] Further circumstantial evidence to that effect was provided by the French Prime Minister, in a Parliamentary debate on May 4, 1954, just before the fall of Dien Bien Phu, when he stated that in previous "military conversations with our Allies, *all* solutions susceptible to improve a situation such as that of Dien Bien Phu had been studied"; but he added, seemingly as an ominous afterthought, that those solutions which "prior to the Geneva Conference included the risk of generalizing the conflict," had been rejected.

When the garrison at Dien Bien Phu, contrary to all expectations, managed to survive the battles for the Five Hills and the first battle for the Huguettes, Giap ordered new supplies from China. Thus the problem of bombing the Communist rear supply lines rather than Dien Bien Phu again came to the fore. Now, contrary to what he had said ten days earlier, Navarre would have been glad to get fifteen to twenty B-29's for the purpose of bombing Road 41 between the Red River and the main Viet-Minh supply point at Tuan-Giao, northeast of Dien Bien Phu. But now, with Britain hanging back, that alternative no longer seemed to be available, either. A brief message from Ely to Navarre noted: "Radford rejects that solution. Everything or nothing."

But while Dulles was still discussing "Vulture" with the French leaders in Paris, the commander of the United States Far Eastern Air

Force, Gen. Partridge, arrived in Saigon. His conversations with the French High Commissioner, Maurice Dejean, and Navarre, revived their hope that American intervention in one form or another was still not altogether excluded. But the rest of the week—as the battle of Dien Bien Phu hung in the balance, and as Communist morale was at its lowest and the morale of the French garrison found a viable equilibrium —turned out to be a dead loss for "Vulture."

Dulles, still acting under the mistaken belief that he had a British commitment for support in his pocket, had called a meeting on April 20, in Washington, of the ambassadors of Australia, Britain, Cambodia, France, Laos, New Zealand, the Philippines, Thailand, and Viet-Nam, for the purpose of setting up the machinery for "united action." Churchill and Eden, unwilling, as the latter termed it, "to endorse a bad policy for the sake of unity," this time stood unequivocally firm. They directed their ambassador in Washington, Sir Roger Makins, not to attend the meeting. That boycott killed the conference. The bitterness and despair of the French government in Paris, caught between the ever more pressing SOS messages from Indochina and the American "roller-coaster" of promises and denials, became profound. Arriving in Paris for a NATO ministerial meeting which was to begin on April 23, Dulles had ample occasion to see his French colleague in private, since he was to stay there for three days, until the Geneva Conference began on April 26. According to a message sent to Eisenhower by Dulles on April 23 at 2000, Bidault had reached a point of nervous breakdown and incoherence. With the conference at Geneva beginning in a few days, it became clear that the Communists in Viet-Nam were attempting to finish off the battered fortress so as to "deliver" its defeat as an opener to their side at Geneva. Hence, any prolongation of its survival to a point in time where at least a temporary cease-fire could be effected in Indochina would be, the French felt, an immense gain. Accordingly, they literally begged Dulles to press for the implementation of "Vulture."

Under firm instructions from Eisenhower, Dulles now held his ground. There would be no American bombing operation near Dien Bien Phu which did not meet the requirement of the mandate of the Congressional leaders of April 3: American air action only within the framework of an Allied force, and only after debating and voting on the proposed joint resolution. Perhaps without realizing it, Lyndon B. Johnson, on April 3, 1954, had made his first crucial decision on Viet-Nam.

By the evening of the same day (the 23rd) and unbeknownst to the French, Dulles had written off Dien Bien Phu altogether. At 2200, Paris time, he sent a briefer message to Eisenhower in which he acknowledged that "the situation here is tragic" but in which he also affirmed that "there is, of course, no military or logical reason why loss of Dien Bien Phu should lead to collapse of French . . ." That assessment was correct inasmuch as only four per cent of the French battle force in Indochina was committed at Dien Bien Phu, but it seemingly did not take cognizance of such aspects as French and Vietnamese combat morale or of the war weariness of French public opinion at home. If Dulles, on April 23, failed to understand what was at stake at Dien Bien Phu, then this is simply one more example of the limitations of many a diplomat in assessing the nonmaterial aspects of a given political problem.

On April 24, Eden also had arrived in Paris for the NATO Council meeting and Adm. Radford personally undertook to convince him of the necessity of at least providing the United States with a symbolic declaration of support. Eden, however, remained adamant and told his American interlocutors that, as in Korea, a policy predicated on air strikes would soon thereafter be followed by commitments of ground troops on the part of the United States. And, as experience had shown, such a commitment would again be followed by American pressure on the allies for "united action"—meaning, the commitment of *their* troops to the battle. The British were grimly determined to give Geneva its chance and Eden flew back to London on Sunday, April 25, to attend a special cabinet meeting to settle the problem once and for all.

All attempts at saving Dien Bien Phu through an America air strike collapsed that weekend. But it remained to put the finishing touches on the historical record all around and to go through the final diplomatic motions. On April 24 in the afternoon, Secretary John Foster Dulles sent Bidault a memorandum drawn up in the course of a meeting at the American Embassy in Paris, whose first sentence (retranslated from the French) makes interesting reading in 1966. "An act of war can only be effected with authorization of Congress." The rest of the letter simply reaffirmed the earlier American position and added to it the new fall-back position that, in fact, Dien Bien Phu was not terribly important, could no longer be saved by air strikes, and in any case already had cost the enemy dearly. Bidault's reply, also dated the same day, began by restating the already known arguments, but added to them the fact that the heavy concentration of the enemy's battle force in the immediate Dien Bien Phu area would permit devastating air strikes which would not only save Dien Bien Phu but could well alter the over-all balance of the war.

There remained one last try—a direct confrontation between the French and the old British leader. It took place in London on Tuesday, April 27; the Western missions had already arrived at Geneva for the purpose of discussing the Korean and Indochinese questions with the Communist Bloc. Late in the morning René Massigli, the French Ambassador to the Court of St. James's, was received by Churchill, but Churchill remained adamant. Britain would not let an opportunity go by at settling the outstanding issues of peace and war with the Communist powers for the sake of a small garrison whose fate, in all likelihood, was sealed anyway.

"Let us not be shaken in our resolution," said the old leader. "I have known many reverses myself. I have held out against them. I have not given in.

"I have suffered Singapore, Hong-Kong, Tobruk; the French will have Dien Bien Phu. . . ."[21]

That afternoon Churchill told a cheering House of Commons that Her Majesty's Government was "not prepared to give any undertakings about United Kingdom military action in Indochina in advance of the results of Geneva."

Operation "Vulture" died a slow death. Brig. Gen. (later Maj. Gen.) Caldera, the commander of the B-29 group at Clark Field, made one more visit to Indochina on April 26, still for the purpose of preparing a variant of the American air raid on Dien Bien Phu. That last variant allegedly provided for eighty-plane raids during three consecutive nights on the surroundings of the valley of Dien Bien Phu and on the Communist depot area at Tuan Giao, this time with mixed American-French crews. Here again, subvariants seemed to have been discussed, involving more accurate daytime raids flown by mixed crews in aircraft bearing the French tricolor. The whole operation was still set to go on a seventy-two-hour alert basis, and a senior French Air Force officer from Saigon had already left for Clark Field to prepare the operation. Perhaps everything was not yet lost.

The final act of that tragedy was an entirely American one. In a dramatic meeting between Eisenhower, Radford, the service chiefs, and several other high level officials on April 29 in Washington, the whole situation was reviewed once more. Of the military present, only Adm. Radford was still in all-out favor of even a unilateral American commitment to stave off defeat at Dien Bien Phu. The Chief of Naval Operations, Admiral Robert B. Carney, and the Air Force Chief of Staff, General Nathan F. Twining, were unenthusiastic about the

operation, but General Matthew B. Ridgway, the Chief of Staff of the
U. S. Army, was dead set against the whole idea. As the former commander of United States forces in Korea, Ridgeway had a clear idea
both of the limitations of air action under such circumstances—in Korea
Operation "Strangle" designed to knock out Communist communication
lines had been a dismal failure—but he also felt, like Sir Anthony Eden,
that the air strikes would in all likelihood be followed by a commitment
of large American ground forces to yet another inconclusive and costly
war on the mainland of Asia. A blue-ribbon U. S. Army team had been
sent by Ridgway to Indochina earlier that year and it had returned
appalled by the conditions under which U. S. forces would have to
operate in case of a ground war there. In this he was fully backed by
Lieutenant General James M. Gavin, the noted airborne commander
of World War II fame and in 1954 the Chief of Research and Development in the Pentagon. More than anyone else, Gavin knew how poorly
the United States was prepared for a limited land war in Asia and he
considerably strengthened Ridgway's adamant stand against a policy
which, in his view, would lead the United States into such a situation.
(In 1966, the now-retired Gen. Gavin still held the same view and
expressed it publicly with regard to committing U. S. forces in Viet-Nam
—and the also-retired Gen. Ridgway in turn backed him.) As the noted
military historian Hanson W. Baldwin reported later, Charles E. Wilson,
the Secretary of Defense at the time, backed Ridgway and Gavin—and
for once, President Eisenhower stood his ground against Dulles and the
other service chiefs.[22] The decision not to come to the help of the French
was about to become final.

The chips now were down. Time stood still for a very brief moment,
not only in Washington, but also at Dien Bien Phu. There, on April 29,
the French lines were holding on the Five Hills, on the southern
Huguettes, and on strongpoint Wieme. Thanks to air-dropped replacement parts, there were still nineteen French 105's. In Hanoi, the 1st BPC
stood ready to be dropped into Dien Bien Phu as reinforcement; and
giant American C-124 Globemasters from the 322nd Air Division were
in the process of air-lifting into Indochina the brand-new 7th BPC.
India, fearful of being accused by Red China and Russia of helping the
hard-pressed French, refused to let the American aircraft fly over Indian
territory or stop for refueling there. The lumbering planes had to make
a vast detour over the Indian Ocean and refuel in Colombo, Ceylon,
which did not raise similar objections. With part of the enemy artillery
obliterated through air raids and with fresh troops thrown into the

battle as constituted units instead of being dribbled in, there still was an infinitesimal chance of surviving long enough to be saved from defeat by a cease-fire. After all, that is what had happened to the encircled Egyptians at Faluja in 1948, when they were saved from utter destruction by the Israelis through a cease-fire imposed by the UN. (If that had not happened, Col. Nasser would have been an Israeli prisoner-of-war.) And with the Communist depots at Tuan Giao badly mauled, the Viet-Minh infantry divisions at Dien Bien Phu would have been, in the middle of the monsoon season, in danger of starvation. That was what, one year earlier, had prompted the Viet-Minh's 308th Division to withdraw from its attack on the Laotian royal capital of Luang-Prabang. With or without Britain's approval, the operation was still feasible and also militarily useful. The decision now was entirely Eisenhower's.

That decision, of course, was negative but, curiously, that is never mentioned in the President's memoirs. Instead, he offers an explanation of the considerations that moved him which still has a bearing on the situation in Viet-Nam twelve years later:

> During the course of this meeting I remarked that if the United States were, unilaterally, to permit its forces to be drawn into conflict in Indochina and in a succession of Asian wars, the end result would be to drain off our resources and to weaken our overall defensive position. If we, without allies, should ever find ourselves fighting at various places all over the region, and if Red Chinese aggressive participation were clearly identified, then we could scarcely avoid, I said, considering the necessity of striking directly at the head instead of the tail of the snake, Red China itself.[23]

Therefore, not to attempt to save the French at Dien Bien Phu was ultimately, as it should have been, a wholly *American* decision, and at the highest level, involving the senior Congressional leaders, the Joint Chiefs, and the President. Yet, almost as soon as the decision had been made, there began a hardly subtle process of blaming the whole failure of "Vulture" on Britain. Secretary Dulles personally stated on a nation-wide telecast on June 12, 1954, that like Secretary of State Henry Stimson in the case of Japan's aggression against China in 1931, his own attempts at saving Indochina through united action had been rebuffed by the Allies.

Commenting on that rationalization the following day, James Reston in the *New York Times* stated that

> This picture, omitting any reference to Congressional or White House opposition to using force in Asia either in 1931 or 1954, is

one of the most misleading oversimplifications ever uttered by an American Secretary of State, but it allocates blame and furnishes an alibi.

And in his own incisive article on the subject, Chalmers Roberts noted that, regardless of Allied action or inaction, Congress would in all likelihood have given the President the requested mandate:

> . . . provided he had asked for it forcefully and explained the facts and their relation to the national interest of the United States . . . But the fact emerges that President Eisenhower never did lay the intervention question on the line.

That is precisely what Lyndon B. Johnson—perhaps mindful of his own action of April, 1954—did not fail to do in 1964 and 1965.

The American failure to make an early decision, one way or the other, with regard to Operation "Vulture" was to dog the Eisenhower Administration in curious ways even after the death of John Foster Dulles. The article in *Life* Magazine of January, 1956, which gave rise to the term "brinkmanship" and in which Dulles deliberately laid the blame once more at Britain's feet and even claimed that, prior to Geneva, his "policy of boldness impressed the Communists" and permitted the French Prime Minister and Eden at Geneva "to bargain from Dulles' strength," raised such a storm of protest as to require the Secretary of State to devote a full press conference to defending it.

When, after the death of Secretary Dulles, the first volume of memoirs of Sir Anthony Eden was published, it included several documents flatly contradicting the official American position; President Eisenhower himself, on January 13, 1960, further compounded the earlier confusion existing about Operation "Vulture" by affirming that "there was never any plan developed to put into execution in Indochina." The President then dismissed all the efforts his late Secretary of State in March-April, 1954, had made to hammer out a joint position for intervention at Dien Bien Phu by saying that Dulles had been "a very forceful man. He could very well talk about possibilities that might by then be considered as proposals, when they were not meant as that at all." Obviously by the time his own memoirs were published in 1963, the President had had time to recollect his thoughts on the matter and to adopt a viewpoint that was somewhat less inconsistent with the acual facts.

On April 18, in a message sent via his personal code, Ely approved the Forces, immediately flashed the fact of definite failure of "Vulture" to Navarre, and Navarre immediately drew the full implication of that fact for the garrison of Dien Bien Phu. Operation "Condor" already was under way but the new situation required more desperate measures. By top-secret telegram No. 24, sent in his own personal code, Navarre informed Ely on April 30 that he now was studying

> . . . a sortie of the garrison in direction of Laos . . . which presents enormous difficulties and will, under the best of circumstances, save only a part of the personnel. It will be inevitable to abandon the wounded. That last-chance operation will be dubbed "Albatross."[24]

Fortunately, only a very few Frenchmen are conversant with *The Rime of the Ancient Mariner*.

During this interval, one of the most bizarre by-plays of the whole war was taking place between Navarre and Ely: One of Navarre's intelligence officers had established contact with a member of Ho Chi Minh's government. This event was so secret that Navarre had requested (and obtained) permission not to mention the whole matter to the highest French civilian representative in Indochina, Commissioner General Maurice Dejean.

On April 18, in a message sent via his personal code, Ely approved the pursuing of the contact but urged Navarre to use maximum care to avoid being trapped by the enemy. Ely also told him to consult the government in Paris before making any commitment, and confirmed that Navarre should withhold the information from the Commissioner General's office, which was widely known for its "leaks." Navarre's reply of the following day was short and to the point:

> I took no initiative. Contacts are top secret. My representative can always be disavowed. No results expected before one week.

What happened next, and *who* exactly that high-level North Vietnamese contact was, is still not known publicly to this day. But he did exist and he was important, for on May 12, after Dien Bien Phu had fallen and the Geneva conference had begun, Navarre radioed to Ely:

> Viet-Minh contact now with Viet-Minh Delegation at Geneva. Everything is off. [Talks] may resume if Geneva fails.

There was a six-man Viet-Minh delegation at Geneva: Pham Van Dong, then Foreign Minister, now the Prime Minister of the Hanoi government; Ta Quang Buu, an Oxford-trained brigadier general; Ha Van Lau, a People's Army colonel who since 1954 has been in charge of Hanoi's relations with the International Control Commission; Phan

Anh, a college professor and holder of several senior posts in Ho's government since 1945; Hoang Van Hoan, then ambassador to Peking; and Tran Cong Tuong, then Vice-Minister of Justice and a trained lawyer. It could have been any one of them. But there was no need of resuming the secret contacts. Geneva did not fail, after all.

Initially, "Condor" had been planned as early as December, 1953, as an operation designed to pursue, in connection with the French forces at Dien Bien Phu, Viet-Minh siege troops supposedly dislocated by a successful French defense of the valley. In its original form, the plan provided for four phases: Phase one—a group of four battalions would destroy the Communist regulars south and west of the Nam Ou River on a thirty-kilometer front between Muong Khoua and Pak Luong (see map, p. 316). Phase two—the "Condor" force would then repeat the operation undertaken by GAP 2 in December, 1953. Phase three—it would progress to Houei Nga Na Song, where it would link up with an airborne battle group of between three to four battalions, to be reinforced by a 75-mm. recoilless rifle battery from the 35th Airborne Artillery and a company of the 17th Airborne Engineers. Phase four—the eight-battalion force would then move in direction of the valley of Dien Bien Phu. At the beginning of the third phase, it would conquer and hold the *Col des Calcaires* (Limestone Pass) between Tay Chang and Ban Na Ti. Upon holding Limestone Pass, the task force would be overlooking the southern flank of Dien Bien Phu and probably see Isabelle.

The plan also provided for a variant in case it proved inadvisable to parachute an airborne group on Houei Nga Na Song or in case Communist resistance west of Limestone Pass did not require the presence of the paratroopers. In that case, the airborne group would be parachuted south of Isabelle once the ground troops had secured Limestone Pass. That variant, in order to stay consistent with the other birdlike code names, was given the code name of "Pivert" (Woodpecker). The total number of troops to be involved in that original version of "Condor" was to be about 5,500.

The trouble with that plan was that it required, just as the original operation "Castor" had, about 115 *Dakotas* a day, or about half that many C-119's and the daily maintenance of that force—in view of the practically nonexistent roads—required sixty tons of airborne cargo space, or the equivalent of twenty-four *Dakotas*—not to mention the fact that those sixty tons would have to be rigged into 600 separate 100-kilogram parcels every day. An operation of that size, in addition to the

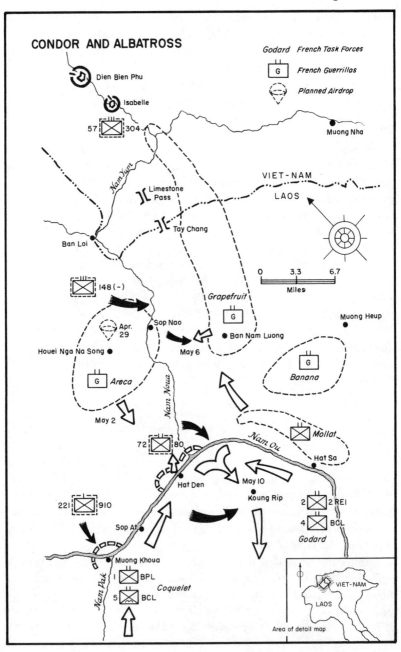

daily feeding of Dien Bien Phu even at minimal levels, simply would have broken the back of the whole air-transport effort. In other words, in order to be successful, "Condor" depended as much on vastly increased American air transport as "Vulture" depended on American bombers.

Hence, when it became clear that "Condor" would become, not an operation to pursue an already defeated enemy, but a last-ditch attempt to save Dien Bien Phu from total destruction, its basic structure was completely changed during the last week of April, 1954. At a conference of senior commanders in Saigon on April 28, the airborne phase of the operation was vastly scaled down, if not eliminated altogether, since the available paratroop battalions would in all likelihood be parachuted into Dien Bien Phu itself. On the other hand, the modified plan now provided for a ground task force of four infantry battalions reinforced by the shadowy infiltrated commando groups of the GCMA.[25] Here again, it had to be the sorely tried commander of Air Transport, Col. Nicot, who threw cold water on even the scaled-down plan. His mathematics were absolutely impeccable: Dien Bien Phu required 150 tons of airborne cargo space a day and the revised version of "Condor" still needed forty-five tons daily.

The other problem in that connection was that the bulk of the C-119's were flown by American civilian crews who had not been initially hired to fly into such a death trap as the doomed valley. There was at the end of April a very good chance that the Americans would suddenly refuse to fly combat-type missions, and in fact, that situation arose suddenly between May 2-6, when both the American and the French civilian crews refused to fly supply missions to Dien Bien Phu unless proper amounts of fighter escort were provided. Nicot on April 28 was fully aware of that situation, which meant that he could lose, at a moment's notice, almost one half of his available transport tonnage. By a fantastic juggling of priorities, Nicot finally agreed that he could provide both Dien Bien Phu and "Condor" with their minimal supply tonnage if *all* of Indochina were to be completely stripped of air transport for six days, save for two C-47's left for the southern Laotian airhead at Seno. But the first phase of "Condor" already had been underway since the day Gen. Navarre had met Col. de Crèvecoeur at Seno two weeks earlier.

Contrary to assertions later made by such diverse sources as Jules Roy, who asserted that "Condor" was more or less a sham,[26] and President Eisenhower, who stated in his memoirs that it merely involved "one relief column of 300 native troops [who] had made a feeble effort to rescue Dien Bien Phu,[27] "Condor"—on the ground, at any rate—was clearly organized to fulfill at least part of its mission. Col. de Crèvecoeur had given over-all command of "Condor" to Col. Then. The latter had at his disposal as of April 13, the 4th and 5th Battalions of Laotian *Chasseurs* (BCL); the 1st Laotian Airborne Battalion (BPL); the 2nd Battalion of the 2nd Foreign Legion (2/2 REI), whose 1st Battalion under Maj. Clemençon was inside Dien Bien Phu; and the Commando Groupment of Lt. Col. Mollat, comprising more than 800 Laotian and Meo tribesmen; for a total of 3,088 men, including 1,682 Laotians. The infantry force, under the command of Lt. Col. Godard[28] was officially known as Mobile Group North (GMN). It was subdivided into two separate forces, Sub-Group East under Maj. Coquelet (5th BCL and 1st BPL) and Sub-Group West, commanded directly by Godard (4th BCL and 2/2 REI).

By April 21, Col. Then had worked out his modified plan for "Condor." As a first step, in order to give Dien Bien Phu a measure of respite, his deployment would be so constructed as to attract, between April 25 and May 15, a maximum of Communist forces to the north flank of the Nam Ou. Once Communist forces had been distracted in that direction, the GMN would leave a light "curtain" of commando forces on that front while the bulk of the force would by-pass the well-known track to Dien Bien Phu via Limestone Pass and instead swing in the direction of Isabelle along a more southern route through Muong Heup. If provided there with four infantry battalions, Col. Then hoped to be able to reach strongpoint Isabelle about May 25.

In order to further confuse the Viet-Minh as to the actual strength of his force, he requested that the French High Command airlift in to him small detachments from French units available in other areas of Indochina. Like John Le Carré's Spy Who Came in From the Cold, these detachments would be deliberately deceived and led to believe that they constituted the advance guard of their own units which were to be moved to Laos as part of the "Condor" force. As members of these detachments became casualties or fell into Communist hands, enemy intelligence would be fooled at least for a time as to the exact strength and location of the French units. Soon, small single-engine *Beavers* and *Nordhuyns* began airlifting those French detachments to front-line units all over northern Laos, to be deliberately offered up to the enemy as decoys. There later was some evidence that, up to a point, the ruse worked.

Finally, Then also requested two airborne battalions. There still existed the 1st and 3rd BPVN's, whom Langlais did not want inside Dien Bien Phu. And for the airlifting-in of ground units on some of the existing small fields he requested C-47's which would be equipped with additional JATO (Jet-Assisted Take-Off) engines to enable them to use the short strips.

While "Condor" began to take shape on paper, its actual execution on the ground was running into trouble. The operation was to take place at a time of brutal heat and in an area which, even during the monsoon season, was extremely arid. On April 17 at 1340, Then had informed Navarre that it was impossible to find 500 human porters "even by force," since much of the population had fled into the mountains, and that 150 mules and the proper pack saddles for them, which were of key importance for logistical transport, also were not available. There also was an important requirement for jerry cans to carry water and for inflatable life rafts to cross the numerous streams. Navarre ordered the airlifting of mules and 500 Vietnamese PIMs into the assembly area, thus adding to the problems of Col. Nicot's air transport plans.

In the meantime, however, Godard had begun to execute phase one of "Condor." The 2/2 REI had begun to move northward along the Nam Ou and on April 21 had intercepted a large Communist cargo pirogue carrying 81-mm. and 120-mm. mortar ammunition. The three captured prisoners explained that they belonged to Company 230, 72nd Battalion, 80th People's Army Regiment, which was composed of 1,200 Lao-speaking Vietnamese and 500 Laotians. On the following day, the Goddard force discovered a Communist ammunition depot at Hat Den containing American mortars, Czech automatic rifles, submachine guns, cartridges, and 205 rucksacks. On April 23, the Legionnaires established a bridgehead north of the Nam Ou between Hat Den and Pak Noua. Pak Noua was a small village at the junction of the Nam Ou and the smaller Nam Noua tributary—and at Ban Loi, 35 kilometers to the northeast, an even smaller river joined the Nam Noua: the Nam Yum. From there, it would only be another 15 kilometers to Dien Bien Phu.

On April 22, intercepted Viet-Minh radio messages showed that the enemy knew about the unleashing of "Condor," first reported by Regiment 148 two days earlier, and that it had correctly identified the purpose of the operation. The radio traffic also confirmed Col. Then's surmise that the Communists expected air drops on Nga Na Song and Sop Nao, the two towns through which Langlais had passed in December, 1953, and which were on the most direct road to Dien Bien Phu. There also were indications that parts of Regiment 148, Battalion 940 of the 82nd Regiment, and elements of Battalion 970 of the 316th Division had received orders to stay put and screen the Dien Bien Phu front against the "Condor" force.

Sub-Group East also had not remained inactive. On April 25 the 1st BPL fell upon that rarity, a Viet-Minh fixed strongpoint two kilometers south of the important river town of Muong Khoua. It took the strongpoint and captured an important booty, including 37 boxes of ammunition and 500 mortar fuses. But the heat was brutal; on that day the battalion reported three deaths from sunstroke. On April 29, the two prongs of GMN were joined at Muong Khoua itself; like all the towns of the Nam Ou Valley thus far reoccupied, it, too, had been completely pilfered and most of the population was suffering from hunger.

The commandos also had not remained inactive. Equipped to move lightly—Lt. Col. Mollat's whole headquarters was composed of one other officer and three sergeants—they already had moved ahead deeply into Viet-Minh territory. They were split into three small groups: Group A under Lt. Mesnier and three sergeants consisted of 320 men; Group B, commanded by Lt. Vang Pao, a Meo tribal leader and a regular French officer, also comprised about 300 men. In the 1960's, Vang Pao, eventually promoted to general in the Royal Laotian Army, was to operate with the American Special Forces in the same area and would be one of the very few Laotian officers to give a good account of himself in guerrilla warfare. Finally, Group C was composed of 200 tribesmen and was commanded by Sgt. Marcellin. There also existed a separate reconnaissance commando No. 610 under Capt. Lousteau, whose job it was to collect intelligence for the French High Command.

In addition to the Mollat commando force, there existed in the area the already-infiltrated GCMA outfits that were directly subordinated to the French High Command in Saigon. Commanded by a lowly lieutenant-colonel, Roger Trinquier, they had progressively taken on greater importance over the past two years and now numbered close to 15,000 men, dispersed in small units all the way from the rubber tree forests northwest of Saigon to the Chinese border. Some, such as the already-mentioned "Cardamum," had been in existence for a fairly long time; others, such as those operating in the spring of 1954 in Laos, were fairly recent. They were the ones who now screened ahead of the whole "Condor" operation and who eventually would pick up the few escapees from Dien Bien Phu and then stay put behind Communist lines to the bitter end. Among the GCMA units involved in "Condor" and "Albatross" were: Group "Alpha," a 300-man force operating from Ou Neua in northernmost Laos; "Gamma," with 650 men, infiltrated west of Muong Té in the northwestern corner of Viet-Nam; "Grapefruit" which operated around Ban Nam Luong 15 kilometers southeast of Limestone Pass; "Banana," stationed near Hat Sa on the Nam Ou River; and, finally, "Areca Tree," in the hills south of Nga Na Song.

As of April 21, Godard had been in touch with "Grapefruit," which was operating ahead of him and would stay with the force until May 8, and "Areca Tree" informed the "Condor" force as of April 29 that the drop zone at Nga Na Song was secured and could be used for air drops. In other words, everything was ready for a successful execution of the second phase of "Condor." To be sure, the troops had been plagued by extremely harsh conditions—the heat had become so intense that the units had to fight their way through extensive forest fires and finally resorted to night marches—but the prospect of marching forward and, at the very least, of bringing a measure of relief, if not salvation, to the hard-pressed defenders of Dien Bien Phu, made them go on.

But elsewhere, where the fate of the war was being decided, things stood otherwise. On April 22, at 2000, Navarre sent a top-secret message to his deputy commander-in-chief, Gen. Bodet (who was then in Hanoi), informing him that the execution of the second phase of "Condor" would be delayed until further order and then would be subject to advance notice of five days. Even the pursuit of phase one would be subject to further messages.[29] Explanation for the delay was never quite clearly given, but a top-secret personal flash message sent by Navarre to Col. de Crèvecoeur on April 29, seems to come close to the truth. In that message, Navarre told the commander of French Union Forces in Laos that the bad meteorological conditions over Dien Bien Phu had made it impossible to provide the fortress with the necessary supply levels without further cuts in the airborne tonnage required to supply the forces of Lt. Col. Godard. That killed all chances of parachuting in a complete Airborne Group. At the earliest, according to Navarre, that GAP could not be made available before seven to eight days. "Under such conditions," added Navarre "I leave you to judge . . ." Strange situation, indeed, where a lieutenant general leaves a lowly colonel in charge of deciding the fate of a whole operation.

After an exchange of messages with his subordinate commanders, Col. de Crèvecoeur decided to at least hold his own for the time being. With the key airborne reinforcement ripped clear out of "Condor," the operation completely changed in character and, in order to confuse the enemy, the modified operation was given the name of an extremely mountainous French district, "Ariège." Far from advancing further in direction of Dien Bien Phu, Mobile Group North was now ordered to establish a defensive position on the north shore of the Nam Ou. Commando Group "Areca Tree" abandoned the drop zone at Nga Na Song on May 2; and the 5th BCL, which had been in contact with Company 221, Battalion 910, of People's Army Regiment 148 since April 27, and which had managed to capture fifteen rifles at the price of losing ten radio sets, fell back to the Nam Ou during the night of May 3, screened by Commando Group "Banana."

On May 6, "Grapefruit" reported a fire fight with Viet-Minh forces near its operations area and reported at 1300 the following day that the inhabitants of Ban Nam Luong said that 10,000 Viet-Minh soldiers from the Dien Bien Phu siege force were expected to move soon from the valley into Laos. In all likelihood it was a reconnaissance force from "Grapefruit" that was watching the agony of Dien Bien Phu from the edge of the valley, although this cannot be fully confirmed at this time.

At 1020 of May 7, 1954, a few hours before Dien Bien Phu fell, de Crèvecoeur sent a message to Gen. Cogny in Hanoi, asking him that he be immediately informed by flash radio message "in case of grave event concerning GONO." Cogny replied a few hours later by providing de Crèvecoeur with a code phrase which, in the form of the so-called "personal messages" sent by the BBC during World War II to the European resistance forces, would be transmitted in clear so as to be sure that all units concerned would be informed in time. The code phrase covered the fall of Dien Bien Phu itself but did not provide any guidance for further action to be taken by the "Condor" force. As Hanoi explained it to the French commander in Laos whose troops in the Dien Bien Phu area were under tactical control of Gen. Cogny, that action would be an immediate and complete retreat at utmost speed, abandoning everything, for there would be no help, no air support, no reinforcements, until Godard's troops reached the already established airhead at Muong Sai, almost 85 miles downstream from Muong Khoua. By the sort of tastelessness to which military staffs are prone when they run out of ideas, that ignominious retreat was given the code name of Emperor Napoleon's most shining victory: "Austerlitz."

On May 8, at 1305, all elements of Operation "Ariège" heard the code phrase: "The fruit are ripe." Dien Bien Phu had fallen. A few minutes later, there also flashed the second part of the message— "Austerlitz." A few minutes later, a little Morane *Cricket* from the 23rd

Air Observation Group at Muong Sai dropped a written copy of the withdrawal order onto the command post of Lt. Col. Godard. Almost simultaneously the outposts began to report heavy enemy contact in several places at once. Fortunately, Godard had had one day's advance warning and had begun to mine the trails leading away from the Nam Ou. With the 5th BCL acting as rear guard, the "Condor" force began to fall back, leaving the mines set to go off at ten-minute intervals. And again, Godard did the correct thing in jungle warfare (a rule that seemingly is forgotten only too often in South Viet-Nam in recent years) : instead of retracing his own earlier steps, he ordered his column to hack a new trail across the hills at Koung Rip. The Viet-Minh, expecting the French to retrace their own steps, had sent an ambush force ahead of them which was to close in on the old path on May 10. Instead, the French column passed the ambush point during the night of May 8 to 9, thus for once catching the Viet-Minh off-balance. In the ensuing fire fight, the 4th BCL was badly mauled, losing almost two companies; the 5th BCL also had some losses, but the rest of the "Condor" force returned to the strongpoint zone with no further losses but with a bitter taste in the mouth. Even the very restrained official reports speak of the bitterness of the officers and troops of Lt. Col. Godard who had suffered extreme hardships for the sake of their comrades at Dien Bien Phu and who felt that the northern command in Hanoi, for selfish reasons, had deprived them of a chance to help their comrades at a moment of dire need. One-fourth of the total strength of the 1st Laotian Airborne Battalion deserted after the battle was over, and another sixty-seven men deserted from the 4th BCL. And thus ended the last-ditch attempt at saving Dien Bien Phu from the outside.

The failure of "Condor" also determined the failure of "Albatross." Officially, Navarre entrusted the preparation of the breakout attempt to the operations staff of Gen. Cogny only on May 3, 1954.[30] While the details of the operation and, above all, the exact date of it, were left to the discretion of Gen. de Castries, the over-all outline of "Albatross" was as follows: The general direction of the breakout was to be southeastward in the direction of Muong Nha and Muong Heup, with French screening forces from Laos to be pushed in that direction at the very last moment in order to avoid detection by the Viet-Minh.

The breakout of the garrison from the battle line inside the valley was to be supported with a maximum effort of all artillery pieces and mortars still available, and all combat aircraft. All wounded would be left behind and all lightly disabled soldiers would provide fire cover for the men of the breakout force. The breakout would take place at the end of the day in order to permit the troops to reach forest cover very rapidly. Only hand weapons and four days' combat rations would be carried. The minimal estimate for the arrival in place of the various elements of "Condor" was then estimated at May 15. When Gen. Cogny in turn communicated the basic outline of "Albatross" to Gen. de Castries in a long radio message on May 4, that estimate had already been stretched to May 20, and Cogny added in a last paragraph that it was "well understood that until further orders the commander of GONO will consider his mission to be to resist on the spot without thought to falling back."

On May 5 at 1615, de Castries answered Cogny:

> The tracks leading to the south do not permit a sufficiently rapid flow-through for 6,000 men. The only thing that is feasible is the simultaneous breakout in various directions. In view of the difficulties in preserving secrecy even when using code . . . I insist upon not revealing my intentions. I must ask you to trust me.

The whole concept of "Albatross" found a great many critics in Hanoi. Cogny's chief-of-staff, Col. Bastiani, went on record that, given the difficulties of the terrain, the strength of the enemy, and the state of total exhaustion of the garrison, "Albatross" would only result in a complete rout and in the piecemeal extermination of the breakout force, from which little if anything militarily usable would be saved. In addition, such an ignominious end would only add a blemish to what thus far had been a gallant defense.

On May 4, one of the senior staff officers working on the details of "Albatross" wrote a terse appreciation of "Albatross" which well summed up the feeling of most of its colleagues:

> Such an operation is both impossible and inconceivable. It strangely resembles the battle of Sedan (1870).
> GONO must continue to resist. It continues to tie down Viet-Minh troops.
> Any command authority[31] in Indochina which would sign such an order to take flight would dishonor itself.

And in a final line that was obviously a reproach to the senior generals who had conceived, planned, and directed the Battle of Dien Bien Phu, the note ended with the sentence:

"One must know how to accept the consequences of one's acts."

Finally, on May 7 at 1000, as the Communist assault forces were within 200 meters of his command post and his last reserves had been smashed in an all-out defense of the last positions on the eastern hills, de Castries decided to attempt "Albatross." The dialogue between him and Gen. Cogny over the radio-telephone link was taped in its entirety. The part referring to "Albatross" reads as follows:

> ". . . And then *mon Dieu,* I'll attempt, if circumstances permit, to have the maximum of what I've got left scram southward."
> "Okay, understood. That will be at night, probably?"
> "What?"
> "At night."
> "Yes, General, at night, of course."
> "That's all right, yes."
> "I need your approval to do it."
> "I approve, old man."
> "You are giving me that approval."
> "I give you that approval."
> "Well, I . . . I'll hold . . . I'll try to hold here as long as possible with what is left over . . ."

They briefly spoke of other matters, and then Cogny returned to the subject of the breakout:

> "Okay. Well, about the withdrawal southward? How do you see it? Is it toward Isabelle or simultaneously in many directions?"
> "Well, General, in any case they must push southward beyond Isabelle, isn't that it?"
> "Yes, that's it."
> "But I'll also give Isabelle the order to attempt to break out, if they can."
> "Yes that is understood. Well, keep me informed so that we can help you with a maximum of aviation for that business."

There is, then, no question but that at the last moment de Castries did decide to attempt "Albatross" but, of course, the order came far too late to be executed in an organized manner, and surviving senior officers told me that de Castries, anxious not to induce panic, had until the last moment refused to inform even many of the battalion commanders of the existence of such a plan.

Isabelle, by virtue of its location closer to the southern edge of the valley, would have had a better chance at making good its escape. In its case there was last-minute hesitation on the part of Col. Lalande once he saw the destruction of the main position of Dien Bien Phu, and, once more apparently, there also was a last-minute attempt on the part of Hanoi to avoid taking responsibility. At 2100 of May 7, there was a radio message from Col. Lalande to the command aircraft No. 545-YA, piloted by the commander of the North Vietnamese Bomber Group, Lt. Col. Dussol himself. The circling command aircraft had been acting as radio relay between Isabelle and Hanoi since the destruction of de Castries' own powerful radio sets at 1700. In his message, Lalande requested Hanoi to tell him whether the southern itinerary was still considered better, since, from his vantage point, a due-west dash in the direction of Ban Loi seemed more favorable. In spite of repeated queries from the command aircraft, Hanoi never answered the question. A few minutes past midnight on May 8, 1954, the remnants of T'ai Sub-Groupment Wieme, and of 12th Company, 3rd Battalion, 3rd Foreign Legion Regiment, made a break for the hill line to the south. They got as far as the southern rim of the valley and that is where "Albatross" died.

Castor Dies

Saturday, April 24, 1954

WITH THE DEFINITIVE loss of Huguette 1, one half of the whole airstrip had fallen into Communist hands for good. Henceforth, there would be even less space for the supply drops, and the French and American pilots who flew the murderous supply runs would have to take even greater chances. During the night of April 23 to 24, another seventy-two volunteers had been parachuted into the main position, including replacements for the crews of the remaining tanks, who were being disabled at a faster rate than the vehicles in which they fought. This was to hold true again: three sergeants and one private came in as tank-crew replacements that night, but on April 26 one sergeant and two soldiers became casualties and on April 29, "Douaumont" sustained a direct hit from a 105-mm. shell, which killed one man and wounded two. Among the latter was Pvt. Lecry. He had been among the four tank crew replacements parachuted in on April 24.

That night also, 117 tons[1] of supplies had been parachuted into the valley, of which about 99 tons fell into French lines. The lucky drop permitted the garrison to raise its supply level for most units to two days of food and about five days of ammunition—but at the price of numerous feats of heroism on the part of the transport crews, and notably the American pilots of the "Flying Boxcars." In view of the ever-shrinking drop zones, the largely American-piloted C-119's had been compelled to fly lower and lower through the flak, and during the previous night one of the "Boxcars" had been hit by two 37-mm. shells from a Soviet antiaircraft gun. It had become common knowledge among the troops at Dien Bien Phu that the American civilian pilots were in many cases taking greater chances than the transport pilots of the French Air Force flying mostly C-47's, and while the American pilots were being paid roughly $2,000 a month for their dangerous job, their contracts had not explicitly stated that they were to fly in an outright combat situation. It was therefore understandable that upon returning from their missions that day they refused to continue to fly the Dien Bien Phu run. This decision was to have disastrous results not only upon the battle of Dien Bien Phu itself, but also upon Lt. Col. Godard's "Condor" force groping its way toward Dien Bien Phu through the Laotian jungles. Cogny, as ground-force commander in the North, did not have jurisdiction over the transport air force, yet he immediately requested Gen. Navarre's permission to transfer French crews from the C-47's to the "Boxcars." For reasons known only to the military bureaucracy, Navarre's authorization to do so reached Cogny only on April 26 at 2330. In the meantime, supply drops on Dien Bien Phu radically fell off. They averaged barely sixty tons a day during the next three days, and April 28—a miraculously clear day in the midst of the monsoon season—was to provide the garrison of Dien Bien Phu with the depressing experience of receiving no supplies whatever.

Saturday also was a day of stock-taking for the exhausted garrison and its commanders. And the picture which was transmitted in the form of an absolute-priority telegram at 1400 showed that there were exactly 3,250 infantrymen left in some sort of fighting condition. In many cases, this meant that the men had lost one eye and even one arm. Isabelle reported 1,400 riflemen still fit for combat. At Dien Bien Phu, Maj. Grauwin's original 44-bed hospital had, with the help of the Moroccan combat engineers, spread its blood-soaked tentacles in all directions; a total of 878 seriously wounded men were now being cared for in the battalion dressing stations, in the hospital annexes manned by the Airborne Surgical Teams, and in lightless burrows and shafts hastily dug along the communications trenches. Another 117 such wounded competed for living space on crowded Isabelle with the garrison, its field-pieces, its ammunition depots, and its tanks.

By now, then, the almost 15,000 men of the garrison fell into three fairly equal parts: the infantrymen, the artillerymen and support troops from the various services (for to redistribute *by hand* over 100 tons of supplies a day and to care for 1,000 litter cases required a large number of noncombatant personnel) and, finally, the last third of the garrison of Dien Bien Phu—the dead, the men who had fallen into Communist hands, and the "Rats of the Nam Yum."

That morning also, Intelligence had provided Dien Bien Phu with a revised estimate of the enemy's strength. Thanks to massive transfers of raw recruits Gen. Giap had succeeded in making up for most of his losses of the previous two months. Some of the new men (and the French were to take prisoners as late as May 2) had enlisted or had been drafted in mid-March and had walked all the way to Dien Bien Phu in small 100-man reinforcement groups. Upon their arrival in the valley they had been paired off with two veterans each, and these four-man "cells" had become the basic element of the reconstituted units, with the veterans in each cell being responsible for the on-the-spot combat training of the raw recruits. To be sure, such reconstituted units were far from having the deadly effectiveness of the Viet-Minh assault outfits of mid-March, but Giap now again fielded 35,000 infantrymen against the French, or about ten of his soldiers against every one of the gaunt and bone-weary Frenchmen, Vietnamese, and North Africans huddling in the mudholes of the French forward trenches. And as both the French staff and its Communist counterpart knew, a three-to-one superiority of the assailant over the defender was a sufficient margin for victory in an assault.

Another piece of bad news also had become available that morning. The French Air Force's 80th Overseas Reconnaissance Squadron had taken a full set of aerial photographs of the valley on the previous day at 1230 and the fully interpreted photographs had been successfully dropped on de Castries' headquarters. They clearly showed a strong tightening-up of the deadly ring of 37-mm. antiaircraft guns and of .50-caliber flak machine guns, particularly on the northeastern rim of the valley. A new battery of 105-mm. howitzers revealed itself on Anne-Marie and several new batteries of 75-mm. howitzers were sighted two to three kilometers east of Isabelle. New Communist batteries also had shown up behind Old Baldy and Phony Mountain on April 23, when they suddenly intervened with devastating effect on the paratroopers counterattacking on H1. On the other hand, no 120-mm. heavy mortars had been fired at Dien Bien Phu since April 19; probably, something had gone wrong with the ammunition supply. This temporary lull did not particularly reassure the French, for they had been told by Communist prisoners taken in recent days that "special guns" had been expected to arrive soon in the siege area. Some special 60- and 120-mm. shells had been picked up around Dien Bien Phu, but they had thus far not given French Intelligence any clue as to what was to come. The solution to the mystery was still about ten days away.

There also remained some unfinished business from the aborted

counterattack by Maj. Liesenfelt's 2nd BEP. The remains of 1st and 2nd
BEP formed the merged Foreign Legion Composite Paratroop Battalion
under Maj. Guiraud which was assigned to the defense of what was left
of Huguette, along with a company of 140 Moroccans of the 1/4 RTM
under Capt. Nicod. The badly mauled II/1 RCP was again regrouped
on the Eliane hills, but left a company of light wounded on Juno. Since
its arrival during the first week of April, the battalion had lost 56 dead,
35 missing (ten of whom were presumed dead), and 267 wounded.
Particularly its 3rd and 4th Companies had lost so many men that
Bréchignac decided that morning to merge them into a single *Compagnie
de marche* (Composite Company) under Lieutenant René Leguère.

The loss of H1 also had had an effect upon strongpoint Opéra on
the other side of the airfield. Opéra had been specifically created to
provide flanking protection for the northern segment of Huguette and
now found itself completely outflanked in turn. Langlais and Bigeard
therefore decided to evacuate it before its small garrison suffered the
fate of all the other overexposed strongpoints. In silence, French combat
engineers mined Opéra during the night of April 23 to 24 as its garrison,
a company of the 5th Vietnamese Paratroops under Capt. Bizard, slowly
pulled back inside the airfield drainage ditch to a new fall-back position
150 meters to the north of D4. In the words of Maj. Pouget, "the position
had no name—perhaps because it was unnameable."[2] Indeed, the
monsoon rains had transformed the airfield drainage ditch into a veritable
canal filled in many places with waist-deep water. Yet, with the
Dominique hills on its right and Huguette 1 on its left under enemy
control, it was sheer madness to attempt even to raise one's head above
the rim of the ditch. Any man who was wounded had to be propped
against the crumbling walls of the drainage ditch and any man who died
immediately sank out of sight. In that incredible place, Bizard and his
men, wet to the bone, worked like beavers in the most literal sense of
the term, trying to dig firing positions into the soft mud and to construct
a few sandbag bunkers in the ditch itself. Much of what they built that
day was swept away the following night in a torrential rainstorm. Again
like beavers, Bizard and his Vietnamese reconstructed their strongpoint
in the quagmire. They were to hold it through the last day of the battle.

The day also witnessed an exchange of icily correct messages between
Navarre and Cogny. The latter still argued that the vital Red River Delta
was in mortal danger of being overrun, while Navarre felt that the
situation, while critical in the Delta, was no more critical than that
prevailing in the rest of Indochina. In a tone intended to be an ironical

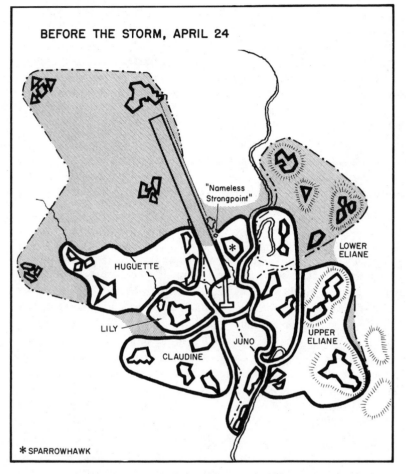

BEFORE THE STORM, APRIL 24

"Nameless Strongpoint"

LOWER ELIANE

HUGUETTE

LILY

JUNO

UPPER ELIANE

CLAUDINE

✳ SPARROWHAWK

allusion to Cogny's preoccupation with Tonkin alone, Navarre informed the latter that he "could be sure that I have informed Government of exact situation from general Indochina viewpoint and not exclusive viewpoint Tonkin."

In a no less biting style, Cogny replied later that day that he

. . . would not doubt that you have informed Government of over-all Indochina viewpoint and not exclusively Tonkin's. That is why, in order to complete said information, I have insisted re-affirming personal view believed to be different from yours on major points.

Cogny once more argued the case for urgent reinforcements for Tonkin as the preservation of the Red River Delta was vital for any future negotiation, regardless of the eventual fate of the garrison of Dien Bien Phu.[3]

At 2220, Navarre sent yet another urgent message to Cogny, asking him to answer four precise questions: his estimate as to how long Dien Bien Phu could hold out with or without reinforcements, considering the enemy's current tactics; whether Cogny was in favor of reinforcing Dien Bien Phu; whether, should he be so inclined, he would advocate such reinforcements to take the form of individual volunteers or of constituted airborne battalions; and, finally, whether Cogny was still in favor of carrying out Operation "Condor" in spite of his reservations concerning the amount of respite it would bring to Dien Bien Phu. Cogny was to give his answer on the following day.

Sunday, April 25, 1954

At 0235 Capt. Bizard reported suspicious noises and digging around the blocking position north of the crossroads where strongpoint Opéra used to be. And in the early dawn, the outposts both of D4 and of the nameless strongpoint in the drainage ditch began to report enemy infiltrations. But the terrain in that swamp was dishpan-flat, and soon the French artillery pieces from Claudine began to hammer away at the enemy. The attacking force simply disappeared in the midst of geysers of mud; in all likelihood more men drowned from the resulting panic than died from actually being hit by the shells.

Despite the driving monsoon rains which had fallen almost all night and whose waters had cascaded into every dugout and trench in the valley, the enemy had been extremely active. At 0330 Bréchignac's II/1 RCP had reported intensive mortar shelling on top of E1, intermingled with hand grenades thrown by Viet-Minh infantrymen in the forward trenches. By six o'clock in the morning the enemy mortars gave way to Communist artillery, which now took over the destruction of the last remaining bunkers on top of E1. Here also, the bone-weary French artillery and heavy mortar crews had to rush out into the open gun pits and lay down an intensive counterbattery fire which finally somewhat slowed the cadence of Giap's guns. But the slim reserves of French artillery shells were running out fast. The remaining two 155's fired fifty of their precious shells, the heavy mortars fired 200, and 750 shells were expended by the 105-mm. howitzers.

The supply situation had now become catastrophic. A total of sixty-three tons of supplies (instead of the necessary minimum of 125) had been dropped in along with fifty-one reinforcements. One French-piloted C-119 (the American crews having been withdrawn from the Dien Bien Phu run) misdropped its whole cargo of badly needed ammunition on the Communist side. Hence, when news came from the outposts on the Eliane hills that the Viet-Minh was installing new firing positions on Phony Mountain, Dien Bien Phu's artillery commander, Col. Vaillant, decided against shelling them. He would need all the ammunition he had on hand to fend off a serious attack, if it were to occur.

In the midst of the shelling, the most exposed line units had to be relieved so as to permit them at least to have a warm meal, if not a moment of relative peace. On top of what was now called *Eliane Haut,* or Upper Eliane, and which comprised hills Eliane 1 to 4, Bréchignac had regrouped what was left of the II/1 RCP, two companies of the 5th Vietnamese Paratroops, two companies of Bigeard's old battalion, and Maj. Coutant, who commanded what was left of the 1/13 Foreign Legion, too over the defense of E2 under the jurisdiction of Bréchignac. Over at Huguette, the Foreign Legion paratroopers under Maj. Guiraud also were frantically digging in, as infiltrations during the past night had shown that the Viet-Minh were going to attempt the same tactics of stealthily digging forward that had already served them so well on the other Huguette positions.

In the southwestern corner Maj. Clémençon also was using that Sunday to consolidate his positions on Claudine. Captain Bienvault, who had become surplus when his company of the 1st BEP had been dissolved for lack of troops, had taken over the command of the 3rd Composite Company of the 1/2 Foreign Legion on the previous day, and had taken a position at Claudine 4. Captain Capeyron's 2nd Company of the 1/13 Foreign Legion, which had been detached from its battalion now stationed on Eliane, took over the defense of C5. All night long, much of the forward positions of Claudine had been under severe fire from mortars, grenade launchers, and snipers, and the diligent Communist trench diggers had again done their work despite the fact that the Foreign Legionnaires had plastered them with hand grenades and 60-mm. mortar shells. When dawn broke, the enemy had dug itself clear through the first line of barbed-wire entanglements and was hard on the second (and last) barbed-wire fence. Claudine nonetheless was under relatively less pressure than any of the other major strongpoints and its patrols still succeeded in slipping through the enemy's siege ring into the open country. During the night of April 24-25, one of the patrols of the 1/2 Foreign Legion had gone as far as Ban Co My—three kilometers southwest of Dien Bien

Phu. One may well wonder at the thoughts of those patrols as they looked back from the silence and darkness of their patrol area on the flame-limned swamp that had been their home now for over fifty days. Such patrols were to continue until April 30, and a Communist soldier was made a prisoner during the course of a patrol as late as May 1.

In Paris, the *Journal Officiel*—a daily government publication which fills the role of both, the American *Congressional Record* and the *Federal Register,* and which had published on Saturday the official promotion to the next higher rank of most of the officers at Dien Bien Phu—this day carried the text of Decision No. 18, dated April 17, citing the whole garrison of Dien Bien Phu in the dispatches of the French Army and awarding it the *Croix de guerre* with palms for overseas operations. Those men who would survive the battle would henceforth be able to wear a blue-and-red *fourragère* as a sign of that unit citation. The final paragraph of the citation read as follows:

> United in the will to win, officers, noncommissioned officers, corporals, and soldiers deserved the admiration of the Free World, with the pride and gratitude of France. Their courage shall remain an example forever.

In his reply to Gen. Navarre's message of the previous day, Gen. Cogny estimated that Dien Bien Phu could last another two to three weeks if it received reinforcements and if the enemy should decide not to launch a general attack. If the reinforcements were to be stopped, Cogny estimated that resistance would collapse within eight days because of the drop in combat morale. He also recommended that for the week to come, reinforcements be limited to individual volunteers, and that a full parachute or Foreign Legion battalion be dropped in later. Cogny considered "Condor" useful if it were to be initiated without delay.

But he again disagreed with his commander-in-chief as to the usefulness of continuing the agony of Dien Bien Phu at the expense of the reinforcement of the Red River Delta. In his own words: "I absolutely reject the hypothesis [of reinforcing Dien Bien Phu] simply to increase the moral value of the sacrifice." Cogny based his estimate of the situation on the simple fact that the moral value or the psychological benefit derived from a prolonged resistance of Dien Bien Phu would mean very little in the context of a general deterioration of the situation, particularly in the key Red River Delta.

Both commanders were caught, each one at his own level, in an irreconcilable dilemma. The agony in full public view of the garrison of Dien Bien Phu at least served as a painful prod to France, the United

States, and Great Britain that something had to be done about the Indochina problem, whether at the conference table or through direct American military intervention. The very drama of the situation called for quick decisions that the unspectacular deterioration throughout the rest of Indochina had until now permitted the West to avoid, even if, in the long run, it was potentially far more dangerous than the fall of Dien Bien Phu itself. Hence, to Navarre, who had to see the situation from the over-all viewpoint and who had to remain responsive to the views of Paris, Dien Bien Phu at the moment was more important than the Red River Delta, because the former represented a capital of political leverage that the latter simply did not possess. On the following day, Navarre again was to attempt to explain this to his reluctant commander in the North.

As night fell that Sunday over Dien Bien Phu, the headquarters staff at Dien Bien Phu began, as always, to transmit its routine reports on the supply situation. As usual, there was an urgent need for more medical corpsmen to take care of the ever-growing hordes of seriously wounded. There were serious shortages of medical supplies of all kinds. In the past, bottles of fresh blood, which had been parachuted in packs of dry ice and had been misdropped, deteriorated and became unusable before they could be found; but on April 15 and 18, Dien Bien Phu received two parachuted "blood banks" which at least permitted the doctors to draw blood directly from volunteers in the garrison. There was also the routine request for trench periscopes, since direct daytime observation had become a hopelessly lethal occupation, now that Dien Bien Phu was tightly surrounded by enemy snipers and recoilless rifles. Once more, also, Supply pleaded for flak jackets for the unprotected artillery crews.

At 1800, as almost every night, the enemy began his pounding of the French artillery positions and of what was left of E1. And at 1820, Dien Bien Phu informed Hanoi that Communist radio traffic seemed to indicate that troops were being relieved on the southwestern flanks, probably preparatory to a new push.

In all, it had been a quiet Sunday. It was the last quiet Sunday the garrison of Dien Bien Phu was to experience.

Monday, April 26, 1954

It also had been a relatively quiet night at Dien Bien Phu, except for the deadly accurate enemy flak. A strong patrol from the 1/2 REI, reinforced by recoilless rifle teams from the 35th Airborne Artillery, had pushed north as far as the ford on the road to Gabrielle. On the ground at least, the enemy seemed to have relaxed its grip for a time. In the air, the situation was different, however. With the American C-119 crews gone, Dien Bien Phu was slowly starving and bleeding to death. Instead of the 80 reinforcements expected that night, four French-piloted C-47's dropped only 36 men, and instead of the 150 tons of promised supplies, a total of 91 tons were dropped—with a thirty-four-per-cent loss rate. That evening at 2330, Navarre was to give his authorization to transfer French Air Force crews from the C-47's to the C-119's.

In the meantime, with fewer targets to shoot at, the Viet-Minh flak had a field day. Fifty airplanes were hit that day over Dien Bien Phu and three shot down. At 1030, two F6F *Hellcats* of French Navy Fighter Squadron 11 were flying wing to wing on a low-level strafing run across Dien Bien Phu in an attempt at suppressing or at least diverting the enemy antiaircraft artillery which was creating havoc among the defenseless transport craft. Both pilots, Ensign Campredon and Petty Officer Robert, were experienced flyers. Campredon had flown twenty missions over Dien Bien Phu, and this was Petty Officer Robert's ninth. Both planes were about to pull out of the strafing run when the new batteries of .50-caliber antiaircraft machine guns from Anne-Marie opened up on them. Campredon's aircraft, though hit, remained controllable, but Robert's *Hellcat* was hit so badly that the pilot immediately lost control. By a sheer miracle he succeeded in opening his parachute and was seen by the garrison of Dien Bien Phu landing in the enemy-occupied hills to the west of Anne-Marie—too far away to be rescued by a French ground party.

Eight years later, I was to see in Hanoi a brief filmstrip on the capture of Petty Officer Robert by the Viet-Minh a few minutes later. The film showed an obviously shaken, very young man (at twenty he was the youngest fighter pilot of the squadron), still clad in flying suit, inflatable life vest, and white American flying helmet, standing at rigid attention before a stern-looking Viet-Minh officer seated behind a table and who was obviously lecturing him. Robert was being accused of having committed "barbarous acts," and was told he deserved to die for them. All that the young pilot could think of saying is that he had not wanted that war.

"Well, then, why did you fight in it?" asked the Communist officer.

Robert's reply was one that was to become a classic for that sort of situation and could still be heard in 1967 from the lips of American pilots shot down over North Viet-Nam:

"I am a soldier. I obey orders."

What happened a few minutes later was even more worrisome. A French B-26 bomber, flying at 2,900 meters (9,000 feet) was shot clear out of the sky by Russian-made 37-mm. guns. No parachutes were seen. And at 1800 another B-26 bomber was shot down by Communist flak southwest of Dien Bien Phu, but this time three parachutes were seen to open. None of them fell near enough to the French lines for a rescue attempt. This plane also had been flying at 9,000 feet. The news of the day's disaster in the air sounded in Hanoi like the crack of doom. Was it possible that the enemy now had received radar-guided antiaircraft artillery? Or had the less experienced Vietnamese crews been replaced by Chinese flak gunners? In any case, it became obvious that the puny French bomber force with its forty-five aircraft could not sustain such losses without disappearing in a matter of days. Not that aircraft aplenty were not available in the United States. The problem was still the shortage of bomber crews. Hence, Lt. Col. Dussol, the northern bomber commander, had to make do with what he had on hand. Even so, by incredible feats of ingenuity of the maintenance mechanics and endurance of the pilots, his forty-five B-26's flew a total of 1,629 sorties between March 13 and May 7, 1954.[4] In his final report on the role of the bombers in the battle of Dien Bien Phu, Dussol noted that the Viet-Minh flak was better than the Nazi flak of World War II. That may have been considered at first as an exaggeration, or an attempt at explaining away what was after all, above all, an air-power failure.

However, independent American appraisals bore out his view. In a report in October, 1955, by Fairchild Corporation, the builder of the C-119, both the American civilian pilots who flew the Dien Bien Phu run and the Fairchild field service representatives agreed that the flak encountered at Dien Bien Phu exceeded in intensity that met in Korea and "was as dense as anything allied pilots had encountered over the Ruhr during World War II."

On the following day, the commander-in-chief of the French Far Eastern Air Force, Gen. Lauzin drew the only logical conclusion from the new situation: absolute priority was assigned to flak-suppressing missions, at the expense of ground support and of the bombardment of Viet-Minh supply lines. *This* could have been air power's finest hour at Dien Bien Phu. With sixty American B-29's standing by in the Philippines and about 400 jet fighters and light bombers standing offshore on the American aircraft carriers ready to intervene, it would have been possible for the French to concentrate on resupplying the garrison and on keeping

Operation "Condor" alive. But that was not to be.

Instead, as night fell, Dien Bien Phu resumed its litany of routine complaints:

> Insist once more upon getting as soon as possible some medical corpsmen, trench periscopes, and bulletproof jackets for artillery personnel . . . don't parachute in local auxiliaries . . . request immediate reinforcements for White T'ai . . . also need one lieutenant for 1/2 Foreign Legion and one lieutenant for 1/13 Foreign Legion . . .

A short while later Dien Bien Phu noted a sudden intensification of Communist artillery fire on the tortured artillery positions. Then, at 2030 there came one single brief message from Dien Bien Phu whose terseness in no way hid its impact upon the garrison: "We lose another 155-mm. gun." That left one single medium fieldpiece in the valley, with about 300 rounds. For all practical purposes, French counterbattery—inasmuch as it ever existed—now was dead.

Hundreds of miles away from the valley between the northern headquarters at Hanoi, where Gen. Cogny ruled, and the GHQ in Saigon where Gen. Navarre held forth, the icily polite exchange of teletype messages continued—each message covering under a thin mantle of administrative directness and military courtesy the feelings of pure hatred that both men now harbored for each other. To Cogny, Navarre was nothing but a narrow-minded armchair general who, for the sake of being unwilling to admit that he had erred in holding on to Dien Bien Phu, was going to sacrifice the key Red River Delta with its 180,000 troops, its 9,000,000 industrious people, and its almost 3,000,000 tons of precious rice. To Navarre, Maj. Gen Cogny, from a loyal subordinate, had become a self-seeking opportunist who was now totally disloyal to his commander, sabotaged his decisions at every turn, and made use of his long-standing good relations with the press corps to short-circuit his own commander's decisions and to make his own viewpoint heard everywhere. On either side, what was said or written now was for the sole purpose of establishing a record for a later duel on a grand scale before a board of inquiry, public opinion, courts of law, and history.

Navaree's answer was extremely long and detailed. In contrast to Cogny, whose messages had become more and more involved and unclear as the situation deteriorated, Navarre's, who had been fairly unsure of himself at the beginning of the battle, now showed that he apparently again felt at home. The tactics of the situation were almost of no importance whatever; what counted were elements of information that belonged to the field of high-level political and military intelligence in which Navarre had spent much of his active life. In simple and clear terms, often reading like a professor's comment on a student's mildly obtuse term paper, Navarre went over the basics of the situation as it now stood. Contrary to Cogny's opinion ("if I understood you correctly . . .") that Dien Bien Phu no longer was worth an additional sacrifice of troops, Navarre felt that the over-all situation warranted such sacrifices. At Geneva, the delegates of the forthcoming conference on Indochina were gathering that day and perhaps could produce a cease-fire which could save Dien Bien Phu from annihilation. Or, conversely, the conference could fail altogether and could thus bring about an American last-minute intervention and save Dien Bien Phu literally on the brink of disaster.

Navarre also demolished Cogny's other pet project of bringing relief to Dien Bien Phu by launching an offensive across the enemy's rear communication lines hundreds of kilometers away from Dien Bien Phu. Using facts and figures found in Cogny's own study of the operation, Navarre clearly demonstrated to him that the operation would have no immediate effect on the situation in Dien Bien Phu itself and would deprive the Delta of part of its present reserves, who in turn would have to face the onslaught of about eighteen Communist battalions already assembled in the area. And lastly, the whole operation would impose on the rest of Indochina a drain of key troops and aircraft that would have "catastrophic" effects elsewhere without bringing relief of any kind to the embattled Dien Bien Phu garrison.

Finally, Navarre told Cogny that, contrary to the latter's advice, he would maintain the principle of carrying out Operation "Condor." With that kind of total gap between the commander-in-chief and his key subordinate commander, any further dialogue was totally fruitless. Yet, to the last day, the exchange of messages continued, icily polite and totally unlikely to sway the recipients from their preconceived opinions, both of the situation and of each other.

And to this day both men have continued to hate each other: before the French government's Commission of Inquiry, before the Courts of Paris for a derogatory passage about Cogny in Navarre's book, before authors writing about Dien Bien Phu, and in the press. Cogny maintained in public his statement to Jules Roy that on April 2 at about 1700, he had said to Navarre: "If you weren't a four-star general I would slap you in the face."[6] And Navarre in another published communication very transparently accused Cogny of having conspired, in Algeria, to murder the then commander-in-chief there, General Raoul Salan, with a bazooka.[7]

Tuesday, April 27, 1954

The combination of incredibly bad monsoon weather and enemy flak reduced the night drops of April 26-27 to a shambles. Only fifty volunteers were dropped in as reinforcements for the garrison. The high-altitude drops from C-119's with the help of powder-train delay fuses proved, in the very words of the official supply report of that day, "disastrous. One third of the cargo was found by us; the rest fell into Communist hands." But at long last, that part of the cargo which had fallen inside the French lines contained 200 flak jackets, while that same night another 100 fell on strongpoint Isabelle. They were rapidly distributed to what was left of the artillery crews and also to the paratroopers and Legionnaires who were standing watch in the shell craters of Upper Eliane. Captain Clédic's men received one flak jacket for every two men, and they immediately saved the lives of Sgts. Caron and Vlado. They had dug a small niche into the trench wall and had hung the jacket over the entrance in curtain-like fashion. A mortar burst right in front of the opening shredded the jacket, but the two men survived without a scratch.

At 0400, for the first time since the battle had begun in March, the din of the battle itself was temporarily overshadowed by the roar of what must have been hundreds of Communist trucks north of the airfield. Taking advantage of the miserable flying weather, the Viet-Minh had pushed its precious trucks all the way to the valley of Dien Bien Phu to bring in ammunition and push new artillery batteries closer to Dien Bien Phu itself. They could have been a tempting target for the French artillery, but the latter had to carefully husband its shells and the last remaining 155 was so worn out that its shells would drop to the ground after only a few hundred yards, making a tired "ploof" sound in the soggy ground. The Communists also attempted to renew their infiltrations around the ill-defended positions of Lily, C5, and H4. Enemy artillery maintained a steady bombardment on outlying C5 and one of its patrols, out on ambush in the no man's land, was in turn ambushed by the Viet-Minh and sustained some losses.

By noon, a new set of aerial photographs showed that the Viet-Minh was pushing forward additional connecting trenches in the Huguette area and around E3. By now, Communist sappers had worked out their siege tactics to the fine rhythm of a well-trained ballet. The lead element would dig a hole deep at the bottom of the trench and pass the earth to the rear where it would be immediately used to fill sandbags. In the meantime, logs and wooden beams which were somewhat wider than the mouth of the trench would be brought forward and laid across the trench, thus providing the diggers almost immediately with fairly adequate overhead cover. And thus the trench would extend its almost invisible underground tentacle toward the French wire entanglements and often would simply dig underneath a French mine field. Over on Eliane, Bréchignac's men now could clearly pick up the noise of Communist sappers digging deep under the hill. Thanks to their crude geophones, which were composed simply of a combination of French Army wine canteens and medical stethoscopes, the scraping and digging could be heard without difficulty just as it could be heard by the Germans atop Messines Ridge in Flanders almost forty years earlier, when miners from Wales were digging away under it to blast the Germans out. The difference was that the Germans did have the possibility of counter-mining. On Eliane the garrison was busy enough simply trying to stay alive and keep a few of the remaining firing positions and bunkers in shape.

In fact, this was not a bad day for the French at all, as in the morning a strong Foreign Legion patrol once more wound its way through the mine fields south of Huguette and west of Claudine across the main Viet-Minh circumferential trench and on to Ban Co My. There was surprisingly little Communist resistance in that direction and it is likely that these patrols, even if they did not know it, were in fact reconnoitering the most suitable escape routes from Dien Bien Phu, should Operation "Albatross" be given the green light. The French were also lucky in another sector. On top of the Elianes, Captain Marcel Clédic had put together an assault team for a strong reconnaissance in the area between E1 and E4. Mounted by volunteers from the II/1 RCP and 2nd Company, 5th Vietnamese Paratroops, the raid succeeded beautifully.

The Vietnamese paratroopers blew up three Viet-Minh bunkers, twelve enemy soldiers were killed by both the Vietnamese and the French, and three bewildered *Bo-Doi* were brought back into camp alive for interrogation. They confirmed what French Intelligence already had relayed to Hanoi and Saigon and what could be simply termed a crisis in Viet-Minh combat morale. That this was in fact so, and not simply a morale-boosting operation of some French staff officers in dire need of reporting something cheerful in the midst of an otherwise gloomy period, was finally confirmed in March, 1965, by the enemy itself. In a small study issued in Hanoi and dealing with the battle of Dien Bien

Phu as seen from the North Vietnamese viewpoint, there appears an entry under the dateline of April 27, whose text reads as follows:

> In Dien Bien Phu, after discovering erroneous tendencies which affected the fulfillment of our tasks, the Front Military Committee held a conference of Party for secretaries of divisions and regiments to launch a campaign for moral mobilization and "rectification" of Rightist tendencies.[8]

In plain English this meant that once more some of the Communist Vietnamese unit commanders were beset by doubts: Perhaps there was more to Operation "Condor" than appeared at first glance and at least part of the Dien Bien Phu siege force would have to be diverted to face it. Moreover, the Western press was full of rumors, some from highly authoritative sources, about the possibility and even likelihood of an American air intervention around Dien Bien Phu. If such an intervention were to occur, it would literally catch tens of thousands of the Viet-Minh's best infantrymen in the open and would surely also result in the total destruction of the huge Communist supply depots in the Tuan-Giao region. Also, a perfectly sound Communist division commander could argue, a prolonged resistance of Dien Bien Phu could well be in the process of achieving what the French had wanted to achieve: to buy time to organize the defense of the vital Red River Delta while drawing away the bulk of the enemy's battle force to a jungle valley in the middle of nowhere. Dien Bien Phu perhaps was expensive to the French in terms of the strain it represented on a notoriously weak logistical support system but, as Navarre was to point out repeatedly, the garrison represented only four per cent of the total French Union Forces available in Indochina. And that small fraction of the French forces kept tied down for almost half a year five Communist divisions; *i.e.*, sixty per cent of their total main battle force and almost one fifth of all their military manpower, part-time guerrillas included.

It probably took all the eloquence and authority that Giap could muster to "rectify" the views of the doubters. And the divisional and regimental political commissars who had come to the meeting of the Front Military Committee and who now had to return to their units, must have pondered at the difficulty of their situation since, as it turned out, it would now be their task to ask the troops and the subordinate military commanders to make yet one more desperate effort to finish off the grimly determined French resistance on the blood-soaked hills and in the filth-laden valley bottom of Dien Bien Phu.

Wednesday, April 28, 1954

The monsoon now prevailed in full force, making the parachuting of personnel and supplies almost impossible. It did not, of course, stop the effectiveness of the Viet-Minh antiaircraft artillery, which was simply firing at the obligatory course that all aircraft had to fly on approaching Dien Bien Phu. As a result, only one 24-man "stick" of Foreign Legionnaires succeeded in landing between 0015 and 0200—and not at the main position, but at Isabelle only. For totally incomprehensible reasons, the Air Force then decided to stop the dropping of supplies altogether. Isabelle received perhaps a total of 22 tons; Dien Bien Phu, on that particular day, received nothing.

As dawn came, a thick blanket of clouds, solidly anchored against all the hills surrounding the valley, made tactical air support impossible. No fighter or bomber flew over the position on that day: Dien Bien Phu had never been as alone as on April 28. The French tanks continued their duel with the enemy's recoilless rifles atop Dominique, and Lieutenant-Colonel Hubert de Séguin-Pazzis, who had become de Castries' chief of staff on April 23 as a replacement for the ailing Ducruix,[9] told Col. Bastiani, Cogny's chief of staff, on the radiotelephone that the parachuting of reinforcements was imperative at Dien Bien Phu for the next night and for Isabelle on the night of April 29-30. Bastiani promised to do his best. On the following day Cogny sent a message to Gen. Navarre requesting permission to use C-119's on low-level missions over Dien Bien Phu.

For once, a note of humanity crept into the communications between the two generals as Cogny pleaded: "The very existence [of Dien Bien Phu] is at stake. I have the honor of requesting an extremely urgent decision in the matter."

That evening, at 2200, Guiraud's paratroopers from H4 crawled through the barbed wire in direction of the first Viet-Minh approach trenches, overwhelmed the enemy sentries in one swift movement, killed the occupants of the trench, and returned to their own lines with only three wounded of their own. At least twenty Viet-Minh were killed.

Among the remnants of the crack units holding out on the perimeter, there was still hope. The troops knew about Crèvecoeur's column in Laos and they also knew about the negotiations in Geneva. There was more contempt than discouragement in their reaction to what they considered the failure of the outside world to support them.

Thursday, April 29, 1954

The rains again fell all night and a short message to Hanoi reported as a matter of course that the average depth of mud in the trenches now reached one meter (three feet).

At 0025 Bréchignac from atop Eliane unleashed an artillery and mortar barrage on Communist trench diggers to the east of E2. The barrage was followed up by patrols who reported that about forty dead Viet-Minh were found in the trenches.

At dawn, the deplorable results of the monsoon on the supply and troop reinforcements began to show up in the headquarters reports: less than 30 tons of supplies had arrived and, contrary to the promises made, not a single soldier had been parachuted.

At dawn, it was the turn of Maj. Tourret's 8th BPC on Sparrowhawk to request a barrage on Communist trench diggers. It, too, was followed by an infantry counterattack from both Sparrowhawk and the unnamed strongpoint in the drainage ditch, which succeeded in filling in a few yards of freshly dug trenches. As the battle seesawed around Sparrowhawk, a small explosion suddenly shook the air in front of E2: a lone Foreign Legion volunteer from the 1/13 Half-Brigade had crawled down the shell-pocked slope of E2 with a rucksack of plastic explosives and had blown up a Communist forward bunker.

This finally led Giap to react. An intensive Communist artillery bombardment began to cover the whole center of Dien Bien Phu and within a few minutes found its mark. A shell from the ubiquitous 75-mm. recoilless rifles on Dominique killed M/Sgts. de Cia and Mitri of the Air Force detachment, while elsewhere in the camp eight other men were killed and twenty-six wounded. And as always, when all of Dien Bien Phu was blanketed by heavy Communist fire, the depots were hit. On April 26, 200 daily food rations had been lost when a shelled food depot burned, and now with an ear-shattering roar 600 artillery shells and a truck blew up, leaving a ghastly crater (which soon was to form a lake, of course) and depleting even more of the slim ammunition reserves of the fortress. With the absence of parachuted supplies the garrison, except for the seriously wounded, went on half food rations. Not that it mattered. Most of the Frenchmen were now, like the Vietnamese, living on rice and *nuoc-mam*—the pungent Vietnamese fish sauce—which, when mixed with a small can of French Army corned beef (referred to among the connoisseurs, because of the somewhat undefined origin of its contents, as "monkey meat") proved to be over the short run an acceptable diet.

At 0940 the already heavy Communist fire reached a new crescendo as yet another five Viet-Minh 75-mm. recoilless guns revealed themselves on the western face of Dominique. What was new about them was that they did not fire from the top of the hill, nor were they positioned in an open gun pit. After days of patient digging, the Viet-Minh coolies had dug long mine shafts *through* the whole hill from the protected reverse slope, and the gunners could hit the whole French position with impunity from almost totally invisible gun ports.

There was an incident of nonmilitary nature which preoccupied the senior commanders at Dien Bien Phu that day also. On April 23, the highly respected French daily *Le Figaro* had published an article under the title of "Could 100 Airplanes Save Dien Bien Phu?" The gist of the article was that while 100 additional planes could perhaps not guarantee a permanent survival of the French garrison, they could in all likelihood insure the garrison's survival for several more weeks and perhaps through the forthcoming negotiations. The article, obviously based on French government "inside information," stated quite accurately that France simply no longer had the potential to provide the airlines and crews, and forecast—again, quite accurately—that the United States, who could provide those airplanes and crews, would not do so. Within a few days clippings of the article began to appear in the mail that the troops received from home, and parts of it also had been read over *Radio Hirondelle,* the French Army broadcasting station in Hanoi which was regularly listened to throughout the garrison.

In his message on the subject, de Castries—they may have been, in fact, Langlais' words but over the signature of the fortress commander—complained bitterly of the "catastrophic effect on the morale of the combatants" of that article and others in a similar vein, and added: "Why don't you get censorship to work on that?"

While the request was understandable under the circumstances, it was of course impossible to carry out. It would have meant opening and searching every single piece of mail going to Dien Bien Phu with resulting delays in delivery; and in the absence of any other contact with the outside world, the air drops of mail constituted a far too precious boost to morale to be lightly tampered with. In any case, it is somewhat doubtful that the newspaper articles in themselves had a determining influence upon the combatants on the firing line. The chief surgeon at Dien Bien Phu, Dr. Grauwin, tells the story of one paratroop volunteer who had jumped into the fortress late in April and who had handed him the French newspaper whose front page carried a banner headline calling

Dien Bien Phu an incredible tactical and political mistake.

"And you came anyway, after having read this?" asked Grauwin.

"Well," said the newly parachuted volunteer, "you don't really think that I'm going to 'bug out' because of some stuff printed in some rag?"[10]

Also, on April 29, at 1800, Lt. Geneviève de Galard was ordered to report to the command post of GAP 2. Weeks ago, Geneviève had abandoned her French Air Force coveralls for a more practical paratroop uniform cut down to her size. Since the GAP 2 was near the hospital, she had in the past received such invitations and considered a visit with the paratroopers a welcome break from the depressing routine of the underground hospital. But when she lifted the blackout curtain and entered Langlais' dugout, an unexpected scene awaited her. There were, in addition to Langlais, Gen. de Castries, Lt. Col. Lemeunier, and Majors Bigeard and Vadot, rising from benches and chairs as she entered.

De Castries stepped forward, picked up something and said: "Geneviève, I've got something for you." And he then pronounced the French ritual formula to be used when a high decoration is being awarded: "By virtue of the powers conferred upon me . . ." and pinned a *croix de guerre* with palms and next to it, the white enamel cross with the blood-red ribbon of the Knight's Cross of the Legion of Honor.

It had not been easy to hold that ceremony, for almost no one had any medals at Dien Bien Phu. Langlais himself managed to find a battered *croix de guerre* in one of his own footlockers,[11] and one of his lieutenants kindly lent his recently awarded Legion of Honor for the ceremony. There was no one at Dien Bien Phu who did not feel that Geneviève de Galard had earned her decorations.

Out in the falling darkness, where the battle continued, tank "Douaumont," which had been dueling with the recoilless rifles of Dominique, sustained a direct hit by a 105-mm. shell. Its whole crew became casualties and the pierced hulk was dragged over to Huguette 3 to serve as a fixed bunker. That left exactly one tank, "Auerstaedt," from Sgt. Ney's old platoon, in full working order.

Friday, April 30, 1954

That Friday was the holiest of holidays for the 2,400-odd Foreign Legionnaires in Dien Bien Phu's main position as well, and it well-nigh turned out to be a holiday for almost everybody. For that was the day when the American air crews from CAT decided, in view of the desperate straits of the Dien Bien Phu garrison, to return to their "Flying Boxcars."

The French Air Force had promised them that it would make a more determined effort to suppress enemy flak (a promise it failed to keep), and thus the sky above Dien Bien Phu was filled with the drone of almost 100 aircraft as the total supply tonnage carried to Dien Bien Phu that day reached the almost all-time high of 212 tons. One element, however, troubled that bright picture. The C-119's now were kicking out their loads at an altitude of 10,000 feet, with a corresponding loss of precision in the drops. The allegation was made later by one source that the drops "were landing with surprising accuracy on a DZ only 330 yards square,"[12] but the French Air Force officially conceded that almost one third of the day's drop, or about 65 tons, had fallen into enemy territory. On the ground, Dien Bien Phu claimed that almost one half of the total load had fallen into enemy hands. The likely fact of the matter was that several tens of tons of supplies technically fell into friendly hands but in places where they could not be collected—mine fields, barbed-wire entanglements, or in areas completely beaten by Communist fire.

One such situation that day was to have humorous side effects. At 2200, de Castries' headquarters reported to Hanoi a successful raid on the Communist trenches and fortifications south of E2 by Maj. Coutant's 1/13 Foreign Legion. One Viet-Minh blockhouse was completely destroyed with plastic charges and two others were severely damaged. In addition at least ten enemy soldiers were killed and other were wounded, while there were no friendly losses to report. The communiqué, however, failed to stress that the idea of the raid originated in the fact that two complete crates of "Vinogel" wine concentrate had fallen into no man's land east of the Eliane ridgeline held by the Legionnaires. The Legionnaires, who thus far that day had had to celebrate Camerone with exactly one bottle of wine per platoon, were not about to let that precious booty fall into enemy hands. A commando of volunteers was organized (as one non-Legionnaire observed: *everybody* would have volunteered for that raid) and as soon as night fell pushed off into no man's land. The main objective was rapidly secured, the knocking out of the enemy bunkers being a mere tactical necessity incident to the success of the operation.

But Camerone was also celebrated elsewhere in Dien Bien Phu. On battered Claudine, not even "Vinogel" was available and the diary of the 1st Battalion, 2nd Foreign Legion, noted tersely: "A Camerone without wine or blood sausage"—a traditional dish for that holiday.[13]

But the main ceremony was at the command post of the 13th Half Brigade, with Lt. Col. Lemeunier acting as the host in his capacity as both the most senior Legionnaire in the fortress and the Legionnaire with the longest service in all of North Viet-Nam. Lemeunier, miraculously impeccable in a full-dress uniform with perfectly shined shoes, read the traditional Camerone proclamation over a radio hook-up that could be heard throughout the fortress and then proceeded with the honorary induction into the Foreign Legion of a few non-Legionnaires—another ancient tradition which permitted the person so honored to wear his Foreign Legion rank insignia, no matter how exalted his real rank was. According to tradition, each person so honored is presented to the Legion by a Legionnaire who acts as his "godfather" and whose serial number, followed by the suffix *bis,* would become his own. That morning, de Castries and Langlais became honorary corporals of the Half-Brigade and Bigeard and Geneviève de Galard became PFC's. Mademoiselle de Galard's "godfather" was Maj. Vadot's batman. As she walked out, she turned to him and said: "If we ever get out of this alive, I'll pay you a bottle of champagne no matter where we meet." In 1963, she was riding in an automobile in Paris with her husband when she recognized the Legionnaire walking along the sidewalk. She stopped, embraced him, and made good on her promise.[14]

Along the perimeter, however, there were signs of increased Communist activity. Between 0600 and 0630, a small Viet-Minh force raided Maj. Chenel's Algerian company on D3. Three Algerians were killed, but twelve Communist bodies were left on the barbed wire. South of Juno, the small strongpoint held entirely by the Air Force detachment, a few tribesmen, and 400 wounded, Communist activity was reported for the first time within a distance of 800 meters. A reconnaissance which that night attempted to push to Ban Co My made contact with the enemy at Ban Pa Pé, a good kilometer closer to Dien Bien Phu.

But the enemy was also taking a measure of punishment. During the "wine raid" around E2, the Legionnaires had found a thoroughly frightened sixteen-year-old cowering in a forward trench and had brought him back with them. When interrogated by Intelligence, he turned out to be a raw recruit who had been drafted into the People's Army on April 8 and who had arrived at Dien Bien Phu only a few days earlier. He did not even know what unit he belonged to and stated that French air raids on the Viet-Minh depots and convoys along Road 41 were devastatingly effective in destroying many trucks and killing a great many coolies.

Perhaps another hundred aircraft *would* have made a difference at Dien Bien Phu.

Saturday, May 1, 1954

This first night of May brought with itself surprisingly little antiaircraft fire but much probing on the ground. A total of only forty-three volunteers jumped in, however, and the heavy transports, now back to full strength, kept up a steady drone of aircraft engines over the valley. By the end of the day, 197 tons had been loaded aboard the aircraft for Dien Bien Phu, but at 1630, Third Bureau (Operations) reported to its counterpart in Hanoi with a note of despair that something must have gone wrong with the powder-train delay fuses:

> 50% of the air drops are parachute failures due to premature opening. Two C-119's just turned around without even dropping their loads.

On the ground, in the meantime, Battalion 227 of Infantry Regiment 322,* People's Army Division 308, attacked the Foreign Legion Paratroopers who had been holding on to H5 now for over a week.

But Guiraud's paratroopers knew only too well that would happen if the Communists were left to get organized on their position. The battalion began its counterattack in a driving rain at 0230 and immediately called for protective artillery fires from the howitzers of the III/10 RAC of Capt. Libier at Isabelle. By 0600 the Communist penetration was disintegrating, but a few hardy elements still hung on close to the edges of H5 and a reserve company from the 1/2 REI took the "subway" northward to reinforce the counterattack.[15] By 0800, even the approach trenches to H5 had been cleared in bloody hand-to-hand fighting, and at 1000 the situation could be considered fully established. When the second wave of supply drops, which had begun at 1200, ended at 1415 without much interference from the flak, everybody became convinced that something serious was afoot. There were other indications, moreover. From listening in on enemy radio traffic, French Intelligence believed that six battalions had been involved in the various probes of the last two days. Particularly on the eastern flank, signs of an imminent attack by major forces became ominous. A prisoner captured that day near E1 declared he belonged to the 812th Company of Battalion 88, of Regiment 176 of the 316 People's Army Division. He had been at Dien Bien Phu exactly three days. And another prisoner captured on D3

---

* The unit number shown does not correspond to that of any unit in the 308th Division or of any other enemy division at Dien Bien Phu. The information came from a severely wounded prisoner and may have been garbled in transmission; or perhaps the French were being deliberately misled by their prisoners in some cases.

declared that he had been a member of Battalion 166, Regiment 209 of the 312th Division.

But just as April 30 had been a holiday in the valley of Dien Bien Phu, May 1 was a holiday in the hills around it. It was Labor Day throughout much of the Western world (except in the United States) and in all of the Communist countries, and Giap's army celebrated it accordingly. There were thousands of blood-red Labor Day flags flying over all the Communist positions, sometimes stuck in the ground and in other cases hung on trees, and in a few cases waving from rifles held high above the trench works. Music could also be heard from loud-speakers installed in the Communist positions.

But as the day wore on it became clear that the enemy was on the move. The forward observers with their high-powered field glasses could see Communist infantry reinforcements moving forward; even artillery pieces were being moved about in full view, despite the fact that the B-26's of the French Air Force were operating over the valley for the first time with new American "Hail" bombs—a new type of fragmentation bomb filled with razor-sharp steel shards designed especially to be used against personnel caught in the open. As there had been on Saturday, March 13, there was in the air a deadly smell of general attack. And this time the French knew that they would not be able to resist it.

Inside Dien Bien Phu, Supply and Personnel were lining up their facts and figures as far as food and ammunition were concerned: the last two days of record drops had been a godsend. There were now again three days of food available, 275 rounds of 155-mm. ammunition, 5,000 rounds of 120-mm. mortar ammunition, and 14,000 rounds of 105-mm. shells for the howitzers. That might sound like a lot of ammunition—except for the fact that as the French knew from the dire experiences of the general attacks of March 13 and March 31, once the battle was engaged, those stocks would melt like butter in the sun. During the thirty-six hours of fighting on March 13-14, the French artillery had fired 14,300 rounds of 105- and 13,000 rounds of 120-mm. ammunition, and in one single day of fighting on March 31, the 105-mm. howitzers had expended 13,000 shells and the heavy mortars, 3,000. In other words, if the new attack was to be as ferocious as the others—and there was every reason to believe that, if anything, it would be worse—then the French would either run out of ammunition altogether within twenty-four hours or simply would have to keep an iron lid on ammunition consumption no matter how urgent was the begging for fire support on the firing line. To be sure, a new maximum effort could be asked from the Air Force;

that is, provided it could find the necessary air crews to fly the missions and provided the bad monsoon weather did not make air action altogether ineffective.

In the Personnel dugout, the head of that service, Lt. Col. Trancart, also had a few telling figures. From April 17 to April 24, Dien Bien Phu had lost a total of about 1,000 combatants, either dead or seriously wounded, and had received a total of 432 parachuted reinforcements. It had therefore lost a net of 568 men. From April 24, which marked the beginning of the period of relative calm, until the morning of May 1, the fortress had lost another 82 dead and 345 seriously wounded, for a total of 427. During that period it had received a total of 251 parachuted reinforcements. And these losses did not yet include the very heavy casualties of the counterattacks launched during the night of April 30 to May 1, both at Isabelle to retake strongpoint Wieme and on the main position to clear up the Communist penetration on H5. Isabelle reported 4 killed and 18 wounded, and the Foreign Legion Composite Paratroop Battalion had lost 12 killed, 68 seriously wounded, and 8 missing. In other words, there were probably less than 2,900 first-line combatants left at Dien Bien Phu, about one third of what had been available on March 13, and they were haggard remnants of once-proud units burned to a hollow shell in forty-nine days of fighting.

The bare statistical facts told a more eloquent story than any long report. The French at Dien Bien Phu were doomed in case of a massive enemy attack unless massive reinforcements, and not dribbles of men, became available immediately. It was obvious that the feeding-in of 600 isolated individuals who had never met each other and who did not know their platoon leaders, let alone their battalion commanders, was not the equivalent of supplying a 600-man battalion that could be thrown into the battle as a constituted unit, even if the state of individual training in both groups was equal. This was the sense of a long and almost incoherent radio message that Col. Langlais sent at 1700 to Col. Sauvagnac, the commander of the paratroop rear base in Hanoi. Langlais demanded the immediate dropping-in of fully constituted airborne units. The end of the message gives a good idea of the whole:

> We will win the battle without you and in spite of you. This message, copy of which I shall transmit to all airborne battalion commanders here, will be the last I shall address to you.

But a few minutes before the message was tapped out by the radio operator, the thunderous roar of a hundred or more field guns had filled the air, and a few seconds later the ground had begun to shake on Claudine and Huguette, in the command posts and the hospitals, among the wounded on Juno and the open holes of the PIM camp. General Vo Nguyen Giap's final attack on Dien Bien Phu had begun. His artillery was laying down the first preparatory fires.

On Upper Eliane, Maj. Bréchignac had spent the day shifting his few remaining paratroop companies for maximum effectiveness. His command post, as Bigeard's before him, was installed on E4, and Capt. Botella of the 5th BPVN now was his executive officer. As for the 5th itself, it had ceased to exist as such. Captain Bizard had a small company with him in the drainage ditch north of Sparrowhawk, and up on E1 there remained a small eighty-man company of Vietnamese paratroopers under a Vietnamese officer, Pham Van Phu. He was twenty-one years old and had just received a battlefield promotion to the rank of captain.

On E1, Capt. Clédic, after two hellish days atop the hill, moved to the rear with the remains of his company, while Lt. Leguère relieved him with the 3rd Company and Lt. Périou's 1st Company went on counterattack alert. On E2 the 1/13 of Maj. Coutant was also holding firm. Plowed under beyond recognition, the hill had held throughout the battle and the enemy had developed an almost superstitious fear of what it called "A-1" or "the Fifth Hill." That night, Sgt. Kubiak was on guard at the southernmost bunker of E2 when, in the greenish light of the parachute flares there appeared what seemed to be a ghost in no man's land— a human figure all draped in white. One of Kubiak's Legionnaires without further ado jumped over the parapet and grabbed the apparition. The man, a Vietnamese draped in a white nylon parachute, allowed himself to be taken without the slightest resistance and walked with his escort to the French bunker. As he came closer Kubiak gave him a brief glance and then jumped him, knocking him to the ground. The Vietnamese was a Viet-Minh "death volunteer" and a walking human bomb. The bulky parachute hid heavy loads of explosives affixed to his back and chest which he was to detonate upon reaching the French position. When he was interrogated, he told the French that the little bunker had considerably hindered the Communist advance on Eliane, and that he had volunteered to immolate himself to destroy it.

By nightfall the Communist fires on the central position shifted to D3 and E4 and simply boxed in what was left of the garrisons on the slopes of the northern part of Upper Eliane. And at 2000, the better part of two Communist divisions, the 312th and the 316th, began to storm

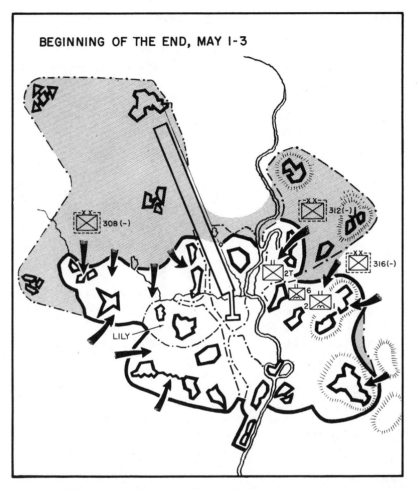

BEGINNING OF THE END, MAY 1-3

the two hills. On Dominique 3, Chenel simply never had a chance with his rag-tag force of T'ai tribesmen and demoralized Algerians barely "stiffened" by the one company of Maj. Thomas' 6th BPC. Still, now that they knew that the fate of Dien Bien Phu depended upon them, the Algerians also fought to the end. At 0200 of May 2 it was all over for Dominique 3. It was out of ammunition and covered with the dead and dying of its own garrison, and there were no reserves or spare ammunition to be had anywhere in the fortress.

On E1, these were the final minutes for the 2nd Battalion, 1st French Parachute Regiment. Lieutenant Leguère grimly held on to the top of E1 in hand-to-hand combat but at 2015 requested reinforcements, and

Bréchignac ordered Lt. Périou's 1st Company to join Leguère and his men.

But the attack was now unfolding in the northwestern sector as well. Four completely new Communist batteries, totaling sixteen 105-mm. howitzers, positioned in full view a mere three kilometers from the center of Dien Bien Phu, now opened up on Huguette and were soon reinforced by a deluge of shells from the heavy 120-mm. Communist mortars, which had re-entered the battle that day. After some diversionary probes on Lily 2 and some small infiltrations between Huguettes 2, 3 and 4, the burden of the Communist attack suddenly concentrated again on outlying Huguette 5. There, after a day's intermittent shelling and an hour's intensive artillery preparation, Lt. de Stabenrath had only 29 able-bodied men left when the first assault waves of the 308th People's Army Division rose out of the trenches. At 2005, Dien Bien Phu reported H5 as fallen. Lieutenant de Stabenrath, who already had been wounded before, was wounded once more before H5 was submerged. He died a few weeks later in a Communist prison camp.

Long before midnight, the senior commanders in Dien Bien Phu knew that the final assault had come, and that, short of a miracle, they would not be able to resist it. The message sent at 2005 simply reeled off the obituary of strongpoints fallen or attacked, and of units destroyed, and added the comment:

> No more reserves left. Fatigue and wear and tear on the units terrible. Supplies and ammunition insufficient. Quite difficult to resist one more such push by Communists, at least without bringing in one brand-new battalion of excellent quality.

That later point was again stressed in a personal message sent by Castries to Cogny at 2345: ". . . in any case extremely heavy losses require as of tomorrow night a solid new battalion. Urgent reply requested."

That night Gen. Cogny made up his mind. The last battalion of the Airborne Reserve, the 1st Colonial Parachute (BPC) of Captain Guy de Bazin de Bezons, would be dropped into Dien Bien Phu during the night of May 2. General Cogny originates from Normandy, a province whose people are known in France for their proverbial caution in making up their minds. In fact, Cogny, as already mentioned earlier, would invoke that Norman trait of prudence in explaining some of his actions.[16] In the present case, the commitment of his last parachute battalion was a prudent measure, indeed. But it had come a few days too late.

In France, U. S. Air Force "Globemasters" of the 62nd Troop Carrier Wing, under the command of Major Michael F. Robinson, began to airlift 450 French paratroops issued directly from the paratroop training schools at Pau and Vannes to Indochina. It was a grueling trip half around the earth—and it was made in vain. They arrived in Indochina on the day Dien Bien Phu fell.

Sunday, May 2, 1954

As the night wore on it was clear to Bréchignac that he would not receive any additional reserves to hold on to E1, but neither was it possible to disengage what was left of its garrison. It was being massacred man by man: Lt. Leguère was wounded sometime after midnight and Lt. Périou was killed shortly after the arrival of his company on the hill. At 0207 Dien Bien Phu reported E1 and D3 as completely fallen, and H4 under attack. H4 was held by a mixed company of Foreign Legion paratroopers under Captain Jean Lucciani, the same officer who had held Eliane 2 for over sixty hours at the beginning of April. Huguette was being strangled by Communist approach trenches. Communist snipers seemed to be everywhere in the triangle between H2, H3, and H4 and, for all practical purposes, Lucciani's little band seemed to be cut off from the rear. But the enemy had taken frightening losses as well and his aggressiveness definitely slackened off at 0200.

At 0250, the Viet-Minh resumed its attack, but this time with an emphasis on the Foreign Legionnaires on top of E2. And at 0305 the night's second attack began on H4, but Coutant, Guiraud, and Lucciani all stood their ground. On E2, the fight developed into hand-to-hand combat in the forward trenches around the south bunker, while on H4 the last remaining movable tank and a mixed force of Legionnaires from H3 and Moroccans from Maj. Nicholas' strongpoint Lily 2 reoccupied the trenches covering the rear of H4. By 0625 all penetrations on E2 and E4 had been cleared, and H4 was again holding. But the price for the night had been frightening. On Upper Eliane the loss of Dominique 3 and Eliane 1 was an irreparable tragedy; the remaining hill positions, E2, E3 and E4, were hopelessly outflanked; and with the loss of D3 every shred of Dien Bien Phu was under permanent observation of the enemy and under his direct fire. And the human losses were of the kind that simply forbade the kind of counterattacks which, one month earlier, still succeeded in clearing E1 and E2. As Trancart added up the losses for that one night, they told a story eloquent beyond words: 28 known killed, including an officer, 168 wounded in French hands, including an officer;

303 missing, including six officers. One battalion had been lost and, if it was very lucky, Dien Bien Phu would receive a battalion to replace it in the course of the following night. But Dien Bien Phu was not lucky. Instead of a battalion, it received at 0250 of May 3 the 107 men of Lieutenant Marcel Edme's 2nd Company, 1st Colonial Paratroop Battalion. Edme had started his military career as a Free French member of the elite commandos of the British Special Air Service (SAS) and still wore the distinctive dark red beret of his British unit. Colonel Langlais had been his commander a year earlier, in France, and knew him well. He also knew that Edme's wife, a nurse in Hanoi, was expecting a baby any day. Langlais scribbled out a short message for her, indicating that Edme had arrived safely, and then assigned him to reinforce the Legionnaires on E2. Having received a total of 107 troops as reinforcements, the French were to lose about 420 men that day.

At 1020, Dien Bien Phu reported that it was regrouping its units under light artillery fire and added: "No more reserves left, extreme fatigue and weariness of all concerned." By 1220, the units had been regrouped and E10 and E12, which were now on the firing line, had been reinforced with wounded who had been scraped together in the various underground hospitals. A decade later, Dr. Grauwin still recalled his amazement at the sight of heavily-bandaged men requesting to be returned to their units. "If we've got to croak, we might as well croak with our buddies," was a view which they expressed very often. Captain Lucciani was a good example of what was meant: wounded three times, he was now commanding H4 with a heavy bandage over one of his eyes, which had been removed.

The only good news of the day was that far to the south, Isabelle had succeeded in retaking strongpoint Wieme; but at Dien Bien Phu the garrison was again treated to the sight of distressingly poor supply drops. At 1400, two C-119's dropped their complete loads of six tons each into enemy lines and much of the rest, perhaps as much as fifty per cent, fell into places where it could not be retrieved.

Yet as always, part of the battle took place far away from Dien Bien Phu, on the airfields of North Viet-Nam, and in the staff offices of the Hanoi citadel, where the headquarters of the Northern Command was located.

On the three key airfields in the Red River Delta and aboard the two available aircraft carriers, the situation had reached the breaking point. On April 30, Capt. Patou's aircraft carrier *Arromanches* had been relieved by Capt. Mornu's newly arrived carrier *Belleau Wood*, which the United States had lent the French Navy for service in Indochina and which now was manned by a French crew. It had brought from France Squadron 14F (Lt. Menettrier) equipped with American *Corsair* dive bombers and was to take over from the *Arromanches* the pilots of Squadron 11F, who had been in combat over Dien Bien Phu for the past four months.

But then the *Arromanches'* doctors stepped in and requested the grounding of the squadron, with the exception of two recently arrived pilots, on medical grounds: of twenty pilots, at least six had been shot down; three of the latter had been killed and one taken prisoner. All the others had either seen their plane seriously damaged or had had to crash-land them at least once. In the words of the report presented by Capt. Patou, the remaining pilots had simply "reached the limit of physical and nervous wear and tear." Permission was granted to withdraw 14F from combat on May 1. While the decision was, of course, inevitable, it left the French fighter force over Dien Bien Phu seriously depleted at an important moment.

As Gen. Dechaux's air staff for North Viet-Nam prepared the flight missions for May 2, the following picture emerged: A total of twenty-eight fighters were available that morning, supplemented by twenty-eight B-26 light bombers and five 4-engine *Privateer* bombers of the French Navy. One additional B-26 was detached for reconnaissance missions and seven *Bearcats* were part of Overseas Reconnaissance Squadron 80. The 21st and 23rd Artillery Air Observation Groups based at Muong Sai clearly showed how deadly the battle had become above Dien Bien Phu—although there were nineteen Morane *Crickets* available that morning, there remained only eight crews to man them. The same was true for the five helicopters available that morning for medical evacuations in Laos—there were five aircraft available, but only two pilots.

On the transport side, Col. Nicot was also in trouble. His American civilian pilots had returned to the Dien Bien Phu run, but now his French civilian pilots spoke of refusing to fly the dangerous war missions. Here again the figures spoke for themselves: Out of a total of forty-three Flying Boxcars available in North Viet-Nam, thirty-four were reported ready that morning to fly on Dien Bien Phu. However, only fourteen completed their mission that day, with the others turning back for a variety of reasons; and during the next two days (when the French civilian pilots really walked out as they had threatened) the number of effectively completed C-119 missions dropped to two out of thirty and seven out of thirty-four, respectively. On the other hand, the score for

the C-47's piloted by French Air Force crews during the period of
May 2-5 stood at 17/17, 18/25, 16/29, 22/27, and 25/29.

The orders for the day provided for three principal combat missions
on Dien Bien Phu. A total of thirteen bombers and six fighters would
fly in direct support of the defenders of Dien Bien Phu; four bombers
and four fighters would attack Communist artillery batteries but could
also be diverted to close air support in case of need on orders of the air
liaison officer at Dien Bien Phu, Maj. Guérin; finally, ten fighters, four
B-26's and two *Privateers* were to fly flak-suppressing missions in support
of the transports. Of the 128 tons parachuted that day, probably less than
65 tons were found by the Dien Bien Phu garrison.

In Hanoi, more fuel had been added to the flames of the Navarre-
Cogny dispute. Cogny, who enjoyed excellent relations with the press,
had during the preceding days given open vent to his pessimism as to
the ultimate fate of the garrison at Dien Bien Phu, and with sufficient
detail to permit Navarre to conclude that the information must have come
from Cogny himself or from his closest associates. As was later confirmed
by the journalists involved, the information had indeed come from Cogny
himself; but at the time, the northern theater commander refuted
Navarre's admonition in several lengthy communications.

In turn, Navarre sent Cogny on May 2 a terse message:

> Received your messages . . . to which no answer will be given.
> My position will be entirely maintained. Orders have been given
> to military security services to investigate indiscretions.

Monday, May 3, 1954

It rained again at Dien Bien Phu in heavy, steady downpours which
now drowned defenders and besiegers alike. In fact, some of the senior
officers at Dien Bien Phu now argued that the rains perhaps were a
blessing in disguise for the garrison. For, as had become evident from
interrogations of recent POW's, the enemy forces were also experiencing
supply shortages as even the coolies now were slowed down on the
slippery slopes of jungle paths, and the progressive flooding of the low-
lying Communist trenches facing Claudine and Huguette now compelled
the enemy to come out in the open for direct assault, thus becoming an
easy target for the still very effective French automatic weapons and
mortars. Apparently, the old military saying that "when it rains on you,
it also rains on the enemy," still held true. Except that the Viet-Minh
units, when badly mauled or exhausted from life in the forward trenches,
were rotated without difficulty to safe rest camps deep in the forest only

a few kilometers away, whereas the French had to stay put under the constant pounding of Gen. Giap's artillery. If the latter was bothered by the rains, it certainly never showed it.

At 0135 the air drop of the lead elements of the 1st Colonial Parachute Battalion (BPC) began.

While the last men of Capt. Edme's company assembled in the darkness below, the supply drops also began. But the poor weather and the absence of the French civilian crews began to have a telling effect. Instead of the more than 100 tons required to break even, a total of 53 tons were dropped and probably about 45 tons were collected. When eight C-119's aborted their mission because of "poor weather conditions," the message was greeted by howls of derision inside the fortress. But already on the previous day, Col. Nicot, the head of the Air Transport Command, had warned Col. Sauvagnac that the difficulties of resupplying Dien Bien Phu were rapidly increasing:

> . . . My pilots experienced difficulties in finding the DZ and in seeing its markers. . . . It is difficult to maintain a split-second course and to fly at night at only 300 meters above the bottom of the valley.
>
> The pilots are subjected to automatic weapons fire coming from all directions, and bursts of tracer bullets converge on the pilots who are also blinded by Viet-Minh illuminating shells, searchlights, and Bangalore torpedoes. The planes also are severely buffeted by the shock waves of the exploding enemy shells and by the friendly shells that are being fired.
>
> That type of acrobatic mission has become par for the course . . .

Yet, taking advantage of the bad weather, the infantry remained active. One offensive patrol slipped out of C3 and headed for Ban Pa Pé, but it was stopped within 350 yards of its own position. On E2, Coutant's Foreign Legionnaires remained as aggressive as ever. A commando patrol slipped out of the position shortly after midnight and soon a loud explosion proclaimed the success of its exploit: the Legionnaires had once more succeeded in blowing up a Communist bunker with explosive charges. Still, Coutant was worried, for deep below E2, the digging and scraping of the Communist miners had almost completely stopped. If they were really digging a mineshaft to blow up E2, then the moment must have come for them to begin to fill it with explosives.

As dawn broke on May 3, French artillery began to lay down harassing fires on recently lost E1, which the Communists were now actively fortifying. On Claudine, where C5 in particular now was strongly surrounded and under constant artillery and mortar bombardment, Capt. Bienvault, a paratroop officer on loan to the Foreign Legion who commanded on C4, was wounded for a second time, and stayed at his post: The underground hospitals were filled to the rafters anyway. His men and Capt. Krumenaker's garrison of Moroccans, T'ai, and Legionnaires on C5, began to transform the drainage ditch into a combat trench connecting both strongpoints. Here, as in the drainage ditch near Sparrowhawk, men would soon fight in water up to their belts.

In the northeastern corner of the fortress, the mixed band of paratroopers from the II/1 RCP, the 6th BPC, and the 5th Vietnamese Parachute Battalion, now could clearly see enemy troop movements on what used to be D6 and E1, but there was too little ammunition around to provoke a firefight. And the rains that day had a devastating effect even on the hill positions. On E4 all hands were preoccupied with digging drainage ditches to keep the position from flooding altogether and to shore up the crumbling dugouts, which were disintegrating under the combined effect of the monsoon and Giap's artillery.

In Hanoi, this was the moment for last-minute decisions. In the course of a staff conference in Gen. Navarre's Hanoi office, Gen. Cogny, Col. de Crèvecoeur, who had flown in from Laos, and their staff officers were faced with some hard choices. According to the notes taken by Cogny's chief of staff, Col. Bastiani, Navarre decided to parachute the whole 1st BPC to reinforce the garrison at Dien Bien Phu in the hopes that its defense would thus be prolonged until the Geneva Conference arrived at a cease-fire in Indochina.

If, however, that proved to be impossible, the French government had given him orders that there would be no capitulation at Dien Bien Phu; that is, no formal act of surrender such as had finally taken place at Corregidor, Singapore, and even at Stalingrad. But Navarre still hoped that with the help of Operation "Condor" and the small commandos of mountain tribesmen and French cadres a breakout of the able-bodied survivors would have a fighting chance. One question that was held in abeyance was whether the now-arriving new parachute battalions, the 7th BPC and the 3rd BEP, who had been brought to Indochina by the U. S. Air Force airlift of huge *Globemasters,* should also be committed to Dien Bien Phu or should rather be used to reinforce Col. de Crèvecoeur's units in Laos.

Cogny was, from the beginning, dead set against Operation "Albatross." He felt that any kind of sortie in the present exhausted state of the garrison could only lead to its total destruction and would in any case be

branded as a rout. According to Roy, Cogny also thought that a prolonged resistance of the garrison would provide his own Red River Delta
with the side benefit of tying down the Viet-Minh divisions far from it
and of leading them a little farther.[17] In 1963, Cogny was still convinced
that his position on a breakout had been correct under the circumstances.
He termed Operation "Condor" a "sinister comedy" and asserted that a
decision to resist on the spot to the end was to be credited to him:
". . . There will be neither capitulation nor rout under the pretext of a
sortie. On the other hand those units whose leaders would still think
the capable of it, would be given a chance to slip through" the siege
ring.[18]

As has been shown earlier, that decision in fact was no decision at all,
since both Navarre and Cogny now left it up to Gen. de Castries and his
battalion commanders to decide when to attempt a breakout. And when
de Castries finally made up his mind to try it, it came too late to become
a rout as Cogny feared. But it also came too late to save any significant
number of French fighting men from the doomed garrison.

In a short memorandum prepared to back up his commander during
the conference, Col. Bastiani stated that the "defenders of Dien Bien
Phu have up to now covered themselves with glory and are an object of
admiration for the Free World."

The price of that unsullied glory came to 5,000 dead, 10,000 prisoners,
and a lost war.

Tuesday, May 4, 1954

A total of seven out of thirty-four available C-119's and sixteen out of
twenty-nine C-47's braved the monsoon and enemy flak that night
to bring succor to Dien Bien Phu. The amount of supplies they managed
to drop amounted to fifty-seven tons with a forty-per-cent loss rate,
but at least they managed to bring in Captain François Penduff
and a small headquarters element of the 1st Colonial Parachute
Battalion and the 125 men of the complete 3rd Company of the battalion,
under Captain Jean Pouget.

Jean Pouget deserves a special mention in the history of Dien Bien
Phu for a variety of reasons. A regular cavalry captain of the French
Army and a graduate of the French Military Academy, Pouget had later
requested a transfer to the paratroops in Indochina. Handsome and well
built with the sharply chiseled features of an Indian chieftain, he had
belonged during World War II to the toughest of all the French *maquis*
outfits in Savoy. After the liberation of France, he had returned to his

branch of origin, the French Armored Cavalry, and had belonged, like de Castries, to the unit commanded by Navarre. Little wonder, then, that upon the latter's appointment to Indochina in May, 1953, he would choose Pouget as his aide-de-camp. And for months thereafter official photographs would record, at a discreet distance behind the commander in chief, the tall and well-uniformed figure of the young officer.

To be the aide of a senior commander is never an easy job—not because of the work load itself, which often is crushing, but because of the seemingly unbridgeable gap that opens between the man who lives in the shadow of the commander and his former associates. Past a certain point, the officer must make the decision either to tie his further career to the fortunes of the commander or to strike out for himself and accept the rebuffs of his associates until they realized that he again had become "one of them." Pouget (though I know him personally, I did not want to ask him that question) apparently made his choice: in January, 1954, he requested a transfer to the 1st BPC. Navarre had given him his transfer without a word of opposition. But when the battalion, on February 13, 1954, made a combat jump to secure Muong Sai, Navarre managed to be on the airfield at Séno to see Pouget off.

Later on, it was alleged that Pouget had jumped at Dien Bien Phu to "atone" for his commander's mistakes and there is no doubt that some of his friends in the valley would ask him jokingly whether he did not now regret to have left his "cushy" job as Navarre's aide. But Pouget had made his choice long before Navarre's star was waning, and, in coming to Dien Bien Phu he simply shared the fate of his own battalion. What Pouget saw at Dien Bien Phu was to leave a deep imprint for the rest of his life. When, after the end of the Algerian war, he felt that his concept of what the French Army should be no longer matched that of the French government, he made another clean break with the past and left the Army in order to be able to write about it.[19]

But on May 4, 1954, at 0200 Pouget simply was another reinforcement for Dien Bien Phu. He had no trouble in finding the command post of the GAP, where Bigeard told him to await dawn to assemble his company and then to take command of E3 with the primary mission of supporting the Foreign Legionnaires on E2. In the meantime, Pouget followed the underground corridor to the Dien Bien Phu headquarters bunkers where he met Séguin-Pazzis and de Castries. The chief of staff, also a former cavalryman before he became a paratrooper, walked barefoot in the deep mud. De Castries used his cane to help himself pull his feet out of it at every step.

As both men and some of the officers of their staff stood around the new arrival and asked him the same questions that all new arrivals were asked at every level—What was going on at Geneva? How far away was the "Condor" force? Could large reinforcements be expected? Would the Americans help?—their discussion was suddenly interrupted by a call from H4. That strongpoint, held by Capt. Lucciani and an eighty-man company of Legionnaires and Moroccans, had been under attack since 0020; and it was probably the largest single enemy attack ever thrown against any of the strongpoints at Dien Bien Phu. Under the command of General Vuong Thua Vu of the 308th People's Army Division, all of Regiment 36 (Lt. Col. Manh Quan), three more battalions from Regiments 88 and 102, and an additional battalion of the 312th Division, supported by the howitzers of Artillery Regiment 34—in all, a force of over 3,000 men—had struck the tiny outpost. At the same time, the French artillery on Isabelle, which had begun to lay down a barrage around H4, was being blanketed by enemy interdicting fire.

Incredibly, two hours later H4 still held, although with serious losses. But the losses on the Communist side were enormous as hundreds of Viet-Minh bodies covered the barbed wire west of H4. At 0300, the French radio operators at Dien Bien Phu began to pick up clear signs of confusion and panic on the Viet-Minh side. The fact that both sides used American radio sets also played in favor of the French. According to the messages, the commander of the attack force, code-named "Tinh," was being replaced by another commander named "Ha." There also seemed to be shifts in the case of one regimental combat team commander and of one battalion commander. Still, the respite was enough to save H4. At 0335 the officers assembled in de Castries' underground head-quarters became the silent witnesses to the end on H4 as a young lieutenant from the Moroccan platoon, apparently the last able-bodied officer on the position (Lucciani himself had sustained a severe head wound a few minutes earlier) shouted into the radio set that there were still about ten fighting men in the positions but that the Viet-Minh were penetrating his trench. His death cry, as the enemy assault teams shot him down, was clearly audible over the radio set.

"You see," said de Castries to Pouget. "There goes another strong-point. There is nothing we can do about it. We are just constantly shrinking."

But on Huguette, Maj. Guiraud was not giving up easily. Now, as experience dictated, was the best moment for a counterattack. The Viet-Minh infantry did not yet know the conquered position too well, its artillery had not yet registered its new defensive fires and was afraid of hitting its own men; on the French side, there was the rage at seeing one's own good friends die and, with the growing daylight, the hope of getting close air support to replace the blanketed artillery and to neutralize at least part of the enemy's fire power. At 0600, the counter-attack began with paratroopers and Moroccans hastily scraped together from the remaining strongpoints of Huguette, supported by tank "Auerstaedt." But a counterattack of 100 men, no matter how fanatically motivated, against an enemy force of over 2,000, doesn't stand a chance. The sheer miracle of it was that the small band managed to fight its way forward through the communications trenches from H3 to H4 and actually reach the fringe of H4 before it was beaten back with heavy losses by a curtain of Communist fire. As Gen. de Castries had foreseen, H4 had been lost for good. Its loss cost the French 14 killed including two officers, 58 wounded, and 150 missing, including one officer. On Isabelle, the day cost two dead and thirty wounded, including two officers. And there were now 1,260 seriously wounded soldiers in the underground hospitals.

As dawn came, Pouget wearily assembled his men in the open trenches of the 8th BPC on Sparrowhawk for the march across the battlefield and through the Nam Yum to E3. He had been observed by the enemy and his progression was straddled by artillery salvos. It would take 3rd Company six hours to cover the short mile to its new position. It found E3 to be another "walking hospital." There were 300 wounded lying in the various combat bunkers under the care of an Airborne Surgical Team. The least-wounded men were manning the automatic weapons. In grim silence the new arrivals began to dig their own firing positions as the driving monsoon rain continued to fall on their shoulders and helmets.

In the meantime, the senior officers at Dien Bien Phu also had drawn their conclusions from the events of the last four days. Obviously the outside world as it affected them (that is, Gen. Navarre in Saigon and Gen. Cogny in Hanoi) still had not made up its mind as to what to do with Dien Bien Phu. The trickle of airborne supplies and reinforcements indicated that there was no intensification of the air effort. As for the "Condor" force, its radio messages still came from the same location in Laos where it had been a week earlier. Only for the purpose of boosting morale was the rumor allowed to circulate that every day a strong French column from Laos was coming closer to bring relief and, perhaps, victory to the hard-pressed men at Dien Bien Phu. As for the American

air strikes, there had been no word of them in official communications for
ten days. In other words, the commanders at Dien Bien Phu knew on
May 4 that the garrison was doomed, and the messages sent from Dien
Bien Phu to Hanoi took on a brutal frankness which they had hitherto
lacked and also dealt with general questions which had not been broached
before. Like Navarre and Cogny, de Castries also intended to put on
record his view of the Battle of Dien Bien Phu.

> When the Air Force talks to me about the risks encountered by
> the air crews, while every man here faces infinitely larger risks,
> there can't be any double standards. Air drops must henceforth
> begin at 2000 instead of 2300. . . . The considerable intervals be-
> tween each plane flying night drop missions has ridiculous results
> [in terms of tonnage dropped]. . . . Quantities which are dropped
> already represent only a fraction of what I request. That situation
> cannot go on much longer.
>
> I insist once more that I also be given a fairly large credit for
> decorations. I can't do anything to boost the morale of my men who
> are being asked to accomplish superhuman efforts. I don't even
> dare go see them with empty hands.

But that was exactly what de Castries had finally done. Together with
his chief of personnel, Lt. Col. Trancart, and Col. Langlais, de Castries
had visited Dr. Grauwin's underground hospital complex after weeks
of being invisible to anyone but a few senior officers. Apparently, now
that the decision-making at Dien Bien Phu was reduced to problems of
day-to-day survival, de Castries began to reassert himself. Originally, the
visit to the underground hospitals was to be limited to a perfunctory
inspection of the main dugout. There, de Castries asked Grauwin to
show him his most seriously wounded cases for the purpose of decorating
them. Grauwin's answer was simply that everyone in here was "most
seriously wounded," whereupon de Castries overruled the objections of
Trancart and Langlais and undertook to visit literally every wounded in
the hospital complex, no matter how remote the dugout or niche. He had
no medals to hand out; thus, the "decoration" ceremony was simply one
of touching the man's shoulder and telling him that the citation would be
entered in his record. Trancart walked silently next to the commander,
taking down names and citations. The visit finally took all day. Among
the last persons he saw was Lieutenant René Leguère, one of the few survivors of the Viet-Minh attack on E1 two days earlier. Leguère had
received a shell fragment in his brain and Grauwin had removed from
his skull almost a cupful of destroyed tissue. But there he was, alive, his

eyes blinking intelligently, but hemiplegic and mute. The less-wounded men of his own company were taking care of him. At first, after his operation, Leguère had violently refused to be placed into a wall niche. With his remaining movable arm he had clawed his way out and was found several times lying in the mud of the communications trench.

He was among the wounded directly evacuated from the battlefield after May 7, and miraculously survived. Months later Grauwin met him in Saigon at Grall Hospital, where Leguère was being trained like a small child to speak again. Grauwin asked him why he had repeatedly tried to leave his niche. Leguère looked at him with his expressive eyes and said, slowly enunciating the syllables as if he were speaking a foreign language: "Because it was like a tomb—and I didn't want to die."

The radio message which de Castries sent after his visit to the hospital, clearly showed the impact of this experience upon him. In a long communication sent during the night of May 4-5, he first detailed the troubles he was again having with the air drops but then added:

> One must add to all this the continuous rain which causes the complete flooding of the trenches and dugouts. The situation of the wounded is particularly tragic. They are piled up on top of each other in holes that are completely filled with mud and devoid of any hygiene. Their martyrdom increases day by day.

Indeed, that day nearly every battalion reported that its dugouts were collapsing under the rain, and the men of the 31st Engineers were busy shoring up the surgical block of Airborne Surgical Team No. 5. To do this, the Engineers now resorted to the dangerous game of crawling out every night on what was left of the airfield and tearing up the now-useless pierced steel plates. Little is said in the records of their activity during that period and even their own diary shows nothing but terse entries describing what would be normal engineering activities—until one remembers that those described here were being carried out under constant heavy artillery fire. On May 1, seven engineers were killed while collecting air-dropped supplies. On May 2 three mining crews were laying a mine field and booby-trapping bunkers on H4, and the Engineers with one unarmored bulldozer towed one of the disabled tanks from one position to another under constant fire. On May 5, the Engineers would once more enlarge the main hospital and dig new depot bunkers and on May 6, under constant artillery and small-arms fire, they laid down new planking on both the Bailey bridge and the wooden bridge crossing the Nam Yum. And 21st Company of the 31st Engineers, whose special charge was the electrical equipment, miraculously managed to keep electric power going day after day throughout the camp, rebuilding generator after generator from the parachuted spares or from salvageable parts of destroyed equipment. The same could be said for the signal personnel, who were constantly repairing smashed telephone lines and broken radio aerials. To the end, Dien Bien Phu did not suffer from lack of communications.

At 1600 that afternoon two French B-26 bombers again were hit by enemy flak. One was shot down over enemy territory; the other crash-landed in Laos. The C-119's immediately gained altitude; as a result three out of four of them dropped their complete six-ton loads into enemy lines.

That day, also, one last "civilian" telegram message reached Dien Bien Phu. It was addressed to the wounded Captain Michel Désiré on Isabelle by Mme. Geneviève Désiré-Vuillemin, his wife and a noted African specialist (in fact, they had met a few years earlier in the Sahara where he, as a lieutenant with the camel riders, tried to stop her from going off all by herself with a nomadic tribe). Mme. Désiré-Vuillemin informed her husband that she had given birth to a little girl. As they had agreed in advance, the little girl was given the name of the strongpoint for which Capt. Désiré had fought with the tribesmen of 3rd BT— Anne-Marie.

Wednesday, May 5, 1954

Shortly after midnight, Artillery had provided Supply with the account of shells fired during the previous day: 2,600 rounds of 105-mm., 40 rounds of 155-mm. and 1,180 rounds 120-mm. mortar shells. At that rate of fire and the present level of air drops, Dien Bien Phu would run out of artillery ammunition on the following day. And the rhythm of air drops already announced another disasterous day. The rains were falling with the desperate regularity of the biblical floods and by 0005 only two C-119's succeeded in making air drops under good conditions, with all the others misdropping their loads. Finally, only about forty-odd tons of supplies actually fell within the perimeter.

But there remained the parachute drops of personnel. Keyed up to the limit, Capt. de Bazin and his battalion had now been sitting at Hanoi airport for three days, awaiting a "massive" drop on Dien Bien Phu. Instead, the battalion was being dribbled in by bits and pieces, losing cohesion and combat morale. But that night, it had been de Bazin's turn and at 0240 five French Air Force C-47's finally dropped seventy-four men into the rain-drenched furnace of the battlefield. They represented de Bazin's battalion headquarters and a few elements of 4th Company under Captain Jean-François Tréhiou, yet another Breton paratrooper. As dawn came, Langlais assigned de Bazin and his staff, along with the elements of 4th Company which had arrived, to join Capt. Clédic on E4. But de Bazin never had a chance to take over his new command; a few hours later an enemy shell crushed one of his legs. Captain Pouget became the acting commander of the 1st BPC at Dien Bien Phu.

In fact, while de Bazin and 4th Company went to E4, Pouget was ordered by Bigeard to relieve the remnants of Coutant's 1/13 Half-Brigade on E2, while the wounded paratroopers, reinforced by some remaining Moroccans from the 1/4 RTM under Capt. Nicod would take over at the still-quiescent E3.

At about 1100—usually the quietest hour of the day because that was when the Viet-Minh relieved *its* troops and fed them their mid-day meal —Pouget finally met Coutant in the wine cellar on top of E2. Long ago E2 had lost all resemblance to anything human, and an incredible stench cloaked the whole hill like a thick blanket. As Coutant was to explain to his successor, there were probably 1500 Viet-Minh churned up on its few acres, not to speak of several hundred French paratroopers and Foreign Legionnaires. It will be recalled that tank "Bazeille," shot to pieces during the attack of April 1, had crowned the hill with its distinctive shape. After a month of continued shelling and rain, it had begun to sink into the ground and now formed a convenient bunker.

With the departure later that day of the remaining Legionnaires (with the exception of Coutant himself who stayed overnight with Pouget) E2 had now become the exclusive responsibility of 2nd and 3rd Companies of the 1st Colonial Parachute Battalion. Captain Edme and his men had taken over the southeastern corner of E2 with its small bunker, while Pouget and 3rd Company held on to the summit of E2. Somewhat below the crest of the hill, another bunker, deeply embedded among the roots of the banyan tree (which miraculously was still alive and seemed to be the last living shred of nature on E2), covered the line of communications which led from E2 via E3 to the Nam Yum. Here, also, a Viet-Minh trench tentacle had begun to grow in the direction of the banyan tree, and three Communist "death volunteers" loaded with explosives had been shot down by French marksmen at the last moment and were now rotting in no man's land. In fact, in the upside-down world that the front-line trenches of Dien Bien Phu had become in the early days of May, it had become a "sport" for a

Legionnaire or paratrooper to crawl out into no man's land and bring back safely the fifty or sixty pounds of high explosives attached to the cadaver of one of the death volunteers. Not that anything could be done with the explosives on the French side—indeed, they had to be prudently reburied far away from any of the combat positions. It was a gesture of pure bravado, of gratuitous defiance of fate, and duly appreciated as such by all concerned.[20]

There remained the problem of the mine shaft under E2. Captain Pouget was to say later that Capt. Coutant never informed him of the existence of the mine shaft. But according to a report written later by Staff Sgt. Chabrier of Capt. Edme's 2nd Company (under whose position the mine shaft was precisely located), at least 2nd Company had been informed of the existence of the mine and of the fact that the Viet-Minh had ceased digging in it for the past two days. But at dawn on May 5, Chabrier again heard them digging and was very happy about it. Obviously the Viet-Minh were not yet ready to blow the mine shaft. Here again, a significant event, seen by two observers, has left different memories. Captain Pouget, in his important work, does not recall that he had done anything to head off the explosion of the mine shaft on E2. On the other hand, Sgt. Chabrier recalls in detail that, because of losses due to enemy fire, Pouget's 3rd Company took over part of the lower E2 area where the mine shaft was located, and Pouget sent out a small commando patrol to attempt to blow up its entrance. According to Chabrier, that patrol was led by Sgt. Clinel; it was caught in the open by a Communist outpost and destroyed to the last man. Clinel himself, according to Chabrier, managed to drag himself back to the French trench, only to die there.[21]

To the west, on Claudine, a small event that night was to have grave consequences. Since April 25, Capt. Schmitz of the 2/1 REI had held strongpoint C5 with his 2nd Company, reinforced by one platoon of Moroccans from the 1/4 RTM. That night of May 5, the morale of the Moroccans finally broke. Five of them, on guard duty in the forward trenches of C5, simply cut open the two separate systems of barbed-wire entanglements in front of their position and slipped through them into the Communist lines. Within minutes after their arrival, and before the Legionnaires were aware of what had happened, Communist automatic weapons began to take the breach under constant fire. M/Sgt. Kosanovic, Sgt. Lunquick of 3rd Company, and the whole platoon of Legionnaires facing the gap desperately tried closing it as they knew that, if it were to remain open, it would surely cause the eventual loss of C5. Kosanovic and seven other men died in the attempt and Lunquick and twelve other Legionnaires were wounded—but the deserters' breach in the barbed wire remained unclosed. In a cold rage the Legionnaires disarmed the remaining Moroccans and kicked them out of their position. They promptly joined the Rats of the Nam Yum in their burrows.

At de Castries' command post, the day had been one of relative calm, and even apathy. With all infantry reserves fully committed and with ammunition levels at their lowest, there simply was nothing left to plan and direct, except the eventual breakout from Dien Bien Phu, for which Hanoi's authorization was required and had not yet been given. Such plans as had been made for "Albatross" were not discussed in order to preserve a maximum of secrecy and also in order to discourage any thought of not resisting at Dien Bien Phu until there existed no further hope of usefully holding out.[22] But during the day, Dien Bien Phu reported without further comment that more and more underground dugouts and shelters were now collapsing from the rain. The command post also noted matter-of-factly that "C-119 air drops [were] particularly bad in spite of almost total absence of antiaircraft fire."

In the afternoon, Lt. Col. Vaillant, the artillery commander, decided to spend some of his remaining precious ammunition to disperse a strong concentration of Viet-Minh infantry east of E1, which seemed to be on the verge of launching a massive attack on the lowland positions of E10 and E12. The wounded Lt. Weinberger from the 1/2 REI had taken over command on E12 that day and held the position with two weak platoons drawn from the least-wounded Legionnaires of his battalion. The French artillery paid for this brief activity with a steady Communist counterbattery fire which began at 1812 and lasted four hours. By the end of the day Dien Bien Phu had lost fourteen killed and forty-eight wounded. And there were the five fateful deserters from Claudine.

On quiescent Juno, now also occupied by some of the remaining Legionnaires of Capt. Coutant's 1/13 Half-Brigade, Sgt. Kubiak late in the afternoon crawled into the "subway" of the covered communication trenches to the signal depot near de Castries' command post in order to obtain spare batteries for the remaining radio sets of his battalion. He got them, along with an electrifying piece of news: Col. de Crèvecoeur's "Condor" force was only 50 kilometers away and would surely break through to Dien Bien Phu in a matter of days! Overjoyed, he retraced his steps back to Juno, shouting the news as he went along. On Juno itself, his own comrades did not seem to care. Happy to be away from the hell of E2, they were sleeping.[23]

Sergeant Kubiak's buoyancy was not simply due to a naïve young soldier's blind belief in what his superiors were telling him, Lieutenant-Colonel Trancart, who witnessed the events from the vantage point of the command headquarters but without being directly involved in them, confirmed that the weeding-out process of the bitter final battle had produced a combination of extraordinary physical misery and high combat morale among the remaining combatants. There was a clear realization that they, the last 3,000 men—the French and Vietnamese paratroopers, Foreign Legionnaires, and African cannoneers—literally represented all that stood between defeat and stalemate in the Indochina War. The main theme repeated throughout the shrinking fortress was "they simply can't let us lose the war." That was to hold true to the very last minutes of the battle. Certain units simply refused to believe that it was all over, and there was a justified fear among the higher commanders that the battle would end in a general massacre of the garrison. There may have been another, more prosaic, reason for the high morale of the remaining defenders. In view of the progressive lack of replacements for the casualties, many of the men remained on duty for days on end and were taking "Maxiton," the French equivalent of benzedrine.

Finally at 2100, de Castries received a brief personal message from Gen. Cogny. It authorized de Castries to attempt a breakout when he felt that on-the-spot resistance had become hopeless. In the third paragraph, Cogny, in spite of the personal character of the telegram, employed a tone more likely to fit a later open record than to be of comfort to a beleaguered commander compelled to make an agonizing decision under pressure:

> I need not underline inestimable value in every field, and per-
> spectives offered, by prolonging resistance on the spot, which at
> present remains your glorious mission.

Thursday, May 6, 1954

May 6 began with the largest supply drop in almost three weeks. The French civilian pilots who had refused to fly the Dien Bien Phu runs on May 3, now had returned to their airplanes and the supply run was flown at almost maximum strength—twenty-five C-119's out of thirty-six available that day and twenty-five out of twenty-nine C-47's. The results were correspondingly high, as a total of 196 tons of supplies were dropped on Dien Bien Phu. Of course, they came by and large too late to do any good. Dien Bien Phu was now, as President Eisenhower aptly phrased it in his memoirs, "reduced to a size no larger than a baseball field," and the supplies were largely falling outside the perimeter. Still, after the harsh remarks made during the previous days about the air drops, there seemed to be a certain amount of warmth in a brief message from Dien Bien Phu to Hanoi at five minutes past midnight, in which the fortress simply said that now "six C-119's launched their cargos quite correctly."

That left the personnel drop for the night. It began at 0412 in the face of extremely heavy Communist flak. A dozen or so of Air Force C-47's were slowly circling the flaming valley, waiting for a momentary lull to dive into the circle, drop four or five men, and gain altitude again. These were still Frenchmen and Vietnamese of Headquarters Company and of the 2nd, 3rd, and 4th Companies of the 1st Colonial Parachute Battalion. At 0520, a total of ninety-one men had succeeded in parachuting in, but the rest of them, including all of 1st Company under Capt. Faussurier, now returned to base. It had become too light to risk further personnel drops. In four nights of air drops, the 1st BPC had succeeded in bringing in 383 men out of its total strength of 876 paratroopers. Here, also, the number of Vietnamese included even in those last desperate jumps was impressive: out of the 383 men who made the jump, 155 were Vietnamese. The 91-man contingent that jumped into Dien Bien Phu at dawn of May 6 was the last to reach it before the fortress fell.

But early on the 6th of May the situation inside Dien Bien Phu seemed far from desperate. A weak Communist probe against E3 had been easily repelled by a company of the 6th BPC. A more serious attack against H3 and H5 had been contained by the Foreign Legion paratroopers of Maj. Guiraud. In two successive counterattacks they cleared the enemy out of their forward trenches and held on to their whole position.

But as the morning wore on it became clear that Gen. Giap was preparing his troops for a major attack. The latest set of aerial photographs clearly showed new approach trenches radiating out of D3 in the direction of what was left of the Elianes; and another net of new approach trenches emanating from Old Baldy and Phony Mountains, now gnawed away at the southern tip of E2. The mine shaft under E2 now had reached a total length of forty-seven meters; the scraping and hammering of the sappers had stopped altogether as long lines of unarmed coolies began to transport into the gaping hole almost 3,000 pounds of TNT.

In the air also, the morning of May 6 had been favorable to the French. The rains had stopped for a while and with both the American and French civilian pilots flying the supply runs, the French Air Force and French Navy bombers and fighters could concentrate entirely on flak suppression. Dien Bien Phu had never seen so many planes: forty-seven B-26 bombers, eighteen *Corsairs,* twenty-six *Bearcats,* sixteen *Helldivers,* and even five 4-engine Navy *Privateers.* This large aircraft deployment now effectively beat down the Communist flak and for once, the transport pilots willingly accepted the directions of Maj. Guérin's Air Traffic Control Center inside Dien Bien Phu. That morning, many of the Communist guns found it prudent to remain silent so as not to reveal their positions, but, finally, the day of reckoning had also come for the gallant Americans from Civil Air Transport who were flying the supply runs. Piloting a C-119, Captain James B. McGovern had become a legend in Indochina just as he had been a legend in China during World War II. A bearded man and so huge—his nickname was "Earthquake McGoon" after a character in the *Li'l Abner* comic strip— that he used a specially built pilot's chair, McGovern that morning flew a full load of ammunition. His co-pilot was Wallace Buford, another American, and the rest of the crew was French. Both men knew the Dien Bien Phu run well; in fact, that morning McGovern was flying his forty-fifth mission over the valley and his wing man, Steve Kusak (with whom this writer had flown supply missions in Indochina in May, 1953), was equally experienced. Thus far that morning, no plane had been hit seriously and for once there was plenty of flak suppression from the military aircraft. Yet, as McGovern eased in for the final run over the drop zone, Steve Kusak suddenly heard his voice over the radio saying: "I've got a direct hit."

Indeed, one of the engines was squirting oil badly and Kusak saw McGovern feathering it quickly. While serious, that incident was not as such fatal, since the C-119 is built with sufficient reserve power to keep on flying for a time on one engine. But another Soviet 37-mm. flak shell hit the stricken plane in one of its tail booms and now the plane was badly out of control. With its six tons of ammunition aboard, the airplane was indeed a gigantic bomb and its crash and explosion inside Dien Bien Phu would have been a major disaster. As McGovern and Buford wrestled with the controls of their plane, McGovern's voice could be heard asking Kusak to point out a low ridge, but it already was too late for any further maneuvering.

It was difficult to tell later whether the words "looks like this is it, son," which Kusak heard from McGovern's plane, were addressed to him, who survived, or to Wally Buford, the co-pilot who died with McGovern a few seconds later when the heavily loaded plane cart-wheeled and exploded in Viet-Minh territory.

At 1000, Col. Langlais called together as many of the battalion commanders and other staff officers as possible for a briefing. The ammunition situation was serious in spite of the fact that on this day no less than seventy tons of infantry ammunition and fifty tons of artillery ammunition (the latter largely 120-mm. mortar shells) had been slated for air drop. But with a few exceptions, nothing could be collected until nightfall because of the constant enemy machine-gun fire and artillery harassment. And if the Communists were to attack by then, the French would never have a chance of collecting that ammunition. Langlais once more emphasized the external aspects of the battle: the Geneva Conference was progressing and a cease-fire could occur any day; the "Condor" force was almost within reach; and the French Air Force, if not boosted by a direct American intervention as expected under Operation "Vulture," nevertheless had received a great many new aircraft whose effect was bound to make itself felt on the enemy's front-line infantry as well as his supply system. Captain Noël, the Intelligence officer, carefully detailed the staggering personnel losses suffered by the Viet-Minh divisions. But all this did not change the situation inside Dien Bien Phu. As of the time of the briefing, Lt. Col. Vaillant's artillery had less than one day's normal reserve, which usually could be fired in three hours if the going got rough. And there were no personnel reserves —not one platoon of thirty men. To be sure, there were the Rats of the Nam Yum. But if they were used on the line they would simply run away and leave a gap somewhere at the wrong moment, just as the deserters had done the night before on Claudine. If only the 493 remaining men of the 1st BPC could be air-dropped during the following night and the Viet-Minh general attack could be held off long enough to collect a large part of the artillery ammunition, there was a chance yet of surviving the onslaught just as Dien Bien Phu had survived the attacks on Beatrice, on Gabrielle, on the northern Huguettes, and on Dominique. If one held this time, perhaps the Viet-Minh would again take two weeks to reconstitute its units for yet another major attack. All that Dien Bien Phu now needed was another twelve hours of relative quiet.

Just as the meeting was about to break up, a top-priority message arrived from Hanoi. Noël read it and passed it over to Langlais, who in turn read it aloud to the assembled officers. French Intelligence had a few months earlier succeeded in infiltrating the innermost circle of advisers around Ho Chi Minh himself and had in recent weeks received remarkably accurate intelligence on crucial decisions made by the enemy. That important source had now informed the French that the general attack with the purpose of completely ending all French resistance at Dien Bien Phu was to take place as of the evening of May 6. Dien Bien Phu would not have twelve hours to collect its ammunition and receive fresh airborne reserves.

Captain Hervouët, the commander of the little tank squadron who had had both forearms fractured during earlier operations, quickly walked over to Dr. Grauwin and asked to have both plaster casts removed from his arms. He wanted to fight his last battle in the last remaining operational tank. Langlais and Bigeard, wearing red berets and no helmets, together crossed the bridge across the Nam Yum to inspect one last time the key defense positions on Elaine. Langlais, known throughout the whole theater for his love of strong spirits—almost every paratroop officer who had jumped into the valley had seen to it that his vast pockets would contain a small propitiatory flask for the commanding officer of GAP 2—had brought along with him a small bottle of cognac which he now passed around in the command-post dugout on E4 where Bréchignac and Botella were commanding the whole eastern flank.

As the final battle now approached the commanders once more reviewed the order of battle: In the far north Maj. Tourret and the remnants of the 8th Parachute Assault Battalion were holding Sparrowhawk, D4, and the nameless strongpoint in the drainage ditch. In the northwest, Maj. Guiraud and perhaps 160 Foreign Legion Paratroopers of the Composite Foreign Legion Parachute Battalion were holding on to the last shreds of Huguette, H2 and H3. Due west, Maj. Nicolas still held Lily 1 and Lily 2 with a mixed bag of Moroccans and watchful Legionnaires; while in the southwest Maj. Clémençon and Capt. Coldeboeuf were holding on grimly to all of Claudine, having thus far yielded nothing to the enemy. Due south lay Juno, the "hospital strongpoint." It was now commanded by Capt. Charnod of the French Air Force and Capt. Duluat (also referred to affectionately as *"Tonton* [Uncle] Carabine"). The actual fighting element on the position consisted of the still deadly quad-fifties of Lt. Redon, the shrinking Air Force detachment fighting as infantry, a small company of White T'ai tribesmen of Duluat's old unit, and a small remnant of Capt. Coutant's 1/13 Half-Brigade whose primary mission was to come to the immediate support of Eliane in case of a catastrophe there. And then, of course, there were the now 602 wounded lying in Juno's dugouts and trenches. Conveniently enough, Juno was located directly next to Dien Bien Phu's cemetery.

But is was on the Elianes that Langlais and Bigeard had lavished their best remaining troops and commanders. On E4, Bréchignac and Botella, in addition to commanding the whole area, also commanded the last remaining shreds of the 5th Vietnamese Parachute Battalion and the II/1 RCP. They were reinforced by the Headquarters Company of the 1st BPC under Capt. Penduff and the same battalion's 4th Company under Capt. Tréhiou. On E2 Capt. Pouget commanded both the 1st BPC, the strongpoint, and his own 3rd Company, while Lt. Edme and his 2nd Company held the key southern bunker and trenches of E2. Eliane 3, that morning, was still held by Legionnaires of the 1/13 and a North African platoon of the 1/4 RTM, soon to be reinforced by the rest of the battalion from Juno; while the Lower Elianes, E10, 11, and 12, were held by a mixed force of paratroop remnants from the once-proud 6th BPC, regrouped around Maj. Thomas on E10. E11 and 12 were held by combat engineers, some T'ai from 2nd BT and some Algerians, under Maj. Chenel. At noon, there were on the line on top of the Upper Elianes about 750 paratroopers who had been told that they could not expect any infantry reinforcements from inside the fortress, that there would be very little artillery fire to support them, and who were not even assured that there would be enough infantry ammunition if the fight were to go on for any length of time. With a heavy heart, knowing full well that some of their adieus would be final, Bigeard and Langlais returned to their own command post.

It was about 1200. With clear skies overhead and the situation temporarily as well in hand as could be, Dien Bien Phu enjoyed a rare moment of respite, as if time had stopped. General de Castries used the time to reply via French radio channels to a telegram which President Eisenhower had sent him two weeks earlier to congratulate him and his troops for "defending the cause of human freedom" and for "demonstrating in the truest fashion qualities on which the survival of the Free World depends." The failure to even attempt the implementation of Operation "Vulture" in one form or another gave the words of the American President a certain hollow ring which de Castries' reply perfectly matched:

> I have been deeply moved by the expression of admiration, of gratitude, and of confidence that President Eisenhower was kind enough to send me on behalf of the American people. The Free

World may be assured that the defenders of Dien Bien Phu, whatever their origin, conscious of the fight they are waging, are determined to do everything in their power to continue to deserve this
confidence and to fulfill right to the end the mission which has
been entrusted to them.

With the suddenness of an earthquake, a howling screech filled the air
over Dien Bien Phu, followed within seconds by a series of explosions
which rocked even the deepest remaining dugouts. Electric lights began
to fail throughout the underground trenches and in dozens of places
wounded and bleeding men, their clothes torn off their bodies by the
strength of the blasts, were frantically clawing at the beams and planks
of collapsed shelters as they tried to dig themselves out or to dig their
friends out before they died of asphyxiation. The echo of the first salvo
had barely died down when a new ear-bursting screech filled the air,
followed by yet another series of shattering explosions. For the first time
in the Indochina War, the Viet-Minh were using Soviet-made *Katyusha*
six-tube field rockets, which the Russians already had used with devastating effect on the Germans during World War II. A crude weapon by
today's standards, the *Katyusha,* fired from mobile launching racks, has
a terrifying blast effect upon troops caught in the open but would not
normally be dangerous to troops in solid entrenchments. At Dien Bien
Phu, the field fortifications had never been good and those which had not
yet fallen victim to Communist conventional artillery had been very
badly undermined by the monsoon. Upon them and upon the remaining
non-European French troops, who had never heard a noise approaching
that of the field rockets, the effect was devastating. Throughout the camp,
depots began to explode and to burn, all the major medical stocks were
destroyed that afternoon; uncollected ammunition packages from the air
drops added their secondary explosions to those of the rockets, and by the
end of the afternoon Claudine 5 reported that three fourths of all its
bunkers had been completely destroyed and that its trenches had been
smashed flat or buried under the explosions.

At 1730 the conventional Communist artillery began to lay down a
heavy barrage on E4 and E2. On both hills all men save those in the most
essential outposts burrowed deep into trenches and bunkers. There was
nothing else to do now but to await the assault. At 1730, the main position at Dien Bien Phu had exactly one more day to live.

The Last Night

A remnant of daylight still hung over the hilltops of Eliane when the final attack began. As the barrage increased in intensity, Bréchignac had radioed Pouget that the attack would in all likelihood aim at E2 first. "But don't worry," said Bréchignac. "You've got at your disposal whatever there is left of the artillery; and I might even get you a small company of reinforcements."

Lieutenant Robin, the artillery forward observer on E2 who had served an incredible continuous three weeks on it and knew the area well, meticulously went over his fire charts. There were too few shells around to waste through errors of calculation.

At about 1845 the whole eastern slope of E2 suddenly seemed to come alive as the first wave of 1,000 *Bo-Doi* emerged from the approach trenches. For that key attack, Gen. Giap had chosen Lt. Col. Vu Yen's Infantry Regiment 102 of the 308th People's Army Division, the "Iron Division" of his army. The 102nd was indeed the crack regiment of perhaps the whole Viet-Minh army and proudly bore the title of "Capital Regiment" which it had earned for its stubborn defense of parts of Hanoi against masses of French troops and armor from December, 1946, until March, 1947. It now had a key role to play face to face with Capt. Pouget's small band of elite French Paratroopers and it was going to play it to the hilt.

On the French side there was a moment of total silence. In Pouget's dugout the voice of Lt. Robin could be heard clearly as he asked for the laying down of the artillery barrage, and just as clearly one could hear in reply the voice of the fire-control officer a few hundred yards away beginning a reverse count: "Ten—nine—eight—seven—six—five—four . . ."

With seemingly a single roar the remaining howitzers and heavy mortars of the main position fired a salvo into the unprotected mass of humanity on the slopes of E2. Several more salvos slammed into Regiment 102; then the forward observer called for a halt. When the smoke cleared, the Viet-Minh assault wave had vanished. From E4 and E2, the paratroop outpost's field glasses counted at least 200 bodies lying still on the churned-up ground. As Pouget would put it later, the thought of that massacre would keep the paratroopers cheered up as they now steeled themselves to face the reprisal artillery bombardment that was sure to come. And it came indeed. With a vengeance, the whole gamut of enemy artillery, from 75-mm. recoilless rifles and 81-mm. mortars to medium howitzers and Soviet rocket launchers, now began to lay down its devastating fire on the whole French central position. Within a short time, three of the remaining 105-mm. howitzers were destroyed and their gun crews killed. At the same time, the enemy batteries near Isabelle began to hammer away at the latter strongpoint's guns. By 2300, Col. Lalande reported eight of his nine howitzers as destroyed. With them disappeared all chances of effective defensive fires for strongpoints Claudine and Huguette. The results of the bombardment became particularly obvious on Claudine 5, already badly mauled by the artillery barrage of the previous hours. Caught in the open, unable to find even the modest protection offered on Eliane by the reverse slopes, 3rd platoon of 2nd Company, 1/2 Foreign Legion, began to pull back its outposts from the deserters' breach in the barbed wire at about 1900. By 2200, C5 was disintegrating and its last remnants attempted to hold the communications trench system west of C2 and C4. The battalion commander, Clémençon, decided to strip the remaining position of every man who could be spared in order to hold C5 as long as possible. Captain Philippe, who commanded a mixed company of remnants of the 3/13th on Claudine 4, sent a platoon over to C5. But in the absence of any artillery support, there was very little that it could do. It soon found itself engulfed in the general debacle of 2nd Company. But then, the platoon of sappers of the 1/2 REI pushed forward. In a Foreign Legion parade, which is colorful enough, the sappers themselves represent an unforgettable sight: chosen from the tallest and biggest men in the outfit, they all wear full beards and a gleaming white leather apron and, in addition to their weapons, carry a long-handled ax. In combat, of course, they wear the same uniform as everyone else, but their special skills in the handling of different weapons and explosives make them a sort of shock troop for their battalion. Even in as desperate a situation as Claudine was during the night of May 6, the impact of that small band of elite troops was not lost. Led by the Foreign Legion sappers, the scattered elements of 2nd Company and of the 3/13 platoon fought their way back into C5. The sight of the bare-chested and bearded giants was too much even for the tough Viet-Minh assault troops of the "Iron Division." By 2230, the Legionnaires were back inside the featureless hollow filled with shell craters and dead bodies that used to be C5. It fell for good at 0200, its garrison dead or wounded.

But while Pouget had won the first round of his fight on E2 and Clémençon had broken even on Claudine, the enemy was now concentrating on E4 and the tiny E10 which was covering its left flank. If E10 fell, Bréchignac and Botella on E4 would be completely outflanked and the approach to the Bailey bridge would be under direct control of the Viet-Minh. The defenders of E2 and E3 would be completely sealed off and the enemy would be in control of the whole hill position. All that

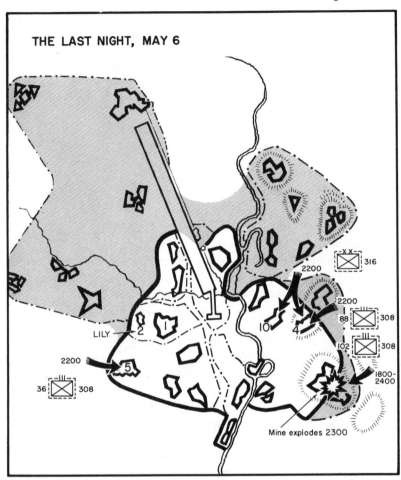

THE LAST NIGHT, MAY 6

LILY

Mine explodes 2300

would be left of the French fortress of Dien Bien Phu would be a series of half-flooded mud flats filled with wounded and dying and the wreckage of what once were artillery pieces and tanks. If Dien Bien Phu was to survive to see another day, let alone live long enough to be saved by a cease-fire, the Upper Elianes would have to be held literally to the last ditch, the last cartridge, and the last man.

At 2200, the attack began both on E10 and E4. It was a massive attack, led probably with the better parts of two regiments of Division 312 and 316. The first brunt of the attack fell upon its northeastern flank, held by the 2nd Company, 5th Vietnamese Parachute Battalion, which counted barely thirty men. It was not by accident that the Viet-Minh chose to attack a Vietnamese unit first, in the hope that it would be most likely to crack. Not only did the little Vietnamese paratroopers fail to crack, but they fought with the cold ferocity that one finds when brother fights against brother. But there were too many enemy troops to be contained by that handful of men. At 2230, Capt. Botella pulled out the remnants of 3rd Company under Capt. Phan Vam Phu from the second line and the southern flank of the strongpoint, and reinforced with them the threatened northeastern flank. At the same time, Bréchignac asked Langlais to provide him immediately with whatever forces he could scrape together. Since the northern face of Dien Bien Phu—Huguette and Sparrowhawk—had thus far been spared from enemy attack, Langlais decided to take a calculated risk by gutting them of the bulk of their troops. Two platoons of Foreign Legion paratroops under Lt. Lecour-Grandmaison and Lt. Fournier began the dangerous trek across the whole width of the fortress via the dimly lit tunnels of the "subway," past the command post of the GAP, de Castries' headquarters, across the battered Bailey bridge and through ghostly E11, which, since it was still theoretically covered by E12 and E10, seemed to have no garrison except some wounded and what appeared to be a pack of Rats of the Nam Yum.

While the Vietnamese had stood off the first enemy attack on E4, the end now had come for Bigeard's own beloved 6th BPC on E10. There, Maj. Thomas and his few remaining officers and men were fighting a hopeless holding action. Lieutenant Allaire's mortars were out of ammunition and his surviving men were fighting as infantry. Yet the most agonizing decision of the last night had to be made by young Lieutenant René Le Page, another paratrooper from Britanny. Le Page's small company held the northern flank of E10 when the first Communist attack smashed into the strongpoint and he had immediately requested a flare ship to light up the battlefield around him. In the absence of effective artillery fire, the few remaining howitzer shells were husbanded for *really* critical situations; the parachute flares were absolutely essential to give maximum effectiveness to the machine guns and recoilless rifles laying down final protective fires.

But high above Dien Bien Phu the troop transport aircraft had begun their nightly rounds with reinforcements for Dien Bien Phu. There was still the better part of the 1st BPC to be dropped in, notably the whole 1st Company of Capt. Faussurier. However, it would have been sheer suicide to begin the air drop of the paratroopers while the whole battlefield was illuminated *a giorno*. The choice then was between paratroop reinforcement and darkness for two hours, at the risk of losing E10 and perhaps also E4 or parachute flares over the battlefield and effective defense of the strongpoints, at the risk of running out of defenders later. The only person who could make that judgment was the officer who was facing the threat on the line. Bigeard, as commander of all counterattack operations, personally called the young officer on the radio:

"Le Page from Bruno. Our friends are above you in the air. We've got to stop the 'fireflies' to drop them. Can we do it?"

There was a brief silence interrupted only by the empty crackling of the voice transmitter, as Le Page surveyed the situation beyond his parapet. The Viet-Minh were within grenade throwing distance. Then his answer came firmly over the air, punctuated by the noise of the battle around him:

"Priority to the 'fireflies.' Out."

Langlais accepted the verdict and now proceeded to scrape together from strongpoint Sparrowhawk the reinforcements for the 6th BPC which it would need in order to survive. The 8th Parachute Assault had to surrender two small companies (in fact, platoons) of forty men each, commanded by Lt. Jacquemet and Lt. Bailly. Major Guiraud on Huguette was bled of another sixty-man company under Lieutenant Michel Brandon to reinforce E4. The gaping holes in the defenses of Huguette were now filled by most of the remaining gun crews from the artillery, fighting as infantry. For although Dien Bien Phu still had seven field pieces, there were only about 600 rounds of ammunition left for them by 2300. On the other hand, faraway Isabelle had 2,000 rounds of artillery shells, but only one single 105-mm. howitzer left to fire them.

By 2300, the remnants of the 6th BPC were cornered in three small bunker systems. Major Thomas was with Lieutenants Jean Elise and Michel Datin, as well as Captain Lucien Le Boudec. Le Page was still holding on to the northeast corner next to the road. Captain Trapp and Lt. Courbineau faced west near Eliane 12, which was still held by a few platoons of the 31st Engineers under Capt. Fazentieux. To the north of Le Page, Lieutenant André Samalens had held off the enemy for almost an hour with a small platoon. But now he was overrun and dying. Courbineau was killed a short while later. By 0300, May 7, Maj. Thomas and twenty men held the communications bunker of E10, the last foothold in the strongpoint.

The end had now come for the garrison of Eliane 2. There, the fighting had stopped for almost three hours, and Pouget's men had used them to dig deeper along their trench line and to distribute the last remaining ammunition. Two sergeants from Capt. Edme's 2nd Platoon,

Bruni and Ballait, had climbed into the smashed hull of tank "Bazeilles" facing the southern slope of E2, and manned the .50-cal. machine gun which was still in operating order. The name Bazeilles means nothing to Americans, but to the French, who are inordinately fond of hopeless last-ditch situations in which totally senseless bravery can best be displayed, just as a pearl is best set off by a background of black satin, the name means a great deal. For on September 1, 1870, in the course of the Franco-Prussian War, a French Marine Infantry force encircled in a farm near the small eastern French village of Bazeilles fought to the proverbial last cartridge. The incident did not change the outcome of the battle but it gave rise to a great many inspirational stories in school textbooks and at least one maudlin painting, naturally named "Last-Cartridge House." And with the morbid logic of the same type of military mind that made the Foreign Legion's defeat at Camerone a Foreign Legion holiday, Bazeilles was promptly made into the traditional holiday of the French Marines. At Dien Bien Phu, the name of Bazeilles was to preside over the destruction of French paratroop battalions bearing the old anchor insignia of the French Marine forces.

At 2300 sharp, strongpoint Eliane 2 blew up. There are three contemporary accounts by survivors: on the French side, those of captain Pouget, who commanded all of E2, and Sgt. Chabrier, who was with Capt. Edme's 2nd Company under which the mine exploded; and on the Communist side, the account of Huu Mai, an officer from Regiment 102 of the 308th People's Army Division. They agree on all the facts— except that Huu Mai states that the mine shaft blew at 2000, thus ignoring the first attack that evening, which E2 had successfully beaten off.

Shortly before 2300, Pouget was sitting in the cellar of the former French Governor's house which still served as battalion command post on E2. He thought that the Viet-Minh, in view of the huge losses on E2 earlier that evening and the heavy fighting in progress on E10 and E4, would leave E2 alone for the moment, or perhaps try to outflank it. On southern E2, Sgt. Chabrier, who, with a small fire team still covered the *Champs-Elysées* slope against Communist infiltrations, was almost captured by a lone *Bo-Doi* who suddenly jumped into his trench without having been seen by anyone and called for Chabrier's surrender. He was killed at the last moment by a French paratrooper standing behind him, whom he had not seen. A few minutes before 2300 Chabrier had withdrawn his last outposts from the *Champs-Elysées*, which was now being churned under by Communist artillery and field rockets.

On the Viet-Minh side the division commander himself was watching the final preparations for the blowing of the mine shaft and the subsequent breakthrough of three infantry battalions. His political commissar stood next to him and again reminded him of the fact that the Geneva conference would begin in two days, on May 8, and that it was imperative that Dien Bien Phu be in Viet-Minh hands by then.

The commander answered with his own version of Mao Tse-tung's saying that power grows out of the barrel of a gun:

"Negotiations with the imperialists should be effected by means of bayonets, explosives, and cannon. Tonight we will 'negotiate' with them . . ."

The political commissar agreed with him and said with a smile:

"That's right. President Ho has said 'Our soldiers are the best diplomatists. . . . After Dien Bien Phu, surely the conditions imposed by the enemy will change.' "[24]

At H-hour minus ten minutes, the radio operators of division headquarters began to check their connections with the three infantry battalions of the assault force. Although they now had a sufficient amount of American-made radio sets for fairly efficient radio communications with their forward units, the Viet-Minh relied extensively on rapidly strung-out telephone cables, and at H-hour minus five minutes the telephone operator handed the division commander the telephone receiver with an open line to Regiment 102's headquarters so as to get immediate news of the results of the mine blast. A few seconds before 2300, the commander turned to his deputy chief of staff.

"Give orders to fire the petards," he said quietly, then left the trench with the political commissar in order to see the explosion for himself. He, like everyone around him, expected to hear an enormous noise from the explosion. But the H-hour passed and nothing was heard. Had the mine failed to explode? The political commissar turned to the division commander with a quizzical look, but at that very moment they could hear, against the background of the battle itself, a dull rumbling and feel an ever so slight tremor. Over the open line, the 102nd reported that a bright flash followed by smoke had been seen over E2 but that it was not certain that the whole load had actually exploded.

The puzzlement of the Viet-Minh was of course understandable. They had never blown a deeply buried mine shaft, and as far as the noise of explosives was concerned, they had only that of French 1,000-lb. aerial bombs to go by. Those of course exploded close to the surface, whereas their own mine shaft was deeply buried in the hill.

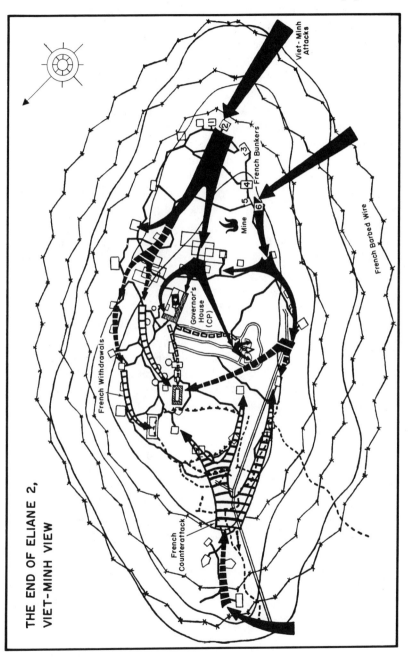

THE END OF ELIANE 2,
VIET-MINH VIEW

Viet-Minh Attacks

French Bunkers

French Barbed Wire

Mine

Governor's House (CP)

French Withdrawals

French Counterattack

After another moment of prudent reconnoitering, the lead battalion of Regiment 102 (probably the 69th Infantry Battalion) rose out of the approach trenches.

Pouget also felt the exploding mine at first merely as a profound tremor, just as a ship which has received a deadly wound from an enemy torpedo still continues on its normal course for an instant before sinking. The same was true for Chabrier, whose position was literally at the rim of the crater created by the explosive charge. He saw a huge geyser of black earth and smoke rising up in the sky and he, realizing in a flash what was happening, threw himself into the nearest bunker. This saved his life as the huge chunks of blown-up earth, weapons, and bunkers began to rain down on E2. Captain Edme's 2nd Company disappeared, buried in the rubble, torn apart by the explosion itself, or stunned into total paralysis.

But when the smoke lifted and the battlefield became visible again in the shadowless light of the parachute flares, the last remnants of 2nd Company took advantage of the moment of hesitation on the Viet-Minh's side to carry forward their remaining automatic weapons. The advancing Communist assault waves found that the rain-soaked earth of the crater was as slippery as oil and progress agonizingly slow. Sgt. Chabrier and his handful of men—he had five with him, including three wounded—fired clip after clip into the mass of bogged-down humanity below them. E2, hacked to pieces by fifty-five days of constant artillery fire and now blown apart by a mine, was still holding fast. All it needed now was some ammunition and a handful of reinforcements. If they could be found, the chaos created by the mine blast could in fact become a boon to the defense. Three hours later, having been promised the small paratroop force of Lt. Lecour-Grandmaison, Pouget himself counterattacked southward over the top of E2, pushing the infiltrated enemy soldiers back from bunker to bunker and hole to hole into the crater.

The men of the 102nd knew that if they did not now push the paratroopers off E2, all their sacrifices, the whole miserably difficult work of digging the mine, would have been vain. And Pouget also knew that if he failed that night the French fortress at Dien Bien Phu would be dead tomorrow. At 0300, with the northern part of E2 now almost completely bereft of troops and no trace of Lecour-Grandmaison and his Foreign Legion parachutists, Pouget returned to his CP in the cellar to contact GAP 2 by radio. He could no longer make contact with it, but could clearly hear Bréchignac speak to his companies on E4. He also clearly heard Clédic, hard-pressed on the northeastern flank of E4, asking Lecour-Grandmaison to hasten his approach, and he heard the latter's reply that he was hindered by the deep mud and by hand grenades thrown at him from all sides. Pouget knew this meant that he would not receive any reserves.

What happened to the various small companies scraped together under fire by Langlais was normal. The first unit to go, Jacquemet's, had been caught in the open as it crossed the Nam Yum and had been destroyed. The bodies of its dead were added to those of hundreds of others that were now lying in the water in such numbers that it was possible to cross the river on them.[25] Bailly's company from the 8th Parachute Assault had fought its way across with some losses and had reached E10 at 0300, where Maj. Thomas was still holding out. There the situation was apocalyptic. A handful of men under Lts. Le Page and Datin were still counterattacking in order to keep the approach to the Bailey bridge open. Captain Le Boudec, who had also held out on E10 until now, collapsed with an arm smashed by shell fragments. Finally, 0330, Lt. Weinberger collected two small platoons of walking wounded Legionnaires on E12 and had come to shore up the defenses of E10.

But Lecour-Grandmaison had the farthest to go in order to reach E2, and the whole route now was under enemy fire. For almost two agonizing hours he attempted to climb E2, but in preparation for the general attack, Viet-Minh artillery had the strongpoint perfectly boxed in. After informing Langlais of the situation, the rapidly melting band of paratroopers received orders to move to E4, where Bréchignac and Botella were again in the process of mounting a counterattack. By a miracle M/Sgt. Robert and two of the Vietnamese PIM's managed to get through to E4 with six boxes of hand grenades, and the counterattack succeeded. At dawn, E4, save for a small chink of perhaps twenty meters in depth on the eastern flank, was again totally in French hands. Of the small unit that had followed Lecour-Grandmaison on E4 there remained only the officer himself, his radio operator, and a Vietnamese and a Foreign Legion paratrooper.

Of all this, however, Pouget on E2 was fully ignorant. He could not understand why, after the incredibly successful defense of E2 thus far, headquarters would abandon him and his companions to their fate.

He remembered that Coutant had left behind his own radio set with which he could reach Col. Lemeunier, the senior Foreign Legion commander in de Castries' headquarters.

Lemeunier's chief of staff, the tall Major Michel Vadot, picked up the microphone to answer. Vadot, during the fifty-five days of the battle, had established a solid reputation as being completely "unflappable." While others would curse over the radio waves or give vent to despair in the headquarters bunker, Vadot would go quietly about his business, shifting the last remaining units about on the acetate overlay of his large-scale map, asking a mortar battery here or a remaining howitzer section there to expend its last shells on a particularly critical target. But on May 7 in the early hours of dawn even he was at the end of his rope. At 0200, Dien Bien Phu's ammunition stocks were perilously low. There were exactly 100 rounds of 120-mm. mortar ammunition left and the remaining seven 105's together owned up to 300 shells, while the last 155, now firing directly 300 meters ahead of itself into Dominique at that moment, had exactly eleven shells. When Clédic on E4 discovered a large concentration of enemy infantry facing him on the slopes of E1 and asked Artillery to give him the kind of fire concentration which earlier in the evening had broken up the first Viet-Minh attack on E2, he got three rounds of artillery support.

Pouget was now once more pleading for reinforcements and ammunition. The calm voice of Vadot sounded like that of an old teacher trying to explain a difficult problem to a somewhat obtuse student:

"Come on, be reasonable. You know the situation as well as I do. Where do you want me to find a company? I can't give you a single man or a single shell, my boy."

But that moment, at about 0400, Captain Jean Pouget had about thirty-five men left alive and in fighting condition on the whole hill. Obviously, he thought, further resistance under such circumstances would be completely pointless and he requested from Vadot permission to abandon E2 and to break out in the direction of E3. There are two versions of what followed next. According to Jules Roy, Vadot is supposed to have said: "You're a paratrooper. You are there to get yourself killed." According to Pouget himself, Vadot said, after telling him that he had to fight on: "After all, you are a paratrooper and you must resist to the death—or at least until morning."[26]

There was nothing else to be said between the two men. Dien Bien Phu could no longer do anything for martyred Eliane 2, and Pouget, whose radio operator had been killed, no longer had any need for a transmitter.

"Understood. Out. If you have got nothing to add, I'll destroy my set," said Pouget.

The calm voice of Vadot seemed very far away, much farther than merely 400 meters of shell-pocked mud which actually separated the two men. Vadot also stuck to French Army radio protocol. "Out for me also."

"Don't destroy your radio set just yet," said a Vietnamese voice in French. "President Ho Chi Minh offers you a rendition of the *Chant des Partisans*." It was the voice of a People's Army radio operator listening in on the French command channel. And the beloved words which the French Resistance sang in the dark days when it fought against the Nazi occupier could be clearly heard on the command channel. Pouget listened to it, from the first verse which spoke of the black crows—that is, the foreign occupiers—flying over the land, to the very last verse which speaks of black blood drying tomorrow on the roads, and ends on the haunting line: "Companions, Freedom is listening to us in the night . . ."

Then Pouget fired three bullets into his set and walked out of his command post.

Outside, there was a strange silence settling over Eliane 2 as, one by one, the last survivors of 2nd and 3d Companies, 1st Colonial Parachute Battalion, were running out of ammunition or were overwhelmed by the slowly advancing Viet-Minh infantry. By now, both sides were mostly fighting with hand grenades. As per orders, Pouget stayed on E2, slowly falling back northward, past the hulk of tank "Bazeilles." He had pulled out the safety ring from his last hand grenade and held the grenade in his right hand. Finally he was cornered in a trench element. His last handful of men piled all the bodies in the trench as a sort of barricade on one side for a final stand against the approaching Viet-Minh. When they were at a distance of five meters, Pouget threw his last grenade and was knocked down by arriving enemy concussion grenades. When he awoke, he was a prisoner.

That still left Sgt. Chabrier and his small band. He was kneeling in a trench giving first aid to a badly wounded sergeant from 3rd Company when the Viet-Minh assault force jumped into his trench. As he was being led away he all of a sudden heard, in the silence around him, the throaty and slow cough of a .50-cal. machine gun. In the burned-out hulk of tank "Bazeilles," Sergeants Bruni and Ballait were still firing at the oncoming enemy. It was 0440 of May 7, 1954. They were firing the last cartridges of Eliane 2.

The Last Day

When May 7 dawned over the valley of Dien Bien Phu, it turned out to be another messy monsoon day, with rain squalls and low-hanging clouds shrouding the surrounding mountain chains. None of the sixteen

C-119's available that day succeeded in making the run to Dien Bien Phu, but twenty-two C-47 *Dakotas* kept on flying supply runs until 1700. The French Air Force seemed to be determined to give Dien Bien Phu a rousing send-off. In addition to the sixteen French Navy fighter-bombers and one heavy *Privateer,* twenty-five B-26's and thirty fighters occasionally pierced the low cloud cover and dropped their deadly loads on friend and foe alike. For now Viet-Minh and French positions were so tightly interwoven that it was difficult to hit one without hitting the other, and the whole immediate rear of the Viet-Minh positions were now filled with the French prisoners from the units overrun during the previous nights. Major Thomas and Lts. Clédic and Lecour-Grandmaison were almost killed later that morning by French bombs after having escaped Communist bullets for fifty-six days. They were marching, with their hands tied behind their backs, in the slippery mud east of Eliane in the direction of the deep forest.

On what was left of the French position on E4, the situation was indescribable. There were now on the shell-scarred hill almost all the surviving heroes of the French paratroops: Bréchignac, Botella, Clédic. Pham Van Phu, Makoviak, Le Page, and many others. They had withstood the last enemy attack on the east flank at 0530 and had held on in the north and south. But now, like Pouget on E2, they were running out of ammunition. And there were the wounded. Incredible as this may seem, E4 also housed Airborne Surgical Team No. 6 under Dr. Vidal and the first-aid stations of the II/1 RCP under Dr. Jourdan as well as that of the 5th Vietnamese Paratroops, under Dr. Rouault. If possible, the plight of the wounded in the niches and burrows on the reverse flank of E4 was even worse than that of the combatants, who at least had fresh air in adequate amounts and stood a chance of dying swiftly from a bullet instead of being buried alive in the collapsing bunkers. Dr. Jourdan was seriously wounded around 0630, and so were Captains Guilleminot and Pham Van Phu and Lt. Latanne, of the Vietnamese Paratroops. Yet, the stunned survivors could see a fresh battalion of Viet-Minh troops assembling in full view on neighboring E1 for another assault. They knew they would not survive it.

At de Castries' headquarters, the bad news of the night was being rapidly collated so as to provide Hanoi with a clear picture of the situation. Everybody realized that the situation was bad, but it was not yet judged as desperate. As far as Langlais and Bigeard could see at about 0700, E4 and E10 could be held and E2 would have to be retaken temporarily, if every remaining clerk typist and mechanic had to be given a rifle to do it. In fact, Lt. Col. Lemeunier, the commander of the Foreign Legionnaires in the fortress, showed up at 0700 in full battle gear, having scraped together all the Foreign Legionnaires he could find. He was going to join Clémençon on Claudine in order to seal off the threatening gap between strongpoint Lily and C2, according to one version,[27] or reinforce E4, according to another.[28] But Langlais stopped him and told him to wait for the counterattack on E2. If only E2 could be retaken and held, operation "Albatross" would be tried the following night. But the counterattack on E2, blasted apart by the mine and covered by dead and dying men of both sides, never came off. General Giap had decided against giving the French any respite.

At 0805 began the final Communist attack on Elianes 4 and 10. At 0900, the Communist commander-in-chief called up the commander of the 308th Division, General Vuong Thua Vu, and told him:

"There are signs of confusion among the enemy ranks. They may surrender in numbers but they also made a sudden attempt at breaking through. Give orders to your men to stick closely to the enemy and not to let any of them escape."[29]

Finally, a few minutes after 0900, the northeastern flank of E4 finally caved in as screaming hordes of fresh Viet-Minh troops, now completely dressed in brand-new French camouflaged paratroop uniforms and American steel helmets (no doubt from equipment drops fallen on the enemy side), submerged what was left of E4. Undeterred, Lt. Makoviak and a handful of paratroopers held on to the communications trenches around the strongpoint's command post.

At about 0930, Bréchignac communicated once more with Bigeard and Langlais. The conversation, interrupted by clearly audible shouts of the last defenders and the screams of the wounded on E4, was of the same tenor as Capt. Pouget's earlier conversation with Maj. Vadot. There was no ammunition and no more reserves on E4 and none to be had elsewhere. The battalion commanders on the hill, Bréchignac and Botella, would stay with their men in the position. Dr. Pierre Rouault would also stay on. Such able-bodied officers and men as would still be capable of it would break out via E10, which was also about to be overrun. Using for the last time the cover nicknames they had adopted for their voice radio communications, Bréchignac spoke first:

"Brèche calling Bruno [Bigeard]. It's the end. Don't clobber us [with artillery]. There are too many wounded here."

Then it was the turn of Captain André Botella:

"Dédé calling Bruno. It's all over. They're at the CP. Goodby. Tell that guy Pierre [Langlais] that we liked him a lot."

Than a third, younger voice, was heard over the set. It was Botella's remaining staff officer, Monaco-born Lieutenant Jean Armandi. Armandi also had refused to abandon his chief and his wounded comrades on E4 and was going to go down with them as a ship's commander goes down with his vessel.

"I'm going to blow up the set," said the young voice on E4, and then the radio waves from Eliane carried for the last time the war cry of the French paratroopers:

"Hip-hip-hip-hurray! . . ."[30]

But it also had been too late for the able-bodied survivors to break out from E4. Lieutenant Lecour-Grandmaison and his handful of men stayed on with Bréchignac on the hill. They were too exhausted for yet another race with death across the fire-beaten approaches to the Nam Yum. Total exhaustion indeed had become a daily phenomenon, and Dr. Grauwin now began to report cases of men who suddenly died at their post without showing signs of combat-induced wounds. They had died of fifty-five days of not sleeping, not eating, and not resting. But the indefatigable Clédic of the II/1 RCP tried to make a run for it. Flanked by his two remaining lieutenants, Albéric Pottier and Charles Césarini, and a handful of paratroopers, he literally slid down the muddy slope of E4 into the communications trench leading to E10, but too late. On E10 the Viet-Minh had also overwhelmed the last remnants of Bigeard's own 6th BPC under Maj. Thomas. A hand grenade burst near Clédic, stunning him and wounding Césarini, and Viet-Minh soldiers immediately pinned them down. A few minutes later they joined the officers of the 6th BPC in captivity.

Lieutenant Pottier was luckier. Having lagged behind during the descent from E4, he was behind a bend in the trench when Clédic was captured, managed to scramble out and find his way to the Bailey bridge, where two disabled but movable tanks were holding a small bridgehead opened with the help of the quad-fifties from Sparrowhawk. Another lucky man was Lt. René Le Page, of the 6th BPC. He and two of his paratroopers had crawled through the air hatch in the roof of a bunker on E10 and had jumped across a trench filled with enemy troops. Rolling through the mud of the approaches to the Nam Yum, they had eluded capture. A few seconds later they staggered into Bigeard's dugout, caked in mud from head to toe, and collapsed. Langlais, who had lived side by side with Bigeard throughout the whole battle and who had seen him

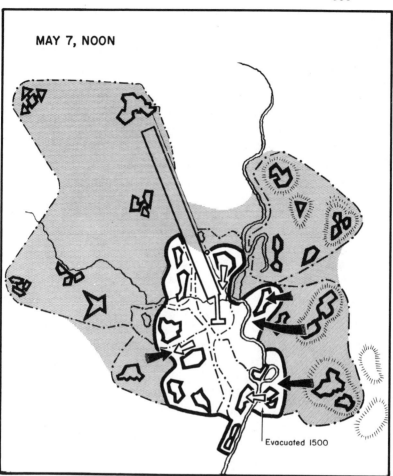

MAY 7, NOON

Evacuated 1500

accept unflinchingly the worst setbacks, for the first time saw him react
with a sense of personal loss. His beloved 6th Colonial Parachute
Battalion, which he had led from the hell of Tu-Lê, where it had been
offered up for sacrifice in 1952 to slow down the Viet-Minh advance in
northwestern Tonkin, and with which he had on March 28 taken the
enemy flak west of Claudine, had died.

Bending down over one of the mud-covered bodies whom only he
could recognize, Bigeard took its hand and said quietly: "Le Page, oh
oh my poor Le Page."

In Dr. Grauwin's hospital, there also had been a sudden influx of
hallucinating mud statues, some of them with one leg, all of them naked

or almost completely naked under the dirt. One of them was Dr. Alphonse Rivier, from the 6th BPC, and the others were some of his wounded. And here again, the enemy had shown some of his surprising front-line chivalry. As the Viet-Minh overran the first-aid station, they made the wounded get out from among the dead and dying and told them: "Get back to the hospital and tell your doctor that we are coming soon." And as the Viet-Minh cleared the remaining trenches and bunkers in bitter hand-to-hand fighting, an enemy soldier suddenly entered the bunker with a hand grenade the pin of which already had been drawn. The French wounded in the bunker began to scream and one sergeant, lying paralyzed on a stretcher, frantically waved his two bandaged hands in the air and yelled in French: "We are wounded! We are wounded!" The enemy soldier nodded, turned around, and threw the hand grenade into the open trench outside.[31]

Now came the trial of the low-lying Elianes 11 and 12 and E3, to the south. Of those, only E3, again held by Legionnaires of the 1/13 Half-Brigade under Capt. Coutant, could be counted on to offer a prolonged defense. On E11 and 12, the remaining tribal T'ai of Maj. Chenel and the Moroccan Engineers under Capt. Fazentieux, were, after the destruction of the paratroopers, in no shape to resist the Viet-Minh. A few minutes after 1000, Fazentieux noted grimly that some of his Moroccans in the forward trenches were waving white towels knotted around their rifle barrels. They were to be overrun at 1210.

At 1000, de Castries spoke to Gen. Cogny over the radiotelephone. Although that conversation, as well as the last contact around 1700, was tape-recorded, there exist several conflicting versions as to what was said that day. And charges were made that the tapes were tampered with later on.[32] Existing written transcripts which this writer has seen also differ from the available tape recordings. However, there were sufficient outside witnesses to the conversation at Hanoi, including the American reporter David Schoenbrun from the Columbia Broadcasting System, that it is possible to affirm that the sum total of the differing records available indeed gives the full picture of what was said that day.

In terse fragments of phrases, his voice pitched even higher than usual, repeating himself and frequently stumbling over his words, de Castries gave Cogny a brief account of the situation in the valley. Most of the time, Cogny simply acknowledged the bad news by a grunted *"oui."*

"The following strongpoints have fallen: E2, E4, E10. The 6th BPC, the 2/1 RCP, and what was left of the Algerian Rifles."
"Oui."

"Anyhow, might as well write them off."
"*Oui.*"

For one instant, de Castries lapsed back into an aristocratic mannerism that consists in beginning every possible phrase with the formulation "*N'est-ce pas?*" ("Isn't it?")

"*N'est-ce pas?* There remains at present, in very weak shape of course, because we have pulled out everything we could on the western flank to shore up the east——"
"*Oui.*"
"——There remain just about two companies each [correcting himself], two companies in all for the two BEP's together."
"*Oui.*"
Three companies of the Moroccan Rifles, but which aren't worth anything, *n'est-ce pas?* . . . they weren't worth anything . . . that have collapsed."
"*Oui.*"
"Two companies of the 8th Parachute Assault . . ."
"*Oui.*"
"Three companies of BT2, but that's only normal because, as always, it is the Moroccan Rifles and the BT2 which have the most men left because they don't fight."
"Sure."
"*N'est-ce pas?* And there are about two companies left at the 1/2—at the 1/2 Foreign Legion. And there are just about two companies at the 1/13 Half-Brigade. It's . . . they are companies of 70 or 80 [men]."
"*Oui.* I understand."
"Well—well, we're holding on claw, tooth, and nail."
"*Oui.*"
"We're holding on claw, tooth and nail and I hope, I hope that by using our means to the maximum [static—de Castries probably said "We should be able to stop the enemy . . ."] on the Nam Yum."
"Hello, hello," shouted Cogny.
"Hello," said de Castries, "can you hear me, General?"
". . . that by stretching your means to the utmost?" repeated Cogny.
" . . . would be to stop the enemy at the Nam Yum."
"*Oui.*"
"*N'est-ce pas?* Even so we have to hold on to the eastern river bank[33] or we would be without water."
"*Oui.* Of course."

"*N'est-ce pas?*"

Then de Castries described to Cogny his proposal for the breakout plan for the following night and described to him what he knew of the enemy's order of battle: There seemed to be now the whole 312th and 316th Divisions engaged in the attack on the eastern flank, along with Regiments 88 and 102 of the 308th Division, with only the Regiment 36 of that division remaining on the western flank.

Then came the part of the conversation dealing with Operation "Albatross," cited earlier. Cogny, who had been specifically given authorization by Gen. Navarre on May 5 to approve the breakout whenever de Castries felt that it became necessary, approved it without any of the hesitations he later was said to have had about it. General Pierre Bodet, Navarre's deputy, remained at Cogny's side throughout that day. He heard Cogny's decision and transmitted it at 1330 to Navarre, who happened that day to be in the ancient Vietnamese imperial capital of Hué.

At Dien Bien Phu, de Castries now had to face up to the hardest part of his conversation with Cogny—that dealing with the fate of that part of the garrison which could not even attempt a breakout: the wounded, the service troops unused to jungle warfare, and the Rats of the Nam Yum.

"Well then, *mon Dieu,* I'll keep here, well—those units which don't want any part of it."

"That's it, yes."

"Then—well, how shall I put it, [there are] the wounded, of course; but many of them are already in the hands of the enemy because they were on the strongpoints Eliane 4 and Eliane 10, those wounded . . . ?"

"Of course, yes."

"*N'est-ce pas?* And then, I'll keep all that under my command."

"*Oui,* old boy."

"That's it then."

"*Au revoir,* old boy."

"I'll still be able to telephone you again before [there was a moment of hesitation and faltering in de Castries' voice]—before the end."

"Come, come—*au revoir,* Castries, old boy."

"*Au revoir,* General."

"*Au revoir,* old boy."

At 1115, Cogny sent a brief message, which apparently was not received or acknowledged, to Col. Lalande on Isabelle. The message, interestingly enough, again contained an ambiguity about whether the "Albatross" breakout should be attempted, as if Cogny had not given Dien Bien Phu the authorization to attempt it just one hour earlier:

> It is understood that I leave it to your initiative to decide when "Albatross" should be executed. Stop. Keep me informed of your intentions. Stop. Inform me of any request you deem useful. Stop. If you are without further communication with GONO [the main position at Dien Bien Phu] you come directly under my orders. Stop.

But while de Castries and Cogny were speaking, Dien Bien Phu itself was disintegrating. Miraculously, the quad-fifties of Lt. Redon were still firing and still provisioned with ammunition, for they constituted by now the last fire base available to the garrison. Virtually buried under the mounds of spent cartridges, their throaty and regular "blam-blam-blam" clearly dominated all other sounds on the French side as they hacked away at the Communist assault troops now massing on the eastern bank of the Nam Yum.

In the west, Claudine was also cracking. At dawn, Capt. Coldeboeuf had established a last blocking position between Lily, where the last Moroccans of Maj. Nicolas were holding on, and C4. Every able-bodied soldier was being used, for if the western flank also broke wide open, there would be not enough left of Dien Bien Phu to even attempt a breakout during the following night. Also, Claudine was the strongpoint that was the closest to the western hills. Until then, it had been the least densely encircled of all the strongpoints. Any attempt at a breakout would have to go over Claudine or Juno.

To the north, the end now was near for Maj. Tourret on Sparrowhawk and for Capt. Bizard's little force still holding on to the nameless strongpoint in the drainage ditch. At 1030 they received orders to pull back to a new blocking position just north of de Castries' own command post; Bizard, in fact, was told to remain ready for the planned counter-attack on E2.

The news that a breakout was to take place that evening had now spread across the camp like wildfire. It also became known that only the cream of the remaining troops would be allowed to attempt it, those in best physical condition and who had shown in the past their ability to fight well. Each man was to take a double load of ammunition, two days of emergency rations, and a tent-half. Although one doctor, Lieutenant Patrice de Carfort, from the 8th Parachute Assault, would make the break with the column, no wounded would be taken along and all casualties sustained during the breakout would be ruthlessly abandoned.

During the morning, one by one, the breakout elements began to assemble on Juno. In many cases, the choice had been agonizing and meant leaving behind many officers and men who had fought magnificently. While no one could have stopped him from coming along, it was obvious that Col. Langlais, for one, would have collapsed from sheer exhaustion within the first few kilometers—assuming that he would have survived the fighting of the breakout. Sergeant Kubiak, who had been selected to be among those who would attempt the breakout, went to say good-bye to his wounded comrades from the 1st Battalion, 13th Foreign Legion Half-Brigade, who would stay behind. Some of them cried, not for fear of their fate, for it was known by then that the Communists did not massacre prisoners, but out of shame that they would have to surrender to the enemy. Kubiak remembered one soldier in particular who argued desperately that he could make the trek: one of his legs had been amputated.

What the soldiers and lower-ranking officers at Dien Bien Phu did not know was that a large part of the breakout force was to be deliberately offered up for sacrifice to insure the passage of at least a small part of it. As the situation developed when "Albatross" was first actively considered on May 5, the only path which offered even a remote chance of success was a westward dash into the mountains, provided enough enemy troops could be tied down by other French forces heading toward certain destruction in the direction where the Viet-Minh expected them; that is, southward where Col. de Crèvecoeur's "Condor" force was still holding its own. Lalande's column on Isabelle could be counted upon to head southward in any case. But in the main position of Dien Bien Phu a life-or-death choice would have to be made. Bigeard proposed a simple system, which Langlais accepted. Two columns would be formed—one of paratroopers under Bigeard and one of "Legs" (as their American counterparts would call nonjumpers) under Maj. Vadot. When the decision would be made to break out, the commanders would simply draw straws to determine their own fate and that of their troops: a long straw meant a dash toward the nearby mountains in the west and a chance of survival after a fairly grueling march through 100 kilometers of jungle. A short straw meant a deliberately suicidal attack in the wrong direction in order to give the winners a chance at surviving.[34] At 1200, Langlais called the remaining available unit commanders for a final conference in his CP bunker: Bigeard, Tourret, and Guiraud from the paratroops; Lemeunier, Vadot, and Clémençon from the Foreign Legion. Many of the officers had not had anything warm to eat in days. Langlais served them warm soup brought over from the nearby hospital kitchen. Just before they had begun to eat, a French Navy F4U *Corsair* fighter had roared low over the camp, as it had almost every day at noon and had dropped a bag of mail and, above all, an eagerly awaited new set of aerial photographs taken the previous day by the French Air Force. Langlais and Bigeard had rapidly looked them over as the conference now began.

In a few words, Bigeard explained once more the plan of the breakout, which he had dubbed Operation *"Percée de Sang"* [Bloodletting]. However, the aerial photographs dropped by the Corsair had added a new element of desperation to the already hazardous plan: three new Communist trenches now barred the last open stretch of terrain south of Juno. Even by offering up a maximum of troops, it was doubtful that anything more than a handful of scattered survivors would ever leave the valley. To make that kind of all-out assault against the strongly fortified enemy position with troops as exhausted as those now left at Dien Bien Phu would lead to a pointless butchery. One by one, the battalion commanders confirmed that none of their units was in such shape as to mount, let alone survive, such an assault. That ended all thoughts of implementing "Albatross."

What remained now was to consider the alternatives. At first glance, there seemed to be two: to capitulate, as the British had at Singapore, the Americans at Corregidor, and even the Germans at Stalingard; or to fight on, asking for no quarter, as Botella, Bréchignac, and Pouget had done on the Elianes, as the Americans had at the Alamo, or the Foreign Legion at Camerone.

"You can do Camerone with a hundred guys, not with 10,000." It was probably one of the Foreign Legion officers present who dropped that remark. Indeed, it was all well and good for the able-bodied men to fight on heroically but not at the expense of those thousands who now were drowning in the mud of the open trenches surrounding the hospital and whom Grauwin and the last remaining Airborne Surgical Teams no longer could accommodate. Now that a breakout was no longer possible, to resist throughout the next night at the expense of killing or wounding another 300 to 500 men was worse than useless. There was a third way to end the fighting without abandoning the garrison to total chaos and yet without striking the flag in a formal capitulation. And that was to inform Gen. Giap that the main position of Dien Bien Phu would cease firing at 1730. At 1300 the conference broke up and Langlais, accompanied by Bigeard, Lemeunier, and Vadot, went to see de Castries.

Outside, where the monsoon weather had temporarily cleared, the Viet-Minh were now massing for the final assault across the Nam Yum. A new assault force appeared to have joined them; troops who until now must have been held in reserve and who wore brand-new French uniforms. A small group of about 100 Communist soldiers tried to wade across the Nam Yum south of E3 where only the wounded from Juno were defending their position. Sergeant Kubiak, who had just returned from E3, noticed with amazement an automatic-rifle team firing point-blank into the Communist assault wave. The rifleman wore an extensive blood-soaked bandage around his waist, leaving a bloody print on the ground every time he shifted position. Passing him the loaded ammunition clips was a one-armed soldier who also wore a bandage around his chest. This enemy attack was stalled by the infantry fire from Juno, and for a time it seemed as if the tiny strongpoints E11 and E12, which covered the approaches to the Bailey bridge, and E3, which still covered Juno and the wooden footbridge, would hold out until nightfall. At 1439, there still seemed some stubborn hope somewhere in the valley that a break could be made, as Supply sent a curt message to Hanoi: "Can we, yes or no, count today on low-altitude drops of ammunition? Reply urgently needed."

But at 1500, with the most battleworthy Foreign Legionnaires having been pulled out for "Albatross," the remaining Moroccans on E3 were panicking. Waving white towels or their own unrolled turbans, they crawled out of the trenches in the direction of the oncoming enemy. Apparently, that gave Gen. Giap the cue that the French were no longer determined to hold the other side of the Nam Yum and that in all probability they had given up any idea of prolonging their resistance beyond the following night. Therefore he departed from his extremely conservative attitude and at 1500 ordered the siege force to pursue its attack relentlessly from both the eastern and western flanks. He re-emphasized the importance of a tight encirclement of the French so as not to let any of them escape.[35]

In de Castries' bunker, his meeting with the senior troop commanders was brief and dignified. The troop commanders told de Castries what he already knew: that the main position of Dien Bien Phu could not hold until nightfall and therefore they could not attempt to execute an organized breakout. They also told him that it would be necessary to contact the enemy and inform him of the fact that resistance would cease at a given time, so as to forestall a partial massacre of the disarmed wounded and of the units which had run out of ammunition. In view of the time required to contact some of the now isolated forward elements by radio, and also the desirability of avoiding the chaos that would surely ensue if resistance would cease in the dark, 1730 was chosen as the time to cease resistance. It would be Langlais' GAP 2 that would contact the enemy by radio.

There was little left to say. De Castries was preoccupied by what would happen to Bigeard, whose very name was hated by the Viet-Minh. There were many accounts to be settled between Bigeard and his 6th Parachute Battalion on one hand, and the enemy on the other. Turning to him, de Castries said:

"My poor Bruno, you should try and get away now with a few of your men. The Viets would only be too happy to get you."

Bigeard refused and said something to the effect that he would attempt to get away only if it meant a general breakout, but not if it meant leaving his men behind. In that case, he would prefer to attempt an evasion later. For the last time he rendered a formal military salute to de Castries, then shook his hand, and left the room with all the other officers save Langlais. Upon arriving in his dugout, Bigeard destroyed all his remaining personal effects and notes and then carefully rolled a silk escape map of the northwestern mountain region around one of his ankles; it might come in handy later. At about the same time, Lt. Col. Séguin-Pazzis called Col. Lalande over the radio. In a calm voice, without giving any indication as to what was going on at Dien Bien Phu, he gave the commander of Isabelle the choice of the alternatives which the senior officers at the main position of Dien Bien Phu had just faced up to: to break out, to fight to the last ditch on the position, or to cease fire at a given hour. Lalande opted for the breakout.

All this seems a great deal more orderly than it really was, for many of these events took place simultaneously and Dien Bien Phu did not speak to Hanoi with a single voice, since, as has been shown earlier, several other radio transmitters at Dien Bien Phu were capable of contacting their opposite numbers "on the outside." Thus, the radio transmitter with the call letters 9-DMO of the 31st Engineers informed the Northern Engineering Command at 1555 that all mail for Maj. Durieux, its commander, should be destroyed. And at 1610, it asked its correspondent in Hanoi to send telegrams of good health to all the families of the battalion's members in France.* Apparently, the 31st Engineers already had been informed of what was coming or acted on the basis of its role under "Albatross," for it informed Hanoi at 1615 that "by order of Commanding General, GONO, Engineering Battalion shall remain on the spot in view of eventual re-establishment of airstrip and for de-mining purposes."

At the headquarters of the Northern Command in Hanoi, where all those various messages were collated, a staff officer noted in the head-quarters journal that "We have the impression that General de Castries is no longer in control of the situation [. . . *ne commande plus* . . .]," as his headquarters canceled the request for ammunition which it had passed earlier and now requested exclusively a drop of food rations. At the same moment, Supply repeated its earlier request of "yes or no, are we going to get ammunition?" while the Air Controller at Dien Bien Phu, Maj. Guérin, reconfirmed to his superiors that ammunition was still a top priority item. But the contradictions were mostly due to the time lag between the arrival of the messages at their various destinations in Hanoi and their centralized collation at headquarters. In fact, Guérin had been called in personally by de Castries a few minutes before 1600 and had been told to call for a complete stoppage of aerial combat support as of 1700 and a switching to food rations as of 1600, with cancellation of ammunition drops already under way.

Shortly after 1600, the end came for E11 and E12, the last bridge-heads east of the Nam Yum. A brief message was heard from Lt. Allaire—the same officer who had been looking for his mortars in the valley of Dien Bien Phu ages ago, on November 20, 1953, when the French had first landed there. Allaire simply said: "They're coming at us without shooting." On Sparrowhawk, the last heavy mortars of Lt. Bergot had run out of Ammunition and as he looked behind him at the nearby central command post of Gen. de Castries he could see dark billows rising above it, and smaller ones at other places throughout the camp: "The black smoke of panic," he would call it later.[36] Over on Claudine, where the Foreign Legionnaires were still holding on to their rain-swamped trenches, a Vietnamese interpreter with the Legionnaires, Sgt. Kim, already noticed at 1500 that the remaining riflemen from the T'ai battalions were putting on civilian clothes. Incredible as it may

---

* Such telegrams sent by the rear bases of units committed at Dien Bien Phu were to have tragic consequences later when it turned out that men who had been killed at Dien Bien Phu during the bitter fighting of the last few days still were listed as the authors of such telegrams. Up to May 5, however, Personnel at Dien Bien Phu had carefully radioed the names of all casualties to Hanoi.

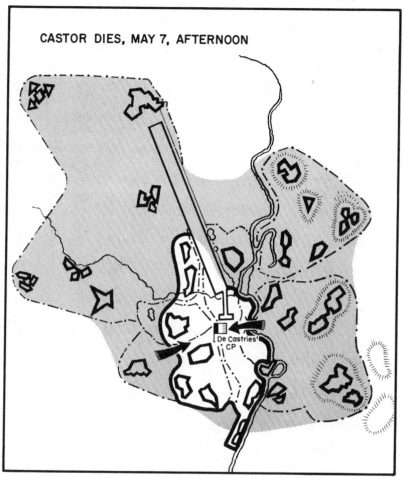

CASTOR DIES, MAY 7, AFTERNOON

De Castries' CP

seem, there were still 200 civilians, including women and children, in the fortress and they were now attempting to flee southward in direction of Ban Co My. With them were the twenty-nine native members of Dien Bien Phu's Intelligence detachment. They knew what would happen if they fell into enemy hands.

There also was on Claudine the Foreign Legion's field brothel. The five Vietnamese girls and their madame had been caught in the battle like everyone else and had lived through it in underground bunkers as auxiliary nurses, like the Algerian prostitutes who had also been unable to leave and had stayed on Dominique. If ever there was a "redemption" on earth of wayward girls, in the biblical tradition, it had taken place here at Dien Bien Phu. Often the women were seen in the water of a trench up to their hips, waiting to help the wounded in a strongpoint. In one case, a shell-shocked soldier had developed a fixation that he was a small child and had to be fed by his mother; one of the Vietnamese prostitutes came to his dugout every day to feed him. As the news spread that Dien Bien Phu was to cease fire late in the afternoon, Capt. Coldeboeuf, upon returning to C4, ran into the madame of the Vietnamese brothel. Considering the puritanical attitude of the Communists, it was very likely that she and her girls would spend an indefinite period in a Viet-Minh "re-educational labor camp" from which their chances of release or even survival would be slim.

"What are you going to do?" said Coldeboeuf to the woman. The madame, looking incongruously "normal" in the apocalyptic environment of a dying fortress, looked at Coldeboeuf with her wise and weary eyes, shrugged her shoulders, and said:

"Oh, I'll just tell them that we have been kidnapped by the Legion in Hanoi and brought here by force."

Perhaps the ruse worked. Perhaps it did not. In any case, the Vietnamese prostitutes were never seen again. Of the eleven Algerian prostitutes, four were killed during the battle. Most of the others eventually went to live with the Rats of the Nam Yum, and all of them later shared the hardships of the prisoner trek. One of them, known as "Mimi-des-Oulad-Naïls," married a fellow Algerian prisoner in the hospital camp and had her first child in Communist-ruled Hanoi.[37]

On Juno, Coutant's small band was firing its last cartridges. Looking out of his trench, Sgt. Kubiak thought he saw a huge white flag flying on Gen. de Castries' command post. In actual fact, it was one of the large white cargo parachutes which had been hanging for the last three days on a well-known tree stump left standing near the command post. Contrary to what was affirmed later by one French source,[38] both the other survivors *and* Gen. Giap, as will be seen later, are in full accord that the only flag which flew over Dien Bien Phu an hour later was the gold-starred red flag of the siege force with the Vietnamese inscription *"Quyêt Chien—Quyêt Thang"* [To Fight and To Win] that had been the motto of the enemy.[39] In any case, that was the last Sgt. Kubiak was to see of the battle. An enemy shell exploded nearby, mangling his right leg, and he collapsed in the mud-soaked trench. At the very same moment an enemy soldier of the first assault wave jumped across the trench, stopped, looked down on him and walked back. He slowly raised his submachine gun to the firing position, but as he was to pull the trigger the ear-shattering staccato of another tommy gun exploded nearby and the Communist soldier, killed by another Legionnaire, collapsed directly on top of Kubiak. The body of the dead Viet-Minh protected Kubiak from further harm until he was collected next morning by Viet-Minh stretcher bearers.

In Dr. Grauwin's underground hospital, the news of what was going to happen had first come via Maj. Tourret from the 8th Parachute Assault, as he was returning from a last call on de Castries before the end.

"That's it, Doc, it's all over. . . . At 1730 we cease firing, we cease all resistance. Those who can will destroy their weapons and will blow up the ammunition depots."

Like many other officers in that hour, there was a veil of tears over Tourret's eyes. Grauwin turned to his personnel and told them to put on standard uniforms (most of them, including Grauwin, had been working in the stifling heat in nothing else but shorts) with Red Cross arm bands to properly identify them, as required by the Geneva Conventions. Otherwise, their work continued, as if nothing had changed. Grauwin was to recall later that his very last surgical patient before the end of the fighting had been Capt. Le Boudec from the 6th BPC, who had been dragged back across the river in the afternoon. Le Boudec was lying under sedation on the operating table when the first Viet-Minh soldiers entered the hospital. On hearing the commotion, he suddenly awoke and asked groggily: "Are our reinforcements coming in?" No one answered him.

At the central command post, two events now took place simultaneously. In his own bunker, Lt. Col. Séguin-Pazzis at 1630 began to personally call every strongpoint to inform them now of the impending cease-fire and patiently waiting in every case for the full acknowledgment:

"By order of the Commanding General, the cease-fire will be effective as of 1700. All equipment and supplies will be destroyed."

In some cases, notably on Claudine, it was later distinctly remembered that he had added a phrase formally forbidding the raising of white flags. The tone employed by the chief of staff in his last message was deliberately terse and curt. That was the only way he could communicate without letting his listener hear that he was crying.

On the secret Z.13 ultrashort-wave transmitter, de Castries was now engaged in a last conversation with Hanoi. He was at first speaking to Gen. Bodet alone, then to Bodet and Gen. Cogny together, and lastly to Cogny alone. At the Dien Bien Phu end of the line the witnesses were Col. Langlais, who was listening in on the second earphone, and de Castries' own radio operator, Sgt. Millien.

At first, de Castries gave Bodet a full picture of the situation at Dien Bien Phu as of 1700:

"We're submerged. The three strongpoints east of the Nam Yum have now fallen. I don't know anymore where my wounded are and my unit commanders are trooping around me asking what to do next. We're now under the fire of the 'Stalin Organs.'* My men are simply automatons falling apart from lack of sleep."

General Bodget then replied: "Let the battle 'die' and let Lalande make a try for 'Albatross.' We won't let you down. Thanks for the handsome defense."

There was a silence at the other end and then the air waves crackled again and de Castries said, harking back to the days of 1940 when he several times parted ways with his German captors: "One can also escape from the Viet-Minh."

Then de Castries explained that at 1730 he would contact the enemy and inform him that tomorrow there would be Red Cross aircraft coming with supplies for the wounded.

It is probably in connection with de Castries' suggestion to send somebody over to the Viet-Minh at 1730 under what obviously would have had to be a white flag of truce that the conversation between Cogny and de Castries turned to the problem of not hoisting a white flag. In view of the divergence of the existing records, only a joint declaration by all the witnesses to the conversations on both ends would establish ultimate reliability of what exactly was said.

According to the official *Agence France-Presse* of May 8, 1954, Gen. Cogny is supposed to have said: "You will fight to the end. There is no question about raising the white flag over Dien Bien Phu after your heroic resistance."

According to the information received by the French writer Jules Roy from Gen. Cogny himself, that same phrase (although it allegedly was cut from the authoritative magnetic tape of the conversation) ran as follows:

"Don't mess up [your magnificent defense] by hoisting the white flag. You are going to be submerged, but no surrender, no white flag."

According to Maj. Pouget, who had been Gen. Navarre's aide and who had received from him the transcript made by Gen. Bodet, the conversation ran as follows:

"Tell me, old boy, this has to be finished now, of course, but not in the form of a capitulation. That is forbidden to us. There can be no

---

* French Army nickname for the Soviet multiple-rocket launchers used by the Viet-Minh.

hoisting of the white flag, the fire has to die of its own, but do not capitulate. That would mess up all that you have done that is magnificent until now."

"All right, General. I only wanted to preserve the wounded."

"Yes; however, I do have a piece of paper. I haven't got the right to authorize you to capitulate. Well you'll do as best you can—but this must not end by a white flag. What you have done is too fine for that. You understand, old boy?"[40]

General de Castries understood. There are several versions as to the very last words of the official radio traffic between Dien Bien Phu and the outside. According to the French press agency the conversation ended with an inspirational:

"The transmitter shall be destroyed at 1730. We shall fight to the end. *Au revoir, Général. Vive la France!*"

But it places a final brief exchange of words at 1730 precisely, in the course of which de Castries said: "I'm blowing up all the installations. The ammunition depots are already exploding. *Au revoir.*" There is an indication in the Headquarters journal that a short conversation of that kind may well have taken place at 1730. All other sources seemed to agree that the conversation ended on a banal: "Well then, *au revoir,* old boy." It was General René Cogny, the French commanding general in North Viet-Nam, who had said those banal words as a fitting epitaph for the dying fortress.

But a few instants after 1730 the assembled generals and other observers in Hanoi heard a voice with which they were unfamiliar. It was that of Sgt. Millien who, after seven months of total anonymity, was signing off and thus entered history:

"In five minutes, everything will be blowing up here. The Viets are only a few meters away. Greetings to everybody."

And the background crackling of the transmitter ceased. In the staff room in Hanoi the heat was stifling, and that was fortunate, for it was impossible to distinguish the sweat from the tears which were running down everybody's face. The one American present, David Schoenbrun, who had been a keen observer of the French scene for almost a decade and who had met with Ho Chi Minh shortly before the Indochina War had broken out, distinctly felt that what he was witnessing here, as day turned into dusk on May 7, was the end of the French adventure in Indochina and, indeed, the end of the French Empire.[41]

But, somehow, this was not the last message to come from Dien Bien

Phu. Prosaically, the Combat Engineers were still passing their traffic to the last minute. According to the records, it was at 1750, or eighteen minutes after the last message from de Castries' transmitter, that 9-DMO signed off with a quiet:

"We're blowing up everything. Adieu."

Dusk

At the news that fighting was to cease at 1730, a veritable orgy of destruction had seized the remaining able-bodied members of the garrison. Each carefully maintained infantry weapon was being fired with the barrel stuck into the ground, thus bursting it. The crew of tank "Auerstaedt" drained the oil out of the tank's engine and then raced it until it died, its insides destroyed beyond repair. The Viet-Minh would later succeed in putting one tank back in operation by cannibalizing parts from all ten of them—but even that one tank had no combat value: its gun had no breechblock. In the gun pits, the African gunners were methodically smashing all optical equipment and dumping into the deep mud the breechblocks of their pieces. Wherever possible, a white-phosphorus hand grenade was thrown into the gun barrel to literally melt its inner lining so as to make the piece permanently unusable. In any case, there was little of the artillery left in a usable state. As we have seen, the American 105's which the French had at Dien Bien Phu were known for their extremely vulnerable hydraulic counter-recoil mechanisms, which the slightest mortar fragment could pierce, making the whole gun unusable. That is how Isabelle had lost the night before eight guns out of nine inside two hours, and in the afternoon of May 7, there was exactly one single 105 in the main position of Dien Bien Phu capable of firing. The dispersion of the remaining artillery ammunition in the main position solved the problem of its destruction. A total of only about 300 shells finally fell into enemy hands, and those were stacked too close to a strongpoint to be safely exploded.

At the central command post itself, a strange kind of silence had settled down now that all the transmitters were smashed. A few telephone lines still functioned, connecting mainly the CP with the hospitals, the artillery, and GAP 2. The electricity still functioned (it was never to cease functioning entirely over the next few days, as the Viet-Minh realized how important it was for the normal functioning of the camp, whether the French or they themselves were in control of it). After the radio conversation with Cogny had ended, Langlais and de Castries looked at each other in silence. There had been many a day in the past fifty-six when the scrawny, hard-drinking paratroop colonel from Brittany had argued with the handsome lisping aristocrat, who was his nominal commander but who was seemingly content to let Langlais run the battle by himself with the help of his small mafia of battalion commanders.

But in the last few days of the siege, when there was nothing to command and where the higher courage consisted simply in accepting one's fate with fortitude, de Castries had again come to the fore as a man who was perhaps better than his reputation. These were the last moments of freedom and, perhaps, of life, for both men if the enemy proved unmerciful. They embraced and then shook hands before Langlais returned to his dugout to burn his personal papers, his official documents, and, finally, his beloved red paratroop beret, which he traded against the anonymous hat of an infantryman. In full defiance, Bigeard kept his beret high on his head for everyone to see. If they, the Viet-Minh, hated the paratroops, so be it. He was one of them to the end.

As the firing died down over the main position—artillery rumbling could be heard, and flashes and geysers of dust could clearly be seen rising over faraway Isabelle, which was still fighting—the swift thumping noise of sandal-clad feet could now be heard on the roofs of the dugouts, followed shortly thereafter by a hasty "flick-flock" in the mud of the communication trenches, and a few seconds later an Asian head, covered with a flat helmet adorned with grass or branches, would show up in the doorway of a bunker. Probably both sides were amazed to find that the other was human at all after what had happened here for months. The little Asian, often barely a shade over five feet tall and hardly ever looking more than fifteen years old even when he was twice that age, would wave a Russian-made submachine gun with its curved ammunition clip and say *"Di, di, mau-lên!* [Go, go, quick!]" or he would say in guttural French: *"Sortez!* [Get out!]" and a new group of Frenchmen, Africans, Legionnaires, or Nationalist Vietnamese (but weren't those who had defeated them also entitled to the word "Nationalist"?) began their apprenticeship as prisoners of the Viet-Minh.

The command bunker was taken almost precisely at 1730. A small five-man assault team armed with automatic weapons and commanded by a Captain Ta Quang Luat and followed by the squad leaders Van and Chu Ba Thé, stormed into the command bunker, shouting excitedly the name of de Castries. They finally found him in his dugout, standing erect and impeccably dressed in a clean tan uniform with his bright red Spahi cap and one row of medal ribbons. It is not clear whether he wore his general's insignia or the stripes of a colonel. Some who saw him that day affirmed that he wore colonel's insignia—in the forlorn hope perhaps that the Communists did not know they were capturing a French general. Soon de Castries' whole staff of twenty-three officers and men was assembled around him. What was said on either side remains somewhat fuzzy as memories play tricks. Hearsay information picked up in the prison camps becomes confused with what one heard firsthand; and the desire to sublimate a harrowing experience becomes evident in every survivor. De Castries is said to have exclaimed either, "Don't shoot me!" or, "Don't shoot!"

But we also have a remarkable non-Asian source on the other side: the Russian film reporter Roman Lazarevich Karmen. Karmen had been sent to Dien Bien Phu by his government to help the North Vietnamese make a cinematographic record of the battle, but had been delayed en route by French bombings of the supply lines. However, he had arrived on the battlefield just a few days after the fight was over and had spoken to the young Viet-Minh company commander. According to Karmen—and under the circumstances this seems a likely question— the Viet-Minh captain looked at the assembled Frenchmen and asked: "Which one of you is General de Castries?"

De Castries identified himself and, apparently as he had planned earlier, asked the enemy officer whether he could tell his own troops to cease fighting. Ta Quang Luat answered with the assurance of the victor, to which he was clearly entitled:

"That's superfluous. They've already given up without your order. We've won."[42]

In silence, the staff began to file out of the command bunker. In the disintegrating sandbags atop its curved steel roof, three Viet-Minh soldiers, including platoon leader Chu Ba Thé, were planting the gold-starred red flag. That a red flag flew over the command bunker at Dien Bien Phu at about 1740 of May 7, 1954, is absolutely certain. Thousands of men saw it, and many of them mentioned it to me. None of them saw a white flag on top of the bunker and not once did even Communist propaganda invent one. A few days later, the planting of the red flag was re-enacted by the Viet-Minh for the Soviet cameraman Karmen. They could just as well have re-enacted a white flag fluttering over the bunker, being eventually replaced by the victorious red flag. I personally saw the film in Hanoi in its uncut version: nowhere was a white flag in sight. Dien Bien Phu had *fallen* to the enemy, but it had *not capitulated*.

In the failing daylight, the valley of Dien Bien Phu represented an incredible mixture of complete human misery as friend and foe alike made their way through the deep mud, and of pristine luxury as in some places mounds of rotting dead, the agonizing wounded, and foul-smelling trenches were covered with the immaculate whiteness of the last misdropped parachutes. A total of 82,926 parachutes had been dropped into the valley, including 3,763 huge cargo parachutes. Dien Bien Phu was the first battlefield in history in which not only the dead combatants but even the ground itself wore a white silk shroud.

The western flank of the fortress was the last to be occupied by the Viet-Minh, since its positions were still covered by extensive mine fields and barbed-wire entanglements. Some of the strongpoints on Claudine were occupied as late as 1820. One of the last to be occupied was strongpoint Lily, still held by a handful of Moroccans under Major Jean Nicolas. As Nicolas looked out over the battlefield from a slit trench near his command post, a small white flag, probably a handkerchief, appeared on top of a rifle hardly fifty feet away from him, followed by the flat-helmeted head of a Viet-Minh soldier.

"You're not going to shoot anymore?" said the Viet-Minh in French.

"No, I am not going to shoot anymore," said Nicolas.

"*C'est fini?*" said the Viet-Minh.

"*Oui, c'est fini,*" said the French major.

And all around them, as on some gruesome Judgment Day, mud-covered soldiers, French and enemy alike, began to crawl out of their trenches and stand erect as firing ceased everywhere.

The silence was deafening.

Finale

Isabelle's Night

AT 1755 OF MAY 7, 1954, Gen. Cogny contacted Col. Lalande on Isabelle and asked him what his plans were for the night, without making any reference to the fate that had already befallen the main position at Dien Bien Phu itself. But, smothered by heavy artillery fire as they were and unable to raise any of their usual radio contacts in the main position, the men on Isabelle knew very well what fate had befallen the garrison. While it may look inspirational in history books, there is no evidence that Gen. de Castries at Dien Bien Phu had requested that the last remaining artillery piece at Isabelle fire directly on his bunker during the last phase of the Viet-Minh attack on the central position. It is, however, likely that the lone howitzer continued to fire its normal supporting mission on Claudine but was told to cease firing at 1700. At about 1900, Isabelle destroyed its last heavy equipment, including Lt. Henri Préaud's tank *"Ratisbonne."*

Colonel Lalande had some misgivings about the southern itinerary. While he for obvious reasons had not participated in the discussions that had led to the planning of Operation "Bloodletting," he was well aware of the fact that the Viet-Minh would expect him to break out southward. But the fighting around Isabelle of the last few days seemed to show that the more daring northward operation would perhaps meet with greater success. What Lalande had in mind was to dash northward in the direction of Dien Bien Phu up to the village of Ban Loi; that is, just below the siege ring around the main position. Particularly with the main French position already in enemy hands, chances were that the trench system would be poorly manned and certainly not prepared for a French attack from Isabelle. At Ban Loi, then, Lalande planned on pivoting straight west across the Nam Yum and into the nearby forest north of Ban Co My. The plan was eminently sound and might even have had a chance of success. But, Gen. Cogny's headquarters in Hanoi remained mute when questioned by Lalande via the radio relay of the command plane circling overhead. In the face of that silence—there is no evidence from the existing radio message logs that an answer to that query was ever given—Lalande then decided to attempt the originally planned breakout in a southerly direction.

At 2140, Lt. Col. Dussol reported from command aircraft No. 545 "Yankee Alpha" a series of continuous explosions on Isabelle, which he identified as its depots being blown up. At 2200 the Air Force radio operator inside the aircraft, in charge of monitoring the channel of the SCR-300 radios of the infantry units inside Isabelle, suddenly overheard a conversation in Vietnamese. Since he was not sure whether they were radio operators from Vietnamese units inside Isabelle (there were none) or of Viet-Minh units on the siege ring using captured American radio sets, he addressed the radio operators in French. The conversation broke immediately and a guttural voice said: "What do you want, Monsieur?" The Air Force operator did not reply. The other two radio operators were from the enemy side. And they were openly operating on Isabelle's infantry channel.

And now Isabelle's breakout began. Scouting in the lead were the tough little tribesmen of Mobile Auxiliary Companies 431 and 432 of Lt. Wieme, followed by the 12th and 11th Companies of the 3/3 Foreign Legion under Maj. Grand d'Esnon. Lieutenant Préaud's tank crews, with the exception of two wounded men who had to be left behind in the infirmary, marched as a platoon with 11th Company. Behind them came Isabelle's headquarters unit, the remaining T'ai of Maj. Thimonier's 3rd BT, and Capt. Jeancenelle's 2nd Battalion, 1st Algerian Rifles. Here again, mythology must give way to history: there was no bayonet charge, as has been variously asserted, but there was no capitulation on Isabelle, either. On the contrary, Isabelle's garrison made the only organized attempt at breaking out from the doomed valley. And it almost succeeded.

The sortie was undertaken in three waves. The first, made up of 12th Company and Wieme's tribesmen, quietly slipped southward along the winding riverbed of the Nam Yum and covered nine kilometers before it ran into a Communist blocking position at Pom-Lot at around 0200 of May 8. Had there been more strength in that spearhead force, chances might have been good for more men to break out. In the ensuing fire fight, the small force was destroyed and Wieme was captured, but ten of his tribesmen and Sgt. Béguin, and two of the Legionnaires from 12th Company, managed to slip through.

The rest of the column never had a chance. The platoon formed by the tank crews, along with 11th Company, fell into a double ambush just one kilometer south of Isabelle. The Algerian riflemen who followed behind were barely out of the barbed-wire entanglements when they were attacked. And since they, in turn, were followed by a horde of walking wounded and other unarmed service personnel who had refused to be left behind, all discipline suddenly collapsed as part of the men attempted to go forward while others, including now Col. Lalande and his staff, attempted to regain the bunker line for a last stand. But the very chaos of that last battle, in total darkness except for the occasional glare of flare shells, gave those units who had retained some sort of cohesion a small chance. The tank crews veered sharply to the west into the nearby dark hills with a speed that surprised the enemy. Lieutenant Préaud and two of his men were captured, but the rest of the platoon managed to break away as a unit. Although they were to suffer casualties later, 2nd platoon of Composite Squadron, 1st Regiment of Armored *Chasseurs*, was the only unit to leave the valley as an organization rather than as a mob of individuals.

From where Algerian Lt. Belabiche was trying to keep the eighty men of his 8th Company together, the situation looked completely hopeless. He could not even order his men to shoot for fear that the shadows in front of him were friendly rather than enemy. The Viet-Minh seemed to have a similar problem, what with its troops now swarming all around the French, and it became suddenly clear to Belabiche that the Viet-Minh were no longer shooting at the men but rather were aiming over their heads. It would not be surprising that, as Jules Roy indicates, a small group of Viet-Minh officers under a flag of truce found it extremely difficult to make their way through that compact mass of humanity in order to meet Lalande and tell him to cease fighting, as further resistance was useless.

At 0150, the command aircraft picked up the very last message a Frenchman would send from Dien Bien Phu:

> Sortie failed—Stop—Can no longer communicate with you—
> Stop and end.

It was the end, indeed. The end of the Indochina War. The end of France as a colonial power.

Later that night, a *Privateer* four-engine bomber of French Navy

Squadron No. 28-F was shot down while bombing Viet-Minh communication lines along Road 41. Its pilot, Ensign Monguillon, and its crew of eight warrant officers and petty officers were the last Frenchmen killed in combat in the Battle of Dien Bien Phu.

Outside, May 7, 1954

There is a time-zone difference of seven hours between Paris and Dien Bien Phu. It was 1030, Paris time, on May 7, when the red flag was hoisted atop de Castries' command bunker at Dien Bien Phu. The news probably reached the French government around noon.

At 1630, the French government informed the National Assembly, France's major legislative body, that the Prime Minister would present it with an important communication. At 1645, the sixty-five-year-old Joseph Laniel, the bull-necked Norman who had become prime minister in June, 1953, mounted the tribune, escorted by several of his cabinet ministers. The Prime Minister was dressed entirely in black. The news of the disaster already had reached Paris and the hemicycle was filled with legislators. Every seat in the visitors' gallery and in the press section was taken.

The Prime Minister said in a voice which he vainly attempted to control and which was at first so low as to be barely audible even with the help of the public address system:

> The Government has been informed that the central position of Dien Bien Phu has fallen after twenty hours of uninterrupted violent combat.

As he said those words, his voice broke. There was an audible gasp in the audience, and in a clatter of seats, the legislators, the visitors, and the press rose to their feet, with the exception of the ninety-five Communists and M. Charles de Chambrun, a legislator from the Progressive Party allied with the Communists.

In the dead silence which followed, punctuated only by the loud sobs of a woman legislator, Laniel continued:

> Strongpoint Isabelle is still holding. The enemy has wanted to obtain the fall of Dien Bien Phu prior to the opening of the conference on Indochina. He believes that he could strike a decisive blow against the morale of France. He has responded to our goodwill, to France's will for peace, by sacrificing thousands of [his] soldiers to crush under their number the heroes who, for fifty-five days, have excited the admiration of the world . . .

. . . France must remind her allies that for seven years now the Army of the French Union has unceasingly protected a particularly crucial region of Asia and has alone defended the interests of all. All of France shares the anguish of the families of the fighters of Dien Bien Phu. Their heroism has reached such heights that universal conscience should dictate to the enemy—in favor of the wounded and of those whose courage entitles them to the honors of war—such decisions as will contribute more than anything to establish a climate favorable to peace.

The news of the disaster covered France like a thick blanket. Maurice Cardinal Feltin, the Archbishop of Paris, ordered a solemn Mass to be said for the dead and prisoners of Dien Bien Phu. The Paris Opéra, which was to be the host for the first time since the end of World War II to the Moscow Opera Ballet, canceled the whole series of Russian performances. French television—in France both radio and television are government-controlled—canceled its programs for the evening and the three radio networks canceled all entertainment shows and replaced them with programs of French classical music, and notably Hector Berlioz' *Requiem*. It was the only Requiem which the thousands of dead of Dien Bien Phu were ever going to get.

In Nice, on the French Riviera, the Chief of State of the non-Communist Vietnamese regime, Bao Dai (whose name, in translation, means "Keeper of Greatness," but who preferred the life of the French Riviera to the chores of facing a war in Viet-Nam), issued a statement of his own in which he thanked the French for the sacrifices they had made:

> Now that France has recognized the independence of Viet-Nam, no one can have any doubts as to the unselfish nobleness of her defense of the Vietnamese people and of the Free World . . . The French can be assured that Viet-Nam shall not forget the sacrifices of France.[1]

In Saigon, there was a double rush. On one hand, a call-up of 120,000 young Vietnamese had brought in only 7,000 draftees, of whom 5,000 were declared unfit for service.[2] And the news of the defeat brought an avalanche of Vietnamese and French bank transfers to Hong Kong, where the Vietnamese piaster suddenly rose from a black market rate of about sixty to the U. S. dollar to eighty-five.*

The news of the fall of Dien Bien Phu hit the United States too late

---

* At the beginning of 1966 the South Vietnamese piaster would be worth 180 to the dollar.

for the morning newspapers of May 7—but that is precisely what makes them doubly interesting. For Dien Bien Phu had in fact disappeared as front-page news a great deal earlier. While the French were dying on the Elianes, America was glued to its television sets, watching the now-deceased junior senator from Wisconsin grilling the Secretary of the Army and an Army general as to why an obscure Army dentist with alleged left-wing leanings had been routinely promoted from captain to major. At the very moment when the Viet-Minh mine gallery blew up Eliane 2, Dien Bien Phu made page 6 of America's most respected newspaper.

On the day that Dien Bien Phu fell, Senator McCarthy challenged the right of the Executive to keep secret data from Congress, and Dien Bien Phu rated page 3. However, a senator from Texas, Lyndon B. Johnson, made a speech before the annual Jefferson-Jackson Day Democratic dinner in Washington, in the course of which he clearly showed the beginnings of a deep interest in Viet-Nam, which was to grow after he became President:

> What is American policy on Indochina?
> All of us have listened to the dismal series of reversals and confusions and alarms and excursions which have emerged from Washington over the past few weeks.
> It is apparent only that American foreign policy has never in all its history suffered such a stunning reversal.
> We have been caught bluffing by our enemies, our friends and Allies are frightened and wondering, as we do, where we are headed.
> We stand in clear danger of being left naked and alone in a hostile world.
> . . . This picture of our country needlessly weakened in the world today is so painful that we should turn our eyes from abroad and look homeward.[3]

Coming after his crucial intervention of April 3, the May 6 speech of the future president committed him to a certain position on the Viet-Nam problem. Once president, Lyndon B. Johnson, contrary to the opinions of those who have denied him a deep knowledge of foreign affairs, acted in accordance with the lessons he had learned from Dien Bien Phu: there would be no American Dien Bien Phu as long as he could help it.

At 2130, EDT, Secretary of State Dulles gave an account of recent events to the American people, in which he paid brief homage to de Castries and his men:

The French soldiers showed that they have not lost either the will or the skill to fight even under the most adverse conditions. It shows that Viet-Nam produces soldiers who have the qualities to enable them to defend their country.

In his speech, Secretary Dulles was also careful to lay the blame for American failure to act both on British Prime Minister Churchill's failure to agree to united action in Viet-Nam prior to the Geneva Conference, and upon the U. S. Congress as well. Here again, what Dulles had to say was of crucial importance in the shaping of the American commitment to Viet-Nam a decade later:

> In making commitments which might involve the use of armed force, the Congress is a full partner. Only the Congress can declare war. President Eisenhower has repeatedly emphasized that he would not take military action in Indochina without the support of Congress. Furthermore, he has made clear that he would not seek that unless, in his opinion, there would be an adequate collective effort based on genuine mutuality of purpose in defending vital interests.

In other words, the French defeat at Dien Bien Phu would be written off and the negotiations at Geneva would be allowed to take their preordained course.

It was left to *Life* magazine to find at least something of a bright aspect to the end of the fortress. "The single ray of hope over the graves of Dien Bien Phu," said the periodical in its issue of May 17, 1954, "is the fact that one obstacle to united action—the heroic stubbornness of France—has been removed."

Saturday, May 8, 1954

May 8 was the ninth anniversary of VE-day—the victory of the Allies over Nazi Germany, and it now also became the anniversary of a new French defeat. The evening before, at the main position of Dien Bien Phu, the Viet-Minh had rounded up and herded together their French captives in long columns. They had looked with empty eyes at Gen. de Castries and some of his senior staff officers being driven past them in jeeps. It was the 308th "Iron Division" which had taken control of the battlefield, and its commanding general, stocky, gray-haired Vuong Thua Vu, had established his command post in de Castries' command bunker.

At 2000 of May 7, Dr. Grauwin received a visit from Dr. Thai, the chief surgeon of the 308th, accompanied by four younger doctors from the division. Thai was tall for a Vietnamese and very thin and pale. He had walked along with his division for more than 600 miles from the Chinese border and he, like Grauwin, had spent the last three months day and night at the operating table. A graduate of the French University of Bordeaux and the medical school of Montpellier, he spoke excellent French. In silence, he had walked through the nightmare of the over-crowded hospital bunkers enveloped in the stench of the dead and the dying, and had sat down on a small stool in Grauwin's niche-like room, while Grauwin himself sat down on his own bunkbed. The Communist medical officer looked at his French counterpart and said:

"We have seen, as we passed through, your bunkers crammed with wounded. We've recognized that odor. We understand what you must have gone through, but there is nothing we could do about it. That's all I can tell you."[4]

Grauwin looked up in surprise: the enemy turned out to be human, too. Within a short time, the doctors agreed that first of all, all the wounded would have to be taken out from the underground dugouts and transferred to open-air hospitals and dressing stations. With the super-abundance of nylon parachutes lying about all over the camp, the erection of temporary tents would present no difficulty whatever. The French doctors and medical personnel would be able to stay at their jobs under the supervision of Viet-Minh medical personnel. The Viet-Minh medics would, on the other hand, be able to borrow surgical equipment and, above all, antibiotics which were almost nonexistent on the enemy side. Grauwin had foreseen the latter request and had care-fully hidden part of his small store of precious antibiotics in camouflaged sewage drains inside the bunkers. In the meantime, however, he was greatly relieved as to the fate of his wounded and grateful for the under-standing shown by his captors. Matters were to change two days later, when the political commissars took charge of everything.

On Isabelle, the early hours of dawn were spent in collecting the French prisoners. The fact that Isabelle's last stand had taken place in the dark of night immediately made matters more difficult all around. Also, the 304th People's Army Division, which was in charge of Isabelle and which was largely recruited from the Red River Delta and had some long-standing scores to settle with the French, seemed to have decided to treat the enemy more brusquely. At 0600, as the soldiers of the 2/1 Algerian Rifles sat under tight Viet-Minh guard along the road leading northward out of Isabelle, they were bypassed by Col. Lalande and his staff, walking northward under heavy guard with their hands tied tightly behind their backs.

But now began for the enemy the fantastically complicated job of sorting close to 10,000 enemy troops of various nationalities. From the outset, the enemy decided to separate the prisoners by national backgrounds and to split them into fifty-man groups: Frenchmen would walk with Frenchmen, and Algerians, Moroccans, and Vietnamese would also form specific units. The Foreign Legionnaires in turn were subdivided according to their national origins into German, Italian, Spanish, and East European groups. Noncommissioned officers would be separated from the lower ranks, and the officers from all other groups. That way, the bulk of the prisoners would become a totally leaderless mob in the hands of their captors. That process of sorting out took several days. It is during that period that most of the successful escapes took place.

The officers were immediately segregated and faced with prolonged interrogations about every detail of the defense of Dien Bien Phu. Their every word was recorded not by one, but by several French-speaking stenographers and sometimes tape-recorded. Often, the same officer was questioned several times about the same subject by the French-speaking interrogators. Particular attention was paid to officers of non-French descent, such as the Algerians. When Lt. Belabiche was brought in for interrogation, he noticed with shock that the interrogating officer was in possession of a perfectly accurate large-scale map of Isabelle showing the exact positioning of every unit inside the French strongpoint. The Viet-Minh was interested not only in what the French actually did do, but also in the various contingencies that could have arisen: possible counterattacks, alternate fields of fire, etc. The enemy interrogator also had Belabiche's personal file, probably found among the papers which his battalion headquarters had failed to burn, and saw his citation for the Legion of Honor. He looked up at Belabiche and said: "You are an Algerian. Are you going to stay with us to struggle for the liberation of your country?" When Lt. Belabiche refused, the interrogator's whole attitude changed. To him, Belabiche had become just another "lackey of the imperialists." Eight years later, Belabiche was a captain in the Algerian National Liberation Army, training young Algerian officers at what had been the French officers candidate school at Cherchell, west of Algiers.

In Hanoi, the French Army had, as every year, planned a VE-day parade and on May 7 Vietnamese workers had put up French and

Vietnamese national flags along the main avenue leading to the war memorial and had mounted a reviewing stand for the Vietnamese and French VIP's, including Gen. Cogny, who would attend the ceremony.

It was probably the grimmest victory parade ever held, made up, as it was, of the Hanoi-based remnants of the units that had been destroyed the day before at Dien Bien Phu: headquarters and depot units of the 3rd Foreign Legion Regiment, the 1st Company of the 1st BPC, and a few isolated paratroopers who had missed the last jump into Dien Bien Phu for the good reason that they had been wounded elsewhere and had just left the hospital. Several of the paratroop officers limped noticeably as they filed by the reviewing stand.

They wore their full battle gear and their alignment was impeccable, but to many observers they looked as dejected as their comrades-in-arms must have looked as at that very moment, across 300 kilometers of mountains, they were forming into groups for the march to the Communist prison camps. Even the French population of Hanoi had deserted its army. Of the half million Vietnamese and perhaps 10,000 French citizens in Hanoi, only three or four hundred had shown up to watch the parade.[5]

Now began the agonizing wait for news by the families of the men who were missing at Dien Bien Phu. Mme. de Castries, who had spoken briefly to her husband over the official radiotelephone as late as 1600 on May 7, and who until now had been freely available to journalists, had locked herself in her hotel room. On the morning of May 8, she drove to Lanessan Military Hospital to visit with the wounded from Dien Bien Phu who had been flown out with the last ambulance aircraft in March. A young blond woman, very thin but obviously pregnant, was also seen piloting her bicycle into the headquarters of Gen. Cogny in the Hanoi citadel. The bicycle was equipped with a small rear seat holding a baby. The woman was Mme. Millien, the wife of de Castries' radio operator. Other families were anxiously clinging to their radio sets where the illegal transmitter of the enemy forces had begun to give the names of the captured survivors. The French Army, however, soon began to jam the transmission. The effect of the interminable recital of names was judged to be too demoralizing on everybody.

But that morning also, Radio *Hirondelle* [Swallow] had transmitted a brief message from Gen. Navarre to his forces. Labeled "Order of the Day No. 9," the message underlined that the garrison, fighting against a 5-to-1 superiority, had fixed thirty enemy battalions for five months, "thus saving Upper Laos from invasion and preserving the Tonkinese

Delta." Navarre blamed the fall of Dien Bien Phu on Chinese Communist aid which "suddenly allowed the enemy to inaugurate a type of modern warfare that was entirely new to the Indochinese theater of operations."

The defenders of Dien Bien Phu, Navarre said, had added to the long history of the French armed forces one of its "most glorious pages" and had given the French forces in Indochina and the Vietnamese Army "a new pride and a new reason for fighting, because the struggle of the free peoples against slavery does not end today.

"The fight continues."

On the Communist side, President Ho Chi Minh waited until May 13 to issue a victory proclamation, followed by one of General Vo Nguyen Giap. Ho's was a typical mixture of the determination and modesty in tone for which he is known:

> Let me first of all express to you my affectionate solicitude to the wounded and to all of you . . .
>
> The Government and I have decided to recompense you. But in what way? As far as the present circumstances permit, we shall do so because we attach great importance to it . . .
>
> We have the intention of distributing to each of you the insignia of "Combatant of Dien Bien Phu." Do you agree with this?
>
> Once more, let me advise you to be modest in your victory. Do not underestimate the enemy and remain ready to accomplish everything the Party and the Government might ask of you.
>
> I embrace you affectionately,
>
> > Your uncle
> > Ho Chi Minh

I saw the round red-starred brass button with the inscription *Chien-si Dien Bien* ("Combatant of Dien Bien Phu") on many a shirt in Hanoi almost a decade later. It is still being worn proudly.

Giap's proclamation widely differed in tone from Ho's. It was, like the man himself, doctrinaire and proud:

> The Dien Bien Phu victory is the most prestigious which our Army has ever achieved . . . In liberating this strategic northwestern region of our country we have further expanded our zone of resistance and contributed to the success of the land reform.
>
> . . . We have brought failure to the Navarre Plan and struck a rude blow against the intrigues of the French colonialist warmongers and the American interventionists who wanted to expand

the Indochina War. . . . If our troops have been victorious at Dien
Bien Phu, this is due to the enlightened guidance of President Ho
Chi Minh, of the Central Committee of the Party; and of the
Government.

It is also due to the heroism, the courage, the endurance of all
the cadres and of all the combatants at the front—their spirit of
sacrifice and their will to win.

It is due even more to the ardor and the enthusiasm of the
People's Porters of the population in the North-West and of the
rear areas. In the name of the Army I warmly thank all the porters
and the whole population . . .

The General, Commander-in-Chief
Vo Nguyen Giap

The last funeral oration to be said officially over Dien Bien Phu was
delivered on May 8 at 1615 in the League of Nations Palace overlooking
an expanse of magnificently manicured lawns extending down to the
quiet shores of Lake Geneva. There, after having ineffectually debated
about the reunification of Korea for over two weeks while Dien Bien Phu
was agonizing, the West was now ready to meet the Communist bloc on
the matter of peace in Indochina and under the effect of the shattering
defeat of the day before. It fell to the French Foreign Minister, Georges
Bidault, to make the opening statement. The small, intense man with
the unruly parted hair falling on his forehead, looked awful after weeks
of harrowing negotiations and travels. Like his prime minister when he
addressed the French Parliament the day before, Bidault was almost
toneless at first. And while his premier at least had the consolation of
addressing a largely friendly audience at home, the French Foreign
Minister now had to acknowledge France's defeat not only under the
glaring camera lights of the world's press but also under the close
scrutiny of the victorious Communist leaders: Chou En-lai of Red China,
Vyacheslav Molotov of the Soviet Union, and Pham Van Dong, the
Foreign Minister (and later Prime Minister) of the Communist Vietnamese regime. And there simply was no way out; there was no possibility
of *not* speaking of Dien Bien Phu at that particular moment in history.
The defeat, no matter what would happen later, was too important to be
ignored.

And Bidault, like France herself, stood there alone. The delegations
of the three little Indochinese states of Cambodia, Laos, and Viet-Nam,
were of little help at that juncture. The British Foreign Secretary,
Anthony Eden, was the co-chairman (with Russia) of the conference

and, in view of Britain's role in the Indochina conflict during the recent weeks, barely on speaking terms with his French colleague. As for the United States delegation, the Secretary of State, in one of his repeated confusions between the appearance and the reality of American prestige, had preferred to return to the United States and leave the American delegation in the capable but less prestigious hands of his Under Secretary, General Walter Bedell Smith. Bidault was reported to have said to an associate that he had come to Geneva with "a two of clubs and a three of diamonds" as his only diplomatic cards.[6] As he looked around him before he began to speak, at his fellow Western diplomats and their embarrassedly downcast eyes and at the Communist diplomats staring at him unblinkingly, he was the very picture of France's loneliness in her defeat.

Addressing the British Foreign Secretary, who was in the chair for this inaugural session, Bidault said:

> Mr. Chairman, at the outset of this Conference I should like to describe its dramatic prelude in the most cruel battle in a conflict which has been going on for seven years . . . It was not our side which wished, while peace was being discussed, an intensification of combat going as far as a refusal to allow evacuation of the wounded contrary to the laws of war and to the principles of the civilized world.
>
> The issue of the Battle of Dien Bien Phu was announced yesterday by the Commander-in-Chief in these words: "The garrison of Dien Bien Phu has fulfilled the mission assigned to it by the command." The French Delegation cannot conceal here its deep emotion and its pride in the face of the heroism of the combatants of France, of Viet-Nam, and of all of the French union who had resisted beyond human endurance . . .

Bidault, who had been the civilian leader of all the French Resistance forces inside Nazi-occupied France, choked as he spoke those words, and then, mercifully, the text switched to the normal diplomatic details of the French position and Bidault regained his composure. Buried in the last third of the text was a short four-line paragraph which, in the rapid-fire French delivery of the Foreign Minister, seemed no more important than the previous or the following, but which indeed contained all that there was to be said:

> We propose that the Conference should, first of all, declare that it adopt the principle of a general cessation of hostilities in Indochina based upon the necessary guarantees of security, the terms

of the principles thus enunciated being inseparable in our mind and
in our resolution.

In effect, one day after the loss of Dien Bien Phu, France had sued
for peace in Indochina.

In Paris also, this had been VE-day and French officialdom was tradi-
tion-bound to make the pilgrimage to the Tomb of the Unknown Soldier
at the Arch of Triumph at the top of the Champs-Elysées. But instead of
being joyful, the large crowd behind the reinforced police cordon
looked sullen.

Even the popular French figurehead president, René Coty, got only a
scattering of perfunctory applause. Premier Joseph Laniel did not fare as
well as he rode past, followed closely by Defense Minister René Pleven.

Some people cried out: "Send 'em to Dien Bien Phu!" while others
cried out the familiar French threat to unpopular politicians: "*Au
poteau!*" ["To the firing squad!"]

After the official ceremony was over a simple black Citroën car drove
up and out of it stepped an extremely tall and heavy sixty-five-year-old
man in the light-tan uniform of a French brigadier general. Although he
was retired both from the Army and from politics, a French military band
awaited him at the Arch of Triumph and a huge crowd had remained
behind the police barriers for his appearance.

The tall general walked in silence to the Tomb of the Unknown
Soldier, saluted the French flag, bowed his head in meditation, and then
walked back to his car.

As he looked at the cheering crowd with his myopic eyes and gave it
his characteristic bent-elbow wave, cheers of "*Vive de Gaulle!*" and
"*De Gaulle au pouvoir!*" ["De Gaulle to power!"] could be heard
everywhere.

The tall brigadier general heard. And he would not forget.

The Wounded

On the battlefield itself, the major problem remained the disposition of
the hundreds of seriously wounded who now were captives of the enemy.
It was obvious that the Viet-Minh did not have the medical or transport
facilities to care adequately for them on the spot or to transport them to
his own rear areas. Unless a battlefield truce could be obtained almost
immediately, many of the seriously wounded prisoners would die. Both
sides knew this and the enemy, aware of the public pressure on the French
to retrieve the wounded prisoners in some way or another, now sought to
extract the maximum in concessions from the French.

French reconnaissance aircraft maintaining a constant vigil over the battlefield had noticed the raising of the parachute tents in the valley, followed by the laying out of an immense Red Cross on a field of white parachutes—a sign that the enemy was not going to use the valley for military operations.[7] This encouraged the French to continue to drop four airplaneloads a day of food, drugs, and ice into the valley, in the hopes that at least a small part of the supplies would be used for the wounded prisoners. A small part was used. And on the afternoon of May 11, Gen. Navarre had a personal message to Gen. Giap parachuted into the valley, followed up by a repetition of the same message over the French military transmitter in Hanoi. Addressed to "The Commander-in-Chief, General Vo Nguyen Giap," Navarre asked the enemy commander to let him know how arrangements could be made to evacuate the French wounded from Dien Bien Phu.

At 1830 of May 11, came the answer from the Viet-Minh. Giap authorized French representatives to come to Dien Bien Phu directly in order to negotiate the release and transfer of the wounded prisoners. A helicopter with Red Cross insignia would be authorized to land on the northern part of the Dien Bien Phu airstrip, below where Huguette 6 used to be.

Navarre immediately appointed as head of the French mission a man who, beyond a doubt, was the most qualified in all of Indochina to lead such a negotiation. He was Dr. Pierre Huard. Huard was dean of the Hanoi University Medical School, president of the French Red Cross in Indochina, and a reserve colonel in the French Army Medical Corps. He had, by then, been living in Viet-Nam for twenty years, was married to a Vietnamese woman, spoke Vietnamese almost perfectly, and in the 1930's had protected many a Vietnamese nationalist or Communist fire-brand against the rigors of the French colonial administration. As head of the Red Cross throughout the Indochina War, he had impartially maintained contacts with the Viet-Minh Red Cross organization and had, even in the midst of the Indochina War, traveled across the lines into Viet-Minh territory to arrange for the exchange of sick or wounded prisoners of both sides. He also had seen to it, as far as was possible, that the French and Vietnamese military treated Viet-Minh prisoners in their hands in accordance with international rules of war. A tall and thin figure with kind eyes, without any insignia on his tropical uniform and always wearing the kind of pith helmet that had gone out of fashion three decades earlier, Huard looked like a sort of Asian Dr. Schweitzer. Accompanied by a Major James from the French Army and a Major

Roger from the French Air Force, Huard flew on May 12 to the Laotian capital of Luang-Prabang, where a helicopter awaited him. On Thursday, May 13, at 1100 he and his small team landed at Dien Bien Phu.

The negotiations covered several extremely difficult points. First of all, it was necessary to define who was a severely wounded soldier and who was not, and who was to make the selection of those prisoners. Then, a decision had to be made as to the type of airlift that would be instituted to remove the wounded: fixed-wing aircraft that could pick up eighteen litter cases at once but whose use was limited until the airfield could be reconstructed, or helicopters which, considering the type then available in Indochina and the long distances involved, could carry only a few wounded at a time but could begin their job almost immediately. The most serious problem in the negotiations was the counterconcessions demanded by the enemy.

These included not only the nonintervention of the French Air Force within a radius of ten kilometers of the valley of Dien Bien Phu, but also the immunity from bombardment of large tracts of Road 41. The latter point was the most important to the Viet-Minh, and the most dangerous to the French. For if there remained a shred of military rationality to the whole Battle of Dien Bien Phu, it was that the prolonged defense of the valley had tied down a considerable part of the enemy's main battle force far away from the Red River Delta and that the Viet-Minh would find it extremely difficult to turn the whole massive siege force around and bring it back into attack position around the Delta before Gen. Cogny had received the additional reinforcements needed to contain such an attack. All depended upon whether the major transportation arteries of Road 41 and, to a lesser extent, Road 7 from Laos, could at least be partially interdicted or their use made as expensive as possible to the enemy. With understandable logic, Gen. Giap now decided to use the approximately 10,000 prisoners in his hands in the same way the Japanese used Allied prisoners on their supply ships during World War II. In the latter case, Allied prisoners would be placed in clearly visible positions on the main decks of Japanese transports carrying raw materials back to Japan, with the consequence that Allied aircraft or submarines faced the quandary of either letting a Japanese ship return to Japan with a precious cargo of raw materials or destroying the ship and with it hundreds of their own comrades. In the case of Dien Bien Phu, the Viet-Minh decided to intersperse its own infantry and artillery columns with convoys of French prisoners. That way, French bombers seeking to interdict the strategic roads would be faced with the problem of having to kill their own comrades as they attacked. The Viet-Minh explained that their own wounded—and there were, of course, thousands of them—would also travel over those roads, so that there was a direct *quid pro quo* between opening the Dien Bien Phu airfield to French planes and keeping the roads open to Communist trucks. The French had no choice but to accede.[8] To do otherwise would have meant sacrificing the lives of perhaps 1,500 seriously wounded men for the sake of a nebulous short-term military advantage. Aroused public opinion at home and abroad probably would not have stood for it.

The problem of the selection of the wounded to be evacuated was perhaps less crucial but in human terms just as difficult. As Dr. Grauwin knew, nearly *all* the prisoners were physically in no condition to march 600 kilometers through the jungle; in many cases, men who had had relatively light wounds but who had lost a great deal of blood were in worse condition to undertake the trek than others who had suffered perhaps a more serious wound, such as the amputation of an arm, but who had recovered from it. Also, there was the problem of the wounded from the Vietnamese National Army who had fallen into Viet-Minh hands. The Communists considered their own nationals who had fought on the French side as traitors and at first refused to include them among the wounded to be selected for evacuation. Again the French were confronted by a terrible quandary: if the whole evacuation process were to be jeopardized for the sake of a small percentage of Vietnamese wounded, French public opinion at home would be incensed. Yet, if the Vietnamese wounded, who had fought valiantly side by side with the French, were to be abandoned to the untender mercies of the Viet-Minh, the ensuing demoralization among the already badly demoralized Vietnamese Army troops outside of Dien Bien Phu would lead to a massive military crisis in Indochina itself. The negotiations were stopped and Col. Huard returned to Hanoi for consultations with the French High Command.

What followed in the next few days was a neat example of sound psychological warfare. Even though the negotiations had not yet brought about a positive result, the Viet-Minh High Command authorized the removal via helicopter of a limited number of wounded from Dien Bien Phu. Their arrival in Laos and Hanoi, with ensuing tales of horror and misery from the valley, immediately produced an increased amount of pressure on the French to be less adamant. Huard and his mission returned to Dien Bien Phu on May 16 and signed the following day an agreement providing for the evacuation of 858 wounded, to be selected according to medical criteria alone, regardless of nationality. But the French had to pay a heavy price for that minor concession: there would be no neutral inspection of the valley or of the POW convoys leaving it, and the French Air Force would refrain from bombing the road until the evacuation of the wounded was completed.[9] The French military knew that they had yielded a significant military advantage, but under the circumstances there seemed to be no other way out. With the preliminary accord in his pocket, the enemy now began the clearing and reconstruction of the Dien Bien Phu airstrip at a snail's pace but allowed French helicopters and single-engine planes to come in to pick up a few wounded at a time.

By May 25, the airfield still was not cleared for C-47's, and the Viet-Minh, who had until now refused the help of French de-mining experts to clear the field, now requested that such experts be flown in. In the meantime, the pressures had also mounted inside the camp, as Viet-Minh political commissars began to take their own doctors in hand. The wounded were "reclassified" according to what was called their "democratic urgency" rather than their medical urgency, with the non-Europeans of the lowest ranks being given preferred medical treatment over the European soldiers, and the latter being treated earlier or better than their noncommissioned officers and officers. When several parachute defects resulted in the crashing into the camp of some loads of medical cargo, the Viet-Minh forbade such air drops but allowed the evacuation helicopters and small aircraft to bring in whatever supplies they could carry with their small payloads.

And above all, since the French medical staff in the camp had no idea as to the results of the negotiations that were under way, it was put under heavy pressure to sign appeals for "clemency" for the sake of obtaining the release of their wounded. Two female political commissars were especially assigned to Mlle. de Galard, the French nurse, to make her sign a series of special appeals, because of their particular emotional impact coming from the single Frenchwoman at Dien Bien Phu. Dr. Grauwin later described in detail how she resisted for ten days but then gave way on his orders (he also signed a separate appeal) because of their fear that it would be the wounded who would have to pay the price of her fortitude.[10]

All these appeals had to be written and rewritten several times until they fit the propaganda requirements of the victors, and they were of course immediately used for propaganda purposes and appeared in the world press.[11] Mlle. de Galard thus wrote a letter to Ho Chi Minh on the occasion of his 64th birthday on May 19, in which she thanked him for his clemency toward the wounded prisoners and in which she promised that upon her return to France she would attempt to create "among the young people who surround me an atmosphere of greater understanding between our two peoples so as to help, in my way, to re-establish peace." Once she had written that letter, she was informed by her two commissars that she would be released but that she must write yet another letter to Ho Chi Minh and another to the women's organization of the Viet-Minh. In her second letter, she held out for something that was dear to her heart—the release of her companions on the medical teams, and while again covering the same ground about struggling for peace upon her return to France, she also added that

> . . . while my joy to return home is great, it would be very imperfect if I were to leave alone, leaving behind me the other medical personnel, doctors as well as attendants, with whom I have worked ceaselessly to care for our wounded. Thus, I ask you not to forget them and I am sure that no one ever appeals in vain to your clemency . . .

A few days later, Ho Chi Minh himself showed Mlle. de Galard's letter to the Russian film journalist Karmen and added: "General de Castries also speaks for peace now. Before [the battle] he didn't speak about peace."[12]

Unfortunately, on May 22, at 1500 three French Air Force planes bombed and strafed Road 41 two kilometers south of Conoi, wounding and killing many French prisoners along with their captors. In reprisal, the Viet-Minh removed the remaining French medical personnel, including Dr. Grauwin, and sent them on the POW trek on Road 41. It was a neat psychological trick. They marched for days like the other prisoners, but then were loaded on trucks, shipped back to Dien Bien Phu, and released with the last wounded in the first week of June, 1954.

Another airlift awaited the most complicated cases. The United States, as a last charitable gesture, offered to treat them at military hospitals in the United States and soon, Operation "Wounded Warrior" was under way, airlifting survivors from Saigon half around the world to Westover Field, Massachusetts. Ten years later, Warrant Officer Liedecke of the Foreign Legion, stationed at one of the last French forts in the Sahara, at In-Ekker, recalled with pride how he had been taught English by American co-eds from Mount Holyoke College, an institution near Westover, once they had found out that the French and Legionnaires from Dien Bien Phu were, in Liedecke's words, "humans like all other humans."

As for Mlle. de Galard, she was released as promised, on May 24. The young woman arrived in Hanoi at 2030, still wearing her cut-down camouflage uniform of the French paratroops. She had made an effort to be as clean as she could, but as she stepped off the plane her jungle boots were still covered with the brown mud of Dien Bien Phu. When she left for France a few days later, Geneviève de Galard-Terraube had spent over four years in Indochina and had flown 149 medical evacuation missions, including forty to Dien Bien Phu.

Madame de Castries had left Hanoi on May 23 for Paris, where she arrived on May 26 at 1155. The French Secretaries of State for Indochina Affairs and for National Defense, Marc Jacquet and Pierre de Chevigné, were awaiting her at Orly Field. She wore a beige coat and a white, close fitting bonnet, and for once refused to speak to the press. A Citroën automobile of the French General Staff, driven by a gendarme, carried her off to the city.

Also on May 24, a seriously wounded master sergeant was lifted out of the valley of Dien Bien Phu to the Laotian capital of Luang-Prabang. He was a Hungarian by the name of Beres and had served with the 1st BEP on Huguette. On May 19, while the Viet-Minh were celebrating Ho Chi Minh's birthday, Beres had dragged himself into the tent of a nearby Viet-Minh command post, where he had previously noticed a Foreign Legion guidon that apparently had fallen intact into enemy hands. It was the fanion of 4th Company, 1st Battalion, 13th Foreign Legion Half-Brigade, which had been destroyed during the very first assault on Beatrice on March 13. Sergeant Beres grabbed the green-and-red guidon with its gold stitching and quickly stuffed it under his shirt. Luckily he was not too closely searched on his departure and, no doubt for reasons of "face," the Viet-Minh never acknowledged that any prisoner—and particularly a severely wounded prisoner—could have eluded its surveillance sufficiently to steal a flag. Thus, the Foreign Legion became the only outfit at Dien Bien Phu to have saved one of its battle flags from destruction or capture.[13]

The Prisoners

According to admittedly incomplete French Army statistics (see Appendices A and B), the garrison of Dien Bien Phu counted on May 5 a total of 8,158 able-bodied or lightly wounded men. It had suffered since November 21, 1953, a total of 8,221 casualties, including 1,293 known dead. No statistics are available for the last three days of the battle, as units were completely wiped out with their battalion records.

However, 165 men of the 1st Colonial Parachute Battalion had been parachuted in on May 5 and 6, which brought the cumulative total of the Dien Bien Phu garrison to 16,544 men, not counting the 1,916 T'ai and Frenchmen of the Lai-Chau force who had attempted in November, 1953, to march from that city to Dien Bien Phu, or the 2,440 PIM's who had been airlifted in.

In view of the violence of the last battles, it is commonly agreed among the French commanders that there were in all likelihood at least another 600 to 800 dead and at least as many wounded. The high proportion of dead during the final phase was due to the fact that most of these casualties were from the heavy artillery bombardment rather than from small-arms fire. Total French casualties can be conservatively estimated at close to 9,000, of whom 885 (including 27 unwounded medical personnel) were handed over to the French under the battle-field truce of May, 1954. This, aside from a handful of escapees of whom more will be said later, left almost 7,000 troops as prisoners on May 8. Many of them were far more seriously wounded than those who were finally selected for transfer to the French, but they already had left the battlefield in compact groups of fifty on the 500-mile-long trek to the prison camps north of the Red River or southeastward to the camp complex in Thanh-Hoa Province. For the exhausted and mostly wounded survivors of the battle of Dien Bien Phu, this became a death march.

This writer has elsewhere covered in detail life in Viet-Minh prison camps,[14] and will therefore deal here only with events pertaining to the fate of the prisoners taken at Dien Bien Phu. Two facts stand out about the prisoners from Dien Bien Phu: first of all, their sheer numbers and the necessity of transporting them far away from areas where they could be liberated by the French, posed an incredibly difficult problem to the primitive logistical system of the Viet-Nam People's Army; second, other French prisoners had usually fallen into Communist hands after only a few days of fighting and, save for the seriously wounded, were not in a state of general physical breakdown. Thirty to sixty days of march at a rate of twenty kilometers a day, while carrying rice rations for the column and the numerous litter cases, simply proved too much for most of the men. The food rations allocated to them by their captors did the rest: fourteen ounces of rice a day and ten peanuts every tenth day.[15] Unboiled water and, on a few occasions light tea, constituted the sole drink available. In many cases the arid countryside near Road 41 limited the availability of water. Dehydration due to continuous dysentery and abnormal perspiration soon transformed the POW's into "walking skeletons" reminiscent of German concentration-camp photographs.

Before the march began, the prisoners still had to undergo a final humiliation. They acted as bit players and manipulated stage props in the re-enactment of their own defeat. While some film footage had actually been shot by the Viet-Minh during the Battle of Dien Bien Phu, certain major attacks, such as the conquest of Eliane 2, for example, had taken place either at night or in the absence of qualified Vietnamese combat cameramen. The presence on the scene of the Russian camera-man Karmen now helped to remedy this. On May 14, all the walking prisoners were herded together in carefully segregated units and paraded past the whirring cameras like the defeated barbarians of 2,000 years ago being paraded through Rome by Caesar. No one was spared this humiliation, from Gen. de Castries to the last Vietnamese auxiliary. But when it came to playing the role of surrendering paratroopers, the para-troopers themselves took their cue from Bigeard. When his captors ap-proached him with the demand that he play his own role by walking out of his command bunker with raised hands, Lt. Col. Bigeard had looked his captors in the eye and had said quietly: "I'd rather croak."

Thus, the Viet-Minh picked largely the now leaderless North Africans to replay part of the Battle of Dien Bien Phu, dressed in the camouflage battle dress of the French paratroopers. Exactly ten years later, on May 8, 1964, Col. Bigeard, before a fascinated nationwide television audience in France, commented on the Communist-made film on the Battle of Dien Bien Phu and picked out the obvious errors that had been incorpo-rated in its making. There was a scene showing a tank-supported infantry attack punctuated by what appeared to be heavy artillery fire—but the somewhat unsophisticated moviemakers had forgotten to eliminate from their film the white-painted medical plane that had brought Dr. Huard to Dien Bien Phu after the battle was over and whose presence in the picture clearly dated it. Likewise, another scene which purported to show the conquest of Beatrice, which had been held entirely by Foreign Legionnaires of European extraction, shows the battlefield littered with brown-skinned North Africans. In another sequence, two French tanks could be seen rolling into combat directly behind each other with only inches to spare. That was due to the fact that the Viet-Minh, with the help of some of the captured tank crews, had been able to put back into operation only one tank engine—the other tank was simply being towed by its brother.

It was said, when the film was projected in France in 1964, that some French officers had deliberately volunteered to become "technical ad-

visors" to the camera crews of their captors precisely in order to intro-
duce into the film technical mistakes that would brand it as an obvious
falsification.[16] If such was their intention, they succeeded, although no
one but a very sophisticated audience is likely to spot the errors. To this
day, the Dien Bien Phu film is being shown to all the recruits in the
Algerian People's Army, and probably to every soldier of the North
Vietnamese Army, as an encouraging example of what even primitive
guerrillas can do to a modern Western force, provided they are willing
to fight and to make sacrifices.

For a short while, various groups of French specialists were culled out
from the hordes of prisoners in order to keep some of the essential facilities of Dien Bien Phu in working order, such as the water purifiers and
the power plants, while some of the others were used to salvage some of
the war booty found on the battlefield or to remove some of the mine
fields. The latter work was never completed. Ten years later, here and
there mines would still explode and kill a stray buffalo or maim an un-
wary farmer's child.

A few men were singled out as potential "war criminals": the intelligence officers; officers who had worked in the tribal areas, such as Col.
Trancart; and the Air Force officers. The Viet-Minh, totally deprived of
airplanes, had a particularly deepseated hatred for the airmen and for
the casualties which they invariably caused to the civilian population.
When they identified among the prisoners the commander of the Air
Base Detachment, Capt. Charnod, they marched him to a grave mound
near Ban Co My, three kilometers south of the main position, where they
had buried the civilian victims of a badly aimed French air raid. One
by one, Capt. Charnod had to unbury the mangled bodies in the blazing
sun; look at them, and rebury them. Then he was marched off to the
camps.

A few days later, as he stumbled numbly along the road, a jeep came
to a screeching halt next to him. A Viet-Minh officer stepped out of,
looked him over, and said in flawless French, using the "thou" form:

"Don't you remember me? I'm ——, and we attended the *Lycée*
together in Montpellier."

Charnod now recognized the face under the strange flat helmet, but he
could not recall the name of his Vietnamese classmate who had grown up
into an enemy officer.

"Come on," said the Viet-Minh officer, "I'll take you along. You don't have to walk." The officer exchanged a few words with Charnod's guards, and Charnod changed hands without further formality. He rode to the prison camp in the comparative luxury of a jeep—even de Castries and his staff rode in trucks—without ever finding out the name of his benefactor.

But for most of the other prisoners, the march to the camps was a nightmare, with its scenes of human frailty and incredible fortitude. Major de Mecquenem, who had been captured early in the battle on Gabrielle, recalled later how the Viet-Minh, even in the temporary POW camps prior to the end of the battle, had played off one group of prisoners against the other, and with some success.

He particularly remembered in his camp a group of Foreign Legionnaires of German extraction who had decided, correctly enough, that this was not their war anyway and that what now counted most was to stay alive until the conclusion of the cease-fire. They informed the camp commander that they had turned "progressive" and were immediately given a preferred status within the camp, along with improved food rations. Every morning part of the ceremonial consisted in a lecture by the camp's political commissar on the previous day's victories in the Battle of Dien Bien Phu, and it became the role of the "progressives" to provide a suitable cheering section for the announcement of such victories. They cheered or gustily sang the *Internationale* for the defeats of the 3rd BT on Anne-Marie and of the Algerians on the Dominiques. They also had no objections to applauding the destruction of Moroccans and Vietnamese paratroopers on Eliane 1.

But then came the bitter battles of mid-April for the Northern Huguettes. One morning the Viet-Minh camp commander read the rousing news that the Foreign Legion infantrymen and paratroopers who had held the Northern Huguettes had been overwhelmed and that part of the vital airstrip was now in the hands of the People's Army. There was a dead silence among the assembled prisoners and, in contrast to established habit, the cheering section of the "progressives" also had remained silent. In an annoyed voice, the camp commander turned to them and said: "Come on, sing! What are you waiting for?"

The Foreign Legionnaires looked at each other in silence and then began to sing. There was an instant gasp of shock among the assembled French prisoners—until they recognized the German song: *"Ich hatt' einen Kameraden, Einen bess'ren findst du nicht . . ."** The turncoat Legionnaires were singing the beautiful song with which Germans have

---

*"I once had a comrade / you couldn't find a better one . . ."

honored their war dead since the Napoleonic wars of 1809. It was one thing to cheer at the demise of the other "strange" units fighting in the valley; it was another to betray the Foreign Legion. The "progressives" were stripped of their special privileges and returned to the rice-and-water diet of the other prisoners.

The officers of the headquarters of Dien Bien Phu were being transported eastward by truck with their hands tied behind their backs and their bodies packed so tightly that the smallest bump of the deeply rutted jungle road threw them helplessly against each other, hour after hour. In their midst were also the war reporters Pierre Schoendoerffer, Daniel Camus, and Jean Péraud. Unable to move, they had seen kilometer after kilometer of jungle forest go by and they knew that with every minute, with every kilometer, they were going farther away from any chance of escaping. Péraud, who had already served a long stretch in a Nazi concentration camp for his activities in the French Resistance, was particularly despondent. He said to Schoendoerffer, "I've just got to get out of this. I can't do it twice. This time I'm sure I wouldn't come out of it alive."

Standing back to back they searched each other's pockets for an object which could help them to escape. Finally, Péraud found that Schoendoerffer still had his Swiss pocketknife in his pocket. At the price of agonizing contortions he succeeded in reaching it and opening its saw blade. Once this was done, it was not difficult to cut each other's bonds, but the problem arose as to the choice of the proper jumping-off point. Since they were not in the last truck of the convoy, the driver and guards of the following truck would surely see them. Therefore they would have to wait for a particularly sharp turn which would force the following truck to slow down enough to be behind the other side of the turn while they were jumping from their own truck. The occasion finally presented itself at the steep crossing of the Black River at Thakhoa, almost midway between Dien Bien Phu and Hanoi.

As they had calculated, the steep turn forced the truck behind them to an almost complete halt, and with the other prisoners blocking the view from the cab of their own truck, Péraud and Schoendoerffer jumped off and headed for the forest at the roadside. They found an almost solid wall of fully grown bamboo. For incredibly long seconds they frantically clawed at it, trying to find an opening wide enough to let their bodies through. Péraud finally succeeded just as the truck was coming around the bend, but Schoendoerffer, who had slipped in a puddle of water, was immediately seen by the Viet-Minh guards. Shots rang out in all directions as the guards furiously tried to catch up with Péraud while others clubbed the prone Schoendoerffer into unconsciousness and loaded him again on his truck. All his photos of the Battle of Dien Bien Phu, which he had hoarded, were taken from him. Péraud was never seen again, although some rumors have it that he was later murdered in the forest by a greedy tribesman or even that he was later on seen in Communist-held Hanoi in the company of a T'ai tribal princess who had been caught in the siege ring at Dien Bien Phu. But all this is hearsay. As far as the French Army is concerned Sergeant Jean Péraud, of the French Press Information Service in Indochina and attached to the 71st Headquarters Company at Dien Bien Phu, disappeared forever somewhere along Road 41 in May, 1954. As he had wanted it, he did not have to go through the humiliation of a prison camp twice in his young life.

Along other points of this incredible calvary, small groups of men were fighting off death as best they could. The Foreign Legionnaires, with their fair skins, were least equipped to withstand the murderous climate, and their highly individualistic attitude led them to let each man fend for himself, although, of course, in many cases they helped men of their own units or their own nationality. The mainland Frenchmen were hardly better equipped for such a march but displayed a psychological quality for which they already had been known in Nazi prison camps during World War II: a great amount of group cohesion and of devotion to their wounded and sick comrades. This was particularly true in the case of the paratroop units, who would grimly carry their wounded or sick comrades as long as they were physically able to, often carrying even their dead until the next rest stop so as to be able to bury them with some sort of decency. There are hundreds of well-documented cases on file with the Office of the French Army Surgeon General, attesting to what went on during the trek. One Foreign Legion chief warrant officer cut off his own gangrenous arm with a knife, without anesthesia, and survived the march thanks to his comrades. A paratrooper, blinded by shell fragments, was half dragged and half carried for forty-five days through the jungle. Four men died because of the gangrene caused by telephone wire tightly wrapped around their bound arms. An Algerian rifleman, operated on for mortar fragments in the chest and liver on March 15 and captured on May 7, marched for forty-five days to a prison camp, holding together his wound with his unrolled turban. These were the lucky ones who had friends to care for them.

The doctor of the 1st Foreign Legion Parachute Battalion, Lieutenant Jean-Louis Rondy, was later to recall the pathetic sight of a soldier whose legs had been amputated to the thighs and who, abandoned by everyone, was dragging himself on his hands and the stumps of his legs to the enemy transit camp at Tuan Giao.[17]

The results of this sort of treatment of the prisoners was self-evident. Not a single POW with severe injuries of the abdomen, chest, or skull survived captivity. In June and July, 1954, eleven per cent of the inmates of Camp 128 died of the ordeal of the march from Dien Bien Phu. Finally, after the war ended on July 20, the Viet-Minh began to repatriate the prisoners. Of the total of 36,979 POW's captured by the Viet-Minh since 1946, a total of 10,754 (or 28.5%) were repatriated. Of those, 6,132 required immediate hospitalization. A total of 61 of them died within the next three months. Of these, 49 had been captured at Dien Bien Phu.

For fear of arousing French public opinion, the extent of French losses at Dien Bien Phu has never been made public, but a simple computation makes it possible to arrive at a close estimate of the actual losses. From the foregoing, it is obvious that the losses on the Dien Bien Phu trek were probably far higher than those suffered by the prisoners captured in earlier engagements. By placing the returnee rate at a conservative one third, including those captured since the beginning of the battle, it is possible to estimate that about 3,000 men (including the 885 directly repatriated from Dien Bien Phu) out of a total of 16,544 eventually returned from Dien Bien Phu. Over 3,000 died in the battlefield area and a few hundred others, of whom more will be said later, disappeared in Eastern Europe. But the rest, close to 10,000 men, died on the trek or in the prison camps in less than three months' time.[18] This is a hard statistical fact which cannot, and should not, be overlooked.

The Viet-Minh clearly realized that the survivors of Dien Bien Phu constituted a choice prize in the sense that they had been the center of attention in the Western world for several months and also constituted the cream of the French Army. The same was true for the native soldiers from northern and tropical Africa. Ideas planted now in the Viet-Minh prison camps would have time to germinate later once they had returned home. The noted French novelist and reporter Jean Lartéguy gives an excellent account of the North Vietnamese brainwashing methods in his novel *The Centurions*.[19] They made roughly two sets of converts: the North Africans, that is, mainly the Algerians; and the right-wing French junior officers. In the case of the Algerians, the reason was obvious. The French colonialists were in the process of losing the war in Indochina and would doubtless be incapable of resisting another anticolonial rebellion.

The argument used on the Algerians was devastatingly simple in its application. Once segregated from their leaders, the Algerian soldiers were congratulated by their captors for their heroic attitude during the battle. But the conclusion that was hammered into them, often by other Algerians or Moroccans who had been trained in Peking or who had been taken prisoner earlier, was: "And since you are such good soldiers, why do you fight for the colonialists? Why don't you fight for yourselves and get yourself a country of your own?" For the officers or non-commissioned officers of Algerian origin, the argument was somewhat more sophisticated but it was simply too potent to be effectively resisted. Almost ten years later a former Algerian prisoner who had been captured not at Dien Bien Phu but elsewhere in North Viet-Nam, told me what made him change his opinion. "One colonial war was enough for us," said he. "The moral commitment between the colonial power and the colonized people was broken forever." In the French Army in Indochina, the man had been a lieutenant. In newly independent Algeria, he was Lieutenant-Colonel Slimane Hoffman, the Director of the Algerian Ministry of Defense.

Some of the North Africans volunteered to serve in the armed forces of their captors, but the Viet-Minh politely refused.

"We are victorious," they would say to the Algerians, "not because there are so many of us, but because we are fighting in our own country among our own people. We do not need Algerians to fight for Viet-Nam. You Algerians must fight in Algeria."

The Algerians listened and learned. On November 1, 1954, the Algerian rebellion broke out. It was to last even longer than the Indochina war and there would be no Dien Bien Phu. But the Algerians won anyway.

Another group of prisoners was the subject of special attention—the Eastern Europeans. Contrary to the accepted myth that the Foreign Legion was made up largely of "former SS troopers," many of the Foreign Legionnaires came from the East European countries overrun by the Soviet armies in 1945. (Since the average age of the Foreign Legionnaire was about twenty-three in 1954, most of them had been small boys in 1945.) Many of the German Legionnaires had come originally from East German areas and now became the object of particular pressure by the Viet-Minh political commissars to return to East Germany as walking propaganda exhibits. The Soviet Union admitted that Foreign Legionnaires of Eastern European nationality who had "volunteered" to return to Eastern Europe had been returned there by Soviet aircraft. In December, 1954, after the repatriation of all French Union prisoners officially listed as such had long since been completed, an organization of Eastern European exiles in New York issued a list of about 1,000 Foreign Legionnaires from Eastern European countries who had allegedly been compelled to return there.[20] What their eventual fate was in their Communist homelands is anyone's guess. A certain number of prisoners of French nationality who were known to be alive at the time of the cease-fire refused to return to their homeland, just as a handful of United States prisoners defected to Communist China after the Korean War.

But beyond a doubt the most interesting victims of brainwashing were the staunchly Catholic and conservative junior officers of the French Army. As far as they were concerned, their whole world, the whole code by which they had lived and fought, had crashed about them on the blood-soaked hills of Dien Bien Phu. They had fought as best they knew how. They were at least as well trained and far better equipped than their Communist counterparts. Yet they had lost. When everything was said and done, it remained a fact that the anti-Communist Vietnamese simply had not fought like the Vietnamese on the Communist side. The non-Communist guerrilla forces in the hills around Dien Bien Phu had not succeeded in cutting off or interfering with the Viet-Minh supply lines, as they were supposed to have done. Even the French troops, though they had fought honorably in many cases, had not—with the exception of the paratroop battalions—fought with the fanaticism of the enemy.

Was it not Gen. Navarre himself who, in his later memoirs, said of his own army that "they were good and devoted men but they were not exactly the soldiers of the French Revolution"? Had not a senior officer from Dien Bien Phu been overheard to say in the prison camp that "we were fighting for our professional honor and in the end, for our skins. But they, the enemy, were fighting for their country . . ."?

Obviously, there was something else to the war in Viet-Nam and the Battle of Dien Bien Phu than professional competence or an error in strategy on the part of Gen. Navarre. That would give far too little credit to what every French officer had witnessed for himself thirty times over throughout the Battle of Dien Bien Phu and what made an old army sergeant major like Abderrahman Ben Salem admire an enemy who made him walk over the dying bodies of his own men. It was that kind of fanaticism which the French Resistance had possessed. The Communists very willingly provided the answers to their captive's question. They were all contained in cheap-looking little booklets written in Chinese but also published in English and French and now laboriously retranslated into Vietnamese. They had mostly been written by a Chinese leader about whom most of the officers had hardly heard, even though they were fighting a war right next to his country: Mao Tse-tung. Others were written by the general secretary of the Vietnamese Communist Party, Truong Chinh. They all dealt with one and the same subject, which they called "Revolutionary Warfare." It was not, as the French officers had thought, simply a newer method of fighting small wars, and it had almost nothing to do with fighting as they knew it. But all those writings, just as the lectures of the political commissars to the prisoners, emphasized the importance of what they called "the people"—the huge mass of illiterate peasants from which their army was drawn.

With a sort of horrified fascination, the French Army officers watched the process work on the lesser-motivated NCO's and particularly on the non-French soldiers among the prisoners. There was in fact little brutality, but there was a fantastic combination of repetitive assertion of certain half-truths combined with methodical rewards for lessons learned well and mild punishment for resistance to the learning process in the true Pavlov tradition. Maximum emphasis was on "group learning" and "group discipline." Since for every individual resistance to the learning process, the whole group was liable to such punishment as, say, withholding of quinine pills essential to resisting malaria, or of a mail distribution known to have arrived in the camp, or of the Red Cross packages that provided a slight improvement in the camp diet, there soon developed selective pressure by the prisoners themselves on the recalcitrants among them who refused to accept the common discipline. Those who proved to be totally unamenable to persuasion soon found themselves transferred to the ill-famed Lang-Trang reprisal camp from which no one ever returned. It was Father Jeandel, a chaplain with the 6th BPC who had been taken prisoner in 1952, who summed up the experience of indoctrination in one single but eloquent sentence: "The worst wasn't to die, but to see one's soul change."

It was this "soul-changing" which was to leave its most indelible mark on the French officers who survived Dien Bien Phu. Not that any of them became convinced that Communism was the way of the future and that the West was philosophically inferior, but they were now firmly convinced that what was needed was the ruthless application of what one Soviet writer called the "rape of the masses" and their deliberate and methodical conditioning for the revolutionary tasks ahead. Had there been a few years of respite between Viet-Nam and Algeria, these officers might have been able to digest their experience, but this was not to be the case. Within months after their liberation from the prison camps in Viet-Nam they were plunged into yet another "national liberation war" in Algeria, a few hundred miles from home—and this time, they believed, they were playing the game for keeps. With cold ferocity both the Algerians and the French who were survivors of the Communist indoctrination sessions began to use the newly learned science against each other. And when it seemed that the French people at home refused to accept the idea of yet another two decades of counterinsurgency in Algeria, those deeply dedicated officers decided to apply Mao Tse-tung to their own country.

But they had misread Mao Tse-tung. The French officers who had joined what was called for a while the "Secret Army Organization" (OAS) had mistaken one million frightened French Europeans living in Algeria for the kind of mass population necessary to support a revolutionary warfare operation. They forgot that, in Algeria, nine million Moslems would not support them and that, in France, there were forty-eight million Frenchmen who did not share their ideas. But before they were defeated for a second time, they had almost engulfed France in the kind of revolutionary war about which they had learned in the camps east of Dien Bien Phu.

The Escapees

While 10,000 prisoners marched westward away from Dien Bien Phu, a handful—seventy-eight, to be exact—clawed their way through the jungle to freedom. Their experience showed conclusively that, if one wishes to escape from the enemy in Indochina, one is better off being a native, and preferably from the area itself. Of the total number of escapees, there were only nineteen Europeans. Of the Asians, twelve of the fourteen NCO's were tribal T'ai and of the forty enlisted men, thirty-two were tribesmen; that is, they blended in perfectly with the surrounding population. The other eight non-Europeans were lowland Vietnamese.

The European escapees were an even more curious lot. Only one single officer made a successful escape, although several others tried it: it was the indomitable Lt. Makoviak of 3rd BT. Makoviak had fought with the paratroopers on Eliane to the last day, but when they were about to be overrun he decided that there still was a chance to survive and fight again. Speaking perfectly the tribal T'ai language, he did not find it difficult, in the chaos of the camp's conquest, to slip through the enemy lines and to begin his trek westward. On May 31, somewhat the worse for wear but in fighting shape, Makoviak ran into one of the French guerrilla units operating in nearby Laos.

The other French escapees were even more surprising, for they included, above all, combat engineers from the 31st Battalion, and tank crews. There were also some Foreign Legionnaires (almost all of them from Isabelle), but only a very few paratroopers succeeded in breaking out. This was probably due to the fact that they were more heavily guarded than most other prisoners, and because they had been in constant heavy combat throughout the battle and were therefore in bad physical shape to resist the extreme hazards of an escape. There may well have been hundreds of men who tried to flee the marching columns and who no doubt were captured or killed by greedy tribesmen desirous to collect a bounty from the Viet-Minh or to ingratiate themselves with them. Many others probably died of exhaustion somewhere in the jungle without ever having been heard from again.

The men who beyond a doubt fared best in the escape from Dien Bien Phu were the tank crews from Isabelle. They stayed together throughout the escape, French and Vietnamese alike, helping each other, and, even though none of them had had any jungle training, came through with flying colors. On May 10, a small but still-armed troop encountered an enemy patrol but succeeded in shaking it off at the price of leaving one prisoner, Gunner Balcon, in Viet-Minh hands. Reinforced by a few Legionnaires from Isabelle, they continued in a southwesterly direction, only to be intercepted again on May 13 by a new Viet-Minh force. In the ensuing firefight they lost part of their men, but Sergeants Re and Tai, Corporals Gung, Talmont, and Menay, and Vietnamese Pvt. Van Thu again succeeded in breaking through. They finally reached Meo tribal villages; the Meos, unlike the T'ai, were hostile to the Viet-Minh. The Meos helped them find rafts and even gave them armed escorts, and by the end of May, the survivors of the armored platoon reached Muong Sai. They had covered 160 kilometers on foot in twenty days.

Two other sergeants, Villers and Ney, from the tank squadron at the main position, managed to escape from the column of prisoners along Road 41 on May 14. Ney, as we have seen earlier, had been wounded at Dien Bien Phu but nevertheless preferred to attempt the escape rather than rot in a prison camp. For seven days they marched by themselves in a vast northeasterly arc around the valley of Dien Bien Phu until, on May 21, they met a small group of combat engineers at the village of Houei Kang hard on the border between Viet-Nam and Laos, overlooking the Nam Noua River which they knew would guide them to freedom. Their meeting with the engineers resulted in one of the more spectacular escapes from Dien Bien Phu.

The engineers had been ordered to stay on at Dien Bien Phu to provide for essential technical services in the camp. The Viet-Minh had at first ordered them to march on into the prison camps, but as early as May 9, the Communists became aware of the fact that they could not, without grave risk, de-mine the valley without having recourse to specialists. Master Sergeants Ryback and Cable and Sergeants Jouatel and Leroy volunteered for the job, which permitted them to circulate in many areas of the camp. On May 13, the Engineers were informed that their mission had been fulfilled and that they would continue to follow the prisoner-of-war trek on the following day. As far as the Engineers knew, their best chance of escaping was about to disappear. Fortunately, M/Sgt. Ryback had found that day a good French Army road map among the debris, and one of the other sergeants had stolen some biscuits and combat rations elsewhere. At 0200 of May 14, the four men disappeared westward into the hills.

Six days later the small group had reached a village named Ban Loi—not to be confused with a locality of the same name near Dien Bien Phu—located about thirty kilometers southwest of Dien Bien Phu on the Nam Yum. To their horror, they found what appeared to be a Viet-Minh soldier in the village, but he turned out to be a Laotian recruit in the Viet-Minh forces who was not at all eager to engage the French in a fight and who sold them fish and rice and showed them the path to Houei Kang. On May 21, they arrived at Houei Kang, only to find Villers, Ney, and a Foreign Legion paratrooper named Horst Kienitz, as well as a few T'ai tribal soldiers, under the guard of one lone Viet-Minh regular armed with a French MAT-49 submachine gun. The Viet-Minh motioned the engineers to sit down and eat with him and the prisoners. That good deed did him no good because the Frenchmen, after the meal, jumped their guard, knocked him out, and took his tommy gun.

From then on they took no chances. Leaving the Nam Nua valley they struck out straight west through the jungle, crossed another tributary of the Nam Nua and attempted to bypass the T'ai tribal villages, known to be occupied by sympathizers of the Viet-Minh, in the hope of finding Meo villages known to be friendly to the French. But late on May 22, at Houei Vang, seventy kilometers northwest of Dien Bien Phu, they were seen by local inhabitants and soon two Viet-Minh soldiers armed with a rifle and a tommy gun came running after them. The French wounded both men and took their weapons, but they were exhausted. Very fortunately they came upon a small Meo hamlet where they found a former soldier from the 6th Laotian Infantry Battalion who warned them from entering nearby Muong Khoua, which had again fallen to the Viet-Minh, and told them to strike out for Muong Sai. There was no doubt but that Muong Sai still was in French hands—but it was almost 150 kilometers away and each one of those kilometers was covered with high-stand jungle and most areas were overrun with Communist patrols or hostile T'ai tribesmen.

Ryback and the other men set out for Muong Sai via the brutally difficult paths where the ridge-running Meos live. On May 26, the escapees crossed the Nam-Hou. There a former Laotian soldier promised them to take them to Muong Sai for a sum of 3,000 piasters (then about $90.00), of which they were to pay him one half immediately and one half on arrival; but as was often the case, the tribesman was not too sure of his road and also took fright at being caught with French troops. He marched with them for two days but then abandoned them at the Meo village of Lai-Tiak. By now, most of the escapees had reached the end of their physical tether. Their clothes were in rags and most of them had lost or worn out their shoes. The only ones who felt capable of continuing the march were Ryback and Villers, who decided to continue towards Muong Sai. The Meos treated the remaining French very well and on May 31, Sgts. Cable, Jouatel, and Leroy felt well enough to continue in the direction of Muong Sai with the help of two Meo guides. Sergeant Ney and Pfc Kienitz, however, were too ill to continue with them.

On June 1, the sergeants crossed the Nam-Pak and knew now that they were only about two days' march away from Muong Sai. Unless they were completely out of luck now, they were absolutely sure of reaching safety. Here and there, indeed, the presence of the French already made itself felt: local villagers would confirm that French patrols had been seen recently and also one could hear an occasional drone of a French transport or reconnaissance aircraft. Finally, at 1530 of June 3, the characteristic "flub-flub" of helicopter rotors could be heard and above them appeared an American-built H-19 helicopter of the French

Air Force, piloted by Lt. Blouin. Waving wildly and screaming at the top of their lungs although it was certain that the pilot could not hear them over the noise of his machine, the sergeants attempted to follow the path of the helicopter. It seemed not to have seen them, but suddenly it stood still in mid-air and then began to lose altitude slowly in a cloud of churned-up leaves and dust. A few hours later the rest of the group was picked up.

Untrained and unequipped for jungle warfare, M/Sgt. Ryback and his men had covered almost 200 kilometers in less than three weeks. In addition, Sgt. Ney had managed to take along with him his camera and thus became the only Frenchman to have brought out of the battle photographs of Dien Bien Phu's agony and of the escape itself. Ironically, *Le Monde* of May 27, 1954, had listed all of them as confirmed prisoners.

Other escapees had different experiences. Gunner Georges Nallet, of the 35th Airborne Artillery, escaped from his POW column during the night of May 15 and walked westward until he reached the Nam Meuk thirty kilometers north of Dien Bien Phu. He built a bamboo raft and paddled up the Nam Meuk in a southwesterly direction. On May 21, he came upon a friendly Meo village and the tribesmen guided him from village to village until on May 24 Nallet came upon four sergeants, including Sentenac from Bigeard's own 6th BPC. They were taking the northernmost route to Muong Sai, but were totally unimpressed by the 200-kilometer-long trek that was ahead. They deliberately rested for two weeks, reconnoitering the area in which they were, and then, on June 8, began the march southward. They were picked up without the slightest hitch by a French helicopter on July 2. Sergeant Sentenac was in such good shape that he refused to be evacuated, preferring to stay with a *maquis* force of Meo tribesmen. Sentenac survived the Indochina war with seven wounds, thirteen citations for bravery, and was knighted in the Legion of Honor. And when Bigeard received the command of a Marine parachute regiment in Algeria, Sentenac again served with him. Master Sergeant Sentenac was killed on November 21, 1957, at Timimoun, at the edge of the Sahara, in a firefight with Bedouin tribesmen loyal to the cause of Algerian nationalism.

"Of all of us," Colonel Bigeard was to say of him, "it was he who had the greatest amount of luck, for he succeeded in dying the way he should have after having led the tormented life that he had chosen."[21]

The Asians among the escapees obviously blended in better with the environment and therefore stood a better chance of getting away.

Thus, two Vietnamese corporals and two T'ai tribesmen corporals, instead of marching into Laos, resolutely struck out for the Red River Delta—and reached it without trouble by July 10. One can imagine the utter amazement of the post commander of Vinh-Yen as Corporals Hoang Van Tuyet and Duong Van Nhien reported to him after crossing almost 300 kilometers of solidly held enemy territory.

Pfc Tra Nhon of 2nd Company, 8th Parachute Assault, escaped on May 11 along with a master sergeant, a corporal and six Vietnamese paratroopers. Surprised by the Viet-Minh on May 16 at a watering point ten kilometers north of Dien Bien Phu, Tra Nhon and one paratrooper escaped but now stayed away from all villages. They marched for five days without food until they found a tribesman who sold them two pounds of rice for 600 piasters ($18.00) and indicated to them a friendly Meo village six days' march away. They arrived in a state of total exhaustion but were lucky enough to be picked up at the beginning of June by a French-led *maquis* force.

And finally, there was the case of Sergeant Hoang Van Tieng. Tieng was an interpreter with French Intelligence, and the Viet-Minh understandably were far from tender with any Intelligence personnel. As soon as it was evident, on May 7, that Dien Bien Phu would fall, Tieng and his other associates had dressed in T'ai tribal clothing in the hopes of being mistaken for local tribesmen cut off inside the fortress. To add to his camouflage, Tieng had taken along on his flight one of the Laotian women who had been the wife of a dead tribal soldier, and both had begun the long trek westward. But the Laotian woman was simply not up to the rigors of the march through rivers and across mountains with little, if any, food. She grew weaker and weaker and one day could go on no longer. But by then, Sgt. Tieng was certain that he had reached friendly territory and that he no longer needed the Laotian woman as a camouflage. He left her to die and reached Muong Sai a few days later without trouble.

And there was Sgt. Béguin, who had been a private on January 4, a corporal on March 1 and a sergeant on May 1, and who had been wounded twice in the cesspool of strongpoint Wieme. He had escaped on May 8 and had walked for nineteen days by himself southwestward in the direction of the Mekong. He almost made it, but on May 28 he was captured by the Viet-Minh only eighty kilometers from Luang-Prabang. He weighed exactly eighty-one pounds when he was turned over to the French by his captors on August 26, 1954.

The Dead

The bodies of about 8,000 Viet-Minh troops and of over 2,000 French Union troops are buried in the reddish earth of the valley of Dien Bien Phu.

But no imposing monument, either French or Viet-Minh, honors the 10,000 men who died here and who may have done more to shape the fate of the world than the soldiers at Agincourt, Waterloo, or Stalingrad. To be sure, there is a small Viet-Nam People's Army cemetery with about 500 bodies at the foot of Eliane, and there are two small monuments, one on Beatrice and the other on ill-fated Eliane 2. The one on Eliane is placed at the foot of the still-surviving banyan tree.

But the French cemetery, bulldozed out near Dr. Grauwin's hospital and used as long as burying one body did not cost two more lives, has disappeared altogether under a succession of monsoon floods and tropical underbrush. The crosses—for there had been crosses planted on the graves at least during the earlier part of the battle (and later there had been short stakes with at least a scrawled Army serial number)—have been slowly used up for firewood by the local population, not as a gesture of hatred but simply as a matter of convenience.

In a strange way, the dead of Dien Bien Phu were the first victims of the Second Indochina War. The cease-fire agreement signed in July, 1954, at Geneva provided that both sides would be authorized to use graves registration teams in each other's zone for the purpose of regrouping the war dead in appropriate cemeteries. A special accord was signed later which provided for the creation of permanent cemeteries by both sides in both South and North Viet-Nam. For Dien Bien Phu, Accord No. 24 provided for the creation of a vast ossuary—a charnel house— in the valley. The French, in view of the technical means available to them, also undertook to regroup the enemy bodies which they would find in the valley, just as the vast Verdun cemeteries in France provide an honorable resting place for the enemy also.

In May, 1955, exactly one year after the end of the battle, the North Vietnamese authorities permitted Captain Paul Belmont of the French Army and Lieutenant Nguyen Van Sai of the South Vietnamese Army to return to Dien Bien Phu and to begin there the preliminary registration and surveys necessary for the regroupment of the tombs. At that time, the traces of the battle were still fresh and, with the help of information provided them by the surviving French unit commanders, the two officers were able to identify 639 graves very rapidly. With the

help of local labor provided them by the adversary, the two officers began
to lay the groundwork for an ossuary that would contain 5,000 bodies.
For a while it seemed as if the battlefield of Dien Bien Phu would,
thanks to the understanding of the People's Army High Command and
the devotion of the French, take on the aspect of a "hallowed ground,"
as befits a place where the fate of one nation and the world role of
another had been forever shaped.

But a new spirit now reigned in Saigon, where the newly divided
but fully independent South Vietnamese state had taken form. Its leader,
Ngo Dinh Diem, whose government had not signed the Geneva cease-
fire, unilaterally decided that Viet-Minh graves registration missions
would not be authorized to circulate in South Viet-Nam and that the
cemeteries of their forces and the monuments erected to honor their dead
would be razed. This was but a minor violation among the many violations of the cease-fire provisions that both sides were guilty of and which
were to lead to the Second Indochina War.

With total predictability, the North Vietnamese immediately used
Saigon's action to deny the French graves registration team the right to
continue its work in the valley. Thus the 10,000 dead of Dien Bien Phu
were left to rot just as they had fought and died—inside or in front of
the shattered bunkers on Beatrice, around the trench lines and the fort
of Gabrielle, on the nipple-like protrusions of breast-shaped Dominique,
on the slopes and in the crater of Eliane, the collapsed dugouts of the
"subway," the swampy lowlands of Huguette, Claudine, and Isabelle,
the gun pits of the artillery, and the smashed cockpits of the downed
aircraft. Most of the French dead are, like royalty, swathed in silk
shrouds. Parachute nylon, like courage, was one of the common items at
Dien Bien Phu, and on both sides.

When Jules Roy remarked to Gen. Giap in 1962 that something
should have been done for the fallen in the valley, the Communist
commander-in-chief promised that an effort would be made to gather
the French dead and that the French would be authorized to erect a
monument in their honor. Nothing has come of it, but Giap may yet
make good on his promise.

After the end of the Second Indochina War.

XII

Epilogue

As IN MOST lost battles, the most fascinating part of the struggle for Dien Bien Phu is the series of "might-have-beens" which can be derived from the reports of the surviving senior officers.

Each one of them seems to feel that a particular deficiency in logistical support or a minor tactical error constituted the decisive blunder which finally doomed Dien Bien Phu. In addition, there are the myths promulgated by outside observers.

One of the most common is that the French "didn't know what they were doing," *e.g.*, that their intelligence was faulty. As we have seen, the French High Command knew within *ten per cent* what the enemy's infantry strength was going to be.

Another widely accepted myth keeps referring to the "17 battalions of [French] infantry" faced by "40,000 men altogether."[1] As was shown earlier *four* battalions disappeared from the battle map inside of forty-eight hours (3/13 Foreign Legion, 3rd BT, and for all practical purposes 2nd BT and the 5/7 Algerian Rifles), and the airborne replacements were fed in understrength and piecemeal over a period of three months. Seventeen battalions *passed through* Dien Bien Phu—but there never were more than ten deployed simultaneously. On the other hand the Viet-Minh maintained an almost constant strength of four divisions in the battle area.

Lastly, there is the myth of Dien Bien Phu as a "German battle," in which the Germans were said to have "indeed made up nearly half the French forces."[2] The statistical appendix will lay this to rest for good. On March 12, 1954—the day before the battle began in earnest—there was a total of 2,969 Foreign Legionnaires in the fortress, out of a garrison of 10,814. Of the almost 4,300 parachuted reinforcements, a total of 962 belonged to the Foreign Legion. Even if one wrongly assumes (there were important Spanish and Eastern European elements among the Legionnaires at Dien Bien Phu) that 50 per cent of the Legionnaires were German, then only 1,900 men out of more than 15,000 who participated in the battle could have been of German origin. But old myths, particularly when reinforced by prejudice, die hard.

The Viet-Minh, however, far exceeded French intelligence estimates in the number of artillery pieces and artillery shells which they succeeded in bringing to the valley. Each Viet-Minh infantry regiment was known to possess one battery of four 75-mm. mountain howitzers and one battery of four 120-mm. heavy mortars. It was also known that the 351st Division could field three artillery battalions of 105-mm., composed of three batteries for four field guns each. In reality there were 144 field pieces available to the enemy at Dien Bien Phu, not including at least thirty 75-mm. recoilless cannon, some thirty-six heavy flak pieces, and, in the last few days of the battle, between twelve to sixteen of the six-tube *Katyusha* rocket launchers.

A more fateful error in French intelligence estimates occurred when the *Deuxième Bureau* estimated the Viet-Minh's artillery ammunition capability at a total of 25,000 rounds and counted on the French Air Force to prevent further sizable amounts of ammunition from reaching the battlefield. While some of the Viet-Minh ammunition figures cited later reached an unbelievable level of 350,000 rounds,[3] it seems clearly established from French artillery observations that the enemy fired a total of 103,000 shells of 75-mm. caliber or bigger, of which a depressing 12,000 were misdropped French-American supply loads. For comparison, the French more or less wasted 38,500 shells during the pre-siege period of November, 1953 - March 13, 1954; and they fired a total of 93,000 shells of similar caliber during the period of actual battle. The French, to be sure, were outgunned three to one on the ground, but possessed airborne firepower and ten tanks. It is, therefore, not quite accurate to say that the French lost Dien Bien Phu simply because they had placed themselves in an area where the enemy's firepower far outclassed them. There were many things that went wrong at Dien Bien Phu. The imbalance in firepower between the two adversaries was not the worst of them.

On the other hand, there can be no doubt that the French completely lost the logistical battle. They proved incapable (and in this there was a terribly important lesson for the Americans who fought in Viet-Nam in 1965-67) of interdicting the flow of Communist supplies to the valley. The Viet-Minh had at its disposal a total of 600 Russian *Molotova* 2.5-ton trucks for which barely passable roads and river ferries had to be built by tens of thousands of coolies. But the mainstay of the supply system were the tough bicycle-pushing human supply columns. Carrying often 200 kilos (440 pounds) of supplies on a standard bicycle whose seat had been replaced by a short holding stick and whose handlebar had been extended by another stick permitting the vehicle to be easily guided even when heavily loaded, 8,286 tons had been shipped over 600 miles of jungle from China to Dien Bien Phu: 4,620 tons of petrol products, 1,360 tons of ammunition, 46 tons of spare weapons, and 2,260 tons of consumable goods, including 1,700 tons of rice of which 400 were eaten by the carrier columns on the trek. In contrast to what goes on in the Second Indochina War, where the Ho Chi Minh trail does not start at any one particular place and, above all, does not end at one particular point (as was the case of the supply system at Dien Bien Phu), the French Air Force was in a position to concentrate its supply interdiction effort upon a relatively well known and fairly well circumscribed route. Its failure to hamper Communist supply operations in any significant manner surely was in part due to the small amount of aircraft and bomb tonnage that could be spared by the pitifully small French Air Force for this work. But it must be remembered that, barely a year earlier, the mighty United States Far Eastern Air Force (FEAF) had also failed to bring the Chinese Red and North Korean supply systems to their knees, despite the fact that hundreds of American heavy and medium bombers were engaged in a year-long, round-the-clock interdiction effort dubbed "Operation Strangle."[4]

On the French side, estimates of supplies parachuted on Dien Bien Phu from March 13 to May 7 varied from 6,410 to 6,900 tons, and daily figures from 117 tons to 123 tons; but actually received usable supplies reduced this to about 100 tons per day. While this was not enough, it was a great deal more than any besieged fortress had received during World War II, from Corregidor to Stalingrad. In fact, in its post-mortem on the battle, Quartermaster asked whether, "In the last analysis, the real bottleneck was not more in the primitive supply-collection capability" of the besieged fortress than in the limited amount of supplies it received. That point warrants closer examination, as similar situations are likely to recur in other wars of this type. Considering the ever-shrinking size of the defense perimeter and, therefore, the extremely limited amount of usable air space above the fortress that was available for supply drops, it would have at first glance seemed wise to drop the largest possible loads from the largest available plane. However, it is perfectly obvious that, with the increase of well-aimed artillery fire over the whole surface of the fortress, it became impossible to move even electric field generators weighing one ton, let alone single five-ton "palette" loads, which the "Flying Boxcars" could have easily handled. Dien Bien Phu was caught in a vicious circle in which the maintenance of wider supply drop zones would have required the presence of larger troop reserves, and in which the presence of larger troop reserves would have required a further upward spiraling of supply requirements.

But here we now come to the more important variables of the might-have-been Battle of Dien Bien Phu. There had been inside Dien Bien Phu at least 3,000 to 4,000 "internal deserters"—tribesmen, Vietnamese, North Africans, and also some Frenchmen and Foreign Legionnaires—who decided to sit out the battle in the rat holes along the banks of the Nam Yum. Ten years later, Col. Bigeard still believed that with the same number of troops that were available at Dien Bien Phu, but of first-class quality, the French could have survived the battle. "If you had given me 10,000 SS troopers," said Bigeard to this writer ten years after the battle, "we'd have held out."

Here, it is impossible to absolve Gen. René Cogny, the French commander of North Viet-Nam, of responsibility. As we have seen, he had never been enthusiastic about the idea of Dien Bien Phu and he considered the Red River Delta, with the core cities of Hanoi and Haiphong, its three million tons of rice and nine million people, far more vital to the French cause than the forlorn valley at the very periphery of his command. He had been reluctant to deprive himself of his best troops and best commanders for the sake of strengthening Dien Bien Phu and had repeatedly underlined to Gen. Navarre that the Battle of Dien Bien Phu had to be conducted at the level of the whole Indochina theater rather than at that of Tonkin alone. The available evidence does not show that Gen. de Castries was particularly aware of his own personnel problem or even alarmed by it. At first, as long as Dien Bien Phu was to remain a mooring point for offensive operations deep into the T'ai highland jungle, there was ample justification to keep the T'ai tribal units around even if they were of dubious fighting value. As for the North Africans, many of the French officers, including de Castries and Langlais, had commanded them in the past and prided themselves in knowing them well. The North Africans had fought well for France for a hundred years and they had fought well elsewhere in Indochina. There was no reason to believe that they would crack now. But crack they did—simply because it had been a terribly long and bloody war, and they were tired of it. It was a war very far away from home, and they had been frequently the object of intensive propaganda appealing to them to quit fighting France's colonial wars.

Many of the surviving senior commanders at Dien Bien Phu argued bitterly that an additional group of two good battalions could surely have saved strongpoints Gabrielle and Anne-Marie in mid-March, both of which covered the vital airfield; and that even one reserve battalion available on March 30 could have retaken Dominiques 1 and 2 from a stunned enemy and held them just as long as Eliane—thus covering the center of Dien Bien Phu from flat-trajectory fire.

In their report, the survivors of the Armored Squadron argued that a full-strength unit of seventeen tanks, instead of ten, could easily have maintained communications with Isabelle and Gabrielle (no one thought much, apparently, of outlying Beatrice, which probably should never have been occupied to begin with); could easily have retaken Dominique 2 and protected the airstrip; and could have, as the Americans often did in Korea and in the Philippines against the Japanese, been used in close combat against the entrenched Communist artillery. Veritable "hunter-killer teams" could have been organized with a combination of tanks and dive bombers to hunt down Communist battery positions. As the successful breakout of March 28 showed, such well-coordinated stabs could have destroyed much of the feared light enemy flak that hampered the supply drops so much and rapidly made the airfield unusable. Whether such an enlarged tank squadron would really have tilted the balance of the defensive battle may well remain one of the most tantalizing "might-have-beens" of the whole struggle for the valley.

Another failure—and it seems to have been both a French and American failure—was the total underestimation of the enemy's antiaircraft gunmanship. Since the Korean War had ended only a few months before the battle for Dien Bien Phu began, it probably was impossible by then to fully evaluate the deadly effectiveness of flak there, which finally accounted for 816 "kills," as against 147 Allied planes lost in air-to-air combat. And in Korea, as was to be the case at Dien Bien Phu, "the flak-suppression strikes usually drove enemy gunners under cover but seldom destroyed enemy weapons."[5] Yet the myth that conventional light flak and even a "fire curtain" of massed small arms could not seriously hurt high-performance aircraft was so strongly anchored in the minds of American air-power strategists that as late as 1962, addressing themselves to the new Viet-Nam problem, they strongly affirmed that "jungle rebels are not equipped with ack-ack or interception capability, so that air superiority is practically assured."[6] Recent aircraft losses over Viet-Nam have probably disabused them of that notion. But in 1953-54 the French fully believed their American teachers. They paid for that error with a total of 48 aircraft shot down over the valley, another 14 destroyed on the ground at Dien Bien Phu, and 167 damaged over the valley by enemy flak. Considering that these losses were inflicted in five months upon an air force which never had more than 100 supply and reconnaissance aircraft and 75 combat aircraft available for Dien Bien Phu, they were extremely heavy.

Dien Bien Phu, like almost all other besieged fortresses, eventually died from its supply deficiencies. This book clearly shows several instances in which successful counterattacks were interrupted because there was no ammunition available to sustain them. In the end, the Elianes, which had weathered every enemy infantry assault, weeks of intensive artillery bombardment, and even underground mining, finally fell because their garrisons had run out of ammunition. If any particular group of enemy soldiers should be considered indispensable to victory, then it must be the Viet-Minh antiaircraft gunners and their Chinese instructors.

When everything has been said about the many major and minor errors which led to the French debacle at Dien Bien Phu (the poorly planned counterattacks, the flimsily built field fortifications, the underestimation of the enemy flak, and even the choice of the battle area itself) one single fact stands out above all others. *Air power on a more massive scale than was then available could not have changed the outcome of the Indochina War, but it would have saved Dien Bien Phu.*

French observers of the battle, regardless of their own service loyalties, appear to be in agreement on this. The chairman of the French Government Investigating Commission on the Battle of Dien Bien Phu, Army General Catroux was to say later—and there is little question that his statement reflects the general tenor of the still top-secret report—that the

> . . . sole chance of salvation of the heroic garrison rested on a massive intervention of a fleet of American bombers based both on aircraft carriers of the U.S. Navy and in the Philippines. Undertaken by some three to four hundred heavy aircraft, that operation would have, in the view of the experts, smashed the Viet-Minh [siege] organizations and would doubtlessly have reversed the course of events.[7]

At a press conference held by Gen. de Castries upon his return from captivity, the commander of the fallen fortress also declared that a massive American air intervention would have "in all likelihood" permitted him to retake the initiative.[8]

And, finally, Gen. Ely, who succeeded Navarre after the latter had been relieved from command and who is known to this day as one of the most pro-American of all French senior officers, judged the role of the lack of air power at the crucial moment in the following terms:

> I truly believe that, had I been commander-in-chief at the time, I would not have made the same decision as General Navarre, but I would be quite incapable of saying today what would then have happened to the situation in Laos and in Tonkin. On the other hand, had, by some unexpected chance which often plays a decisive role in war, Dien Bien Phu not fallen—if only the fortress had been disengaged [from enemy encirclement] by American aerial intervention—would not then the choice made by Navarre be considered to this day as a stroke of genius? And wouldn't those who have condemned him since, attempt to share with him in the authorship of the operation?[9]

These various viewpoints give rise to two additional questions: (1) Why did France herself not provide her armed forces in Indochina with an adequate air force? (2) Why did the United States, knowing full well what was at stake, fail to provide the lacking air power, after all?

As shown earlier, the answer to the first question goes back in part to the whole French military structure after World War II. France, defeated and occupied by the Germans from 1940 to 1944, had built up a Free French Air Force in Great Britain, North Africa, and Italy—and, eventually, even in Russia—which included, as its mainstay, 330 American light and medium bombers (the largest type being the B-26) and 723 American-built fighters. To this force must be added a few Free French squadrons armed with British *Spitfires* and two fighter groups operating on the Russian front with Soviet-built *Stormoviks*.

When the Indochina War began it was at first thought to be of the classical colonial kind and thus only transport planes and a few fighter squadrons were assigned to it. When it became obvious that bombers would be required, it turned out that France's mission within the new NATO structure did not provide for the building up of a specifically French bomber force but assigned to France an exclusively passive role in the field of tactical support and air defense. In fact, during the early years of NATO, only the United States and Britain possessed bomber forces. With the exception of two French Navy squadrons of four-engine

Privateers, the French did not even possess any aircraft capable of providing a training nucleus for heavy-bomber crews. In that particular sense
(and the argument is now often invoked by French officials opposed
to the "subordination" of French national interests to the over-all
requirements of the NATO alliance) the very modernization of the
French fighter force within NATO into an all-jet force, prevented the use
of that force in Indochina, since there were practically no airfields available in that country which were capable of providing for the efficient
maintenance of a large jet force. It took the incredibly huge American
military and industrial deployment of 1965-66 to provide South Viet-Nam
alone with that kind of infrastructure.

In addition, even the senior French officials involved admit that both
the military and the French government of the time had made some
crucial mistakes. On the military side, the importance of bombers in that
kind of war had been grossly underestimated until very late, and the use
of jets had been considered, in view of their high speed, as totally un-
economical, if not unfeasible. Edouard Frédéric-Dupont, a long-time
French conservative member of Parliament and Minister for the Associated States of Indochina during the crucial 1954 period, later accused
the French military of both tactical blindness and excessive timidity in
stating their requirements:

> Four years had to go by before it was understood that this sort of
> war required riverboats and helicopters.
> Heavy bomber aircraft, whose lack resulted in the [defeat of]
> Dien Bien Phu, had never been requested by the responsible author-
> ities from the legislators who went on missions to Indochina.
> And when we finally got aircraft, it was found that the necessary
> training fields and repair crews were lacking.[10]

While that assertion no doubt contains a large grain of truth, Gen.
Charles Lauzin, the commander of the French Far Eastern Air Force at
the time of the Battle of Dien Bien Phu, in his first top-secret sum-up
of the battle, was to remind his superiors in France that he had reported
the serious deficiencies in aircraft and air force personnel prevailing in
Indochina as soon as he had taken over his Indochina command on June
30, 1953, and that the French Parliament had turned down a modest
$18.4-million budget request for airfield construction and improvement
in Indochina for the fiscal year 1953-54.[11] The net result of that combination of French errors of judgment and conflicting NATO obligations
was that the French were unable to deploy fully the obsolete aircraft
which became available to them through last-minute intensive American

aid. In addition, and that was also the price the French now had to pay for their own defeat in World War II, there were very few French senior officers who had had sufficient command experience to make intelligent use of the available air power.

This was clearly felt by the air commanders in Indochina. General Lucien-Max Chassin, Lauzin's predecessor, wrote in his own end-of-mission report of June 14, 1953 (*i.e.*, six months before the beginning of the Battle of Dien Bien Phu), that the French High Command in Indochina, which was totally dominated by ground-force officers, regularly committed "two capital errors" in the use of its aviation. One was that aircraft were always requested on a piecemeal basis with the result that every ground commander finally operated with his own "personal" air force; and the other was that neither the Air Force nor the Navy ever actually participated in the over-all planning of the war itself. Just as the French had not known how to use their tanks in 1940, they did not know how to use their air force in 1954. A good part of the reason why Dien Bien Phu was lost lies right there.

But even so, less than 100 combat aircraft, no matter how well deployed and how aggressively used and led, could not have changed the fate of the Indochina War or even of the valley of Dien Bien Phu. A small comparison with the situation prevailing in Korea from 1950 to 1953 and during the Second Indochina War in 1965-66, make this abundantly clear. In Korea, by July, 1953, the United States Far Eastern Air Force had jurisdiction over 1,536 American and Allied aircraft. By mid-1966, the United States had deployed for use in Viet-Nam approximately 1,700 helicopters (most of them armed), about 700 fixed-wing support aircraft (transports and reconnaissance planes), 400 U. S. Navy combat planes and about 1,000 U. S. Air Force combat aircraft in the country itself. To those aircraft must be added the 400-plane Viet-Nam Air Force and 35 Royal Laotian Air Force aircraft, the latter operating against Communist supply lines crossing Laotian territory. In addition, close to 90 heavy B-52 bombers support the Viet-Nam war from their base in Guam.

What this means in terms of actual performance can be easily guessed at. Throughout the total of 167 days of the siege of Dien Bien Phu from November 20, 1953, to May 8, 1954, a total of 10,400 air missions were flown in behalf of Dien Bien Phu. Of those, 6,700 were supply or troop-transport missions and 3,700 were combat missions. Of the latter, 1,267 were flown by the French Navy. At the beginning of 1966, the *weekly* sorties flown by American aircraft in Viet-Nam often *exceeded* the

25,000 mark! One single example from the Second Indochina War
clearly illustrates what can be done when air power is available in well-
nigh unlimited quantities. During the battle around the totally unim-
portant Special Forces camp at Plei Mé, a triangular mud fort manned
by 300 mountain tribesmen and twelve Americans, friendly combat aircraft flew 240 sorties a day. Dien Bien Phu, with its 15,000 men, considered itself extremely fortunate if a total of forty combat missions were
flown in any 24-hour period.

The question, then, arises as to whether a major American air effort
around Dien Bien Phu in 1954 would have achieved a desirable military
result and, hence, a worthwhile political result at Geneva. The answer
is yes. For example, the incredible saturation of American air power
in South Viet-Nam in 1965-66 saved American and Vietnamese troops
from disaster on several occasions when they were being badly mauled
by far more battle-experienced and jungle-wise South Vietnamese Viet-
Cong or North Vietnamese People's Army troops.

Even in the restricted field of aerial supply, an enlarged American
effort of limited proportions would have permitted the simultaneous
maintenance of Dien Bien Phu's supply levels and the adequate reinforcement of Col. de Crèvecoeur's "Condor" force clawing its way
through the Laotian jungles in the direction of the valley. That supply
force could have been American without even entangling the United
States in an enlarged Indochina war. Dozens of ground actions were
fought in South Viet-Nam in 1965-66 in which the sudden reinforcement
of a position by an air-landed battalion, or the near-total destruction
of enemy depots by a flight of B-52's, changed the issue of the local
battle. One can imagine what a fleet of American B-29's could have
done to the Viet-Minh depot area at Tuan-Giao or to the Communist
artillery batteries west of Claudine; and to the hordes of Viet-Minh
infantry emerging out of the trenches below Dominique and Eliane.

Ten years later, Georges Bidault, who had been France's Foreign
Minister at the time of Dien Bien Phu and who now was in exile in
Brazil for his subversive activities against the French government of
General de Gaulle, commented acidly in his memoirs that the calculated-
risk policy of the late Secretary of State Dulles had been one which
"involved a great deal of calculation—but no risks," and that the present
risks the United States now must shoulder almost alone in Viet-Nam
"come from there."[13]

While this may well be an oversimplification of the situation, there
is little doubt that it was the French defeat at Dien Bien Phu which gave

the whole situation in the Indochina peninsula its especially unstable character. Other colonial nations had withdrawn from former possessions under situations of duress, and still others (including France in Algeria and Britain in Cyprus) finally evacuated colonies after fighting prolonged and bloody wars to inconclusive ends. But only at Dien Bien Phu was a colonial power recently defeated on the open field of battle by the subject nation. For the sacrifice of Dien Bien Phu did not even save the Red River Delta, which Gen. Cogny wanted to preserve at all costs: There were enough People's Army forces left around the Delta itself to begin the dreaded counteroffensive that would deliver it to the enemy as the war's major prize. On June 28, 1954, Gen. Ely ordered the evacuation of the whole southern part of the Red River Delta, including the two stalwart Catholic bishoprics of Phat-Diem and Bui-Chu; the whole French position on North Viet-Nam now was reduced to a narrow corridor on either side of the Hanoi-Haiphong lifeline. In South Viet-Nam, for the first time, the situation was also deteriorating rapidly, with Vietnamese army units deserting in many places and French hospitals overflowing with the wounded pouring in from the about-to-be-abandoned zones.

Dien Bien Phu had been a Viet-Minh military victory over the French as well as a political victory over the United States. As this writer has pointed out elsewhere in great detail,[14] American policy would have been more consistent with practical realities of the postwar era, and with the long-standing ideals of anticolonialism which the United States has continuously professed, if at least as much pressure had been put on France to come to an early understanding with Vietnamese nationalism as was put, for example, on the Netherlands with regard to Indonesia and on Britain with regard to India. Contrary to a prevailing misunderstanding of the facts—easily cleared up by a reading of the published State Department papers of the time—that seemingly lenient policy with regard to France was due neither to excessive Francophilia in the State Department nor to fears of French obstreperousness in NATO. The latter was created only in 1949, at a time when the Indochina War had already hardened into a major conflict; and the same fears of obstreperousness could have arisen in connection with Holland or Britain, but did not stop the United States, for example, from being at total loggerheads with Britain over the latter's Palestine policy.

I must give credit to the noted commentator and specialist in French affairs, David Schoenbrun, for having personally drawn my attention to the particular aspect of the Viet-Nam crisis which differentiates it from the other postwar decolonization wars: By the time the United States became seriously interested in the Indochina struggle, mainland China had fallen to the Communists and Washington was in frantic search of allies—*any* kind of allies, including the French colonials in Indochina and the British colonials in Malaysia—to man a second-line blocking position in the Far East. Secretary of State Dean Acheson's "Crisis in Asia" speech of January, 1950, marked that change of policy from one of total aloofness from the Indochina War to one of all-out support of the French, regardless of the obvious errors of their policies. As the Korean War added its problems to the gloomy picture of the West's positions in Asia, the United States further encouraged the French to commit themselves to what had now become a "crusade against Communism"— and, in the process, committed herself increasingly to their support with money, weapons, supplies, and advisers, and, as we have seen, at the very least with combat aircraft.

That commitment was an entirely *American* option, in which additional commitments by other European or Australasian allies played by no means an essential part—just as they did not in August, 1964, when President Lyndon B. Johnson committed the United States to an open-ended defense of South Viet-Nam and Thailand (and perhaps the rest of Southeast Asia), regardless of the policies or attitudes of other allies. The decision, then, in April, 1954, to let events at Dien Bien Phu take their course and to make any kind of American intervention the object of prior approval by other allies, was likewise unilateral. Under the circumstances, it put the United States in a position where, for the first time in her whole history, she would abandon an ally to his fate while the ally was fighting a war that the United States had encouraged him to fight to a point far beyond his own political objectives* and most certainly far beyond his own military means. In that sense, there can be no doubt but that Dien Bien Phu, far from being a purely French defeat, became an *American* defeat as well.

That is why the magic name of Dien Bien Phu is conjured up whenever North Viet-Nam is exhorted by its leaders to stand fast under the deluge of American bombs that rain down on the country. And it is Dien Bien Phu (along with Suez) which comes to the mind of French military commanders and politicians when General de Gaulle avers that, in a crisis not involving her directly, the United States cannot be counted upon with full certitude. From 1965 onward, the United States was willing to go to war for the sake of preserving what her President calls

*See Chapter IX.

her "national honor." In 1954, one hundred airplanes could not be found to save 15,000 French troops at Dien Bien Phu.

Even so, Dien Bien Phu played a strategically useful role for the United States. It faced her squarely with the reality that, along with the Chinese People's Army, there would now be another major Communist military force in Southeast Asia: Dien Bien Phu signaled in an unequivocal manner the coming of age of the Viet-Nam People's Army. In doing so, it compelled the United States to make later on the choice which the Republican administration and the Democratic Congressional leaders, Lyndon B. Johnson and John W. McCormack, had successfully avoided making under perhaps less unfavorable conditions in 1954.

Future historians will tell whether it was necessary for the West to suffer a defeat at Dien Bien Phu in 1954 in order not to have to face one in South Viet-Nam in 1967; or whether, had a decisive defeat at Dien Bien Phu been avoided in 1954, Viet-Nam's history would have taken a less troubled course. A North Vietnamese Communist state less conscious of its military superiority, and a South Vietnamese state less burdened by the shadow of crushing military defeat, might have been able to work out by themselves a fate which would not have led the world once more to the brink of war over Indochina. And a France which, rightly or wrongly, would not have felt abandoned by two close allies in her direst hour of need, might well have become a stabilizing factor in the Indochina area, just as she has become one in Africa.

American warplanes eventually did come to Dien Bien Phu on July 2, 1965, exactly eleven years, one month, and twenty-six days after Brigadier General Christian Marie Ferdinand de la Croix de Castries had walked out of his bunker, a prisoner.

With an ear-shattering screech, twenty-four American jet-powered F-105 *Thunderchiefs* and A-4 *Skyhawks* attacked a North Vietnamese military barracks area in the Dien Bien Phu valley three miles to the south of the main airfield, near where strongpoint Isabelle used to be, and they also cratered the airfield and a group of twelve adjoining buildings, located just about where the French had fought for strongpoint Opéra, the nameless strongpoint, and Sparrowhawk. The new Communist airfield was longer than the one the French had built, and formed a light-angled X with the old strip, thus covering with a thick layer of concrete the dead from the Huguettes.

In less than fifteen minutes, the American jets expended twenty-nine tons of 750-lb. high-explosive bombs, 2.75-in. rockets, and Bullpup airborne missiles on the new target. There was, as eleven years earlier, a great deal of enemy flak. But no enemy planes were sighted and all American aircraft returned safely to their bases.

The pilots who flew the mission reported that the weather had been perfectly clear that summer day over the valley.

Postface—
Where Are They Now?

GENERAL NAVARRE retired soon after his return from Indochina, wrote a book, and was sued by General Cogny—a suit that nobody won. He now runs a brick factory on the Riviera. General Cogny, after holding a "paper command" for some years in Paris, retired in 1964. General de Castries for a time commanded the 5th French Armored Division in Germany and, after a car accident with his wife, retired in 1959 and now is the president of an industrial consortium for the reuse of waste paper. General Gilles, already afflicted with a heart condition when he jumped into Dien Bien Phu, died literally of a broken heart in 1961 when one of his sons was killed in Algeria. General Vo Nguyen Giap, the enemy commander at Dien Bien Phu, is now, in addition to being the commander-in-chief of the Viet-Nam People's Army, the Minister of Defense and Vice-Premier of North Viet-Nam.

Langlais, now a brigadier general, commands the 20th Airborne Brigade at Pau in the Pyrenees Mountains near the Spanish border. It is part of the 11th *Division Légère d'Intervention,* a new French division especially designed for rapid deployment overseas. The new commander of the division is Brig. Gen. Lalande, the former commander of strongpoint Isabelle. The 25th Brigade of the division is commanded by Col. Bigeard, and many of the junior survivors of Dien Bien Phu still serve together, twelve years later, in the 11th Division. Hubert de Séguins-Pazzis, Dien Bien Phu's last chief of staff, is now a brigadier general and deputy commander of the *Ecole Supérieure de Guerre,* the French war college, in Paris. Trancart ended his military career in 1964 as subdivision commander in Marseilles, with the rank of brigadier general; Chenel, of 2nd BT, served under him as a colonel. Vadot, the imperturbable Foreign Legion chief of staff, now is the colonel commanding the 1st

Foreign Legion Regiment at Aubagne and Coldeboeuf, from the 1/2 Foreign Legion Infantry, serves with him as a major.

Guérin, the Air Force commander at Dien Bien Phu, in 1966 served as a colonel in the NATO Standing Group in the Pentagon in Washington. Colonel Nicot, who had commanded the air transport for the fortress and was later a major general in Algeria, served time for his involvement in an attempted antigovernment putsch in 1961 until amnestied on Christmas Day, 1965.

Alliou, who commanded an artillery battalion at Dien Bien Phu, now runs a cellulose factory in independent Algeria. Guiraud continued to command paratroops in Algeria, including the famous 1st Foreign Legion Parachute Regiment, dissolved in 1961 for its participation in a mutiny. It cost him his career. Lieutenant Wieme, now a major, served for a long time as military adviser to the Malagasy Republic, and is currently working on a thesis on African labor unions. Sergeant Béguin, who served with him in the tribal auxiliaries, now has a trucking business in Savoy. Erwan Bergot, whose Airborne Mortar Company held off the Viet-Minh until the end, is still a captain and works in the French Army Public Information Office, having written a book on Dien Bien Phu as seen through the eyes of a private. Roland de Mecquenem and Jean Nicolas, who commanded North African battalions at Dien Bien Phu, now are instructors at senior French service schools.

Bréchignac, like many of his colleagues dissatisfied with the fate of Algeria, left the army to enter business. He now runs a cement factory in Valence, north of Marseilles. Tourret left the army as a colonel to enter business. Major Jean Pouget, despite brilliant prospects, preferred to leave the service to write. His own book on Dien Bien Phu is excellent. Warrant Officer Franz Josef, formerly of Claudine, now lives close to French military history as a supervisor at the Invalides Memorial, where Napoleon is buried. John Verdi, one of the Americans who flew the "Boxcar" missions over Dien Bien Phu, returned to the Marine Corps, where he now serves as a major with Marine Aircraft Group 12.

Father Guidon, the chaplain on Isabelle, returned to his civilian missionary work and was last heard from in Ubon-Rajthani in northeastern Thailand, working among Vietnamese refugees. Dr. Grauwin also stayed in the Far East and now runs his own private hospital in Phnom-Penh, Cambodia. Geneviève de Galard-Terraube married an officer who had not been at Dien Bien Phu, moved with him to Madagascar, and recently returned with him and their children to France. Abderrahman Ben Salem, the Algerian master sergeant who saw the beginning of the end on top of Gabrielle, is now a member of the Algerian Parliament, after having fought against the French for six years. Mimi (her real name was Myriam) and her husband Saïd, who is now a sheet-metal worker, have settled down in the Parisian working-class suburb of Aubervilliers with their two children.

And there is Michel Désiré, who survived the prison camps in spite of his severe wounds which left him too disabled for a troop command. Promoted to major, he now works at the French Military Archives in the Château de Vincennes near Paris. One of his main jobs is to put the Far Eastern files in good order. Dien Bien Phu is still very much with him.

Notes

Chapter I: Natasha

1. In 1966, American troop commanders in South Viet-Nam often preferred to undertake an operation without the help of available Vietnamese troops rather than have to share the details of the operation with the Vietnamese officers, since security was always considered extremely slack.
2. Gilles (Gen.), Jean, "Comment et pourquoi fut créé le camp de Dien Bien Phu," *Le Figaro* (Paris), May 6, 1954.
3. Fall, Bernard, *Street Without Joy: From the Indochina War to the War in Vietnam* (4th rev. ed., Harrisburg: Stackpole Books, 1964), pp. 144–73.
4. *Ibid.*, pp. 61–77.
5. Burchett, Wilfred, *North of the 17th Parallel*, 2nd enlarged ed., (Hanoi: Red River Publishing House, 1957), pp. 27–29.
6. The difference between the theoretical strength of 911 men and the actual jump strength of 722 is accounted for by soldiers who were in hospitals, on leave, in training programs, and administrative personnel.
7. Friang, Brigitte, *Les fleurs du ciel* (Paris: Robert Laffont, 1955), p. 306.
8. They were from the 35th Light Parachute Artillery Regiment (RALP, in French).
9. Langlais (Gen.), Pierre, *Dien Bien Phu* (Paris: France-Empire, 1963), p. 13.
10. The command organ was known as the *Elément Divisionnaire Aéroporté* (EDAP), or Airborne Division Command Element.
11. Bourdens, Henri, *Camionneur des nuées* (Paris: France-Empire, 1957), p. 126.
12. Fall, *op. cit.*, pp. 61–70.
13. Roy, Jules, *La bataille de Dien Bien Phu* (Paris: Julliard, 1963), pp. 66–67. (Although an English-language version of the same book exists, references are to the more complete original French edition.)
14. Some sources have erroneously translated the code name "Castor" into the English equivalent "Beaver." This is an error. As the second code name "Pollux" clearly indicates, the planners meant to refer to the twin brothers of Greek mythology, Castor and Pollux, to emphasize the twin aspect of the landing at Dien Bien Phu and the evacuation of Lai Chau.
15. *Le Monde* (Paris), November 22–23, 1953.

Chapter II: Base Aéro-Terrestre

1. Dejardin, "L'Armée de l'Air en Indochine" MS (Versailles: French Air Force Historical Service, 1961), 689 pp.
2. For a thorough study of the T'ai tribes, see Roux (Col.), Henri, "Quelques minorités ethniques du Nord-Indochine," *France-Asie*, No. 92–93 (Special Issue) (Saigon, January-February, 1954).
3. For an appraisal of the battle of Na-San, see Randon, Georges, "Le rendez-vous de Na-San," *Indochine—Sud-Est Asiatique* (Saigon, February, 1953), pp. 16–23.

4. Rénald, Jean, *L'Enfer de Dien Bien Phu* (Paris: Flammarion, 1955), p. 11.
5. Directive No. 40 of December 30, 1952 (803/EMIFT/TS).
6. Fall, *op. cit.,* pp. 77–106.
7. Olivier, Max, "Portrait du Général Navarre," *Indochine—Sud-Est. Asiatique* (February, 1954).
8. Cogny (Gen.), René "La libre confession du Général Cogny," *L'Express* (Paris), December 6, 1963.
9. Charpy, Pierre, "Responsable, Oui—Coupable, Non," *Le Nouveau Candide* (Paris), October 17–24, 1963. (Italics in original.)
10. This writer personally witnessed part of an incident which took place in Hanoi on Bastille Day, 1953, in the course of which Cogny insisted upon ceremonial precedence over the local French civilian representative. His own troops often referred to Cogny as "Coco La Sirène" for his excessive use of siren-blowing motorcycle escorts.
11. Olivier, Max, "Un portrait du Général Cogny," *Indochine—Sud-Est Asiatique* (April, 1954).
12. Roy, *op. cit.,* p. 20.
13. Cogny, *L'Express, loc. cit.,* November 21, December 6, 1963.
14. For biographies of de Lattre, see Salisbury-Jones, Sir G., *So Full a Glory* (London: Weidenfeld & Nicolson, 1954), and the detailed study by Darcourt, Pierre, *De Lattre au Viet-Nam* (Paris: La Table Ronde, 1965).
15. Berteil was to later write a small book on military tactics. He retired as a brigadier general.
16. Cogny, *L'Express, loc. cit.,* November 21, 1963, p. 22.
17. *Ibid.*
18. Navarre (Gen.), Henri, *Agonie de l'Indochine* (Paris: Plon, 1956), p. 63.
19. Laniel, Joseph, *Le drame indochinois, de Dien Bien Phu au pari de Genève* (Paris: Plon, 1957), p. 20.
20. Navarre, *op. cit.,* p. 338. See also Stéphane, Roger, "En un combat douteux," *France-Observateur,* July 30, 1954. Stéphane's article was a frighteningly exact rendition of the top-secret deliberations of the National Defense Committee. The French government was torn between the temptation of publicly denying the article (thus attracting further attention to it), and requesting an official inquiry, and the hope that total silence would minimize the enemy's attention to it. It seems, however, that the Viet-Minh *did* take the matter seriously and Navarre later asserted that the subsequent attacks on ill-defended Laos were prompted by the "leaks." One year later, the "Affaire des fuites" [The "Leaks Affair"] became a public scandal, but no high-level political figure was ever indicted.
21. Catroux (Gen.), Georges, *Deux actes du drame indochinois* (Paris: Plon, 1959), p. 142.
22. No. 563/EMIFT/3/0/TS of July 25, 1953. "Préparation de la bataille d'automne." The order was signed by Adm. Auboyneau, the naval commander in Indochina, rather than Air Force Gen. Bodet, the official deputy to Navarre, because Auboyneau held date-of-rank seniority.
23. The staff was known by the initials EMIFT *(Etat-Major Interarmées et Forces Terrestres,* or Joint and Ground Forces General Staff).
24. Navarre, cited in *Le Nouveau Candide* (weekly) (Paris) October 17–24, 1963.
25. *Directive Particulière d'Orientation* (Special Guidance Directive) No. 852/Ops/TS.

26. The document was drawn up by Col. Bastiani, Cogny's chief of staff; Lt. Col. Denef, his deputy for operations; and their direct subordinates.
27. Luang-Prabang is the royal residence town of Laos, while the more secure Vientiane is the administrative capital. During the first Viet-Minh offensive against Laos, in the spring of 1953, the aged monarch, King Sisavong Vong, refused to leave his capital and stood in grave danger of becoming a prisoner if the city fell. Hence the defense of Luang-Prabang assumed political overtones going far beyond the military importance of the area.
28. Roy, *op. cit.*, p. 39: ". . . if it succeeds, Cogny would be able to take credit for it, and if it failed, the reservations he had expressed would protect him."
29. Laniel, *op. cit.*, p. 23.
30. Cogny, *L'Express, loc. cit.*, November 21, 1963.
31. IPS 886/3/Ops/TS of November 14, 1953.
32. No. 739/FTNV/3/TS. FTNV stands for *Forces Terrestres du Nord Viet-Nam,* the Ground Forces Command in North Viet-Nam, headed by Gen. Cogny. The otherwise very complete study by Roy fails to mention this change in missions.
33. Radio message TO No. 3/114/03/TS of November 26, 1953.
34. Those alternate plans fill all of file box No. 51 in the French Army Historical Service files in Vincennes.
35. Vanuxem, then the commander of a mobile regimental combat team in the Red River Delta, was one of the best-liked French commanders in Indochina. Later promoted to major general in Algeria and France, he was arrested and removed from command in 1962 for his alleged sympathies with "French Algeria" proponents.
36. Cogny, *L'Express, loc. cit.*, November 21, 1963.
37. Fall, *op. cit.*, pp. 77–106.
38. Navarre, *op. cit.* p. 167 *n.*
39. IPS 949/EMIFT/3/TS. See also Catroux, *op. cit.*, p. 154.
40. Navarre, *op. cit.*, p. 279 *n.*
41. *Ibid.*
42. Fall, *op. cit.*, pp. 185–250.
43. *L'Humanité* (Paris), October 30, 1953.
44. Catroux, *op. cit.*, pp. 158–59.
45. Giap (Gen.), Vo Nguyen, *Dien Bien Phu* (Hanoi: Foreign Languages Publishing House, 1959), pp. 29–30. (Italics in original.)
46. LeGall, Jean-Marie, "Dien Bien Phu raconté par Giap," *Regards* (Paris, February, 1955).

Chapter III: Sorties

1. Roy, *op. cit.*, pp. 78–79.
2. Langlais, *op. cit.*, p. 15. Roy (p. 425) attributes the command of the December 5 reconnaissance to Langlais. The latter, however, by a personal letter to this writer, dated December 10, 1964, confirmed that he had remained immobilized in Hanoi until December 12, 1953.
3. Very little is known about the GCMA's. For references, see Trinquier (Col.), Roger, *Modern Warfare: A French View of Counterinsurgency* (New York: Frederick A. Praeger, Inc., 1964), and Fall, *op. cit.*, pp. 267–79.
4. ZONO stands for *Zone Opérationnelle Nord-Ouest,* or Northwestern Operational Zone. The area centered around Lai Chau and was commanded by Lt. Col. Trancart.

5. *Time* (December 21, 1953).
6. Later, in Algeria, Vaudrey became one of the leading members of the Secret Army Organization (OAS) and was cashiered from the French Army.
7. For a novelized account of the agony of the tribal units, see Schoendoerffer, Pierre, *La 317e Section* (Paris: La Table Ronde, 1964). Schoendoerffer himself was taken prisoner at Dien Bien Phu. He later became a film director and the film made from his book became an overnight hit.
8. No. 567/FTNV/3/TS of December 8, 1953. The operations involved in the order were to include raids on Tuan Giao. Ban Keo Lom, Sop-Nao, Muong Muon.
9. In fact, no other book on Dien Bien Phu seems to have considered the aborted sorties of December as an integral part of the battle of Dien Bien Phu. Yet, with the failure of the sorties, Dien Bien Phu ceased to fulfill the role which had been the reason for its creation.
10. Fall, *op. cit.,* pp. 116–30.
11. Friang, *op. cit.,* p. 334.
12. See Peers (Brig. Gen.), William R., and Brelis, Dean, *Behind the Burma Road* (Boston: Atlantic, Little, Brown, 1963); Ralo, Charles, *Wingate's Raiders* (London: Harrap, 1944); and Ogburn, C., *The Marauders* (New York: Harper & Brothers, 1956).
13. See Appendices at the end of the book. Yet even the chief of staff of the U. S. Army at the time, Gen. Matthew Ridgway, later stated in his memoirs that the Dien Bien Phu garrison was made up "mainly from the mercenaries of the French Foreign Legion."
14. There are no physical differences between Black T'ai and White T'ai. The colors refer to certain items of clothing that the tribes wear.
15. IPS 187/Ops/EMIFT of January 21, 1954.
16. IPS 189/Ops/EMIFT of January 29 and 192/Ops/EMIFT of January 30, 1954.
17. Radio message TO 1127/EMIFT/3/Ops/TS of February 2, 1954.
18. Fall, *op. cit.,* pp. 144–73.
19. Note (Personal and Secret) 10.193/FTNV/3/TS of February 17, 1954.
20. 2nd BT and 3rd BT, as well as the 301st BVN. The 301st was relieved before the siege began.

Chapter IV: Siege

1. Interview with Col. Sudrat in Paris, August, 1963.
2. In his IPS 949/EMIFT/3/Ops/TS of December 3, 1953, on the "Conduct of Operations in the Northwestern Zone of Tonkin," Gen. Navarre envisaged an "attack phase which might last *several days* . . . and which should end in the failure of the Viet-Minh offensive." (Italics added.)
3. IPS 10.141 FTNV/3/TS of February 3, and 10.151 of February 5, 1954.
4. Note No. 194/GONO/TS of February 15, 1954.
5. No doubt for heightened drama, *Time,* on May 15, 1964, referred to the "foul drinking water" of Dien Bien Phu.
6. 18/GONO/TS of December 12, 1953.
7. An artillery group is the equivalent of a battalion, with normally three batteries of four artillery pieces each, plus attached service, headquarters, and fire control elements. In the French Army, three groups form an artillery regiment.
8. The Composite Mortar Companies *(Compagnies Mixtes de Mortiers)* had

both 81-mm. and 120-mm. mortars. The Heavy Airborne Mortar Companies (*Compagnies Parachutistes de Mortiers Lourds*) were entirely equipped with 120's.

9. Noël was relieved on February 26, 1954, by a Capt. Dumoussand.

10. On March 13, 1954—the day of the first assault—Dien Bien Phu had on hand 27,400 rounds of 105-mm. howitzer ammunition, 22,000 rounds of 120-mm. heavy mortar shells, and 2,700 rounds of 155-mm. ammunition for its four medium counterbattery guns.

11. Catroux, *op. cit.*, p. 189.

12. Roy, *op. cit.*, p. 153.

13. For Graham Greene's view of Dien Bien Phu, see his article, "Decision in Asia: The Battle of Dien Bien Phu," in *The Sunday Times* (London), March 3, 1963. It was part of a series entitled "The Great Blunders of the Twentieth Century."

14. Eisenhower (Gen.), Dwight D., *Mandate for Change* (New York: Doubleday & Co., 1963), p. 344.

15. Chaffard, Georges, *Les carnets secrets de la décolonisation* (Paris: Calmann-Lévy, 1965) pp. 159, 193.

16. Pouget (Maj.), Jean, *Nous étions à Dien Bien Phu* (Paris: Presses de la Cité, 1964), pp. 256–59, *passim*.

17. Grauwin wrote two books dealing with his experiences in Indochina, one of which was translated into English: *Doctor at Dien Bien Phu* (New York: The John Day Company, 1955).

18. Dr. Rives was rotated out of Dien Bien Phu before the battle began and replaced by Dr. Le Damany from Lt. Col. Lalande's Mobile Group 6.

19. See Appendix A for all units stationed at Dien Bien Phu.

Chapter V: Assault

1. In comparison, the French expended 95,000 rounds of 105-mm., 38,000 rounds of 120-mm., and 8,500 rounds of 155-mm. ammunition. Of course, their targets were a great deal more dispersed than those the Viet-Minh had to fire at.

2. Guigues, C., "Logistique Viet-Minh," *Indochine—Sud-Est Asiatique* (March, 1953).

3. Giap, *Dien Bien Phu* (rev. ed., 1964), pp. 104–07, *passim*.

4. Roy, *op. cit.*, p. 77, among others, raises the point that "nobody believed in the strategic mobility and the logistics of the Viet-Minh." The Guigues article cited in note 2, above, published six months before Dien Bien Phu began and based on French intelligence estimates available in Saigon, clearly shows the opposite.

5. See No. 039/Air/EO/2/TS of May 27, 1954, the preliminary report on the air force aspects of the battle of Dien Bien Phu by Maj. Gen. Charles Lauzin, the commander-in-chief of the French Far Eastern Air Force.

6. Squadron 28F was commanded by Lt. Marcel Leclercq-Aubreton, French Navy.

7. The aircraft sorties involved 288 by F8F's, 27 by B-26's, 49 by F6F's, and 3 by *Privateers*.

8. Giap, *op. cit.*, p. 103.

9. Rénald, *op. cit.*, pp. 95–96.

10. Kubiak (Sgt.), "Opération Castor . . . Verdun 1954," *Képi Blanc* (Sidi-bel-Abbès and Marseilles, October, 1962), p. 36.

11. Langlais, *op. cit.,* pp. 23–24.
12. Vu Cao, "Breakthrough at Him Lam," in *Return to Dien Bien Phu and Other Stories* (Hanoi: Foreign Languages Publishing House, 1961), pp. 97–112. See also Tran, Do, *Récits sur Dien Bien Phu* (Hanoi: Editions en langues étrangères, 1962), pp. 45–51.
13. Burchett, *op. cit.,* pp. 49–51.
14. Personal interview with Abderrahman Ben Salem (now a major in the Algerian National People's Army) in Algiers, July, 1963. He added: "We were pretty impressed."
15. Pouget, *op. cit.,* p. 225. As will be seen later, however, the rest of the weeded-out battalion was to fight on with great courage to the last day of the battle.
16. The radio message from de Castries to Hanoi, requesting a replacement for Piroth was sent on March 20, 1954, at 0920.
17. One of the brothels was staffed with Vietnamese women, the other with girls from the Oulad Naïl tribe in Algeria.
18. Roy, *op. cit.,* p. 476
19. *Ibid.,* p. 228.
20. Radio message TO 87/40/TS of March 19, 1954, at 1500.
21. Report on the activities of the *Groupement de Formations d'Hélicoptères* (GFH), by its commander, Maj. Marceau Crespin, of March 11, 1955.
22. Roy, *op. cit.*
23. Langlais, *op. cit.,* p. 249.
24. *Note de Service* GONO No. 284/3B of March 24, 1954, effective March 27 at 0000.
25. Interview with Col. Bigeard in Paris, August, 1963. See also his 69-page MS on the battle of Dien Bien Phu (Saigon, September, 1954). The counterattack took place, as indicated, on March 28, 1954, and not, as published elsewhere, on March 26.
26. On March 30, Supply at Dien Bien Phu reported that it had on hand 8,879 "ration consumers" but only 6,150 "combatants." The difference between the two numbers is accounted for by the wounded, the maintenance units, and, of course, the "internal deserters."

Chapter VI: Strangulation

1. FTNV, Intelligence, *Règlement d'Infanterie Viet-Minh: Le Bataillon et la Compagnie d'Infanterie dans l'attaque d'une position fortifiée.* (Hanoi: September, 1953).
2. *Ibid.,* p. 8.
3. The rest, about one and a half companies, was placed in the airfield drainage ditch near the newly constructed Sparrowhawk strongpoint and on D5.
4. Langlais, *op. cit.,* p. 79.
5. Pouget, *op. cit.,* p. 260.
6. Langlais, *op. cit.,* p. 109. He errs, however, when he asserts that Maj. Nicolas fell back at 2000, an error repeated by Roy (p. 246) on the basis of Langlais' assertion. Radio traffic shows that Nicolas still held his position until midnight. He confirmed this in a personal interview in Paris, September, 1963.
7. Lts. Gaven and Marquèze were killed; Lt. Delobel, wounded.
8. Pouget, *op. cit.,* p. 264.
9. Roy, *op. cit.,* p. 248.
10. This was due, not to neglect or some defect in the supply system from Hanoi, but simply to the constant shelling of the drop zones which made the gathering

of supplies increasingly difficult. The mortar shells lay for three days on the drop zones before they were finally found.

11. Giap, *op. cit.*, p. 123.
12. Mai, Huu, *The Last Stronghold* (Hanoi: Foreign Languages Publishing House, 1963), pp. 100–101.
13. Bergot (Capt.), Erwan, *Deuxième classe à Dien Bien Phu* (Paris: La Table Ronde, 1964), p. 68. Langlais and Pouget also refer to that situation.
14. Radio message, G-2 (Intelligence) GONO to G-2 FTNV, April 1, 1954, at 1830.
15. Radio message from Gen. de Castries to FTNV, April 26, 1954, at 0151.
16. Frédéric-Dupont, Minister for the Associated States for a while in 1954, later wrote in his book, *Mission de la France en Asie* (Paris: France-Empire, 1956), p. 200, that the volunteers included 800 mainland Frenchmen, 350 North Africans, 350 Foreign Legionnaires, and 200 Vietnamese.
17. Langlais (p. 159) says that Viard's company was committed first; Pouget (p. 276) and Roy (p. 262) say it was Clédic's company; Clémençon in his own report stated that it was Lt. Bailly's company, with Viard in second position and Clédic in third. Bigeard also believes that Clédic's unit was first.

Chapter VII: Asphyxiation

1. Giap, *op. cit.*, pp. 124–26, *passim.*
2. According to French estimates, at least 3,500 105-mm., 4,000 75-mm., and 7,000 mortar shells were misdropped into enemy lines. In the final days of the battle, the Viet-Minh would have run out of its own 105-mm. ammunition had it not been for the French misdrops.
3. Langlais, *op. cit.*, p. 118. This method, in fact, was used in South Viet-Nam by an inventive French commando leader, Sgt. Marcel Georges. See his book *Mon ami Sinh* (Paris: France-Empire, 1963).
4. Langlais, *op. cit.*, p. 176.
5. Bigeard, *op. cit.*, pp. 49–51.
6. Radio message from G-2, GONO, to G-2, FTNV, April 15, 1954, at 1310.
7. Pouget, *op. cit.*, p. 293.
8. The "Lazy Dogs," or LD's, are large bomb containers filled with razor-sharp steel shards whose effect upon human beings caught in the open is devastating. They are still used in Viet-Nam in 1965–66.
9. Langlais, *op. cit.*, p. 177. Cogny had to bear the brunt of Intelligence's complaints about Langlais' behavior with its local representatives, and Cogny finally warned de Castries to put a rein on Langlais as far as Hébert and GC 8 were concerned.
10. According to official German statistics (see Helmut Heiber, ed., *Lagebesprechungen im Führerhauptquartier* [Munich: Deutscher Taschenbuch Verlag, 1963], p. 67), the German *Luftwaffe* provided the 220,000 troops in Stalingrad with 6,591 tons of airborne supplies over a period of 76 days (or 94.1 tons per day). In 56 days of siege the 16,000 French troops at Dien Bien Phu received a total of 6,410 tons (or 117 tons per day). Obviously, the German 6th Army inside the siege perimeter of Stalingrad must have had substantially more reserve supplies than did the French at Dien Bien Phu.
11. Radio message 07/01/TS of April 14, 1954.
12. The problem of getting the French, during World War II, to understand that Quartermaster and other supply units were just as important as fighting men is excellently described by the late Marcel Vigneras in his official "U. S. Army in

World War II" volume, *Rearming the French* (Washington: Government Printing Office, 1957).
13. Grauwin, Paul, *Seulement médécin* (Paris: France-Empire, 1956), p. 27.
14. Bergot, *op. cit.*, pp. 115–18.
15. *Le Monde*, April 20, 1954.
16. Castelbajac, Bertrand de, *Sauts OPS* (Paris: La Table Ronde, 1959), p. 85.
17. Fall, *op. cit.*, pp. 48–60.
18. Fiedler, Arkady, *Im Lande der wilden Bananen* (Leipzig: Brockhaus, 1957), pp. 165–74.
19. Pouget, *op. cit.*, p. 302.
20. Kubiak, *Képi Blanc* (December, 1962), pp. 36–37.
21. Langlais, *op. cit.*, pp. 171–72.
22. CIPE stood for *Compagnie Indochinoise de Parachutistes Etrangers*, or Foreign Legion Indochinese Parachute Company. Each non-native parachute battalion in Indochina had one company composed of men from the various ethnic groups found in the whole area: Cambodians, Laotians, tribesmen, etc. That way, the battalion was never completely alone in unfamiliar terrain. This method would still be useful today. Information available today shows that not a single Cambodian survived captivity. The hatred that exists between the Vietnamese and the Cambodians probably accounts for that.
23. Roy, *op. cit.*, p. 286.
24. Giap, *op. cit.*, pp. 131–35, *passim*. (Italics in original.)

Chapter VIII: Isabelle Alone

1. An excellent American film on the subject, *Paths of Glory*, was not cleared for showing in France on the grounds that it "infringed upon the honor of the French Army." \
2. Interview with Capt. Belabiche, Algerian National People's Army officers' training school at Cherchell, Algeria, in July, 1963.

Chapter IX: Vulture, Condor, and Albatross

1. With the notable exception of the U. S. Air Force's clearing of some data pertaining to Gen. Caldara's mission, there appears to be a total blackout of information on any and all of the American aspects of the Dien Bien Phu problem, going so far as a refusal to confirm facts or events that were part of the public record in 1954 when they occurred, or were made part of the public record later by such high authorities as President Eisenhower.
2. Eden, Sir Anthony, *Full Circle* (London: A. S. Cassell & Co., 1961), and the already cited works of Laniel, Catroux, and Navarre, as well as the important book by Gen. Paul Ely, *L'Indochine dans la tourmente* (Paris: Plon, 1964).
3. Notably: "How Dulles Averted War" (the article that made "brinkmanship" a household word) by James Shepley in *Life,* (January 16, 1956); "We Nearly Went to War Three Times," by Fletcher Knebel, in *Look* (February 8, 1955); "The Day We Didn't Go to War," by Chalmers Roberts—by far the best of the three—in *The Reporter* (September 14, 1954); and the memoirs of Gen. Ridgway and of President Eisenhower; as well as the contemporary articles by Hanson W. Baldwin in *The New York Times*.
4. Fall, B., *The Two Viet-Nams* (rev. ed.; New York: Frederick A. Praeger, Inc., 1965), pp. 123–24.
5. Laniel, *op. cit.*, p. 17.

6. In actual fact, the bulk of the matériel supplied still was American-made and captured either in Korea or from the Chinese Nationalists.
7. Eisenhower, *op. cit.* (Signet Book edition), p. 409.
8. *Washington Post,* January 20, 1957.
9. French National Assembly, *Journal Officiel* (March 10, 1954), pp. 768–69. Speech by M. Daladier.
10. Laniel, *op. cit.,* pp. 79–80.
11. Ely, *op. cit.,* p. 66.
12. Roy, *op. cit.,* p. 254. The point has been recently confirmed in full by the then French Foreign Minister and at present an anti-de Gaulle and pro-American exile, M. Georges Bidault, in his *D'une résistance à l'autre* (Paris: Les presses du siècle, 1965), p. 198. Bidault states that he turned to French Ambassador Jean Chauvel, whose English is excellent also, and restated Secretary Dulles' question in full, to be sure he had understood him correctly, and he asserts that he turned down Dulles' offer (if that is what it was), saying that in the event that A-bombs were used near Dien Bien Phu, the "defenders will suffer as much as the assailants," and if the bombs were to be used on the communication lines "at their source in [Red] China, there's a risk of generalized war. . . ." It is now up to official American sources to confirm or deny that version of what transpired.
13. Pouget, *op. cit.,* p. 378.
14. Based on sources cited in note 3, above, plus a press conference held by John Foster Dulles, of January 18, 1956, after the "brinkmanship" article appeared. The Department of State Historical Division, queried on October 29, 1965, was unable to release even the list of persons who attended this decisive conference.
15. *Life* (January 16, 1956) also speaks of the carrier *Philippine Sea,* but it was under way from Pearl Harbor to Yokosuka, Japan, and was not involved. But the carriers *Wasp* and *Oriskany* and the escort carrier *Rendova* were in the South China Sea area and could have become rapidly involved. The *Oriskany* in fact was to be involved—but ten years later.
16. Communication from Senator Russell to the author on June 7, 1966. On the other hand, the Senator denied a *New York Times* story (May 1, 1966), which quotes him as having said,, of the April 3, 1954, meeting: "I sat there listening to him [Dulles] talk about sending American boys off to fight in a war like that and suddenly I found myself on my feet shouting at the Secretary of State, 'We're not going to do that!' "
17. Eisenhower, *op. cit.,* p. 420.
18. Reston, James, *New York Times,* June 13, 1954.
19. Tournoux, J. R., *Secrets d'Etat* (Paris: Plon, 1960). See also note 12, above.
20. Eden, *op. cit.,* pp. 51-54. It is noteworthy that a French right-wing legislator and former general, Auméran, on October 24, 1953 (see *Journal Officiel,* p. 4541, of that date) proposed to lay a "radioactive belt" along the Sino-Vietnamese border to seal off Chinese supply routes. The radioactive material was to be obtained from the U.S. *Life (loc. cit.)* also referred to a U. S. offer "to provide weapons for instant retaliation, if it should prove necessary . . ."
21. Tournoux, *op. cit.,* p. 57.
22. *New York Times,* November 25, 1954. A recent study by a British specialist fully agrees with my view of events during that crucial period. See Warner, Geoffrey, "Escalation in Vietnam: The Precedents of 1954," in *International Affairs,* The Royal Institute of International Affairs, London (April, 1965), pp. 267–77.

23. Eisenhower, *op. cit.*, pp. 428-29

24. Pouget, *op. cit.*, p. 415.

25. No. 401/EMIFT/TS of April 27, 1954; 244/Ops/TS of April 12, 1954; and Radio message 250/Ops/TS of April 22, 1954.

26. Roy, *The Battle of Dien Bien Phu* (New York: Harper & Row, 1965), pp. 234, 238, 244.

27. Eisenhower, *op. cit.*, p. 428.

28. Godard, in Algeria, became a member of the Secret Army Organization and was later arrested, tried, and convicted for conspiracy.

29. Radio message EMIFT to FTNV, 250/Ops/TS of April 22, 1954, at 2000.

30. No. 145/EMIFT Forward to FTNV, of May 3, 1954, and No. 103/CP Forward/Laos, same date.

31. The French term was *commandement,* rather than *commandant* (commander).

Chapter X: Castor Dies

1. Official French Air Force figures. Pouget (p. 406) states a total of 139 tons.

2. Pouget, *op. cit.*, p. 406.

3. Roy, *op. cit.* (French edition), p. 536.

4. Dussol (Lt. Col.), "Les B-26 dans la Bataille de Dien Bien Phu," MS (May 22, 1954).

5. Wadell, L. S., "Phase-Out for Charlie One-One-Nine," *Pegasus* (The Fairchild Corp., Hagerstown, Md.) (October, 1955), p. 4.

6. *Paris-Match* (September 21, 1963). In a subsequent communication to the magazine, Navarre denied that the incident happened, but Cogny maintained his version of the facts, and Navarre did not take further action.

7. *L'Express,* February 20, 1964.

8. "Contribution à l'histoire de Dien Bien Phu," *Etudes Vietnamiennes,* Special Edition, No. 3 (Hanoi, March, 1965), p. 175.

9. Ducruix was to die in a Viet-Minh prison camp in June, 1954.

10. Grauwin, *J'étais médécin à Dien Bien Phu,* p. 270. Langlais, *op. cit.*, p. 181, also complained about the "defeatist attitude" of Radio Saigon.

11. Langlais, *op. cit.*, p. 178. In the English translation of Roy (p. 256), the French word for "footlocker"—*cantine*—is rendered as "canteen," which has an entirely different meaning in English. The error does not, of course, occur in the original.

12. Wadell, *loc. cit.*, p. 4.

13. Maj. Coldeboeuf, in a personal interview at the Foreign Legion headquarters at Aubagne, near Marseilles, told me that the entry had been his own.

14. Interview with Col. Vadot at Aubagne, August, 1963.

15. The incomplete set of radio messages shows this to be as indicated. The war diary of the 1/2 REI, lost at Dien Bien Phu but reconstituted later, indicates that Capt. Bourges led the company (or two platoons of it) to E12. The latter, however, was not under attack that day, but H5 was.

16. Cogny, *L'Express, loc. cit.*, December 6, 1963. Speaking of his hesitant telegram to Navarre, Cogny said: "Under such circumstances wouldn't a Norman be tempted to say neither 'yes' nor 'no', or rather 'yes *and* no'?"

17. Roy, *op.cit.*, p. 551.

18. Cogney, *L'Express, loc. cit.* Cogny also called the idea of a breakout with abandonment of the wounded a "degrading solution."

19. Pouget, *op. cit.* He also participated to some extent in the writing of the first part of Jean Lartéguy's *The Centurions.*

20. *Ibid.,* pp. 334-35.
21. Langlais, *op. cit.,* pp. 206-07.
22. Interview with Brig. Gen. Langlais at Pau (Pyrenees), September, 1963.
23. Kubiak, *Képi Blanc* (January, 1963), p. 57.
24. Mai, *op. cit.,* p. 285.
25. Kubiak, *Képi Blanc* (March, 1963), p. 50.
26. Pouget, *op. cit.,* p. 338. Col. Vadot confirmed the dialogue to me.
27. Roy, *op. cit.,* p. 317.
28. Langlais, in a personal interview.
29. Giap, Vo Nguyen, "Quelques souvenirs de Dien Bien Phu," *Etudes Viet-namiennes, loc. cit.,* p. 136.
30. Langlais, *op. cit.,* pp. 221-24. Some details are added from personal interview with Bigeard.
31. Such instances of front-line chivalry of the enemy were confirmed by Langlais (p. 223), Rénald (p. 187), and Grauwin (p. 370).
32. The French edition of Roy's book included a small plastic record of the tape, but in his comment he mentions several deleted passages. Pouget (p. 345) rebuts this, and the official French press agency, AFP, transmitted on May 8, 1954, from Hanoi a written text which included the passages missing on the Roy recording.
33. The word "eastern" may well be an absent-minded mistake, for what was left of Dien Bien Phu now was entirely on the *western* bank.
34. In a combined interview with Bigeard and Nicolas (who had commanded the Moroccans), in Paris in September, 1963, it turned out that Nicolas had not learned until that day that he was to be part of the group which was to have been deliberately sacrificed.
35. Giap, *Dien Bien Phu,* p. 139, and *loc. cit., Etudes Vietnamiennes,* p. 205.
36. Bergot, *op. cit.,* p. 136. He himself had been wounded on April 26, 1954.
37. Vautier, René, "Sur le marché de la chair," *Jeune Afrique* (Tunis, August 7, 1966).
38. Roy, *op. cit.,* p. 331 (French edition); p. 283 (U. S. edition).
39. Giap, *Dien Bien Phu,* p. 140.
40. Pouget, *op. cit.,* pp. 344-45.
41. Schoenbrun, David, in "End of an Empire," a Columbia Broadcast System telecast, April 15, 1962, 1800-1830 E.S.T. (Reprinted by permission.)
42. Karmen, Roman Lazarevich, *Viet-Nam srazhaetsia: zanikh sov'etskovo kino-operatora* (Moscow: Biblioteka soldata i matrosa, 1958), pp. 73-74.

Chapter XI: Finale

1. High Commissioner of Viet-Nam in France, *Viet-Nam* (bi-weekly French-language bulletin) (Paris), May 15, 1954, pp. 18-19.
2. *Paris-Match* (May 12, 1956), p. 26.
3. *New York Times,* May 7, 1954.
4. Grauwin, *Seulement médécin,* p. 17.
5. Bodard, Lucien, "Dramatique attente à Hanoi après Dien Bien Phu," *France-Soir,* May 11, 1954.
6. *Le Monde,* May 9-10, 1954.
7. *Ibid.,* May 14, 1954.
8. United Press, in *Chinese World* (San Francisco), May 17, 1954.
9. *Le Figaro,* May 19, 1954.
10. Grauwin, *Seulement médécin,* pp. 54-55.

11. *Le Monde,* May 6-7, 1954.
12. Karmen, *op. cit.,* pp. 44-45.
13. *Le Monde,* May 25, 1954, and *Vert et Rouge,* No. 93 (Foreign Legion periodical) (Marseilles, 1954), p. 32.
14. Fall, *Street Without Joy,* pp. 295-311.
15. *New York Times,* July 16, 1954.
16. *Le Nouveau Candide,* May 13-20, 1964, p. 5.
17. Jeansotte (Gen., French Medical Corps), *Report* No. 7091/DSS/EO/FT/S, of December 28, 1954, and subsequent reports by Maj. Martin, M.D., Professor of Medicine, Marine Forces; and by Lt. Col. Chippaux, M.D., Professor of Medicine, Marine Forces.
18. Dr. Stanley L. Falk's standard work on the Bataan death march, *Bataan: The March of Death* (New York: Norton, 1962), permits some comparisons. The total Bataan march covered 65 miles, and only 650 Americans died on the trek. Filipino losses are variously estimated as between 5,000 and 10,000.
19. (New York: E. P. Dutton, 1961.)
20. *New York Times,* December 19, 1954.
21. Bigeard (Col.), Marcel, *Aucune bête au monde . . .* (Paris: La Pensée Moderne, 1959).

Chapter XII: Epilogue

1. Heilbrunn, Otto, "Another Dien Bien Phu?" *Army* (October, 1965), p. 36.
2. O'Ballance, Edgar, *The Indo-China War, 1945-54* (London: Faber & Faber, 1964), p. 237.
3. Farran, Jean, "La leçon de Dien Bien Phu," *Paris-Match,* (May 12, 1956); O'Ballance, *op. cit.,* p. 230.
4. Futrell, Robert F., *et al., The United States Air Force in Korea* (New York: Duell, Sloan, and Pearce, 1961).
5. *Ibid.,* p. 416.
6. Witze, Claude, "USAF Polishes Its New COIN," *Air Force and Space Digest* (June, 1962).
7. Catroux, *op. cit.,* p. 213.
8. *Le Monde,* September 18, 1954.
9. Ely, *op. cit.,* p. 97.
10. Frédéric-Dupont, *op. cit.,* p. 193.
11. Report 039/Air/E0/2/TS of May 27, 1954, p. 20.
12. *New York Times,* January 23, 1956. Interview of Congressman John W. McCormack.
13. Bidault, *op. cit.,* p. 200.
14. Fall, *Viet-Nam Witness, 1953-66* (New York, Frederick A. Praeger, Inc., 1966), pp. 5-8.

Appendix A: Order of Battle*

I. On December 6, 1953: 4,907 troops.

Airborne

HQ, Airborne Divisional Element (EDAP)
2nd Battalion, 1st Parachute *Chasseurs* (II/1 RCP)
1st Colonial Parachute (1 BPC)
1st Foreign Legion Parachute (1 BEP)
5th Vietnamese Parachute (5 BPVN)
8th Parachute Assault (8 BPC)
17th Airborne Engineers Company
35th Airborne Artillery Regiment (2 batteries) (35 RALP)
1st Foreign Legion Heavy Airborne Mortar Co. (1 CEMLP)
342nd Parachute Signal Company (elements)

Infantry

3rd T'ai Battalion (BT 3)

Artillery

Laotian Autonomous Artillery Battery (BAAL)

Engineers

3rd Company, 31st Engineers (31/3 BG)

II. On March 13, 1954: 10,814 troops.

A. UNITS

Headquarters

71st Hq. Co. (for all of Dien Bien Phu)
HQ, GAP 2 (for all airborne units at first, then, in fact, the whole defense)
9th Command & Service Co. (Foreign Legion)
6th Command & Service Co. (Isabelle)

Infantry	Assignment
1/13 Half-Brigade, Foreign Legion (1/13 DBLE)	Claudine
3/13 Half-Brigade, Foreign Legion (3/13 DBLE)	Beatrice
3/3 Algerian Rifles (3/3 RTA)	Dominique
5/7 Algerian Rifles (5/7 RTA)	Gabrielle
1/4 Moroccan (1/4 RTM)	Eliane
1/2 Foreign Legion (1/2 REI)	Huguette
2nd T'ai Battalion (BT 2)	Eliane

*Unless otherwise indicated, all units listed are battalions. French designations are in parentheses.

Infantry (continued)	*Assignment*
3rd T'ai Battalion (BT 3)	Anne-Marie
1st Foreign Legion Parachute (1 BEP)	HQ Reserve
8th Parachute Assault (8 BPC)	HQ Reserve
3/3 Foreign Legion (3/3 REI)	Isabelle
2/1 Algerian Rifles (2/1 RTA)	Isabelle
T'ai Partisan Mobile Group No. 1	Françoise and
(11 companies) (GMPT 1)	other strongpoints

Artillery	*Assignment*
3rd Group, 10th Colonial Artillery (III/10 RAC):	
2 batteries of 105-mm.	Isabelle
1 battery of 105-mm.	Claudine
2nd Group, 4th Colonial Artillery (II/10 RAC):	
2 batteries of 105-mm.	Claudine
1 battery of 105-mm.	Dominique
11th Battery, 4th Group, 4th Colonial Artillery	
(11/IV/4 RAC):	
4 medium howitzers, 155-mm.	Claudine
I Battery, North Viet-Nam AAA Group (FTA-NVN):	
1 section of 2 quad-.50 mounts	Dominique 4
1 section of 2 quad-.50 mounts	Huguette 1
1st Foreign Legion Heavy Airborne Mortar Co (1 CEMLP)	Claudine
1st Foreign Legion Composite Mortar Co. (1 CMMLE)	Gabrielle
2nd Foreign Legion Composite Mortar Co. (2 CMMLE)	Anne-Marie

Armor	*Assignment*
Composite Squadron, 1st Regiment of Armored Cavalry	
(1er RCC):	
1st and 3rd Platoons (7 tanks)	Main position
3rd Platoon (3 tanks)	Isabelle

Service Units	*Assignment*
31st Engineer Battalion (31 BG):	
2nd Company (31/2 BG)	Eliane 10
1st Company (31/1 BG)	HQ area
5th Foreign Legion Medium Repair Company	HQ
29th Mobile Surgical Detachment, French Union Forces	HQ
44th Mobile Surgical Detachment, Viet-Nam Nat'l Army	HQ
342nd Parachute Signal Company	HQ
2nd Company, 822nd Signal Battalion	HQ
2nd Company, 823rd Signal Battalion	HQ
403rd Postal Detachment	HQ
730th Gasoline Supply Company, Depot No. 81	HQ
3rd Ammunition Supply Company (detachment)	HQ
1st Quartermaster Operational Exploitation Group	
3rd Legion, *Garde Républicaine* and *Gendarmerie*	
(detachment)	HQ

Intelligence	*Assignment*
8th Commando Group, Composite Airborne Cdo. Groups	

Intelligence (continued)   Assignment
(GC 8/GCMA) and detachments of *Sécurité Militaire,*
DOP, and 6th Section (French Central Intelligence)   HQ Area

French Air Force and Army Aviation   Assignment
Fighter Group 1/22 "Saintonge" (GC 1/22)   Airfield, DBP
21st Aerial Artillery Observation Group   Airfield, DBP
23rd Aerial Artillery Observation Group   Airfield, DBP
Airbase Detachment 195   Airfield, DBP
Air Force Signal Company 21/374   Airfield, DBP

B. ETHNIC COMPOSITION

Nationality	Officers	NCO's	EM's	Totals
French Mainland	180	477	755	1,412
Foreign Legion	97	309	2,563	2,969
North Africans	2	167	2,438	2,607
Africans	–	8	239	247
Vietnamese Regulars	1	97	2,053	2,151*
Vietnamese Auxiliaries	–	105	1,323	1,428*
	280	1,163	9,371	10,814

*Of the combined total, 2,575 were tribal T'ai.

III. From March 13 to May 6, 1954: Airborne reinforcements, 4,291 troops.

A. CONSTITUTED UNITS PARACHUTED IN: 3,507 TROOPS.

1st Colonial Parachute (incomplete) (I BPC)
2nd Battalion, 1st Parachute *Chasseurs* (II/1 RCP)
2nd Foreign Legion Parachute (2 BEP)
5th Vietnamese Parachute (5 BPVN)
6th Colonial Parachute (6 BPC)
35th Airborne Artillery Regiment (elements)
3rd Airborne Surgical Team (ACP 3)
5th Airborne Surgical Team (ACP 5)
6th Airborne Surgical Team (ACP 6)

B. ETHNIC COMPOSITION

Nationality	Officers	NCO's	EM's	Totals
French Mainland	92*	303	1,003†	1,398
Foreign Legion	31	131	800	962
North Africans	–	1	29	30
Vietnamese	10	68	1,823	1,901
	113	503	3,655	4,291‡

*8 were air-landed.
†6 were air-landed.
‡A total of 680 non-qualified volunteers were parachuted in.

IV. *Combined total of II and III, above: 15,105 troops plus 2,440 PIMs.*

V. *On April 24, 1954: Combat units, 5,300 troops.*

Strongpoint	Unit	Commander	Effectives
Huguette	Foreign Legion Parachute Composite Bn.	Maj. Guiraud	600
Huguette	1 Co. 1/4 Moroccan	Maj. Guiraud	140
Claudine	1/2 Foreign Legion	Maj. Clémençon	400
Lily	1/4 Moroccan (remnants)	Maj. Nicolas	250
Juno	White T'ai, Air Force	Capt. Duluat	180
Sparrowhawk } Opéra }	8th Assault; 1/5 BPVN Quad-50's, 1/BT 2	Maj. Tourret	530
Upper Eliane	II/2 RCP; 5 BPVN (–) 1/13 DBLE (–); 6 BPC(–)	Maj. Bréchignac	1,150
Lower Eliane } and D3 }	BT 2(–); companies of 3/3 RTA; 6 BPC	Maj. Chenel	650
Isabelle	3/3 REI; 2/1 RTA; remnants of BT 3, 5/7 RTA	Col. Lalande	1,400
		Total:	5,300

Appendix B: French Losses

I. From November 21, 1953 to March 12, 1954

Nationality	Killed				Missing				Wounded				Totals
	OF's	NCO's	EM's	Total	OF's	NCO's	EM's	Total	OF's	NCO's	EM's	Total	
French	4	10	25	39	2	4	4	10	20	34	65	119	169
Foreign Legion	3	6	21	30	—	3	24	27	8	23	206	237	294
North Africans	—	1	27	28	—	—	10	10	—	21	169	190	228
Vietnamese	—	2	16	17	—	2	39	41	1	16	235	252	347
GRAND TOTALS:	7	19	125	151	2	9	77	88	29	94	675	798	1,037

II. From March 13 to May 5, 1954

Nationality	Killed				Missing				Wounded				Totals
	OF's	NCO's	EM's	Total	OF's	NCO's	EM's	Total	OF's	NCO's	EM's	Total	
French	33	79	157	269	26	59	95	180	68	271	635	974	1,423
Foreign Legion	18	56	244	318	19	64	655	738	41	120	1,105	1,266	2,322
North Africans	—	19	172	191	1	31	401	433	1	66	916	983	1,607
Africans	—	2	13	15	—	—	1	1	—	2	51	53	69
Vietnamese:													
French Union	—	15	246	261	—	4	152	156	—	42	913	955	1,372
ARVN	3	3	40	46	—	—	57	57	4	8	98	110	213
Auxiliaries	—	2	40	42	—	—	41	41	—	11	84	95	178
GRAND TOTALS:	54	176	912	1,142	46	158	1,402	1,606	114	520	3,802	4,436	7,184

III. *Casualty Totals Prior to May 8, 1954*

	Dead	Wounded	Missing	Totals
Operation "Castor" (Nov. 20, 1953)	11	52	0	63
Operation "Pollux" (Dec. 10–22, 1953)	?	?	1,916	1,916
Nov 21, 1953–March 12, 1954	151	798	88	1,037
March 13–May 5, 1954	1,142	3,802	1,606	7,184
May 5–May 8, 1954	900?	1,800?	?	2,700?
TOTALS	2,204	6,452	3,610	12,900
French Air Force	15	6	94	115
French Naval Aviation	21	4	7	32
American civilian pilots	2	1	–	3
GRAND TOTALS	2,242	6,463	3,711	13,050

IV. *Prisoners taken on May 7–8, 1954: about 6,500 men.*

V. *Combined total of III and IV plus "Condor" losses: about 20,000 men.*

VI. *French Hospital Statistics**

	3/13–3/26	3/27–3/31	4/1–4/16	4/17–4/26	4/27	5/7	Totals
Admissions	784	369	751	412	899	3,000†	6,215
Operations	145	43	310	241	?		739
Evacuations	312	12	0	0	0		324
Deaths	62	58	76	56	?		252
GRAND TOTALS	1,303	482	1,137	709	899	3,000	7,530

*Covers only main hospitals.
†2,100 wounded reported by battalion stations.

NOTE: The total number of admissions exceeds the total number of wounded because many men were wounded several times or because severely wounded cases were logged in both at their battalion stations and, later, at the main hospital. They also include wounded PIMs not listed as combatants.

Appendix C: The Role of Airpower

Fighters

Fighter Group 1/22 "Saintonge" } Fighter Group 2/22 "Languedoc" }	F8F *Bearcats* (U.S.)
3rd Carrier Assault Flotilla (On *Arromanches* until April 30)	SB-2C *Helldivers* (U.S.)
11th Carrier Fighter Flotilla (On *Arromanches* until April 30)	F6F *Hellcats* (U.S.)
14th Carrier Fighter Flotilla (On *Belleau Wood*, replacing decimated 11th Flotilla on May 1)	13 F4U *Corsairs* (U.S.)

Bombers

Bomber Group 1/25 "Tunisie"	B-26 *Marauders* (U.S.)
28th Bomber Flotilla (French Navy)	PB4Y2 *Privateers* (U.S.)

Transports

Transport Group 1/64 "Béarn"	C-47 *Dakotas* (U.S.)
Transport Group 2/64 "Anjou"	C-47 *Dakotas* (U.S.)
Transport Group 2/63 "Franche-Comté"	C-47 *Dakotas* (U.S.)
Transport Group 2/63 "Sénégal"	C-47 *Dakotas*; C-119 *Packets* (U.S.)

Reconnaissance

80th Overseas Reconnaissance Squadron	RF8F *Bearcats* (18)
21st Aerial Artillery Observation Group	Morane-500 *Crickets* (French)
23rd Aerial Artillery Observation Group	Morane-500 *Crickets* (French)

Liaison and Medical Evacuation

1st Light Medical Evacuation Helicopter Company which merged later with Helicopter Formations Group (GFH)	Sikorsky S-55's Sikorsky S-55's
53rd Air Liaison Squadron (ELA 53)	DHC2 *Beavers*, L-19 *Bird Dogs*, Siebel NC-701 *Martinets* (German), and Morane-500's.

Civilian Aircraft

The following airlines flew chartered flights into Dien Bien Phu or participated in the subsequent supply drop operations:

Aigle-Azur	Air Outre-Mer
Civil Air Transport (Taiwan)	COSARA
Air Viet-Nam	CLCT (Laos)

Additional transports flown: British Bristol 170 Freighters, Boeing 307B *Stratoliners*, Curtiss C-46 *Commandos*, DC-4 *Skymasters*, and S. O. *Bretagne*.

Appendix D: Viet-Nam People's Army

I. Order of Battle, March 13–May 8, 1954

COMMANDER-IN-CHIEF: *Vo Nguyen Giap*
CHIEF OF STAFF FOR THE DIEN BIEN PHU FRONT: *Hoang Van Thai*

308th Infantry Division: *Vuong Thua Vu*
    36th Infantry Regiment
    88th Infantry Regiment
    102nd Infantry Regiment

312th Infantry Division: *Le Trong Tan*
    141st Infantry Regiment
    165th Infantry Regiment
    209th Infantry Regiment
    154th Artillery Battalion

316th Infantry Division: *Le Quang Ba*
    98th Infantry Regiment
    174th Infantry Regiment
    176th Infantry Regiment (incomplete)
    812th Heavy Weapons Company

304th Infantry Division: *Hoang Minh Thao*
    57th Infantry Regiment
    345th Artillery Battalion
    (other infantry regiments not present)

148th Independent Infantry Regiment: *(not available)*
    910th Battalion
    920th Battalion
    900th Battalion (incomplete)
        523rd Signal Company
        121st Weapons Company

351st Heavy Division (Reinforced): *Vu Hien*
    151st Engineer Regiment
    237th Heavy Weapons Regiment (40 82-mm. mortars)
    45th Artillery Regiment (24 105-mm. howitzers)
    675th Artillery Regiment (15 75-mm. pack howitzers and 20 120-mm.
        mortars)
    367th Antiaircraft Regiment (20 37-mm. AA guns and 50 .50 caliber AA's)
    Field Rocket Unit (12–16 Katyusha rocket launchers)

II. Estimated Losses: 22,900 troops.

Unit	Strongpoint attacked	Killed
304th Division	Isabelle	490
308th Division	Gabrielle	2,000
	Eliane 2	350
	Huguette 1	300
312th Division	Beatrice	590
	Huguette 6	30
	Dominique	800
	Huguette (4/4)	750
316th Division	Ban-Loi (3/21)	50
	Elianes (April)	1,200
148th & Miscellaneous	Condor and valley	340
All units	Final assault	1,000
	Total killed:	7,900
	Wounded (estimated):	15,000
	GRAND TOTAL:	22,900

Appendix E: French Military Abbreviations

While abbreviations are a barbarism in any language, they have become well-nigh unavoidable, particularly when one is dealing with the contemporary military scene. In that respect, French military terminology is no different from that of France's Anglo-American allies, and historical accuracy demands that it be employed wherever it does not interfere with the actual comprehension of the text. No one at Dien Bien Phu called the 1st Foreign Legion Parachute Battalion *"le Premier Bataillon Etranger de Parachutistes"* when it could be conveniently (and euphoniously) called *"le Bep."* Below is a list of some of the abbreviations most likely to be encountered in this volume, arranged numerically for the reader's convenience, although text references occasionally vary in form.

Abbreviation	French Name	English Translation
1 GAP	Groupement Aéroporté	Airborne Battle Group
1 GMPT	Groupement Mobile de Partisans T'ai	T'ai Partisan Mobile Group
1 BEP	Ier Bataillon Etranger de Parachutistes	1st Foreign Legion Parachute Battalion
1/2 REI	Ier Bataillon, 2e Régiment Etranger d'Infanterie	1st Battalion, 2nd Foreign Legion Infantry Regiment
1/4 RTM	Ier Bataillon, 4e Régiment de Tirailleurs Marocains	1st Battalion, 4th Moroccan Rifle Regiment
1 BPC	Ier Bataillon de Parachutistes Coloniaux	1st Colonial Parachute Battalion
1/13 DBLE	Ier Bataillon, 13e Demi-Brigade de Légion Etrangère	1st Battalion, 13th Foreign Legion Half-Brigade
2 BEP	(as above for 1 BEP)	
2 GAP	(as above for 1 GAP)	
II/1 RCP	IIe Bataillon, Ier Régiment de Chasseurs Parachutistes	2nd Battalion, 1st Parachute Light Infantry Regiment
II/4 RAC	IIe Groupe, 4e Régiment d'Artillerie Coloniale	2nd Battalion, 4th Colonial Artillery Regiment
2 CMMLE	2e Compagnie Mixte de Mortiers de Légion Etrangère	2nd Composite Mortar Company, Foreign Legion
2/1 RTM	(as above for 1/4 RTM)	
BT 2	2e Bataillon T'ai	2nd T'ai (tribal) Bn.
2/1 RTA	2e Bataillon, Ier Régiment de Tirailleurs Algériens	2nd Battalion, 1st Algerian Rifle Regiment
BT 3	(as above for BT 2)	
3/3 RTA	(as above for 2/1 RTA)	
3/1 RCC	3e Escadron, Ier Régiment de Chasseurs à Cheval	3rd Squadron, 1st Armored Cavalry Regiment
III/10 RAC	(as above for II/4 RAC)	

Abbreviation	*French Name*	*English Translation*
3/3 REI	(as above for 1/2 REI)	
3/13 DBLE	(as above for 1/13 DBLE)	
IV/4 RAC	(as above for III/10 RAC)	
5 BPVN	5e Bataillon de Parachutistes Vietnamiens	5th Vietnamese Parachute Battalion
5/7 RTA	(as above for 2/1 RTA)	
GM 6	6e Groupe Mobile	6th Regimental Combat Team
6 BPC	(as above for 1 BPC)	
8 BPC	8e Bataillon de Parachutistes de Choc	8th Parachute Assault Battalion
GC 8	8e Groupement de Commandos	8th Commando Group
GM 9	(as above for GM 6)	
21 GAOA	31e Groupe Aérien d'Observation d'Artillerie	21st Aerial Artillery Observation Group
31 BG	31e Bataillon du Génie	31st Engineer Battalion
35 RALP	35e Régiment d'Artillerie Légère Parachutiste	35th Airborne Light Artillery Regiment
EROM 80	80e Escadrille de Reconnaissance Outre-Mer	80th Overseas Reconnaissance Squadron (French Air Force)
301 BVN	301e Bataillon Vietnamien (T'ai)	301st Vietnamese Army Battalion (tribal T'ai)

Bibliography

The books listed below deal specifically with the Battle of Dien Bien Phu or contain items of general interest or background information of special relevance.

Amouroux, Henri. *Croix sur l'Indochine.* Paris: Domat, 1955.

Bator, Victor. *Viet-Nam: A Diplomatic Tragedy.* Dobbs Ferry: Oceana, 1965.

Barjot (Adm.), Pierre. *Histoire de la guerre aéronavale.* Paris: Flammarion, 1961.

Bergot (Capt.), Erwan. *Deuxième classe à Dien Bien Phu.* Paris: La Table Ronde, 1964.

Bourdens, Henri. *Camionneur des nuées.* Paris: France-Empire, 1957.

Bidault, Georges. *D'une résistance à l'autre.* Paris: Les Presses du Siècle, 1965.

Bornert, Lucien. *Dien Bien Phu.* Paris: Documents du monde, 1954.

Burchett, Wilfred. *North of the 17th Parallel.* Hanoi: Red River Publishing House; 2nd ed., 1957.

Castelbajac, Bertrand de. *Sauts OPS.* Paris: La Table Ronde, 1959.

Catroux (Gen.), Georges. *Deux actes du drame indochinois.* Paris: Plon, 1959.

Chassin (Gen.), Lucien Max. *Aviation Indochine.* Paris: Amiot-Dumont, 1954.

Devillers, Philippe, and Jean Lacouture. *La fin d'une guerre: Indochine, 1954.* Paris: Le Seuil, 1960.

Donovan, Robert J. *Eisenhower: The Inside Story.* New York: Harper & Brothers, 1956.

Eden, Sir Anthony (Lord Avon). *Full Circle.* London: A. S. Cassell & Co., 1961.

Eisenhower (Gen.), Dwight D. *Mandate for Change: The White House Years 1953-1956.* New York: Doubleday & Co., 1963.

Ely (Gen.), Paul. *L'Indochine dans la tourmente.* Paris: Plon, 1964.

Etudes Vietnamiennes (periodical), "Contribution à l'histoire de Dien Bien Phu," Special Edition, No. 3 (Hanoi: March, 1965).

Faber, Franz. *Rot leuchtet der Song Cai.* East Berlin: Kongress-Verlag, 1955.

Fall, Bernard B. *Street Without Joy.* Harrisburg: Stackpole; 5th rev. ed., 1966.

―――. *The Two Viet-Nams.* New York: Frederick A. Praeger, Inc.; 3rd rev. ed., 1966.

Frédéric-Dupont, Edouard. *Mission de la France en Asie.* Paris: France-Empire, 1956.

Fiedler, Arkady. *Im Lande der wilden Bananen.* Leipzig: VEB Brockhaus, 1957.

Friang, Brigitte. *Les fleurs du ciel.* Paris: Robert Laffont, 1955.

Giap (Gen.) Vo Nguyen. *Dien Bien Phu.* Hanoi: Editions en Langues Etrangères; rev. ed., 1964.

―――. *People's War, People's Army.* New York: Frederick A. Praeger, Inc., 1962.

Gras (Maj.), Yves. "Deux revers du C.E.F. en Indochine―Cao Bang et Dien Bien Phu" (Manuscript). Paris: Ecole Supérieure de Guerre, 1961.

Grauwin (Maj.), Paul, *Doctor at Dien Bien Phu.* New York: The John Day Company, 1955.

―――. *Seulement médécin.* Paris: France-Empire, 1956.

Guillain, Robert. *La fin des illusions: Notes d'Indochine, février-juillet 1954.* Paris: Centre d'études de politique étrangère, 1954.

Jensen, Fritz. *Erlebtes Vietnam.* East Berlin: Dietz Verlag, 1955.

Juin (Marchal), Alphonse. *Trois siècles d'obéissance militaire.* Paris: Plon, 1963.

Kelly, George A. *Lost Soldiers: The French Army and Empire in Crisis, 1947–1962.* Cambridge: M.I.T. Press, 1965.

Karmen, Roman L. *Vietnam srazhaetsia: zanikh sov'etskovo kinoöperatora.* Moscow: Biblioteka soldata i matrosa, 1958.

Lancaster, Donald. *The Emancipation of French Indochina.* Oxford University Press, 1960.

Langlais (Gen.), Pierre. *Dien Bien Phu.* Paris: France-Empire, 1963.

Laniel, Joseph. *Le drame indochinois, de Dien Bien Phu au pari de Genève.* Paris: Plon, 1957.

Lartéguy, Jean. *Les Centurions.* Paris: Presses de la Cité, 1960.

Mai, Huu. *The Last Stronghold.* Hanoi: Editions de langues etrangerès, 1963.

Marchand (Gen.), Jean. *L'Indochine en guerre.* Paris: Les Presses Modernes, 1954.

Navarre (Gen.), Henri. *Agonie de l'Indochine.* Paris: Plon; 2nd rev. ed., 1956.

O'Ballance (Maj.), Edgar. *The Indo-China War, 1945–1954.* London: Faber & Faber, 1965.

Paillat, Claude. *Dossier secret de l'Indochine.* Paris: Presses de la Cité, 1964.

Palu, Marie-Thérèse. *Convoyeuses de l'air.* Paris: Ed. du Siamois, 1957.

Pouget (Maj.), Jean. *Nous étions à Dien Bien Phu.* Paris: Presses de la Cité, 1964.

Rénald, Jean. *L'enfer de Dien Bien Phu.* Paris: Flammarion, 1954.

Roy (Col.), Jules. *La bataille de Dien Bien Phu.* Paris: Julliard, 1963. (U.S. edition, abridged, Harper & Row, New York, 1964.)

Ridgway (Gen.), Matthew B. *Soldier.* New York: Harper & Bros., 1956.

Seeger, Bernhard. *Sturm aus Bambushütten.* East Berlin: Volk and Welt, 1956.

Thong, Nguyen Van, et al. *Return to Dien Bien Phu and Other Stories.* Hanoi: Foreign Languages Publishing House, 1961.

Tournoux, J. R. *Secrets d'Etat.* Paris: Plon, 1960.

Tran, Do. *Récits sur Dien Bien Phu.* Hanoi: Editions en langues etrangères, 1962.

Trinquier (Col.), Roger. *Modern Warfare: A French View of the Counterinsurgency.* New York: Frederick A. Praeger, Inc., 1963.

Index

Other titles of interest